About This Book

Teach Yourself the Internet in a Week shows you how you can c tools to satisfy your own interests and research needs—all farthest reaches of the Internet, in every corner of the worlc

Over the course of its 21 chapters, you'll learn the major Internet tools—and more importantly, you'll combine these tools to sift through the Internet's truly staggering amount of information. By the time you finish, you'll have everything you need to make the Internet your own.

Who Should Read This Book

Anyone interested in learning more about the Internet should read this book. Beginners will find the basics they need to get started on the Internet, learning its tools, its resources, and its rules. More advanced Internetters will find advice on how to combine the tools at their disposal to pursue their interests or needs in specific areas.

How the Book Is Structured

Teach Yourself the Internet in a Week consists of 21 chapters. Each day, you'll work through three chapters. On Day 1, you'll learn about the Internet, its origins, and how to get started. After Day 1, however, you'll spend the rest of the week learning about the Internet tools available to you, how to use them, and where you can go on the Internet.

Conventions

Text that you see onscreen is indicated by a `monospace` font.

Text you type is indicated by a **`bold monospace`** font.

Italic typeface is used when new terms are introduced and also for emphasis.

Note: A Note box presents interesting pieces of information related to the surrounding discussion. It also contains extra information that is helpful for you to know.

Tip: A Tip box offers advice or teaches an easier way to do something.

Caution: A Warning box warns you about potential problems and helps you steer clear of disaster.

Task

Throughout the course of each day's lesson, you'll perform many tasks and take numerous excursions to places on the Internet. Think of these as field trips designed to show you first-hand a particular Internet tool or technique in action.

Teach Yourself the Internet

in a Week, Second Edition

Teach Yourself the Internet in a Week, Second Edition

Neil Randall
John December
Carol DeVrieze
Celine Latulipe
Colin Moock
Marion Muirhead
Karin Trgovac
Stephanie Wunder

201 West 103rd Street
Indianapolis, Indiana 46290

International Standard Book Number: 0-672-30735-9

Library of Congress Catalog Card Number: 94-66281

98 97 96 95 4 3 2 1

Interpretation of the printing code: The rightmost double-digit number is the year of the book's printing; the rightmost single-digit, the number of the book's printing. For example, a printing code of 95-1 shows that the first printing of the book occurred in 1995.

Composed in AGaramond and MCPdigital by Macmillan Computer Publishing

Printed in the United States of America

Publisher *Richard K. Swadley*
Acquisitions Manager *Greg Wiegand*
Development Manager *Dean Miller*
Managing Editor *Cindy Morrow*
Marketing Manager *Gregg Bushyeager*

Acquisitions Editor
Christopher Denny

Development Editor
L. Angelique Brittingham

Production Editor
Kitty Wilson

Copy Editor
Marla Reece
Bart Reed
Joe Williams

Technical Reviewer
Bruneau Babet

Editorial Coordinator
Bill Whitmer

Technical Edit Coordinator
Lynette Quinn

Formatter
Frank Sinclair

Editorial Assistant
Sharon Cox

Cover Designer
Tim Amrhein

Book Designer
Alyssa Yesh

Production Team Supervisor
Brad Chinn

Production
Angela D. Bannan
Michael Brumitt
Terrie Deemer
Ayanna Lacey
Kevin Laseau
Paula Lowell
Nancy C. Price
Brian-Kent Proffitt
Bobbi Satterfield
SA Springer
Susan Van Ness
Mark Walchle

Overview

Contents

Day 2: Conversing/Communicating 65

Sams.net
Learning
Center
sams
net

Sams.net
Learning
Center
sams
net

Sams.net
Learning
Center
sams
net

Acknowledgments

I have many people to thank. Too many, in fact, and I'm desperately afraid of forgetting someone. Nevertheless, here goes.

I wish to thank the readers of the first edition of *Teach Yourself the Internet*, for making it successful enough to guarantee this second edition. Mark Taber, as usual, has been extremely helpful in getting the book through to its conclusion, in making suggestions to improve the book further, and in assigning me to two other books since the first edition was released. I'm extremely grateful to several people at *PC/Computing* magazine, who gave me enough assignments to get me listed as a contributing editor, and to Sebastian Rupley, now with *PC Magazine*, for giving me my first work with both magazines. And thanks as well to John December, because our *World Wide Web Unleashed* helped the success of this book.

Next, my contributors. From the first edition, Marion Muirhead remains, along with Carol DeVrieze and Stewart Lindsay, and I thank them again for their fine contributions. Celine Latulipe also remains, and she's worked with me since, as co-author of *Plug-n-Play Internet for Windows*, and I continue to marvel at her reliability and her consistency. Karin Trgovac helped me on *The World Wide Web Unleashed*, and I thank her again for kicking in at the last minute here. Colin Moock came in at the last second as well, and to him my thanks as well. The most sustained outside contributions to the second edition come from Stephanie Wunder, whose high-quality work and complete reliability have impressed me through the last several months. She, too, gets my heartfelt thanks.

On a more personal front, thanks again to David Wade, who came very close to launching the best Internet magazine on the planet (unfortunately, it got stopped) and who let me help work on it. He remains a great friend, as does Guy Kay, whose perspectives on the Internet have helped me see the technological issues more clearly, and whose superb recent novel helped me get through the final stages of preparing this edition. I have a host of people from the University of Waterloo to thank, including Bill Macnaughton, Dave Goodwin, and Keith McGowan. And more thanks to Carrie Pascal, who escaped the university for Microsoft but who inspired me more than she knows.

One more time, and more deservingly than ever, I thank Michelle and Catherine, for being about as perfect as daughters can be, and Heather, whose patience and support continues to amaze me.

About the Authors

Neil Randall

Neil Randall (`nrandall@watarts.uwaterloo.ca`) teaches English at the University of Waterloo in Waterloo, Ontario. He offers courses in professional writing and rhetorical theory, and he conducts research in issues surrounding the Internet. He is the co-author of *The World Wide Web Unleashed* (Sams) and *Plug-n-Play Internet for Windows* (Sams). He is a contributing editor with *PC Computing*, and he has published articles and reviews in several magazines, including *PC Magazine*, *Windows*, *Compute*, *Amiga World*, and *Computing Canada*.

John December

John December (`john@december.com`) is a doctoral candidate in English at Rensselaer Polytechnic Institute in New York. He is the co-author of *The World Wide Web Unleashed*, and the maintainer of the immensely popular Internet Tools Summary and Internet Web Text. He is founder and editor of *CMC Magazine*, a Web-based publication focused on the growing field of computer-mediated communications.

Carol DeVrieze

Carol DeVrieze is a high school teacher in Kitchener, Canada. Although she'd heard of some of the K–12 Internet activity in the United States and Canada, it wasn't until she began exploring the resources fully that she realized what was happening out there. More than any other contributing author in this book, because of the staggering amount of information available, Carol first became awestruck and then quickly overwhelmed by the possibilities. As soon as her eyes stop burning from staring at the screen for hour after late evening hour, she'll move quickly to bring these possibilities into her classrooms.

Celine Latulipe

Celine Latulipe is completing a degree at the University of Waterloo, Canada, with a major in economics and a minor in computer science. She is the co-author of *Plug-n-Play Internet for Windows*, and she has contributed to *The Net* magazine. She has become, over the past year and a half, an Internet expert par excellence.

Colin Moock

Colin Moock is a graduate student in English at the University of Waterloo, Canada. A long-time user of MUDs and MOOs, he has conducted research into MUDs and newsgroups for his courses, and has been developing and maintaining a MUD over the past several months.

Marion Muirhead

Marion Muirhead, the main writer in Chapter 14 ("Traveling with the Net"), is a doctoral candidate at the University of Waterloo, Canada. She uses the Internet for a variety of different purposes, travel information being just one of them. She is also extremely interested in the development of electronic texts and books.

Karin Trgovac

Karin Trgovac is on staff as a computer support assistant with the Electrical and Computer Engineering Department at the University of Waterloo, Canada. She has established the department's Web site, and she offers several other interesting connections to her life and interests in her personal home page at `http://coulomb.uwaterloo.ca:80/~ktrgovac/`. A long-time Internet user, she has parlayed that knowledge into articles for *The Net* magazine, and she contributed to several chapters in *The World Wide Web Unleashed.*

Stephanie Wunder

Stephanie Wunder is a fourth-year student in the Professional Writing program at the University of Waterloo, Canada. She came to the Net as a relative newcomer in early 1995, but emerged a few months later as an Internaut of considerable expertise. She assisted in the preparation of several chapters of the second edition of *Teach Yourself the Internet,* contributing new material to Chapter 5, "Newsgroups," and her vast experience in non-virtual shopping helped considerably in her writing of the entirety of Chapter 16, "Electronic Commerce: Shopping on the Internet."

Introduction

Let's face it—this isn't the first Internet guide on the market. There are others, and some are excellent. In fact, I've used a number of them myself, and I continue to recommend them to my friends.

Their strengths are clear. They guide you, step-by-step, through the sometimes bewildering variety of tools you need to know if you want to become Internet-savvy. They explain them in varying degrees of thoroughness, and they make it possible to work through the Internet at all. What they don't do—nor are they meant to—is show you how you can combine the tools to satisfy your own interests and research needs.

Teach Yourself the Internet in a Week attempts to do just that. Over the course of its 21 chapters, you'll learn the major Internet tools, and more importantly you'll combine these tools to sift through the Internet's truly staggering amount of information. By the time you finish, you'll have everything you need to make the Internet your own.

And that's the point—making it *your* Internet, using it for *your* purposes, getting it to satisfy *your* needs and *your* curiosity. Like any technology, the Internet will be valuable to you only if you—and any people you care about—can put it to good use. If you're interested in technologies for their own sake, the Internet has a lot to offer. If you want your technologies to somehow make your life better (and what else are technologies for?), well, that's where the Internet shines. That's what this book helps you do.

Two other points about this book. First, I designed it so that you can get a great deal out of it without actually being on the Internet. Read it in a coffee shop, or on a plane, or in front of the TV, and you'll get a good idea of what the Internet has to offer. Second, I wanted users of Microsoft Windows or the Macintosh to feel at home. While the text examples are taken from UNIX accounts, all of the screen captures are from my own Windows machine in my study, and Mac screens look similar. This was important to me, because Mac users have been in the Internets foreground for a long while, and Windows users are the fastest growing group of Net-connected people.

Since the first edition of the book was published, the Internet has grown explosively, and in many ways it has changed a great deal. Gopher is no longer the major browsing tool, although it certainly was at the time of the first edition's publication. In fact, new Gophers have almost disappeared in the wake of the enormous growth of the World Wide Web, and Web browsers in many ways are becoming the Net's major interface. Fourteen months ago, electronic commerce was barely a gleam in the credit card companies' eyes; now those companies themselves are racing to bring full payment systems directly to the Net. And more; much, much more. You can expect even more changes as the next few months go by, and the Net has even become a part of the mainstream. If you don't believe it, just ask Sandra Bullock.

How the Book Is Structured

Teach Yourself the Internet consists of 21 chapters, each representing a day of activities. In Chapter 1, you'll go on an all-too-brief tour of the Internet and learn some Internet basics, then you'll spend the rest of the first day learning how to get connected and logged on. The next three chapters (Day 2) take you through the Internet's communications programs, and in Day 3 you'll work with traditional Internet tools that let you download software, search the Net for files, and maneuver through the myriad easy-to-use Gophers. Chapters 10-12 (Day 4) introduce you to the vast and hugely popular World Wide Web, and soon you'll be a master of Mosaic, Netscape, and fascinating things like the World Web Worm.

Beginning with Day 5, "The Internet at Home," you'll be ready to make the Internet work for you. In Chapter 13, for example, you'll make use of all the Internet tools to explore resources in entertainment, while travel and art await you in the remainder of Day 5. Day 6 is devoted to using the Internet for work or business, with chapters on getting a job, doing business, and that most intriguing of activities, using the Web to buy things. The final three chapters take you through some possibilities for the Internet at School, with education and learning including learning the Net itself forming the major theme.

When you've completed all 21 chapters, you'll be more than ready to branch out on your own, combining the Internet tools to track down information about topics of your own particular interest. In fact, by that time you'll probably already have started. Once you get going, and you see items on a Gopher menu or a World Wide Web site that interest you, you'll be so tempted to explore them that you'll almost certainly set this book aside and do some "surfing" on your own. I encourage you to do so, but I also encourage you to pick the book back up. There's more to learn in each succeeding chapter, and you can put all of it to use in your own detailed searches and retrievals.

The Role of the Contributors

Not only will you explore the Internet through a variety of topics, you'll also do so from a number of different viewpoints. To demonstrate first-hand that the Internet is a collaborative venture, I enlisted a number of contributors to write the basis of several of the chapters. A high school teacher, for example, leads you through the K–12 education scenario, while an art enthusiast examines the Internet's archives of digital art. An enthusiastic shopper looks at buying stuff over the Web, a job-hunter shows what's available along the lines of finding a career, and a veteran of many newsgroups shows you how to get the most out of the huge newsgroup system. I'm on the Internet many hours per day, but I can't pretend to be an expert at all of it. The Net is too big for one person to know fully, and it's getting bigger every hour.

My Internet Address

At various points in this book, you'll see my Internet address revealed in its full, multipart glory—`nrandall@watarts.uwaterloo.ca`. Here's an invitation to use it. If you have any comments about *Teach Yourself the Internet*, send me a message. If you have a question, I'll try to answer it. A small warning, however; the answers will be brief, and I may not get back to you immediately (I have a day job).

After You Finish Reading

This book isn't a one-time item. It will continue to evolve along with the Internet itself, and I invite you to be part of that evolution. As you read this, and once you're comfortable with the World Wide Web, visit the Web site at `http://randall.uwaterloo.ca/`, where you'll find a link to a suite of interconnected pages designed specifically for readers of *Teach Yourself the Internet in a Week*. Here, you'll find links to additional resources, comments, and frequently asked questions from readers, and whatever other information becomes important. Please join us, and please let us know your Internetting needs.

DAY

1

For Starters

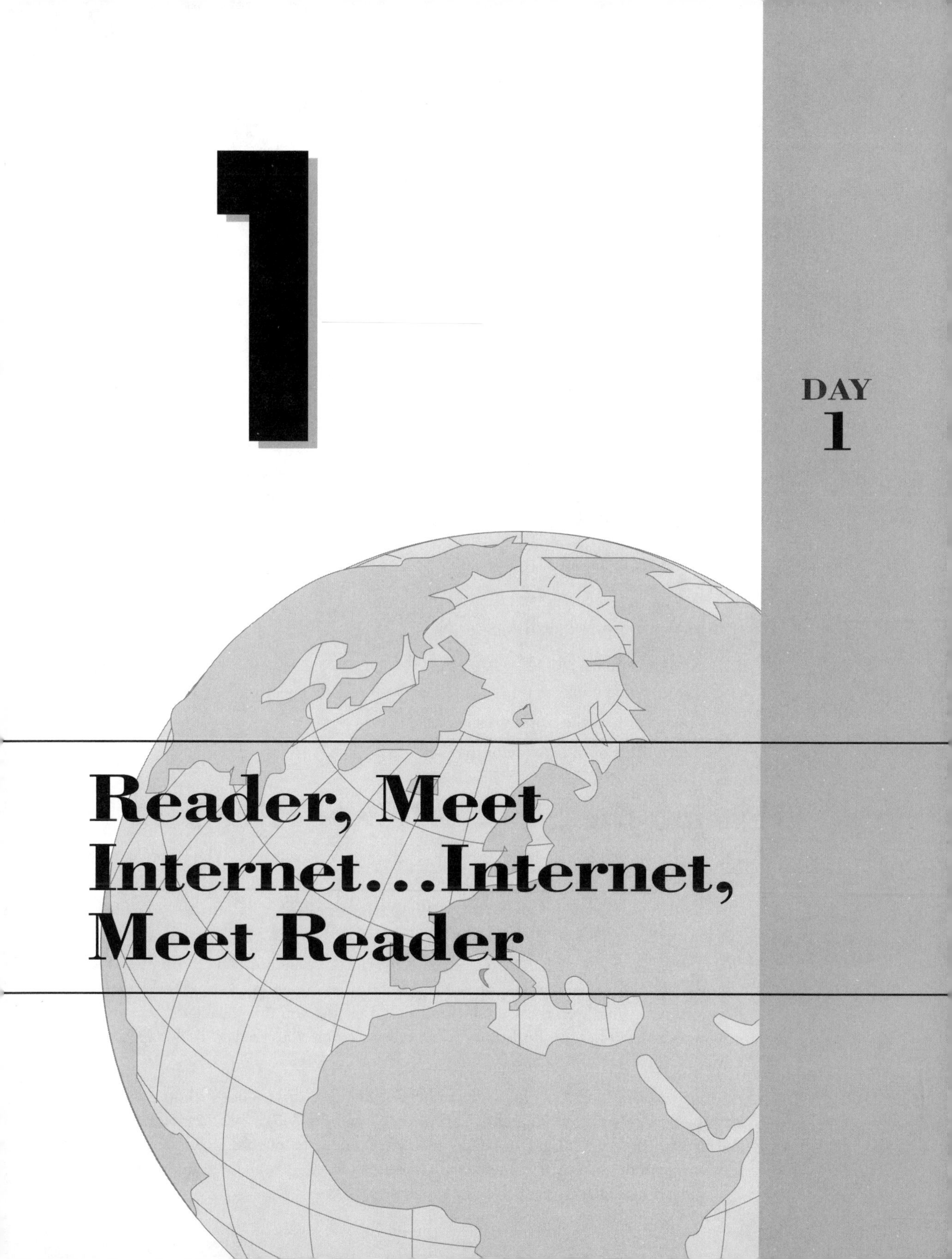

1

DAY 1

Reader, Meet Internet...Internet, Meet Reader

You're about to embark on something that will almost certainly change your life. I realize that sounds like the opening sentence of a self-help book, but to some extent that's what *Teach Yourself the Internet in a Week* is. You want to learn about the Net, and you need a place to start. Over the next seven days, you'll do precisely that.

To be completely honest, you don't have to go through this chapter if you don't want to. It's an introduction to the Internet, and it's designed to show you the Net's global scope, fascinating past, and the pieces of which it's composed. It also offers a short pictorial tour of the Internet, as a means of getting your bearings. But if you think you already know this stuff, or if you just want to leap right in, by all means skip to Chapter 2. (You'll miss some really superb writing, carefully crafted by a deeply caring artesan to capture the richness and the subtletly of the Net, but, hey, what's a week or so of intensive labor among friends?)

If you are in fact new to the Net, context helps, and that's what this chapter is all about. So kick off your shoes, grab a soda or a cup of tea, and spend the next few minutes looking at the Net from outside. When you get to the next chapter, you'll be ready to dive in.

Task List

In this chapter, you will do the following:

- ☐ Get an overview of the Internet as a whole
- ☐ Learn what people do on the Internet
- ☐ Take a tour of the world via the Net
- ☐ Learn some of the history of the Net

Putting the Net in Perspective

The Internet is big. So big, in fact, that it's hard to get a handle on it. You've probably read things about how many computers are hooked up to how many networks, with how many users in how many countries. Doesn't mean much, though, does it? The whole thing is just too huge. So let's knock it down a bit.

Inside your computer is a hard drive. Most likely, the drive contains several hundred files; if you run Microsoft Windows 3.1 or higher, for example, you've got a couple hundred right there. How do you keep track of all these files? Usually, you don't have to, because your programs know where to find things themselves. When you need to find a specific file, however, you can laboriously do so yourself, or you can get some software to do it for you.

As long as you have only one moderately-sized hard drive—80–120 megabytes, for example—finding files isn't much of a problem. Upgrade to 240 or 340 megabytes, however, and locating that one elusive file gets a bit dicier. Looking through directory after directory quickly becomes tedious, so you'll start to make use of the file-search programs provided with any number of new software packages.

Even so, it's no big deal. You've got a hard drive, and you can find what's on it. Everything's fine.

Now add a second hard drive. Start filling it with program files, graphics files, multimedia files, all the stuff you can find. Suddenly, it's no longer even an option to search for a specific file on your own. You need that file-search program, and you want one with enough features to help you narrow down your search.

As soon as you have those two drives under control, add a few more. A hard-card, for example, and a couple of daisy-chained SCSI drives. Ridiculous? Hardly. That's what I have, and I'm not alone. But forget about realism for a bit. Picture your computer with five hard drives, together totaling over two gigabytes of storage space. Any guesses how long it would take to find one single, solitary text file? Especially on a DOS machine, with its dopey file-naming convention? You need that file-search program more than ever. In fact, you can hardly operate without it.

Now let's get really adventurous. Imagine a system with not just five hard drives, but five million. Imagine that every ten minutes, another hundred or so are being added on. Imagine that you have no control over who puts them there, nor what files are loaded onto them. All you know is that you have access to most of them. Welcome to the Internet!

The Internet is nothing more than a bunch of computers all joined together. These computers have three major functions, as follows:

- First, they let people on one computer send messages to people on another.
- Second, they store files that people might want access to.
- Third, they let people on one computer connect to a remote computer to do things as if they were actually at that site.

That's it. That's primarily what the Internet is.

So why is everybody from the United States government to the British Broadcasting Corporation jumping onto it? Because, quite simply, they want to send messages and access those files. Or, to reverse this, they want to receive messages and provide files that can be accessed by others.

But the Internet's popularity can be even more easily explained. It's huge, and it's global. Get on the Net (as it's called), and you can suddenly exchange messages and files with over a million computers in dozens of countries. Every ten minutes or so, another computer network attaches itself to the Net, which means that those million-plus computers are getting company very quickly. Think about all the users, and think about all the hard drives. Every one of those computers has files you might be interested in, and every one of them also has users you might want to contact.

The only trouble is finding them. To help you, some inventive programmers have developed some equally inventive software.

- **Archie**, for example, is a program that goes out and searches the Net for files, and then builds a huge database of the files that are out there. When you do an Archie search, you're actually accessing this database. The program tells you where to find it; that is, it tells you which computer(s) holds that file. (See Chapter 9 for more details on Archie.)
- **Gopher**, the most popular Internet protocol of all, until recently, provides links from computer to computer. There are always other ways of making these links, but Gopher makes it easy by replacing the Internet's rather arcane commands with numbered lists (or pictured lists if you're working in Windows or on a Macintosh). You may not be comfortable typing `ftp ftp.reston.va.us`, but choosing number 5 from a list is easy enough for anyone. (Chapter 4 deals extensively with Gopher.)
- **World Wide Web** (WWW) is even easier, as long as you're working with a program like Mosaic or Netscape in a graphical environment, such as Windows, the Mac, or UNIX's X Window. Each WWW screen looks like a well-designed page in a document, with some words or phrases highlighted or underlined. Click on one of these, and you'll be taken somewhere else. Through the WWW you can get into Gophers, download files, and access all sorts of other Internet activities. On the Web, in addition, are large directories of resources, organized by subject to help you even further. (For more on the World Wide Web, see Day 4.)

And that's just three pieces of software. Over the course of this book, you'll learn about other software programs, many with exotic and more or less impenetrable names. WAIS, Veronica, ERIC, CARL—all of them are designed to help you find things. The fact that there are so many is testament enough to how big the Net is. Keep in mind that most Internet programs are designed just to help you find whatever you want to find.

The other side of the Net, of course, is the phenomenon known as electronic mail. I can't even imagine the days—not too long ago—when I had no recourse to e-mail at all. A few months on the Internet, and you won't either. Every day I receive at least fifty messages, and sometimes over a hundred. Many of them simply tell me about new stuff on the Net, to be sure, but there is a lot of the person-to-person kind of message as well. Join the Net, and e-mail can quickly become your life.

Is that a good thing? That's probably not the point. Good or bad, it happens. I personally think it can be very good indeed. While it's true that e-mail can become a time-consuming monster, and as a result can be (and is) used as a crutch, it also can be the most important link you have to people that have similar personal or professional interests. Reading your e-mail in the morning can be one the most thought-provoking and even inspiring events of the day, and writing a few quick replies can get you going. It can also bog you down, but that's just a matter of self-management.

I've seen e-mail transform people. I've seen it expand their intellectual and even social horizons. I've helped people use it to propose, negotiate, and submit entire projects. I've also seen it destroy people's carefully planned schedules, but that's been the much rarer event.

The point is that e-mail exists, and it's not about to disappear. You can use it as a tool for sending everything from post-it notes to lengthy documentation, and its sheer flexibility makes it indispensable.

I've already mentioned the World Wide Web, but I'll do so again because it is one of the truly remarkable phenomena of our times. The Web, as it's usually called, has become the centerpiece of computer and business books, and of feature articles in scores of major newspapers and magazines. You gain access to the Web through "browsers," such as Mosaic or Netscape, and even the names of these programs have become famous. Whenever you hear about conducting business over the Internet, or the potential of the Net for on-line education, video-conferencing, or even live concerts by rock bands or symphony orchestras, the World Wide Web is part of the equation. It combines both communication and file access technologies, and as such is becoming the core of the Internet itself.

Because that's what the Internet is: a carefully developed collection of communication and file access technologies. What's so amazing about it is that it exists at all. Try to network three PCs together in the same room, and you'll quickly learn how complex and unforgiving networking technology can be. Extend those problems across oceans and a huge array of operating systems and communications incompatibilities, and you begin to see how Internet researchers have been spending their time. Right at this moment, I'm sitting in front of a 486 PC that is networked through complex transmission scheme to a Cray supercomputer in Illinois, a Macintosh in British Columbia, an IBM mainframe in Australia, and who knows what pieces of old and new technology in Peru, Brazil, the Netherlands, Norway, the U.K., Poland, Italy, Turkey, Singapore, Malaysia, Japan....

You get the idea. It's all pretty impressive.

Statistics: The Facts, Just Give Us the Facts

I really don't want to provide real numbers here, because between the time I finish writing this book and the time it hits the shelves those numbers will change. Here are a few guidelines, just so you have some figures you can pass around at a dinner party.

The Internet began with four host computers in 1969. Now, it incorporates well over 15,000 sub-networks in over 70 countries, and these networks consist, in turn, of roughly two million host computers. In the past year, the number of commercially-based computers has practically overtaken the number of research and education computers on the Net, a trend that only promises to continue. The future has begun, and it's looking quite business-like.

How many users are on the Internet? Nobody knows. Each host, remember, can have a number of individual users. You and your PC or Mac may be an individual host with one user, but a university typically will have several hosts, each with many users. It would be possible to figure it out, I suppose, but at the rate the Internet is growing, it would be futile. As soon as the numbers were in, they'd change. Instead, let's just say that the Internet has several million users. Good enough?

No? Okay, then, let's expand it. Estimates from experts (or at least people we acknowledge to be experts) suggest that by the turn of the century, the number of Internet users will rise to anywhere from 80 million to 300 million (depending on which expert you consult), and that within a decade, it will be as unusual for a person to be without an Internet e-mail address as it is now for a person to be without a telephone number. Businesses, indeed, will have practically no choice but to establish an Internet presence, and it will be little different for personal users as well.

Just look around. Magazine and newspaper ads contain e-mail addresses and World Wide Web locations, while the major TV news and information shows encourage you to use the Net to communicate with them. Pizza Hut lets you order your favorite anchovy-laden midnight snack through the Web, and the Rolling Stones have broadcast a small portion of a live concert over the Net. You can e-mail the president of the United States, you can follow the latest episodes of your favorite TV shows, you can learn how to dissect a frog, you can download entire albums of alternative music, and on and on it goes. The Net is everywhere, and it's getting bigger by the hour, to the point where the whole thing is beginning to seem overwhelming indeed.

Teach Yourself the Internet in a Week will help you get started.

A World Tour via the Internet, with Greetings from Abroad

For the remainder of this chapter, you're going to use the Internet to tour the world. You can either join in by signing on to your Internet account, or you can simply read along and see what the Internet has to offer. In fact, this chapter is designed for anyone who is curious about the Net but who hasn't actually been on it, or who has done a few things on the Internet and is wondering what else there is to know.

What will happen during this tour is known as *net surfing.* You're going to do nothing more than "surf" from one "site" to another, to see what the new site contains. The important thing to keep in mind is that each site is another computer, physically located somewhere else in the world. You'll be using the Internet to connect to a computer in the United States, and then from there to a computer in Canada, and then Mexico. You'll then link back to the U.S., where you'll connect to computers in Europe, the Middle East, Asia, and so on.

When you connect to the remote computer, you'll be looking at a screen that contains information and points to other sources of information. Someone at that location has set up a Gopher directory or a World Wide Web page that anybody on the Internet can access, and this directory or page will display on your monitor. You'll temporarily become part of that remote computer, able to examine whatever its owners have given you permission to see.

Ready? Okay, you're off!

This tour is structured quite simply, and unlike most tour buses this one stops whenever you want it to, and for however long you want. In fact, you can even skip entire continents and return to them later.

Here's what to do. You'll start from the United States, visit a few countries on each continent—unless, of course, the continent has only one, or even none—and end up back in the United States. You'll visit primarily Gopher and World Wide Web sites, because through them you can do pretty much anything else (except send e-mail). Along the way, well, let's just see what happens.

North America

The Internet started in the United States, and this is where most of the activity is taking place. You'd probably expect Japan to be next, but that's not the case. Because of a wide range of concerns and issues, Japan got a late start, but they're picking up steam. Second to North America is Europe, in fact, and we'll go there after our U.S. tour.

Example 1.1: U.S.A.

Let's start with the United States. This is the Internet's birthplace, and with recent Presidential initiatives, it's where the Net will expand most quickly. We'll begin with a significant location, the University of Minnesota, the home of the important browsing program called *Gopher*.

Figure 1.1 shows the result of Gophering to the following address: `gopher.tc.umn.edu`. (See Chapter 8 for details on how to do this.) At the top left of the screen is the main Gopher. We could choose any item from the menu, but let's opt for University of Minnesota Campus Information, the last item listed. This leads us to the long listing on the right half of the screen, with all sorts of interesting choices available. Like all campuses these days, Minnesota offers services for students with disabilities, and to see what this is like, select Disability Information (lower left). This reveals several items (bottom right), including an intriguing "Top Ten Items in Disability Gopher."

Tip: Whenever you encounter a Gopher listing, you'll have these kinds of choices. Each listing leads to another, with the only ending point being an actual document that you can read or download. As you can already see, Gopher browsing can be time-consuming, instructive, and quite addicting.

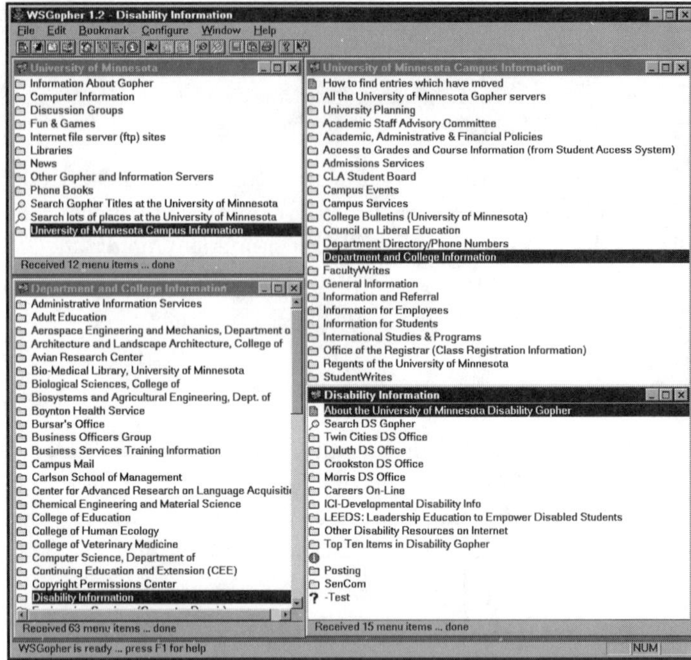

Figure 1.1.
University of Minnesota Gopher servers.

Example 1.2: Canada

Canada, the United States's largest trading partner, began developing its internetworking capabilities soon after the Internet became a reality. So let's go east of Minnesota and into New Brunswick, where we find a World Wide Web site and the University of New Brunswick (`http://www.unb.ca/`—see Chapter 10 for information about how to access WWW sites). Figure 1.2 demonstrates the Web's potential for incorporating graphics and even sound—the little Speaker icon beside the Welcome line is a sound file that we can play if we have the necessary hardware and software. See Chapter 11 for details on WWW audio, video, and viewers.

Example 1.3: Mexico

Far to the southwest of New Brunswick lies Mexico (the third of the NAFTA partners), and that's where we head next. Mexican information is accessible primarily through Gophers, so we return to our Gopher program and see what we find. From the Other Gopher and Information Servers line of the University of Minnesota Gopher we arrive, eventually, at Figure 1.3. Here you see a collection of Mexican Gophers in the middle of the screen, with three additional selections, Gopher Universidad Anahuac, Manuales o Informacion, and the text file Introduccion al Gopher, displayed on the screen as well.

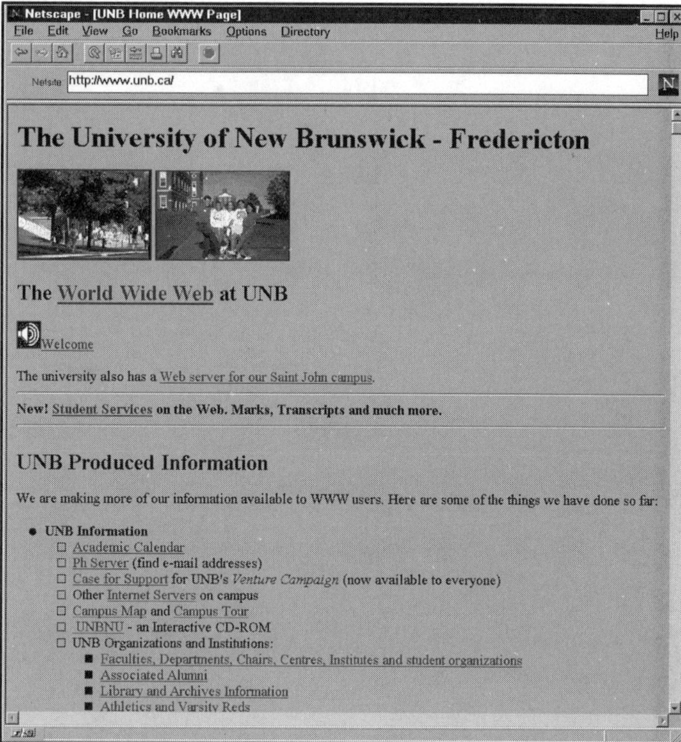

Figure 1.2.
The University of New Brunswick home page.

Note: As you might expect, most of the Mexican information is in Spanish. As you'll also discover, however, a great many Gopher and WWW sites offer English versions. For better or for worse, English has established itself as the *lingua franca* of the Internet, although other languages are starting to appear.

Example 1.4: The Virtual Tourist

Now we're back to the U.S.A., and this time to Buffalo, New York. Here we find an extremely useful bit of Internet technology, the *clickable map.* The Virtual Tourist, shown in Figure 1.4, is a World Wide Web page (`http://wings.buffalo.edu/world`) that allows you to click your mouse pointer on whatever section of the world you'd like; in turn, you'll receive another clickable map. You'll be returning to the Virtual Tourist frequently throughout this book. It's an exceptionally useful guide to the world's Internet resources.

At this point, let me pause the tour to meet your first new contact. Brandon Plewe is Assistant Coordinator, Campus-Wide Information Services, for the State University of New York at Buffalo. He'd like to say hello (see the following sidebar).

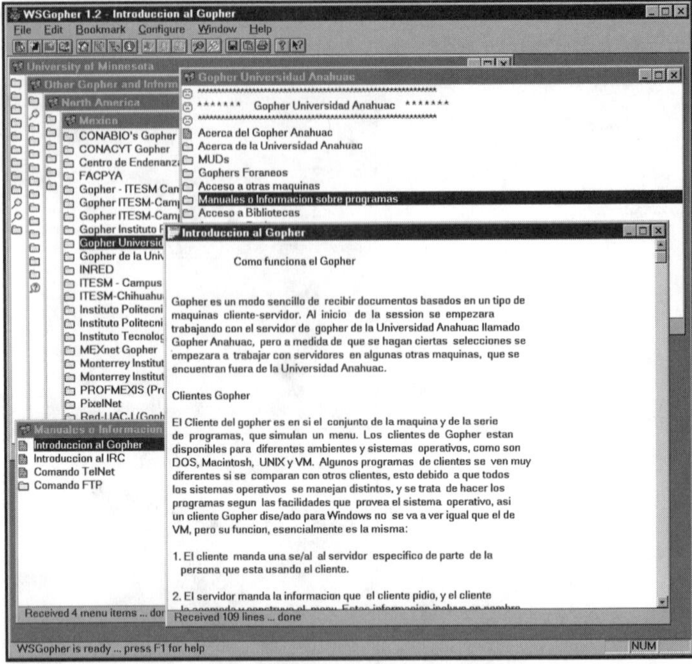

Figure 1.3.
Mexican Gopher servers.

Welcome to the Virtual Tourist. This service has been provided to you by many people around the world who want you to know more about themselves, their lands, and their resources on the Internet. We hope you find it a valuable trailmap as you backpack around cyberspace.

The Virtual Tourist is really two guides in one. The first is a catalog of information about the real world, and the second is a guide to the services in the virtual world of the Internet. You can use the first kind of service to learn more about another country or region, or perhaps even plan a trip there. The second will be useful to you in your travels in cyberspace, by showing you what resources each area has to offer.

Unfortunately, this volunteer effort is far from complete. Perhaps, down the road, you too can contribute to the Virtual Tourist.

Brandon Plewe

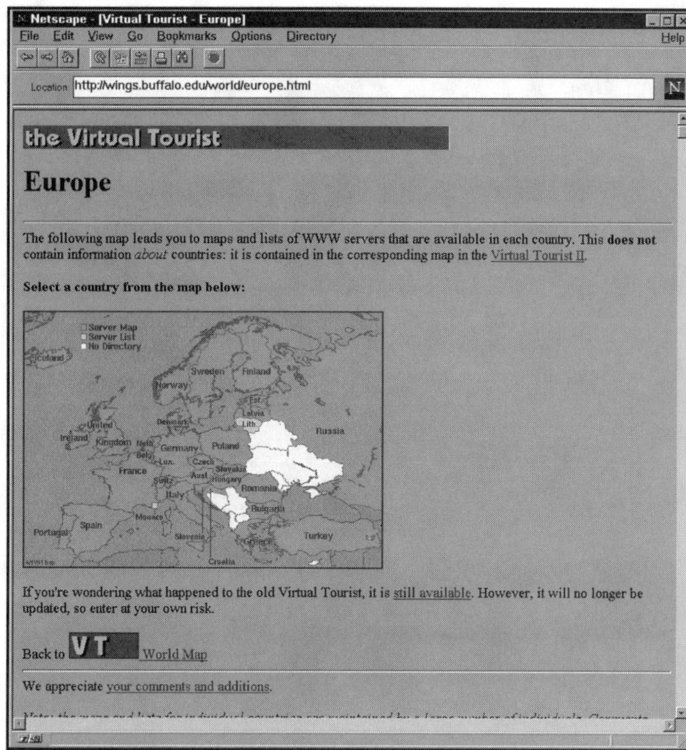

Figure 1.4.
The Virtual Tourist top-level page.

Note: The preceding greeting is just the the first of several greetings from around the world you'll find in this chapter. I located all these people through the World Wide Web, then e-mailed them and asked if they'd provide a short welcome note to put in the book. It's a testament to the sheer power and cooperativeness of the Internet that the messages all arrived within a few days of my request, and that, of all the people I asked, only one turned my request down. I don't know about you, but I find this amazing.

Europe

As far as the Internet is concerned, Europe is already highly developed, with an increasing number of sites appearing almost daily. Figure 1.5 shows the European inset of the Virtual Tourist map, along with the clickable map of Germany that appears if you select that country. As you can see from the map's key, a large number of sites are available, including several that include city information.

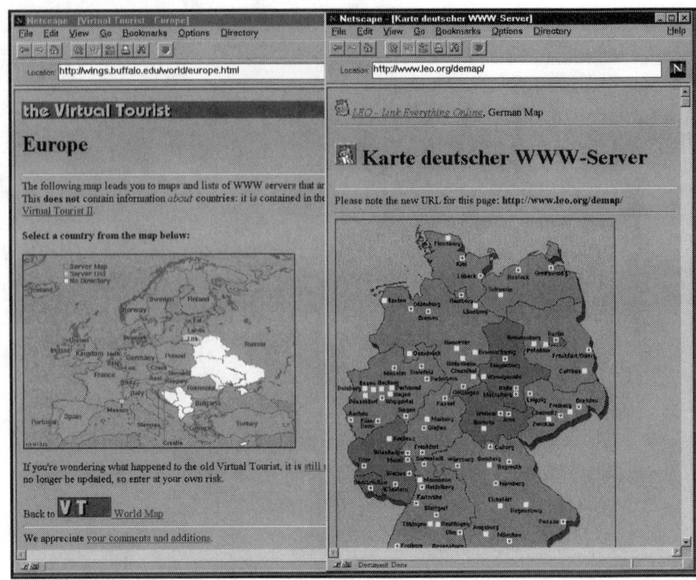

Figure 1.5.
The Virtual Tourist page for Europe.

We won't visit Germany right now, however. Instead, we'll take a quick swing through the U.K. on our way to three smaller places: Switzerland, Hungary, and Sardinia.

Example 1.5: The United Kingdom

The U.K. is the dominant European nation from an Internet perspective, as one glance at the multi-item Gopher menu in Figure 1.6 demonstrates (U.K. Gopher Servers item from `ukoln.bath.ac.uk`). The lower left half of Figure 1.6 shows a small portion of the 89 items in the list, from which we'll choose the venerable University of Cambridge. Once again you'll bypass the serious details, skipping right to information about the Cambridge area (Cambridge area information item from `gopher.cam.ac.uk`). This appears at the bottom right of the screen, which consists primarily of documents. A quick click on the Theatres in Cambridge item would give you information about what's happening there in the world of theater, but again, let's just skip on through.

Example 1.6: Switzerland

Among the more impressive Internet sites in Switzerland is TECFA, Technologies de Formation et Apprentisage, based at the University of Geneva. Figure 1.7 shows TECFA's colorful home page (`http://tecfa.unige.ch`), including links to other educational technology sites.

Once again, let's stop the tour for a quick meeting. Here is Daniel Schneider, "webslave" as he calls himself, from the Faculte de Psychologie et des Sciences de l'Education at Geneva, again with a message written specifically for this book (see the following sidebar).

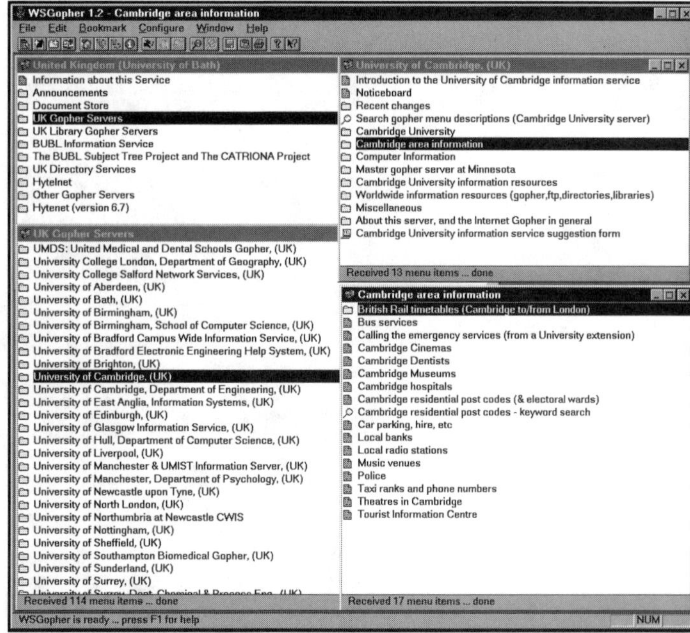

Figure 1.6.
Gopher servers in the U.K.

TECFA is an academic team active in the field of Educational Technology. It belongs to the School of Education and Psychology of the University of Geneva and includes about ten collaborators. TECFA's main research interests are the applications of artificial intelligence to education, the cognitive effects of educational software, and the communication issues with new technologies (distance education, multimedia systems, multimedia courseware, and so on).

The Internet is very important to us. Swiss academia is small and in most fields we lack "critical mass" and therefore we depend very much on international cooperation.

We have access to fairly fast lines (2 mbps). In the near future, we will participate in experimental ATM networks that would enable us, for example, to do full-motion video and 3D animations over long distances and therefore, bring the world still closer.

Daniel Schneider

Example 1.7: Hungary

From Switzerland it's eastward across Austria and into Hungary, where we find another clickable map in Figure 1.8 (`http://www.fsz.bme.hu/hungary/homepage.html`).

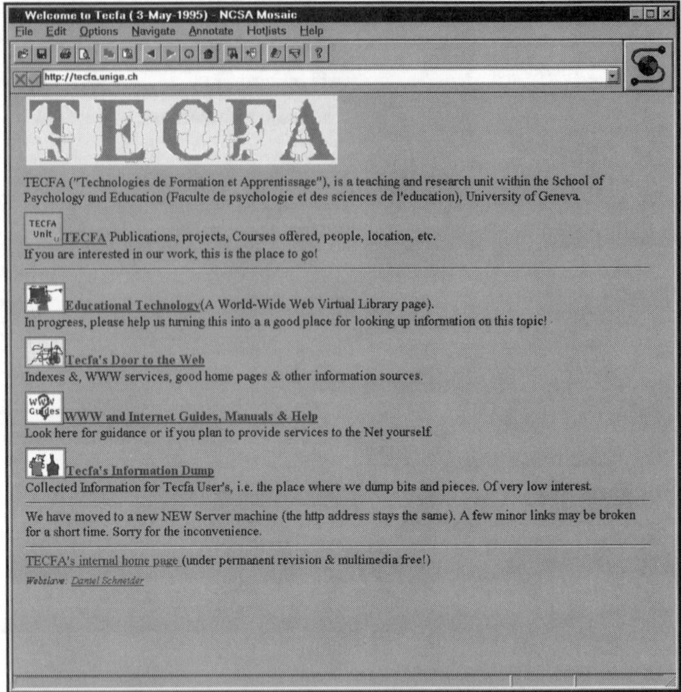

Figure 1.7.
TECFA home page—Switzerland.

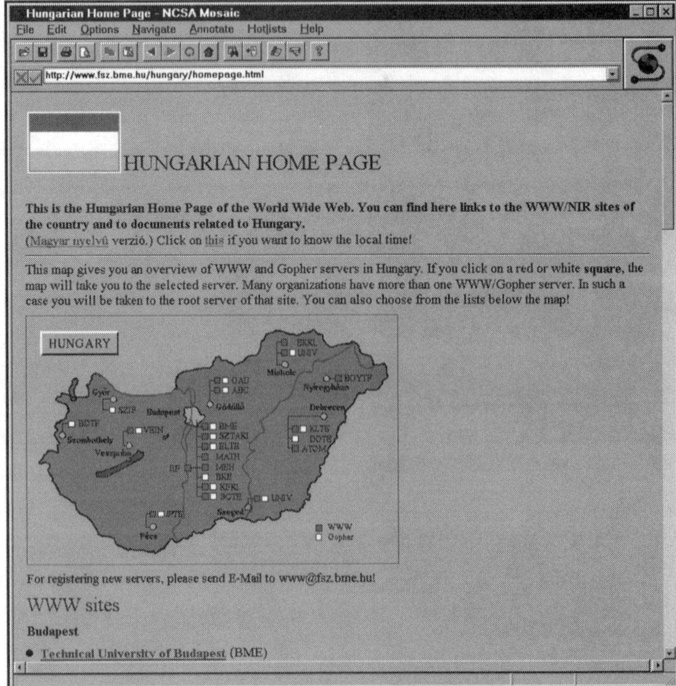

Figure 1.8.
Clickable map for Hungary.

We also find the home page for the Department of Process Control at the Technical University of Budapest (shown in Figure 1.9) at `http://www.fsz.bme.hu/welcome.html`.

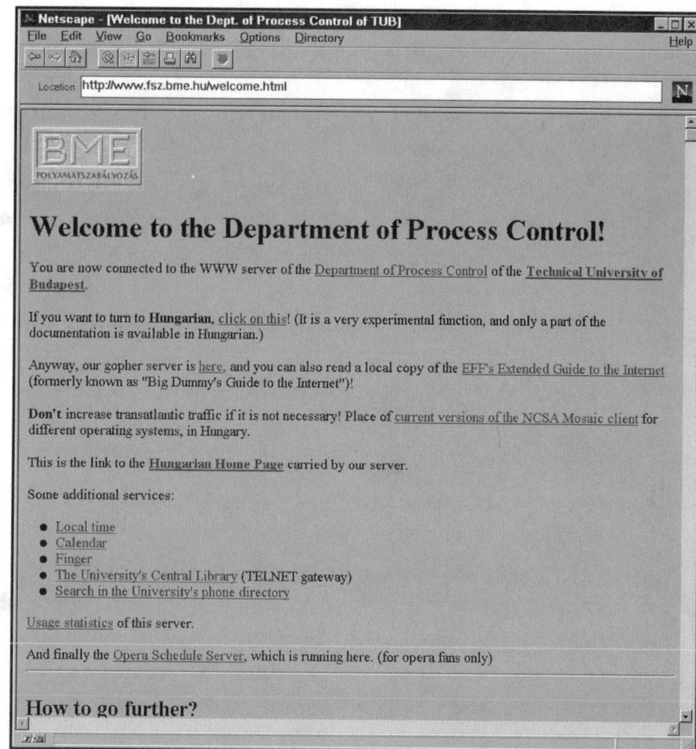

Figure 1.9.
Department of Process Control home page.

These pages are the work, in part at least, of Tamas Maray, who greets you now from his home country (see the following sidebar).

> **Welcome to Hungary!**
>
> This small East European country has been connected to the Internet since 1991, and the first few Hungarian WWW servers are already available to you! So, welcome to the Hungarian Home Page of the World Wide Web, which is carried by the WWW server of the Process Control Department of the Technical University of Budapest (`http://www.fsz.bme.hu/welcome.html`). This server was set up at the end of 1993, among the first in Hungary.
>
> *continues*

At present, there are almost 4,000 computers connected to the Internet in Hungary. Most of the users are from the academic field—researchers, professors, students, and so on—although commercial users have also started to appear. With the required infrastructure in place, the popularity and use of Internet is growing fast. At the moment, WWW technology is very new on the Hungarian Net. The first two WWW servers were launched in 1993, although some new servers have appeared since then.

On the Hungarian home page (`http://www.fsz.bme.hu/hungary/homepage.html`), you will find the (probably) complete list of all the important Hungarian public services available through Internet, such as the WWW and Gopher servers, databases through telnet, and so on. Beyond that, you can retrieve information and data about Hungary, Budapest, and the Technical University of Budapest, and you can reach the Opera Schedule Server (`http://www.fsz.bme.hu/opera/main.html`), which is very popular among classical music lover users of the Internet.

In the future, we would like to improve the database of our server to increase the multimedia information about Hungary and Budapest. We also want to create pages for the Budapest World Expo in 1996. Spreading the WWW culture in Hungary is something we consider to be very important.

Our Web project—supported by the Process Control Department of the Technical University of Budapest—is based on the work of three persons, although we want to draw more people into the project and we want to apply for external support as well. All three of us—Janos Mohacsi, Imre Szeberenyi and I—as young researchers and professors of the University's Faculty of Electrical Engineering and Informatics, are among the first keen users of the Internet in Hungary, and we are doing our best to initiate and spread the wonderful WWW technology in this country.

See you on our server,

Tamas Maray

Example 1.8: Sardinia

Finally in Europe, somewhat out of our way geographically but certainly not on the Net, we come to the island of Sardinia. Here is another burst of somewhat unexpected Internet activity, including some graphically gorgeous work such as the Sardinian history page shown in Figure 1.10 (`http://www.crs4.it/~zip/sardegna.html`).

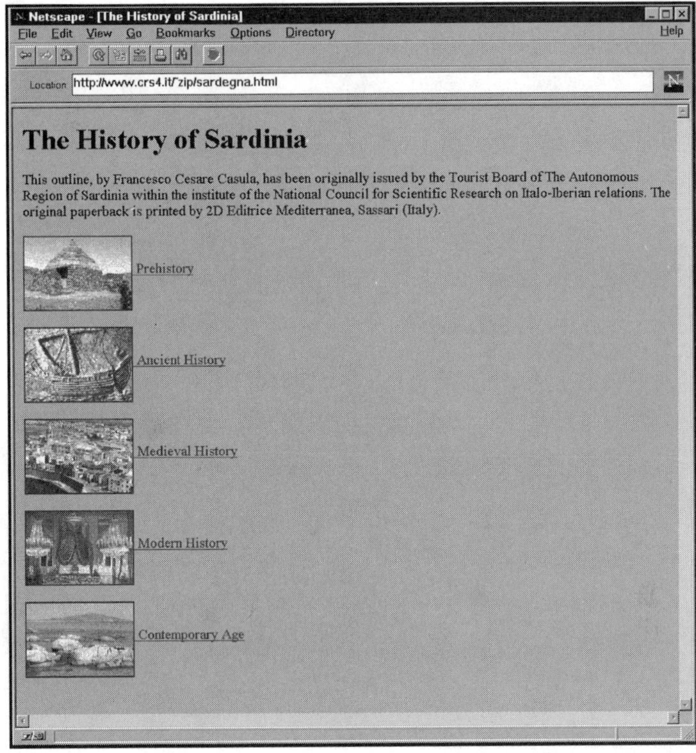

Figure 1.10.
Sardinia—information page on Sardinian history.

Now for something extra special. Pietro Zanarini, Head of Scientific Visualization Group at the Centre for Advanced Studies, Research and Development in Sardinia (CRS4), has prepared not just a welcome message, but an entire welcome page on the World Wide Web! The page is located at `http://www.crs4.it/~zip/sardinia/welcome.html`, and it offers links to all kinds of other Sardinian information. Figure 1.11 shows this page, complete with its attractive graphics.

Here's the message that informed me of the page's existence (see the following sidebar):

> Hi Neil,
>
> I apologize for giving you the CRS4 "Welcome message" after a week, but I worked on it a while, and now I'm quite satisfied. But, of course, you (and your readers) have to like it, so please don't hesitate to give me any kind of feedback.
>
> *Pietro*

Not much problem there, I'd venture to say.

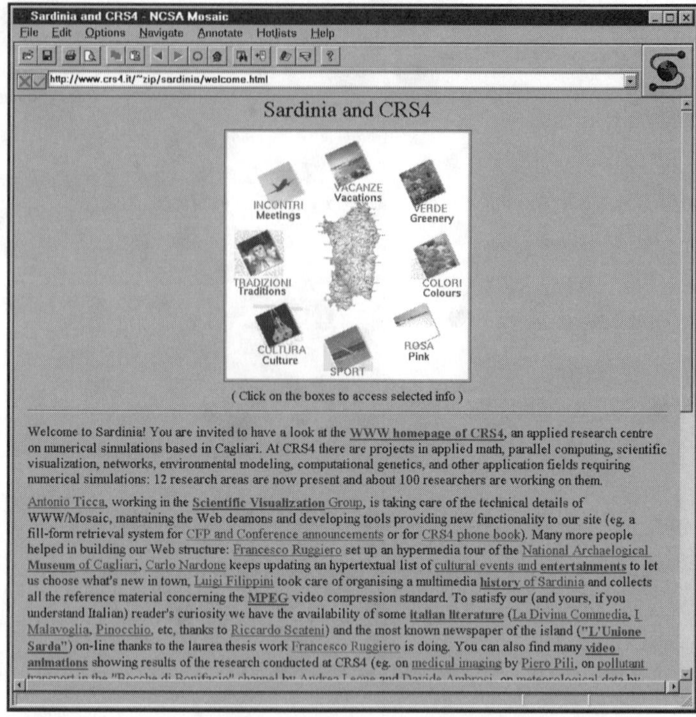

Figure 1.11.
Pietro Zanarini's special welcome page.

The Middle East

Yeah, I know the Middle East is part of Asia, and not a separate continent on its own, but it seems only natural to treat it separately. Partly that's because of the seemingly constant world focus on the area, and partly it's because Internet sites have begun to appear with some frequency. In either case, the Middle East is well worth paying attention to. The other reason is that we'll touch down in Australia later in this book, so that continent won't be featured here.

Example 1.9: Israel

First stop, Israel. Among the more interesting sites here are the Gopher servers shown in Figure 1.12 (`israel-info.gov.il` or `jerusalem1.datasrv.co.il`). From these selections, you could get detailed information about the Arab–Israeli peace process, the Hebron tragedy, and almost anything else you want to know. There are also links to Jewish Internet sites in other parts of the world.

Also in Israel we find the Weizmann Institute of Science World Wide Web site (see Figure 1.13). WISDOM, as this site is creatively called, offers information about the Institute and links to other Israeli Internet locations. Its World Wide Web address is `http://www.wisdom.weizmann.ac.il`.

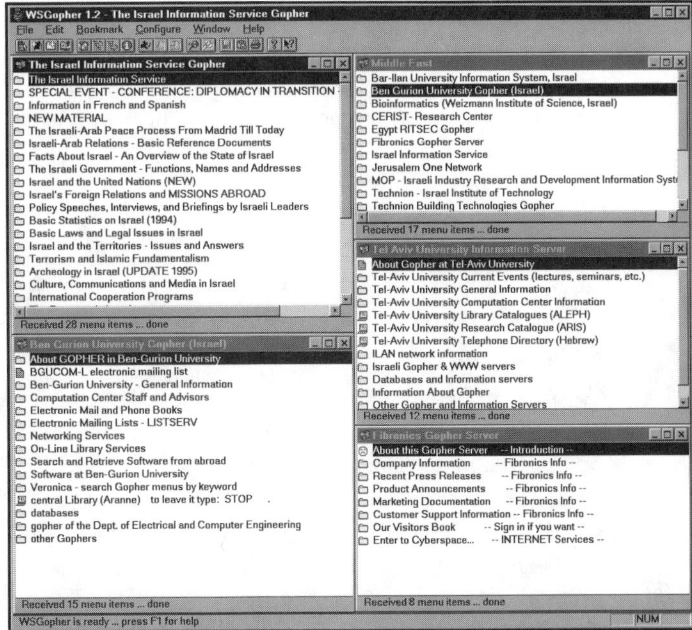

Figure 1.12.
Several Israeli Gopher menus.

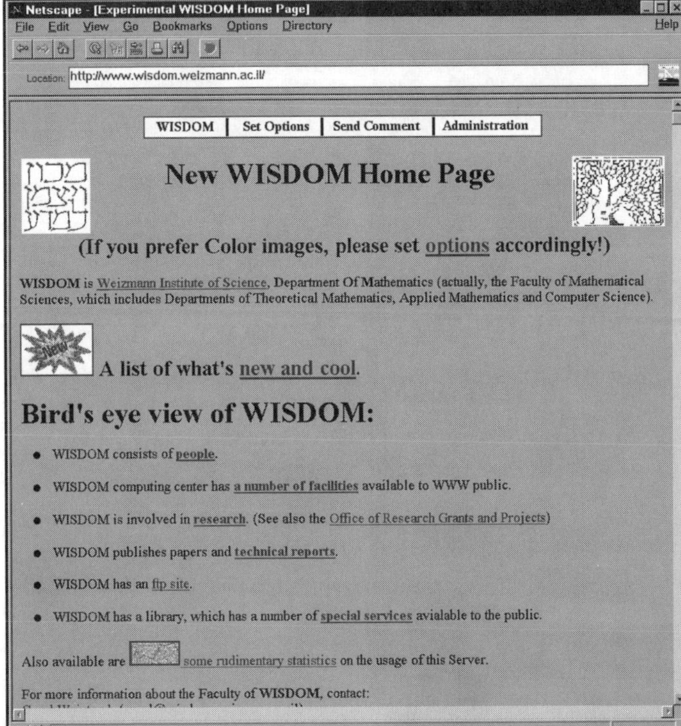

Figure 1.13.
Weizmann Institute of Science page.

Time for another pause—this time to meet Shimon Edelman. Dr. Edelman is Senior Researcher in the Department of Applied Mathematics and Computer Science at the Weizmann Institute. He was the designer of the original WISDOM page (still available at `http://eris.wisdom.weizmann.ac.il/`), and he has prepared the following greeting (see the following sidebar).

> My home page represents a minimal attempt to facilitate access to the information I have to offer over the Net (mainly my FTP archive, and some teaching-related material), by making it both easy and fun. Serious improvements to the looks and to the contents are expected when I finally have the time for this (following my retirement, in a few decades).
>
> My home organization, the Weizmann Institute of Science, was founded in 1934 by Dr. Chaim Weizmann, a distinguished researcher in organic chemistry, and a brilliant politician, who made important contributions to the Zionist cause, and later became the first president of the newly established State of Israel. The Weizmann Institute is devoted to basic research in a wide range of disciplines, from molecular biology and biochemistry to mathematics and environmental sciences. The Institute, along with the six other Israeli universities and a rapidly increasing number of high-tech industrial enterprises, benefits from the instant global communications service provided by the Internet. All my colleagues here use e-mail, and many of us rely on the Net for regular exchange of data with collaborators all over the world.
>
> As to my home country, you may be able to find information on Israel on the Net, but you have to come over and see it to believe it.
>
> *Shimon Edelman*

Example 1.10: Turkey

Leaving Israel, we head northward to Turkey. Ankara, specifically, or at least nearby. This time it's the Middle East Technical University, whose home page, shown in Figure 1.14 (`http://www.metu.edu.tr/METU/MetuHome.html`), points to a substantial archive of material about the institution and its programs.

Here's another hello, this time from Erdal Taner, Information Service Manager at METU. As the Internet would have it, this message appeared exactly as I was finishing off this chapter. Excellent timing, wouldn't you say? (See the following sidebar.)

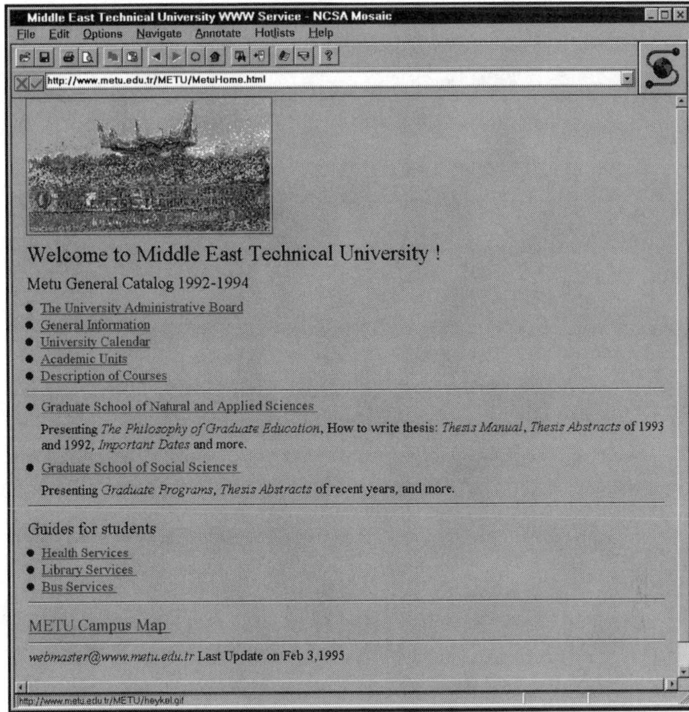

Figure 1.14.
Middle East Technical University, Turkey.

Founded in 1956, Middle East Technical University (METU) is a university campus located seven kilometers west of Ankara. The Campus, located on 11,000 acres of forested land that includes Lake Eymir, has 350,000 square meters of floor space. The campus has been forested entirely throught the efforts of University employees and students since the early 1960s. METU has more than 43,000 graduates and now serves about 20,000 students from all parts of the world.

METU Campus Network (METU-NET) is composed of a fiber-optic 16 Mbit Campus backbone network with departmental LANs tied to the backbone. The METU Computer Center operates both the METU-NET and the national/international connections. It is, in fact, the Internet international gateway for Turkey. The TCP/IP protocol is the common protocol on the METU-NET, making it possible for Internet to be accessed throughout the Campus. For student use, there are five fully LANed PC labs—PCs equipped with necessary software to use all the possible Internet services (telnet, FTP, SMTP, FSP, Gopher, WWW, WAIS, and so on).

continues

As Internet services have become quite common on the campus, some information services have been initiated. The main services for METU (such as METU Archive, METU Home Gopher, and METU WWW Home) are maintained by the Computer Center. The idea of having a Campus Wide Information System in METU-NET has resulted in building such a system on the popular Internet Information Retrieval tools. WWW is the core of the METU-CWIS, and a Gopher server is also being used to facilitate a number of Gopher gateways. In addition, WAIS is used to create a searchable index over some parts of information in the METU WWW Server.

If you want to find more information about METU, point your URL to the `http://www.metu.edu.tr/`.

As the home page shows, it also looks like an excellent campus to visit for real.

Asia

Asia has been a bit late coming to the Internet, but the progress is strong. Here you'll visit a very few sites, but together they'll offer an idea of the kind of activity now occurring.

Example 1.11: Sri Lanka

Our first stop is at Sri Lanka (see Figure 1.15). Actually, this Web site is situated at Stanford University, not on the island at all (`http://suif.stanford.edu/~saman/lanka/sri_lanka.html`), but it offers a look at what the Internet promises for the future in Sri Lanka, and even at this stage it contains a solid amount of information about life in that part of the world.

Example 1.12: Malaysia

Almost due east of Sri Lanka is Malaysia, the long, narrow land mass jutting into Indonesia. Here you find the WWW home page for the Universiti Sains Malaysia (see Figure 1.16), which offers links to information about Penang Island, where this university stands (`http://www.cs.usm.my`).

And, once again, we have a welcome message, this time from the truly lovely Penang Island. Let's hear what Vincent Gregory, Systems Analyst in the Computer Aided Translation Unit, has to say to us (see the following sidebar).

1

Figure 1.15.
Sri Lanka home page, with information on reaching Sri Lankans.

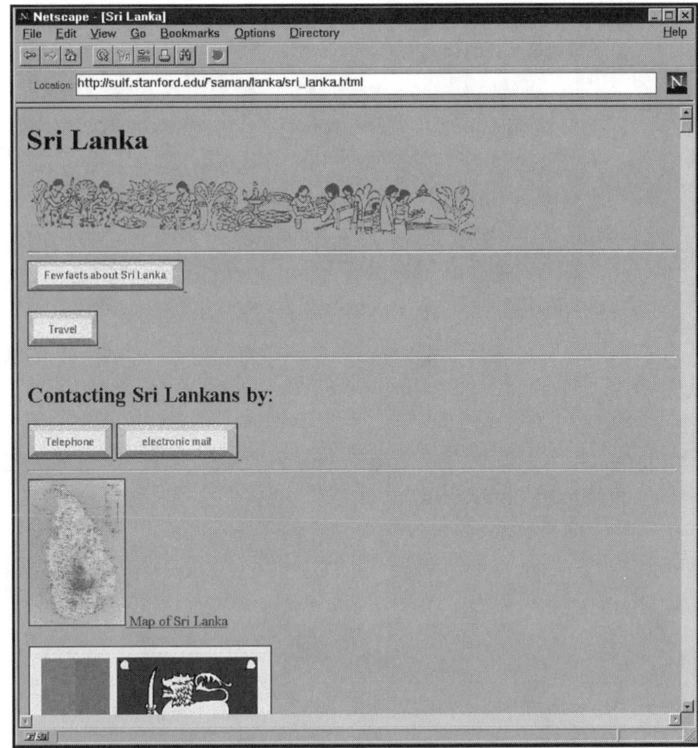

Welcome to Universiti Sains Malaysia (USM), Penang WWW server. The Web server project at USM was initiated by Vincent Gregory and put together by staff at the Computer Aided Translation Unit. The server provides information about the university (details of history, administration, research, and so on), about Penang Island (ideal for tourists), and also links to other Web servers in Malaysia.

Malaysians enjoy Internet connectivity via the local JARING (Joint Advanced Research Integrated Networking) network. The original name of JARING was "Rangkom"—a pilot.

The UUCP-based computer networking project was started by MIMOS (Malaysian Institute of Microelectronic Systems), a government R&D body, at the end of 1986. Full Internet connectivity was established in 1990 with a 64K satellite link to NSFnet in USA. Within the country 64K lines link the various states together with plans for future upgrade to 128K lines.

continues

> Internet connectivity is provided to both private and public organizations plus home users. All universities and major organizations are connected to the network.
>
> Penang Island (the Pearl of the Orient) is located on the northwest of Malaysia and is a popular tourist destination. Information on the Island, tourist attractions, food, culture, languages, maps, pictures, and so on, can be found on the Web server. The information on this server is updated regularly and any comments, feedback, or requests are appreciated.
>
> *N. Vincent Gregory*

If you ask me, it sounds like a must-visit—both virtually and, someday, physically.

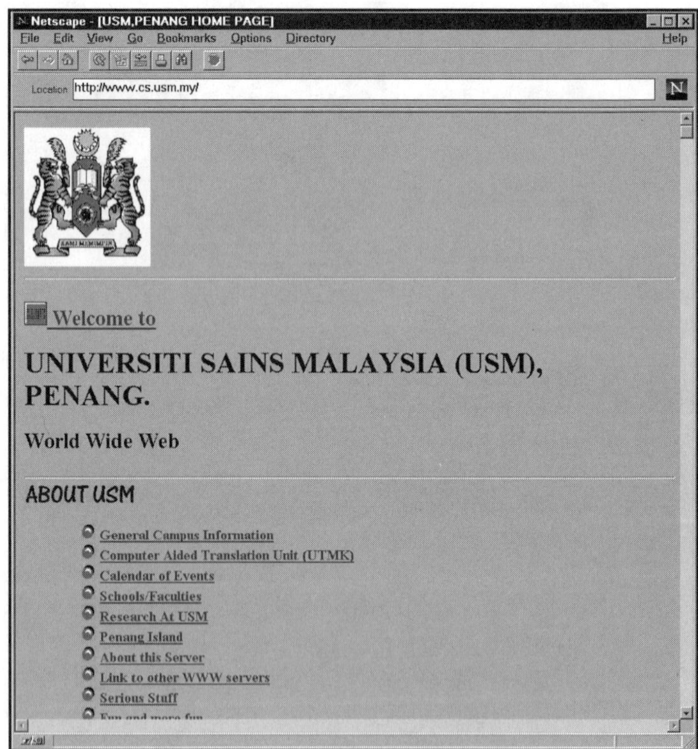

Figure 1.16.
USM Penang home page.

Example 1.13: Japan

Our last stop in Asia is Japan. First we'll take a look at the Japanese clickable map (see Figure 1.17) as a demonstration of how far Internet access has come in this nation, despite a very late start (`http://www.ntt.jp/japan/map/`).

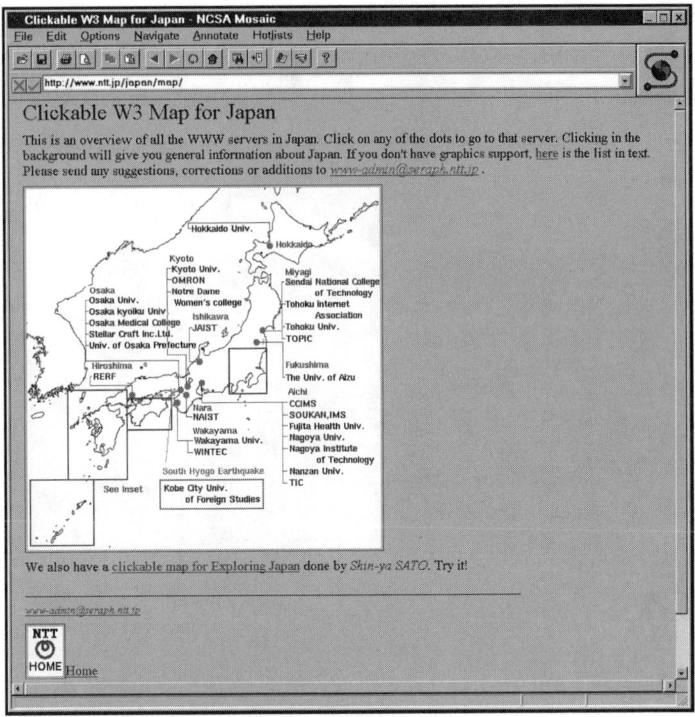

Figure 1.17.
Clickable map of the Japanese islands.

You'll visit Japan a few times during the course of this book. For now, let's head to Tokyo, where Figure 1.18 shows the Tokyo Netsurfing Association's main page (`http://www.eccosys.com/index.html`). One of those responsible for the creation of this innovative page is Joichi Ito, who has also stopped by to say hello (see the following sidebar).

> Hi!
>
> Thank you for accessing Tomigaya. Tomigaya is the name of the district in Tokyo where my HTTP server and I live. Tomigaya is run by the Tokyo Netsurfing Association, a loosely organized group of hackers, musicians, artists, night club promoters, and video gamers. The Tokyo Netsurfing Association is sponsored by Eccosys, Ltd., a virtual company that focuses on Internet evangelical work helping companies set up systems based on ideas that emerge as we hack Tomigaya.
>
> *continues*

Tomigaya is one of the few sites in Japan where artists and young people not working in a research environment can hack Web pages and develop Internet software. Hopefully, the number of cottage IPs will increase over the next year and we'll have more company.

The Internet is just beginning to emerge in Japan. Currently only ATT JENS and IIJ provide commercial Internet service. This number should increase dramatically over the next year. There is still no CIX equivalent in Japan, so University and non-commercial research traffic has to travel all the way to the CIX in the United States to get through to commercial Japanese sites. Bad news for Japanese academics trying to access Tomigaya.

We get our service from PSI Japan, which is setting up in Japan as I write this message.

Hopefully the penetration of the Internet will be another black ship to open the doors of the Japanese information and entertainment industry, as Admiral Perry's black ship opened trade to Japan. Expect to see a lot more stuff from Japan on the Internet soon!

Joi

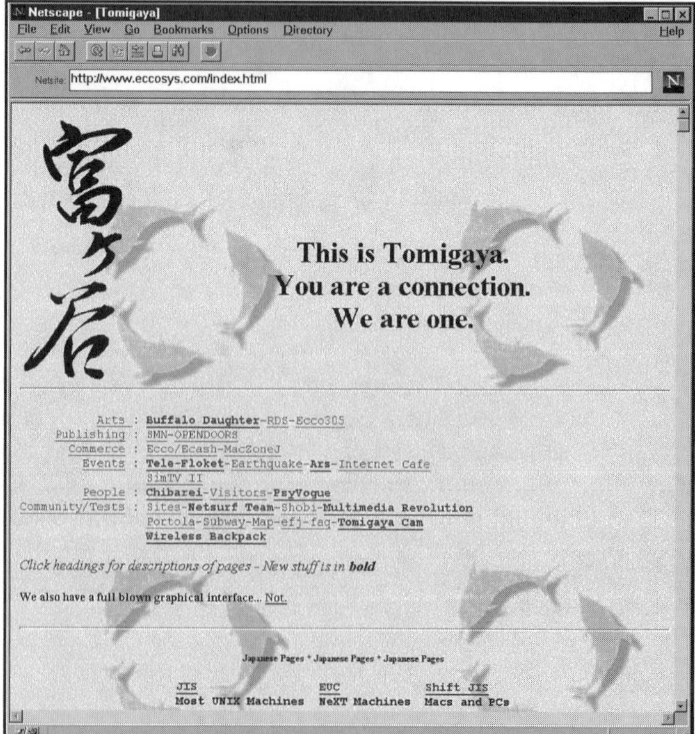

Figure 1.18.
Tomigaya home page.

South America

Across the Pacific lies South America, where Internet access has started slowly but is now well on its way. The continent's largest country, Brazil, also boasts the strongest Net access, but we'll bypass this center in favor of two smaller nations.

Example 1.14: Chile

Entering South America from the southwest, we arrive first in Chile. Figure 1.19 (`http://www.dcc.uchile.cl`) gives you a glimpse of the colorful home page of the Universidad de Chile, particularly its Computer Science department. Here we have links to other Chilean servers, the vast majority of which, at this stage, are Gopher sites.

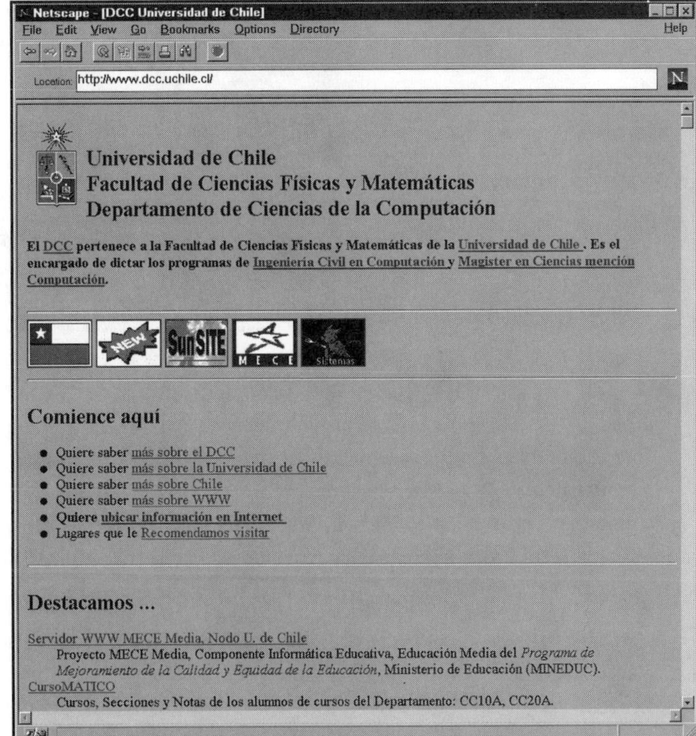

Figure 1.19.
Universidad de Chile WWW page.

Example 1.15: Peru

Peru is a fairly recent addition to the Internet, and the Peruvian Web site shown in Figure 1.20 (`http://www.rcp.net.pe/rcp.html`) provides links to the small but growing number of other Internet sites in Peru. The clickable imagemap at the top of the page is very nicely done, although it does look a bit like a scene from a fantasy role-playing game.

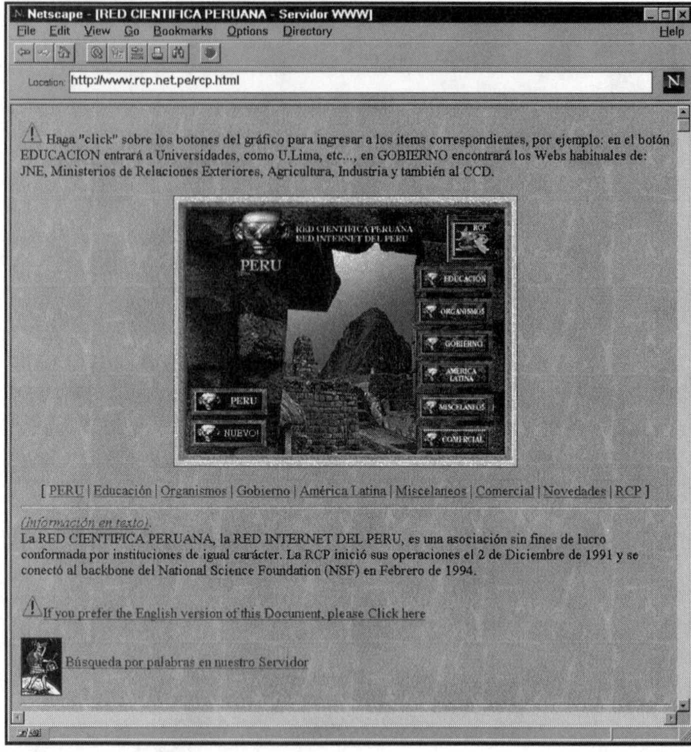

Figure 1.20.
The first Peruvian WWW site.

Back in North America

You're back where you started, in the U.S.A. What better place to tour than a Web page featuring the country's best-known dwelling? Figure 1.21 (`http://www.whitehouse.gov/White_House/Mail/html/Mail_President.html`) offers a fill-in form that enables you to send e-mail to the White House. Further down the form, you can select the subject matter of your comment, the capacity in which you're sending it, and so on.

And, finally, you can visit the Internet Society, the international organization for Internet activities and technologies (See Figure 1.22). Vint Cerf, often called the father of the Internet, is featured on the home page, and if you want, you can join the society and get yourself a card to carry in your wallet. Look carefully, and you might even find a job you're interested in.

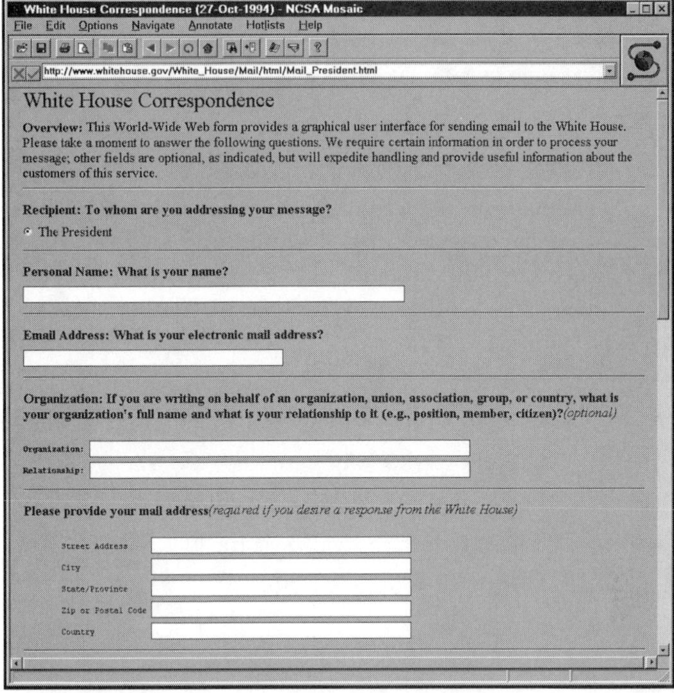

Figure 1.21.
Corresponding with the White House via World Wide Web fill-in forms.

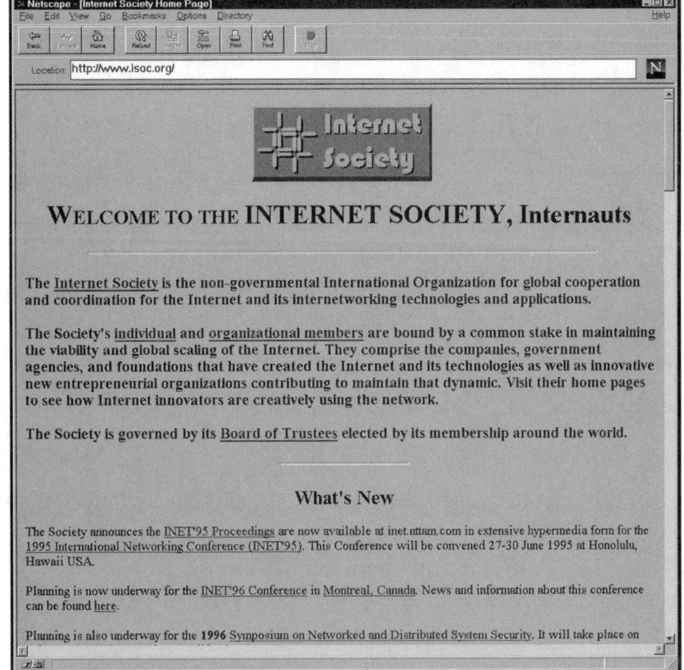

Figure 1.22.
Home page of the Internet Society, with details about events, conferences, and issues surrounding the Net.

Summary

The prerequisite has offered an overview of the Internet. As you enter Day 1 of your exploration of the Net, much of this information is worth carrying with you. You'll find out very quickly that the Internet's global, yet uncentralized structure, offers both advantages and difficulties, and why it's necessary to "master" the Net at all. The Internet is vast and challenging, all because of the way it has been developed over the years, and learning it well demands concentration and effort. But the rewards are endless, and increasing all the time. One thing's for certain: You'll never, ever regret it.

Task Review

In this chapter, you learned how to perform the following tasks:

- ☐ Get an overview of the Internet as a whole
- ☐ Learn what people do on the Internet
- ☐ Take a tour of the world via the Net
- ☐ Learn a bit about the history of the Net

Q&A

Q Who's in charge of the Internet?

A Great question, with only one answer—no one. It's true that, until recently, the U.S.'s National Science Foundation subsidized many of the high-speed links among the supercomputers that form the "backbone" of the Net. It's also true that the U.S.'s Advanced Research Projects Agency (ARPA) performed the same kind of service before NSF involvement. But even those organizations couldn't be termed "in charge" of the Internet. The Net is global, it has no controlling computer, and it has a series of infrastructures that are truly beyond the mandate of any single organization. This is very difficult to understand for almost everyone, but it's a fact. That's why attempts by the U.S. Congress and other national governments to restrict Internet activity is so ironic: users in Spain communicating with users in Australia really don't care what Washington has to say.

Q I read in a magazine that the new Microsoft Network will make the Internet obsolete. Any truth to this?

A No. MSN (the Microsoft Network) promises to be a very good online service, but it has a long way to go to match CompuServe or America Online, let alone the Net. In fact, the battle among the commercial services is much more interesting than the battle between the Internet and anything else, especially since all three services (and Prodigy as well) offer full access to the Net. In other words, MSN is

another network joined to the Internet (albeit a potentially very large one), not a threat to the Internet's existence. There's also no proof, as yet, that Microsoft can actually deliver on a consistently excellent online service. They don't have much experience in that area.

Q I keep hearing and reading that the Internet is basically a huge collection of pornography. Is that really true?

A No, it's not. Not at all. Pornography certainly exists on the Internet, but aside from a few well publicized newsgroups, it's quite difficult to find. Proportionately, in fact, there's much, much less pornography on the Internet than in most magazine stores. What you're hearing is what the media want you to hear: they need stories that sell magazines and newspapers, and while the Internet by itself is hot news, the Internet as a bad thing is even hotter. That's the real story behind the famous *Time* magazine "Cyberporn" cover feature of 1995, which was based on a study that has been roundly denounced by a host of researchers. But no amount of refutation could possibly undo the damage done by a magazine as widely distributed as *Time*, and it remains to be seen how that issue will affect the Internet as a whole. Certainly it's lent considerable strength to those in favor of the U.S.'s Communications Decency Act and other legislation like it, and that can't possibly mean good things for the vast majority of users.

Extra Credit

Some people—me, for instance—like to know where their technologies came from. Your first extra credit section, therefore, takes you through the Internet's history.

So Where Did the Internet Come From, Anyway?

Although the Internet has only recently been making headlines, it's been in existence—in one form or another—for over two decades. The following short history offers a bit of background that will help you understand some of its strengths, weaknesses, and idiosyncrasies.

ARPANET: There's This Nuclear Problem, See...

The Internet began as the ARPANET, back in early 1969. Funded by the U.S. Advanced Research Projects Agency (ARPA, hence the name), ARPANET was designed to let researchers communicate and share information with each other. Also high in the design goals was this: the network should be able to survive even if part of it was physically destroyed.

This was 1969, remember, and the threat of nuclear attack was still on everyone's mind.

Basically, then, the idea was this: build a network for researchers around the United States to use in their day-to-day activities and, in the process, make sure that blowing up a machine in one location doesn't stop the network from functioning.

Four ARPANET sites were established as test locations: the University of Utah, the Stanford Research Institute, and two University of California sites, Santa Barbara and Los Angeles. In September 1969, the ARPANET was switched on. Compared with the coverage of Woodstock and the first moon landing only a few weeks before this, the new network didn't get a whole lot of press. Who cared?

A few years later, many people did. Over a thousand people watched ARPANET's first public demonstration in the fall of 1972, and that, effectively, is when the whole idea of a national—even international—network began to take hold. Everyone started developing reasons why they needed to be part of it, and what such a network could do for them. This isn't to say, mind you, that ARPANET was ever implemented with this goal in mind. From its beginnings, it was apparently designed to be small, with only a few key research sites participating.

Two Major Technologies: Breaking Up is Easy To Do

If there were two single technical decisions that allowed the network to function at all, it was the development of packet-switching technology and the design of TCP/IP.

Packet-switching makes it possible for data from different machines to share common transmission lines. Without it, dedicated lines linking one computer directly to another would be necessary, or at least preferred. With it in place, the network could be built with lines linking node to node (that is, one machine or network to another machine or network), with data routed through the nodes depending on its origin and destination.

Essentially, packet-switching technology breaks data down into little *packets*, each with a code showing its destination and instructions for putting the packets back together again. The packets move individually through the network, joining up again when they all reach the destination. It's a bit like the days when hitchhiking was still considered a safe practice. If four of you were trying to hitchhike somewhere, it wasn't likely you'd get a ride. Instead, you'd split up, each find your own ride, and agree to meet at a specific place. In effect, you were being packet-switched without knowing it.

TCP/IP means Transmission Control Protocol/Internet Protocol, but it's doubtful you'll ever need to know that. You'll need to remember the initials, however, because any computer that hooks onto the Internet must make use of TCP/IP. This technology, developed in the mid-70s, provides the standard means by which computers can talk to each other. Just like

social protocol with its rules that everyone adheres to (you don't tell your boss's husband that his suit would look better on someone who weighed considerably less), computer protocol establishes procedures to allow effective communication to take place. TCP/IP became and remains the standard, and it allows the Internet's connectivity to happen.

NSFNET and NREN: A Plot for Breeding Acronyms?

ARPANET lasted until 1990. In the meantime, it had been split into two networks. MILNET handled military affairs, while ARPANET carried data for research into networking and other fields. Universities scrambled to join, and the networks began to attract non-scientists and non-technologists as well. In the mid-80s, the National Science Foundation linked six U.S. supercomputer centers in a network called (not surprisingly) NSFNET, with data speeds increased from 56,000 bits per second (your modem probably runs at 9600 bps or 14.4 kbps, by comparison) to 1.5 mbps. This type of connection, called T-1, remains in place, but in 1990, the T-3 specification was introduced, allowing connection speeds of 45 mbps. (Anyone still working with a 2400 bps modem may want to stop reading for a few minutes and calmly smash the thing to bits.)

In the late '80s, the NSF turned the funding and management of NSFNET over to the a nonprofit group of universities called the Michigan Educational Research Information Triad (MERIT). MERIT worked with MCI and IBM on expanding and improving high-speed national access, and eventually the three organizations formed Advanced Network Services (ANS), created to run NSFNET. This was important: the NSF had established an *acceptable-use policy* (called AUP, naturally) that allowed no commercial access to NSFNET, but now corporations were beginning to get involved. The look of the network was starting to change.

By 1990, NSFNET had taken over from ARPANET, and the latter was discontinued. In 1991, President George Bush signed the High Performance Computing Act, which essentially established a new network, the National Research and Education Network (NREN). NREN was to use NSFNET as its basis (initials getting to you yet?), and ironically has some research goals similar to those of the original ARPANET. Importantly, however, NREN was specifically established to join governmental and commercial organizations, which means that NSFNET's non-commercial policy is, for the most part, gone.

Other Networks: Because It Was Time

While all this was going on, there were other organizations interested in global networking. The Computer Science Network (CSNET) was established by the NSF to help universities that couldn't access NSFNET get onto what was slowly coming to be called the Internet. The only tool this new network could use, however, was electronic mail, so it had its limitations. Enter another new network, BITNET. This one was created "because it's time," (B-I-T—get it?), offering e-mail, mailing lists, file transfer capabilities, and other

options. Unfortunately, BITNET didn't use TCP/IP, so it had to develop another way of sharing information with NSFNET.

Eventually, BITNET and CSNET realized they were trying to do much the same thing (that is, connect to NSFNET), so they formed the Corporation for Research and Educational Networking (CREN). As they complete their merge—the technical difficulties are considerable—they also will be working to integrate more completely with NREN. Now, if CREN and NREN ever get together completely, we can only assume they'll change the name to WREN. Then it'll really fly (sorry).

Not to be outdone, of course, other parts of the world decided to hook into the emerging network. Canada established CA*NET and NETNORTH, the former corresponding roughly with NSFNET and the latter with BITNET. European networks began to form as well, with EARN and EUNet being the primary examples. With South America, the Middle East, Australia, and the Pacific Rim taking an active interest in the Internet, it's only a matter of time until more nationally- and continentally-based networks join in. The term *Internet* originally referred to ARPA's experiments in internetworking, but it's quickly becoming the abbreviation for international networking (popularly, at least, if not officially).

2

DAY 1

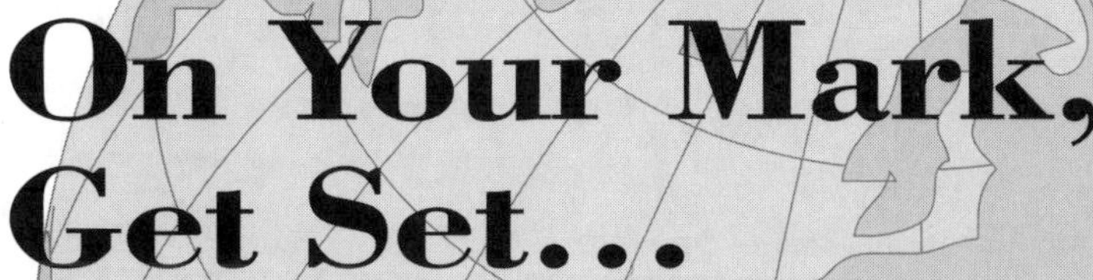

On Your Mark, Get Set...

Getting started on the Internet is much easier now than it was even a year ago. Internet *service providers*, companies who provide Internet access, are cropping up all over the country, while the traditional providers, universities and corporations, have tools at their disposal that make access much more user-friendly. In addition, the major online services—CompuServe, America Online, Prodigy, Delphi, and GEnie—are all beginning to offer full Internet access, and both IBM and Microsoft have created online networks that not only feature access to the Net, but which ship with the new versions of their operating systems (OS/2 Warp and Windows 95, respectively).

This chapter is a bit different from all the rest. Here, the goal is to get onto the Internet, only after which your actual tasks kick in. If you already have an Internet account, you can skip directly to Chapter 3, which covers some Internet basics and a few essential UNIX lessons. Even if you do have an account, you'll likely find something of interest here. Among other things, you might want to change your type of access to get better speed or quality, and several possibilities are covered.

Task List

In this chapter, you'll perform the following tasks:

- ☐ Determine the type of computer you need.
- ☐ Determine the type of Internet connection you need.
- ☐ Determine the service provider you wish to use.

Three Steps to Getting onto the Net

To connect to the Internet, you need the following three major items:

- ☐ A computer
- ☐ An account with an Internet service provider
- ☐ The right software

Depending on the type of connection, you might also need the following:

- ☐ A modem
- ☐ A dedicated line

That's it, really. As long as you have a computer, an account with an organization that provides Internet access, the appropriate software for your operating system, and a means of connecting your computer to your Internet account, you can be on the Net. The problem is, there's any number of ways to do all this. Sorting them out can be difficult, and getting the right kind of Internet access is important.

Step 1: Get a Computer and (Maybe) a Modem

You might already have a computer you're happy with: if that's the case, skip down to step 2, Choose an Internet Provider. If you don't have a machine, or if you're thinking of upgrading, here are some points to keep in mind.

2

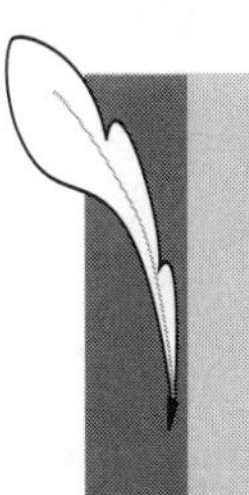

Note: For the sake of consistency throughout this book, I'll refer to the main computing platforms as PC, Macintosh (or Mac), UNIX, and OS/2.

- **PC**—A computer that runs some version of DOS and probably Microsoft Windows 3.1 or 3.11, or, recently, Windows 95. These were formally known as IBM-PCs or IBM-compatibles. Note that, although the same computers can run the OS/2 operating system, I'll refer to OS/2 machines as a separate category.
- **Macintosh**—A computer, usually manufactured by Apple Computer (but clones are beginning to appear), running the Macintosh operating system.
- **UNIX**—UNIX machines run the UNIX operating system, which is available in many different "flavors." Typically, these are significantly more expensive than PCs or Macs, and consequently are found in large organizations or technical firms. A PC or a Macintosh can run UNIX operating systems, but typically UNIX is run on more powerful workstations.
- **OS/2**—OS/2 is IBM's operating system for PCs. It runs on the same machines as those that run DOS and Windows, but because it is an entirely different operating system, I will refer to OS/2 separately.

- If you're connecting to the Internet through your organization, you probably won't have a choice of computer systems. You'll likely have one computer—PC, Macintosh, or UNIX—and it will probably be linked via local area network (LAN) to other computers in the organization.
- PCs outnumber all other computers. If you choose a PC, you'll have access to an enormous number of applications, utilities, games, and specialty items. Internet software, both commercial and free, is being developed for PCs at a faster rate than for any other platform. On the other hand, PCs are generally more difficult to configure than Macs, so this is a consideration if you don't like tinkering. Much of the configuration difficulties are disappearing with advanced software and, importantly, the Windows 95 operating system, but they remain an issue at least for now.

- Macintosh computers are famous for their ease of use, their ease of configuration, and, until recently, their overly high prices. Clones are now appearing, which should drive down the price, and a substantial amount of Internet software is available and under development. If you already have a Mac, there's no reason to change to a PC. On the other hand, if you don't have a computer and you're planning to base much of your computing activity on the Internet, you might well be better served by a PC, especially if your plan is to keep up with all the latest Internet software releases. The Mac is more powerful than the PC in several important application areas, but the Internet isn't one of them.
- OS/2 can be installed on a PC alongside DOS and Windows (and even Windows 95 with some work), so it's not really an issue of choosing OS/2 over another system. Still, the OS/2 operating system requires a powerful computer with a lot of memory and hard disk space, so it requires a commitment if you want to use it regularly. The system comes stocked with solid Internet software, however, including full Internet access to the IBM Network, so it's an excellent choice for many novice Internetters. Unfortunately, despite OS/2's technological excellence, software developers are *not* producing many OS/2 applications. This is something you *must* keep in mind as you decide which computer and operating system you want to use.
- UNIX is, in many respects, the operating system that underlies the Internet. It is rich, powerful, and endlessly configurable, but it is also complex and, for many, intimidating. Learning some UNIX is essential to complete mastery of the Internet, but you don't need to own a UNIX machine to do this. In fact, it's unlikely you'll ever actually go out and *buy* a UNIX box (as they're called), because they're expensive, somewhat difficult, and unsuited for standard computer tasks, such as word processing, spreadsheeting, and game playing. If your organization places a UNIX machine on your desk, however, don't turn it down, especially if it's capable of running the popular graphical interface X Window. Many important Internet applications begin their lives as X Window applications, and having such a machine takes you to the heart of Internet development.
- No matter which platform you intend to use, you want a computer with a lot of memory, a lot of hard disk space, the fastest processor, and the largest and clearest monitor you can find. If your machine contains less than 8 megabytes of memory (RAM), it simply won't do very much, and if your hard disk is smaller than 240 megabytes, consider upgrading immediately (and get 500 megabytes while you're at it). OS/2, Windows 95, and Macintosh System 7.5 run best with at least 12 megabytes RAM, and UNIX typically needs much more. Applications take far more disk space than they used to, and you'll be downloading many of them—as well as graphics, sound, video, and text files—as you explore the Net. As far as the monitor goes—well, it's the visual interface between you and Internet, and you'll

find yourself staring at it for hours at a time. Lousy monitors can hurt your eyes or, worse, weaken your vision.

- Modems are necessary for many types of Internet access (see the section, "Methods of Access," later in this chapter). If you're connecting through a UNIX shell account (see the section, "Indirect Access," later in this chapter), you can get reasonable results from your trusty old 2400 bps modem, but for anything else, you should consider 14,400 bps (often called 14.4 kpbs) the minimum. Increasingly, Internet providers are offering 28,800 bps (28.8 kbps) connections, and because of the multimedia developments of the Internet, this is far preferable. Expect to pay $30 to $40 for a 2400 modem, $90 to $100 for a 14.4, and $250 to $400 for a 28.8. Many good brand names (such as Hayes, U.S. Robotics, Zoom, Practical Peripherals, Supra, and so on) are available, and you really do get what you pay for. Don't cheap out on the modem because it's the single most important item in the connection.

Step 2: Choose an Internet Provider

You can't just buy a cable for your computer and hook up to the Internet. The Net is designed so that access is available through regional providers, who usually turn that function over to local providers. Essentially, it works like this: you establish an account with a local provider, who in turn is connected to a regional provider, who in turn is connected (maybe a stage or two later) to the "backbone" of supercomputers that are connected together via ultra high-speed access.

As the Internet has increased in popularity, software manufacturers have included Internet access with their packages. Netmanage's Chameleon, Spry's Internet in a Box, and Quarterdeck's Internet Suite all offer this kind of installation-based choice of providers, and so do packages such as Netscape Navigator Personal Edition. Since these packages were designed with the service providers' cooperation, access is reasonably easy, and if you don't have a provider you should consider starting with one of these. Often, the software becomes considerably harder to set up when you opt for a non-listed provider.

Methods of Access

Typically, you access the Internet through one of the following organizations:

- **Universities, Colleges, and Schools:** Most universities and colleges are hooked up to the Internet, as is an increasing number of high schools and even K–8 schools. If you attend one of these institutions (or work at one), contact your systems people about Internet access. Often, access from home is possible through the institution, as well.

- **Government Institutions**: Many institutions at all levels of government have good Internet access. Contact your systems people about getting hooked up. Often, access from home is possible through the institution as well.
- **Corporations and Small Businesses:** Access to the Internet has become increasingly important for corporations and smaller businesses. Check with your systems people to see if you have access. Often, access from home is possible through the institution, as well.
- **Local Service Providers:** If you have no other Internet access, or if you have work access but you want an account for personal activities, you can contact one of a growing number of local providers. You'll need a computer, a modem, and (usually) a credit card.
- **Bulletin Boards:** Local computer bulletin boards (BBSs) frequently offer Internet access. In most cases, this is limited access, but not always. Check with your BBS SYSOP (system operator) for details on the type of access available. BBSs usually charge much less than service providers. To connect to a BBS, you'll need a modem.
- **Commercial Online Services:** CompuServe, America Online, Prodigy, Delphi, and GEnie all offer Internet access. If you're already a member of one of these services, it is extremely easy (in most cases) to access the Net without doing anything special at all. In addition, the OS/2 Warp operating system ships with built-in connectivity to IBMNet, with full Internet access, and Windows 95 ships with built-in connectivity to the Microsoft Network, also with Internet access. But *beware*: while connections through these services are quite easy, it's often more expensive than through a dedicated Internet provider. Prodigy access to the World Wide Web, as just one example, can cost nearly $3.00 per hour, up to six to eight times as much as the hourly rate for a service provider. To connect to a commercial online service, you'll need a modem.

Types of Access

There are two essential types of Internet access. They go by a variety of names, but let's cut through everything and call them the following (even though there are variations of each):

- **Indirect Access:** This is the most common type of access. Your machine essentially is a terminal attached to a main computer (sometimes via a modem), which in turn has direct access to the Internet. Often, services and capabilities are restricted by the owner of the main computer.
- **Direct Access:** This is the most desirable type of access. Your computer is an individual node on the Internet, capable of doing whatever it's possible to do on the Net. Your machine has its own IP (Internet protocol) number, and you can establish it as an FTP, World Wide Web, Gopher, or telnet site, if you want.

> **Note:** As mentioned previously, there are other terms for type of access. Among the most common is *dial-up access*, in which you dial into a server through a modem, and *dedicated access*, in which your machine is hooked up to the Net through dedicated connection, such as a separate high-speed line. The problem is that the terms overlap. Some providers offer dial-up access that, through SLIP or PPP, essentially gives you dedicated access. Furthermore, your firm can have dedicated access, but through its local network you have what sometimes is called *terminal access*, meaning that your computer is just a terminal on the machine that is hooked up directly. I've used *direct* and *indirect* because they distinguish between being a node on the Net and being connected to a machine; that is, in turn, a node on the Net.

Indirect Access

If you're connecting to the Internet through a commercial, governmental, or educational institution, you likely already have indirect access. You'll know this as soon as you try to access a favorite newsgroup (newsgroups are covered in Chapter 5), which suddenly isn't available to you any more even though you know it's still operating.

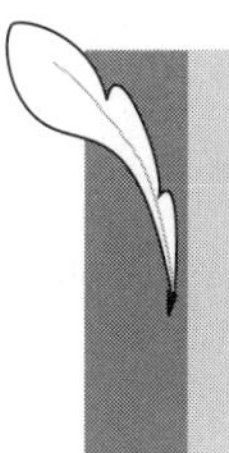

> **Note:** In many cases, this is reasonable: the owners of the main computer want you to work, not read irrelevant news or play addictive games, so they simply remove the temptation (it's their computer, remember). In other cases—many of them covered in the press—such restrictions are tantamount to blatant censorship; these are often referred to by euphemisms, such as institutional responsibility.

You may already have indirect access. If you're working for a large company, or if you're a student, staff, or faculty member at a university (or, increasingly, a K–12 school), check with your systems people to see what kind of access you have. Be persistent; sometimes systems people come up a bit short on the information-giving process, often because they're too busy putting out high-tech fires.

When you hook up to a host UNIX machine, you'll be opening a *shell* connection. This means, basically, that your computer is a terminal on that machine, and that you're using a UNIX shell as your main interface.

Despite the overwhelming trend towards direct access, UNIX shell connections remain common. Many Internet users either link to the Net through shell connections at work, or they dial in to a UNIX machine and enter the shell that way. With this type of connection, you'll have an account on the host machine, and you'll be allocated a limited amount of that system's resources (typically, a megabyte or so of hard disk space). That machine normally will be part of a local network (often through Ethernet), which in turn will be connected to the Internet.

You also can get indirect access through electronic bulletin boards (BBSs). Check out the local BBS scene by heading down to a good computer store, or find a locally produced computer newspaper. If you know college students, have them check the bulletin boards (the real ones, with all the thumbtacks and sublet notices, not the electronic ones); information is available here as well.

Warning: Access through these services is often partial. A BBS might offer e-mail capabilities, for example, or a combination of e-mail, newsgroups, and FTP. Rarely do they offer the full range of possibilities. Still, it's a good way to get started.

Direct Access

Direct Internet access means that your computer has access to all available Internet functions. Instead of being a terminal on a host, your computer is an individual node on the Internet. That means that you can establish yourself as an FTP, Gopher, World Wide Web, or Archie site, or anything else you want to be. Whether you want to do that depends on your needs, your computer's power, and the speed of your connection.

If your organization is directly connected to the Internet through a high-speed, dedicated line, you might be able to arrange direct access. This will be handled through your systems people. In most cases, your computer will already be part of an internal network (usually an Ethernet system), that in turn connects via high-speed line to the Internet.

Note that this is different from being simply a terminal on the main computer. Here, you're a separate machine, dependent on the main computers for such things as shared software and shared files, but fully capable of existing on your own. In the terminal-only type of connection, your machine is entirely dependent on the main computer's software (which is why these connections are often referred to as dumb terminals).

Warning: Although you may have all the tools in place for a direct Internet connection, don't think for a minute that it's an inalienable right. Many firms simply don't allow it, for all kinds of reasons. Sometimes it's security, sometimes it's lack of knowledge and/or lack of systems support (these connections consume technical resources), or sometimes it's a matter of them not knowing the benefits.

Another form of direct access is through SLIP or PPP connections. *SLIP* (Serial Line Internet Protocol) is the most common PC or Microsoft Windows connection, while *PPP* (Point to Point Protocol) is common to the Macintosh (but they're not respectively restricted).

SLIP and PPP enable you to essentially directly access the Internet through a modem. You're still dependent on a host computer, however, which itself has direct, high-speed Internet access.

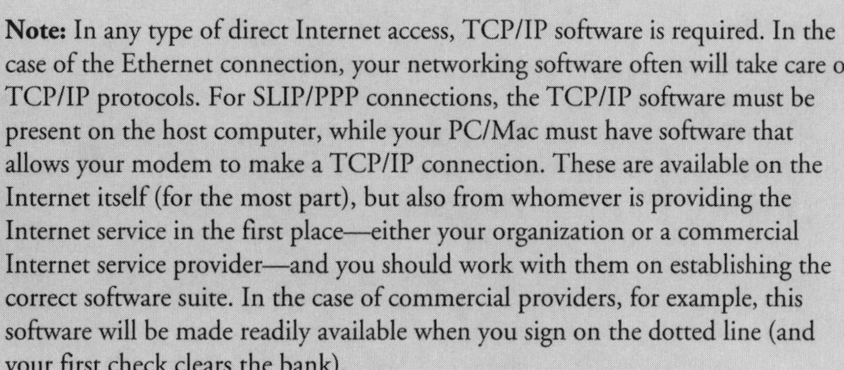

Note: In any type of direct Internet access, TCP/IP software is required. In the case of the Ethernet connection, your networking software often will take care of TCP/IP protocols. For SLIP/PPP connections, the TCP/IP software must be present on the host computer, while your PC/Mac must have software that allows your modem to make a TCP/IP connection. These are available on the Internet itself (for the most part), but also from whomever is providing the Internet service in the first place—either your organization or a commercial Internet service provider—and you should work with them on establishing the correct software suite. In the case of commercial providers, for example, this software will be made readily available when you sign on the dotted line (and your first check clears the bank).

SLIP/PPP connections have the following two major disadvantages:

- They're slow, because they rely completely on the speed of your modem. Don't even bother connecting at less than 9600 bps; 14.4 kbps should be your minimum consideration.
- You're not always connected to the Internet. When you shut down the modem connection, you're off the Net. So make sure you don't establish yourself as an important Gopher, FTP, or WWW site, because unless you leave your modem on all the time (and remember that costs are usually associated with the number of connect-time hours), you won't be accessible.

On the other hand, SLIP/PPP connections have one huge advantage:

- They're cheaper, by a long shot, than dedicated direct access. I pay my commercial service provider $300 per year for full Internet access, which gives me 90 hours per month (and 50 cents per hour after the first 50 hours). By comparison, a direct line would cost thousands of dollars per year.

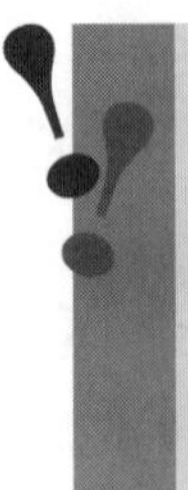

Warning: SLIP and PPP software must be present on *both* your computer and the host computer. Just because your Mac has PPP software on its hard drive, or your Windows machine has the necessary SLIP software, doesn't mean you can dial in to a host computer and get onto the Net. The other machine has to run software to make the connection happen. As before, SLIP/PPP connections are dependent on systems resources (including systems personnel) at the host computer site.

Step 3: Install the TCP/IP Software

Computers don't do anything without software. To access and use the Internet, you need a variety of software tools. Many programs are available, and more are under development at all times. Software is one thing you won't run out of.

The one, single unifying factor about Internet access is that you *must* use the TCP/IP protocol. To do so, you'll need software that contains TCP/IP "stacks." Several options are listed here.

- If you have a UNIX shell account, all you need is a telecommunications program to dial into the remote machine. Many of these are readily available, as commercial software, shareware, or freeware. DOS users have programs such as Procomm or Q-Modem (shareware), while Windows users have Terminal built right in (Windows 95 users have HyperTerm). Mac users can choose from an equally strong variety, and packages such as ClarisWorks offer built-in communications software. These are but a few of the myriad choices. Note that, in this case, the UNIX machine itself contains the TCP/IP software; your computer is simply one of many terminals on that machine.
- If you're accessing the Net through your organization's local area network, talk to your systems people about getting the appropriate software. In some cases, you'll need to install TCP/IP software directly on your hard drive; in others, the LAN will offer all users TCP/IP connectivity.
- If you've chosen OS/2 Warp (or the full version of OS/2 3.0) as your operating system, your TCP/IP software and your modem dialer are built right in. All you need is an Internet connection, either through IBMNet or a local provider.
- If you have a Macintosh and a direct connection, you'll need MacTCP, which is included in System 7.5, or available separately in many books and software packages, plus MacPPP (usually included with MacTCP or available over BBSs and the Net). Both then must be configured to your service provider's (or LAN administrator's) specifications. Several Internet books, available at your bookstore, offer the software needed to hook your Mac to your existing service provider, and several provide easy access to service providers if you don't have one (see, for example, *Plug 'n' Play Internet for Macintosh*).

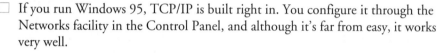

- If you work with Microsoft Windows 3.1 or 3.11, many TCP/IP choices are available to you. Essentially, you need to install Windows Sockets ("Winsock") software, which contains the TCP/IP protocol. You can download Microsoft's TCP/IP stacks from CompuServe, America Online, or over the Net via Microsoft's FTP site (`ftp.microsoft.com`—see Chapter 7 for details on using FTP). Alternatively, you can choose from one of a growing number of software suites that provide their own TCP/IP software and other applications as well: a selection includes Spry's Internet in a Box, Netmanage's Chameleon, and Frontier's Superhighway Access for Windows. Additionally, a number of books contain all the necessary software, including my own *Plug 'n' Play Internet for Windows.*
- If you run Windows 95, TCP/IP is built right in. You configure it through the Networks facility in the Control Panel, and although it's far from easy, it works very well.
- If you have Internet access through a commercial online service, you usually won't have to worry about configuring TCP/IP; the service will offer direct access through its own software.
- If you have any other operating system, TCP/IP software is usually available through BBSs, user groups, or over the Internet. I haven't actually seen TCP/IP for the Vic-20 or the Coleco Adam, but presumably someone, somewhere has developed it.

Warning: TCP/IP can be difficult to configure. You'll need to acquire information about IP addresses, gateways, domain name servers, host names, and server IPs from your service provider. Fortunately, recent software releases have made this process easier, and a good service provider will help you get started. Don't expect to be up on the Internet five minutes after you open your software package, however. Often, it can take a whole week to shake things out.

Summary

This chapter has introduced you to the various types of Internet connections, as well as the major hardware and software options for getting started. You need an account to do anything at all on the Net, and you need to understand the different types of access and types of service providers in order to make informed decisions about your account. At this stage in your Internet explorations, you're ready to make those decisions.

Task Review

In this chapter, you did the following:

- ☐ Determined the type of computer you need
- ☐ Determined the type of Internet connection you need
- ☐ Determined the service provider you want to use

Q&A

Q My friend told me that setting up SLIP or PPP access was extremely complex. How do I find out about this?

A Your service provider can help you. To set up your SLIP or PPP software, you'll need to know such items as your IP number, your mail and news server names, various domain names, and often some other information. All this is exclusive to the service you're receiving, and you can get this information only from your provider.

Usually, the service provider will give you software on disk or via download that will include all this information (as well as your password); or, you'll receive it by phone or in a letter. Then you'll be guided through the initial setup. Yes, it's complex, but a good service provider will make sure you get up and running as quickly as possible.

Q Seriously, how much will the Internet cost me?

Good question. If you're at an organization that provides access, probably nothing, at least not directly. If your access is through a commercial provider, count on $1 to $3 per month, depending on how much and what type of Internet activity you intend. Through a local service provider, typical charges are between 35 cents and $1.50 per hour, depending on the package you select. If you're running a business, and you choose high-speed connections, expect $250-$3,000 or higher per month.

Q Does it really matter which service provider I choose? Aren't they all basically the same?

A It does, and they're not. In fact, nothing is more important than finding a service provider you're happy with. Some service providers offer 28.8 kbps modem access, while others have 14.4 kbps as their top speed. If you're using one of the commercial services, you might find 9600 or even—gasp!—2400 bps as a connection in your area. Some service providers block "objectionable" newsgroups, while others let you make your own decisions (either approach might appeal to you). And some tell you that busy signals in the evening are common, while others insist that you get in the first time every time. Shop around. It does make a real difference, and not just in price.

3

DAY 1

...Go!

You have your account, and you're ready to get going. In this chapter, the real work—and the real fun—begins. You'll start with a quick look at the basics of "netiquette" (just so you don't get on the Net and immediately make enemies), and then you'll log into your "shell" account to learn some basic UNIX commands that will come in extremely handy. Even if you don't regularly use the UNIX shell portion of your account (it comes standard with most, but not all, Internet accounts), working through "UNIX in Brief" will still be valuable. Many Internet tasks are based on the UNIX operating system, and understanding even a tiny portion of UNIX can only help in your Net activities. And, believe me, a tiny portion is all this section provides.

In this chapter, you'll perform the following tasks:

- ☐ Learn the basics of netiquette
- ☐ Log on to your account
- ☐ Learn a basic set of UNIX commands
- ☐ Telnet to remote computers

Getting Started: Points to Keep in Mind

The Internet is an exciting place, partly because it's largely a free-for-all. You do what you want, when you want, and how you want, and the people and resources are available in huge numbers. But it's important to keep a few things in mind before you start.

First, Internet access isn't a right, at least not yet. You can be kicked off by the local access provider if you start offending people or doing stupid things. In other words, there's such a thing as Internet etiquette, which has become, in Internet terminology, *netiquette.*

Netiquette is based on the following several important assumptions:

- ☐ The Internet is a cooperative venture.
- ☐ The Internet is open.
- ☐ Nobody owns or polices the Internet.
- ☐ Nobody wants people around who don't play nice.

It's also based on the following two crucial technological facts:

- ☐ The Internet is a collection of hundreds of thousands of computers linked via a complex series of expensive high-speed connections that handle an almost staggering amount of important data.
- ☐ Your flame (refer to Chapter 4) isn't important data.

As a result of all this, following are a few important rules of netiquette:

- Don't access remote computers for intensive operations, such as FTP or MUDs, during that machine's business hours. Keep a time-zone chart on the wall above your monitor, and pay attention to it. Sometimes you won't be allowed in; other times, you'll simply slow everything down.
- When accessing an Archie, WWW, or other site, try to find the computer with the most direct connection to your own (usually the closest geographically). If you have a choice between doing an Archie search on the computer down the road or the one half-way across the globe, don't choose the latter because it's so cool to be getting stuff from so far away. This needlessly consumes huge gobs of bandwidth—the finite capacity of the Internet's wires to carry networking traffic. On the other hand, it's often a very good idea to access overseas sites, if doing so avoids clogging up local computers during business hours. Again, keep that time chart handy.
- Don't post messages to newsgroups, or send e-mail to mailing lists, that the entire list doesn't need to see. If you're just saying, "Liked your message, Joe," and nothing else, send the thing to Joe, not to everyone on `alt.internet.overkill` or whatever group it was. Messages like this are infuriating to readers, and they quickly destroy your credibility.
- Don't send three messages when one will do. All this uses up bandwidth, and more importantly, from a personal point of view, it clogs mailboxes. If people start seeing your name eight times per day, they'll quickly learn to dread you.
- Don't hide behind your anonymity. Nobody on the Net knows who you are, where you are, what you look like, or anything else about you, but that doesn't mean you can send offensive, degrading, harassing, threatening, demeaning, or just plain idiotic messages.
- Don't send junk mail to entire lists. If you do, prepare to get 50 times as much mail in return, usually in the form of very long messages that will tie up your mailbox forever. This kind of thing can be automated by people who know how.

I could go on, but I won't. Some of this is covered in other chapters. The point is the Internet is available, it's exciting, it's even fun, but it's not a plaything designed expressly for your or my personal enjoyment. Treat it with respect, okay?

UNIX in Brief

UNIX is the basis for the Internet. Today's software largely hides PC, Mac, and OS/2 users from UNIX, but even the most basic familiarization with the powerful operating system will serve you in good stead. You'll see signs of UNIX in e-mail messages, FTP directories, World Wide Web addresses, and many other areas, and you'll make your life considerably easier by knowing at least something about it.

My guess, as I've hinted, is that you don't actually want to know UNIX. Or you have plans to learn it, but maybe a bit later. For now, your real goal is to learn only what you have to in order to get Internetting.

Why do I guess that? Because that's the way I started with UNIX. I'd heard all the horror stories—UNIX is even uglier than DOS, the only good UNIX command is a changed UNIX command, all of them—and I really had no interest. No, I shouldn't say that. I had interest, just as I have interest in all operating systems, but there was that lack-of-time problem to consider.

So I floundered about, learning only what I needed to know. I learned enough about the vi editor to use the e-mail program Elm, and enough about telnet to let me get from one of my accounts to the other. Inevitably, I ran into trouble. Someone attached a WordPerfect file to an Elm message one day, but when I detached it, I had no idea where it went. A local program, called Files, let me see it, but I had no idea what to do from there.

Eventually I learned Kermit, to help me solve that problem and, slowly but surely, a few more UNIX details. Still, I didn't know the most basic stuff, the sort of commands I used with DOS every day of my life. As I found out early, DOS's famous `DIR` didn't do a thing.

Elsewhere in this book, you'll try your hand at telnet, Mail, Elm, and Pine. By the time you reach the end of Day 3, you'll know FTP, Archie, XModem, and Kermit, as well. For now, however, here are the very basic essentials. UNIX is huge, and extremely customizable as well, but it's possible to get by with a minimal amount of knowledge.

Note: No matter how much you think you don't want to know UNIX, keep firmly in mind that UNIX is an extremely powerful, extremely capable operating system. I've talked to all kinds of people who don't like it, or who guffaw at its almost cryptic nature, but most of them simply haven't worked with it very much. Once you work your way into UNIX, and you realize its amazing flexibility and customizability, as well as its multiuser stability and networking capabilities, you'll come to realize why it's the workhorse of the Internet.

To practice with UNIX, log in through your UNIX "shell" account. If your Internet account is through a local service provider, you're almost certain to have one of these. Even if you don't, telnet programs enable you to get into UNIX accounts and work your way around. Internet access through the commercial providers or through Internet providers, such as Netcom or Pipeline, hide the shell account from you, but it's there nonetheless.

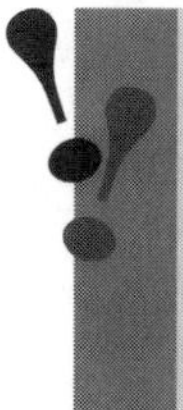

Warning: If you're used to using DOS, one thing to learn right off the bat is that UNIX is case-sensitive. DOS users can type **`dir`** or **`DIR`** and get the same result, but in UNIX, capitalization matters. If a DOS file is named `budget.doc`, for example, you can type `BUDget.doc` in your word processor's file dialog box and it won't matter. In UNIX, however, `budget.doc` and `BUDget.doc` are two separate files.

Task 3.1: Log in to your shell account.

Unless you have specific instructions from your organization's systems administrator for connecting to the Internet, the process is essentially as follows:

1. Get the login prompt on your screen. This will look like one of the following:

```
login:
username:
login name:
```

2. Type your username at this prompt, and then press Enter.

```
login: nrandall
```

Note: You don't have to use your full Internet address here, just the username for the system you've logged into.

3. When the password prompt appears (it does so automatically), type your password.

```
login: nrandall
Password: not4U2knoW
```

4. Wait for system confirmation. You'll either receive another request for your name and password, or you'll be shown a series of login messages (which are useful only because they show you've succeeded), or you'll just receive the UNIX command prompt, which means you're successful.

Note: The UNIX command prompt usually is a dollar sign (`$`) or a percent sign (`%`), but if you want to change it, you usually can do so. Check with your systems administrator, or pick up a good UNIX book, to learn how.

5. You may be asked for a terminal type. The most common seems to be DEC VT100, but you can choose from many other possibilities. You can set up your communications software to emulate specific terminals, in which case you choose the one you've emulated.

```
TERM (unknown): vt100
```

Note: If you want to know which terminals are available to you, press a couple nonsense characters (for example, `ddd`) and press Enter. On most systems, this will generate an error message and a list of available terminal types.

6. You also may be given a choice of protocols. When logging into one of my accounts, I'm given the following protocol list to choose from:

```
Choose Protocol:
1.  Shell
2.  SLIP
3.  PPP
```

Here, if I want a standard UNIX shell account, I type `1` and press Enter. If I want to use my Macintosh (see the preceding account types), I choose Point-to-Point Protocol (`PPP`). Because I'm primarily a Microsoft Windows user, and most Windows software to date uses Serial Line Internet Protocol (`SLIP`) connections, I choose #`2`.

7. Following is what a login looks like on my main Internet account:

```
SunOS UNIX (watserv1)

watserv1 login: nrandall
Password: xxxxxxxxxxxxxxx
Last login: cn-ts1 (ttys9) Tue Apr 19 13:42:30 1994
You have new mail.
TERM = (vt100) vt100

[51]%
```

(At this point, I know I'm on.)

8. Once you're logged in, you can do whatever you want. To check your mail, type **`mail`**, **`elm`**, or **`pine`**. To start an FTP session, type **`ftp`**. (See Chapter 7 for details.) To begin a Talk session, type **`talk`** *`username@full.address`*. To do a telnet or browse a Gopher, see the following sections.

Task 3.2: Try the *ls* and *cd* commands.

The first great UNIX mystery for anyone coming over from DOS is how to get a directory listing. As it turns out, it's simple, but don't expect UNIX to volunteer the information. The command is `ls`, short for list; like `DIR`, it comes in a variety of flavors.

1. Type **`ls`** at the command prompt. This will give you a basic list of files. On my main account, the result looks like this:

```
[56]% ls
Mail                     interview_andrews      shopping.txt
News                     mail                   interview_johnson
README                   mbox                   whodat
bin                      me                     xmodem.log
catherine.memo           propos.txt
```

There are a couple things to note here. First, the listing is in columns (this can be changed if you want), and no file information is provided. Second, UNIX filenames have far different conventions than DOS's anemic 11-character rule and they more closely resembles the Mac's file-naming system. Knowing this is important primarily when you're FTPing from another site. You will find some incredibly long filenames, and you have to remember to type them exactly as they appear, *including* the exact same case. The file named `README`, preceding, cannot be entered as `readme`. In UNIX, the two aren't the same thing at all.

3

Note: The basic requirements for a UNIX filename are as follows:

- UNIX filenames are case-sensitive; this means you can have several files named `readme`, all using different case combinations—for example, `README`, `Readme`, `ReadMe`, `readme`, `readMe`, and so on.
- UNIX filenames can consist of seemingly any combination of characters: digits, dashes, plus signs, underline characters, or dots.
- UNIX filenames cannot begin with dashes or plus signs.

Task 3.3: Get a detailed directory listing with the *-l* switch.

Often, you'll need detailed information about the files in a directory, such as date, size, and UNIX permissions (such as who can act on the file). The `-l` switch enables you to see those details.

1. Type **ls -l** at the command prompt (be sure to put the space between the **ls** and the **-l** portions of the command). The directory listing from Task 1.2 now looks like this:

```
[57]% ls -l
total 51
drwx------  2 nrandall      512 Apr 12 12:45 Mail
drwxr-x—x  7 nrandall      512 Feb 13 21:40 News
-rw-r----  1 nrandall      757 Mar 24 18:47 README
drwx--s--x  2 nrandall      512 Mar 26  1990 bin
-rw------  1 nrandall        4 Feb 23 12:00 catherine.memo
-rw-r----  1 nrandall     3038 Mar 22 14:02 interview_andrews
drwx------  2 nrandall     1024 Apr 19 09:32 mail
-rw------  1 nrandall    10741 Feb 23 12:03 mbox
-rw-r----  1 nrandall       90 Jan  8 21:09 me
-rw-r----  1 nrandall     5267 Apr  7 20:57 propos.txt
-rw-r----  1 nrandall    15935 Mar 31 14:41 shopping.txt
-rw-r----  1 nrandall     2771 Mar 22 13:54 interview_johnson
-rw-r----  1 nrandall      186 Nov 11  1990 whodat
-rw-r----  1 nrandall     3242 Apr  7 20:59 xmodem.log
```

The file size, in bytes, is shown to the left of the date. Also of importance is the first column, which lists the attributes. It all has to do with who can do what to which file, but for your immediate purposes, only the first character really matters. The rule is if the first character is a hyphen (-), the item is a file; if the first character is a letter `d`, the item is a directory.

Task 3.4: Change directories with the *cd* command.

Before going back to `ls`, here's another command: `cd`. Like the DOS version, this command changes your current directory. In the listing for Task 3.3, you'll see an item named `mail`. You know this is a directory because its attribute column begins with `d`, so you can use `cd` to get into that directory, and then `ls` to get a listing.

1. Type **cd** *mail* at the command line. (Note that *mail* could be any directory.)
2. Type **ls** at the command line. The result is now a listing of the current directory.

```
[59]% cd mail
[60]% ls
amato          courses        infobits       net-happenings  sent-mail
bnr            deutsch        inktank        nii             strangelove
business       education      interesting    oha-list        stuff
```

The new items in the directory are actually the folders I created in the Pine mailer. The point, for now, is that I'm in a different directory. Not that UNIX was about to volunteer that information. I didn't actually get a response to the `cd mail` command. I had to do something further to determine where I was.

Actually, there's another way, and this command, too, is useful. The `pwd` command will tell you what directory you're currently in (for example, your working directory).

3. Type **`pwd`** at the command line to determine your current directory.

```
[66]% pwd
/home/watserv1/nrandall/mail
[67]%
```

Warning: The UNIX directory structure uses the slash character (/), not DOS's infamous backslash (\) to separate directories. This usually confuses converted DOS users for about a year after starting to use the Net.

3

4. Return to the previous directory by typing **`cd ..`** at the command line.

```
[62]% cd ..
```

5. Return to your home directory by typing **`cd`**. It's possible to get lost in a large UNIX system. Fortunately, typing `cd` and pressing Enter will return you to your home directory.

Task 3.5: Finding hidden files with the *-a* switch.

Back to `ls`. One last `ls` switch worth knowing is `-a`. This one shows you all files in your directory, even those that are hidden. In UNIX, a hidden file is simply one whose filename starts with a period (.), and they aren't displayed with the normal `ls` command.

Type **`-ls -a`** at the command prompt.

Note the difference in the following result from that displayed in Tasks 3.2 and 3.3:

```
[58]% ls -a
.                       .oldnewsrc              Mail
..                      .pine-debug1            News
.Xauthority             .pine-debug2            README
.addressbook            .pine-debug3            bin
.cshrc                  .pine-debug4            catherine.memo
.elm                    .pinerc                 interview_andrews
.files                  .pinerc.save            mail
.forware                .pinercbu               mbox
.gopherrc               .profile                me
.gopherrc~              .rnlast                 propos.txt
.history                .rnsoft                 shopping.txt
.letter                 .signature              interview_johnson
.login                  .signature.save         whodat
.newsrc                 .xsession               xmodem.log
```

Files such as .pinerc, .elm, .gopherrc, or .newsrc are configuration files. You can change them manually, but it's usually better to let the software do it for you.

Task 3.6: Delete, copy, and rename files.

1. Type **rm filename** at the command prompt (rm means *remove*) to delete a file from the directory. For example, the following will delete the file interview_andrews:

   ```
   [59]% rm interview_andrews
   ```

Warning: You won't be asked for confirmation, and there are no undelete utilities. The file is gone, pure and simple. Don't use rm unless you mean it.

2. Type **cp** *filename* **new.***filename* at the command prompt to copy a file. For example, you could have copied the previous file like this, resulting in two identical files:

   ```
   [60]% cp interview_andrews really-fascination-interview.cool
   ```

3. Type **mv** *filename* at the command prompt to rename a file. For example, the following command will change the name of interview.andrews to old-andrews.interview.

   ```
   [61]% mv interview_andrews old-andrews.interview
   ```

UNIX in Brief

That's it. UNIX for minimalists. Anything else you truly need will be covered in its respective section, beginning with telnet and rlogin immediately following.

Note: Eventually, you'll want to know more about UNIX because UNIX is the basis for the Internet. Several good UNIX primers are available, but why not start with Dave Taylor's *Teach Yourself UNIX in a Week*, which is in the same series as the book you're reading right now. I realize it sounds like I'm sucking up to my publisher by recommending a book in the same series as my own, but Taylor's book really is excellent. I've been using it to learn UNIX in greater detail as I find the time.

Accessing Remote Computers

Thousands of machines are out there on the Net, all just waiting for you to access them. There are several ways of doing so. You can Gopher to them (see Chapter 8), you can FTP to them (see Chapter 7), or you can use the World Wide Web (see Chapter 10), but the most direct way is to `telnet` into the site, or to use the similar but lesser-featured `rlogin`.

Task 3.7: Telnet to a machine on which you have an account.

The most common use of `telnet` is through Gopher or the World Wide Web, but it's also fairly common from the UNIX command line. Here, its primary function is to log into a remote computer on which you have an account. This will happen, for example, if you're traveling and you find yourself sitting in front of a machine connected to the Internet. You want to check your mail, of course, because about two days after finishing this book, you'll already be an e-mail addict (much like food or drug addiction, except that society looks more favorably on it).

3

In my case, the remote login through `telnet` would look like the following:

```
$ telnet watserv1.uwaterloo.ca
Trying 129.97.129.140...
Connected to watserv1.uwaterloo.ca.
Escape character is '^]'.

SunOS UNIX (watserv1)

watserv1 login: nrandall
Password: NotTelling
Last login: cn-ts1 (ttyp1) Tue Apr 19 19:41:19 1994
You have new mail.

[56]% logout
```

Following are a few things worth noting:

- The `telnet` command is followed by the name of the host machine, not my own Internet address. My address is `nrandall@watserv1.uwaterloo.ca`; the stuff after the `@` sign is the host name.
- The digits on the second line comprise the host computer's IP (Internet Protocol) address. Computers don't do names, they do numbers, which means this is the computer's real name.

- The fourth line says that the Escape character is `^]`. This means, "hold the Ctrl key down and press the closing square bracket (]) key." This is the standard method of canceling a telnet session, and it's extremely valuable. Often a telnet will take many minutes, and there's no point waiting.
- Once in the remote system, you enter the login name and password for that system, not the one you're currently in. These will likely be different.
- Once you've logged in completely, you can do whatever you normally do, including read your mail, transfer files via FTP, enter Gophers, and so on. You can even use your remote system to telnet back to the machine you're currently using. In fact, you can telnet several places in a series of telnet sub-sessions, but make sure you log out of each in succession.

Task 3.8: Telnet to a machine on which you do not have an account.

1. At the command prompt, type **`telnet watarts.uwaterloo.ca`**.
2. When you receive the `login` prompt, type your username.
3. At the `password` prompt, type your password.
4. Keep trying until the remote machine kicks you out.

Unless you were incredibly lucky, you didn't get into my host computer. If you actually have an account on `watarts.uwaterloo.ca`, then you probably logged in okay (and, if so, drop by and say hello), but otherwise the chances are unfathomably remote that your username and password exactly match a username and password on that computer.

Your session probably looked like this one, a real attempt of mine to log into a remote computer on which I don't have an account:

```
[53]% telnet ai.mit.edu
Trying 128.52.32.80 ...
Connected to ai.mit.edu.
Escape character is '^]'.

SunOS UNIX (life)

login: nrandall
Password: NoThingWorKs
Login incorrect
login: nrandall
Password: TRYsomethingFAST
login: nrandall
Password: iFeelUnWanTed
login: Connection closed by foreign host.
```

Typically, you get three tries to get your login name and password right, then you're booted out. Oh well…

Task 3.9: Open telnet without connecting to another machine.

It's not actually necessary to include a host name with a `telnet` command. By just typing `telnet` by itself, you start a telnet session, at which point you can get a list of telnet options by typing `help`. Then, to connect to a remote machine, you use the `open` command with the desired host name.

1. At the command prompt, type **`telnet`**.
2. At the `telnet>` prompt, type **`help`**. This will yield the program's help screen, with explanations of possible commands. The result of both commands will look much like the following:

```
$ telnet
telnet> help
Commands may be abbreviated. Commands are:

close           close current connection
logout          forcibly logout remote user and close the connection
display         display operating parameters
mode            try to enter line or character mode ('mode ?' for more)
open            connect to a site
quit            exit telnet
send            transmit special characters ('send ?' for more)
set             set operating parameters ('set ?' for more)
unset           unset operating parameters ('unset ?' for more)
status          print status information
toggle          toggle operating parameters ('toggle ?' for more)
slc             change state of special characters ('slc ?' for more)
z               suspend telnet
!               invoke a subshell
environ         change environment variables ('environ ?' for more)
?               print help information
```

3. To launch a telnet session, type **`open`** *`host.name`* at the prompt. For example, to reach my machine, type the following:

```
telnet>open watarts.uwaterloo.ca
```

Notice that ending a telnet session requires typing `quit`, or using the Crtl++ combination.

Task 3.10: Telnet into a computer that allows access without an account.

In many situations on the Internet, you can use telnet to connect to a system, and then a series of special login names or passwords to enter permissible areas. Connecting to World Wide Web or to Archie sites through a UNIX shell account is like this, where you normally type `www` or `archie` as the login name, which bypasses the password completely.

One such site (among a great many) is NISS, the National Information on Software and Services, located in the United Kingdom. The following task takes you into the site.

1. At the command prompt, type **`telnet sun.nsf.ac.uk`**.
2. At the `login:` prompt, type **`janet`**.
3. When the `password:` prompt appears, press Enter as per the onscreen instructions.
4. When the `hostname:` prompt appears, type **`uk.as.niss`** to move to the actual information site.

The entire procedure looks as follows:

```
$ telnet sun.nsf.ac.uk
Trying 128.86.8.7...
Connected to sun.nsfnet-relay.ac.uk.
Escape character is '^]'.


SunOS UNIX (sun.nsfnet-relay.ac.uk)

login: janet
Password: [no password, just press Enter]

Welcome to the JANET X.25 PAD Service.

Enter a JANET hostname (i.e uk.ac.janet.news) 'h' for help or 'q' to quit.
hostname: uk.ac.niss
SunLink X.25 PAD V7.0. Type ^P<cr> for Executive, ^Pb for break
Calling... connected...
Welcome to the NISS Gateway

Checking your terminal type...

**** []I S S   G A T E W A Y  ********  M A I[] M E[]U  ****


AA) NISS Bulletin Board              (NISSBB - Traditional access)
AB) NISS Bulletin Board              (NISSBB - Gopher access)
B)  NISS Public Access Collections   (NISSPAC)
C)  NISSWAIS Service  - free text searching of selected databases
D)  NISS Newspapers and Journals Services
E)  NISS Gopher Services
```

Task 3.11: The *rlogin* command.

The `rlogin` command is much like `telnet`, except that it has fewer options. Still, if you have accounts with identical login names on two separate computers, `rlogin` is often more

convenient. `rlogin` often takes you directly to the password prompt, or, depending on the way it's configured, even directly into your second account.

1. At the prompt, type **`rlogin`** *`host.name`*.

   If `rlogin` is installed on your system, and you have an account on the destination machine, you'll be taken to that machine and directly to the password prompt.

2. At the `password:` prompt, type your password. You should now be logged in to your second account.

Note: If you make a mistake on your password in `rlogin`, you'll be asked for a new login name as well, which makes the session very much like telnet.

Warning: `logout` is the proper exit command for `rlogin`. The Ctrl+] combination does not work.

Summary

In this chapter, you've covered the major issues of netiquette, and you've learned some basics of UNIX, including how to log on to your own account and to remote machines. With these tasks completed, you're more than ready to move onto the more complex Internet topics. In Day 1, you've picked up a fair bit, but from this point on, you'll learn more and more all the time. So get some sleep, wave good-bye to your loved ones, and get ready to plunge back in.

Task Review

In Chapter 3, you did the following:

- ☐ Learned the basic rules of netiquette
- ☐ Logged on to your account
- ☐ Learned a basic set of UNIX commands
- ☐ Telnetted to remote computers

Q&A

Q Shouldn't I change my password as soon as I log on?

A Well, that's the general rule, but part of it depends on whether your account has anything worth stealing (that's why I never locked my '83 T-Bird). For the most part, however, you should change your password every few months or so, and much more frequently if you've been alerted to security problems.

To do so, enter the UNIX command `passwd` and follow the prompts. You'll be asked to type the old password, then the new one, and then the new one again to confirm. Your systems people will have regulations or guidelines about what your password should consist of. The rule of thumb is to keep it as complex as you possibly can. Don't, for heaven's sake, use your name, or your username, or your spouse's or dog's name, or anything else that could be easily traced.

Q This netiquette thing isn't for real, is it?

So far, yes. And it shows no signs of changing. Internet users pride themselves on getting along, on exchanging information and ideas quite freely, and on establishing a system whereby nobody bullies or takes advantage of anyone else. Increasingly, these values are taking a beating, because in any community of 20 to 40 million, you're going to find a few idiots. If you want to participate fully in the Net and its offerings, keep the getting-along thing firmly in mind. It might sound naive, but communication on the Net began as a co-operative effort, and "playing nice" is still the most accepted behavior of all. How long this will last is anyone's guess.

Conversing/ Communicating

DAY
2

E-Mail and Mailing Lists

Nothing is more essential to using the Internet than mastering *electronic mail.* Through e-mail you can exchange ideas, concerns, agendas, memos, documents, and files with anyone on the Internet in any part of the world. The Internet was originally designed as a communications tool, and the spread of e-mail has proven the design to be an enormous success. This chapter outlines this flexible and ubiquitous tool, demonstrating its capabilities and offering some important guidelines.

Task List

In this chapter, you'll perform the following tasks:

- ☐ Focus a reader's attention through effective use of the Subject line
- ☐ Create a useful signature
- ☐ Consider the different forms of accepted e-mail etiquette
- ☐ Decide among the three major UNIX mailers
- ☐ Decide whether you need a graphical mailer such as Eudora
- ☐ Attach documents or other files to a message
- ☐ Subscribe to a mailing list

Using E-Mail

Even if you've never been on the Internet, you probably already know about e-mail. Research and military personnel have been sending e-mail messages over the phone lines for decades now, and in the past half-dozen years or so, e-mail has become a staple of online services such as CompuServe, GEnie, America Online, and MCI Mail. Over the same period of time, business computers have become more networked, and for many business employees, e-mail now is an everyday way of life.

It's an everyday way of life on the Internet, too, but the stakes are a whole lot higher.

There's no real difference between Internet e-mail and CompuServe e-mail. There isn't even a significant difference between Internet e-mail and the e-mail that flows through a local business office. Basically, you send messages to other people and groups, and you wait for the answers to arrive. Then you reply to the answers, wait for more responses, and so on. An endless cycle, and in many ways, pretty mundane.

Here's the difference, however. If you're on your company's local network, or even its nationwide or multinational network, you're writing mainly to others in your company (no

matter where they are). If you're an MCI Mail user, you're writing mainly to other MCI Mail users. Essentially, the messages go to MCI Mail's computer, or to your company's computer or network. Once you're on the Internet, however, you can start sending messages to any user on any computer anywhere in the world.

Anyone, that is, who also is on the Internet.

Note: It is, in fact, quite possible to reach a user of MCI Mail, CompuServe, GEnie, America Online, or other commercial online services through Internet mail. See the Extra Credit section at the end of this chapter for details.

Feel like e-mailing your friend who works at a university on the West Coast? No sweat; just type in the full address and let fly. Need to set up a product demonstration with a client in New Zealand? As long as you have the Internet address, you don't even have to worry about whether you'll be getting him out of bed. Trying to organize a frequent research exchange with colleagues in Venezuela, Colombia, Brazil, and three other South American countries? Go into your e-mail program, set them up as a group called `samerica`, and then start sending messages with attached files to all of them at once.

It's easy, it's enjoyable, it's fast, and it's effective. What else could you ask for?

Electronic mail is the most fundamental of Internet applications. It's the one that everyone learns first, and usually the one that draws people to the Internet in the first place. I'm a fairly typical example. For the first three years of my Internet life, I didn't know you could do anything *except* e-mail. Nobody told me about FTPs or Gophers, and the World Wide Web didn't even exist yet. As a matter of fact, I didn't even know that the Internet was the thing I was on.

What I *did* know was that I could keep in contact with a few colleagues who had managed to scatter themselves around the world, and with some who hid in their offices down the hall. That's what I wanted, and that's what I got. I e-mailed infrequently at first, but slowly things started to pick up.

The turning point for me was when I realized how fast it all was. I'd send a message to an associate in the morning, and often he'd reply in less than an hour. When I sent a message late at night (I worked late, he started early), an answer would almost always be waiting for me first thing in the morning. Then I began to realize something else. There's simply no way those exchanges would have happened at all, if we'd been depending on the good old mail services. Not only is snailmail (as it's called) too slow, it's also a completely different activity.

Writing a letter takes time. I'm not about to send a one-sentence response through the mail, so I wait until I have more important things to say. That means a delay. Once I have them, however, there's even more delay. Find a pen, find some paper, do the writing, find an envelope, find a stamp. Then—this one has always been tough for me—remember to actually put the envelope in a mailbox. It isn't unusual at all for a stamped envelope to sit on the front seat of my car for a couple days, and I suspect I'm not alone. More time lost, more delays to deal with.

With e-mail, things have changed. I log in every morning, read my messages, and respond immediately to those that want an answer (delinquency is really noticed in e-mail). Four or five times per day I log in and check again, and usually there's something else to answer. In total, reading and answering e-mail will take you anywhere from a few minutes to a couple of hours a day, and after a short time, you get really good at recognizing and deleting the stuff that isn't of any interest to you. However long it takes you, it's almost invariably time well spent.

Your E-Mail Program

To send and receive e-mail, you need an e-mail program (sometimes called a *mailer*). There are three types, depending on the type of Internet access you have (see Chapter 2 for details on the different types of Internet access). If you have Internet shell access only, you're normally restricted to the e-mail programs that already exist on the UNIX computer you've hooked to. If you have direct Internet access and a Macintosh or a PC, you probably can use the more attractive e-mail programs designed for graphical environments, such as the Macintosh or Microsoft Windows. Finally, if you're hooked into the Net through your company's network, you'll just use the mailer you normally use.

Tip: As always, check with your network administrator to find out what type of Internet access you have. Sometimes, however, there are other possibilities, even though you may not be told about them. Keeping political protocol firmly in mind, explore a bit further with your systems people.

The Three Major UNIX Mailers

A considerable number of e-mail programs have been designed for UNIX systems, but the following three are the best known:

- **Mail**, which, like so many UNIX programs, is full-featured, but comes with an interface that can best be described as brutal. There's actually more than one version of Mail, but the interfaces remain brutal.

- **Elm** is equally full-featured and quite a bit easier to use, although its editor, like Mail's, is anything but intuitive and requires considerable practice. Elm's default editor is *vi*, a standard UNIX editor, and if you decide you don't like it, you can tell Elm to load an alternative by typing **o** (for options) from Elm's main screen and making the change in configuration. But first-time users of Elm will almost invariably encounter vi, and while extremely powerful, it's hardly a walk in the park.
- **Pine** is a somewhat simplified program, but far and away the best one for novices to start with, and maybe for many people to stay with. Pine greatly simplifies everyday procedures such as typing text, saving messages in separate folders, and creating address books with aliases.

Graphical Mailers: Eudora, Pegasus Mail, and Others

The best-known graphical e-mail program for Windows and the Macintosh is *Eudora.* A free version is available on the Net, while a commercial version is available from a company called QUALCOMM for $69. Eudora is easy to use and the commercial version is extremely full-featured, although only that version is continually under development.

4

Product: Eudora for Windows

FTP Site: `ftp.qualcomm.com`

FTP Directory: `/quest/windows/eudora/1.4`

FTP Filename: `eudor144.exe`

Note: Wherever you see software available for download, you'll see that it resides on an *FTP site.* To conduct FTP transactions, see Chapter 7.

Product: Eudora for Macintosh

FTP Site: `ftp.qualcomm.com`

FTP Directory: `/quest/mac/eudora/1.5`

FTP Filename: `eudora152.hqx` (or `eudora152fat.hqx` for Power Mac)

WWW Homepage: `http://www.qualcomm.com/`

The Elements of an E-Mail Message

No matter which e-mail program you use, sending a message is done basically the same way. You address the message, fill in the subject line, type in the message, and then send it. Other options include sending to multiple recipients or groups, and attaching files for the recipient to download.

The *TO*: Line

In the `TO:` line, you type the recipient's address. That, or you type the alias you've created for the recipient. If you want to send the message to more than one recipient, separate the addresses (or the aliases) with a comma (or simply a space with some mailers). You also can include a group name in the same line.

For example, to send a message to Donna Johns (`dcjohns@entropy.cmu.edu`), for whom you have no alias, Suzanne Pelletier (whose alias is set up as "sue"), and all the members of your research team (which you've set up as "research"), your `TO:` line will look as follows:

```
TO: dcjohns@entropy.cmu.edu,sue,research
```

The *CC*: Line

`CC:` means *carbon copy*, a holdover term from the days of, well, carbon paper. By including an address on the `CC:` line, you're copying the message to someone else's e-mail address.

Tip: Why use the `CC:` line when you could just include the address in the `TO:` line? Essentially, for the same reason you'd do so if you were sending a business memo. The `TO:` line contains the addresses of the people you want to alert directly to the message contents. The `CC:` line contains the addresses of people who should see the message, but whose responses—and attention—you're not really requesting. You might even include it for simple filing purposes. Technically, addresses in the `CC:` line can often be given a lower delivery priority, a consideration for network efficiency.

The *ATTACHMENTS*: Line

Just as in a paper letter or memo, you may have some documents you want to include as an attachment. In an e-mail message, this means you want to attach a file to the message, one the recipient will detach, download, and work with. You might, for example, be e-mailing a co-worker about a problem with budget figures, so you attach the Lotus 1-2-3 file you're

working on (you know that she works with 1-2-3 as well). She receives the message, which automatically tells her a file is attached. She then detaches it, downloads it, and opens it in her 1-2-3 program.

Attaching a file differs, depending on your type of Internet access. The idea is the same, however. When you get to this line, you tell the e-mail program to attach a file that's present on your hard drive. The only question is where the file is actually located.

Caution: The ATTACHMENTS: line may not actually be called "Attachments," depending on your mailer. Sometimes it's abbreviated, while on mailers operating on your organization's network you might have an entirely different term. The idea is the same, however; to enable you to send a file through e-mail. Attaching a file, however, depends on standards for allowing this to transpire—the proposed standard is called MIME—and as of yet, this isn't fully implemented. Check with your systems people to see if you can actually transmit a file through e-mail.

If you have direct Internet access, the file is probably on the hard drive of your PC or Mac (or your UNIX station), or on your company's network drive. In Eudora, for example, you select Attach Document from the Message menu, and Eudora presents you with the Windows or Mac file selection box. Double-click the file you want, and then finish your message. Eudora will upload it from your hard drive when you actually send the message. When you receive a message containing an attached file, the reverse procedure takes place.

Tip: You can configure Eudora in a number of different ways through the Configuration dialog box, which you can access from the Special menu. Among other options, you can tell Eudora to download attached files automatically to a specific directory. If you choose this option, it's best to create a separate directory for these downloads, and if you receive your e-mail automatically, be sure to check this directory regularly for downloaded attachments.

If you're working from a stand-alone PC or Mac, however, and you access the Internet through a UNIX shell account, an extra step often is necessary. In these cases, you can't attach a file directly from your own computer's drive. Instead, you have to place it on the host system's drive. To do so, you have to upload the file from your PC or Mac to the host, using the host's XModem or Kermit programs (see Chapter 7 for details Xmodem or Kermit programs). There may be others on your system, but these two are the most common.

After the file is uploaded to the host computer, you can attach it to your message. In Pine, for example, you place the cursor on the ATTACHMENTS: line and press Ctrl+T, as the menu on the bottom of the screen tells you. You'll be shown a list of files on your drive, which you can choose by cursoring to the one you want. You also can change directories from here.

The *SUBJECT:* Line

The SUBJECT: line is the first element of the message that's completely up to you. Make a mistake on the other three lines, and you'll get error messages. On the SUBJECT: line, you're on your own.

Warning: Don't overlook the SUBJECT: line's importance. Many Internet users receive dozens—even hundreds!—of messages every day. They can't possibly read them all, so they rely on two message elements to guide them through.

The first, of course, is the address line: if they recognize the name of the sender, they'll read that message. The second is the subject line.

When readers are faced with several screens of messages in their in boxes, the subject lines are often the only way of determining what's worth reading. So it's very important to give them a subject line that will stop them from pressing Delete. Remember, you may be new to sending e-mail across the Internet, but your recipients probably aren't. They're likely busy, and swamped with stuff to read.

Above all, be sure not to leave the subject line blank. I'm one of many readers who routinely delete—before reading—any message that doesn't have a subject line; unless, of course, I recognize the sender's name.

Doing something with the SUBJECT: line is especially important since it's not required on an e-mail message. You can leave it blank, or you can simply resend the existing line. It's voluntary, but it's important.

The Message Area

There are no rules—you can type whatever you want. There are, however, some guidelines, which are simple and not much different from the ones you know about sending memos. Remember, the idea is to get your point across.

- Write clearly. If you have something to say, write it so the reader will understand.
- Write concisely. You have no interest in receiving a 4-page memo, and your reader doesn't want a 4-screen message. A good rule of thumb is this: if the message is

more than one screen in length (25 lines or so), it's too long. Trim it, unless you can fully justify not doing so.

- Write civilly. Back to an office memo, you wouldn't send a memo swearing at the recipient, or suggesting a questionable parentage, so don't do so here. AND DON'T SCREAM. Words typed in uppercase usually are read as anger rather than enthusiasm, and you'll be seen as an impolite and unsophisticated "flamer."
- Don't send three messages where one will do. This happens especially in mailing lists (see Chapter 5), where one person will get caught up in the discussion and reply to just about everything. If you see four or five messages in one day from the same address, you'll instantly lower your opinion of that person, no matter how thoughtful the messages themselves might be.
- Ask for a response if you want a response. Don't assume that the addressee will read between the lines and figure out what you want. Nobody has time.

All these guidelines, of course, go out the window when you're dealing with personal messages to friends. But not long after getting on the Internet, such messages probably will be the minority.

Using a UNIX Mailer: Pine

The tasks in this chapter are divided among the UNIX mailer Pine and the Windows mailer Eudora. UNIX tasks take up the first group because practically all Internet users have access to at least one of these mailers. Besides, the process of putting together an e-mail message is the same, regardless of the mailer or the operating system, so the actual mailer doesn't really matter.

Sending Messages

If you want to send someone a message, you need two things: an e-mail program and the recipient's Internet address. Internet addresses always have two parts to them, separated by the `@` sign. Mine, for example, is `nrandall@watarts.uwaterloo.ca`: my username (`nrandall`) followed by the computer name and the domain name where my account resides (`watarts.uwaterloo.ca`). As soon as you get an Internet account, call your friends and find out their Internet addresses. That's the way your e-mail network gets started.

Task 4.1: Send a basic message.

Most of the e-mail messages you'll send will be extremely simple, consisting of one recipient and a short sentence or two. This task takes you through the basic steps.

1. At the UNIX command line, type **pine** (followed by pressing Return or Enter, of course). You'll be presented with a screen similar to the one shown in Figure 4.1. Note that you could also type `elm` or `mail` to retrieve those mailers, if you prefer or if you have no choice.

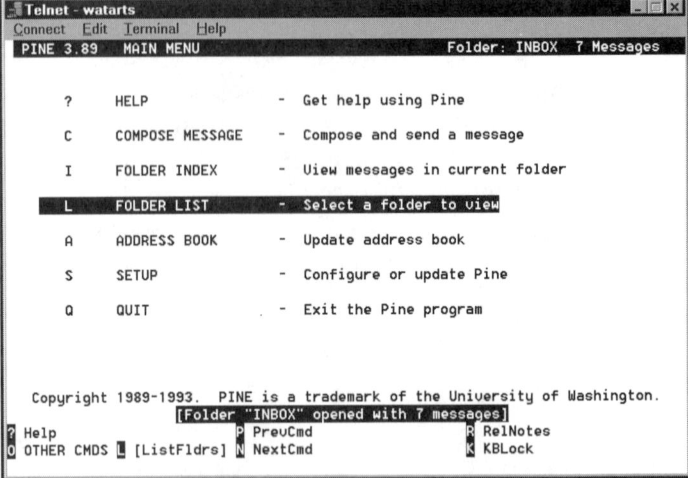

Figure 4.1.
Pine's introductory screen.

2. Press **C** to begin composing your message. The cursor will automatically appear on the `To:` line.
3. Type the recipient's Internet (e-mail) address on the `To:` line. If you can't remember anyone's e-mail address, type **tyi@watarts.uwaterloo.ca**.
4. Press Enter or Return three times to move the cursor to the `Subject:` line.
5. In the `Subject:` line, type **My first message from Teach Yourself the Internet**. Press Enter to move to the Message area.
6. In the Message area, type whatever you want, paying attention to basic rules of netiquette. Note that you do *not* have to press Return/Enter at the end of each line (Pine does word-wrap). When you've finished the text of the message, press Return/Enter a couple times to get to a new line, and then type your name. At this point, the screen will look essentially like Figure 4.2.
7. At the bottom of the Pine screen you'll find a menu of commands. The caret (^) in front of each letter refers to the Ctrl key on your keyboard. For example, the Send command is `^X`, which means you hold down the Ctrl key and press the X key (you don't need the Shift key). Therefore, to send your message right now, press Ctrl+X. Pine will ask if you want to send the message. Press **y** to verify. A message line just above the menu area will tell you Pine is sending the message, and you'll be returned to Pine's main menu.

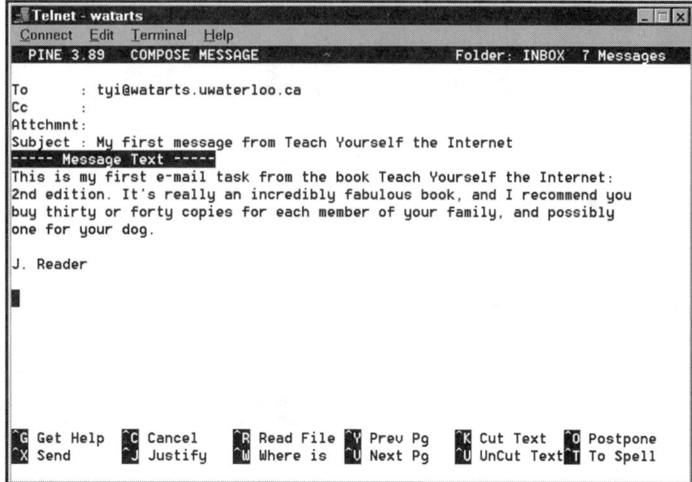

Telnet - watarts
Connect Edit Terminal Help
PINE 3.89 COMPOSE MESSAGE Folder: INBOX 7 Messages
To : tyi@watarts.uwaterloo.ca
Cc :
Attchmnt:
Subject : My first message from Teach Yourself the Internet
----- Message Text -----
This is my first e-mail task from the book Teach Yourself the Internet:
2nd edition. It's really an incredibly fabulous book, and I recommend you
buy thirty or forty copies for each member of your family, and possibly
one for your dog.
J. Reader
^G Get Help ^C Cancel ^R Read File ^Y Prev Pg ^K Cut Text ^O Postpone
^X Send ^J Justify ^W Where is ^V Next Pg ^U UnCut Text ^T To Spell

Figure 4.2.
Filled-in e-mail message in Pine (somewhat biased, perhaps).

Task 4.2: Send a message to more than one recipient.

Often, you'll want your message to go to more than one addressee. Rather than sending separate messages to each one, you can simply add e-mail addresses to the `To:` and/or `Cc:` lines. Each recipient will get the same message.

1. Type **`pine`** and prepare to compose a message as described in steps 1 and 2 of Task 4.1.
2. Type the recipients' Internet (e-mail) addresses on the `To:` line with a comma separating each (some mailers simply require a space). Again, you may use **`tyi@watarts.uwaterloo.ca`** among your recipients if you cannot locate other addresses. Press Enter/Return twice to reach the `Subject:` line.
3. In the Subject line, type **`Practicing E-Mail with multiple recipients`**. Press Enter/Return once to reach the Message Text area.
4. Compose any message you want, but remember—the idea is to get your point across clearly and concisely.
5. To send your message right now type **`^x`** as demonstrated in Task 4.1. Pine will ask if you want to send the messages. To confirm your command, type **`y`**, and your single composition is on its way to multiple sites.

The `To:` line provides a simple and efficient way of transmitting the same message to many recipients, just as if you had composed new messages for each addressee. In some cases, however, you may want to make certain individuals aware of a message that you are sending to another recipient without requesting those individuals' comments or replies. In this scenario, the `Cc:` line would better suit your purpose.

1. Type **pine** as you have in the previous tasks and select the Compose Message command.
2. In the `To:` line, type the address of the main recipient to whom you want to send your message. Press Enter/Return once to reach the `Cc:` line.
3. Type the addresses of the secondary recipients of your message (those who you want to read the message but from whom you do not require a response). Press Enter twice to locate the `Subject:` line.
4. In the Subject area type **Experimenting with pine's Cc: function** and press Enter once to begin composing your actual message. At this point, your screen should resemble that displayed in Figure 4.3.

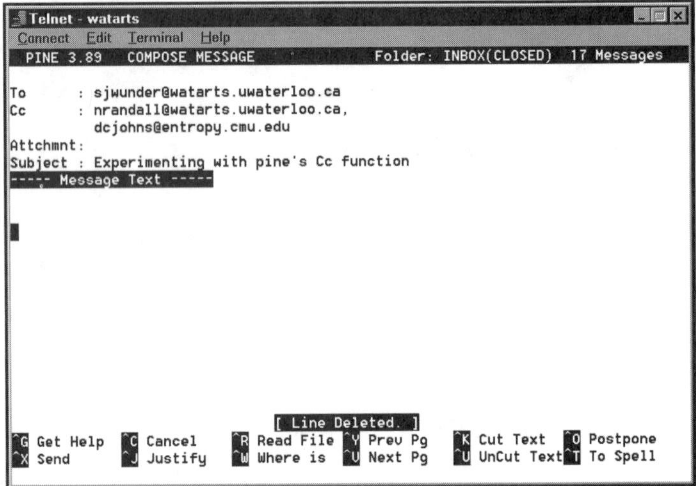

Figure 4.3.
E-mailing to multiple recipients using the `Cc:` *command line.*

5. Type a brief message and type **^x** to send the documents. After confirming your command, Pine will distribute your message to the desired recipients with lower delivery priority given to the secondary addresses.

Task 4.3: Use an alias to send a message.

Aliases (also known as nicknames) are crucial if you e-mail frequently. As you've seen, Internet addresses often are long and complex, and it's hard enough to remember your own, let alone someone you only infrequently send messages to. All e-mail programs enable you to create and save aliases; when you want to send a message to your friend Joseph Worthington at the University of Chicago, for example, you just type the alias (such as **joe**), and the program fills in the full address (such as `jaworthi@dragon.uchicago.edu`).

A good mail program also will enable you to capture the address from an incoming message and assign an alias to it. When you're reading a message in Pine, for example, and you want

to capture the sender's address, you just enter **T**. You're asked for an alias, and then to confirm the person's full name and full address. Pine then tucks the address nicely in your address book, and you no longer have to type the full version again.

You also can use your e-mail program to create *groups*. Groups combine the names of recipients, and when you want to send a message to the entire group, you address it to the group name only. You might have a project team scattered in different locations, for example. Put all the individual addresses into a group called `team`, and then address the messages to `team`. The message will go out to every member of the group.

To create an alias, complete the following simple procedure:

1. At UNIX's command prompt, type **`pine`** and press Enter.
2. From the main menu, select the Address Book item with your arrow keys and press Enter. The resulting screen provides you with a list of all the aliases you've already created (if any), in alphabetical order.
3. To create an alias press `a` (for Add) on your keyboard and Pine presents further instructions directly above the commands featured at the bottom of your screen.
4. First enter the name of the individual for whom you are creating the alias (last name, first name). For example, if I am creating an alias for my friend John Dowe, I would type `Dowe, John` and press Enter.
5. Now type the nickname or alias you want to use for your recipient (make it memorable). Press Enter.
6. Finally, you must enter the correct Internet address for the individual, that is, the electronic mail address you currently use to send the individual messages. Press Enter. Pine indicates that your addition is successful by stating `Addition Complete`, but you may verify the alias by scanning the alphabetical list in the Address Book for its entry.

Task 4.4: Take an address for future reference.

An added benefit of Pine (like most mailers) is that you can easily take addresses from existing messages and store them in your address book.

1. To take down an electronic mail address, type **`t`** while you are reading the message. Pine will then prompt you to create a nickname for the address.
2. Fill in a shortform or nickname for the original sender's address just as you did when creating an alias. Press Enter. Pine will then display the full name of the sender and ask you to confirm.
3. If the name is correct, press Enter once. Pine will then display that person's electronic mail address as displayed in the message you are reading.

4. Press Enter once if the address is correct. To complete the procedure, Pine will update the address book and post a confirmation on your screen. Now when you access your address book, an alias will have been created, which you may use in your electronic mail activities.

Task 4.5: Attach a file to a message.

Sometimes, you'll want to attach a file to an e-mail message, which your recipient will detach and use as a document or program. Usually, these attached files will be formatted binary files, such as graphics files, sound files, spreadsheets, or desktop publishing files, or entire programs if you want. Because they're binary files, they can't be included as part of the message itself.

Most mailers allow you to attach files. Where the problem lies, however, is in the method of *encoding* used by the mailer to get the file in one piece across the Internet. The most common encoding mechanisms are *uuencode*, *BinHex*, and *MIME* (Multiple Internet Mail Extensions). In general, uuencode works best when sending to a UNIX system, while BinHex works on the Mac platform. MIME is more recent, and is developing quickly as a standard, but not every user has access to MIME. Eudora users can select any of the three. Pine doesn't give you any options.

1. At the UNIX command line, type **`pine`** and select Compose Message from the main menu, using the arrow keys (or by pressing **`c`**). Press Enter.
2. Fill in the `To:` line and the `Cc:` line (if applicable) using the skills discussed in Tasks 4.1 and 4.2.
3. In the Attachments space, type **`^j`** to attach a file (as indicated in the menu at the bottom of the screen).
4. Pine will prompt you to enter the location of the file that you want to attach on a line appearing directly above the list of commands (see Figure 4.4). If you know the filename, type it in. If not, type **`^t`** to enter your UNIX file directory. After selecting the correct file, press Enter. Pine will confirm your success by indicating whether or not it could locate the desired file.
5. Fill in the `Subject:` line with an appropriate explanation and press Enter to compose the remainder of your message. The Send command (`^X`) will deliver your composition and the attached file to the addressee.

Figure 4.4.
Pine's attachment prompt.

Note: When using the Attachments feature in Eudora or other PC, Mac, or OS/2 mailers, you take the file from the hard drive of your own machine. For Pine, however, the file must be located on the UNIX machine itself. Often, you must upload the file from your computer to the UNIX machine by using Xmodem or Kermit before attaching it to a Pine message.

Task 4.6: Cancelling a message before sending it.

Once a message is sent, you can't pull it back (unfortunately, sometimes). However, you can easily cancel a message that you're in the process of composing.

1. To cancel a message once you have already begun composing it, type `^C` as indicated in the command list at the bottom of the screen. Pine will inform you that cancelling will abandon the message in order to verify your command.
2. Next, the mailer asks if you want to cancel. Type `y` to delete the message and Pine will return to the main menu from which you may choose any options (see Figure 4.5). The Cancel command is important because simply closing the screen or even exiting the entire system will not delete the message. The next time you attempt to compose a message or access Pine, the mailer will automatically prompt you to complete the interrupted message.

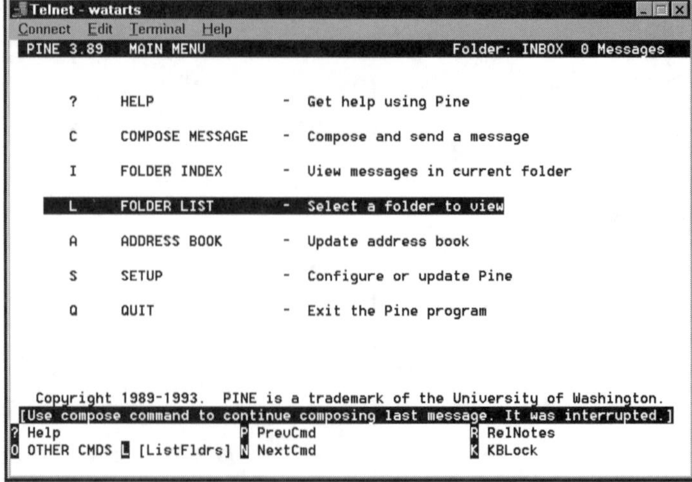

Figure 4.5.
Pine's main menu after exiting the program without cancelling a composition.

Receiving Messages

Knowing how to send well-constructed and useful messages is crucial, but you'll be spending far more of your e-mail time receiving messages that others send your way. If you get only a few, there's not much to do other than read them, but unless you're an unusual Internetter, you'll quickly find yourself deluged with them. Suddenly it becomes important to know how to store them, reply to them, or delete them before even seeing them, to maintain some sense of order.

Reading New Messages

When you fire up your e-mail program, the first thing you're likely to see is how many messages are waiting for you. In some programs, you have to actually request a check for messages, but usually the program does it for you by default. Find your message index or your INBOX, and start reading your mail.

Task 4.7: Access your folder lists and read a message.

1. Using the arrow keys, select Folder List from Pine's Main Menu and press Enter. The resulting screen will present a list of the mail folders contained in Pine's memory with your INBOX first (you can get to the INBOX directly from within Pine by typing `i`. Figure 4.6 shows what my Folder list looked like on the day I wrote this.

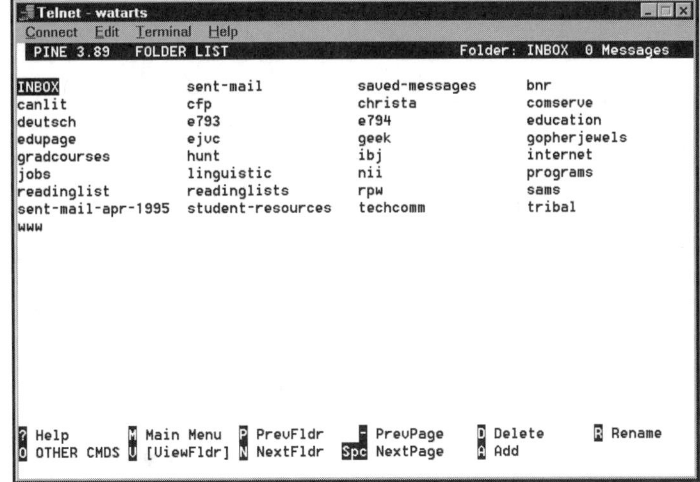

Figure 4.6.
My list of folders, any of which can contain read or unread messages.

2. Choose a folder using the arrow keys and press Enter. Pine will list all of the messages contained in that particular folder.
3. Cursor down to a message and press Enter (or the spacebar, in some mailers). Then settle back and read away.

Actually, you don't even have to go that far if you don't want. The first thing to do is to go through the message index and choose which ones you simply want to delete. Do that, and the list gets much shorter. To delete a message in Pine, highlight the message and type **d** (as explained immediately in the next section).

Deleting and Undeleting Messages

When you have a message on the screen in front of you, a number of options are open. You can delete it, save it, reply to it, forward it, print it, or export it. Or you can just leave it where it is.

Warning: If you receive a large number of messages, you won't want to leave any in your INBOX for long. These things pile up at an unbelievable rate, and soon you won't even know why you wanted to keep it.

Task 4.8: Delete a message.

1. Locate and open a message following the procedure described in Task 4.7.
2. While reading the article, type **d**. In the upper right corner, DEL will appear, signaling that you've flagged the message for deletion (see Figure 4.7). In the message listing for that folder, the message will be preceded by the letter D, again signaling that it has been flagged for deletion.

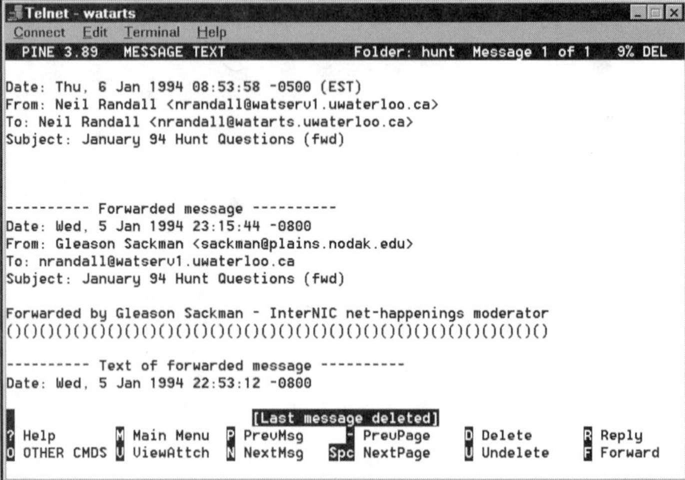

Figure 4.7.
The DEL *characters at top right show that the message has been flagged for deletion.*

3. Delete the message before even opening it for reading by cursoring down to the message and typing **d**. Pine immediately marks the message for deletion and eliminates it when you exit the program.

If you delete a message, you won't immediately lose it. In almost all e-mail programs, you can undelete a deleted message, as long as you do so before exiting the program.

Task 4.9: Undelete the message.

Cursor up to the deleted message (it's marked with a D), and type **u**. If you exit the program before remembering to undelete it, however, it's gone.

Saving Messages

Apart from deleting the message, the action you'll most likely take with an e-mail message is to save it. This is especially true as you start receiving messages from mailing lists, most of which you either can't or don't want to reply to, but which you want to keep for their valuable contents.

Task 4.10: Save a message from your INBOX.

1. Type **`pine`** and open your INBOX to read any messages contained there.
2. To save a message that you are currently reading just type **`s`**. Pine will prompt you with a `Save to folder:` line. If no folder is specified, Pine will automatically save the file in the default folder, saved messages (see Figure 4.8).

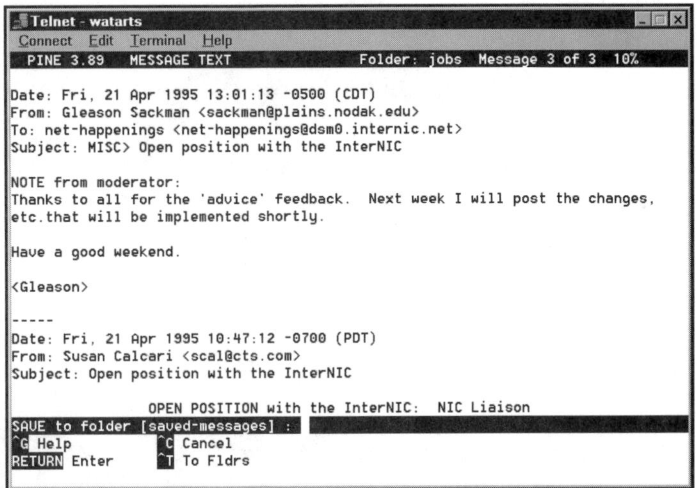

Figure 4.8.
The Save prompt as featured in Pine.

3. Type your desired folder name at the prompt. If the folder doesn't exist, Pine will tell you, and will let you create it on the spot. It will then save the message in the specified folder and delete it from the INBOX.

Tip: The saved-message folders in the mailers are simply files to which you continually append new text. You can FTP one of these files from one account to another if you want to work with the whole folder at once. This especially is useful if you work on a PC or Mac at home and a UNIX machine at work. Simply FTP the folder to your home computer, and then load it into a word processor and take the details you want. Sometimes this is necessary when you're running out of disk space on your office machine.

Replying to a Message

Replying to a message is much the same as sending one, but requires two essential considerations: the span of your audience and the inclusion of the original text.

Task 4.11: Respond to a message in Pine using the Reply command.

1. Decide if you want to send the reply to everyone who received the original. Often this is unnecessary, so don't automatically do so (the e-mail program usually will give you a choice).
2. Determine whether you want to include the original message in your reply. Be careful with this one. While it's useful to include certain lines from the original to refresh the sender's memory, nothing is as infuriating as getting the full text of a long message sent back to you (or across a mailing list). Be selective.
3. While the message is open before you for reading, type **R** (Reply) as indicated by Pine at the bottom of your screen. Pine will ask whether you want to include the original text in the reply message and offers you a series of possible responses—yes, no, or cancel, with no as the default.
4. Type **y** to include the original message. If your message was forwarded from a mailing list or multiple senders, Pine will then ask if you want to use the `Reply to:` address instead of the `From:` address. Type **y/n/^C**, depending on the desired audience for your reply (see Figure 4.9).

Figure 4.9.
Determining your audience through Pine's reply command.

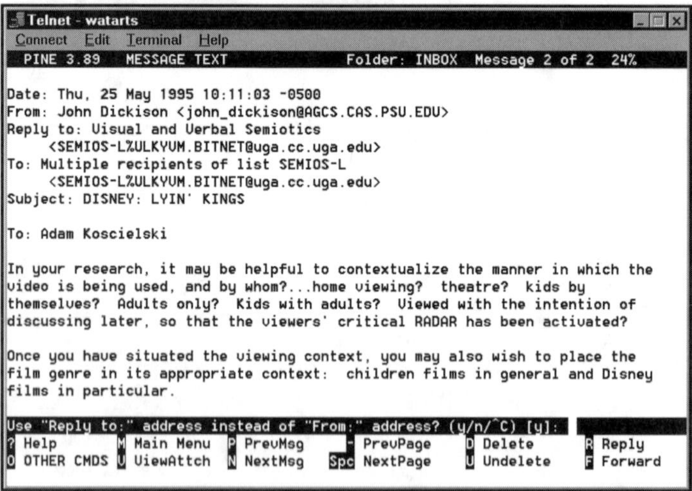

Your screen will now contain a copy of the original message text from which you may delete irrelevant segments or add comments and opinions.

5. Most often, the recipient of your Reply message will not require the entire span of the original message, but only key points to refresh their memory. Using the arrow keys, move to the beginning of a line that you want to delete and type **^K**. Pine will cut that line from your Reply text.

6. Type your message at the end of the original text or intersperse comments throughout the text as you want. The point of the reply message is simply to relate your response as clearly and efficiently as possible.
7. Type `^X` to send the message and confirm your command at Pine's Send Message prompt.

Forwarding a Message

Often you'll receive a message that you want someone else to read. Forwarding a message is like sending an original message, except that the forwarded message is attached to the end.

Task 4.12: Forward a message from your Pine account.

1. While reading a message that you want to forward, simply type `F`. Pine will transform your screen to place the `To:`, `Cc:`, `Attachments:`, and `Subject:` lines at the head of the forwarded message (see Figure 4.10).

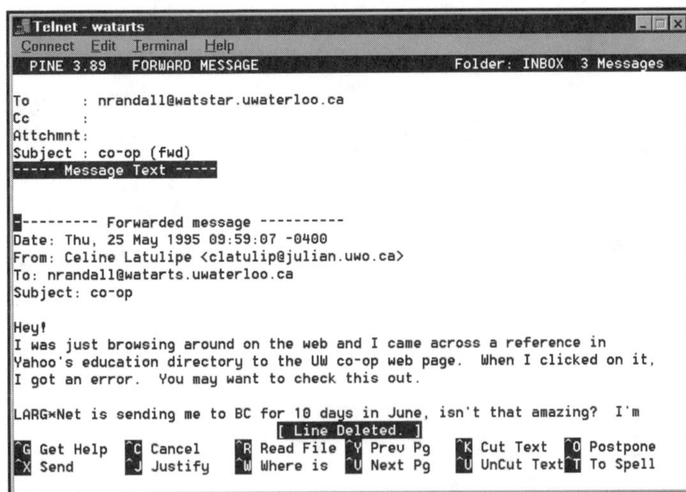

Figure 4.10.
Pine's forwarding screen.

2. You can do the following three useful things to a forwarded message before sending it:
   - **a.** Alter the subject line to make the message's contents clear.
   - **b.** Include an introductory sentence or paragraph at the beginning of the text explaining why you're forwarding it.
   - **c.** Edit the message, cutting out extraneous information, such as the original header and whatever material isn't important to the recipient.
3. To send the forwarded message simply type `^X` and confirm your command.

Exporting a Message

Exporting a message means sending the message as a text file out of your UNIX mailing program and your the hard drive of the machine where your UNIX account resides. When you export a message, it becomes a fully editable text file that you can load into a word processor on UNIX, download to your home system, FTP to another account, or do whatever else you do with text files.

Task 4.13: Export a message from Pine to your computer's hard drive.

1. To export a file that you are reading, type **e** (Export). Pine will ask you which file (in the home directory) to save the message text in.
2. Enter the appropriate filename and Pine will immediately export the message to the indicated file. Pine provides a final confirmation of the task's success and returns to the original message screen. From here, you can delete the mail message itself if you want. Note that the message has not been saved on the hard drive of your PC or Mac, but rather the hard drive of the UNIX machine that contains your account. See Chapter 7 for details on using Xmodem or Kermit to move the file to your PC or Mac.

Using a Graphical Mailer: Eudora

If you use Microsoft Windows, OS/2, or a Macintosh, you'll want to use the graphical interface of your system for your Internet functions as well. Pine and the other UNIX mailers are fast and powerful, but they're just not as graphically appealing as a graphical mailer, nor as carefully integrated with your other graphical applications. Fortunately, strong mailers are available for all operating systems. This section examines the highly popular *Eudora*, available for Mac and Windows in both a free and a (more advanced) commercial version.

Sending Messages

Sending and receiving messages on any electronic mailer involves the same essential steps that were discussed and applied using Pine. The move from a UNIX mailer to a graphical option such as Eudora essentially is one of convenience. Eudora offers many of the same services to its users, but often provides an easier or more user-friendly means of accomplishing those tasks.

Task 4.14: Send a basic message.

Although some minor differences may be highlighted, Eudora's basic message system contains the same essential components as Pine. The following procedure outlines the simple steps required to send a message in Eudora.

1. Click the Eudora (Eudora Local) icon from your main menu to access your graphical mailer. All possible commands are located at the top of your screen, contained in standard Windows pull-down menus. Simply click once on the menu name to reveal the controls and select the option you want.
2. To send a basic message, select New Message from the Message menu. Eudora should present you with the set-up screen shown in Figure 4.11.

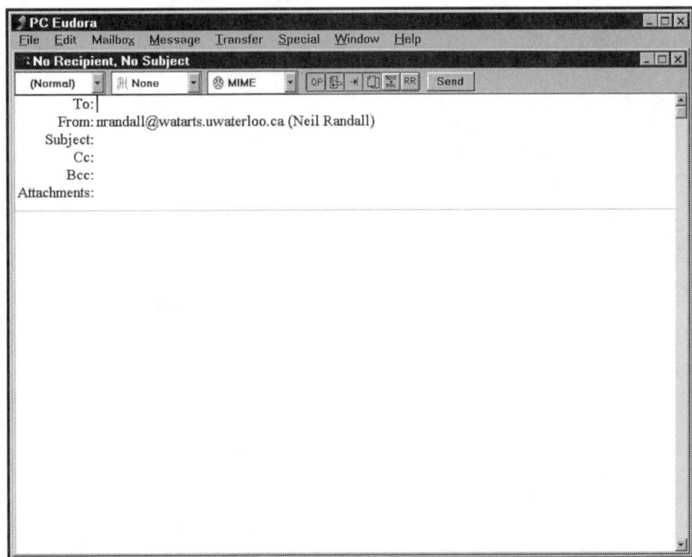

Figure 4.11.
Eudora's New Message screen.

3. Fill in the appropriate headers, according to the directions provided for mailing with a UNIX program—the message structure remains the same. The only difference you may encounter is the `Bcc:` line that sometimes appears below the `Cc:` option. `Bcc:` allows mailers to send messages to individuals without the other recipients' knowledge. When you list names under the `Cc:` line, each recipient's message contains that list so that they know who else has recieved the same message. But when you list names under the `Bcc:` line, this information is not relayed to all addressees. Although the `Bcc:` line may have some valid business applications, it can also be a sleazy thing to do.
4. When you are ready to compose your message, move your cursor to the blank message area and begin typing. You can adjust your font choice to suit your taste.
5. If you do not yet have a signature file created (see the section, "Creating a Signature"), sign your name at the bottom of your message to identify yourself to the recipient(s).
6. To send your message click the Send icon at the top right corner of the New Message screen or choose Send Immediately from the Message menu. Eudora will

display a small rectangular window at the top of the screen that flashes the message's `Subject:` line as it is sent to the desired address. The process is complete when Eudora returns to the main screen from which any command may be chosen.

Tip: You may configure Eudora to queue messages, which is a process that prepares files for sending but holds them until you select the Send Queued Messages command from the File menu. This option enables you to send all your messages at once. Choose the Switches command from Eudora's Special menu and locate the Immediately Send option under the Sending section. Turn the function off by clicking once on the command. Now when you access the New Message function, the Send icon will be replaced by a Queue icon. The Queue option also permits offline use.

Task 4.15: Attach a file to your message.

Attaching a file in Eudora involves the same basic activity as in Pine—you must specify the name and location of the file you want to attach to your message and the mailer will include it when your message is sent. The difference is that Eudora displays the standard File dialog box for your system, which makes locating the file quite easy.

File attachment depends on standards for allowing the document to be sent through electronic mail. Eudora offers three methods of encoding: *MIME*, *BinHex*, and *Uuencode*. Of the three, MIME is the most advanced, while BinHex is designed to allow Mac users to send files, and Uuencode is the same encoding program as that used in Newsgroups and most UNIX mailers. To attach a file, follow these steps:

1. When you come to the `Attachments:` line of your composition, select Attach a document from the Message menu at the top of your screen. Eudora will display the screen shown in Figure 4.12.
2. Type in the name of the file and indicate the directory or folder where it is contained. Or, maneuver through your directories using the mouse. Next, click the OK button. Eudora then will fill in the name of the file in the `Attachments:` line of your new message and append the file to your composition.
3. Type a brief message or introduction to the attachment, instructing your audience what to do with the appended document. Click the Send icon to deliver your message and attachment immediately.

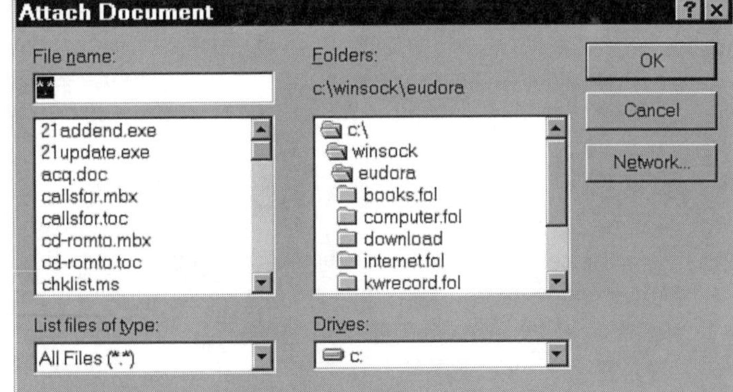

Figure 4.12.
Attaching a document to a simple message in Eudora.

Receiving Mail

Creating mail is one of the most important activities on the Internet, but inevitably, you'll read much more than you send. In this section, you'll go through a series of tasks that will show you how to receive messages and what to do with them.

4

Task 4.16: Check and read your mail.

Reading your incoming mail with Eudora is much the same as with any UNIX mailer, but once again, the process is more graphically pleasing, and additional options are available. To check and read your mail, follow these steps:

1. To check your mail, choose the Check Mail command from the File menu. Eudora will run through the list of all available new messages and automatically update your INBOX and folders.

Tip: For added privacy and security, Eudora allows you to precede the Check Mail command with a prompt that asks for a password. If this option has been selected from the Switches directory, mail may only be checked if your password has been entered. To add the password prompt, choose Switches from the Special menu and click the Save Password option *off.* This forces you to enter a password each time you check your e-mail.

2. To read any of the new messages now made available to you, simply double-click on the desired message block and begin reading. From this stage you can save, print, delete, undelete, reply, or redirect your messages at your own convenience. See Eudora's help file for details, or just experiment with the menus.

Mailboxes and Folders

The feature that sets Eudora above other graphical mailers in terms of advanced efficiency and organization is its complex *mailbox/folder system.* In Eudora, you can design an infinite number of mailboxes to sort and store all saved messages. You can organize your mailboxes by topic, author, or by any other criteria you want. Eudora also allows you to subdivide these mailboxes into more specific topics by creating folders. Folders are like mailboxes within mailboxes, which narrow the range of the original mailbox's subject and simplifies the location of articles.

Task 4.17: Create a mailbox for your incoming messages.

1. To create a mailbox for grouping files in Eudora, first choose New... from the Mailbox menu. Eudora will project the screen shown in Figure 4.13.

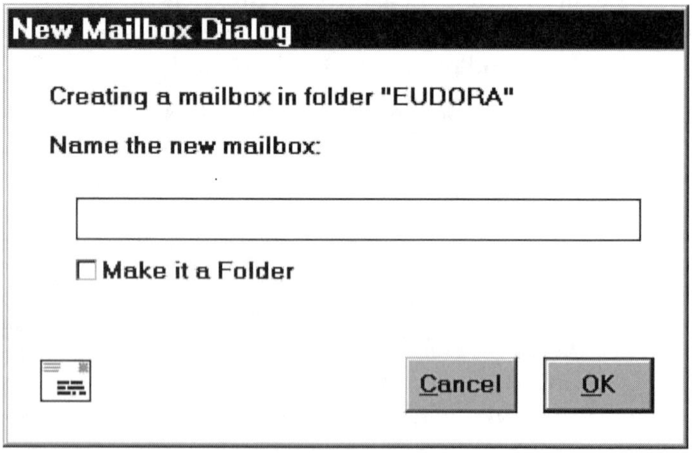

Figure 4.13.
Naming a new mailbox in Eudora.

2. Type the name of the new mailbox in the proposed slot, ensuring that the title is clear, subject-oriented, and concise (the benefit of creating a sorting file such as this is lost if you can't remember which messages belong under which heading).
3. When you have entered an appropriate name, click the OK button and the mailbox will be created. If I receive a large number of computer related messages, for example, I may entitle my new mailbox `computer`. Now, when I select the

Mailbox menu, the mailbox entitled `computer` will be listed below the New... command.

Task 4.18: Extend your mailbox listing to include a folder.

If your mailbox becomes too large or the articles contained in a mailbox could be further divided for easier manipulation, you can create a folder to store goupings of related topics. To extend your mailbox, follow these steps:

1. To create a folder, choose New... from the Mailbox menu, as you did when creating a mailbox. Eudora will project the same screen as shown in Figure 4.12.
2. Type the name of the mailbox in the Name slot, but before clicking OK, click on the Make it a folder option. Then click the OK button. Eudora will then create that mailbox and present you with another New Mailbox Dialog screen.
3. Type the name of the desired folder in the Name slot and choose OK. Again, make sure that the names used are appropriate for locating and using the messages stored under that heading.
4. To verify the success of these operations, click on the Mailbox menu and locate your mailbox name. Then scroll down to the name and highlight it. Eudora then extends the menu to include the list of folders created under that specific mailbox.

To create a new folder under a mailbox that already exists, simply scroll down to the mailbox's name under the Mailbox menu and select New from the extended folder listings. Eudora will then create another folder under that same heading.

Tip: You can create your mailboxes and folders on-the-fly, rather than working through the Mailbox menu. If you're reading a message you want to store in a mailbox, chooser New from the Transfer menu. You'll be presented with a dialog box that enables you to create a mailbox in which to store the message. You also can create folders from this New Mailbox dialog box, after which the dialog box will automatically reappear and ask you to create a mailbox. This is an extremely powerful feature of Eudora.

Filtering Messages

Eudora's mailbox/folder system is quite complex and extends far beyond this minimal application. In fact, you can configure Eudora to save incoming messages to specific mailboxes or folders rather than simply placing them all in your INBOX. This option is designed for those who receive large amounts of e-mail each day and who want to sort the messages automatically.

Task 4.19: Filter incoming messages that contain a specific phrase and originate from a specific user into a particular mailbox.

Note: The filtering feature is available only on the commercial version of Eudora.

Once you have created an efficient and organized mailbox and folder system, Eudora's advanced filtering option comes into play. Eudora offers users the capability to screen messages (incoming or outgoing) and transfer, save, alter the priority, or change the subject line before ever viewing the messages themselves. Essentially, you can configure your electronic mailer to place certain messages directly into their appropriate folders, alter the order of importance in which they are listed, or change the subject line to help you determine which messages you want to read at which time. The following steps show you how to create a specific filter for a specific purpose:

1. From Eudora's main screen, select Filters from the Window menu. Notice that the Filter Messages command under the Special menu activates the filter once it has been created under the Window menu. Eudora presents a set-up screen from which your filtering options may be selected (see Figure 4.14).

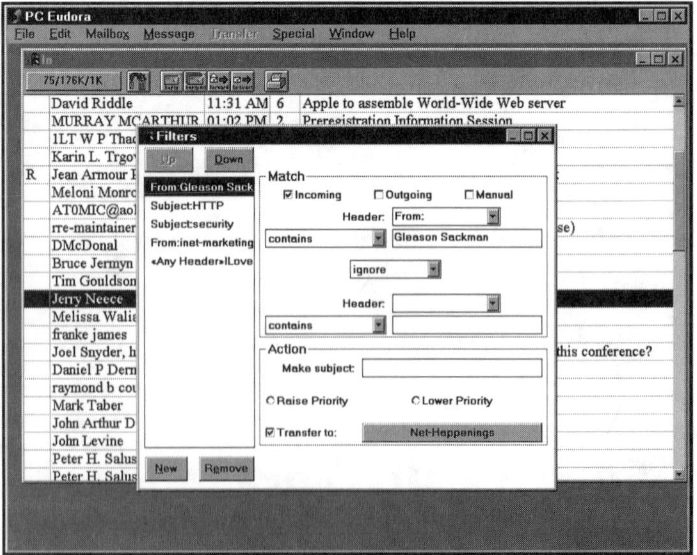

Figure 4.14.
Eudora's introductory filtering screen.

2. The Match portion of the Filters screen determines the type of messages that the mailer will search for or isolate to perform the filtering action on. In this scenario, you want to instruct Eudora to locate all incoming messages from Neil Randall concerning the subject `electronic mail`, and to save these messages in a mailbox called `Teach Yourself the Internet`. Using your mouse, select incoming from the initial options.
3. The second option (Header) determines the information that Eudora will look for in the header of the incoming messages. Because you want to filter messages from Neil Randall, select the From option and move to the next information block.
4. Choose contains from the appended list and type **`Neil Randall`** in the adjacent space. This tells Eudora to isolate messages containing the name `Neil Randall` in the From Header of any incoming messages.
5. Next, choose the second Header. Because you're looking for messages that have `electronic mail` in the subject line, choose Subject from the Header list. Leave contains as it is, and then type **`electronic mail`** in the adjoining box. You've now isolated messages that have `Neil Randall` in the From field and `electronic mail` in the Subject field.
6. Now move your cursor to the Action portion of the filter screen. This is the area in which you tell Eudora what to do with the messages it has matched. Click on the Transfer indicator and, using the New item, create a mailbox called `Teach Yourself the Internet`.
7. When you have inserted the appropriate information, close the filter screen. Eudora will then ask if you want to save the changes to the filtering option. Select Save.

A variety of other filtering options are available and can make your e-mail system increasingly efficient. Explore the various commands and format a filter or a collection of filters that will suit your individual needs. To create a second filter, simply select the New button at the bottom of the screen and fill in the desired options. To remove a filter that is no longer necessary, highlight the filter name from the list provided on the left side of the filter screen and select Remove.

Other E-Mail Considerations

As you might expect, full mastery of e-mail means control of several other variables as well. A few of these are covered here, but as you learn your particular mailer you'll discover even more.

Signatures

At the end of some messages, you'll notice a clever "sign-off" message. This often includes the sender's full name and address, and possibly a phone or fax number, an alternate e-mail address, and even a quote or witty saying. Your own messages, you'll instantly notice, don't have this interesting and appealing feature. Naturally, you'd like to change that.

What you've seen is called a *signature.* It's created by the user in a separate text editor, and then saved to disk and brought in by the e-mail program.

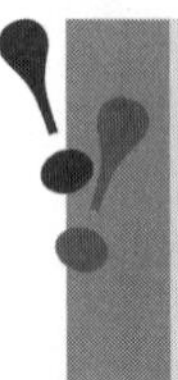

Warning: When subscribing to a mailing list (see Chapter 4), be sure to erase your signature before sending the subscription message. The Listserv software can't process the request if there's anything more than the standard one-line message.

Creating a Signature

To create a signature, you need to develop a separate file that your mailer will look for each time you begin composing a message. In Pine's case, for example, this file is called `.signature` (note the preceding dot); whenever you choose the Compose command from Pine's main menu, the contents of this file will appear in the message area (you can edit or delete it, as with any other message text). You can configure each mailer to look for a specific signature file, but configuring mailers is beyond the scope of this book.

Task 4.20: Create an appealing signature file in Pine.

If you have Pine, you almost certainly have the text editor called *Pico.* If you do not have Pico, you'll probably have an editor called *vi.* Contact your systems people for details on how to create a file with vi (which is more complex than Pico). To create a signature file in Pine, follow these steps:

1. To create your signature file, exit Pine (Q-quit) and type **`pico.signature`** at the UNIX prompt. The `.signature` file consists of a blank screen in which any existing signatures will be listed. Because this is your first signature file, your screen will be empty.
2. Type the signature you want.
3. When you finish, exit Pico by pressing Ctrl+X. Pico will ask if you want to save the "modified buffer." Type **`y`** to save the file.

Now when you compose a message in Pine, you'll see your signature at the bottom of the message area.

Warning: Keep your signature civil, by the way. That means not too long, and not filled with nifty line pictures. And if you include a funny message, remember that most things are funny only once, so change such a signature regularly. In other words, treat your signature file like your answering machine message. Short, informative, and not too cutesy.

Task 4.21: Create a signature file in Eudora.

Creating a signature file in Eudora is incorporated directly into the program itself, revealing the advanced ease of this graphical mailer. To create a signature file in Eudora, follow these steps:

1. Select Signature from the Window menu.
2. Type the signature you want and close the window. Now Eudora will place that signature file at the end of your e-mail messages if you want (select your signature options from the Switches command under Special).

Tip: The commercial version of Eudora also contains an Alternate Signature option that enables you to create another variant signature file. Select the Alternate Signature command from the Window menu and fill in the appropriate information.

Emoticons (a.k.a. Smileys) and Other Questionable Conventions

You've likely heard about *emoticons.* They're the little symbols you type into an e-mail message to convey a subtle emotion or suggestion. The best known are the smiling face (hence the name smileys), `:-)` and the winking face, `;-)`. The first shows that you're trying to convey a happy or good thought, the second that you're letting the reader know that what you just wrote was a bit "wink-wink" humorous. The idea is that your readers tilt their heads to the left so the symbol actually looks like a face. These things have become so numerous that there's even a smiley dictionary available.

Emoticons aren't the only e-mail convention I—and a many other people—find annoying.

Often in a message, you'll see a humorous or ironic statement followed with something like this: `<grin>`. The idea, of course, is that not everyone understands irony, so sometimes it's necessary to do this to prevent misunderstanding, in the same way you'd actually grin in face-to-face conversation. My point is a bit different than this; if your writing isn't good enough to get the idea of irony, humor, or sarcasm across, don't use it. As far as I'm concerned, the `<grin>` symbol is equivalent to the way 5-year olds tell jokes and then keep asking, "Get it? Get it?" It does nothing for your credibility as a writer.

But then, that's just my opinion.

Flaming

Flaming is the practice of sounding off in e-mail messages or on newsgroups. In other words, the practice of yelling and screaming as if you were standing in front of the person you want to tell off.

It's so tempting. You read a message that drives you up a wall, so you fire up your e-mail program and blast away. The sender was stupid, after all, and he deserves to be denounced. And you're the best person to do it.

The only problem is, once you've sent the message, you can't easily get it back. If you write an angry letter, you can wait for a while before dropping it in the mailbox, and then change your mind before it actually goes. Sending a flame is much like picking up the phone and screaming in someone's ear—except that most of us back down when we actually hear the person's voice. It's even worse when you're flaming in public, across a mailing list or a newsgroup. It's rarely impressive, and you usually come across as a prize jerk.

Note: E-mail at its best combines letters and phone calls. Like the latter, it's almost immediate, but like the former you have a chance to formulate an intelligent question or response. At its worst, e-mail combines them badly. As with phone calls, you can scream at someone immediately, but as with letters you can hide behind the fact that you don't see the recipient.

So don't flame. Stop yourself. Believe me, you'll feel better about doing so. And remember that, if someone has written something stupid in public, you won't be the only one who realizes it. The Internet is crammed with intelligent people. If you want to express a defamatory opinion, do so with wit and class instead (reading Samuel Johnson's letters is a good start).

Mailing Lists

Where newsgroups combine personal, professional, and all other topics, *mailing lists* (also called *discussion lists* and *Listservs*, among other names) are designed primarily to be professionally oriented. Many, in fact, are based on academic topics, offering scholars from a wide range of disciplines a place to meet, discuss, and occasionally even socialize. Mailing lists have been established to be used for collaborative classrooms, and even as the distribution method for conferences.

Most mailing lists are moderated. This means that someone is watching over them, to some degree or another. The moderator's function is to keep the list more or less on the topic and to prevent idiocy. Usually, however, moderators have little time to worry a great deal about such things, so the lists tend to moderate themselves. Still, the existence of the moderator is what generally distinguishes mailing lists from newgroups.

Working with mailing lists is easier than working with newgroups, mainly because you don't have to master new software. While effective newgroup participation practically requires you to learn *rn* or *trn*, or one of the graphical newgroup readers, mailing lists are handled exclusively via e-mail. As soon as you know how to send and receive e-mail messages, you're ready to subscribe to mailing lists.

Task 4.22: Discovering mailing lists.

You can find out about the existence of mailing lists in a number of ways. The easiest way is to talk to other Internetters in your office, who probably will be on one or two lists already and who can help you subscribe.

Next easiest is to use Gopher. By connecting to any good Gopher (see Chapter 8 for examples and instructions), you usually can maneuver your way into an item called Internet Resources, or something similar to that. In here, look for a directory or file called Mailing Lists or Discussion Lists. This will give you all you need to get started.

1. Gopher to `cwis.usc.edu` (see Chapter 8 for details on Gopher). Select Other Gophers and Information Resources, and then Gopher Jewels. Select the item Internet and Computer Related Resources, and finally Lists of Lists Resources. From this menu, you can search for specific mailing lists (and newsgroups) by selecting the Search item, or you can browse the information by selecting List of Lists Resources (`misc`). Included are the names of the mailing lists and how to subscribe to them.

The best way to discover *new* mailing lists is, ironically enough, to subscribe to a mailing list.

2. Load your e-mail program.
3. In the `To:` field, type **`majordomo@is.internic.net`**.
4. Leave the subject line blank.
5. In the message area, type **`subscribe net-happenings`**.
6. Make sure you are *not* automatically sending your signature.
7. Send the message.

In a few minutes or (sometimes) hours, you'll receive an acknowledgement, consisting of a message that tells you about the mailing list. *Keep this message.* Here you'll learn how to unsubscribe and other information.

This is a superb mailing list for those who want to keep up with Internet advances. Enjoy.

Task 4.23: Subscribe to a BITNET mailing list.

Some mailing lists are available through Listserv software in BITNET sites, rather than on the Internet itself. To subscribe, you send a subscription message to the Listserv's address. To subscribe to a BITNET mailing list, follow these steps:

1. Open your mail program (Mail, Elm, Pine, Eudora, and so on) and prepare to send a message.
2. In the `To:` line, type **`LISTSERV@`*`ADDRESS`*`.BITNET`** (where `ADDRESS` is the list's address as shown in the information file).
3. Leave the subject line completely blank.
4. In the first line of the message area, type **`subscribe`** ***`LISTNAME`*** *`Your_Name`*. (Use your real first and last name for `Your_Name`, such as Jane Smith.)
5. Be sure not to include a signature in your message.
6. Send the message.

Shortly, you'll receive confirmation of your subscription. This usually consists of two messages: one telling you about computer time used (which you can erase), and another introducing you to the list and explaining other details.

The introductory message tells about the list and shows you how to do the following:

- Unsubscribe
- Stop your mail temporarily
- Restart your mail

- Acknowledge your postings
- Receive once-a-day or once-a week-digest postings rather than each one as it's posted. This is especially useful if you're getting 10 to 20 messages per day (which is hardly uncommon)

Now it's just a matter of sitting back and waiting, and checking your mail every so often for postings.

Task 4.24: Subscribe to a Majordomo mailing list.

In Task 4.21, you subscribed to the Net-Happenings list. This is a *Majordomo* type of mailing list; that is, it is run by software that goes by the name of Majordomo. Subscribing to these lists is a bit easier than to BITNET-based lists. In this task, you'll subscribe to a list that deals with trading and investing on Wall Street.

1. Load your e-mail program.
2. In the `To:` line, type **`majordomo@shore.net`**.
3. Leaving the subject line blank, skip to the message area. Here, type **`subscribe wallstreet`** *`xxxxxx@xxxxx.xxx`* (that is, your e-mail address).
4. A short while later, check your mail and save the verification message.

Task 4.25: Read postings from a mailing list.

The whole point of joining a mailing list is to exchange messages with others who have an interest in the list's subject matter. Often, you'll receive messages several times a day, although some lists are far less active.

To read postings, load your mailer and check your mail.

That's all you have to do, which is why mailing lists are so popular. It's also why some people shun them; mailing lists can easily clog up your mailer, often with postings that interest you very little.

Task 4.26: Post to a mailing list.

You can post to a mailing list according to the instructions in the introductory message, but the usual way simply is to reply to the message. It's nothing but an ordinary e-mail message, after all, with the exception that it's been sent to a group rather than just you. To post to a mailing list, follow these steps:

1. Having read the message, start a Reply sequence (in Elm or Pine, for example, type **`r`**).

2. If your mailing software prompts you, decide whether to include the original message in the reply, and whether to post to the entire list. Type **y** or **n**, as desired.
3. Check the subject line to ensure that it still applies. If you're changing the topic somewhat, change the subject line as well.
4. Send the message. Depending on how the list is set up, you may get a copy of your own message as it's posted to the list.

Before posting your first message, read the following guidelines regarding posting to a mailing list:

- Don't just automatically resend the original message. In fact, don't send it in its complete original form *at all.* If you want to include part of it, include that part and delete the rest. Show that you've actually thought about what you're doing; it enhances your credibility immensely with the rest of the group.
- If you have something personal to say to the sender of the last message, e-mail that person and *not* the entire group (your mail program will prompt you for this option).

Note: The preceding guideline is extremely important! Mailing lists are designed to be more professional than newsgroups; often, they're accessed by people at work. Nobody wants to read a message that says, "Nice work, Barb!", or—much worse—"Glad to hear about Chelsea's sax recital, Bill. Best to Hillary, okay?" Even worse, some people completely forget that the messages are broadcast all over the place, and include *extremely* personal information. I have been hugely embarrassed for people who have outlined their marital problems, their legal problems, and even their prison experiences in what should have been a personal e-mail.

- If you have four things to say, say them in one message, not four separate ones. Nobody wants to see your name appear in their mailer six times a day.
- Be brief, unless you can justify not being brief. One screen of text is more than enough for most people to read.

Summary

Electronic mail is the Internet's most obvious and most instantly useful function. You can send messages to anyone in the world, as long as you know that person's e-mail address—and unlike some commercial online services, the message won't carry a fee. You can create groups of recipients who receive the same message at the same time, you can attach files for

downloading, you can forward messages, and you can keep a message stream going indefinitely.

You also can use e-mail to join special interest mailing lists generated by Listserv software. These lists tend to be more specific and more disciplined than newsgroups, and many have an academic focus. Through these lists, you can find out about current research and upcoming conferences and gatherings, and the lists often lead you to other Internet resources in your topic area.

Many who use e-mail find it the single most effective means of communicating with peers, friends, colleagues, and even clients. E-mail offers the benefits of both letter-writing (considered responses, depth of thought) and telephone conversation (immediacy, brevity, informality), without the inconviences of either. But it can be—and often is—abused. If you find yourself sending out five messages a day to the same person and only getting one in response, ask yourself if you shouldn't step back a bit and reconsider. And if you start seeing 10 messages over 3 days from the same person on a mailing list, ask yourself if you haven't been doing the same thing. It can be annoying, distracting, and counter-productive.

Task Review

This chapter has concentrated on the things to consider when using e-mail, rather than on how to send and receive messages. You now are fully qualified to do the following:

- ☐ Include a useful, readable, and sensible subject line with each message
- ☐ Avoid flaming
- ☐ Think carefully before cluttering your message with smileys
- ☐ Create a sensible, intelligent, and useful signature
- ☐ Decide among the three UNIX mailers: Mail, Elm, and Pine
- ☐ Decide whether you want access to a graphical mailer like Eudora
- ☐ Attach documents or other files to a message
- ☐ Determine whether you should reply to a full mailing list or just the originator of the message
- ☐ Create address books with aliases for easier use
- ☐ Find the important information in a message header

Q&A

Q How do I include two or more names in the `TO:` field?

A The first way is to type all the addresses, separating each with a comma. Note that you can combine aliases and full addresses in the following way:

```
TO:
nrandall@watarts.uwaterloo.ca,tom,carole@office
```

(my full address, the address you've nicknamed `tom`, and `Carole` next door)

If you have a group of two or more people you frequently e-mail, set them up as a group name. In any of the mailers, you can do so as part of the address book (or as part of the Nicknames feature in Eudora). Create the group and include the individual addresses inside it. Note that you can use aliases when creating a group, so that after you've nicknamed a long address as `tom`, you can simply specify `tom` in the group.

Q Do I have to read a message before I delete it?

A Not in any of the UNIX mailers, nor in Eudora. Just press Delete and get rid of it. In older systems, however (I'm thinking of VMS, where I began my e-mail career), you may not always have this option. If that's the case, reading mail becomes an incredible pain, unless you have few correspondents. Try to upgrade if at all possible.

Q Can I send a message to myself?

A Yes. Just fill in the appropriate address.

Q How do I show emphasis in an e-mail message?

A Good question. Don't count on using things like underlining or italics, unless you know that your recipient's system will display them. If you absolutely must emphasize, consider using ALL CAPS, but this practice is heavily frowned on throughout the Net. The best approach simply is to write forcefully, relying on none of these tactics.

Q Is it true that systems administrators can read my e-mail?

A Usually, yes, if they really want to. In fact, there's a series of enormous debates going on as to whether or not e-mail is considered official correspondence (internal or external) for the sake of organizational policy. The best bet is this: if you wouldn't send a memo saying it, don't use e-mail to say it. If you want to communicate personally with someone, phone them in your off-hours, or send them an old-fashioned letter.

Q If I can attach files to an e-mail message, why don't I just type them up using my word processor and attach them, rather than typing directly into the e-mail program?

A With long messages, that's actually a good idea. When you type using a word processor, you usually spend more time organizing and thinking about your writing. But for everyday correspondence, it's just too inconvenient, not only for you but for your recipient. Remember that the person who gets your file has to download it and open it in a word processor. Unless you know your message merits that kind of extra effort, don't count on it being read.

Extra Credit: Sending E-mail Messages to Commercial Online Services

Internet users and those on the commercial online services—CompuServe, GEnie, Prodigy, America Online, Delphi, MCI Mail, and so on—can exchange electronic mail. Everything is the same as sending to another Internet address, except that the `To:` address itself has a few different elements (both from the Net and from inside the commercial service).

Table 4.1 summarizes the address patterns for each service.

Note: Our fictional user for these examples is the poet Virgil, who has an Internet address of `virgil@aeneid.rome.it`.

Table 4.1. Address patterns for commercial online services.

If user is on:	With username:	Address from Net as follows:
America Online	`VirgilR`	`virgilr@aol.com` (capitals removed)
BIX	`virgilr`	`virgilr@bix.com`
CompuServe	`73859,1788`	`73859.1788@compuserve.com` (comma replaced by period)
GEnie	`virgilr2`	`virgilr2@genie.geis.com`
MCI Mail	`Virgil (256-4985)`	`Virgil@mcimail.com` (if there's only one Virgil)
		`256-4985@mcimail.com` (to guarantee no duplicate Virgils)
Prodigy	`virgil3`	`virgil3@prodigy.com`

These are the major services. For others, one of the simplest things to do is have the recipient send you a message first, and then store the return address as an alias for later use.

5

Newsgroups

by Stewart Lindsay, Stephanie Wunder, and Neil Randall

This chapter is devoted to one of the Internet's most continually fascinating features, Usenet. Although begun as a non-Internet network, Usenet has become as much a part of the Net as Gopher and the World Wide Web. No matter what your area of interest, there is probably a newsgroup already in place with participants from just about anywhere. Finding them and subscribing to them is easy, but active participation has its rules and protocols. For more information, refer to Chapter 4.

In this chapter, you will learn how to do the following:

- Access newsgroups using the rn and trn programs
- Read posts on selected newsgroups
- Post to a newsgroup—contributing to the conversation
- Decode and use binary attachments
- Discover the usefulness of graphical newsreaders
- Access newsgroups using News Xpress for Windows

Interacting with People Who Share Your Interests

Despite its obvious strengths, e-mail by itself is not the answer to all your communications needs. It's excellent as long as you know someone's Internet address, but eventually you'll run out of people you know and things to discuss. Those whose addresses you've managed to gather aren't necessarily interested in the same things you are, at least not to the same degree. Even mailing lists have their limitations, because there simply isn't a mailing list for every conceivable topic. Somewhere in the world, someone must share your passion for medieval architecture, or training Cocker Spaniels, or which Australian wine goes best with tripe, or theories of consciousness, or global marketing, or *Gilligan's Island*...

The question is, now that you want more, where do you find it? Where can you find/meet people on the Net who share your interests? Where do you go with questions you might have, to discuss your world and its ongoing development, as well as to discover new worlds and opinions you hadn't thought existed? In short, where is all this global interaction you've heard so much about in the press?

The answer lies in newsgroups, which are lumped in a network technically known as Usenet. In this chapter, you'll learn how to choose from the myriad of newsgroups available, how to access and read them, and how to participate in their conversations.

Introduction to Usenet

Although it is a prominent and much-hyped feature of the Internet, *Usenet* started out as a separate network. It was put into place in the late '70s by a couple of students at Duke

University, and its first connection was to the nearby Chapel Hill campus of the University of North Carolina. As its potential became clear, the network expanded quickly, sites on the Internet began to carry it, and many users got their first Internet experience through it.

The idea behind Usenet is that people have topics they want to discuss, and they want to involve others from anywhere in the world in the discussion. Once you find a newsgroup you're interested in joining, you subscribe to it, and then load a program called a *newsreader* in order to read new messages. With these readers, you can read every message in succession, or you can follow message *threads* (sub-topics) that you're especially interested in. At any point, you can post a reply to a message you've read, or you can start an entirely new discussion.

Usenet newsgroups are classified according to a grouping called *hierarchies*. In general, the hierarchies help you locate groups you're interested in. Following are some of the major categories:

`alt`	Topics about—well, you name it—UFOs, sex, TV, dogs…
`bionet`	Topics appealing to biologists
`bit`	BITNET mailing lists (usually mirrors of the Listserv versions)
`biz`	Topics dealing with business, some on specific companies or products
`clari`	Topics from ClariNet through the UPI wire service
`de`	Newsgroups from Germany (often in German)
`fr`	Newsgroups from France (often in French)
`k12`	Topics appealing to users involved in K–12 education
`comp`	Topics appealing to computer hobbyists and professionals
`misc`	Topics not fitting into the other categories
`news`	Topics regarding new Internet information and events
`rec`	Topics appealing to hobbyists of all kinds
`sci`	Science topics
`soc`	Cultural and social topics
`talk`	Topics lending themselves to debates

Usenet isn't carried by all Internet sites—and even where it is, some sites restrict access to certain hierarchies. It's not uncommon, for example, to have Usenet access but no way of getting the `alt` groups. Talk with your systems people if you want hierarchies or newsgroups added for potential subscription.

Okay, so the Usenet is the means by which you can interact. How do you get there? This part is quite straightforward. Most Net providers use a newsreader program called *rn* or *trn.* Because of the popularity of these programs (they are available at a large percentage of sites), this chapter deals with them exclusively. Other readers are available for UNIX, Macs, PCs, and other platforms, but rn and trn are dominant.

The name rn stands for *Read News,* while trn is *Threaded Read News.* They are, in fact, the same program, but they differ in the way they present the various groups for your viewing.

The rn program is the bare-bones version that presents articles within each group as they are received. That is, in a newsgroup discussing American culture, article 231 could be about the growing problem of gun-based violence, while the next article, 232, could be a request for information on the annual Peach Festival in Georgia. Both articles have to do with American culture, and rn serves them up in chronological order. As explained later in this chapter, you can thread the groups, but you have to do so yourself.

On the other hand, trn offers threading, a very simple way to filter what you want to read from what you have no interest in. It enables you to choose articles, based on their subject line, before you read and without having to wade through several (sometimes hundreds) of articles to find something of interest.

Warning: One thing you always have to remember about Usenet is that, for the most part, it is an unmoderated forum (especially in the `alt` groups; several `soc`, `comp`, and other groups are moderated). Unlike a newspaper or magazine, there is no editor to filter anything; anyone can (and, believe me, usually does) say what they like. You are your own editor on the Net, and using threading is one way to quickly learn to filter out the noise.

Task 5.1: Access your newsgroups.

Note: In this chapter, trn is used for all examples, but if your server has only rn, don't worry: first, bug your Systems Administrator for trn, and if that doesn't work, just get onto the groups as shown here. Things will be pretty much the same, except that you won't have automatic threading from the beginning.

1. To start, type **`trn`** at the UNIX prompt:

   ```
   % trn
   ```

   Because this is your first time, you probably won't be subscribed to any newsgroups, although some servers automatically subscribe you to local newsgroups of interest.

2. You'll be presented with each newsgroup, one by one, asking if you want to subscribe. For now, type **`N`** to stop this process (it might take a while, as rn/trn tells you it's ignoring each one). Even if you have been presubscribed to a newsgroup, for the sake of this task just say no until you see the following message:

   ```
   ****** End of newsgroups — what next? [qnp]
   ```

3. Type **h** to access the Help menu.

Tip: At any time, if you forget what commands are available at any point, just type **h** for help. Also, trn usually will give you a choice of three or four of the most likely commands in square brackets: `[qnp]` means quit, next, or previous. Always remember that besides pressing the appropriate key, you can press the space bar to select the first item (in the preceding case, quit).

After typing **h**, you'll get the following:

```
Newsgroup Selection commands:
t       Toggle the newsgroup between threaded and unthreaded reading.
c       Catch up (mark all articles as read).
A       Abandon read/unread changes to this newsgroup since you started trn.
n       Go to the next newsgroup with unread news.
N       Go to the next newsgroup.
p       Go to the previous newsgroup with unread news.
P       Go to the previous newsgroup.
-       Go to the previously displayed newsgroup.
1       Go to the first newsgroup.
^       Go to the first newsgroup with unread news.
$       Go to the last newsgroup.
g name  Go to the named newsgroup. Subscribe to new newsgroups this way too.
/pat    Search forward for newsgroup matching pattern.
?pat    Search backward for newsgroup matching pattern.
(Use * and ? style patterns. Append r to include read newsgroups.)
l pat   List unsubscribed newsgroups containing pattern.
m name  Move named newsgroup elsewhere (no name moves current newsgroup).
o pat   Only display newsgroups matching pattern. Omit pat to unrestrict.
O pat   Like o, but skip empty groups.
a pat   Like o, but also scans for unsubscribed newsgroups matching pattern.
L       List current .newsrc.
&       Print current command—line switch settings.
Set (or unset) more command—line switches.
&&      Print current macro definitions.
&&def   Define a new macro.
!cmd    Shell escape.
q       Quit trn.
x       Quit, restoring .newsrc to its state at startup of trn.
^K      Edit the global KILL file. Use commands like /pattern/j to suppress
pattern in every newsgroup.
v       Print version and the address for reporting bugs.
```

Tip: The preceding list is extremely useful, so it's probably a good idea to mark this page for future reference (or print it out).

Task 5.2: Subscribe to a newsgroup.

The next step is actually subscribing to a newsgroup, so that you can follow the discussions over time.

1. Type `l` to get a master list of all available newsgroups at your site. This list is extremely long, however, and contains several thousand groups from which to choose. If, at any time, you want to stop reading the list, Press Ctrl+C to escape back to the Newsgroups prompt.

   Typing `l` generates something that looks like the following list. (I have edited out most, but tried to keep a broad section of a variety of newsgroup types to give you an idea what's available.)

```
****** End of newsgroups — what next? [qnp] l
Completely unsubscribed newsgroups:

ab.politics
advocacy
air.unix
alt.abortion.inequity
alt.activism
alt.activism.d
alt.activism.death-penalty
alt.adoption
alt.aldus.freehand
alt.aldus.misc
alt.aldus.pagemaker
alt.alien.visitors
alt.angst
alt.barney.dinosaur.die.die.die
alt.bbs
alt.bbs.ads
alt.binaries.pictures.cartoons
alt.binaries.pictures.d
alt.binaries.clip-art
alt.coffee
alt.current-events.bosnia
alt.current-events.clinton.whitewater
alt.current-events.flood-of-93
alt.current-events.la-quake
alt.current-events.somalia
alt.fan.dan-quayle
alt.fan.dave_barry
alt.fan.rush-limbaugh
alt.fishing
alt.sex
alt.tv.ren-n-stimpy
alt.tv.simpsons
bionet.genome.chromosomes
bionet.immunology
bionet.info-theory
bionet.jobs
bionet.journals.contents
bionet.neuroscience
bit.listserv.catholic
```

```
bit.listserv.cdromlan
bit.listserv.pagemakr
bit.listserv.tech-l
bit.listserv.tecmat-l
bit.listserv.tesl-l
bit.listserv.test
biz.books.technical
de.sci.electronics
de.soc.jugendarbeit
de.soc.weltanschauung
fr.news.distribution
fr.news.divers
k12.chat.elementary
k12.chat.junior
k12.chat.senior
k12.chat.teacher
misc.invest.real-estate
misc.invest.stocks
misc.jobs.contract
misc.jobs.misc
rec.arts.startrek.current
rec.aviation
rec.food.veg.cooking
rec.gambling
rec.humor.d
sci.med.dentistry
sci.med.nursing
soc.culture.burma
soc.culture.canada
soc.culture.jewish
soc.culture.usa

****** End of newsgroups — what next? [qnp]
```

5

As you can see, there are newsgroups for pretty much every topic under the sun.

The first part of the newsgroup name gives an indication of the general category to which that newsgroup belongs (see the preceding list). By far, the most diverse category (or *hierarchy*, in Usenet lingo) is the `alt` (alternative) hierarchy. This is the one you read about in *Time* and *Newsweek*, and is where you find the comical (`alt.humor`), the bizarre (`alt.barney.die.die.die`), and a mixture of both (`alt.jokes.tasteless`). This also is where you find the sexually-oriented topics that cause frequent protests.

So, to avoid being offended, stick with groups you know are to your liking. `alt.fan.letterman` most likely will be about David Letterman (and rumors abound that he, himself, sometimes "lurks," but doesn't contribute); `alt.sex` probably is going to be discussions of a sexual nature. The ones that may surprise you are those with ambiguous names: `alt.motss` isn't about a brand of Clamato juice, but rather is an acronym for "members of the same sex."

2. Write down the names of the groups that interest you. Start with only a few, to get a feel for newsgroups in general.

3. Type **g alt.coffee** (go to the newsgroup alt.coffee, for example). Presumably, this is a general discussion about the nectar of the gods. Your screen will look like the following:

```
****** End of newsgroups — what next? [qnp] g alt.coffee
```

Because you have never accessed the group before, you'll get the following message:

```
Newsgroup alt.coffee not in .newsrc-subscribe? [ynYN]
```

Don't worry about the capital letters just now, just type **y** and you'll get the following

```
====== 1068 unread articles in alt.coffee — read now? [+ynq]
```

This means that you now are in the newsgroup `alt.coffee`. There are 1,068 articles that you personally have not read.

4. You now have a choice. Type **q** to quit, **n** to go to the next subscribed newsgroup (but you don't have any yet) without reading this one, **y** to start reading in chronological order, or **+** to see a threaded list of Subject lines (which you'll do in Task 5.3). You can get the full list of possible actions by typing **h**. The first part of that list looks like the following:

```
y       Do this newsgroup now.
SP      Do this newsgroup, executing the default command listed in []'s.
.cmd    Do this newsgroup, executing cmd as first command.
+       Enter this newsgroup through the selector (like typing .+<CR>).
=       Start this newsgroup, but list subjects before reading articles.
U       Enter this newsgroup by way of the "Set unread?" prompt.
u       Unsubscribe from this newsgroup.
t       Toggle the newsgroup between threaded and unthreaded reading.
c       Catch up (mark all articles as read).
A       Abandon read/unread changes to this newsgroup since you started trn.
n       Go to the next newsgroup with unread news.
N       Go to the next newsgroup.
p       Go to the previous newsgroup with unread news.
P       Go to the previous newsgroup.
-       Go to the previously displayed newsgroup.
1       Go to the first newsgroup.
^       Go to the first newsgroup with unread news.
$       Go to the end of newsgroups.
g name  Go to the named newsgroup.  Subscribe to new newsgroups this way too.
/pat    Search forward for newsgroup matching pattern.
?pat    Search backward for newsgroup matching pattern.
```

Tip: For those without trn, rn will look exactly the same except there is no automatic threading. If you still want to view using subject threads, just type **y** to go to the first article, and then type **_t** to thread the group.

Task 5.3: Display the threaded list of articles.

Now that you've subscribed to a newsgroup and accessed its messages, it's time to "thread" the listing so you can see which messages belong to which topic of discussion.

1. From the `[+qny]` prompt (refer to Task 5.2), type `+` or press the spacebar (since that's the first choice given in brackets). The list will look something like the following (the actual articles, of course, will be different from these):

```
====== 1068 unread articles in alt.coffee — read now? [+ynq] +

Getting overview file..

alt.coffee            196 articles

a Alex Loukes         1  Caffeine's Frequently Asked Questions
b Alwyn Perland       3  >Essentials for Great Coffee!
Tom Bridgeman
Jonathan Linden
John Calling        1  >Essentials for Great Coffee!(porcelain mellita)
d Sarah Rostern       1  >the enviro/social implications
e Matthew Murts       1  favorite bean
f Matthew Murts       1  >DUNKIN' DONUTS
g Matthew Murts       1  CNN & Coffee
i R B Whiteman        7  >Good cheep Coffee
Cob
Robert McDonald
Tom Bridgeman
Rosie
Bob Banks
Bob Banks
j Jaclyn Rand         3  >Starbuck's Rules!
Jeanette Skeller
David Feinstein

 — Select threads (date order) — Top 9% [>Z] —
```

The preceding screen means that within the newsgroup `alt.coffee`, 196 articles are available for viewing. Note that this is less than the 1,068 unread articles shown at the beginning. The reason for the difference is that most sites periodically purge older messages because of space considerations. Because the `alt.` groups tend to be thought of as being not as "serious" as some of the others, they tend to be purged more frequently. Some sites purge `alt.` messages more than two days old, others every week.

Of the articles available for you to read, this screen shows the first 9 percent (bottom right) according to the date in which the first article of the thread occurred. Thus, threads (which essentially are discussion lines) that have been ongoing for some time will be shown first, with newer threads coming later.

Task 5.4: Obtain the FAQ for a newsgroup.

The first article in most newsgroups is a very important one. It is what is known as a *FAQ* (Frequently Asked Question), and many newsgroups are set up to have their particular FAQ

as the first article newcomers get (that is, it never gets purged). It's a good idea to read this post to get an idea of what the group is all about, as well as answer most questions you might have.

To obtain a FAQ for a newsgroup, follow these steps:

1. Using either the down arrow key or the n key, move to the article regarding the newsgroup FAQ.
2. Press Enter to display the article.

Warning: Before doing anything else, be sure to read the FAQ! It will save you from asking a question that is asked of the group every week (which is a good way to get flamed).

Task 5.5: Read a particular thread.

Displaying the messages and threads is useful, but eventually you want to dig into the articles themselves. This task takes you through the necessary steps.

1. To view a particular thread, press the letter preceding it, or move the cursor down to it using the arrow keys and press **+**. To select the CNN & Coffee thread shown in the listing in Figure 5.5 (and which might not be available by the time you actually try this), for example, press **g**. A + will appear next to it. If you change your mind and don't want to read that thread, deselect it by pressing the letter again. In this example, pressing **g** removes the +.

   Notice that some of the thread subjects have a greater than sign (>) in front of them. This means that this is an older thread, and all the articles shown refer to a previous posting. Alwyn Perland (I've changed the names, although the group and all article subjects are genuine) didn't start the discussion on Essentials for Great Coffee, but he and the other two contributors to that thread are continuing the conversation.

   New threads, such as CNN & Coffee, are not preceded by a >.

2. To get to more articles, press the spacebar or the right arrow key.

```
alt.coffee            196 articles

a Stephen Jakes       1  >*** chemicals in flavored coffee?? ***
b Michael Shogan      1  >music with coffee
d Barry Jartolli      2  >Tanzania Peaberry Rules!
Bob Barrie
e Barry Jartolli      3  >Where do you buy unroasted coffee (re:home roasting)
Lawrence Graham
Chris Pearl
```

```
f Barry Jartolli     2  >Iowa City coffee
Sheila Mcdonald
g Barry Jartolli     1  >organic coffee
l John Arnold        1  >The Perfect Coffee House
o John Cherry        2  >Green Card Lottery- Final One?
William Kolb

— Select threads (date order) — 15% [>Z] —
```

You now can see more of the 196 articles available (you've now viewed the first 15 percent). To select articles for viewing, type the appropriate letter.

Note: You can't just select individual articles; you must select the thread. Thus, you can't just view Sheila Mcdonald's post concerning Iowa City coffee, you have to look at Barry Jartolli's as well. But that's not a big problem: it's easy to skip through articles you want only to skim.

3. To view the articles in the selected threads, press Enter at any time. I selected the Essentials for Great Coffee and CNN & Coffee threads, and came up with the following:

```
alt.coffee #938 (4 + 192 more)
From: aperland@kevin.seas.Berkeley.EDU (Alwyn Perland)

Re: Essentials for Great Coffee!
Organization: University of Berkeley
Date: Sun Mar 10 19:28:20 EDT 1994
Lines: 5
Anyone know where you can get a cone filter holder that's NOT made of
PLASTIC? My parents used to have a porcelain one, but glass would also be
OK.
alwyn
End of article 938 (of 1068) — what next? [npq]
```

On this screen, I see the first article of the first thread is article 938 (in case I want to find it again). I have selected four articles and there are 192 more articles that I haven't selected yet.

4. On the last line, I see that there have been 1,068 articles since the inception of the group. I'm also asked what I want to do next. Pressing the spacebar will take me to the next selected article (the one by Todd Bridgeman). After that thread is finished, I will get to the next selected topic, CNN & Coffee.

Using trn enables you to concentrate on a single topic line (although, often there is some "topic drift" within a thread) without having to always think back, "now what was she referring to?" But sometimes, it still is hard to figure out what someone is referring to. That's why responses often have "included text" from the prior post:

```
alt.coffee #1037 (1 + 191 more)
From: jlinden@bill.com (Jonathan Linden)              Re: Essentials for Great
Coffee!
Followup—To: alt.coffee

Date: Sat Mar 16 12:54:20 EDT 1994
Lines: 33

In article <CoB6vI.55L@ihs.com>, Alwyn Perland
(aperland@kevin.seas.Berkeley.EDU) wrote:

>  Anyone know where you can get a cone filter holder that's NOT
>made of PLASTIC? My parents used to have a porcelain one, but
>glass would also be OK.
I can think of two — Melitta (king of the plastic manual—fill drip maker)
makes a porcelain (is that spelled right?!) carafe/cone setup.  Very pretty
looking, I suspect they work great.
I suggest that, aesthetics aside, the plastic cone is superior. Problem with
the ceramic version is that it's quite massive, and is going to cool your hot
water much more than the plastic cone. It's prettier, sure, but more
functional? I think not.
—MORE—(66%)
```

This shows that Jonathan Linden is responding to Alwyn's request, and, to refresh people's memories (especially as this is five days after the original post), he includes part of Alwyn's post (lines preceded by >). Some newsreaders use a colon instead.

Because there is some included text, the post doesn't fit on a single screen. The `--MORE--(66%)` tells you that there is more to the post and that you have already seen 66 percent of it. If you want to view the rest of the post, press the space bar; if you don't want to view anymore, press `n` to go to the next article.

Tip: Press `n` to go to the next article; you don't need to scroll through an entire post before going on. This especially is useful as in some groups, whole programs and magazine texts can be posted.

Note also in the preceding articles that the author of the article (as well as the author of any included text) is shown in one of the *headers.* A header is shown at the top of the article and gives subject, author, date, and, usually, the number of lines in the post. These can be used to send mail directly to an author. This is useful if you're shy about posting to the group, and recommended if it's truly the original sender with whom you wish to converse.

Task 5.6: Catch up with a newsgroup.

When you read an article in a newsgroup, that article is marked as `read` (pronounced "red," as in "it's been read"). Articles marked `read` won't show up next time you view that newsgroup. You don't have to read every article to get rid of them, however; the `catch up` command in newsreaders performs that function for you. `catch up` marks *all* articles as read, offering a means of getting you completely up-to-date without slogging through article after uninteresting article.

1. To catch up a newsgroup, type **`c`** at the `[+qny]` prompt. This tells trn or rn that you don't want to see those postings again. The screen will look much like the following, including the question confirming you want to mark all articles as having been read.

```
alt.coffee          191 articles

a Fred Duckman      1  There's still a city without Starbuck's (thank goodness)
b Fred Duckman      1  SEND US YOUR FAVORITE CAFES!
d K.R.              1  Chickory (sp?)
e Steven Munk       2  Yet Another Mail-Order Coffee place
Bobby Bittman

— Select threads (date order) — Bot [Z>] —
```

2. Press **`c`**.

```
Do you really want to mark everything as read? [yn]  y

****** End of newsgroups — what next? [npq]
```

5

Task 5.7: Search for and subscribe to newsgroups on a particular topic.

This time, when asked what to do next, you'll look for newsgroups with titles that have a keyword of interest to you. For the sake of example, choose the word `culture`.

1. At the `what's next? [npq]` prompt, type **`l culture`**, as follows:

```
****** End of newsgroups — what next? [npq] l culture
```

The following result is a list of any group with the string `culture` in it (including such things as "agriculture"):

```
Completely unsubscribed newsgroups:
alt.culture.hawaii
alt.culture.indonesia
alt.culture.kerala
alt.culture.ny-upstate
alt.culture.oregon
```

```
alt.culture.tamil
alt.culture.us.asian-indian
resif.culture
sci.agriculture
soc.culture.afghanistan
soc.culture.burma
soc.culture.canada
soc.culture.caribbean
soc.culture.celtic
soc.culture.german
soc.culture.greek
soc.culture.hongkong.entertainment
soc.culture.indian
soc.culture.indian.american
soc.culture.soviet
soc.culture.uruguay
soc.culture.usa
soc.culture.venezuela
soc.culture.vietnamese
soc.culture.yugoslavia
trial.soc.culture.czechoslovak
trial.soc.culture.italian
```

Many of the groups have to do with culture (this list shows only a few of them), but suppose that the one that strikes you as interesting right now is `soc.culture.usa`, presumably about American culture.

2. To subscribe to `soc.culture.usa`, type **g soc.culture.usa**, and press **y** (yes) when asked if you want to subscribe:

```
****** End of newsgroups —what next? [npq] g soc.culture.usa
Newsgroup soc.culture.usa not in .newsrc — subscribe? [ynYN]  y
```

3. Place the newsgroup in a position of priority.

   Because this is not your first newsgroup (you've already subscribed to `alt.coffee`), trn/rn will ask where you want to put this new group:

```
Put newsgroup where? [$^Lq]
```

   This means that you're being given the choice of where in your list of subscribed groups you want to put `soc.culture.usa`. Do you want to read this group first whenever you invoke trn? Last? Somewhere in the middle (assuming that you are on several groups)?

4. Press **h** for help:

```
Type ^ to put the newsgroup first (position 0).
Type $ to put the newsgroup last (position 2).
Type . to put it before the current newsgroup (position 2).
Type —newsgroup name to put it before that newsgroup.
Type +newsgroup name to put it after that newsgroup.
Type a number between 0 and 2 to put it at that position.
Type L for a listing of newsgroups and their positions.
Type q to abort the current action.
```

   With only two subscribed groups, placement doesn't really matter. As you keep subscribing, it very well might. You can keep all your science groups together, all your investment groups, and so on.

5. Press **$** or Return to place this group last on your list. Following is the default:

```
Put newsgroup where? [$^Lq] $
===== 25634 unread articles in soc.culture.usa — read now? [+ynq]
```

You now see that there are a total of 25,634 articles in the group. Remember, however, that this is a total number, and groups usually get purged, leaving probably a few hundred articles.

Task 5.8: Locate international newsgroups.

Like many other things on the Internet, most newsgroups originate in the United States. Increasingly, however, other nations are offering their own. The following is a partial listing of a variety of international newsgroups that you may want to take part in. Note, however, that your local site may not carry all these groups. Or it might carry even more.

1. At the `what's next [npq]` prompt, type **`l xxx`** (**`xxx`** refers to the country abbreviation). Country abbreviations often are the same as the Internet's country codes, but not always. A sampling of the available international lists is as follows:

Australia

```
aus.acs
aus.ads.commercial
aus.ads.forsale
aus.ads.jobs
aus.ads.wanted
aus.aswec
aus.cdrom
aus.comms.fps
aus.comms.videocon
aus.computers.ai
aus.computers.amiga
aus.computers.cdrom
aus.computers.linux
aus.education.rpl
aus.flame
```

Chile

```
chile.anuncios
chile.chile-l
chile.chilenet
chile.ciencia-ficcion
chile.comp.mac
chile.comp.pc
chile.comp.sun
chile.compraventas
chile.consultas
chile.economia
chile.futbol
chile.grupos
chile.humor
chile.trabajos
chile.uucp
chile.varios
```

Germany

de.admin.archiv
de.admin.news.groups
de.admin.news.misc
de.alt.buecher
de.alt.comm.mgetty
de.comp.sys.amiga.advocacy
de.comp.sys.amiga.archive
de.comp.sys.amiga.chat
de.comp.sys.amiga.misc
de.markt
de.markt.jobs
de.markt.misc

Finland

finet.atk.kielet
finet.koti.tee-se-itse
finet.koulutus.opintotuki
finet.kulttuurit.venaja
finet.kulttuurit.viro
finet.markkinat.kaupalliset
finet.markkinat.pc
finet.politiikka.yk
finet.uutiset.baltia
finet.viestinta.bbs
finet.viestinta.freenet
finet.yhteiskunta.anarkismi

France

fr.announce.divers
fr.announce.important
fr.announce.newgroups
fr.announce.newusers
fr.announce.seminaires
fr.bio.biolmol
fr.bio.general
fr.bio.genome
fr.bio.logiciel
fr.network.modems
fr.news.8bits
fr.news.distribution
fr.news.divers
fr.news.groups
fr.rec.cuisine
fr.rec.divers
fr.rec.genealogie
fr.rec.humour
fr.rec.oracle
fr.rec.sport
fr.res-doct.archi
fr.sci.automatique
fr.sci.cogni.outil

The Netherlands

nlnet.comp
nlnet.culinair
nlnet.misc

```
nlnet.sport
nlnet.taal
nlnet.tv
```

Task 5.9: Unsubscribe to a newsgroup.

If, after looking at a group, you decide that it's not for you, or you get bored or frustrated with it, you can unsubscribe very easily. To do this, follow these steps:

1. To unsubscribe to a group, press **u**. You can do this when you're reading the group, or at the `read now` prompt. Following is an example of the latter method.

   Just press **u** when in the group. To unsubscribe to `soc.culture.usa`, for example, look at the following:

   ```
   ===== 486 unread articles in soc.culture.usa — read now? [+ynq] u
   Unsubscribed to newsgroup soc.culture.usa
   ```

2. To resubscribe later, follow the subscription method in Task 5.2. In the case of `soc.culture.usa`, resubscribing produces the following message:

   ```
   ****** End of newsgroups — what next? [npq] g soc.culture.usa

   Newsgroup soc.culture.usa is unsubscribed — resubscribe? [yn]  y

   ====== 486 unread articles in soc.culture.usa — read now? [+ynq]
   ```

Notice, first, that you're asked if you want to *re*subscribe, and, second, that you don't see the humongous number of articles you did when you first subscribed. Trn/rn remembers that you have already been there once, and has already "caught up" any purged articles, as well as any articles you may have read the first time.

5

Task 5.10: Save an article.

Sometimes, you may read a post you want to save for later, either to print or to keep on file for future reference. To save an article, follow these steps:

1. While reading the article, press **s**.
2. Press Enter to save the article to a file in your account's `News` directory.

   As an example, to save an article you liked on the `alt.coffee` newsgroup, press **s** and then Enter while viewing the article.

3. You'll be prompted as to whether you want to use mailbox format, which, quite frankly, isn't very useful for any but the most devoted newsgroup addicts. Type **n**. Following is the result:

   ```
   File /u2/slindsay/News/alt.coffee doesn't exist—
   use mailbox format? [ynq] n

   Saved to file /u2/slindsay/News/alt.coffee
   ```

Now, the next time you save an article from the `alt.coffee` newsgroup and press **s** and Enter, rn/trn does *not* create a new file. Instead, it automatically appends the article to the end of the file `alt.coffee`. This is a good way to keep an archive of useful information from a particular group.

If, however, you wanted to save the post to a file of its own, rather than pressing **s** and then Enter, type **s filename** and then press Enter. This saves the post to a file of that name.

```
End of article 1068 (of 1068) — what next? [npq] s coffee.poem

File /u2/slindsay/News/coffee.poem doesn't exist—
use mailbox format? [ynq] n

Saved to file /u2/slindsay/News/coffee.poem
```

You can find the file in the `News` directory of your UNIX account. You also can append other poems to this file by typing **s coffee.poem**. I use this to save interesting FTP sites (see Chapter 7) that people occasionally post to a newsgroup. If you type **s site**, the post is appended to your site file. Note that this works from any newsgroup—you can save a post from `alt.coffee` in `coffee.poem` and then append a post from `soc.culture.usa` automatically by typing **s coffee.poem**.

Task 5.11: Save and use a binary file.

Most posts on newsgroups are text files. But graphics files, sound files, programs, and other formatted files are frequently posted to Usenet. Groups such as `comp.lang.c++`, for example, contain a large number of C++ programming language files.

Binary files, however, cannot be posted as-is to the Net, because newsgroups can handle only text or ASCII type files. In order to be posted to a newsgroup, a binary file first must be coded into a text file. In order to use such a post, you must save it to a file as usual and then decode it.

Most UNIX systems have the capability to code and decode files using UUencode/UUdecode. Decoding programs are also readily available for PCs and Macs, and increasingly are built right into the newsreader (see the section "Newsgroups in a Graphical Environment"). For now, since you're in UNIX, here's how to save and decode a binary file.

1. Subscribe to the newsgroup **alt.binaries.clip-art**.
2. Read the postings until you come to a binary file. It will look much like the following example (from `alt.binaries.clip-art`):

```
====== 25 unread articles in alt.binaries.clip-art read now? [+ynq]  y


Article 479 of alt.binaries.clip-art:
Xref: watserv2.uwaterloo.ca alt.binaries.clip-art:479
Newsgroups: alt.binaries.clip-art
From: jeffc@pcu.teary.com (Jeff Cantor)
```

```
Subject: PCX Clip Art: giraffe 1/1
Date: Mon, 18 Mar 1994 03:45:24 GMT
Lines: 509

This is a hi-quality PCX of a giraffe

section 1 of uuencode 5.22 of file big_neck.pcx    by R.E.M.

begin 644 big_neck.pcx
M"@(!'0""'_'L\""""""""""""""""""""""""""
M"""""""""""""""'!2"!"""""""""""""""
M"""""""""""""""""""""""""""""#__\C_P?__
M_\C_P?___\C_P?___\C_P?___\C_P?___\C_P?___\C_P?___\C_P?___\C_
MP?___\C_P?___\C_P?___\C_P?___\C_P?___\C_P?___\C_P?___\C_P?__
M_\C_P?___\C_P?___\C_P?___\C_P?___\C_P?___\C_P?___\C_P?___\C_
MP?___\C_P?___\C_P?___\C_P?___\C_P?___\C_P?___\C_P?___\C_P?__
M_\C_P?___\C_P?___\C_P?___\C_P?___\C_P?___\C_P?___\C_P?___\C_
MP?___\C_P?___\C_P?_0_\'_P=_U_\'_T/_!_Y?U_\'_T/_!_Y?U_\'_T/_!
M_YGU_\'_T/_!_Y'"_\'_P</Q_\'_T/_!_YS"_\'_!O'_P?_0_\'_A,+_P?\&
M\?_!_]#_P?_!UG_!_\'^'#_P_\'_T/_!_\'6?\'_P?X'/_#_P?_0_\'_P<(?
MP?_!_@!\?^__P?_0_\'_P=H?P?_!_0!\/^__P?_0_\'_P<+!S\'_P?@'P?@'
M[__!_]#_P?_!PT?!_\'X'<'X'^__P?_0_\'_P<!#P?_!^''!\''O_\'_T/_!
M_\'(8<'_P?@!P?`![__!_]#_P?_!P'#!_\'X`\'@`^__P?_0_\'_P<"PP?_!
M^'?!X@?O_\'_T/_!_\'(DG_!X'?!P'?O_\'_T/_!_\'MFC_!X'?!P'_O_\'_
MT/_!_\'@'!_!P'^''^__P?_0_\'_P>"'X'?@!_O_\'_T/_!_\'P3@^"'P@_
—MORE—01%
```

Believe it or not, this is a picture of a giraffe. It is a uuencoded version (you can tell if a file is uuencoded by looking for the `M` at the beginning of each line) of a file called `big_neck.pcx`. (Look after the `begin 644`—this is a uudecode command line). I know that this is a picture of a giraffe in .PCX format. There are several graphics formats, the most common being .JPG (JPEG), .GIF (GIF), .TIF (TIFF) and .PCX (PCX). You need a special viewer for each type (although some viewers can handle several types), but .PCX files are pretty easy to view, as the Windows Paintbrush can use them.

3. Save the binary post to a file, using the **`s`** *`filename`* option. Here, for example, type **`s giraffe`**.

Tip: You may not have to do all the work in the preceding step. Your version of trn or rn may well support the `e` command, which means extract. Extract will look for a uuencoded binary within the posting, and then automatically uudecode it and save it to your disk. In some cases, you'll get binary files that are sent in several parts, and extract can handle these as well. Try it.

```
End of article 479 (of 504) — what next? [npq] s giraffe

File /u2/slindsay/News/giraffe doesn't exist—
use mailbox format? [ynq] n

Saved to file /u2/slindsay/News/giraffe
```

4. Exit rn/trn by pressing **q**, and change to your `News` directory.

   ```
   % cd News
   ```

5. Type **ls** to show the files in that directory:

   ```
   % ls

   alt.coffee   coffee.poem   giraffe   site
   ```

   The list includes all your saved posts (the two coffee posts from earlier in the chapter), as well as your site file of good FTP sites posted in newsgroups.

   To decode the giraffe file—reconvert it from a text file into a binary—type **uudecode giraffe**.

   ```
   % uudecode giraffe
   %
   ```

   Notice that, unlike DOS, UNIX doesn't tell you if the procedure was successful. It will tell you if there is a problem, so, with UNIX, no news is good news.

   Typing **ls** again shows the new addition to your directory:

   ```
   @watarts[105]% ls

   alt.coffee   big_neck.pcx   coffee.poem   giraffe   site
   ```

   The `giraffe` file has been decoded into a binary file named `big_neck.pcx`. You can delete the `giraffe` text file, which you don't need any more, by typing **rm giraffe**.

6. If you can use the file on your UNIX machine, do so. If it's a file for your PC or Mac, download it to your machine using Xmodem or Kermit (see Chapter 7).

Task 5.12: Save and use a multi-part binary file.

For the sake of readability and compatibility, binary files are often split into multiple parts and posted as separate articles. Typically, these contain entries such as 1/8, 2/8, 3/8, and so on, along with the decoded filename, in the subject line. In order to save the entire binary file, you must save all of its parts. To save and use a multi-part binary file, follow these steps:

1. Start rn/trn.
2. Type **l binaries** to find a newsgroup containing binary files. Note that there are many of these, including a horde of `alt.binaries` groups, both decent and indecent.
3. Type **g comp.binaries.ms-windows** to subscribe to a Windows binary group, or **g comp.binaries.mac** for a Macintosh-based group.
4. If you have trn, type **+** to view the threads. You'll be able to tell instantly which postings contain multi-part binary files. The following is an example:

   ```
   comp.binaries.mac          12 articles (moderated)
   a Ross E. Bergman    1   RAM Doubler 1.52 Indicator Patch
   b Jon Gotow          1   Sleeper 1.1.3 Control Panel (part 1 of 3)
     Jon Gotow          1   >Sleeper 1.1.3 Control Panel (part 2 of 3)
     Jon Gotow          1   >Sleeper 1.1.3 Control Panel (part 3 of 3)
   ```

```
d Darmok@eworld.co  1  PowerCheck 2.0.4 (part 1 of 5)
  Darmok@eworld.co  1  >PowerCheck 2.0.4 (part 2 of 5)
  Darmok@eworld.co  1  >PowerCheck 2.0.4 (part 3 of 5)
  Darmok@eworld.co  1  >PowerCheck 2.0.4 (part 4 of 5)
  Darmok@eworld.co  1  >PowerCheck 2.0.4 (part 5 of 5)
e Jeremy Kezer      1  MyBattery 3.0 (part 1 of 3)
  Jeremy Kezer      1  >MyBattery 3.0 (part 2 of 3)
  Jeremy Kezer      1  >MyBattery 3.0 (part 3 of 3)
```

Notice that the five threads (a–e) indicate multi-part files.

5. If you use rn, view files until you find one with a binary attachment and a multi-part indication in the subject line or the message.

   At this point, trn users will want to skip to Step 11, since the extract command (e) is far better than the save commands.

6. While viewing the article containing the part of the binary file, press **s** to save it. Give it a name, such as **testfile**. Say no to mailbox format.
7. Type **n** to move to the next article. If it's the next part of the binary file (check to make sure), press **s** and save it *as the same filename.* Remember that rn will append the second file onto the first.
8. Continue until you have all the parts saved as **testfile**.
9. Exit rn and type **uudecode testfile**.
10. Type **cd News** to move to your News directory. Type **ls** to get a listing of files. You'll find a new directory that goes by the name of the decoded file. Enter that directory and type **ls**. You'll see the decoded file there.
11. If you're using trn, the process is considerably easier. Enter the thread containing the multi-part file you want by pressing Enter to read the first article.
12. While viewing the first article, type **e** and press Return. Trn will decode the file and give you the response **(Continue)**. This signals you that more parts are to follow.
13. View the next article in the sequence, and type **e** once again. This time, trn says (Continued)—the past tense—telling you it's appending this article to the previous one.
14. When you've extracted all the parts of the file, trn will display Done.
15. Exit trn and **cd** to the News directory. There you'll find a new subdirectory containing the decoded file. Use it or download it.

Task 5.13: Post to a newsgroup.

There are two ways to post to a newsgroup, either by using the program Postnews, or by responding to a post while reading a newsgroup. Both ways are quite straightforward. To post to a newsgroup, follow these steps:

1. Find an article to which you want to respond. The following one is from the alt.coffee group:

```
alt.coffee #990
From: mmurts@clear.norman.edu (Matthew Murts)

Date: Mon Mar 11 13:41:04 EDT 1995
Lines: 10

Today (March 11) CNN ran a story on the rebirth (or so they say) of
coffee drinking. They had the owner/ Pres./ head of Coffee Connection on
the story talking about business and a bunch of people explaining their
addiction. Check it out if you wish...it'll probably be on during the day.
```

2. Reply to this article while reading it by pressing **F** (as in Shift+F):

```
End of article 990 (of 1068) — what next? [npq] F
(leaving cbreak mode; cwd=/u2/slindsay/News)
Invoking command: QUOTECHARS='>' Pnews -h /u2/slindsay/.rnhead
This program posts news to thousands of machines throughout the entire
civilized world. Your message will cost the net hundreds if not thousands
of dollars to send everywhere. Please be sure you know what you are doing.

Are you absolutely sure that you want to do this? [ny] y

Prepared file to include [none]:
```

3. If you have composed a response in your word processor and saved it as a text or ASCII file, you can include it by typing the filename here. Otherwise, press Enter.

```
"/u2/slindsay/.article" 26 lines, 633 characters
Newsgroups: alt.coffee
Subject: Re: CNN & Coffee
Summary:
Expires:
Sender:
Followup—To:
Distribution:
Organization: University of Waterloo
Keywords:
Cc:

In article <1994Mar11.174104.28707@orlith.norman.edu>,
From: mmurts@clear.norman.edu (Matthew Murts) wrote:
>
>
>Today (April 11) CNN ran a story on the rebirth (or so they say) of
>coffee drinking. They had the owner/ Pres./ head of Coffee Connection on
>the story talking about business and a bunch of people explaining their
>addiction. Check it out if you wish...it'll probably be on during the day.
>
```

4. By default, trn brings you to the vi editor, loaded with a copy of the post to which you want to respond. If the original article is long, delete as much of it as possible—don't just blindly send the whole thing back to the group! To do this, move the cursor to a line you want to delete and press **d** twice. This will delete that line. To create space after the current line, press **o** (or **O** if you want the open line before the current line).

5. Move the cursor below the included text and press **i** to enter Insert mode and start typing a message.

Note: It is very important to remember that vi, although powerful and useful, is much more difficult than word processors, such as Microsoft Word and WordPerfect. Unlike other word processors, in vi, you have to press Enter at the end of each line.

6. Exit Insert mode by pressing Esc and then press **z** twice. vi answers with the following:

   ```
   What now?  [send, edit, list, quit, write]
   ```

   You now can choose any of the choices by typing it and pressing Enter. It's a good idea to list your posts to review them before posting.

7. When you're ready, type **send** to post your response.

   ```
   What now?  [send, edit, list, quit, write] send
   ```

   You now are returned to trn at the point from which you left.

8. The other way to post an article, either starting a new thread or responding to a previous article, is to type **postnews** at the UNIX prompt:

   ```
   % postnews
   Is this message in response to some other message? y
   ```

   If you are starting a new thread, press **n** for no. Because you are responding to an article, however, press **y**.

   Postnews asks for the newsgroup to post to:

   ```
   In what newsgroup was the article posted? alt.coffee
   ```

Remember that articles are purged periodically. Postnews tells you which article numbers are valid and then asks for the article number to which you want to respond, as in the following example:

```
Valid article numbers are from 873 to 1068

What was the article number? 990

article /usr/spool/news/alt/coffee/990
From: mmurts@abacus.bates.edu (Matthew Murts)
Subject: CNN & Coffee
Is this the one you want? y
```

This is the one I want, so I press **y** for yes.

```
Do you want to include a copy of the article? y
```

If you answer yes to this question, Postnews will include the entire article you are responding to and asks you to trim the text, as in the following:

```
OK, but please edit it to suppress unnecessary verbiage, signatures, etc.
```

You now are taken into vi in the same way as when you responded while reading the newsgroup. Posting proceeds in the same way, except that when finished, you return to the UNIX prompt.

Newsgroups in a Graphical Environment

With each passing minute, Usenet expands and improves, and additional groups and members flood the system with activity while new software continues to make access easier and more pleasurable. Although rn and trn remain the dominant UNIX-based newsreader programs (one or the other is available at the majority of sites), sophisticated newsreaders have been designed to cater to the growing number of Windows and Macintosh users. This section concentrates on one particular Windows-based newsreader (the development of Internet programs in general has simply exploded for the Windows environment), but Mac users are quite well served in the newsreader department as well.

For Windows users, several newsreaders are now available, including Free Agent and WinVN, but this chapter uses a very strong offering called News Xpress, an advanced newsreader written by W.L. Ken, Ng (`kenng@HongKong.Super.NET`), which is available as freeware over the Net.

From UNIX to Windows

The shift from a basic rn/trn newsreader to News Xpress or a similar variant means several notable benefits.

First, rather than you remembering and manually keying in UNIX's coded commands, all Windows newsgroups visually display the system's functions in lists obtained from standard pull-down menus or icons. Subscribing, posting, reading, and saving become simple maneuvers involving a click of your mouse rather than the complex exchange of commands UNIX programs require.

Accessing newsgroups through a Windows newsreader, for example, becomes as simple as turning on and off a light-switch—click the All Groups command once to activate the newsgroups list and a second time to deactivate the function. Using NewsX2 or a similar program, you will never forget a command because they are all listed at the top of your screen.

The second significant benefit of a Windows newsreader involves threading. While trn threads articles and displays those threads, graphical browsers show threads by default, and

do so in a much more visually useful way. News Xpress threads articles by subject and/or reference, according to the individual user's preference. The program sorts posted articles by subject, author, and date, and then places them in their corresponding threads. The threads are displayed much like directories and files in Windows' File Manager, and accessing a thread is simply a matter of double-clicking.

Tip: Adjust News Xpress's sorting function to suit your individual needs by selecting Preferences from the pull-down Config menu. Simply choose the desired options presented for formatting the program from those displayed and click OK.

A major advantage of using a Windows newsreader for PC owners is that the articles are brought directly into your PC when you select them. If you're using a modem, retrieving articles is slower, but if you choose to save an article, it's saved to *your* hard drive, not the hard drive on the remote machine that holds your UNIX account. If a text file interests you, simply save it to the directory you want. This also is true of binary files, and the result is that you no longer have to download them to your PC via Xmodem or Kermit to use them.

Finally, the current crop of graphical newsreaders contains built-in decoding software for binary files. This means that, when you see an article that contains an encoded binary file, you can both download it and decode it with no intervening steps. Downloading a sound file, for example, means clicking on the file (or choosing the multiple parts of the binary), and then telling the newsreader to decode it into a specific directory. This is a major advantage for users who want access to the binary files that increasingly work their way across Usenet.

Using News Xpress

To reiterate, News Xpress is one of several excellent newsreaders for Windows. It's free, however, which is one of the reasons it's been selected to serve as an example here. It is also the first that contained built-in decoding, so it occupies a position of influence.

Task 5.14: Acquire and install the News Xpress program.

First, you need the News Xpress program. Note that this task assumes that you have already established a Winsock connection, either via modem or through your local area network.

1. FTP anonymously to `ftp.cica.indiana.edu`, and enter the directory `/pub/pc/win3/winsock/`. (See Chapter 7 for instructions on anonymous FTP.)
2. Get the program nx10b3.zip. Note that the filename will be different if News Xpress has been updated by the time you read this (almost inevitably).

3. If you used a Windows-based FTP program, the file will not be on your hard drive. If not, use Xmodem or Kermit to transfer it to your PC. (See Chapter 7 for details on Xmodem and Kermit.)
4. Using an unzipping program (either PkZip 2.04g or WinZip 5.6), unzip the file into a new directory (such as `c:\newsx`).
5. In Program Manager, create an icon for News Xpress by using the File/New commands.

Task 5.15: Launch News Xpress.

Now that you have News Xpress on your hard drive, it's time to put it into action.

To launch News Xpress, either double-click on the icon created in Task 5.14 or use File Manager to run the `nx.exe` file in the new directory.

Task 5.16: Configure News Xpress.

As you might expect, just launching an Internet program won't quite make things happen. You need to configure your newsreader to tell it how to find your Internet provider's news server.

1. With News Xpress running, choose Setup from the Configure menu.
2. Fill in the name of the news server to which you're logging in. Often, this will simply be `news`, with the remainder of the name (`news.domain.name`) understood. Check with your service provider for the correct name.
3. Fill in the name of the SMTP server to which you're connected. Often, this will be the same as the domain name in your e-mail address. In my case, for example, the e-mail address is `nrandall@watarts.uwaterloo.ca`, and the SMTP server is `watarts.uwaterloo.ca`. The SMTP server address is needed to send e-mail from News Xpress.
4. Fill in your full name, e-mail address, and, optionally, your organization and signature file. These are needed for e-mail and news postings.
5. The authorization information is rarely needed; check with your service provider to see if you require it.
6. File and Path information is filled in by default. Unless you know of a reason to change it, leave it as is.

Task 5.17: Subscribe to a newsgroup.

With News Xpress able to find the news server, it's time to subscribe to a newsgroup or two.

1. When News Xpress starts for the first time, it will automatically access your news server and download information about available newsgroups. You'll be presented

with a dialog box showing all available groups. Click on the ones you want to subscribe to.

2. Once you've used News Xpress, you can subscribe to new groups by choosing All Groups from the View menu. You'll be presented with a list of all available groups. Click on those you wish to include in your subscribed groups list.
3. Each time you launch News Xpress, it will update your newgroups and display a list of all newly created newsgroups. This feature enables you to subscribe to new newsgroups directly, without having to sift through the complete All Groups list.

Tip: The filter segment that appears at the bottom of all News Xpress screens filters or segregates groups according to the specified topic. For example, to isolate all newsgroups that deal with the Internet itself, type the word **`internet`** in the filter space. The newsreader will immediately alter the All Groups list, as you type, to display only those groups containing `internet` in their titles. You may perform the same function on your subscribed lists.

The numerical count preceding the newsgroup names indicates the entry's current number of unread articles, enabling you to judge the relative activity and size of each Usenet group before accessing the articles themselves. A zero in front of a newsgroup name signifies that no postings have been made to the group and saves you time that you could have wasted sorting through stagnant listings. Nothing is more annoying than selecting a seemingly interesting newsgroup only to discover it contains no entries!

5

Unlike UNIX's trn, News Xpress doesn't force you to subscribe to a group in order to view the articles. You can, instead, read the posts from the initial All Groups screen, by double-clicking on any title. The only advantage to subscribing is that News Xpress then keeps track of which messages have been read; if you don't subscribe, you'll keep seeing old messages whenever you activate that group.

Task 5.18: Subscribe to *news.announce.newsgroups.*

Among your first subscriptions, the following are highly recommended:

```
news.announce.newusers
news.newusers.questions
news.announce.newsgroups
```

These groups offer vital knowledge about Usenet information, content, and conduct that can make your introduction to newsgroups more pleasurable and may save you from being flamed!

To subscribe to `news.announce.newsgroups`, a group in which you'll find details of new newsgroups or those in the process of forming, follow these steps:

1. Select All Groups from the View menu.
2. Scroll down the newsgroup list until you see `news.announce.newsgroups` and click on it. You also could type **`newsgroups`** in the Filter box at the bottom of the screen. If you wish to read some articles before subscribing, double-click on them to see what they offer.
3. Select Subscribe from Group menu/icon, or click in the box at the far left of the newsgroup name.
4. Select All Groups once again.

The result should be a screen with news.announce.newusers listed at the top. News Xpress lists your subscriptions alphabetically.

Task 5.19: Unsubscribe from a newsgroup.

If you want to unsubscribe from a particular newsgroup (perhaps it does not interest you or is not what you expected), do the following:

> Highlight the group's title from your subscribed list and choose Unsubscribe from the View menu. You may subscribe and unsubscribe as often as you want.

Task 5.20: Mark articles read.

Usenet's capacity to overwhelm resides in the massive amounts of information that come through daily, even momentarily! In fact, users direct such vast quantities of information through Usenet each day that most system managers purge their files at regular intervals in order to prevent a backlog of articles and to conserve disk space on the news server.

The last thing you want to see in your newsgroups is old articles. Fortunately, like all newsreaders, News Xpress shows only the headings of articles you have *not* already viewed. When you view an article, News Xpress will automatically mark the submission `read` to prevent the article from appearing the next time you access the newsgroup.

However, News Xpress also offers you the capability to perform this function yourself. You can mark individual articles as read, or you can mark the entire newsgroup as read. To do this, follow these steps:

1. Double-click on a newsgroup to see its articles.
2. Single-click on one particular article to highlight it.

3. Choose Mark Read from the Article menu. The icon next to the article will change to show that it's been read (even though you haven't actually viewed it).
4. Choose Catch Up from the Group menu. All articles in the group will be marked as read, and the group window will close.
5. Now, single-click on another group to highlight it, and then select Catch Up from the Group menu. All articles in the group will be marked as read.

Task 5.21: Post a message to a newsgroup.

To post a message to a specific newsgroup, follow these steps:

1. While reading the articles in a newsgroup, select Post from the Article menu. You can do the same from the Newsgroups list by highlighting a particular newsgroup and selecting Article/Post.
2. Fill in the subject line, any keywords you want, a short summary if you want, and a separate To: address if you want to send it via e-mail to specific users.
3. Attach a file, if you want (see Task 5.24).
4. Close the Post window, and click on the Save button when asked. The message will be posted.

Task 5.22: Follow up a message in a newsgroup.

To *follow up* a message means to post a message response to the newsgroup. To do this, follow these steps:

1. While reading the message, choose Follow-up from the Article menu.
2. Fill in the fields as per Task 5.21, but notice that, unlike the Post command, the subject line is filled in with the same subject as the original message.
3. Edit the message area as you want, keeping only what you need to answer the original effectively.
4. Close the window, clicking on Save when asked.

Task 5.23: Reply to a message in a newsgroup.

To *reply* to a message means to send a response to the original sender of the message, *not to the entire newsgroup.* This is an extremely useful command because it enables you to converse directly with the sender via e-mail. Often, there's no need for the whole group to hear about it. To reply to a message, follow these steps:

1. While reading a message, choose Reply from the Article menu.
2. Fill in the fields as per Task 5.21, but notice that the To: line is filled in with the original sender's e-mail address.

3. Edit the message area as you wish, and then close the window (click on Save when asked) to send the message.

Task 5.24: Attach a file to your message.

If you want to attach a file to your posting, use News Xpress's Attachments feature. To do this, follow these steps:

1. With the message box open (after selecting Post, Follow-up, or Reply from the Article menu), click in the Attachments field to open the Attachments box.
2. Type the path and filename, or click on the button beside the field to browse your drives for the correct file.
3. If it's a text file, leave the Encoding field as is (showing `None`).
4. If you're attaching a binary file, click on the arrow beside the Encoding field and choose uuencode.
5. In the Options box, click on all three items to post the file as smaller, separate messages.
6. Close the window and click on Save when asked.

Task 5.25: Save an article.

As your newsgroup activity increases, you'll soon encounter articles that you may want to save for future reference. News Xpress makes this easy. To save an article, follow these steps:

1. Select Save from the File menu while reading an article. The Windows' Save As dialog box appears.
2. Choose the directory, name the article, and click OK.

Tip: It may be helpful to create a new directory to exclusively store News files. This makes retrieval and manipulation quicker and easier.

Task 5.26: Save a one-part binary file.

The essentials of binary manipulation apply to both UNIX and Windows-based newsreaders—binary files are coded as text files and must be decoded for viewing. The difference between the two systems resides in the means of coding/decoding and the relative ease of the operation itself. To save a one-part binary file, follow these steps:

1. Find and open a newsgroup containing binary files (such as `alt.binaries.clip-art`). (See Figure 5.1.)

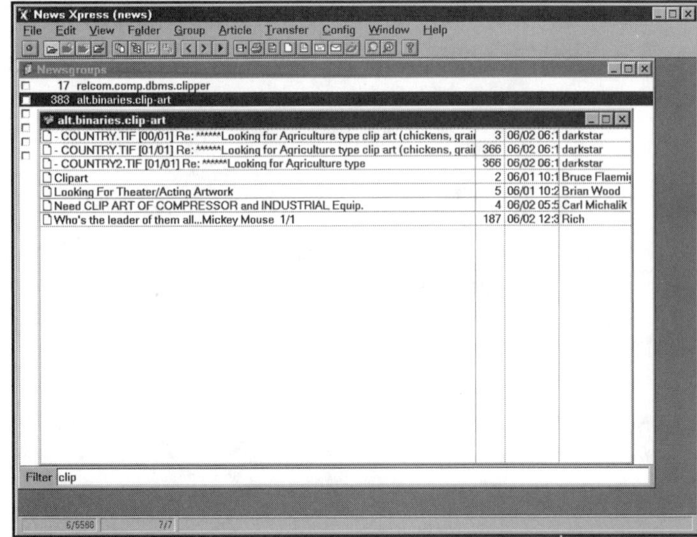

Figure 5.1.
News Xpress showing binary files.

2. Double-click on an article containing a binary file. Typically, these are 150 lines or longer in size, and will often contain an indication in the subject line such as number of parts (1/1) and type of file (.GIF or .JPG). Figure 5.2 shows an article with an encoded file.

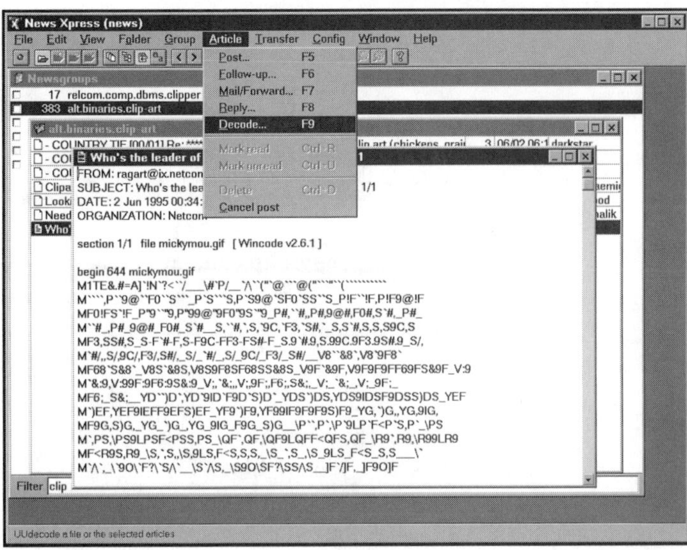

Figure 5.2.
News Xpress showing encoded file within an article.

3. Choose Decode from the Article menu (refer to Figure 5.2).

4. In the resulting UUDecode box, type the name of the directory in which you want the file stored. News Xpress lets you create directories on-the-fly in this manner.
5. When the decoding is complete, use the file in an appropriate viewer, or install it as a program (whichever is applicable).

Task 5.27: Save a multi-part binary file.

Many binary files are posted in multiple parts. Figure 5.3 shows the newsgroup alt.binaries.sounds.tv, which has four multi-part binary attachments (see Figure 5.3). They must be saved and decoded together in News Xpress. To save a multi-part binary file, follow these steps:

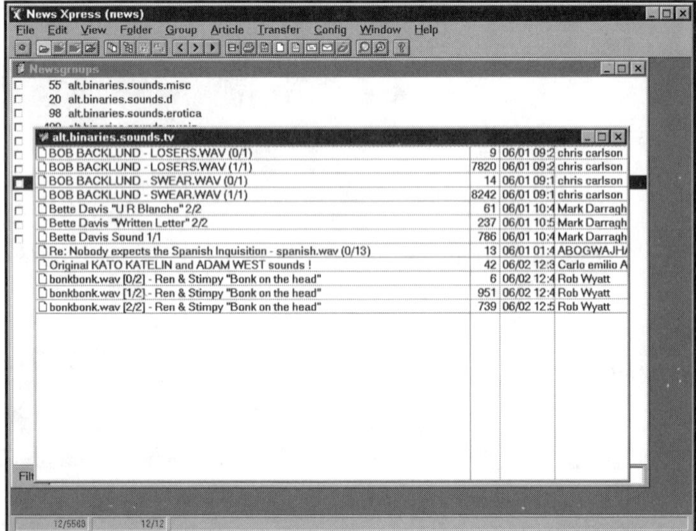

Figure 5.3.
Newsgroup with four multi-part binary attachments.

1. Locate and open a newsgroup containing multi-part binary files. Typically, the subject line will indicate the number of attachments (1/4, 2/4, 3/4, for example), plus the type of file (.GIF, .JPG, .WAV, and so on.).
2. Using the *right* mouse button, single-click on the first part of the binary. The number 1 will appear as a small yellow indicator on the right of that line. Next, again using the *right* mouse button, click on the second part of the binary. A yellow number 2 appears on the right. Continue until all parts of the binary are selected. Be sure you've selected them in the correct order. Figure 5.4 shows a correctly selected multi-part file.

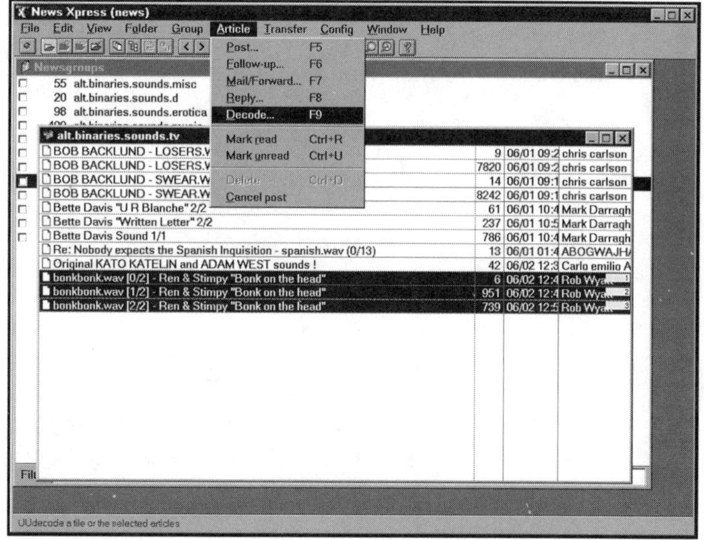

Figure 5.4.
Selecting a multi-part file in News Express.

3. Choose Decode from the Articles menu, and proceed as per Task 5.26.

Note: Newsreaders such as Free Agent and WinVN simplify the process of retrieving encoded files. You need only select the first file, and then tell the newsreader to decode the file. It will find the remaining parts for you. News Xpress might well work this way by the time you read this.

The most frightening aspect of embarking on any new experience is accepting the fact that you just don't know everything there is to know. News Xpress and other Windows-based newsreaders provide users with an interface that makes learning easy, pleasurable, and fast. Before you know it, you'll be trapped by the Internet's addictive powers—just another expert among thousands. Enjoy.

Summary

Newsgroups and mailing lists enable you to communicate with people who share your interests and concerns, on both a personal and a professional level. Using mailing lists requires little more than a knowledge of your e-mail program, but newsgroup participation means learning some new software. Still, they're well worth the effort if you want to see the Internet at its best, as a global communications tool with thousands of interested participants.

Task Review

In this chapter, you learned to perform the following tasks:

- ☐ Access newsgroups using rn and trn
- ☐ Read posts on selected newsgroups
- ☐ Post to a newsgroup—contributing to the conversation
- ☐ Decode binary files from newsgroups
- ☐ Access newsgroups using News Xpress for Windows

Q&A

Q I'm ready to post to a newsgroup but am still a little unsure of myself. What sort of things should I avoid when posting? Are there any big no-nos?

A Good question, and one that far too few people ask. Yes, there are definitely several things to watch out for when posting. In order to avoid being "flamed" (or insulted), try to remember that you are talking to *people*. Many people on the Net get caught up with themselves being (often) alone in the safety of their home, and they think they can say just about anything with impunity. While this is largely true (flames won't actually hurt if you are thick-skinned), you must remember that you aren't completely anonymous, and are still subject to laws of libel, slander, and copyright. Other than these legal caveats, there are things you can do to ensure relatively smooth posting. On the other hand, speaking from personal experience, there are several things you can do that will get you flamed.

Q Can I start my own mailing list?

A Yes, but it takes planning. You'll need to work with your Systems Administrator, who can establish a location for the list and ensure that the Listserv software is available and working. You'll also need to set aside a few hours a week for administrative functions; as "listowner," you'll have to moderate, deal with glitches and irate (or just confused) subscribers, and keep on top of cross-postings and other good and bad possibilities. I've never been a listowner; others, however, tell me it's interesting and enjoyable, but occasionally it can be intrusive and thankless.

DAY
2

MUDs and MOOs: Connecting in Real Time

In Chapters 4 and 5, you learned two ways of communicating with other Internet users: electronic mail and newsgroups. Neither of these, however, is much like face-to-face communication. When you write an e-mail message, you can think about it, change it, and even change your mind about sending it (as long as your software is set up properly). The same goes for posting newsgroup messages. By comparison, think about telephone conversations or eye-to-eye chats: they're spontaneous, rambling, and unorganized—in other words, fun.

In computer-speak, phone and face-to-face conversations are known as *real-time communication.* On the Internet, the primary form of real-time communication takes place in *Multi-User Dimensions,* otherwise known as *MUDs.* MUDs started as adventure games, but they've expanded to become important educational tools in their own right. Classes and conferences have been conducted through MUD-like environments (usually called MOOs, which stands for MUD-Object-Oriented), and the potential is remarkably strong.

This chapter comes to you from the keyboard of a dedicated MUD and MOO user and designer, Colin Moock. Why didn't I write it myself? Because, quite simply, I don't spend much time with MUDs, and Colin—like many other thousands of internauts—does. I spent several years with my Commodore 64 playing adventure games such as Zork, Planetfall, A Mind Forever Voyaging, Brimstone, and many more. When I heard about MUDs, which are really advanced forms of these games (albeit the way they *should* be), I realized that if I got involved, I'd never get anything done. Sadly, I chose the path of greater resolve and decided to stay away.

Warning: MUDs can be addictive. You might have heard about users (particularly students) who get so caught up in MUDs that they sacrifice their entire terms to the great god of adventure games, and while such instances might be rare, they *do* happen. So be careful. Enter at your own risk, and give yourself (and stick to) a definite time limit. If you pay for your Internet account by the hour, this is doubly important, because the last thing you need is an extra $100 per month on top of everything else.

Task List

In this chapter, you perform the following tasks:

- ☐ Learn about MUDs and MOOs
- ☐ Learn where MUDs and MOOs came from
- ☐ Connect to a MUD and MOO
- ☐ Get started with some basic MUD/MOO commands

- Learn some common MUD/MOO terms
- Get a permanent user account on a MUD/MOO
- Learn where to get information about specialized connection software
- Discover how to find the right MUD for you
- Find MUD information sources

MOOs and MUDs

By Colin Moock

Twice in my years of using the Internet, I have been made supremely aware of exactly what it is I am doing when I sit using my computer in my comfortable room in my little Canadian city. Both times, I have been using MUDs. The first time, I was playing a game with "Blackthorn," a user from Seattle, Washington. We were teaming up on killing some evil goblins, when my mother walked in my room and told me to ask my fellow marauder what he thought of Jean Chretien, who at that time had only recently been elected as the Canadian Prime Minister. Blackthorn replied quite innocently, "Who's she?" He thought I was referring to another player in the game, and had misread the French male name "Jean" with the female English name spelled the same.

The second time, I was preparing to write this chapter, and sent a general request out for information and documentation. Within an hour, I had received a long piece of mail with the subject "MUD Frequently Asked Questions." I opened it eagerly only to find that the entire text was in Italian.

All the services available through the Internet cross borders to one degree or another. Most, however, seem eventually to lose their feel of distance both in geographical and in cultural terms. Very little of the character of an Australian is expressed by the domain suffix `.au` in an e-mail address. Likewise, a WWW site somehow always feels to me removed from its HTML author. The one place on the Internet where I get consistently reminded of the *people* behind the computers, is on MUDs.

What is a Multi-User Dimension (MUD)?

MUDs have been described as text-based virtual reality. Essentially, a MUD is a text setting (like a description from a novel) which enables users to interact both with their environment and with other users. Structurally, MUDs are made up primarily of descriptions of real and imagined areas, such as forests, dungeons, offices, universities, cities, rooms, or any other spatially-oriented environment. Users can navigate through and examine these settings, and can communicate with other users within the context and confines of the particular setting of the MUD.

Socially, then, MUDs provide users with a grounded situation in which to interact with others at near real-time speed. Communication commands are modeled on real life, with `say`, `tell`, `whisper`, and `shout`, among the most common commands. Non-verbal communication is also incorporated into the virtual world. A user can, for example, shake hands with, or smile at, another user. Like the description says, MUDs are text-based virtual reality.

Something to note, however: obviously, the authors and programmers of MUDs are rarely famous authors. In fact, very few MUDs exist as commercial entities. For the most part, their creators and administrators work entirely on a volunteer basis. The quality of the virtual experience depends in many ways on the imagination and thoroughness of each individual MUDs creators; the difference in quality has as many variations as there are MUDs.

The History of MUDs

New users of MUDs often encounter a great deal of confusion simply because of the imprecision of the name and its acronym, and because of the sheer number of MUD spin-offs. In general, you should know that *all* MUDs, no matter what their name, have the same foundational premises: on all of them you can walk around a virtual world, and on all of them you can interact with other users. You are safe to call them *all* MUDs, although some will complain about your lack of accuracy. The confusion over the name stems from the origin of MUDs.

Between 1979 and 1980, Roy Trubshaw and Richard Bartle developed a program called *Multi-User Dungeon* at Essex University in England. They called it *MUD1.* Originally, the project was a commercial venture, but students became involved in both playing and programming the game. Some of these students actually created their own versions of MUD1. The first was called *AberMUD* (programmed at Aberstwyth), and was distributed over *JANet* (Joint Academic Network) and the Internet.

Both MUD1 and AberMUD were entirely game-oriented. Remember, the 1980s were the zenith of interest in TSR's Dungeons and Dragons. As in D&D, players of MUD1 were there to explore dungeons, fight monsters, buy swords, and become powerful wizards. However, once MUD1 entered a broader academic forum via AberMUD, it grew once again. From AberMUD came *TinyMUD* and *LPMUD.* This growth marks a crucial change in the world of MUDs: LPMUD continued the gaming tradition of its predecessors, but TinyMUD was developed as more of a social environment than a game. No dragons here, just a place to interact and create interesting things.

Hence, a confusing renaming took place. The "D" in TinyMUD came to mean "Dimension," or "Domain," or "Dialogue," or *anything* that didn't sound like a game. The "D" in LPMUD continued to mean "Dungeon," but eventually also meant "Dimension" when different LPMUDs started to provide gaming settings not based on dungeons and medieval scenarios. To this day, the distinction, and the ensuing confusion, still exists, and there's no

sign of things getting any better: one descendent of TinyMUD now bears the name *MUSH* for *Multiple User Shared Hallucination.*

Tip: As a general rule, MUDs are divided into two categories: 1) games, and 2) purely social environments. Both LPMUD and MUD nearly always refer to a game with some form of combat, while TinyMUD and its descendants, TinyMUCK, TinyMUSH, and TinyMOO, all refer to more socially-oriented MUDs.

MUCK, MUSH, and MOO are all variations of TinyMUD. Each is a step away from the game atmosphere towards MOO, which is the main type of non-game-oriented MUD. If you want to know the whole fifteen year saga, check out Lauren Burka's WWW site at `http://www.ccs.neu.edu/home/lpb/muddex.html`.

Playing Games with MUDs

Although the beginning of this chapter stresses the people *behind* the computers in the world of MUDs, many users of MUDs wish to submerge the reality both of the computer and of the real people working the computers in order to achieve a virtual reality experience. The original creator of MUD1, Dr. Richard Bartle, wrote the following:

> MUA's [Multiple User Adventures (MUDs)] can exert an influence over a large number of...players all out of proportion to that of either a chatline or a game alone. MUA's have an emotional hold over their players, which stems from the players' ability to project themselves onto their game persona, feeling as if the things which happen to the game persona are happening directly to the players themselves....The really exceptional thing about interactive, multi-user computer games of the MUA variety is not that you're chatting to someone miles away (although that can be fun), and it's not that you're competing against a real human instead of a machine (although that can also be fun); it's that you're existing in another world. That's the root of their appeal.

Bartle's observation certainly holds true in the world of games. Although games are not the specific focus of this chapter, you will be able to use all the skills you learn in the next sections within a game context. Remember, all MUDs (Tiny and LP) work on the same principles. Once you learn one, you'll be able to use them all at the basic level.

In most MUD games, you have one central goal: kill things. By killing things, you gain points, and by gaining points you go up levels. Once you have made it through all the levels, you become a wizard. As a wizard, you gain the power to actually create your own area, that is, if you're zealous enough to learn to program. Typically, don't expect to become a wizard in less than a year if you're only going to play for an hour a day. The combat system is designed to be extremely slow in order to prohibit players from shooting up the ranks too quickly, and, hence, from not knowing what to do once they become wizards.

That gives you a skeletal structure. The interesting part is finding out what each individual MUD does to enhance that structure. MUD games can get incredibly elaborate. If you get hurt in a fight, what do you do? Drink alcohol to heal, or cast a healing spell, or drink a potion. If you're drunk from healing, you can't fight, so how do you get sober? Drink some coffee, or sleep it off. Sound familiar? Most MUD games go much further. Choose your race, learn new languages, and speak them only to others who know your tongue. Join players' guilds and gain special powers (telepathy, spells, skill enhancement) from devotion, deeds, and donations. Engage in one on-one-combat with another user, or in full scale multi-user battles. Go on a quest to increase your level. Buy a dog or a hawk from a pet store that follows you around and fights with you. Decide which weapon and armor suits your class: monks can't use weapons because they need their hands free for martial arts. Truly, some MUD games go into seemingly endless detail.

The fun for most users is discovering those details. Therefore, your best bet for getting involved in MUD games is either to jump right in and figure it out as you go, or to follow through the next section to learn some MUD basics: communicating and moving. You then can learn each individual MUD game's style of combat when you get there. Follow the steps in the section "Connecting to MUDs," but you won't have to type `connect guest`. Just wait for the game to prompt you for information. Task 6.8 of this chapter lists a few games for you to try, and gives you information on how to find out about the hundreds more.

Connecting to MUDs

The simplest and most common way to connect to a MUD is to use *telnet.* Because telnet is a generic Internet tool, it can provide only basic screen formatting and text editing. There are connection tools called *clients* (described later in Task 6.7) that provide much neater interfaces to MUDs, but telnet provides usable access that's easy to learn. Many MUDs try to take into account the fact that the majority of their users only have telnet. Those MUDs design special features to make up for what can occasionally be a fairly jumbled and ugly screen display.

Task 6.1: Connect to a MUD.

You will be connecting to a MUD of the MOO type (MOO stands for "MUD-Object-Oriented") called *LambdaMOO.* Remember that MOOs are entirely social environments, so there won't be any game features here, but it can still be fun! LambdaMOO is the largest of all MOOs; in fact, most other MOOs are developed from the basic LambdaMOO program. Most users of other MOOs also have accounts at LambdaMOO, so you can

imagine how busy LambdaMOO can get. Luckily, this means many users will be waiting to assist you. Unfortunately, this also means that your connection will be slow. The amount of time that elapses when you type a command and the MOO responds to it is called *lag*. The lag time can reach as long as 10 seconds on LambdaMOO. To connect to a MUD, follow these steps:

1. Log in to your UNIX shell account.
2. Type **`telnet lambda.parc.xerox.com 8888`**. You *must* have a space between `com` and `8888`. This is your first MUD address.

   All MUD addresses will have either four or five components: a series of either three or four words separated by periods, and a four digit *port number*, in this case `8888`. Sometimes your computer won't be able to convert the words to numbers. If your telnet can't locate the host, you can try giving it the actual numeric address. Most MUD lists provide both. The numeric address for LambdaMOO is `192.216.54.2 8888`. Notice that you still need the port number.

Tip: If you mistype even one digit of an entire MUD address, you will be sent to an unknown machine and asked to log in. If you ever see `login:` when you try to connect to a MUD, you've incorrectly typed the address. Type **CTRL+C** to end the telnet session, and then check that you have all required parts of the address, including the port number.

When you complete step 2, you should see the following output on your screen:

```
% telnet lambda.parc.xerox.com 8888
Trying 192.216.54.2...
Connected to lambda.xerox.com.
Escape character is '^]'.
                          ***************************
                          *  Welcome to LambdaMOO!  *
                          ***************************

                      Running Version 1.7.8p4 of LambdaMOO

PLEASE NOTE:
   LambdaMOO is a new kind of society, where thousands of people voluntar-
ily come together from all over the world.  What these people say or do may
not always be to your liking; as when visiting any international city, it
is wise to be careful who you associate with and what you say.
   The operators of LambdaMOO have provided the materials for the buildings
of this community, but are not responsible for what is said or done in
them.  In particular, you must assume responsibility if you permit minors
or others to access LambdaMOO through your facilities.  The statements and
viewpoints expressed here are not necessarily those of the wizards, Pavel
Curtis, or the Xerox Corporation and those parties disclaim any responsi-
bility for them.
```

```
For assistance either now or later, type 'help'.
The lag is approximately 8 seconds; there are 191 connected.
help
Type 'connect <character-name> <password>'     to connect to your charac-
ter,
     'connect Guest'     to connect to a guest character,
     'create'            to see how to get a character of your own,
     '@who'              just to see who's logged in right now,
     '@uptime'           to see how long the server has been running,
     '@version'          to see what version of the server we're running,
or
     '@quit'             to disconnect, either now or later.

For example, 'connect Munchkin frebblebit' would connect to the character
'Munchkin' if 'frebblebit' were the right password.

After you've connected, type
     'help'              for more documentation.

Please email bug/crash reports (but NOT character-creation requests)
to lambda@parc.xerox.com.
```

3. You are now at the LambdaMOO site, but you are still not connected to the MOO. You are only looking at what is called the *welcome page*. Because you don't have an account on LamdaMOO as a regular user (you'll learn how to acquire one in "Getting a User Account" later in this chapter), you will have to connect as a guest. To log in as a visitor, type **`connect guest`**. You don't need a password. You should then see the following:

```
connect guest
Okay,... guest is in use. Logging you in as 'Ruddy_Guest'
*** Connected ***
```

Some Basic MUD Activities

MUDs, MOOs, and MUSHes offer a wide range of activities. You can move from "room" to "room," you can talk with other MUDders, and you can solve quests by yourself or with others. You can read documents, exchange information, and even—if you get good enough—build rooms of your own to add to the MUD's setting. Here we'll look only at a few basic activities, but keep in mind that each MUD has its own particular events and possibilities.

Task 6.2: Communicate with others and move around the terrain.

1. Immediately after you connect, LambdaMOO will ask you which type of environment you want to enter. You should see the following on your screen:

```
Would you like to start in a noisy or quiet environment? A noisy environ-
ment will place you where you can get help from others and converse; while
a quiet environment will give you a quiet place to read help texts.
[Please respond 'noisy' or 'quiet'.]
```

2. Type **noisy**. This will put you in a place where there are other users. Then you should see the following:

```
The Coat Closet
The closet is a dark, cramped space. It appears to be very crowded in here;
you keep bumping into what feels like coats, boots, and other people
(apparently sleeping). One useful thing that you've discovered in your
bumbling about is a metal doorknob set at waist level into what might be a
door.
There is new news. Type 'news' to read all news or 'news new' to read just
new news.
Type '@tutorial' for an introduction to basic MOOing. If you have not
already done so, please type 'help manners' and read the text carefully. It
outlines the community standard of conduct, which each player is expected
to follow while in LambdaMOO.
```

Tip: Up to this point, everything has probably looked pretty smooth and coherent. However, you're in now: *Do not panic!* Things will scroll by before you can read them; commands may get mixed up with other text; lines may be truncated. You can fix all this. Remain calm.

3. The Closet is the first room in LambdaMOO. Read the description. That's where you are, or more accurately, that's where you should envision yourself being. You can see already that the description provides hints about what you are supposed to do. You might want to open the door. However, if you tried typing something like `I would like to open the door`, or `Please open the door for me`, the computer won't know what you mean. You need to drop all the articles from your speech (the, an, a), and to issue short, terse commands. To open the door, for example, type **open door**. To turn the doorknob, type **turn doorknob**. Also, you might have to keep trying until you get the right phrase. If you type **swivel handle** and nothing happens, it's not because there's no doorknob, it's just because the computer doesn't realize that `handle` is another name for `doorknob`, and `swivel` is another word for `turn`. Try it now. Type **open door**. You should see the following:

```
You open the closet door and leave the darkness for the living room,
closing
 the door behind you so as not to wake the sleeping people inside.
The Living Room
It is very bright, open, and airy here, with large plate-glass windows
looking southward over the pool to the gardens beyond. On the north wall,
there is a rough stonework fireplace. The east and west walls are almost
completely covered with large, well-stocked bookcases. An exit in the
northwest corner leads to the kitchen and, in a more northerly direction,
to the entrance hall. The door into the coat closet is at the north end of
the east wall, and at the south end is a sliding glass door leading out
onto a wooden deck. There are two sets of couches, one clustered around the
fireplace and one with a view out the windows.
You see README for New MOOers, Welcome Poster, a fireplace, Cockatoo,
Helpful Person Finder, The Birthday Machine, a map of LambdaHouse, lag
meter, and Dutch here.
```

6

Not all rooms have such extensive descriptions, but this is the main hub of activity in LambdaMOO, and the place where you can always come for help.

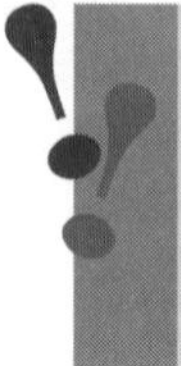

Warning: Once you enter the Living Room, there will be an *enormous* amount of activity. Typically, there are at least ten users in the Living Room all chatting. While this is exhilarating, it can also be overwhelming. Stay calm. This is about as noisy as you'll ever see a MUD get.

4. You probably want to get in on some of this communication. To say something to others in the Living Room, type **`say`**, leave a space, and then type your message. Your message will be sent to everyone in the room. You might type **`say Hi, I've never used a MUD before`**. Everyone else in the room would see `Guest says, Hi, I've never used a MUD before`. The say command is your main communication device. Note that only those in the Living Room will hear you. If you go to another room, only those in that room will hear you.

Tip: Now that you've learned how to talk to other users in a MUD, you should know the most useful command you'll ever learn: `say I'm new...could someone please help me learn to use a MUD?`. People on MUDs are nearly always helpful and will spend their time answering your questions and teaching you the ropes. If you have a specific question, just say it, and watch carefully for the reply.

One of the confusing aspects of the telnet interface is that everything you type gets mixed in with everything else. You will have to get used to this. Don't worry if your typing is dispersed through messages that are coming up on your screen. Your command will still work when you press Enter. A display like the following is common. In this case, Guest is typing the command `say can someone help me learn how to use this MOO?`. Guest's typing is printed in capitals here so you can see it, but when you're really connected, it will all be in lowercase.

```
SAY CAN SOMEONE Bill [to Sally]: the weather is sporadic and crappy, humid
summers and mild winters.
HELP ME LEARN TO USE THIS MOO?
Sally [to Bill]: yep, you said it.
Kelvor [to Shadow]: i'm gonna have to get going here in a second
Silver_Guest [to Mr.jones]: I've just been introduced two days ago. I get
 completely lost in tunnels and cellars.
Mr.jones [to Silver_Guest]: so I've heard...
You say, "can someone help me learn to use this MOO?"
```

Notice how the MUD sends you confirmation of your command all on one line with the sentence `You say, "can someone help me learn to use this MOO?"`. That's how you know your command registered, and the MUD allows you to see what you typed if you can't decipher it through the other users' conversation. Remember, if you're typing and something interrupts you, just keep right on typing. The MUD remembers what you typed, even if you don't!

5. You eventually might want to talk to a user that is in a different room than you, and `say` won't work, and you don't want to go all the way to that user's location. To send a private message to one individual in the room, type `page`, followed by the user's name and then your message. For example, you might type `page Bill Nice to see you again! Bill`, and only Bill would see `You sense that Guest is looking for you.` He `pages`, `Nice to see you again!`.

Note: On LPMUDs and other MUDs the word `page` means `tell`, but the result is still the same.

6. Most MUDs have built-in actions. They are easy to use and enhance the MUD experience greatly. Try typing the following, one at a time:

```
smile
bow
wave
laugh
```

Others will see the action you do in text. Some MUDs have hundreds of actions for you to use.

7. After you've tried talking a little, you'll want to move around. Type **`look`** to get a description of where you are again.

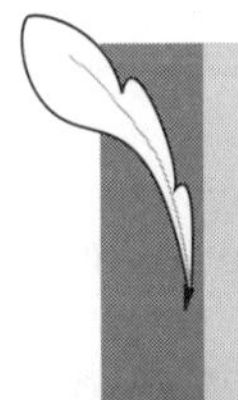

Note: You can always type `look` to get your bearings. The `look` command usually will also tell you the exits you can take to get out of your current location and into another one. Once you have read about the exits, simply type the name of one of them to go in that direction. Typically, MUD exits are based on compass directions, such as north, south, east, and west. Some rooms, however, will have other directions, such as `up`, `out`, `porthole`, `ladder`, or anything else that can be used to move from one place to another. Still, other MUDs work entirely on their own system. The HyperText Hotel MOO is a walk-through fiction, and the main exit type is `follow`.

6

8. The four commands, `say`, `page`, `look`, and `exit-name`, will get you started using MUDs. From there on, the more you learn to control your persona, the more real the virtual reality will feel. To learn more about how to use MUDs, you can and should always type `help`. Finally, your last task will be to take the MOO tutorial on LambdaMOO. This tutorial will help you practice some of the basic commands you have learned, and will teach you more. The tutorial will also help you fix up your screen display. Type **`@tutorial`** to start the tutorial.

Tip: Many commands in MOO are preceded by the `@` sign. This feature is particularly abundant in MOOs in comparison with other MUDs. If a command doesn't work, you might try putting an `@` in front of it. Alternately, if you already have an `@` sign and it doesn't work, you might try excluding the `@` sign from the command. If you get used to MOOs, you'll have to train yourself to omit the `@` when you use other MUDs.

Task 6.3: Fix your screen display (MOOs only).

The LambdaMOO tutorial does a good job of teaching you to adjust your screen display. However, for a general guide to fixing your display, follow these steps. Note that your specific set up may require slightly different parameters. The following are, however, fairly typical.

1. Type **`@linelength 75`**. This prevents lines from getting cut off.
2. Type **`@wrap on`**. This enables word wrapping.
3. Type **`@pagelength 22`**. This prevents text from scrolling by before you can read it. There's a catch, however. You will need to type **`@more`** every time the scrolling pauses. The `@more` command will display the next page of text.

The Jargon of MUDs

Because of the time typing takes, many frequently-used phrases are shortened by users. Often, users type only the initials of common phrases. In addition, MUD users seem to like giving nicknames to things. The following are just a few of the terms you'll see used on MUDs. Expect to also see more general Internet lingo, such as *flame* or *spam*.

`rl`	Real Life, as opposed to the MUD character
`irl`	In Real Life
`afk`	Away From Keyboard. Users might type this if they have to leave their computer for any reason.

btw	By The Way
otoh	On The Other Hand
imho	In My Humble Opinion
brb	Be Right Back
MU*	A reference to all the varieties of MUDs out there. MUDs in general.
to wiz	A verb used to describe a user's graduating to the level of wizard
net-dead	The user is logged in, but his or her connection has been cut
idle	When a user hasn't touched the keyboard for a while
lag	The time that elapses between typing a command and getting a response to it from the MUD
newbie	A new MUD user
emoticons	Be prepared to see many sideways smiley faces :) They're faster than typing `smile`.

Getting a User Account

On some MUDs, you'll automatically be offered a character the first time you log in. Each MUD differs slightly, but most simply ask you to type in your name and the password you want to use. From then on, you type in that same name and password to connect as your old identity. On other MUDs, however, you will have to request a character after you log on as a guest.

To become a registered user on LambdaMOO, for example, type **@request <player-name> for <email-address>**. If you wanted a user to be called `Chris`, and your e-mail address was `csmith@tech.com`, you would type **`@request Chris for csmith@tech.com`**. On more restricted MUDs, you may have to provide more extensive information about yourself in order to be granted an account. If you don't want to give out that information, then perhaps this MUD isn't the one for you.

Once you have used `@request`, your character request will be processed. If you are granted an account, your name and new password will be mailed to you at your real e-mail address. You'll also be mailed instructions on how to connect. To connect to a registered user identity on LambdaMOO, type **`connect`**, followed by your username, followed by your password, as in the following:

```
connect Chris secretpassword.
```

Better than telnet: Information About Client Software

If you've simply had enough of the telnet interface, you might consider getting a *client*. You'll need a decent knowledge of the operating system you're running on, but if you manage to set up a client, you'll love the difference. Clients automatically adjust your screen display, allow you to connect to several MUDs at once, and can separate your input from the MUD output, thus eliminating the jumbled look of telnet.

The most popular UNIX client for Tiny MUDs is *TinyFugue*. You can learn more about setting up TinyFugue (a.k.a TF) at the following WWW site:

```
http://www.tcp.com/hawkeye/tf.html
```

There are clients for nearly every operating system (including Windows, Mac, and DOS) and for nearly every type of MUD. The client FAQ will get you started on setting one up for your system. Visit the following location:

```
http://www.math.okstate.edu/~jds/mudfaq-p2.html
```

To get a free copy of nearly any client by anonymous FTP, check out the following:

```
ftp://ftp.math.okstate.edu/pub/muds/clients/
```

Finding the Right MUD for You

There are probably over a thousand MUDs of reasonable quality set up around the world. Most allow public access. Part of the process of finding a MUD that suits you simply involves visiting several of them and trying them out. In this section, you'll find a short list of the more established MUDs. You can see the variety out there from these few. Many academic institutions are setting up *virtual campuses* for correspondence students. Businesses are creating *virtual offices*. And, of course, eager individuals are still hacking out endless gaming scenarios.

To get a good-looking list of a few hundred MUDs, point your WWW browser to Scott Geiger's home page at `http://www.interplay.com/mudlist`. You can even telnet directly to each MUD right from the Web site if you've got your software set up correctly. Also, for a searchable index sorted by MUD type and theme, try Andrew Wilson's WWW site at `http://paladin.cm.cf.ac.uk/htbin/AndrewW/MUDlist`.

Game MUDs

The first MUDs were adventure games, and today games still comprise the majority of MUDs and their ilk.

Dragon's Den

The Dragon's Den is a venerable adventuring MUD, mainly in the Dungeons and Dragons genre, that just keeps expanding and improving. It has a fairly small user base right now, and is ready to grow. It is a good, fully functional MUD that has a lot of support for newbies.

telnet: `hellfire.dusers.drexel.edu 2222` or `129.25.56.246 2222`

BatMUD

By far, BatMUD is the biggest and most complex gaming MUD around. It has nearly half a million rooms, and hundreds of spells and special skills. Dozens of guilds. Get lost forever. Two hundred players on average, with little lag. Excellent detail (from sunrises to thirst) adds to the atmosphere of the game. Probably the best, but certainly not the easiest. You might want to get your training on other MUDs first. Located in Helsinki, Finland. Check out their WWW site.

WWW: `http://bat.cs.hut.fi`
telnet: `bat.cs.hut.fi 23` or `130.233.40.180 23`

Genocide

Genocide encourages player to player combat. You might want to have some MUD experience before you try Genocide.

telnet: `camelot.shsu.edu 2222` or `192.92.115.145 2222`

6

Future Realms

Closely adherent to the Star Trek theme. Offers a very large realm and an interesting social system based on Star Trek. All your favorite Trekkie toys. Minor combat system. The creators spent a good amount of time on development before opening this growing MUSH to the public early in 1995. Lots of help for newbies.

WWW: `http://www.fc.net:80/~infoteql`
telnet: `dendrite.onramp.net 1701` or `199.1.135.110 1701`

Also try these in the Star Trek genre.

Product: HoloMUD

Telnet: `holo.fc.net 7777`

Product: TrekMOO

Telnet: `aaraaf.ravenet.com 1701` or `204.176.14.4 1701`

TrekMOO will likely have moved by 1996. Send mail to `stm-l@abmsystems.ns.ca` if you have trouble connecting.

Social, Academic, and Non-Gaming MUDs

MUDs started as games, but their communicative potential is so strong that they are now used—often as MOOs or MUSHes—for academic, pedagogical, and social purposes. Here are a few of the strongest of this type.

LambdaMOO

The parent of them all. Huge areas to explore. Decent polish. Hundreds of users. Lag time can occasionally make Lambda nearly unusable.

telnet: `lambda.parc.xerox.com 8888` or `192.216.54.2 8888`

Brown's HyperText Hotel

An attempt to render hypertext fiction into the MUD environment. Interesting pioneering effort. A little unpolished.

telnet: `128.148.37.8 8888`

P(ost) M(odern) C(ulture) MOO

An academic forum for the Arts. Expect to chat, but not necessarily about Jacques Derrida. Users don't necessarily conform to the theme.

telnet: `hero.village.virginia.edu 7777` or `128.143.200.59 7777`

Diversity University

Probably the largest and most elaborate academic project going. A host of interesting adaptations of academia to MUDs. Extensive collaboration with other academic MOOs, and

also connected with the Global Network Academy. Serious tone. Only those involved in education are given permanent accounts. Neat to see, though, even as a guest.

telnet: `moo.du.org 8888` or `192.101.98.5 8888`

BioMOO

A forum for Biology research and graduate students. User access limited to "guest" and legitimate biologists. Not a place to hang around and chat, but certainly an excellent example of the potential for academic research and collaboration in MUDs.

telnet: `bioinformatics.weizmann.ac.il 8888`

Sources of Information About MUDs

If you would like to learn more about MUDs, explore the following sites and services for excellent and thorough information.

Site: Lydia Leong's MUD Central

Address: `http://www.cis.upenn.edu/~lwl/mudinfo.html`

One of the best sites out there. Information about and links to FAQs, MUD Lists, WWW Sites, FTP Archives, and Usenet groups.

Site: Fran Litterio's MUD Page

Address: `http://draco.centerline.com:8080/~franl/mud.html`

A good all-around reference, with links to other reference sites.

6

Site: Yahoo's MUD Page

Address: `http://www.yahoo.com/Entertainment/Games/MUDs_MUSHes_MUSEs_MOOs_etc_`

If you can type the name in correctly, you'll find lots of info here, as well as an annotated list of sites with direct telnet links.

Site: Research Papers

Address: `http://lucien.berkeley.edu/moo.html`

See what's going on in the study of MUD life. Both recent and classic texts, as well as links to other collections.

Usenet Groups

You might also want to subscribe to the following:

Address: `rec.games.mud.announce`
Arbitrated to provide news to the MUD community.

Address: `rec.games.mud.lp`
Discussion of, and information about, combat-style MUDs.

Address: `rec.games.mud.tiny`
Discussion of, and information about, social-style MUDs.

Summary

Hooked yet? If so, you're probably not reading this; you're probably out there in some room or another, conversing with another character or maybe plotting an overthrow of the empire, or exchanging ideas and files with a person who studies the same stuff you do. Or, or, or...

If you're not hooked, don't worry about it. MUDs will be around for a long time, and they promise to get better. You might want to try them again later, or maybe you'll meet someone who enjoys their MUD so much they convince you to join up. Or maybe, like me, you're worried that you'll like them *too* much, and you'd be much better off leaving them alone.

Whatever the case, you can scarcely deny that MUDs and MOOs are fascinating. And just imagine what might happen as these things become increasingly connected with the multimedia capabilities of the World Wide Web.

It's scary, if you ask me.

Task List

In this chapter, you completed the following tasks:

- ☐ Learned about MUDs and MOOs
- ☐ Learned where MUDs and MOOs came from
- ☐ Connected to a MUD and MOO

- Got started with some basic MUD/MOO commands
- Learned some common MUD/MOO terms
- Got a permanent user account on a MUD/MOO
- Learned where to get information about specialized connection software
- Discovered how to find the right MUD for you
- Found MUD information sources

Key Terms

As you work your way into MUDs and MOOs, you'll encounter a brand new vocabulary. Some of the most prevalent terms or references are as follows.

Zork—One of the early text adventure games, available for the Apple II, Commodore 64, Atari 800, and IBM PC. Based on the original Adventure, Zork had you maneuver through a fantasy work with puzzles, items, and computer-controlled characters. Zork had no graphics (the much more recent Return to Zork has plenty), but it didn't need them. One of the most popular computer games of all time, and very much like today's MUDs except for multi-player capabilities.

MUD—Multiple User Dimension (or Multi-User Dimension). Originally Multi-User Dungeon, back where MUDs were primarily fantasy role-playing games. MUDs go by many names, including MOO, MUSH, and others.

Character—Also known as persona (and other things), your character is the role you take on in the MUD itself. You might be a 97-pound weakling in real life, but there's no reason your character can't be built like, say, Dan Connor. Or, maybe more impressively, Arnie Schwarzenegger, or Kathy Ireland (you get the idea). There's also no reason your character can't be an emotional hothead rather than the sane, reasonable human being you are in real life. The problem, of course, is maintaining character in the game situation.

World—The setting of a MUD. Worlds are divided into areas and rooms, and the whole idea is to move from one to the next; unless you get heavily into conversation without other characters, of course, in which case you don't move around much at all.

Q&A

Q Come on, are these things really addictive?

A They can be. If you're not into solving adventure games, they won't be. If you're not into real-time communication over the Net, they won't be. If you just don't like game settings, they won't be. But many people like one, two, or all three of the above, and they are at risk of addiction. If you've ever spent hour after hour at home or work trying to solve some frustrating task once and for all, you'll understand the problem. Just be careful.

Q Couldn't MUDs be used for all kinds of long-distance conversational activities?

A Yes, and they are. If you and three long-distance friends are trying to work out some details about something, there's no reason you can't all log on to your accounts, enter a MUD, head for a room, and carry on your conversation. Find out from the help system if you can even lock the door and keep others out.

Q Why aren't MUD designers incorporating graphics?

A They are. Search through the Yahoo pages for information on Web-assisted MUDs. The problem is that MUDs are designed to make you use your imagination, and graphics could easily detract from rather then enhance the experience. If you're the kind of movie-goer who believes (as I do) that special effects are best left to the imagination, you'll understand why graphics really don't matter. But expect them to enter the scene, primarily because they're so predominant in computer games as well.

Utilitarian Stuff You Should Really Know

7

DAY 3

Utilitarian but Worthwhile: FTP, XModem, and Kermit

The Internet contains files, thousands upon thousands of them. With Archie and the various Web tools, you can locate some of them, but this isn't the only way you'll discover their existence. When you subscribe to newsgroups and mailing lists, you'll begin hearing about files that reside on *FTP* sites, and in this chapter, you'll learn how to bring those files from the remote site to your own machine.

By the time you've read this chapter, you'll have begun what for many is a daily practice—the downloading of files of many types.

Task List

In this chapter, you'll perform the following tasks:

- ☐ FTP a file from another computer to your own account
- ☐ FTP a file from a remote site directly to your PC or Mac
- ☐ FTP a file from within a World Wide Web browser
- ☐ FTP a file using a dedicated Windows or Mac FTP program
- ☐ Use XModem and Kermit to transfer a file from a UNIX machine to your PC

FTP: File Transfer Protocol

FTP (*File Transfer Protocol*) has been around a long time. About as long, in fact, as the Internet itself. It's essentially the most basic command you can perform on the Net, because its only function is to enable you to exchange files with another computer, which was the first activity the Internet was designed to do.

To use FTP fully, you need an account on both machines. Increasingly, however, the most popular form of FTP is *anonymous FTP*. Here, you use your Internet account to get into the "public" area of a remote machine, and then retrieve a file that the remote machine allows you to access. Task 7.1 takes you through the anonymous FTP process.

Task 7.1: Retrieve a file using anonymous FTP through your UNIX shell account.

If you've been on the Internet performing the tasks in the previous chapters, you've probably already heard about anonymous FTP. On mailing lists, in newsgroups, even in MUDs and in Gophers, the term appears more than just occasionally. That's because anonymous FTP is considered as fundamental as e-mail to productive Internet use, and it's a function others on the Net expect you to be able to handle. So you'll see a number of messages with a line that goes something like the following:

```
You can get a copy of the Mosaic licensing document for yourself via anonymous
FTP at ftp.ncsa.uiuc.edu, in the /Web/Mosaic/Licensing directory. It's called
src_rel.doc.
```

What does this statement mean? Basically, it's no different from a co-worker who uses a Pentium telling you that you can find a copy of her memo called `kramer.doc` in the `c:\data\docs\memos` directory of the network drive. As long as you can get into that directory, and as long as the directory hasn't been restricted from your access, you can copy the file to your own system, load it into your word processor, and read it.

In the case of the FTP message, you're being told the following: A file named `src_rel.doc` is stored on a computer at NCSA, the National Center for Supercomputing Applications. The system's FTP address is identified as `ftp.ncsa.uiuc.edu`, and the file is located in the directory called `Licensing`, which is a subdirectory of the directory called `Mosaic`, which in turn is a subdirectory of the directory called `Web`. You can get into the machine using anonymous FTP and retrieve it. To do this, follow these steps:

1. Log in to your UNIX shell account (see Chapter 1 for login details).
2. At the UNIX prompt, type **`ftp ftp.ncsa.uiuc.edu`** and press Enter. You will see the following lines:

   ```
   % ftp ftp.ncsa.uiuc.edu
   Connected to ftp.ncsa.uiuc.edu.
   220 curley FTP server (Version wu-2.4(25) Thu Aug 25 13:14:21 CDT 1994)
   ready.
   Name (ftp.ncsa.uiuc.edu:nrandall):
   ```

3. At this name prompt, type **`anonymous`** and press Enter.

Note: Anonymous FTP means just what it says. You log in with the username `anonymous`. Don't type your actual Internet name here, or the remote computer will treat you as if you have a real account on that system and thus demand a password from you. Later in this chapter, you'll discover that there are other commands you can enter at the `login:` or `Name:` prompt as well.

4. Next, you'll be asked for a password, just as if you were logging into your own Internet account. Here, however, type your full Internet address rather than your regular password. Mine, for example, is `nrandall@watserv1.uwaterloo.ca`. In some anonymous FTP situations, you might be able to get away with typing the password **`guest`**, but this is becoming increasingly uncommon.

5. In a few seconds, NCSA's computer will respond with the following screen:

```
230-Note to HyperFTP users: If you log in, and cannot list directories
230-  other than the top-level ones, enter a - as the first character of
your
230-  password (e-mail address).
230-
230-If your ftp client has problems with receiving files from this server,
send
230-  a - as the first character of your password (e-mail address).
230-
230-If you're ftp'ing from Delphi, please remember that the Delphi FTP
client
230-  requires you to enclose case-sensitive directory and file names in
double
230-  quote (") characters.
230-
230-You are user # 73 of an allowed 130 users.
230-
230-Please read t3he file README
230-  it was last modified on Tue Jan  3 18:54:35 1995 - 156 days ago
230-Please read the file README.FIRST
230-  it was last modified on Thu Jan 12 17:53:58 1995 - 147 days ago
230 Guest login ok, access restrictions apply.
Remote system type is UNIX.
Using binary mode to transfer files.
ftp>
```

Congratulations. You've just received your first FTP message. In it, you'll see special instructions for certain users, and a count of users currently logged in. FTP sites allow only a limited number of simultaneous users, which is the main reason you can't get into them all the time.

6. To get a directory of files, type **dir** and press Enter (not the UNIX `ls`). The response will be similar to that shown here:

```
lrwxr-xr-x   1 12873    wheel         10 Aug  1  1994 Mosaic -> Web/Mosaic
drwxr-xr-x   5 12873    wheel       2048 Jan  5 06:18 PC
-rw-r—r—     1 80       wheel      16557 Jan  3 18:54 README
-rw-r—r—     1 12873    wheel       1933 Jan 12 17:53 README.FIRST
drwxr-xr-x   5 12873    wheel       2048 Oct 31  1994 SGI
drwxr-xr-x   4 12873    wheel       2048 Dec 20 01:49 Telnet
drwxr-xr-x   7 12873    wheel       2048 Aug 24  1994 Unix
drwxr-xr-x   5 12873    wheel       2048 May 22 01:51 VR
drwxr-xr-x  22 12873    wheel       2048 Oct 27  1994 Visualization
drwxr-xr-x   6 12873    wheel       2048 Aug 22  1994 Web
drwxr-xr-x  10 12873    wheel       2048 Aug 22  1994 aff
drwxr-xr-x   2 80       wheel       2048 Aug 22  1994 bin
drwxrwxrwx   2 root     wheel       2048 Apr  6 11:02 cosmic
drwxr-xr-x   4 80       wheel       2048 Sep  8  1994 etc
drwxr-xr-x   8 80       3           2048 Jun  4 21:28 incoming
drwxr-xr-x   2 80       3           2048 Aug 22  1994 lib
drwxr-xr-x  12 12873    wheel       2048 May  4 10:22 misc
drwxrwxrwx  22 root     wheel       2048 May 22 13:50 ncsapubs
drwxrwxrwx   5 root     wheel       2048 Apr 25 16:50 netdev
drwxrwxr-x   9 12984    10          2048 Apr  5 14:14 outgoing
drwxr-xr-x   4 12873    wheel       2048 May 23 08:55 sc22wg5
drwxr-xr-x  14 root     wheel       2048 May 26 08:11 x3j3
226 Transfer complete.
ftp>
```

This is only part of the full listing. If your telnet program enables you to scroll up and down in the listing, you'll have an advantage. Most don't, however, including the one used here. Still, because the e-mail message told you exactly where the file is located, it doesn't really matter.

7. Recall that the message said the file was in the `/Web/Mosaic/Licensing` directory. You can enter that directory by typing **`cd Web/Mosaic/Licensing`** and then pressing Enter, or you can do so one step at a time. To do the latter, type **`cd Web`** (press Enter), type **`cd Mosaic`** (press Enter), and then type **`cd Licensing`** (and press Enter). Why bother with the latter? Often, you'll want to explore each directory as you enter it, so it makes sense to move to the first one and then the next.

8. Once in the Licensing directory, type **`dir`** and press Enter. You'll see the following listing:

```
ftp> dir
200 PORT command successful.
150 Opening ASCII mode data connection for /bin/ls.
total 136
drwxr-xr-x   2 12984    10          2048 Aug 25  1994 .
drwxr-xr-x  10 12873    wheel       2048 Jan  6 19:55 ..
-rw-r—r—     1 12873    other        249 Aug 22  1994 .index
-rw-r—r—     1 12873    10           380 Aug 25  1994 LICENSING.FAQ
-rw-r—r—     1 12984    10           505 Aug 15  1994 read.me
-rw-r—r—     1 12984    10         10202 Aug 15  1994 src_rel.doc
-rw-r—r—     1 12984    10          9728 Aug 15  1994 src_rel.mcw
-rw-r—r—     1 12984    10         23171 Aug 15  1994 src_rel.ps
-rw-r—r—     1 12984    10          7068 Aug 15  1994 src_rel.txt
-rw-r—r—     1 12984    10         10752 Aug 15  1994 src_rel.wri
226 Transfer complete.
ftp>
```

See Chapter 1 for how to read the entire directory. What you're after right now is the file `src_rel.doc`. And there it is, halfway down the list, with a size of 10,202 bytes and a date of Aug 15, 1994.

9. All that's left to do is the actual transfer. First, however, because this is a formatted file and not a plain text file (.DOC tells you it's probably a Word for Windows file), you have to tell FTP to transfer it in *binary* mode rather than *ASCII* mode. If you don't do this, you won't receive the file properly, and you might not get it at all. To change to binary mode, type **`binary`** at the `ftp>` prompt, and then press Enter.

10. Now for the transfer. Type **`get src_rel.doc`** and then press Enter. You'll receive a response much like the following:

```
ftp> get src_rel.doc
200 PORT command successful.
150 Opening BINARY mode data connection for src_rel.doc (10202 bytes).
226 Transfer complete.
10202 bytes received in 0.39 seconds (26 Kbytes/s)
ftp>
```

This tells you that the file has been transferred, and that it took less than half a second to do so. Welcome to the speed of UNIX-to-UNIX over high-speed lines (your transfer might take less or more time).

Warning: If you're not used to working with UNIX filenames, there are a few things to keep in mind. First, they can be much longer than MS-DOS filenames, which must use the annoying 11-character (8.3) convention. Second, they can include underscores and other characters, including multiple dots (periods). Finally—and this is crucial—case matters. If you want to edit, rename, erase, download, or otherwise deal with a file named `README-Before-TRYing`, you must type all upper- and lowercase characters exactly as they appear. Otherwise, the system will respond that it can't find the file.

11. Now it's time to leave the NCSA computer. To do this, at the prompt, type **`quit`** and press Enter. You'll be presented with your home machine's UNIX prompt.
12. At the prompt, type **`ls`** and press Enter (you can't use `dir`, because you're out of the FTP program and back to standard UNIX). You should see the retrieved file sitting there on your account.

That's it. Your first FTP. Kinda felt like stealing, didn't it?

Task 7.2: FTP multiple files from a remote site.

In this task, you'll enter an anonymous FTP site, maneuver around the directories, and then retrieve several files with one command. In the process, you'll also enter two excellent software archives, to which you'll want to return frequently.

1. Log in to your UNIX shell account.
2. At the UNIX prompt, type **`ftp oak.oakland.edu`** and press Enter.
3. At the name prompt, type **`anonymous`** and press Enter, and then at the password prompt, type your full e-mail address. In other words, you're logging in anonymously. Following is the result:

```
230- If you have trouble using OAK with your ftp client, please try using
230- a dash (-) as the first character of your password — this will turn
230- off the continuation messages that may be confusing your ftp client.
230- OAK is a Unix machine, and filenames are case sensitive.
230-
230- Access is allowed at any time.  If you have any unusual problems,
230- please report them via electronic mail to archives@Oakland.Edu
230-
230- You are user #216 out of 400 maximum users on Thu Jun  8 23:44:34
1995.
230-
230- Oak is also on the World Wide Web, URL: http://www.acs.oakland.edu/
oak.html
```

```
230-
230- File searching is now available!  Example command:  site exec index
4dos
230-
230-Please read the file README
230-  it was last modified on Fri Mar 24 18:59:19 1995 - 76 days ago
230 Guest login ok, access restrictions apply.
Remote system type is UNIX.
Using binary mode to transfer files.
ftp>
```

4. Two things are of interest in the FTP message. First, the second-to-last line tells you that this server is already set in binary mode, so there's no need to make the change. Second, near the middle, the message tells you that the Oak archives are also on the World Wide Web. Write down the URL, because you'll use it later in this chapter.

5. Type **`dir`** and press Enter. You'll see the following list:

```
ftp> dir
200 PORT command successful.
150 Opening ASCII mode data connection for /bin/ls.
total 1258
-rw-r—r—    1 w8sdz    OAK            0 Nov 13  1994 .notar
drwxr-x—   2 root     operator    8192 Dec 31 16:44 .quotas
drwx— — —   2 root     system      8192 Dec 30 19:16 .tags
-rw-r—r—    1 jeff     OAK      1120876 Jun  8 03:20 Index-byname
-r—r—r—     1 w8sdz    OAK         1237 Mar 24 18:59 README
drwxr-xr-x   3 w8sdz    OAK         8192 May 29 16:35 SimTel
d—x—x—x     3 root     system      8192 Jan 19 20:26 bin
d—x—x—x     2 root     system      8192 Jul 30  1994 core
drwxr-x—   2 cpm      OAK         8192 Jun  1 16:43 cpm-incoming
d—x—x—x     5 root     system      8192 Dec 30 05:15 etc
drwxrwx—   2 incoming OAK         8192 Jun  8 23:21 incoming
drwxrwx—   2 25913    OAK         8192 Jun  8 23:46 nt-incoming
drwxr-xr-x   3 w8sdz    OAK         8192 Apr 13 19:46 pub
drwxr-xr-x  15 w8sdz    OAK         8192 May 30 23:03 pub2
drwxr-xr-x   8 w8sdz    OAK         8192 May  3 13:24 pub3
drwxr-xr-x   3 w8sdz    OAK         8192 May 29 16:35 simtel
drwxr-xr-x   2 jeff     OAK         8192 Apr 17  1994 siteinfo
drwx— — —  47 w8sdz    OAK         8192 Jun  8 23:03 w8sdz
226 Transfer complete.
ftp>
```

Hmmm. Not just one `/pub` directory, but three! Which one do you choose?

6. As it turns out, none of them. The SimTel archives are one of the most important on the Net (for DOS and Windows users), and this is a good time to try them out. Type **`cd SimTel`** and press Enter.

7. Type **`dir`** and press Enter to get a new directory listing. You'll see three subdirectories: `msdos`, `nt`, and `win3`. Enter the `win3` directory by typing **`cd win3`** and then pressing Enter.

8. Get a new directory listing. This time, it will be long, with subdirectories scrolling past your eyes extremely quickly. The `dir` command doesn't offer a paging switch (like DOS's `DIR /P`), so there's nothing you can do about this. In all likelihood, however, your telnet or telecommunications program has a capture (or logging)

command, which usually puts the scrolling text into your system's clipboard. You can read the entire directory from there.

9. For now, however, one of the directories near the bottom is fine. The `winsock` directory in Windows archives always features Internet programs, so it's well worth a look. Type **`cd winsock`** and press Enter to move to that directory.

10. Get a directory. The result will be much like this:

```
-rw-r—r—    1 w8sdz    OAK      109947 Jan 28  1994 wgopher.zip
-rw-r—r—    1 w8sdz    OAK      123743 Oct 27  1994 winapps2.zip
-rw-r—r—    1 w8sdz    OAK      300288 May 29 22:49 winter13.zip
-rw-r—r—    1 w8sdz    OAK      216548 Jan 18 03:52 wlprs40c.zip
-rw-r—r—    1 w8sdz    OAK       50855 Mar  3 00:52 wrcmdl15.zip
-rw-r—r—    1 w8sdz    OAK       67596 Mar  3 00:52 wrcpdl15.zip
-rw-r—r—    1 w8sdz    OAK      119258 Mar  3 00:52 wrcprs15.zip
-rw-r—r—    1 w8sdz    OAK      146005 Nov  7  1994 wrsh16.zip
-rw-r—r—    1 w8sdz    OAK      190046 Mar  3 00:53 wrshd15.zip
-rw-r—r—    1 w8sdz    OAK      499253 May 19 18:27 ws_cha30.zip
-rw-r—r—    1 w8sdz    OAK      117019 May  3 02:02 ws_ftp.zip
-rw-r—r—    1 w8sdz    OAK      147846 May  3 02:35 ws_ftp32.zip
-rw-r—r—    1 w8sdz    OAK       56635 Jan  8 03:37 ws_ping.zip
-rw-r—r—    1 w8sdz    OAK      195729 Mar  5 17:39 ws_watch.zip
-rw-r—r—    1 w8sdz    OAK      174837 Jan 21 02:36 wsarch07.zip
-rw-r—r—    1 w8sdz    OAK      559460 Apr 14 01:25 wsirc14g.zip
-rw-r—r—    1 w8sdz    OAK      400549 Apr 13 23:39 wsoup081.zip
-rw-r—r—    1 w8sdz    OAK      100074 May 13 22:28 wstbar23.zip
-rw-r—r—    1 w8sdz    OAK      127096 Jan 27 22:41 wtalk12.zip
-rw-r—r—    1 w8sdz    OAK      148789 Jan  4 21:05 wtar14u.zip
-rw-r—r—    1 w8sdz    OAK      285470 Jun  8 00:29 wv169905.zip
-rw-r—r—    1 w8sdz    OAK      303336 Jun  8 00:51 wv329905.zip
226 Transfer complete.
ftp>
```

All these files are compressed; you can tell this by looking at the .ZIP extension. The ZIP program (or any other compression program) makes FTPing much easier by both combining many files into a single file and then compressing those files, that is, making them significantly smaller. They'll all need to be "unzipped" when you get them to your hard drive.

Tip: When you're doing FTPs, it's important to understand how to read the `dir` result (if you're familiar with UNIX, you already know how to do so). This looks a bit confusing, but it's actually quite simple. The only columns you need to pay strict attention to are the first and last, with the date sometimes being useful, and the file size, immediately to the left of the date, even more useful.

The first character in the first column tells you whether the item is a file or a directory. If this character is a `d`, it's a directory; otherwise, it's a file. In this listing, most of the items were obviously directories, and I had to figure out which directory I wanted to enter.

In many anonymous FTP situations, the directory with the most interesting and useful material is called pub (short for public). The list I received displayed pub fourth from the bottom. The command to change directories is cd, again exactly like MS-DOS. The next step was to change to the appropriate directory, and then type another dir command to get a listing there as well.

11. The files ws-ftp.zip, wsarch07.zip, and winapps2.zip look interesting. You could execute get commands for each one separately, or one get command for the lot. For the latter option, type **mget ws_ftp.zip wsarch07.zip winapps2.zip**, and then press Enter.
12. As the files are transferred, you'll be asked to confirm each in turn. Do so by pressing the **y** key. The first two transfers will appear as follows:

```
ftp> mget ws_ftp.zip wsarch07.zip winapps2.zip
mget ws_ftp.zip? y
200 PORT command successful.
150 Opening BINARY mode data connection for ws_ftp.zip (117019 bytes).
        226 Transfer complete.
117019 bytes received in 58 seconds (2 Kbytes/s)
mget wsarch07.zip? y
```

13. Now that you've raided the SimTel site (until you decide to return on your own, which you almost certainly will), it's time to leave and head for a different FTP site. At the ftp> prompt, type **close** and then press Enter. You're now out of the Oak archives.
14. To enter a new site, this time another software site, type **open sunsite.unc.edu** and then press Enter. Log in anonymously, and then enjoy the visit.

Other FTP Commands

There's more to FTP than the commands shown in the previous examples. While the ftp> prompt is displayed, any of the commands in Table 6.1 may be useful to you.

Table 6.1. Other FTP commands.

Command	Description
ascii	Switches to ASCII mode, the mode to be used for copying text files
binary	Switches to binary mode, the mode to be used for copying binary files (ZIP files, .GIF, .HEX, and so on)
cd	Changes the current directory on the remote computer
close	Ends the current FTP session without quitting FTP entirely

continues

7

Table 6.1. continued

Command	Description
dir/ls	Lists the files in the current directory on the remote computer
get	Copies a file from the remote to the local computer
hash	Displays a # on the screen for every 1KB transferred
help	Gets help regarding FTP commands
lcd	Changes the directory on the local computer
lpwd	Displays the current directory name on the local computer
mget	Copies multiple files from the remote to the local computer
mput	Copies multiple files from the local to the remote computer
open	Starts a new FTP session from within FTP
put	Copies a file from the local to the remote computer
pwd	Shows the present working directory (pwd) on the remote computer
user	Restarts the user/password process

File Types

Soon after you start using FTP regularly, you'll discover a wide range of file types available for download. Many will be compressed—that is, reduced in size to save disk space and transfer time—and you'll need the appropriate software on your system to uncompress them so that you can use them. You can find uncompression utilities on the Internet, or as shareware or freeware on BBS or commercial online services, or on floppy- or CD-ROM-based shareware collections for your computer.

Following are the major file types you'll encounter (but there are many, many others). If you're familiar with the types of files you find on your computer, you'll be able to instantly recognize most of those listed in Table 6.2.

Table 6.2. File types.

File Suffix	FTP Mode	File Type
.arc	binary	ARChive (compressed, rare)
.arj	binary	Arj (compressed, usually DOS)
.asc	ASCII	ASCII (text-based) files
.doc	binary	Document (word processor)

File Suffix	FTP Mode	File Type
.gif	binary	Graphics
.gz	binary	GNU Zip; not compatible with Zip
.hqx	binary	HQX (Macintosh)
.jpg	binary	JPEG Graphics
.lzh	binary	LHa, LHarc, Larc (compressed)
.mpg	binary	MPEG (video standard)
.ps	binary	Postscript (formatted text)
.sit	binary	Stuffit (Macintosh)
.tar	binary	Tape ARchive (Unix)
.txt	ASCII	Text file (very common)
.uu	ASCII	uuencode/uudecode, also .uue (compressed)
.Z	binary	UNIX, often seen in combination with .tar
.zip	binary	Zip (compressed; extremely common)
.zoo	binary	Zoo (compressed)

Note: You also will find files that require specific programs. For example, .ppt files require Microsoft PowerPoint, while .wp5 files need WordPerfect 5.0 or 5.1.

FTP via the World Wide Web

World Wide Web browsers, which you learn about in Chapter 10, have become a primary means of doing anonymous FTP, partly because they make it quite easy to do so, and partly because many people prefer using one piece of software to do the majority of their Internet work.

Increasingly, popular FTP sites are making their materials available over the Web. In just about every case, the Web browser makes it easier to locate the files you want, and you don't need to memorize any special commands to make the retrieval happen. Many sites have hyperlinks that start an FTP transaction without even taking you to the FTP directory itself, and this makes the whole thing even more transparent.

The next two tasks take you out onto the Web for an anonymous FTP.

Task 7.3: Access the SimTel software archives through Netscape.

You can access the SimTel software archives through Netscape. To do this, just follow these steps:

1. Launch Netscape (refer to Chapter 11 for details on how to acquire and use this popular browser).
2. Using Open Location from the File menu, go to the following URL: **`http://www.acs.oakland.edu/oak.html`** (see Chapter 10 for instructions on how to do this). Your screen will look like Figure 7.1.

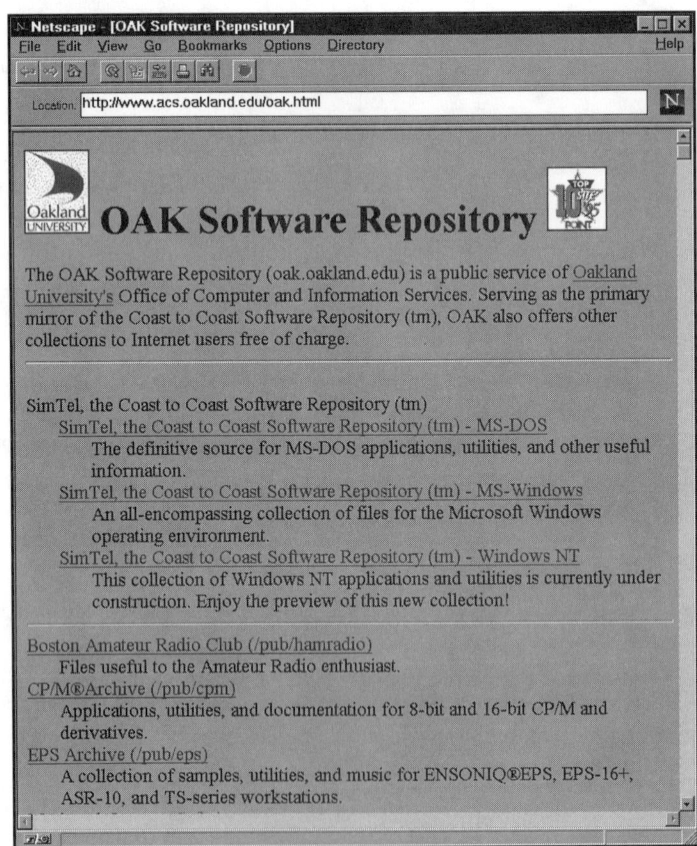

Figure 7.1.
The OAK Software Repository page in Netscape.

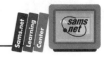

3. Click on the hyperlink labeled `SimTel, the Coast to Coast Software Repository % - MS-Windows`. Figure 7.2 displays the result. This is the same information that you received after changing to the SimTel directory in Task 7.2 and then issuing a `dir` command. One of the main differences here is that you can scroll through the directories easily. Another is that the directories now have descriptive names.

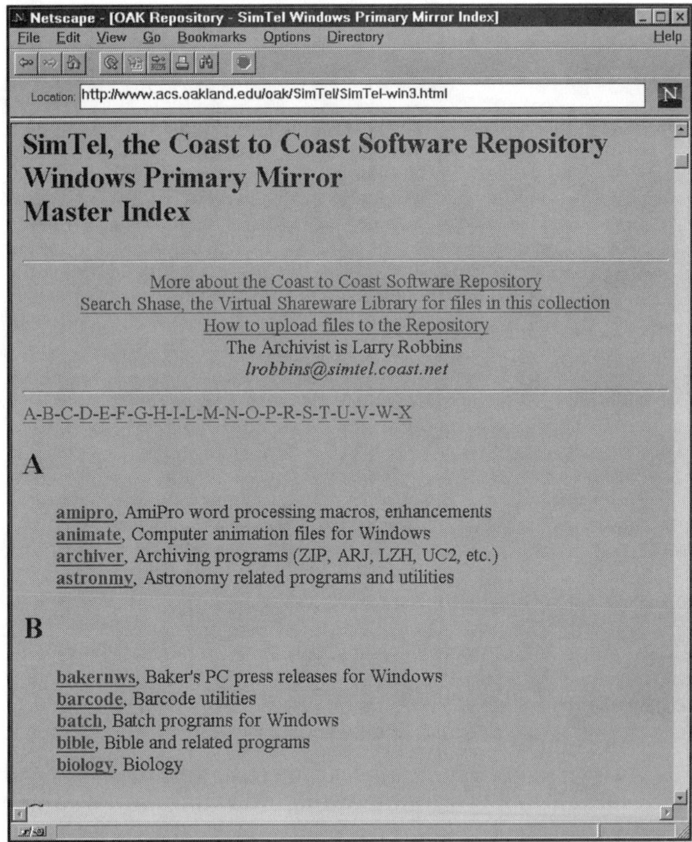

Figure 7.2.
The main directory page of the SimTel archive.

4. Scroll down until you come to the `W` section, and then click on the Winsock hyperlink. The result is shown in Figure 7.3. Again, you'll immediately notice that the directory is now scrollable, and that items have descriptions (however brief) beside them. This is much more informative than the results in Task 7.2.

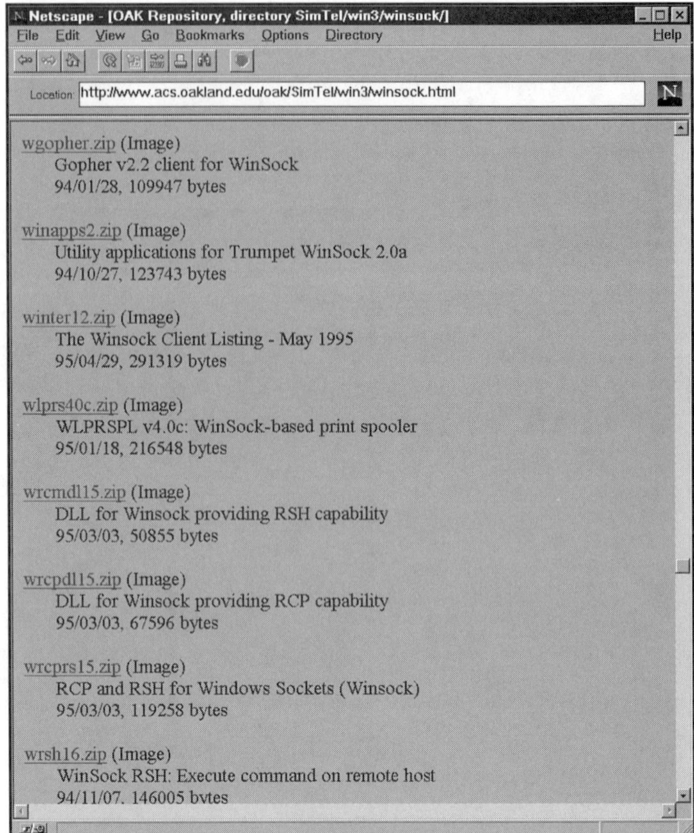

Figure 7.3.
Part of the winsock directory in the SimTel archives.

5. Find the file named `winapps2.zip` and click on the hyperlink. Netscape will ask if you want to save the file to disk, cancel the transfer, or configure a viewer. Click on Save to Disk and tell Netscape in which directory to place the .ZIP file. Notice that, unlike the transfer in Figure 7.2, the file is now on *your* hard drive, not the hard drive of the machine where your UNIX account resides.

Note: Not all FTPs on the Web are this elegant. In many cases, the hyperlink will take you into an FTP directory that gives you the exact same file and directory list as if you entered via standard FTP. You still have the convenience of merely clicking on a hyperlink to download a file, but it isn't nearly as usable as the SimTel page encountered in Task 7.3. As an example, try the Microsoft FTP site at the following URL:

`ftp://ftp.microsoft.com`

(Notice the `ftp://` intro to this URL, rather than the standard `http://`.) You'll notice a considerable difference.

Task 7.4: Find an FTP program for Windows using the Search Shase system.

If you're looking for a specific file, or type of file, some especially useful FTP search tools are available on the Web. One of these is the *Search Shase system*, available from the SimTel page shown in Figure 7.2.

1. Return to the main SimTel page by selecting Back from the Go menu. Or use the following URL:

   `http://www.acs.oakland.edu/oak/SimTel/SimTel-win3.html`

2. In the resulting search form, type **`ftp`** in the first search for box. To make sure you get a relatively new FTP program, type **`950101`** in the be newer than box, to limit the search to 1995 uploads or later. Notice that you could make your search much more specific, but this is good enough for now.
3. Click the Search button. The result appears in Figure 7.4.
4. Click on the file you want to download, and tell Netscape where to put it on your hard drive.

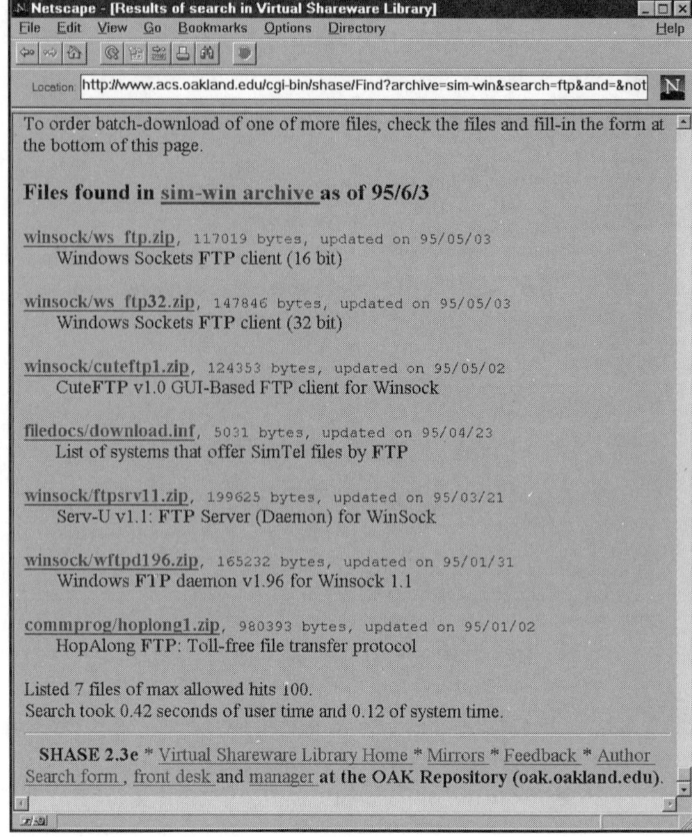

Figure 7.4.
The result of a search for FTP programs in the Virtual Shareware Library.

A Few More FTP Sites

To try another kind of software repository, go to the URL, `http://uts.cc.utexas.edu/~neuroses/cwsa.html`. This is Forrest Stroud's *Consummate Winsock Apps List*, a must for any Windows Internet user.

If you're a Macintosh user, go to the excellent *Well Connected Mac* site at URL: `http://rever.nmsu.edu/~elharo/faq/Macintosh.html`.

OS/2 users should give a try to `http://www.os2bbs.com/`.

For a collection of links to several interesting FTP sites, head for `http://www.bahnware.com/bahnware/gateways/selected-ftp-sites.html`.

FTP with a Dedicated FTP Program

Several excellent FTP programs (clients, technically) are available for all platforms. Macintosh users have easy access to the superb Fetch, available by anonymous FTP at `dartmouth.edu` in `/pub/mac/`. Windows users have a host of such programs, including commercial items included with Internet in a Box, Netmanage Chameleon, and Superhighway Access. Here you'll use the extremely popular Winsock FTP, which you found in the SimTel archives.

Task 7.5: Use Winsock FTP to transfer a file directly to your PC.

1. Anonymously FTP to **`oak.oakland.edu`** and enter the directory **`/SimTel/win3/winsock`**. Retrieve the file called `ws_ftp.zip`, or `ws_ftp32.zip` if you're using Windows 95 or Windows NT.
2. Using an unzip program, install the Winsock FTP program. The truly wonderful WinZip is available in the `SimTel/win3` archives, in the directory `/archiver`. Look for the file `winzip56.exe` (or a higher number), transfer it to your PC, put the file in a separate directory, go to a DOS prompt, and type **`winzip56`** at the prompt. Then launch the program and use File/Open to unzip the `ws_ftp.zip` program.
3. Launch Winsock FTP. Your screen will look similar to Figure 7.5.

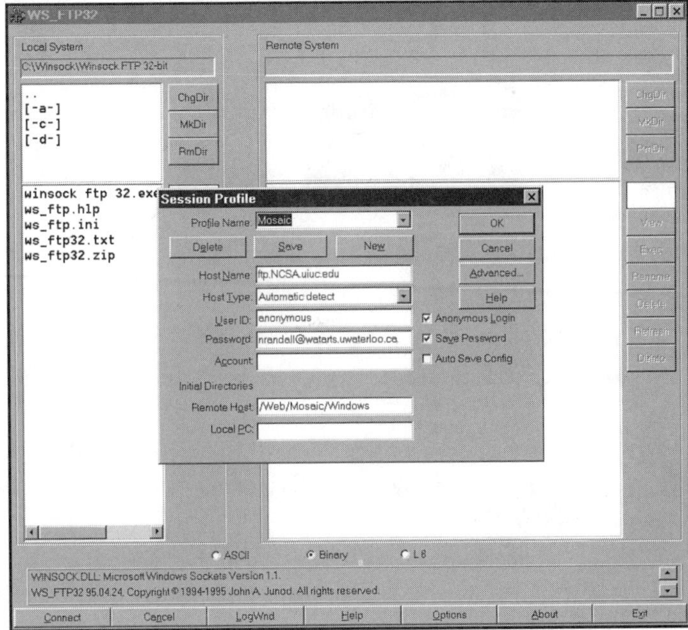

Figure 7.5.
The opening screen for Winsock FTP.

4. Click on the arrow beside Profile Name in the Session Profile box. You'll see an entry for the OAK Archives. Select this by clicking on it.
5. Type **anonymous** in the User ID: field, and type your full e-mail address in the Password: field.
6. Click the OK button. The result is displayed in Figure 7.6.

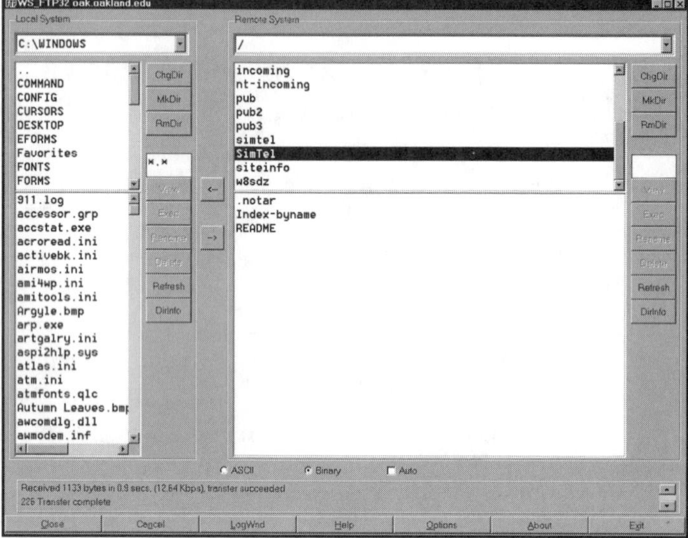

Figure 7.6.
The entry screen for the OAK archives in Winsock FTP.

The screen is divided into four parts. The left side shows *your* computer, with directories in the top portion and filenames in the bottom. The right side shows the remote computer, with (again) directories at the top and filenames below.

7. In the Remote System directory box, scroll until you find the `SimTel` directory, and then double-click on it.
8. Double-click on the `win3` directory.
9. Scroll down to the `winsock` directory and double-click on it.
10. Scroll down to the Remote System file list to find the file called `sticky08.zip` (or a higher number). Click on it *once* to highlight it.
11. On the left side of the Winsock FTP screen, select the drive and directory in which you want this file stored. Note that you can create new directories by clicking the MkDir button.
12. Notice the two arrow buttons on the bar between the two sides of the Winsock FTP window. The left-arrow button transfers files from the remote machine to your PC. The right-arrow button transfers files the other way, primarily useful for

FTPing to your own UNIX account (that is, you need permission to store the file on the remote computer). With the remote file still highlighted, click the left-arrow. Winsock FTP will transfer the file from the SimTel archives to your own computer.

Downloading Files from Your UNIX Account to Your PC

Once you've used FTP to transfer a file from a remote computer to your UNIX account, you aren't necessarily finished. Everything's fine as long as the computer that now contains the file is the one you use regularly, but if you've used UNIX FTP to move a file from a remote machine to the computer on which your UNIX account resides, this probably won't be the case. At some point in your Internet life, you'll almost certainly have to download from your UNIX account to your PC or Mac.

Note: As more people gain direct access to the Internet from their personal computers, this type of downloading will all but disappear. As you've seen so far in this chapter, FTPing from the Web, or via a Windows or Mac FTP program through a SLIP or PPP account, places the file on the hard drive of *your* computer. However, it's still useful to know how to get a file from your UNIX account to your PC, which is what this section is all about.

A huge range of software is available for uploading and downloading files. Two, however, are extremely common: XModem and Kermit. All communications packages for PCs and Macs allow XModem file transfer, and practically all allow Kermit transfer. Check the configuration menus in your particular package.

Note: This section takes you step-by-step through the download process, but only as far as the UNIX machine is concerned. That's because there are far too many communications packages for PCs and Macs to make specific procedures worth specifying. The thing to keep in mind is this: at one point in the download procedure, you'll be told to proceed from your own computer. Do what has to be done locally—either press a keystroke combination or access the appropriate menu—to finish the process.

Task 7.5: Download a text file by using XModem.

In this task, you'll download a text file that exists on your UNIX account. If you performed the first tasks in this chapter, you already have at least a binary file waiting there, and you probably have a text file sitting on your account somewhere. If not, FTP one now to have one available, or just follow along. Note that all the screens are from my own account; yours will look different.

1. Log in to your UNIX shell account.
2. Get a directory of files by typing **ls** and then pressing Enter.

```
% ls
Mail           ftpfaq.txt      porusch.txt
News           gopher1.bin     tribal-interviews
README         interview       whodat
agre.txt       mail            xmodem.log
bin            mbox            xmodemsc.txt
dead.letter    me
```

   Usually, this is enough. In many cases, however, a more complete listing is preferable—one that shows file sizes and dates. For this, type **ls -l**.

```
% ls -l
total 151drwx-  2 nrandall      512 Nov 14 15:27 Mail
drwxr-x—x   7 nrandall      512 Feb 13 21:40 News
-rw-r—    1 nrandall     757 Mar 24 18:47 README
-rw-r—    1 nrandall   63638 Mar  6 00:09 agre.txt
drwx—s—x   2 nrandall      512 Mar 26  1990 bin
-rw——     1 nrandall       4 Feb 23 12:00 dead.letter
-rw-r—    1 nrandall   28487 Mar 24 09:02 ftpfaq.txt
-rw-r—    1 nrandall   51810 Mar 24 18:53 gopher1.bin
-rw-r—    1 nrandall    3038 Mar 22 14:02 interview
drwx——     2 nrandall     1024 Mar 27 09:48 mail
-rw——     1 nrandall   10741 Feb 23 12:03 mbox
-rw-r—    1 nrandall      90 Jan  8 21:09 me
-rw-r—    1 nrandall   15021 Mar  8 09:58 porusch.txt
-rw-r—    1 nrandall    2771 Mar 22 13:54 tribal-interviews
-rw-r—    1 nrandall     186 Nov 11  1990 whodat
-rw-r—    1 nrandall   18113 Mar 25 11:01 xmodem.log
-rw-r—    1 nrandall       0 Mar 27 09:50 xmodemsc.txt
```

3. The desired file in this case is `ftpfaq.txt` (it's a file with a lot of FTP information). To download it, you'll need the `xmodem` command. First, type **xmodem** and then press Enter to get a list of xmodem commands available.

```
% xmodem
Xmodem Version 3.10 (04 Jan. 1991) — UNIX-Microcomputer File Transfer
Facility
Usage:        xmodem -[rb!rt!ra!sb!st!sa][options] filename
Major Commands —
rb <— Receive Binary
rt <— Receive Text
ra <— Receive Apple macintosh text
sb <— Send Binary
st <— Send Text
sa <— Send Apple macintosh text
```

```
Options —
y  <— Use YMODEM Batch Mode on transmit
g  <— Select YMODEM-G Mode on receive
m  <— Use MODEM7 Batch Mode on transmit
k  <— Use 1K packets on transmit
c  <— Select CRC mode on receive
t  <— Indicate a TOO BUSY Unix system
d  <— Delete xmodem.log file before starting
l  <— (ell) Turn OFF Log File Entries
x  <— Include copious debugging information in log file
p  <— Use with SunOS tip ~C command
w  <— Wait before initial handshake
e  <— Supress EOT confirmation
n  <— Allow mid-transfer CAN-CAN aborts
```

4. Your options were to send or receive `ftpfaq.txt` as a binary file, a text file, or a Macintosh-specific text file. Here, you'll choose the text option. Type **`xmodem st ftpfaq.txt`** and then press Enter. Note that, to download a binary file, you'd use the **sb** flag instead.

Note: Although the final destination for a file downloaded from your UNIX account is your own PC, you have to use the command `send` rather than `receive`. Think of the UNIX machine as being egocentric and you'll have no problem. You have to look at everything from its perspective, not your own. This can be confusing, however, because in the case of FTP, the reverse is the case; there, you get the file from the remote machine, while here you `send` the file to your home machine.

```
% xmodem st ftpfaq.txt
Xmodem Version 3.10 (04 Jan. 1991) — UNIX-Microcomputer File Transfer
Facility
File ftpfaq.txt Ready to SEND in text mode
Estimated File Size 28K, 223 Sectors, 28487 Bytes
Estimated transmission time 4 minutes 25 seconds
Send several Control-X characters to cancel
```

5. The file is ready to be downloaded to your PC or Mac. Tell your communications software to *receive* a text file using XModem protocol, and then specify a directory and filename. If the UNIX filename is too long (or incomprehensible), change it to suit.

Task 7.6: Download a file from your UNIX account by using Kermit.

Unlike the standard UNIX XModem, Kermit offers an interactive environment. That is, you actually enter Kermit the way you enter FTP, and then work from there. To download a file from your UNIX account by using Kermit, follow these steps:

1. Log in to your UNIX shell account.

2. Type **kermit** at the prompt.

```
% kermit
C-Kermit 5A(189), 30 June 93, SunOS 4.1 (BSD)
Type ? or HELP for help
```

3. Type **help**. Kermit offers its own internal help system, although learning about the program's actual command takes a bit of further digging.

```
C-Kermit> help
C-Kermit 5A(189), 30 June 93, Copyright (C) 1985, 1993,
Trustees of Columbia University in the City of New York.

Type INTRO for an introduction to C-Kermit, press ? for a list of commands.
Type HELP followed by a command name for help about a specific command.
Type NEWS for news about new features.
While typing commands, you may use the following special characters:
DEL, RUBOUT, BACKSPACE, CTRL-H: Delete the most recent character typed.
CTRL-W:  Delete the most recent word typed.
CTRL-U:  Delete the current line.
CTRL-R:  Redisplay the current line.
?        (question mark) Display a menu for the current command field.
ESC      (or TAB) Attempt to complete the current field.
\        (backslash) include the following character literally
or introduce a backslash code, variable, or function.
Command words other than filenames can be abbreviated in most contexts.
From system level, type "kermit -h" for help about command-line options.

DOCUMENTATION: "Using C-Kermit" by Frank da Cruz and Christine M. Gianone,
Digital Press.  DP ISBN: 1-55558-108-0; Prentice-Hall ISBN: 0-13-037490-3.
DECdirect: +1-800-344-4825, Order Number EY-J896E-DP, US $34.95.
```

4. The most important finding here was the first line, which tells how to get further help on specific commands. Type **?** at the prompt and press Enter.

```
C-Kermit> ?
apc            ask            askq           assign
bug            bye            cd             check
clear          close          comment        connect
declare        decrement      define         delete
dial           directory      disable        do
echo           enable         end            exit
finish         for            get            getok
goto           hangup         help           if
increment      input          introduction   log
mail           msend          msleep         news
open           output         pause          ping
print          push           pwd            quit
read           receive        redial         reinput
remote         rename         return         run
script         send           server         set
show           space          statistics     stop
suspend        take           telnet         translate
transmit       type           version        wait
while          who            write          xif
```

5. While you might scarcely be able to restrain yourself from finding out what `msleep` is all about, why not stick to efficiency and learn how to use `send`. Type **help send** and press Enter.

Tip: While Kermit offers a number of commands, only a few are necessary for simple uploading or downloading. Learn `send`, `receive`, `dir`, `connect`, and `exit`, and you'll be off and running. The rest are for more complex sessions, including those where one computer or the other acts as a host machine for communications purposes.

```
C-Kermit> help send

Syntax: SEND (or S) filespec [name]
Send the file or files specified by filespec.
filespec may contain wildcard characters '*' or '?'. If no wildcards,
then 'name' may be used to specify the name 'filespec' is sent under; if
'name' is omitted, the file is sent under its own name.
```

6. Now that you know how to send a file to your PC, get a directory listing by typing **`dir`** and then pressing Enter.

```
C-Kermit> dir
total 184
drwx——   2 nrandall      512 Nov 14 15:27 Mail
drwxr-x—x  7 nrandall      512 Feb 13 21:40 News
-rw-r—   1 nrandall      757 Mar 24 18:47 README
-rw-r—   1 nrandall    63638 Mar  6 00:09 agre.txt
drwx—s—x  2 nrandall      512 Mar 26  1990 bin
-rw—   1 nrandall        4 Feb 23 12:00 dead.letter
-rw-r—   1 nrandall    28487 Mar 24 09:02 ftpfaq.txt
-rw-r—   1 nrandall    51810 Mar 24 18:53 gopher.zip
-rw-r—   1 nrandall     3038 Mar 22 14:02 interview
drwx—  2 nrandall     1024 Mar 27 09:48 mail
-rw—   1 nrandall    10741 Feb 23 12:03 mbox
-rw-r—   1 nrandall       90 Jan  8 21:09 me
-rw-r—   1 nrandall    15021 Mar  8 09:58 porusch.txt
-rw-r—   1 nrandall     2771 Mar 22 13:54 tribal-interviews
-rw-r—   1 nrandall      186 Nov 11  1990 whodat
-rw-r—   1 nrandall    18592 Mar 27 09:53 xmodem.log
-rw-r—   1 nrandall    32768 Mar 27 09:53 xmodemsc.txt
```

7. In this example, the desired file is `gopher.zip`. Unlike XModem, Kermit doesn't need to be told whether the file is binary or text, so simply type **`send gopher.zip`** at the prompt.

```
C-Kermit> send gopher.zip
Return to your local Kermit and give a RECEIVE command.
```

8. As with Xmodem, tell your communications package to download a file using Kermit protocol, choose the directory and filename, and a few minutes later the file will be on your PC.
9. Exit the Kermit session by typing **`quit`** and pressing Enter.

Summary

File Transfer Protocol is an extremely important part of your Internet activity. Whether you use UNIX FTP, a dedicated FTP program such as Fetch or Winsock FTP, or a Web browser such as Netscape or Mosaic, you'll find yourself performing FTPs frequently. In the case of the Web, you won't always know you're actually doing an FTP, but if you're downloading a file, FTP is part of the action.

Task Review

In this chapter, you performed the following tasks:

- ☐ FTP a file from another computer to your own account
- ☐ FTP a file from a remote site directly to your PC or Mac
- ☐ FTP a file from within a World Wide Web browser
- ☐ FTP a file using a dedicated Windows or Mac FTP program
- ☐ Use XModem and Kermit to transfer a file from a UNIX machine to your PC

Q&A

Q FTP works great, but sometimes when I get a list of files in the directory, the output scrolls way off the top of the screen. Is there any way I can stop it?

A Try the command `ls ¦more` (`¦` is the pipe symbol, two vertical dashes, usually located above the backslash key on standard PC keyboards). This should deliver one screen of details at a time, and then wait for you to press the spacebar. Most systems support this feature.

There are a couple other ways, however. First, select a communications package that has what's called a *screen buffer* or *backscroll buffer* or something similar. These will enable you to see what's gone off the top of the screen (although activating them isn't always as easy as it might be). Second, if you're working on a pure character-based terminal, use UNIX's `script` command. Type **`script filename`** (call the file whatever you want), and then do your directory listings. Type **`exit`** to get out of **`script`**, and then load the file into a standard editor (or word processor). `Script` captures the session in an ASCII file, and you can use it whenever you want to track what you're doing and where you've been.

Q I've tried to download to my PC using XModem, but nothing seems to happen. Should I buy a new communications program?

A If you're using an especially old communications package, you might want to consider upgrading anyway, because the new ones take advantage of faster modems and additional transfer protocols. There are excellent shareware packages available for every computer type, so there's really no excuse for using an old version. One of the things continually tested in upgraded programs is compatibility, and this may well be the problem here.

But not necessarily. Before doing anything, double-check that you've selected the right download protocol in the program on your own computer. There are several varieties of XModem, and while some are faster than others, you should start with the most basic, XModem itself (not XModem-1K or something with a similar extension). Also, make sure that you told the remote computer to send the file rather than receive it (that is, use XModem, st, or sb). Finally, make sure that you, in fact, activate the download. I used to think it just happened automatically, which it often does with other protocols, but XModem needs elbow grease.

8

DAY 3

Navigating with Gopher

This chapter introduces you to *Gopher*, the multi-purpose browsing and searching system. Through Gopher, you can move quickly from computer to computer across the entire Net, viewing and downloading information as you discover it. The resources available via Gopher are many, and more significantly, they're extremely easy to access.

Gopher isn't really a tool. Instead, it's a combination of tools. Gopher provides links to files and directories at local and remote machines alike, and it essentially hides all the details from you (unless you specifically request them). That's what makes Gopher so effortless to use. Rather than using FTP commands to retrieve a file (see Chapter 7), for example, you can simply Gopher to the site, select the file, and download it to your hard drive.

Until 1994, Gopher was the most important information retrieval tool on the Net. Since then, the World Wide Web has overtaken it. But Gopher remains important, especially for users without graphical Web access, and a great deal of information is still available only on Gopher sites. Gopherspace (as it's called) is accessible through all World Wide Web browsers, but dedicated Gopher programs are more versatile. And the Gopher team, led by Mark McCahill at the University of Minnesota, is currently developing an entirely new look for Gopher, which, in conjunction with the Web, will soon offer a three-dimensional hierarchical view of information.

Task List

In this chapter, you'll perform the following tasks:

- ☐ Enter and explore a sample Gopher site
- ☐ Download, save, and mail files from Gophers
- ☐ Bookmark your favorite Gopher sites
- ☐ Explore a number of specific sites in the United States and beyond

Entering and Maneuvering Through a GopherSite

Gopher sites are readily available across the entire Internet. In these sites, you'll find Gopher menus, or directories, presented in list format. Selecting a menu item takes you either to a file—text, graphic, sound, program, video, and so on—or, more commonly, to yet another menu. Eventually, you'll want to arrive at an actual file to read or download, but at first, it's both enjoyable and instructive to move from site to site, simply "surfing" from computer to computer around the world.

To access a Gopher site, you need a Gopher *client* program. If you have a UNIX shell account, your host computer probably has Gopher installed. To check this out, log into your account and, at the UNIX prompt, type **`gopher`**. If a numbered list appears, then you have gopher at your disposal. If not, talk to your systems people about installing Gopher; the software is free over the Net.

If you're a Mac or Windows user with SLIP or PPP access, Gopher clients are readily available over the Net, and also as part of packages, such as Internet in a Box, Superhighway Access, and Netmanage Chameleon. This chapter offers a short overview of Winsock Gopher, a popular (and free) package for Windows, but the main Gopher you'll see on these pages is the standard UNIX version. This is especially appropriate because Gopher's main use today remains with UNIX shell accounts.

Task 8.1: Access the University of Chicago Gopher site (*uic.edu*).

One of the nicest things about using Gopher is that you don't have to remember Internet addresses and the like. As soon as you find a local Gopher, you can usually work your way all around the Internet from that original site. In these lessons, you start at the University of Chicago's main Gopher, and then move from there to a variety of different Gophers. Entering a particular Gopher site simply involves typing **`gopher`** and the Internet address of the specified host. To access the University of Chicago Gopher site, follow these steps:

1. Log into your UNIX shell account (see Chapter 2 for details on logging in).
2. At the UNIX prompt, type **`gopher uic.edu`** and press Enter.

It's as simple as that. A few seconds later, you'll get the following menu:

```
        1.  Gopher at UIC/ADN/
        2.  What's New
        3.  Search the UIC Campus and Beyond/
        4.  The Administrator/
        5.  The Campus/
        6.  The Classroom/
        7.  The Community/
        8.  The Computer/
        9.  The Library/
        10. The Researcher/
  -->   11. The World/

Press ? for Help, q to Quit, u to go up a menu                  Page: 1/1
```

Task 8.2: Select menuitem 11 from the Gopher list.

All basic Gophers consist of a vertical list (usually numbered for easier access), with each item pointing to a file or another site. You can select an item from the list by typing the appropriate number reference or by using the arrow keys. In this case, select item `11`, `The World`.

1. To select `The World (11)` from `uic.edu`'s menu, arrow down to the item's title and press Enter once. If your Gopher presented you with a numbered list, type **11** and press Enter.
2. Once you have cursored to the item or typed the number, a `view item number` line will appear at the bottom of your screen with the number already displayed. Press Enter and your Gopher will provide immediate entry.
3. To verify that the Gopher has received your directions, look at the bottom right corner of your screen. If your commands were successful, the words `Retrieving Directory` (or something similar) appear, indicating that the program is connecting to and retrieving the directory.

Your screen should now look like the following:

```
-->    1.  Other Illinois Gophers/
       2.  University of Minnesota/
       3.  CICnet Gopher/
       4.  Library of Congress (LC MARVEL)/
       5.  The Internet Mall
       6.  Netnews: Usenet, news services, etc (local access only)/
       7.  United States Government gophers/
       8.  Veronica - Netwide Gopher Title Index/
       9.  Gopher Jewels/
       10. InterNIC Information Services/
       11. The World By Subject (from Rice)/
       12. The World by Location (from Minnesota)/
       13. The World By Phonebook (from Notre Dame)/

Press ? for Help, q to Quit, u to go up a menu                  Page: 1/1
```

Note: On a Gopher menu, you'll see a variety of symbols at the end of the menu headings. They are as follows:

```
(none)       0      file
/            1      directory
<)           s      sound file
<Picture>    I,g    image file
<Movie>      ;      movie file
```

```
<HQX>           4       BinHexed Macintosh file
<Bin>           9       binary file
<PC Bin>        5       DOS binary file
<CSO>           2       CSO (ph/qi) phone-book server
<TEL>           8       telnet connection
<3270>          T       telnet connection (IBM 3270 emulation)
<MIME>          M       Multi-purpose Internet Mail Extensions file
<HTML>          h       HyperText Markup Language file
<?>             7       index-search item
<??>         (none)     ASK form
```

These symbols will appear in the Gopher sites you visit. You might want to print them out so you don't have to keep referring to them as you proceed. Each type of file will offer different possibilities as you access them.

Task 8.3: Select an item from The World menu.

A menu item similar to The World exists on practically every Gopher server. Often it's called *Other Gophers Around the World*, or something similar. Its purpose is to move you beyond the local Gopher and into links with Gophers in other places.

The following menu item offers a number of choices, including subject, location, and phonebook directories. Note that item 5 is a text file you could read by selecting it, while the rest of the items all point to other directories. You'll see what else is available in Illinois by choosing item `1`.

1. Your cursor should already be positioned at item `1`, so just press Enter once to select the `Other Illinois Gophers` item. Your screen now shows the following:

```
-->   1. Argggh Gopher Server/
      2. Board of Governors Universities, IL USA/
      3. Bradley University/
      4. Center for Research Libraries [CRL]/
      5. Chicago State University, IL USA/
      6. Chicago-Kent gopher/
      7. College of St. Francis, Joliet, IL, USA/
      8. Concordia University, River Forest, IL, USA/
      9. Dana Victor Gopher Server/
      10. Danville Area Community College, Danville, IL/
      11. DePaul University/
      12. DePaul University Library Services/
      13. ERIC Clearinghouse on Elementary and Early Childhood Education/
      14. Eastern Illinois University/
      15. Elmhurst College/
      16. Goofy Gopher Server/
      17. Governors State University, IL USA/
      18. Illinois Institute of Technology/

Press ? for Help, q to Quit, u to go up a menu                    Page: 1/4
```

Often, access to Gopher menus and documents is a hit-and-miss operation. At times, you may gain entry to sites quickly, with little interference, while periodically the machine may be unable to connect to the selected item. Delays often occur, especially at busy periods of the day, so try again later.

Tip: Sometimes, after selecting a Gopher item and pressing Enter, your computer might get "stuck" trying to access the desination Gopher. You'll see the status line showing `Connecting....` "No problem," you might think, just choose a different menu item. Right? Wrong. Unfortunately, none of the commands listed in most Gopher's help menus can interrupt this connecting (or not-connecting) process. Instead, hold down the Ctrl (^) key and type **c** for cancel. The connecting process will cease and a `quit` prompt will appear at the bottom of your screen, asking you if you really want to exit the system. Type **n** and the program will return you to The World menu and you may select another option.

Task 8.4: Return to the previous menu item.

The result of the `Other Illinois Gophers` selection might be interesting but so are many other tempting items on the previous menu. Gopher presents the most common commands at the bottom of the screen. This line from the `Other Illinois Gophers` menu looks like the following:

```
Press ? for Help, q to Quit, u to go up a menu                    Page: 1/4
```

You can press **?** to get help, which will give you the complete set of Gopher commands, or you can press **q** to quit Gopher completely (you'll be asked to verify your decision). Or, importantly, you can press **u** to move back to the previous menu. Usually, pressing the left-arrow key accomplishes the same function.

1. Because you want to choose another option from the previous menu, type **u** to move back. This basic step returns you to `The World` menu.
2. Press **u** again to move back to the first menu. By pressing **u** repeatedly, you can retrace your path to the beginning of your browsing.

Task 8.5: Page through a long Gopher list.

Not all the menus featured on your Gopher system will be as clear and concise as those you have examined so far. More frequently, selecting an item from a menu opens up expanded lists, files, and documents that you must sift through to locate information.

1. From The World menu, choose item number 11, The World By Subject (from Rice)/. You'll see the following screen:

```
--> 1.   About the RiceInfo collection of "Information by Subject Area"
    2.   More about "Information by Subject Area"/
    3.   Clearinghouse of Subject-Oriented Internet Resource Guides
         (UMich../
    4.   Search all of Gopherspace by title: Jughead (from WLU) <?>
    5.   Search all of Gopherspace by title: Veronica/
    6.   Search all of RiceInfo by title: Jughead/
    7.  Aerospace/
    8.  Agriculture and Forestry/
    9.  Anthropology and Culture/
    10. Architecture/
    11. Arts/
    12. Astronomy and Astrophysics/
    13. Biology/
    14. Census/
    15. Chemistry/
    16. Computer Networks and Internet Resource Guides/
    17. Computing/
    18. Economics and Business/

Press ? for Help, q to Quit, u to go up a menu               Page: 1/3
```

   This menu offers 18 options, most of which point to other sites. No, wait, there are more than 18! This list only goes alphabetically as far as E.

   Notice the bottom line again. At the far right is a page reference, showing the page number you're currently on and the total number of pages in this menu.

2. Press the spacebar to view the remaining screens and browse your choices thoroughly. The result of the first press of the spacebar is the following list:

```
--> 19. Education/
    20. Engineering/
    21. Environment and Ecology/
    22. Film and Television/
    23. Geography/
    24. Geology and Geophysics/
    25. Government, Political Science and Law/
    26. Grants, Scholarships and Funding/
    27. History/
    28. Jobs and Employment/
    29. Language and Linguistics/
    30. Library and Information Science/
    31. Literature, Electronic Books and Journals/
    32. Mathematics/
    33. Medicine and Health/
    34. Military Science/
    35. Music/
    36. News and Journalism/

Press ? for Help, q to Quit, u to go up a menu               Page: 2/3
```

Although it doesn't say on the menu, pressing the spacebar takes you to the next screen, and pressing the hyphen key (-) takes you back up a screen.

Warning: Don't confuse the hyphen key with the u (up) key. Often—very often, in fact—you'll wait a minute or so for a long Gopher menu to appear, spacebar down a few pages, and then press the **u** key when you meant to press the hyphen to move up a page. The result? You're back to the previous menu, completely out of the list you spent so long retrieving. It's enough to drive you to Gophercide.

Working with Files

The whole point of Gopher is to help you find your way around the Internet. So far, your browsing has moved you from list to list, but you have not accessed any actual files. You still haven't opened any tangible information sites. Once you find a site of interest, you'll also want to access files, save or mail information, and print valuable documents.

Task 8.6: Access an article from Gopher *Jewels/* and manipulate the data.

The first step in manipulating any Gopher site is to locate an actual article and read its contents. Remember that the / sign at the end of a menu listing indicates that another menu of choices follows. Only a menu item with no ending symbol points to a file you can actually access.

1. Move back to `The World` menu again, using the u key as described in Task 8.4.
2. This time, select item 9, the fascinatingly-named `Gopher Jewels`. Your Gopher will present the following screen:

```
        1.  GOPHER JEWELS Information and Help/
        2.  Community, Global and Environmental/
        3.  Education, Social Sciences, Arts & Humanities/
        4.  Economics, Business and Store Fronts/
        5.  Engineering and Industrial Applications/
        6.  Government/
        7.  Health, Medical, and Disability/
    --> 8.  Internet and Computer Related Resources/
        9.  Law/
        10. Library, Reference, and News/
        11. Miscellaneous Items/
        12. Natural Sciences including Mathematics/
        13. Personal Development and Recreation/
        14. Research, Technology Transfer and Grants Opportunities/
        15. Search Gopher Jewels Menus by Key Word(s) <?>

Press ? for Help, q to Quit, u to go up a menu                Page: 1/1
```

Note: `Gopher Jewels` is listed on many, many Gophers, and it's well worth visiting regularly. It's continually being updated, and it's the best source of complete Gopher information. You can access it directly by Gophering to `cwis.usc.edu` and following the path, `Other Gophers and Information Resources`, and then `Gopher by Subject`, and finally `Gopher Jewels`. If you're accessing it from a World Wide Web browser, use the following URL:

`gopher://cwis.usc.edu:70/11/Other_Gophers_and_Information_Resources/Gophers_by_Subject/Gopher_Jewels`

3. Having already become entranced by the Internet, select item `8`, `Internet and Computer Related Resources/`. At the very least, it sounds interesting. Because the `/` sign appears at the end of the title, you already know that you will receive another menu to choose from. You should see the following:

```
        1.  A List Of Gophers With Subject Trees/
        2.  Computer Related/
  -->   3.  Internet Cyberspace related/
        4.  Internet Resources by Type (Gopher, Phone, USENET, WAIS, Other)/
        5.  Internet Service Providers/
        6.  List of Lists Resources/
        7.   Jump to Gopher Jewels Main Menu/
        8.  Search Gopher Jewels Menus by Key Word(s) <?>

Press ? for Help, q to Quit, u to go up a menu                  Page: 1/1
```

4. Now choose item `3` from the preceding menu, `Internet Cyberspace Related/`. Your Gopher will present the following menu:

```
        19. Ejournal - Internet World Magazine/
        20. Electronic Frontier Foundation/
        21. Electronic Frontier Foundation (Austin, TX)/
        22. Federal Networking Council Information/
        23. Fins Information Age Library - University of Maryland/
        24. FONOROLA - Directory of Trainers and Consultants
        25. FYI Newsletter - Marketplace Gopher/
        26. Information Infrastructure Sourcebook - Harvard JFK School of
            Gov'../
        27. Information Networks - Inst. of Public Policy Studies, U. Michi
            gan/
        28. Institute for Information Management - Univ. of St. Gallen/
        29. International Telecommunication Union (ITU) Gopher/
        30. Internet Beginners Information - INTERNIC/
        31. Internet Documents - Wheaton College, IL/
        32. Internet Engineering Task Force (IETF)/
        33. Internet Glossaries And Definitions - INTERNIC/
        34. Internet Society (ISOC)/
        35. Internet Timeline v1.3 by Robert Zakon, Indiana Univ. Libraries
  -->   36. Internet Wiretap (Cyberspace)/

Press ? for Help, q to Quit, u to go up a menu                  Page: 2/4
```

5. No question here. Internet Wiretap (Cyberspace) sounds irresistible, so resist no longer. Arrow down to item `36` (or type in the number) and press Enter. Following is the result:

```
 --> 1.  A Cynic Looks at Moo
     2.  Cardozo Law Forum Article on Neidorf
     3.  Case for Telecommunications Deregulation
     4.  Common BBS Acronyms
     5.  Computer Underground (Meyer & Thomas)
     6.  Concerning Hackers who Break into Systems
     7.  Crypto Anarchist Manifesto
     8.  Cyberpunk From Subculture To Mainstream
     9.  Defamation Liability of BBS's
     10. Electropolis (About Internet Relay Chat)
     11. Fight Communists With Cryptography
     12. GAO report on Computer Security
     13. Internet Connectivity in Eastern Europe
     14. JP Barlow: Crime and Puzzlement
     15. James Joyce and the Prehistory of Cyberspace
     16. Lawsuit against Steve Jackson Games
     17. MUD as a Psychological Model
     18. Mindvox: Voices In My Head, Patrick Kroupa

Press ? for Help, q to Quit, u to go up a menu
Page: 1/2
```

6. All the listings are text files (no symbol at the end of the lines), so choose one to read. Type **6** press and Enter. Following is a short paragraph from `Concerning Hackers who Break into Systems.`

```
From such a profile I expect to be able to construct a picture of
the discourses in which hacking takes place. By a discourse I mean
the invisible background of assumptions that transcends individuals
--More-- (5%) [Hit space to continue, Q to quit]
```

   Notice the last line on the screen. You've only seen 5 percent of the article (that is, there are 20 more screens to read). This percentage appears in all files and indicates the approximate length of articles as well as the amount you have read.

7. Following the instructions on this line, press the spacebar to continue reading the document.

Task 8.7: Mail a file to an e-mail account.

When you find a file you want somebody else (or yourself) to read, you can send it to that user via e-mail. To mail a file to an e-mail account, follow these steps:

1. While reading a file in Gopher, press **q** for quit. You'll receive the following menu at the bottom of the screen (the menu also appears if you come to the last screen of the document):

```
Press <RETURN> to continue,
<m> to mail, <D> to download, <s> to save, or <p> to print:
```

Warning: This menu is confusing in one important regard. Pressing Return (or Enter) doesn't actually do what it says. You'd expect to be able to continue reading the article, but in fact pressing Enter takes you back to the menu where you found the article title in the first place. In the case of long files, this can be an extremely frustrating choice, because to read the file again means reloading it from scratch. There is, in fact, no way of continuing to read the article at this point.

8

This menu offers the following choices:

`<RETURN>`	Go back to previous menu
`<m>`	Mail the document to an account (your own, for example)
`<D>`	Download the file (Note that this is Shift+D (uppercase) not just lowercase d)
`<s>`	Save the file to your account's hard disk
`<p>`	Print the file to the specified printer

2. Because you want to mail the document to an account, press `m` and you will see the following screen:

```
+---------------Concerning Hackers who Break into Systems---------------+
|                                                                       |
|                                                                       |
| Mail current document to:                                             |
|                                                                       |
|                                                                       |
|                                                                       |
| nrandall@watarts.uwaterloo.ca                                         |
|                                                                       |
|                                                                       |
|                                                                       |
| [Help: ^-]  [Cancel: ^G]                                              |
|                                                                       |
+-----------------------------------------------------------------------+
```

3. Type the full Internet address into the box (as shown previously). The preceding example shows the file being mailed to my main account. Press Enter to send the document. A small `mail` message will appear in the bottom right corner of your screen that indicates the success of your command and Gopher will then return you to the `Internet Wiretap (Cyberspace)` menu.

Task 8.8: Save the file on your hard drive.

Another choice is to save the account on your hard drive. This means, in almost all cases, that it will be saved as a file on the machine holding the UNIX account itself, not on your own home computer (if you're working from home). You can accomplish the latter through the download feature described in Task 8.9. To save the file on your hard drive, follow these steps:

1. Choose an article from the Internet Wiretap (Cyberspace) menu and open it according to the procedure described in Task 8.6. Press **q** to quit.
2. Type **s** to save the document on your hard drive. The following example shows the filename suggested by the save feature; you can edit it to say whatever you want (within the UNIX filename restrictions).

```
+---------------Concerning Hackers who Break into Systems---------------+
|                                                                       |
|                                                                       |
| Save in file:                                                         |
|                                                                       |
|                                                                       |
|                                                                       |
| Concerning-Hackers-who-Break-into-Systems                             |
|                                                                       |
|                                                                       |
|                                                                       |
| [Help: ^-]  [Cancel: ^G]                                              |
|                                                                       |
+-----------------------------------------------------------------------+
```

3. After you enter an appropriate name for the article, press Enter and the process is complete. Again, Gopher will return you to the `Internet Wiretap (Cyberspace)` menu.

Task 8.9: Download an article to a directory.

The most popular option for those who log in from PCs or Macs (or Amigas or anything else, for that matter) is downloading. The download feature enables you to place the file on your PC's hard drive, using one of the protocols listed in the box. In order to use this, you must know how to use your communications software to download files, and your communications program must be able to handle one of the listed protocols. To download an article to a directory, follow these steps:

1. Open an article and press **q** to reveal the command line.
2. Type **D** (that is, Shift+D) to download the article you have opened and the following screen will appear:

```
+---Concerning Hackers who Break into Systems---+
|                                               |
|  -->    1. Zmodem                             |
|         2. Ymodem                             |
|         3. Xmodem-1K                          |
|         4. Xmodem-CRC                         |
|         5. Kermit                             |
|         6. Text                               |
|                                               |
|  Choose a download method (1-6):              |
|  [Help: ?]  [Cancel: ^G]                      |
+-----------------------------------------------+
```

3. Choose a downloading option by typing the number of the protocol that applies to your system.
4. Once you've chosen your download protocol, instruct the communications software to save the file in whatever directory on your hard drive you want.

Bookmarks

It would be extremely tedious to keep working your way back to a particularly interesting Gopher site, so Gopher quite nicely offers a bookmarking feature. Essentially, your list of bookmarks creates a personal Gopher menu, which you can access at any point in a Gopher session by pressing the `v` (for view) key.

Task 8.10: Create a bookmark for the Internet Wiretap (Cyberspace) menu.

In this task, item `22` from the `Internet Cyberspace Related` menu has been chosen, because you've found `Internet Wiretap (Cyberspace)` worth returning to in the future.

1. Press `u` to return to the `Internet Cyberspace Related` menu where `Internet Wiretap (Cyberspace)` is listed.
2. To create a bookmark, cursor to the item you want and then type `a` (for add). The following shows the resulting screen:

```
+--------------------Internet Wiretap (Cyberspace)--------------------+
|                                                                     |
|                                                                     |
|                                                                     |
| Name for this bookmark:                                             |
|                                                                     |
|                                                                     |
|                                                                     |
| Internet Wiretap (Cyberspace)                                       |
|                                                                     |
|                                                                     |
|                                                                     |
| [Help: ^-]  [Cancel: ^G]                                            |
|                                                                     |
+---------------------------------------------------------------------+
```

3. Gopher suggests a bookmark name, the same as the item name. You can change this if you want.

Note: When you bookmark an item by pressing `a`, you bookmark only that item, not the entire menu on which the item appears. If you want to bookmark the entire menu, press `A` instead (that is, Shift-a). Note, however, that this option is only available on Gopher version 2.0 or higher.

4. With the bookmark chosen, view your bookmark menu by pressing `v`. Following is what mine looks like:

```
Bookmarks

1.  A List Of Gophers With Subject Trees/
2.  Federal Agency and Related Gopher Sites/
3.  Legal or Law related/
4.  Patents and Copy Rights/
5.  Limit search to jobs in the Northeast <?>
6.  SEARCH using any word or words of your choosing/
7.  SEARCH using The Chronicle's list of job titles/
8.  Employment Opportunities and Resume Postings/
9.  Gopher-Jewels/
10. Internet Wiretap (Cyberspace)/
```

Notice item `10`, the site you've just bookmarked.

Getting Technical Information and Searching for Titles

Bookmarking is one way of making a Gopher item easy to get to. Another is to request technical information, which you can use to Gopher directly to the site. Yet another way is to search for a specific known site by initiating a Gopher search.

Task 8.11: Request technical information on a Gopher site.

You can receive technical information by cursoring to any menu item and pressing the equal sign (=). This command is listed in the `Other Commands` section of Gopher's Help Menu. To request technical information on a Gopher site, follow these steps:

1. Locate the Gopher Jewels site on `The World` menu where you began surfing, and scroll down to the numbered entry.
2. Type `=`. Here is the technical information for the `Gopher Jewels` menu item on the University of Chicago menu.

```
#
Type=1
Name=Gopher Jewels
Path=1/Other_Gophers_and_Information_Resources/Gophers_by_Subject/
➥Gopher_Jewels
Host=cwis.usc.edu
Port=70
URL: gopher://cwis.usc.edu:70/11/Other_Gophers_and_Information_Resources/
➥Gophers
_by_Subject/Gopher_Jewels


Press <RETURN> to continue,
   <m> to mail, <D> to download, <s> to save, or <p> to print:
```

From now on, you could reach Gopher Jewels by typing `gopher cwis.usc.edu` at the command line and selecting `Other Gophers and Information Resources`, and `Gophers by Subject`, and then `Gopher Jewels`.

Note: As with bookmarks, you receive information only about the item you're about to select. If you want information about the entire directory you're currently viewing, press ^ (Shift+6) instead.

Task 8.12: Conduct a search of Gopher menu titles.

The last major Gopher feature worth knowing about is searching titles. Searching titles operates on the same basis as a Find... command used to locate documents and files on your system. In this case, if you've encountered a multi-page Gopher list, you don't have to keep pressing the spacebar to find a specific item. Instead, pressing the slash key (`/`) will yield a search box.

1. Using the techniques discussed in previous tasks, locate `The Arts` menu following this path:

   `/uic.edu (home menu)/The World/The World by Subject(from Rice)/Arts/`

   You should receive the following screen:

```
--> 1.  About this directory
    2.  Back up to RiceInfo Information by Subject Area/
    3. ACM SIGGRAPH Online Bibliography Project/
    4. ASCII Bazaar/
    5. About this directory
    6. Algonquin College Of Applied Arts And Technology/
    7. American Furniture
    8. ArchiGopher (University of Michigan)/
    9. Art History Inf. Facility (Heidelberg U,Germany)/
    10. Art and Architecture/
    11. Art and Art History Department, Rice University/
    12. Art and Images (Texas Tech University)/
    13. Art:  UCSB Library Reference Guide
    14. ArtFBI Gopher & Boutique/
    15. Artbase:  Bibliography of Arts Online
    16. Artliaison Virtual Gallery/
    17. Arts And Humanities Gallery/
    18. Arts Gopher sub-tree at Rice U./

Press ? for Help, q to Quit, u to go up a menu            Page: 1/11
```

2. Your cursor is placed at the first item on the menu, which contains 11 pages in total; however, you just want to locate any titles containing the `Grateful Dead` in them. To conduct a search for those titles, type `/`. Gopher will present the following search screen.

```
+--------------------------------Arts-----------------------------------+
|                                                                       |
| Search directory titles for:                                          |
|                                                                       |
|                                                                       |
|                                                                       |
|                                                                       |
|                                                                       |
| [Help: ^-]  [Cancel: ^G]                                              |
|                                                                       |
+-----------------------------------------------------------------------+
```

3. Type **`grateful dead`** in the search block and press Enter. If the search locates a title, you'll be taken directly to the first item containing the search string. Here, your search for `Grateful Dead` leads you to item `71`, four screens down:

```
      66. From ritual to romance: paintings inspired by Bali **HTML**/
      67. From ritual to romance: paintings inspired by Bali **HTML**/
      68. Go M-Link (Music)/
      69. Gophers in the humanities/
      70. Gothenburg University faculty of Arts/
  --> 71. Grateful Dead/
      72. Griffithiana

Press ? for Help, q to Quit, u to go up a menu                Page: 4/11
```

Note: After your search has been successful, you can request the next item of the same search string by typing **`n`** (for next).

Commands for Gopher for UNIX

The following list shows the available commands in the Internet Gopher Information Client v2.0.15, which is a recent version of the Gopher program typically found on UNIX systems. The following list is, in fact, a reprint of the Help menu:

```
Quick Gopher Help
                         ---------------

Moving around Gopherspace
-------------------------
Use the arrow keys or vi/emacs equivalent to move around.

Right, Return .......:  "Enter"/Display current item.
```

8

```
Left, u .............:  "Exit" current item/Go up a level.
Down ................:  Move to next line.
Up ..................:  Move to previous line.
>, +, Pgdwn, Space ..:  View next page.
<, -, Pgup, b .......:  View previous page.
0-9 .................:  Go to a specific line.
m ...................:  Go back to the main menu.

Bookmarks
---------
a : Add current item to the bookmark list.
A : Add current directory/search to bookmark list.
v : View bookmark list.
d : Delete a bookmark/directory entry.

Other commands
--------------
q : Quit with prompt.
Q : Quit unconditionally.
s : Save current item to a file.
S : Save current menu listing to a file.
D : Download a file.
r : goto root menu of current item.
R : goto root menu of current menu.
= : Display technical information about current item.
^ : Display technical information about current directory.
o : Open a new gopher server.
O : Change options.
/ : Search for an item in the menu.
n : Find next search item.
g : "Gripe" via email to administrator of current item.
!, $ : Shell Escape (Unix) or Spawn subprocess (VMS).

Gopher objects:
Item tag    Type      Description
--------------------------------------------
(none)        0       file
/             1       directory
<)            s       sound file
<Picture>    I,g      image file
<Movie>       ;       movie file
<HQX>         4       BinHexed Macintosh file
<Bin>         9       binary file
<PC Bin>      5       DOS binary file
<CSO>         2       CSO (ph/qi) phone-book server
<TEL>         8       telnet connection
<3270>        T       telnet connection (IBM 3270 emulation)
<MIME>        M       Multi-purpose Internet Mail Extensions file
<HTML>        h       HyperText Markup Language file
<?>           7       index-search item
<??>        (none)    ASK form
```

Graphical Gophering: Winsock Gopher

As you become more involved in Internet explorations, Gopher will prove nearly indispensable, assisting you daily in your browsing activities. For the growing number of Windows users, several Gopher programs are available, but one of the oldest, and the one that seems to undergo the most continual development, is *Winsock Gopher.* Currently in version 1.2, Winsock Gopher provides excellent Gopher control throughout, and single-handledly demonstrates why it's better to use a dedicated Gopher client rather than your World Wide Web browser to access Gopherspace.

Gophers designed for Windows-based systems (or any other graphical user interface system) display all commands and options in the standard Windows pull-down menus or icon toolbars featured at the top of every screen. Users no longer have to rely on their memory or the Other commands/Help screens for lists of coded UNIX commands. Instead, simply point to the options you want to use and click your mouse button to access them.

Another significant benefit of the graphical format involves the visual screen display. With most Windows-based Gophers, the path you follow to locate a certain menu item is displayed in cascading site lists at the top of your active screen. No more wondering how you got to a site or what the previous menu was called, it's all right in front of you.

Task 8.13: Acquire and install Winsock Gopher.

1. FTP to **`sunsite.unc.edu`** and go to the directory **`/pub/micro/pc-stuff/ms-windows/winsock/apps/`**. Get the file named `wsg12.exe` (the numeral might be higher by the time you actually read this).
2. Move `wsg12.exe` into a new directory, called something like `c:\wsgopher`. Using the Run command in Program Manager, launch `wsg12.exe` (you also can do so from a DOS prompt). The files will uncompress into that directory.
3. Create an icon for Winsock Gopher inside a program group of your choice.
4. Double-click on the icon to launch Winsock Gopher.

Task 8.14: Set up your home Gopher.

You probably want Winsock Gopher to connect to a specific Gopher site each time you launch the program. If your campus or office has a local Gopher server, this would be the most obvious starting point, because it normally will be accessible. In fact, in Winsock Gopher, you can specify two home servers if you want. If the first doesn't connect, the program will try the second.

After you select an appropriate home Gopher, use the following procedure to help you set up the site for automatic connection:

1. Select the Home Gopher Server... option from the Configure menu. This will yield a dialog box allowing you to establish your home Gopher site(s) (see Figure 8.1).

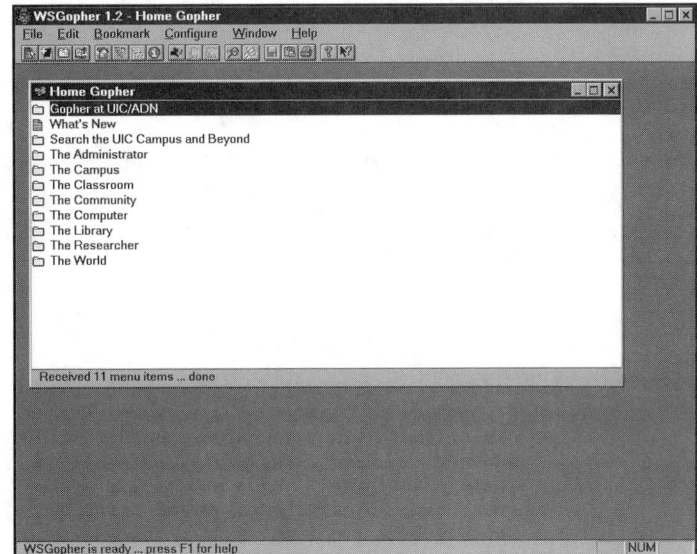

Figure 8.1.
Setting up the home Gopher servers in Winsock Gopher.

2. Type the host name in the appropriate box. If you know of a different port and a requirement for Gopher, fill in the appropriate boxes as well. For most Gopher servers, however, these boxes can be left blank.
3. Click OK to submit your entry.
4. To verify the success of this operation, select Home Gopher from the File menu. Your Gopher program should connect to the site you entered in the dialog box and will automatically connect to this site each time you enter the system.

Task 8.15: Enter a site and manipulate files.

The first thing that you'll notice about Winsock Gopher is its clear, colorful layout. The second is the ease with which many of the operations you've practiced on your basic Gopher systems may be performed. Now that you have your Home Gopher menu before you, you can explore some standard Gopher browsing techniques.

Tip: The /, ?, and . markings in UNIX Gopher that indicated whether a menu item lead to another menu, a search file, or a document do not apply for Winsock Gopher. Instead, this Gopher illustrates each entry's features with icons that precede the menu's titles. A yellow square box indicates that the menu item leads to another menu, a square gray icon with its corner folded points to an actual document, and the magnifying glass icon leads to a search file. Figure 8.2 shows these icons, from the Winsock Gopher help system.

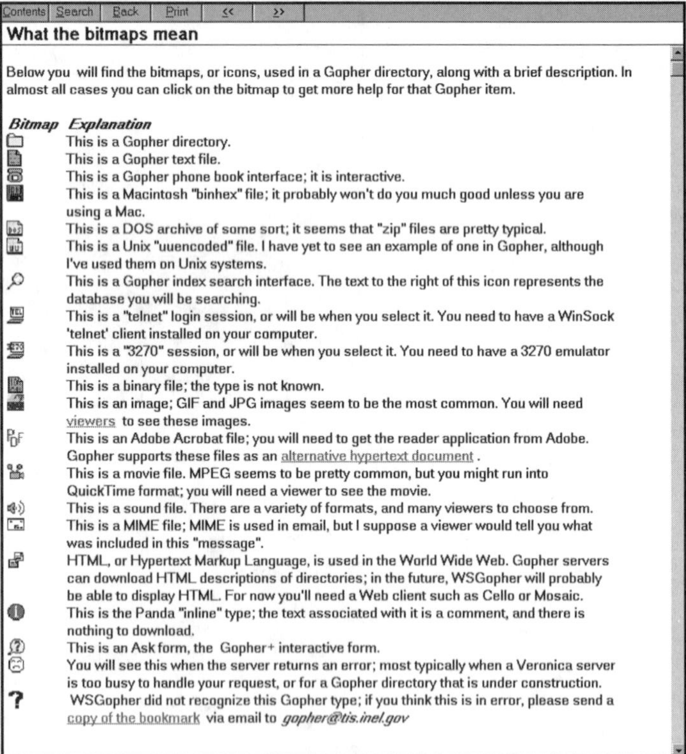

Figure 8.2.
The menu icons from Winsock Gopher's help files.

1. To enter a site, move your mouse to the appropriate title name and double-click. Winsock Gopher will flash two messages, informing you that it has first connected to the Home Gopher and has then sent the request to the site. The result is a screen that looks like Figure 8.3.
2. Moving from screen-to-screen and menu-to-menu with a Windows-based Gopher requires little effort. If you want to return to a previous screen to select another option, simply click on the screen you want, or select it from the Window menu.

Winsock Gopher opens each directory in a separate window, and you can manipulate the windows as you would in any Microsoft Windows program.

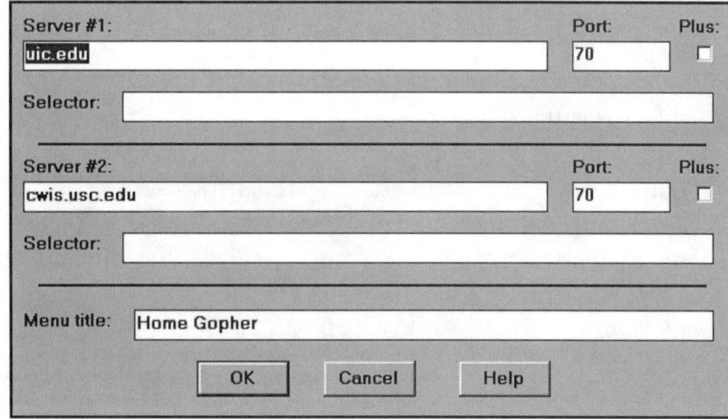

Figure 8.3.
The home Gopher site (`uic.edu`*) in Winsock Gopher.*

3. To page through long Gopher lists, simply scroll down the menu using the vertical scroll bars.

Task 8.16: Save a text file.

To save a text file you've found in your Gopher browsing, select Save Item from the File menu. This will yield Windows' standard Save dialog box, which you can use to save the file to a specified directory on your hard disk.

Notice that, unlike UNIX Gopher, the Save command places the file on *your* hard disk, not the disk of the UNIX system on which you have an account. This is a major benefit of a Windows or Mac Gopher program.

Task 8.17: Download a binary file.

You can easily save a binary file on your hard drive using Winsock Gopher. In this example, you'll save a graphics file in TIFF format.

1. Enter the home Gopher (**`uic.edu`**).
2. Double-click on `The World`.
3. Double-click on `Gopher Jewels`.

4. Double-click on `Education`.
5. Double-click on `Social Sciences, Arts and Humanities`.
6. Double-click on `Arts and Humanities`.
7. Double-click on `Lute Files - Dartmouth College (Music)`.
8. Finally, double-click on `Pictures`. Your screen should look like the screen shown in Figure 8.4.

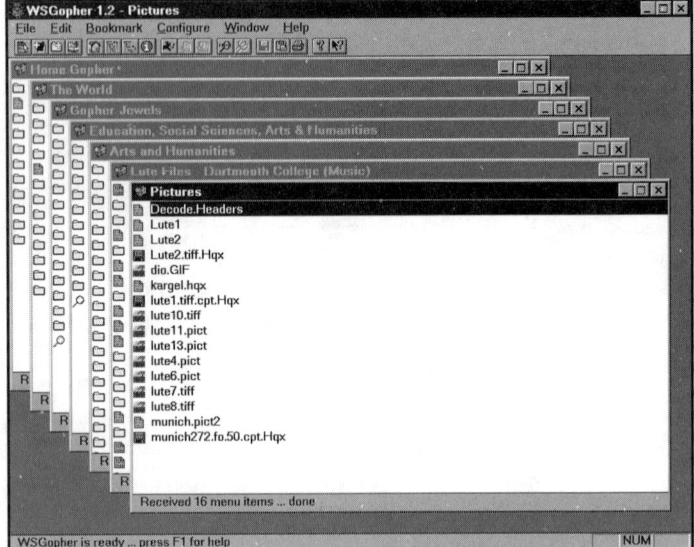

Figure 8.4.
The Picture directory from Dartmouth College's Lute file collection.

9. In the Local Directories dialog box from the Configure menu, tell Winsock Gopher the directory to which you want to download files. If you don't do this, the file will be saved, by default, into Winsock Gopher's own directory (which is fine for many users).
10. Double-click on the item named `lute11.tiff` (the icon to its left tells you that it's a graphics file). You'll see the progress window shown in Figure 8.5.

When the transfer is complete, the file is on your hard drive. Note that you can configure Winsock Gopher to launch a "viewer" (such as a graphics program) as soon as the download is complete, or to simply save the file to your hard drive.

In addition to its ease of use, Winsock Gopher offers an extensive, superb bookmarking system. You can create as many bookmark categories as you want, and the program ships with a great many already in place. This feature is worth exploring in detail as you continue your gophering activities.

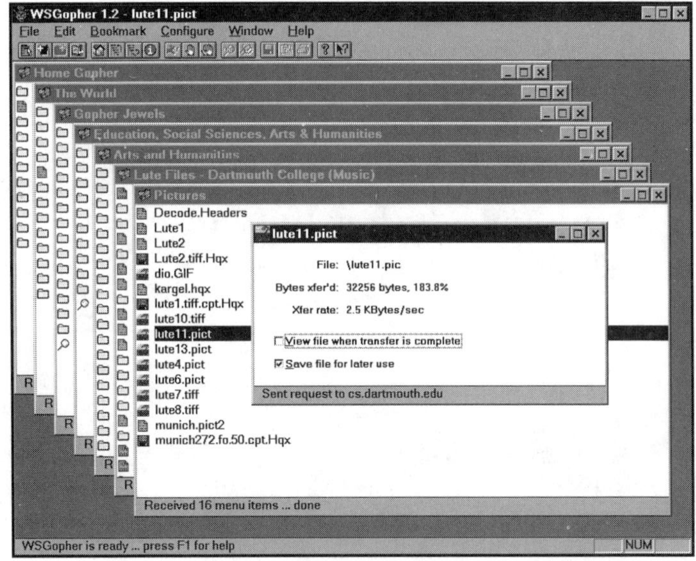

Figure 8.5.
The download progress dialog box in Winsock Gopher.

Exceptional Gophers from Around the World

There are Gophers and then there are Gophers. Some offer only one or two menu items, and usually a link to other larger Gophers. Others, however, are complete in themselves, with hordes of subdirectories, files, and all sorts of well-designed links. This section looks at some of the best and most established Gophers, to get a sense of what's available on a Gopher tour of the world.

Excursion 8.1: Gopher Jewels (*cwis.usc.edu*).

You've already encountered Gopher Jewels. However, it's such an extensive resource that we'll take another quick look at it now.

Gopher Jewels, as its name suggests, is a fully-organized listing of many of the best Gophers on the Internet. It is under development primarily by David Riggins at the Texas Department of Commerce in Austin, Texas, who also maintains a mailing list to let you know regularly about new Gopher offerings.

To subscribe to the Gopher Jewels mailing list, send an e-mail message to **`LISTPROC@EINET.NET`** (leave the subject line blank) and, in the message area, type **`SUBSCRIBE GOPHERJEWELS`** *`FIRSTNAME LASTNAME`* (remember *not* to include your signature file). Shortly after, you'll start to see Riggins' name appear in your mailer almost daily, each time with another worthwhile Gopher site to visit.

Every so often, you'll also receive a message summarizing what's new on Gopher Jewels, what's to come, and how the Gophers are currently arranged.

Gopher Jewels is available from a large number of Gophers. Enjoy it—it's exceptional.

Excursion 8.2: The University of Minnesota Gopher (*gopher.tc.umn.edu*).

Like Gopher Jewels, this site also is accessible from any number of Gophers worldwide. Because it is the original home of the Gopher, why not take a look? You can find it at `gopher.tc.umn.edu`.

```
1.  Information About Gopher
2.  Computer Information
3.  Discussion Groups
4.  Fun & Games
5.  Internet file server (ftp) sites
6.  Libraries
7.  News
8.  Other Gopher and Information Servers
9.  Phone Books
10. Search Gopher Titles at the University of Minnesota
11. Search lots of places at the University of Minnesota
12. University of Minnesota Campus Information
```

There's nothing really sensationally noteworthy here, until you select `Other Gopher and Information Servers`. This yields the following menu, which practically has become a commonplace link on Gophers around the world:

```
-->  1.  All the Gopher Servers in the World/
     2.  Search All the Gopher Servers in the World <?>
     3.  Search titles in Gopherspace using veronica/
     4.  Africa/
     5.  Asia/
     6.  Europe/
     7.  International Organizations/
     8.  Middle East/
     9.  North America/
     10. Pacific/
     11. Russia/
     12. South America/
     13. Terminal Based Information/
     14. WAIS Based Information/
     15. Gopher Server Registration <??>
```

From here, you can link to a huge variety of Gophers in just about any nation you can think of. The only thing missing from this list is the extremely useful item called `New Gophers`, from `liberty.uc.wlu.edu`, in the path `Finding Gopher Resources`, `All Gopher Sites`, and then `New Gophers`. This isn't being updated nearly as often as it once was, however. Why not? Check item `#2` in Example 8.3 (immediately following), to discover that many Gophers have transferred their information onto the World Wide Web instead.

Excursion 8.3: The Rice University Gopher (*riceinfo.rice.edu*).

For an example of an extremely well-developed campus Gopher, try RiceInfo (`riceinfo.rice.edu`). Here you'll find directories pointing to Rice itself, to Houston, and to a range of other Gophers.

```
-->  1.  About RiceInfo
     2.  BETTER VERSION OF RICEINFO FOR WWW USERS <HTML>
     3.  More About RiceInfo and Gopher/
     4.  Calendars and Campus Events/
     5.  Campus Life at Rice/
     6.  Computer Information/
     7.  Health and Safety at Rice/
     8.  Houston Information/
     9.  Information by Subject Area/
     10. Library Services/
     11. Other Gopher and Information Servers/
     12. Research Interests and Opportunities/
     13. Rice Campus Directory/
     14. Rice Course Schedules, Admissions and Continuing Studies/
     15. Rice University and Departmental Policies/
     16. Search all of RiceInfo gopher by title/
     17. Weather/
```

Surf through this Gopher and you'll find a huge number of resources organized similarly to Gopher Jewels. Under `Information by Subject Area`, you're also presented with a range of search tools, as shown by the following partial menu:

```
1.  About the RiceInfo collection of "Information by Subject Area"
2.   More about "Information by Subject Area"
3.   Clearinghouse of Subject-Oriented Internet Resource Guides (UMich)
4.   Search all of Gopherspace by title: Jughead (from WLU)
5.   Search all of Gopherspace by title: Veronica
6.   Search all of RiceInfo by title: Jughead
7.  Aerospace
8.  Agriculture and Forestry
9.  Anthropology and Culture
10. Architecture
```

Excursion 8.4: The Electronic Frontier Foundation Gopher (*gopher.eff.org*).

The Electronic Frontier Foundation specializes in issues dealing with freedom in cyberspace. As the following list shows, many of the directories on the main Gopher menu here demonstrate this commitment:

```
-->  1.  About the Electronic Frontier Foundation's Gopher Service
     2.  About the Electronic Frontier Foundation
     3.  ALERTS! - Action alerts on important and impending issues/
     4.  Electronic Frontier Foundation files & information/
     5.  Links to EFF WWW Resources <HTML>
     6.  Computers & Academic Freedom archives & info/
     7.  Other Similar Organizations and Groups/
     8.  Net Info (EFF's Guide to the Internet, FAQs, etc.)/
     9.  Publications (CuD, Bruce Sterling, Mike Godwin, etc.)/
     10. Search all of Gopherspace using Veronica - 4800+ servers/
     11. 00-INDEX.pub
     12. Frequently Asked Questions & Answers about EFF's FTP Site
     13. Other Gopher and Information Servers around the World/
     14. README.WWW
     15. Recent Changes to EFF Online Resources
```

Note, for example, the `Publications` item, which offers directories for several well-known organizations and people all concerned with similar issues. Part of the menu is as follows:

```
-->  13. Bruce_Sterling/
     14. CuD/
     15. Dan_Brown/
     16. David_Farber/
     17. David_Johnson/
     18. David_Post/ 16. EFF_newsletters
     19. E-journals/
     20. EFF_Frontier_Files/
     21. EFF_Net_Guide/
     22. EFF_misc_authors/
     23. EFF_newsletters/
     24. EFF_papers/
     25. Esther_Dyson/
     26. FAQ_RFC_FYI_IEN/
     27. Jerry_Berman/
     28. John_Gilmore/
     29. John_Perry_Barlow/
     30. Mike_Godwin/
     31. Misc/
     32. Mitch_Kapor/
     33. Net_guidebooks/
     34. README
     35. Shari_Steele/
     36. William_Gibson/
```

Excursion 8.5: The Nova Scotia Technology Network Gopher (*gopher.nstn.ca*).

Another strong site is the Nova Scotia Technology Network Gopher, located at `gopher.nstn.ca`. The main menu demonstrates some of the directories being developed here.

```
       1.  ----------- NSTN's CyberMall Gopher Server ---------------
       2.  About This Site/
       3.  NSTN CyberMall -  Internet Storefronts/
       4.  NSTN CYBRARY - The Internet Public Library/
-->    5.  NSTN CyberMall - Information Kiosks/
       6.  NSTN Service Centre/
       7.  ----------------------------------------------------------..
       8.  New to the Internet?  Start Here!/
```

The CyberMall and Cybrary are of interest, but so is the New to the Internet area, which yields the following menu:

```
-->    1.  ----------- NSTN CYBRARY - The Internet Public Library -----------..
       2.  Beginner's Corner (Internet Guides)/
       3.  Library Catalogues Worldwide/
       4.  Internet Information by SUBJECT/
       5.  Internet READING Room (News, Magazines, Books)/
       6.  Internet SEARCH Facilities/
       7.  Canadian Government Information/
       8.  United States Government Information/
       9.
       10. -------------------- Space for Rent! ----------------------------..
       11. This space is being made available for commercial advertising.
       12. For information on obtaining this space, email sales@nstn.ca.
```

Excursion 8.6: The U.K. Office for Library and Information Networking Gopher (*ukoln.bath.ac.uk*).

Directly across the Atlantic from Nova Scotia (well, more or less) is the Jolly Old U.K., and a very strong Gopher site at UKOLN (`ukoln.bath.ac.uk`). The main menu is short, but it leads to a range of very useful sites.

```
-->    1.  Information about this Service
       2.  Announcements/
       3.  Document Store/
```

```
        4.  UK Gopher Servers/
        5.  UK Library Gopher Servers/
        6.  BUBL Information Service/
        7.  The BUBL Subject Tree Project and The CATRIONA Project/
        8.  UK Directory Services/
        9.  Hytelnet/
        10. Other Gopher Servers/
        11. Hytenet (version 6.7)/
```

Among the best here are the BUBL Information Service and UK Gopher Servers items, the latter of which yields a huge menu looking, in part, like this:

```
-->  1.  About this list of gopher servers
     2.  ALMAC BBS, (UK)/
     3.  Action for Blind People, (UK)/
     4.  Aston University, (UK)/
     5.  BUBL Information Service, (UK)/
     6.  Bristol Maths and Stats Gopher Service, (UK)/
     7.  British Library Network Services - Portico/
     8.  British Library of Political & Economic Science (BLPES), (UK)/
     9.  Brunel University, (UK)/
     10. CSAC Ethnographics Gallery, (UK)/
     11. Cambridge University Press, (UK)/
     12. Colloid Group, Department of Chemistry, University of Surrey, (UK)/
     13. Communications Research Group, Nottingham University, (UK)/
     14. Cranfield Institute of Technology, (UK)/
     15. Daresbury Laboratory, (UK)/
     16. De Montfort University Gopher Server, (UK)/
     17. Decanter Magazine, (UK)/
     18. Dundee University Library, (UK)/
```

This is the first 18 of over 100 items, and each is a directory to another Gopher. If you want to know what's happening on the Internet in the U.K., there's no better place to start.

Excursion 8.7: The Australian National University Gopher (*info.anu.edu.au*).

Because you entered the U.K. from one former British colony, Canada, it's only natural that you exit by heading to another former colony. At the Australian National University, you find a very carefully developed Gopher, with a main menu that looks like the following:

```
-->  1.  About ELISA (Electronic Library Information Service at ANU)
     2.  What's New on ELISA/
     3.  ------------------- LIBRARY SERVICES -------------------
     4.  ANU Library Services/
```

```
5.  Other ACT Library Services & Catalogues/
6.  Australian Library Catalogues/
7.  Worldwide Library Catalogues/
8.  ----------- NETWORKED INFORMATION SERVICES --------------
9.  The Electronic Library - Internet Resources by Subject/
10. ANU Networked Information Servers/
11. Australian Networked Information Servers/
12. Worldwide Networked Information Servers/
13. ----------------- INDEXES & DIRECTORIES -----------------
14. Phone and Email Directories/
15. Internet Information/
16. Search Gopherspace: Jughead & Veronica/
```

From the `Worldwide Networked Information Servers` item, you get the following menu, showing the (quite natural) Asian focus of ANU's efforts:

```
-->  1.  Search for Gophers by Name or Internet Address <?>
     2.  All the Gophers in the World via ANU/
     3.  Australia/
     4.  Gopher Jewels /
     5.  Gophers of Scholarly Societies/
     6.  Hong Kong/
     7.  India/
     8.  Japan/
     9.  Korea/
     10. Library Gophers/
     11. Malaysia/
     12. New Zealand/
     13. Services in the Pacific Region/
     14. Singapore/
     15. Taiwan/
     16. Thailand/
     17. WAIS Based Information/
     18. links to all New Gophers in the World [by name] (WLU,USA)/
```

One link along, Japan, will show how much information is to be gained by exploring these sites. Here is the Japanese portion of the ANU Gopher, with, of course, additional links to other sources:

```
-->  1.  DNA Data Bank of Japan, Natl. Inst. of Genetics, Mishima/
     2.  Dept. of Applied Molecular Sci., IMS, ONRI, [Okazaki, Aichi]/
     3.  JPNIC (Japan Network Information Center), Tokyo, Japan/
     4.  Japan Organized InterNetwork (JOIN)/
     5.  Keio University, Science and Technology campus gopher (Japan)/
     6.  Matsushita Electric Group, Japan (gopher.mei.co.jp)/
     7.  National Cancer Center, Tokyo JAPAN/
     8.  National Institute for Physiological Sciences [Okazaki, Aichi]/
```

```
9.  Reitaku-University(Computer System Center) Chiba, JAPAN/
10. Saitama University/
11. TRON Project Information, Univ. of Tokyo, Japan/
12. University of Electro-Communications(UEC)/
13. World Data Center on Microorganisms (WDC), RIKEN, Japan/
```

It's pretty clear by now that the amount of information to be obtained through Gopher surfing alone is enormous. Go to any of these Gophers and start choosing menu items. I guarantee you'll never exhaust the possibilities.

Warning: Gopher servers are still important sites for information, but increasingly, the efforts of the information providers are being turned to the World Wide Web. As you move through the world's Gopher sites, check to see that the information you receive is up to date before using it for anything important. And read what the Gopher sites themselves have to say about migrating to the Web.

Summary

Gopher is the easiest and the most accessible Internet browsing tool available. Furthermore, hundreds of sites have constructed hundreds of Gophers filled with thousands of documents all available for retrieval, so Gopher isn't just easy, it's also both highly useful and extremely exciting. Its only downside is that it's both overwhelming and addictive. If you can resist the urge to just surf, and actually sit back and explore one or two sites completely, you'll have a much better start at taming information overload. And that, in a nutshell, is what Gopher is trying to do. The fact that Gopherspace is being largely superseded by Webspace is no reason to avoid this immense source of information and resources.

Task Review

In this chapter, you learned how to do the following:

- ☐ Enter and explore a sample Gopher site
- ☐ Download, save, and mail files from Gophers
- ☐ Bookmark your favorite Gopher sites
- ☐ Explore the benefits of graphical Gopher programs
- ☐ Explore a number of specific sites in the U.S. and beyond
- ☐ Enter the huge world of Gopher

Q&A

Q How are Gophers constructed?

A Essentially, here's what happens. First, the host computer must run the appropriate Gopher software, available from the University of Minnesota (you can find this information at Minnesota's Boombox Gopher, at `boombox.micro.umn.edu`). Basically (and oversimplified), Gopher is told to look for a specific directory on the local network. When that directory is linked to Gopher, Gopher then displays its contents as a menu. Depending on the Gopher software you're running, it will be a numbered list or will display icons next to the entries. Directories appear differently than do files, and so on. As a Gopher maintainer, your job is to set up the directories, subdirectories, and files within those directories so that they're in the order you want and so that they will display the names you want them to display. And, of course, you can specify links to other Gophers as well. It's not difficult, but if you want to build a useful Gopher, the process can be time-consuming.

Q If Gopher is so powerful, why bother with anything else?

A Gopher is extremely powerful, but it's not the be-all and end-all of Internet access. For one thing, a Gopher menu is just that, a menu. Menus aren't always nearly as well designed as they might be, and they often obscure their own contents. That's how the World Wide Web can help, at least in part. Another point is that, while Gopher does telnet and FTP commands (and others), if you already know how to do these tasks, there's no reason to dig through Gopher menus to accomplish them. In fact, advances in individual pieces of software aren't necessarily reflected in Gopher automatically. Still, the advantages of Gopher are so strong that, to many users, these are minor concerns. For a number of people I know, in fact, Gopher and e-mail used to represent everything they needed on the Internet. Many are turning to the Web, but others remain convinced that Gopher is a viable resource.

Q Does Gopher offer *any* advantages over the Web?

A Yes. Gopherspace is organized hierarchically. Information is logically placed under headings and subheadings. Webspace is much less carefully organized, and although it's more easily browsed, its information is often harder to locate. The Gopher team at the University of Minnesota is working with the Mosaic team at the University of Illinois to develop Gopher as a three-dimensional, hierarchical information storage area (GopherVR is already available for the Power Macintosh), and in this way, they hope to merge Gopher's organizational strengths with the Web's presentational excellence.

DAY 3

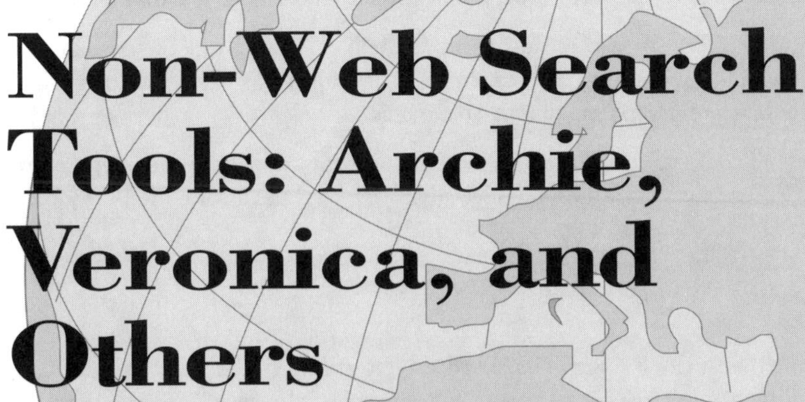

Non-Web Search Tools: Archie, Veronica, and Others

In the first two days of your Internet exploration, you learned all about communicating with others and browsing the Net for information. But a major problem remains: how do you efficiently find Internet users in order to communicate with them, and how can you locate files without simply firing up your Gopher or Web browser and surfing until you get lucky? This chapter offers some solutions to this problem by introducing you to Finger, Whois, and the various search tools through Gopher. These tools are used much less these days than the World Wide Web search engines (covered in Chapter 12), but they're still important for a complete Internet knowledge, and especially important if you don't have easy Web access.

Task List

In this chapter, you'll perform the following tasks:

- ☐ Use Netfind, Whois, and Finger to locate people on the Internet
- ☐ Use Archie to locate documents on FTP sites
- ☐ Use Veronica to search for items in Gopher menus

Finding People: Netfind, Whois, and Finger

Just about all Internet users, early in their Internet life, want to find out if friends, relatives, or former acquaintances or colleagues are on the Net as well. Filled with hope and even excitement, they turn to the Net for help. The result, almost always, is disappointment.

Simply put, there *is* no easy way to find a user on the Net. There isn't even a reliable way to do so. The old joke about the Internet remains true to this day: if you want to find out someone's e-mail address, phone that person and ask.

If phoning isn't an option, a few tools exist to help, at least a little. Sometimes, you might even get lucky. But don't count on it, especially if you need the information for something important.

Netfind

Netfind is the closest you'll come to reliable discovery of Internet addresses, but it's far from perfect, and unlikely to do what you want. It's worth a try, however, and you learn how to do it in Task 9.1.

Task 9.1: Search for a name using Netfind.

1. Telnet to **`ds.internic.net`** (refer to Chapter 2 for telnet instructions).
2. At the login: prompt, type **`netfind`**. You'll get the following prompt information:

```
*****************************************************************************

               Welcome to the InterNIC Directory and Database Server.

*****************************************************************************


Top level choices:
        1. Help
        2. Search
        3. Seed database lookup
        4. Options
        5. Quit (exit server)
-->
```

3. Type **`2`** (Return) to begin your search.
4. Type a name, followed by a set of keywords. The name can be a first name, last name, or user name (you can try only one name per search). The keywords should try to specify the user's location, as precisely as possible. For example, try the following search:

   `randall waterloo canada university`

You'll receive a series of possible domain names in a numbered list. Choose a number to start your search, and see what happens. If you're lucky, you'll find me.

That's the essence of Netfind. It's useful to a degree, but phoning is still easier (and maybe cheaper, depending on how much you're paying for your Internet service). It can be fun seeing who's out there, though.

Whois

Whois seems somewhat more reliable than Netfind at locating users; only by a bit, however. The advantage is that Whois is extremely easy to use, and very fast as well.

Task 9.2: Search for a name using Whois.

1. Telnet to **`rs.internic.net`**.
2. At the `login:` prompt, type **`whois`**.
3. At the `INTERNIC>` prompt, type the last name of the person you're trying to find. For example, type **`randall`**. The result will be a list of people with the name Randall. For whatever reason, I won't be one of them.

4. You also can find organizations this way. Try typing **inforamp** at the prompt, for example, and you'll get extensive details about a specific Internet service provider. Or try IBM, for an entire listing of servers.

If you want to know more about Whois, type **help whois** at the prompt. This will tell you how to use Whois more extensively.

Finger

Finger is an old Internet utility, and it remains a useful one. It has two functions. First, it tells you about specific users. Second, it tells you who is currently logged on to a given host. Not all organizations allow Finger transactions, so don't be surprised if you receive no information.

Task 9.3: Use Finger to get information about a user.

1. Log in to your UNIX shell account (there are several Finger clients available for Windows and Macintosh, as well).
2. At the command prompt, type **finger** *username@domain.name*. For example, try **finger nrandall@watarts.uwaterloo.ca**. The result will be something like the following:

```
[watarts.uwaterloo.ca]
Login name: nrandall                      In real life: Neil Randall
Office:     CY 285, 4759                  Home phone:
Directory:  /u/nrandall                   Shell: /bin/csh
On since:   Jun  4 00:53:11 on ttype from cnts4p08.uwaterloo.ca
New Mail:   Sun Jun  4 00:56:33 1995     Last read:  Sun Jun  4 00:52:05
1995
```

   Notice the information here. Finger tells you that I'm currently on system (`On since:`), and when I last read my e-mail. Finger is an excellent way of gauging a user's activity, and of discovering whether an intended recipient has read the mail you sent them.
3. Now try typing **finger**. If the command works on your system, you'll be informed of which users are currently online.

Finger is limited, but at times it's extremely useful. Sometimes it's out of date, however, especially the non-Internet information given. That information is entirely dependent on whether the user has updated the details lately, and most people never get around to it. The Internet has no way of tracking people down in real life.

Finding Information: The Growing Arsenal of Search Tools

As the amount of information on the Internet grows to staggering proportions, it becomes more difficult to find exactly what you want. Sure, surfing is enjoyable, but if you have a task to perform, the last thing you need is three or four hours of moving from Web site to Gopher site to FTP site and back again, looking for that special graphics or sound file or piece of crucial data.

Fortunately, Internet users have long recognized the need for assistance in tracking down material. Some of the more helpful of these users have written search programs to offer that assistance. Here, you'll look at a few of them in detail, and pointers will lead you to others with which you can experiment.

Archie

Archie was the first of the important Internet search tools. It was designed to produce and maintain a database of directories and files found in FTP sites across the Internet. Archie sites hold copies of the database, and you enter these sites to search it.

Note: When you do an Archie search, it's important to realize that you're not actually scanning the Internet or files. Instead, you're searching through the Archie database at the Archie site. This database is updated frequently, but—with the exception of the moment of updating—it is never completely current. If you enter a specific FTP site frequently, it's quite possible that you'll be more up-to-date for that particular site than the Archie database will be. Archie's value is that it keeps tabs on a whole host of FTP sites.

Warning: Several locations hold the Archie database. One of the best-known is Rutgers University. Because Archie is so commonly accessed, however, this site frequently gets jammed with users. As soon as you can, find an Archie site near you (your own host might be such a site) and use it instead. In the first example, following, I was able to connect to the Rutgers site, but my searches kept timing out.

Table 6.3 is a partial list of Archie sites, as retrieved by typing `servers` while engaged in an Archie search (you can get the same list by typing **`archie -L`** at the command prompt). Note the country address; it's important to choose the site nearest you.

Table 6.3. Archie sites.

Host Name	IP Address	Country
archie.au	139.130.4.6	Australia
archie.edvz.uni-linz.ac.at	140.78.3.8	Austria
archie.univie.ac.at	131.130.1.23	Austria
archie.uqam.ca	132.208.250.10	Canada
archie.funet.fi	128.214.6.100	Finland
archie.th-darmstadt.de	130.83.22.60	Germany
archie.ac.il	132.65.6.15	Israel
archie.unipi.it	131.114.21.10	Italy
archie.wide.ad.jp	133.4.3.6	Japan
archie.kr	128.134.1.1	Korea
archie.sogang.ac.kr	163.239.1.11	Korea
archie.rediris.es	130.206.1.2	Spain
archie.luth.se	130.240.18.4	Sweden
archie.switch.ch	130.59.1.40	Switzerland
archie.ncu.edu.tw	140.115.19.24	Taiwan
archie.doc.ic.ac.uk	146.169.11.3	United Kingdom
archie.unl.edu	129.93.1.14	USA (NE)
archie.internic.net	198.48.45.10	USA (NJ)
archie.rutgers.edu	128.6.18.15	USA (NJ)
archie.ans.net	147.225.1.10	USA (NY)
archie.sura.net	128.167.254.179	USA (MD)

Task 9.4: Find files about NAFTA using Archie.

The first step in an Archie search is to telnet to the Archie host. You may use any of those listed previously, but the example here will show the fairly popular `sura.net` site, logging in by using the username `archie`.

1. Telnet to the Archie host.

```
% telnet archie.sura.net
Trying 128.167.254.195...
Connected to yog-sothoth.sura.net.
Escape character is '^]'.

SunOS UNIX (yog-sothoth.sura.net)
```

2. Type **archie** at the `login:` prompt.

```
login: archie
Last login: Mon Jun  5 12:03:06 from raiz.uncu.edu.ar
SunOS Release 4.1.3 (NYARLATHOTEP) #3: Thu Apr 22 15:26:21 EDT 1993

                                Welcome to Archie!
                                  Version 3.2.2

SURAnet is pleased to announce the release of archie with a new version of
archie software.

If you need help with the interactive client type 'help' at the 'archie>'
prompt. If you have any questions, please read help >>FIRST<<, then if
your question was not answered send e-mail to 'archie-admin@sura.net'

archie-admin.

# Bunyip Information Systems, 1993, 1994

# Terminal type set to 'vt100 24 80'.
# 'erase' character is '^?'.
# 'search' (type string) has the value 'sub'.
archie>
```

3. Set the search type.

   On the last line of the response, the search type is listed as `sub`. This means that the search string you type will try to find filenames that contain that string, and that upper- or lowercase doesn't matter. Other search types include `exact`, where the search string must match the filename exactly, and `subcase`, which is the same as `sub` except that it will match case as well. You can use the `set search` command from the `archie>` prompt to set the type to your liking. For now, leave the search type as **sub**.

4. Ask the system for help.

   Before performing the actual search, why not ask for help to learn Archie better? As with Kermit, typing `help` actually led me to the real help, the question mark.

```
archie> help
These are the commands you can use in help:
               .    go up one level in the hierarchy
               ?    display a list of valid subtopics at the current level
done, ^D, ^C        quit from help entirely
        <string>    help on a topic or subtopic
Eg.
        "help show"
will give you the help screen for the "show" command

        "help set search"
Will give you the help information for the "search" variable.

The command "manpage" will give you a complete copy of the archie manual
page.
```

9

5. Type **?** at the help> prompt to get a list of possible commands.

```
help> ?

# Subtopics:
#
#   about                help              regex
#   bugs                 list              servers
#   bye                  mail              set
#   compress             manpage           show
#   domains              motd              site
#   done                 nopager           stty
#   email                pager             term
#   exit                 path              unset
#   find                 prog              version
#   general              quit              whatis
#
help>
```

While inside an Archie search, you can obtain help for navigating through the program by typing **h**. The result:

```
                    SUMMARY OF HELP COMMANDS FOR ARCHIE

     Commands marked with * may be preceded by a number, N.
     Notes in parentheses indicate the behavior if N is given.

  h  H                 Display this help.
  q  :q  :Q  ZZ        Exit.

  e  ^E  j  ^N  CR  *  Forward  one line (or N lines).
  y  ^Y  k  ^K  ^P  *  Backward one line (or N lines).
  f  ^F  ^V  SPACE  *  Forward  one window (or N lines).
  b  ^B  ESC-v      *  Backward one window (or N lines).
  z                 *  Forward  one window (and set window to N).
  w                 *  Backward one window (and set window to N).
  d  ^D             *  Forward  one half-window (and set half-window to N).
  u  ^U             *  Backward one half-window (and set half-window to N).
  F                    Forward forever; like "tail -f".
  r  ^R  ^L            Repaint screen.
  R                    Repaint screen, discarding buffered input.
  /pattern          *  Search forward for (N-th) matching line.
  ?pattern          *  Search backward for (N-th) matching line.

  NOTE: search commands may be modified by one or more of:
        !  search for NON-matching lines.
        *  search multiple files.
        @  start search at first file (for /) or last file (for ?).

  n                 *  Repeat previous search (for N-th occurrence).
  N                 *  Repeat previous search in reverse direction.
  ESC-n             *  Repeat previous search, spanning files.
  ESC-N             *  Repeat previous search, reverse dir. & spanning
                       files.

  g  <  ESC-<       *  Go to first line in file (or line N).
  G  >  ESC->       *  Go to last line in file (or line N).
  p  %              *  Go to beginning of file (or N percent into file).
```

```
    {                  *  Go to the } matching the (N-th) { in the top line.
    }                  *  Go to the { matching the (N-th) } in the bottom
                          line.
    (                  *  Go to the ) matching the (N-th) ( in the top line.
    )                  *  Go to the ( matching the (N-th) ) in the bottom
                          line.
    [                  *  Go to the ] matching the (N-th) [ in the top line.
    ]                  *  Go to the [ matching the (N-th) ] in the bottom
                          line.
HELP -- Press RETURN for more, or q when done
```

Pressing the spacebar moves you to the next help screen (there are plenty more commands). Pressing **q** gets you out of this help screen, but take note of the commands before you do so, especially the forwards and backwards commands.

6. Get help on the `find` command by typing **`find`** at the prompt.

```
help> find

The 'find' command (also known as the 'prog' command)
 allows you to search the database for a specified pattern.

 The usage is:

    find <expression>

 where the interpretation of <expression> depends on the
 current value of the 'search' variable. Searches may be
 performed in a number of different ways. See the help
 section on the 'search' variable for a full explanation.

 The output of find can be sorted in different ways,
 depending on the value of the 'sortby' variable. See help
 for the 'sortby' variable for a full explanation.

 The output format of the results can be changed through
 use of the "output_format" variable.

 The search criteria can be further specified to be restricted
 on domain names and pathname components. See the "domains"
 command and the "match_domain" and "match_path" variables.

help>
```

7. Type **`done`** to exit help. Try **`quit`** or **`bye`** if you don't believe this, but you'll find they're restricted to exiting from Archie itself. Weird.

8. Now for a search. At the Archie prompt, type **`find nafta`**.

```
archie> find nafta
# Search type: sub.
# Your queue position: 84
# Estimated time for completion: 4 minutes, 3 seconds.
working... 0
```

Notice the estimated time. the `0` in the `working` line alternates with a `=` to let you know your request is still being processed.

Very soon, you'll have a staggering amount of information. The following is only a small portion, but enough to give you an idea of what you're likely to find if you do a fairly general search on a well-studied topic:

```
Host nic.funet.fi    (128.214.248.6)
Last updated 05:21 12 Apr 1995

    Location: /pub/doc/literary/gutenberg/etext93
      FILE    -rw-r--r--  176233 bytes  22:00  7 Nov 1993  naftarif.txt.gz
      FILE    -rw-r--r--  140747 bytes  22:00  7 Nov 1993  naftannx.txt.gz


Host ftp.gmd.de    (129.26.8.84)
Last updated 06:13 17 Apr 1995

    Location: /documents/etext/etext93
      FILE    -r--r--r--  140747 bytes  18:00 23 Sep 1993  naftannx.txt.gz
      FILE    -r--r--r--  176233 bytes  18:00 23 Sep 1993  naftarif.txt.gz


Host cocoa.contrib.de    (192.109.39.10)
Last updated 01:52 11 Apr 1995

    Location: /t4/pub/text/etext/Gutenberg/etext93
      FILE    -rw-rw-r--  176233 bytes  18:00 22 Sep 1993  naftarif.txt.gz
      FILE    -rw-rw-r--  140747 bytes  18:00 22 Sep 1993  naftannx.txt.
```

Notice the `Host` line. This tells you where you can find each file. In this case, two of the files are on German computers (`de`), while the third is in Finland (`fi`). The `Locations` line tells you the path to follow when retrieving the file via FTP (refer to Chapter 7).

And that's what Archie does. It tells you exactly where to find the files you need. Once you have this information, you can use FTP to transfer them to your own account. Archie is far more powerful and configurable than noted here, but the simple substring search is the one you'll do most often. Good luck.

Tip: To get the full value from your Archie results, set your communications program to "capture" the text as it appears, either to your printer or to a file. Then, when you turn to FTP to retrieve some of these files, you'll have the host sites, directories, and filenames right in front of you.

Task 9.5: Conduct an Archie search on the Web.

Like most things these days, Archie has moved to the World Wide Web. Conducting a search through the Web looks much nicer, but in addition it gives you better control over the results. To conduct an Archie search on the Web, follow these steps:

1. Launch your Web browser and go to the URL **http://pubweb.nexor.co.uk/public/archie/servers.html** (refer to Chapter 10 for entering URL addresses).
2. Select the Archie server located closest to you.
3. Enter the search string in the search box, such as winword.
4. Choose your search type, means of sorting the results, and which Archie server you want to search. Leave the impact choice on `nice`, unless you know why you want something different (it has to do with how many Internet resources you want to consume), and restrict the search as you want. Finally, click on the Submit button.
5. Read the result of your search.
6. Now, here's where Web-based Archie shines. Because the Web handles FTP, there's no need to launch an FTP program to retrieve your file. Simply click on the file you want, and tell your Web browser to save it to your hard disk.

Veronica

If you want to conduct a search through your Gopher program, the most likely candidate is *Veronica.* Veronica was designed from the beginning as a Gopher-based search tool, and that remains its strength today.

Task 9.6: Conduct a search through Veronica.

Conducting a Veronica search means entering a Gopher site with a Veronica menu item, selecting that item, and entering the search string in the resulting box.

1. Gopher to **uic.edu**, the same Gopher site you visited in Chapter 8.
2. Select item `#3, Search the UIC Campus and Beyond`. You'll see the following menu:

```
        1.  Search UIC/ADN Gopher Item Titles <?>
        2.  UIC Campus Unit Listings/
        3.  UIC Faculty, Staff, Student, Department Directory <CSO>
        4.  Computer Center INFORM Document Library/
    --> 5.  Veronica: Netwide Gopher Menu Search/
        6.  Internet file server (ftp) sites (from Urbana)/
        7.  Directory of WAIS (Wide Area Information Server) Databases/
        8.  Search Many Internet Databases/
```

3. Choose item `#5, Veronica: Netwide Gopher Menu Search`. The following menu will appear:

```
    --> 1.  How to Compose Veronica Queries
        2.  Search Gopher Directory Titles at NYSERNet             .. <?>
```

```
     3.  Search Gopherspace at NYSERNet                                      .. <?>
     4.  Veronica at University of Nevada at Reno/
```

4. Select item #2, `Search Gopher Directory Titles at NYSERNet`. The following search box will appear:

```
+-Search Gopher Directory Titles at NYSERNet                                   -+
¦                                                                               ¦
¦ Words to search for                                                           ¦
¦                                                                               ¦
¦ Beatles                                                                       ¦
¦                                                                               ¦
¦ [Help: ^-]  [Cancel: ^G]                                                      ¦
+-------------------------------------------------------------------------------+
```

5. Enter the word **`Beatles`** in the search box. Obviously, you can enter whatever word you want, but why not make it interesting?
6. The result of your search will appear as a Gopher menu, such as the syntax that follows:

```
Search Gopher Directory Titles at NYSERNet                                  : ...

 --> 1.  beatles          (bobcat.bbn.com)/
     2.  rec.music.beatles/
     3.  Beatles/
     4.  beatles/
     5.  _beatles Folder/
     6.  beatles          (A:Postings about the Fab Four & their music.)/
     7.  Beatles/
     8.  Beatles/
     9.  beatles/
     10. beatles/
     11. beatles/
     12. beatles/
     13. beatles/
     14. beatles/
     15. Beatles/
     16. The Beatles (Wiener)/
     17. The Beatles: A Bio-Bibliography (McKeen) 1989/
     18. The Beatles: A Bio-Bibliography (McKeen) 1989/

Press ? for Help, q to Quit, u to go up a menu                          Page: 1/2
```

7. Select the item you want (or press the spacebar to move to the next page). You also can save this result as a bookmark.

Note: You can conduct Veronica searches on the World Wide Web because the Web is compatible with Gopher. Fire up your browser, type **`gopher://uic.edu`** in the URL box, and follow the items into Veronica. You'll see a Web-based search box, and the results will be the same.

Summary

Finding information on the Internet remains a challenging task, despite the proliferation of search tools now at your disposal. To get started, however, the tools covered in this chapter will help. You can locate information in Gopher sites by using Veronica, and you can find files on the Net's many FTP sites through an Archie search. To find people, Netfind, Whois, and Finger will give you a start, but none of them is perfect. The fact is that the Internet is still far from organized, and if you want to find information, you'll need any number of search tools to assist you, but you'll also need to do a great deal of plain old browsing. Good luck.

9

Task Review

In this chapter, you learned how to perform the following tasks:

- ☐ Use Netfind, Whois, and Finger to locate people on the Internet
- ☐ Use Archie to locate documents on FTP sites
- ☐ Use Veronica to search for items in Gopher menus

Q&A

Q I did an Archie search for some Internet tools for my Macintosh, and I found the same programs in many different sites. Should I just use the first one I find?

A No. Make sure to examine the dates, and select the most recent one. A program like Eudora, for example, is scattered all over the Net, which is good for accessibility, but bad for ensuring the latest upgrade. There are old versions of just about every program in largely forgotten directories, and the last thing you want to do is retrieve an old version. You might even wind up with an old alpha or beta version (that is, an incomplete test version). Be on guard against this.

Q I keep hearing (and seeing on my local Gopher server) references to Hytelnet, ERIC, CARL, and other tools that seem to be for searching. What are they?

A Excellent question. In the interest of space, this chapter covered only the most significant and best-known search programs, Archie and WAIS, but there are plenty of others. Hytelnet is essentially a feature-rich version of the standard telnet, enabling you to select from menus in a manner somewhat similar to Gopher. ERIC and CARL are especially interesting to educators (at every level); both are extensive databases offering a wide range of material. Veronica is a search program that many prefer to Archie, because instead of just giving you a list of documents, it also enables you to FTP them from that list.

While all these programs can be launched from the UNIX prompt, it's far easier to use them from within a Gopher. Practically every Gopher contains a menu line for Veronica searches, and if you find the line that reads something like `Other Information Sources` (I've seen few Gophers without such a line), you'll almost invariably see a menu item for ERIC, CARL, and Hytelnet. Usually these screens offer small how-to files as well, to help get you started.

Q Wait a minute! I just realized this. Is Veronica any relation to Archie?

A Actually, yes. One of computing's more enjoyable contributions to our culture is its variety of naming systems, and Internet tools are no different. Archie originally was a shortened version of Archive, which is what the program reflects. This name, of course, suggested the famous comic book character to another designer, who promptly selected the name Veronica, one of Archie Andrew's two girlfriends. Whether the idea that the character Veronica was richer and prettier than Archie had anything to do with the naming is impossible to say. To carry the comic book thing further, there is currently a Jughead search program available; if anyone ever does a Miss Grundy, I suggest it's time we quit and start over.

DAY

4

The World Wide Web

10

DAY 4

The Web, Mosaic, and Netscape

The *World Wide Web* (WWW) offers a hypermedia environment for accessing the Internet. It is the first Internet tool—or perhaps better termed a *toolkit*—that takes full advantage of the graphical user interface standards of XWindow, Microsoft Windows, and the Macintosh. Unlike other Net tools, it displays graphics, plays sound, and even runs movies, as long as you have the equipment to support it. Creators of WWW pages are taking advantage of the Web's multimedia nature to design fully interactive materials across a huge range of subjects.

Tip: To learn much, much more about the Web, pick up a copy of *The World Wide Web Unleashed.* Co-authored by myself, John December, and a collection of Web experts, this book is nearly 1,400 pages long and contains extensive write-ups of Web software, Web sites, and Web design issues. My accountant thanks you.

In this chapter, you'll perform the following tasks:

- ☐ Learn about the World Wide Web
- ☐ Use Mosaic to discover the benefits of multimedia
- ☐ Examine the Web design advantages available through Netscape

The Web and the Net: Made for Each Other?

At some point in about the middle of 1994, "Internet" became a household word. Suddenly it was everywhere—in newspapers and magazines, on television and radio, in the courts and in Congress, and in schools and businesses, as well. Everybody was on the Net, it seemed, and even if they weren't they were talking about it.

But it wasn't Gopher, or e-mail, or even good old, controversial Usenet that was causing all the excitement. What people were talking about, instead, was the World Wide Web. And not even the Web, in fact, but rather a program called *Mosaic.*

The World Wide Web offers a hypertext view of the Internet—not all of the Internet, but much of the material that the Internet contains. And what's a hypertext view? Basically, a *hypertext document* is one that contains built-in links to other documents; when you select one of these links, you're taken directly into the linked document. Navigating the Web is every bit as easy as navigating Gopher lists, but rather than going from directory to directory, you move straight from document to document.

There's more to the Web's popularity than hypertext, however. Unlike the rest of the Internet, the WWW is colorful, and because of that, it offers its own brand of excitement.

When you access a Web page—they're called pages, and often in fact they resemble book or magazine pages—you find colorful logos, artwork, photographs, and even backgrounds. While you browse Gopher for the sake of information, it's entirely possible to browse the Web merely for the excitement of visual appeal.

And the Web doesn't stop at graphics. On any number of Web pages, you'll find multimedia files that offer sound and even video. Click on a sound file, and you can hear what the site has to offer. Click on a video file, and you can watch things in motion. At this point, as on Mac and Windows computers themselves, sound is stronger than video, but the gap will close over the next few months.

So what's the downside? A couple, actually. First, accessing the Web's multimedia takes a relatively fast connection. The bare minimum is a 14.4 kbps modem, while a 28.8 kbps modem is quickly becoming indispensable. For reasonable video, 28.8 kbps simply won't cut it, as it won't for high-quality audio (although one product covered in this chapter helps a great deal).

The other downside is that the Web is becoming crowded, and it's often impossible to find the information you need. Chapter 12 features several search tools and subject lists for the Web, but even with these you can easily spend an hour or more (sometimes a couple of days) in a detailed search for information.

But the Web is versatile, and so far, reasonably democratic, and as a result, it has earned its immense popularity. Any tool that lets you access complex scientific research papers one minute, update your stock portfolio the next, and then track your Federal Express package and order a pizza after that, definitely deserves attention.

What Exactly Is the World Wide Web?

Unlike FTP and telnet, the Web is not a program. Unlike Archie and Veronica, it's not a search tool. Unlike Gopher, it's not a specific information browser. Instead, the Web refers both to the way in which we can access information and to the network of information itself. In other words, the Web is in the position of becoming almost synonymous with the Internet itself.

This makes some sense, after all. William Gibson and other cyberpunk authors have given us terms like the *matrix* to work with, and when we think of the matrix, we think of all the linked electronic information that's out there. The World Wide Web's name evokes the same kind of information morass. Somehow, incredible amounts of available data have linked one piece to another, in an almost web-like structure. It's a great name, mysterious and yet familiar, and probably the best name of all the Internet tools.

Actually, calling the WWW a tool isn't right, either, because the Web provides access to all the other major tools. Once on a Web page, you easily can Gopher or FTP, and in fact, most Web pages provide automatic links to a number of Gopher and FTP sites. You also can use the Web to telnet to other machines, and search tools such as Archie and WAIS are extremely Web-friendly as well. If you have access to a graphical version of the Web, you'll quickly find it at the center of your Internet activities. It's that intuitive and powerful.

Why the Web Is So Popular

A WWW page takes advantage of the fact that all our lives, we've been interacting with the printed page. A Web page looks like a page from a book or magazine; rather than lists, paragraphs and graphics often are dispersed throughout. Some pages are tasteful, others quite garish; some are clearly professional, others bear the stamp of the amateur.

The only difference—and it's a huge one—is that a Web page contains links to other Web pages, Gopher servers, FTP sites, and so on. When you're reading a book and you see an interesting reference to another book, your only option is to head to the library and hunt the book down, which means that most of the time, of course, you don't bother. On a Web page, referenced information areas are highlighted; the reference is underlined and usually a different color than the standard text. Move the mouse to the highlight until the cursor changes shape, and then click. Presto! You're taken to the referenced site.

Note: These links are hypertext, in fact the most powerful demonstration to date of the concept of hypertext. If you've ever used the help system of a GUI environment such as the Mac or Windows, using the Web will be instantly familiar. Those systems also use hypertext: from the Contents page you just click the topic you want, and a new page will pop up, usually with other hypertext links. The Web is precisely the same idea, except that rather than just making the link on your hard drive or CD-ROM, it can fire its link request halfway around the world. No matter how jaded you get about all this global network stuff, watching the WWW do its thing remains pretty awesome for a long time after you've started using it.

The nice thing about a Web page is that the linked reference can be placed anywhere on the page. Some Web pages are designed like the Contents pages on a GUI help screen, but others are simply free-flowing prose with highlighted words or phrases, and with graphics that may themselves be links to other locations. It's not uncommon, for example, to see a single paragraph with three or four separate highlights and illustrated with two or three small graphics, all the features working together in a comfortably readable design. Like printed prose, you can simply read past the links if you want, getting a good sense of what's available before branching out into the great digital unknown.

And the operative word is *unknown.* While you'll get to know some Web pages like the back of your hand, you'll never get to know them all. Like Gophers, Web pages are proliferating at an almost unbelievable rate, because they're fairly easy to design and implement. Commercial Internet providers often provide their own Web page, and dedicated Webbers quickly will become familiar with the pages at the National Center for Supercomputing Applications (NCSA), home of the famous WWW software Mosaic. The NCSA maintains a What's New page that gives you at least some idea of what's been added recently, and one look at it is a rather sobering experience. Just when you think you might be on top of the information world, along comes another dollop of new WWW pages, each of which points to all kinds of other stuff to know.

10

But that's the bad news. The good news is that the Web makes that material more manageable than does any other current Internet tool. You may not be able to access everything, but at least you have a sense of what's being made available, which is something that not even Gopher can do.

Accessing the Web Through Mosaic

If you have a Mac or Windows machine, you have several strong World Wide Web browsers (technically called *clients*) at your disposal. The two major browsers, both available free off the Net, are Mosaic and Netscape. This section deals with Mosaic, probably the most influential—and hyped—piece of software in the 1990s.

Mosaic exists in several versions. The official version is called *NCSA Mosaic*, and comes to us from the National Center for Supercomputing Applications (NCSA) at the University of Illinois at Urbana-Champaign (`uiuc.edu`). This is the version used in this chapter, in particular, release 2.0 beta 4. Several versions of Mosaic are appearing on the market, most of which are licenced versions of Spyglass's Enhanced Mosaic, which offers technical support and advanced security features. One popular version of Enhanced Mosaic is SPRY Mosaic (formerly Air Mosaic), which is included in the Internet in a Box software suite. Several others are available, either independently or as part of software collections.

Mosaic was originally released in early 1993. Designed by a student at NCSA named Marc Andreesen, the program appeared first for UNIX's X Window system. Later in 1993, the Macintosh version appeared, and near the end of that year Windows users had a version for themselves. The versions are officially called NCSA Windows for the XWindow System, NCSA Mosaic for the Apple Macintosh, and NCSA Mosaic for Microsoft Windows.

Ironically, Marc Andreesen is largely responsible for Mosaic's biggest competitor (in fact, its conqueror, depending on whom you believe), Netscape Navigator. Netscape is covered later in this chapter.

Note: This chapter deals with the Microsoft Windows versions of Mosaic and Netscape, although there will be notes for Macintosh users. Mac users, please forgive, and keep in mind that Mac software is always easier to install and work with anyway. Actually, using the software is very similar, and in Netscape's case, nearly identical. And the sites themselves look identical in any case.

Task 10.1: Acquire and install Mosaic.

To acquire and install Mosaic, just follow these steps:

1. FTP to **`ftp.ncsa.uiuc.edu`** (refer to Chapter 7 for FTP instructions). Enter the directory **`/Web/Mosaic/Windows`**. Macintosh users enter **`/Web/Mac/Mosaic`** instead.
2. Transfer the file named `mos20fb.exe` to your hard drive. By the time you read this, it might bear a slightly different name.

Note: NCSA Mosaic is a 32-bit program, which means that it needs the 32-bit Windows extensions to work. Check your hard drive for a directory called `c:\windows\system\win32s`—if you have it, you're probably running the extensions. If you're running Windows 95, you have no need of them (Win95 is already 32-bit). If neither of these cases applies, you have to download them from the NCSA site as well—the file name is `w32s125.exe` (or similar)—and install them on your hard drive. If you have no room for them, an older version of Mosaic is available in the `/Web/Mosaic/Windows/old` directory, but it lacks many current features.

3. Move `mos20b4.exe` to a separate installation directory. Then go to a DOS prompt, enter this new directory, and type **`mos20fb`**. The file will unzip itself into many files.
4. Using Program Manager's Run command (in the File menu), launch the Setup program contained in this directory. Follow the prompts to complete the installation of Mosaic.
5. Create an icon for Mosaic in a Program Manager group.

Note: If you're a Mac user, your life is predictably easier. Your FTP program (Fetch, probably), will automatically decompress the file and possibly even launch the installation routine. In any case, double-clicking on the decompressed file will install Mosaic properly, into an appropriate folder.

10

Task 10.2: Launch Mosaic and enter the Mosaic home page.

To launch Mosaic and enter the Mosaic home page, just follow these steps:

1. Double-click on the Mosaic icon (identical procedure for Mac or Windows users).
2. Once Mosaic has loaded, select Open URL from the File menu. In the resulting box, type the following URL address, *exactly* as it's shown here (including capitals, slashes, dots, and spaces):

   `http://www.ncsa.uiuc.edu/SDG/Software/Mosaic/NCSAMosaicHome.html`

Note: World Wide Web site addresses are called *Uniform Resource Locators* and are always abbreviated URL. URLs can be long and difficult to type, and for the most part, you won't have to do so at all (you'll simply click on a hypertext link). But learning how to enter them is useful because you'll often see URLs in magazines, newsgroups, mailing lists, and other resources. That's why it was dealt with early here.

Mosaic should now look like Figure 10.1.

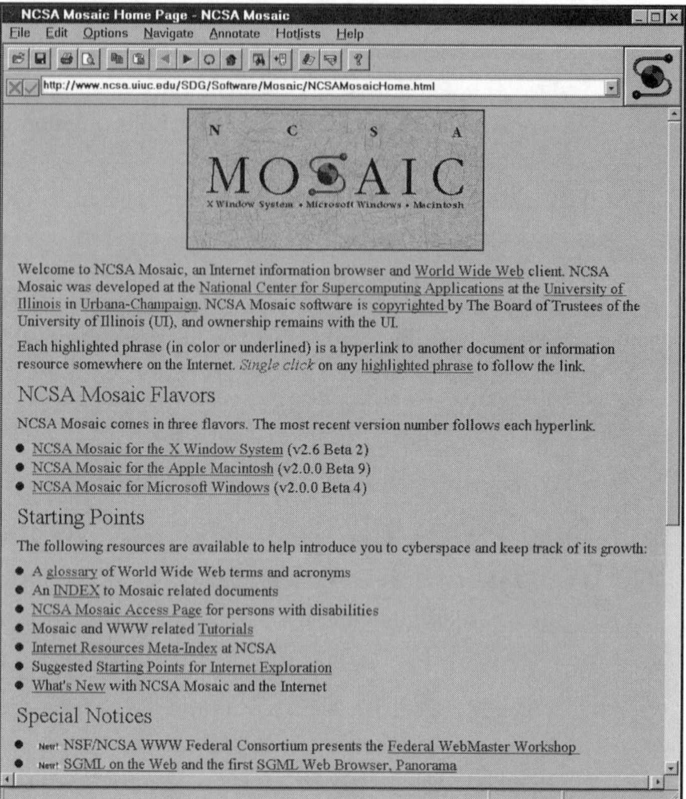

Figure 10.1.
Mosaic showing NCSA Mosaic home page.

Task 10.3: Move to the NCSA What's New page.

One of the most popular pages on the World Wide Web is the NCSA What's New page. Every few days, this page offers links to new Web sites and resources, and as you try to keep up with the Web it will quickly become an indispensable companion. To move to the NCSA What's New page, follow these steps:

1. On the NCSA Mosaic home page (loaded in Task 10.2), locate the line labeled "What's New with NCSA Mosaic and the Internet." Depending on your screen size and resolution, you might have to scroll down the page, using the vertical scroll bar at the right of the Mosaic window.
2. The first two words in this line are highlighted (probably with a blue color) and underlined. The highlighting tells you that this is a hyperlink. Using the mouse, move the arrow to the `What's New` hyperlink. The arrow will change to a small hand with a pointing index finger. Click *once* to engage the hyperlink.

   Mosaic will now load the What's New page. You'll see text first, with several rectangles labeled `Image`. On the status line at the bottom of the Mosaic window,

you'll see Mosaic running through a series of activities, connecting to pages and transferring image files. One by one, these *inline images* (as they're called) will appear on the screen, until the page looks like Figure 10.2.

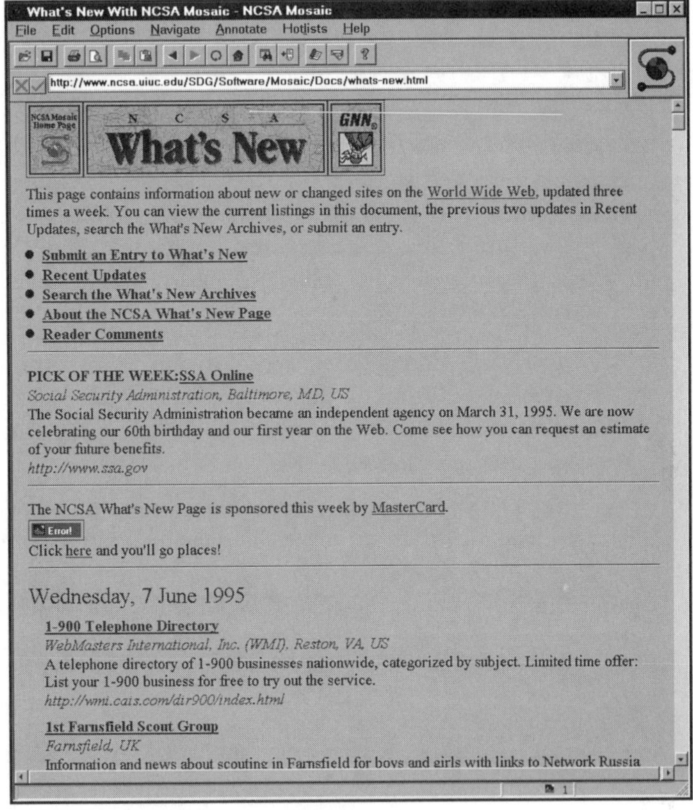

Figure 10.2.
NCSA What's New page fully loaded, with inline images along the top.

Tip: You don't have to wait for the entire page to load before clicking on a new hyperlink. One of the most useful habits you can get into as a Web user, especially if you're working through a modem, is loading only the first portion of the page, and then scrolling through the page as the remainder is loading and clicking on the next desired hyperlink. Netscape works better than Mosaic at this, but both offer this feature.

3. Notice in Figure 10.2 that the small graphic in the center of the page displays as `Error`. This isn't unusual, and there's nothing wrong with your Web browser. The image might be faulty, or the computer on which it resides might be down. If you

want to see it, move the arrow to the image, *right*-click (that is, click with the right mouse button, not the left one), and see if Mosaic loads it properly this time. If not, don't worry about it.

Task 10.4: Reload an entire Web page, and set the cache.

This seems like a weird thing to do so early in your Web life, but it's important (and, besides, it gets you using Mosaic's Preferences menu). Mosaic and Netscape use a disk "caching" system to store Web pages on your hard drive. They do this because downloading takes time, and it's much faster to get them off your drive than the drive of the remote computer. The problem is that the page at the remote site might be different from the cached version, because Web pages are frequently updated. To reload an entire Web page, and set the Cache, follow these steps:

1. To ensure you have the most up-to-date version of the current page, reload it by selecting Reload from the Navigate menu. This will cause Mosaic to go back onto the Net and retrieve the same page, updating text and graphics alike. It will cache this new version over the old.
2. You can set the caching yourself. To do so, select Preferences from the Options menu, and then click on the Cache tab. Figure 10.3 shows the results of doing so.

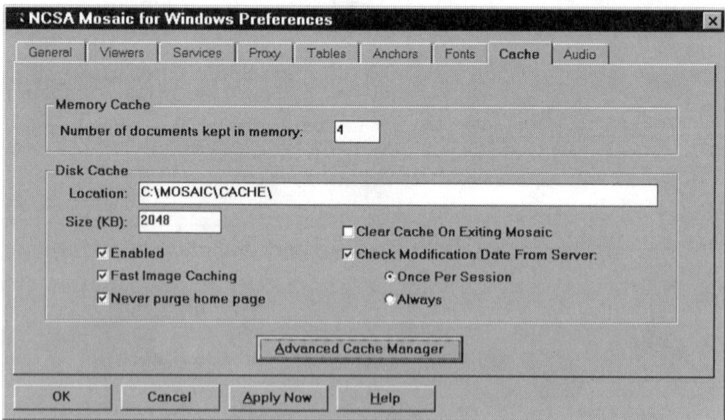

Figure 10.3.
The Preferences menu in Mosaic, here focused on Cache.

3. Click in the box labeled Check Modification Date From Server (in Figure 10.3, it's already clicked). Click on the Once Per Session radio button to turn it on. This tells Mosaic to go out to the server when you load that page, ensuring it's up to date. It will do so only once per session, however; until you close the Mosaic program, the only way to update the page is through the Reload process. Note that you can control a great many additional cache settings here as well.

Task 10.5: Click on a hyperlinked graphic and an imagemap.

You've already clicked on a text hyperlink (the What's New link from Task 10.3). But graphics can also be hyperlinks. In this task, you'll access Web pages via graphical hyperlinks and imagemaps.

1. At the top of the What's New page, next to the big NCSA What's New logo, is the logo for GNN, the Global Network Navigator. Move the arrow to this logo—it will become a small hand—and click the mouse. You will move to the GNN home page, as shown in Figure 10.4.

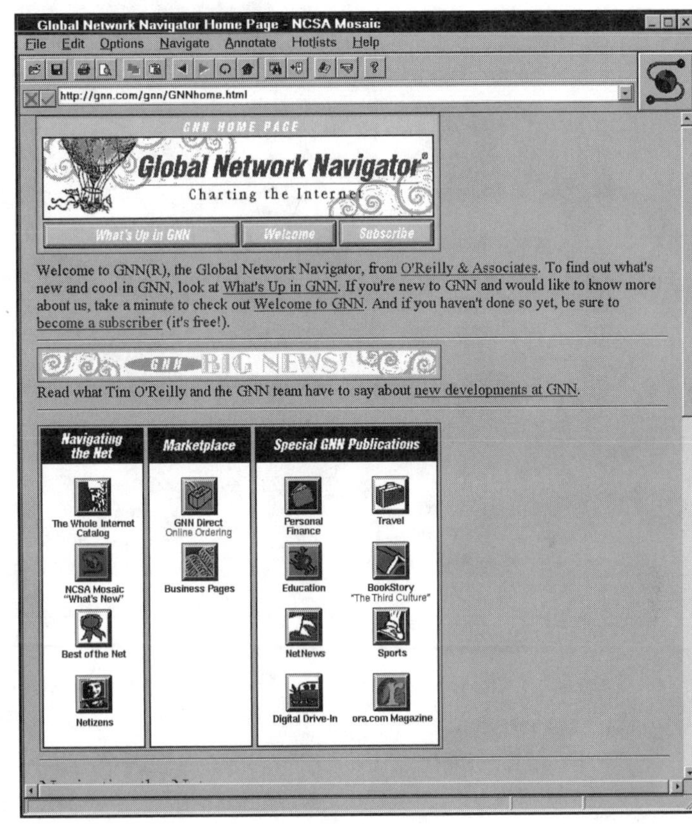

Figure 10.4.
GNN home page at `http://gnn.com/gnn/GNNhome.html`.

2. The GNN logo was a graphical hyperlink that pointed to only one destination. Another type of graphical hyperlink is the *imagemap*, a single image that can point to many differnet locations. The large graphic near the bottom of the GNN home page is an imagemap containing links to over a dozen separate pages (they look like labeled buttons here, but they're not really). Move the cursor over the imagemap

and watch the status line. No matter where you move the small hand, the destination address (shown in the status line) does not change. This tells you you're dealing with an imagemap. Now, move to the button labeled The Whole Internet Catalog, and click. Your screen will now look like Figure 10.5.

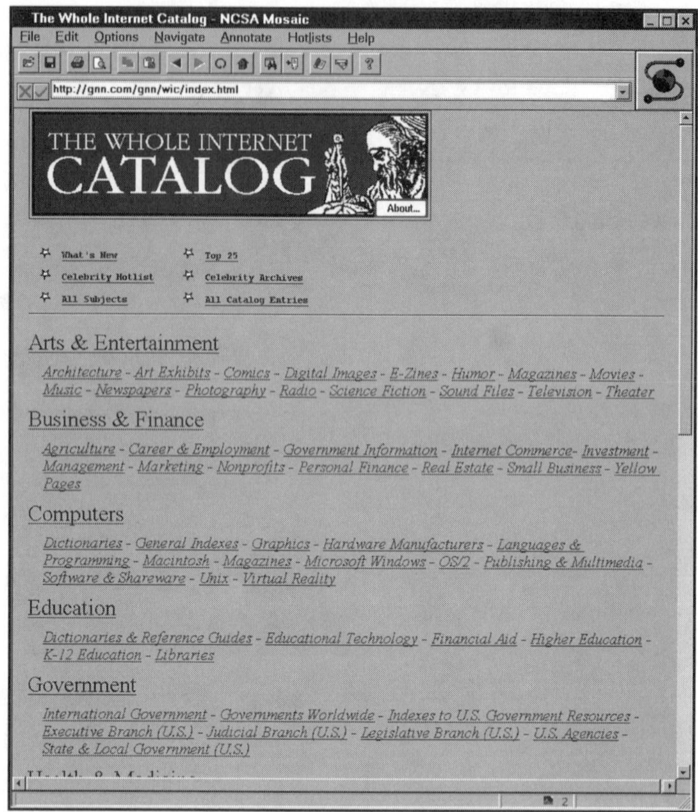

Figure 10.5.
The home page for the Whole Internet Catalog (`http://gnn.com/gnn/wic/index.html`).

Task 10.6: Access two World Wide Web meta-lists.

The Whole Internet Catalog is an important Internet resource. It is one of several "meta-lists" on the Web, essentially a directory of items organized by topic. As Figure 10.5 shows, the WIC is divided into major topics and sub-topics, each of which is a hyperlink pointing to a more detailed set of documents and further subtopics. To access two World Wide Web meta-lists, follow these steps:

1. Locate and click on the hyperlink under Education named K–12 Education. This will take you to a page of links of interest to K–12 educators and students.

2. From here, click on the CIA World Fact Book link and browse to your heart's content.
3. Now move to a second meta-list, the highly popular `Yahoo` directory. To do so, select Open URL from the File menu and type the following URL:

   ```
   http://www.yahoo.com
   ```

   Your screen will now resemble Figure 10.6.

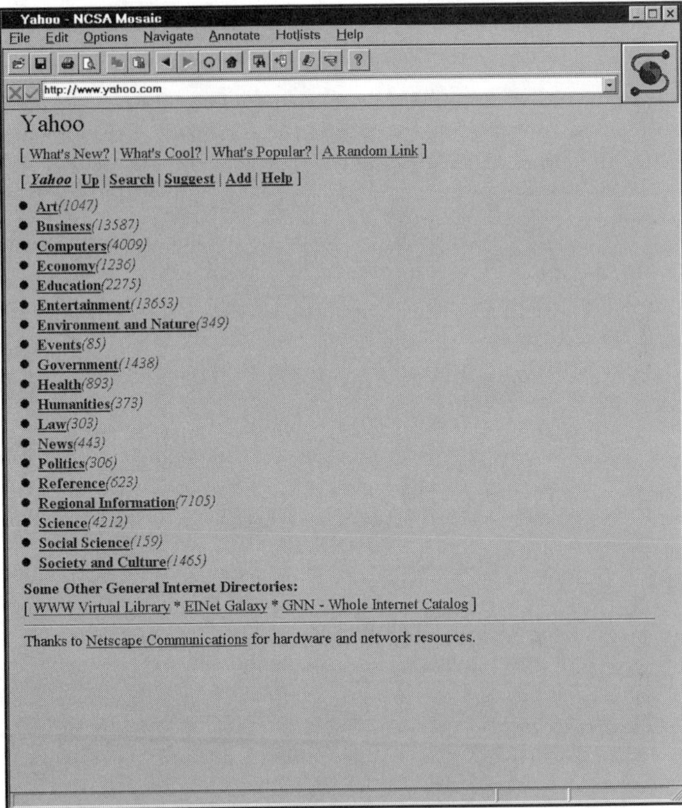

Figure 10.6.
The Yahoo home page, with links to other meta-lists at bottom.

4. At the bottom of the Yahoo home page are links to several other lists, including the Whole Internet Catalog you just visited. Ignore these for now, however, and click on the Society and Culture link. Notice that beside the link are the number of links you'll find within that category (including all sub-links). Society and Culture offers well over a thousand, but Entertainment has nearly ten times as many!

Task 10.7: Tour an online museum through Mosaic, and use Mosaic's history list.

Museums and exhibits have become extremely popular on the Web. For real-world institutions, the Web provides an opportunity to give a global audience a chance to see what they offer, in the hopes of attracting visitors to the site in the future. For others, the Web offers a chance to be seen, to show collections or designs that otherwise would go unnoticed. Here you'll enter a couple of museums via Mosaic hyperlinks.

1. From the Society and Culture page of Yahoo (`http://www.yahoo.com/Society_and_Culture/`), click on the Museums and Exhibits link.
2. On the resulting page, click on Museum of New Zealand. This will take you to a computer in New Zealand, and a page entitled Te Papa Tongarewa (`http://hmu1.hmu.auckland.ac.nz:80/400CAE30/Cmonz`).
3. Click on the link called The Museum of New Zealand Te Papa Tongarewa. This will bring you to the museum's home page, from which you can select Ground Floor, First Floor, or Side Entrance.
4. Click on First Floor and you'll get a floor plan of the exhibits area. Click on the section at the top of the imagemap, "History, Mystery, and the Wolf," and you'll be taken to a screen that tells you when you can visit the exhibit.

   You aren't actually shown anything, however, and this is one of the frustrations of the Web. Any number of sites do what this museum has done, drawn you in but given you little. Many other sites, however, offer extremely useful information, and we'll visit one now.
5. If you wanted, you could get back to the Yahoo Museums and Exhibits page by clicking repeatedly on the left-arrow icon in the program's toolbar, or by selecting Back repeatedly from the Navigate menu. There's a better way, however. Select History from the Navigate menu. The resulting window will be similar to Figure 10.7.

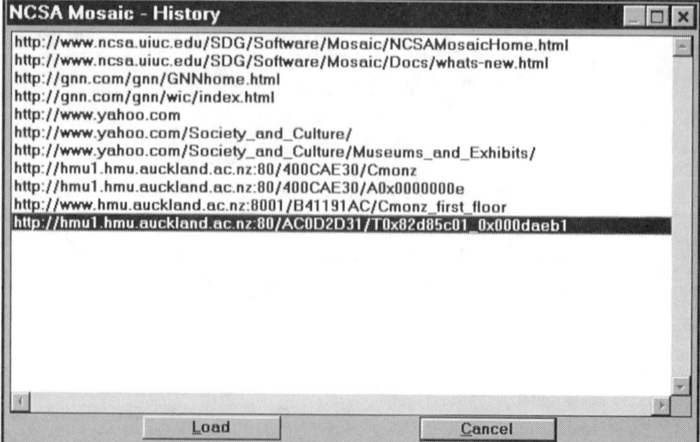

Figure 10.7.
Mosaic's history window.

6. The history windows show URLs, not document titles (unfortunately). Here, double-click on the URL for Yahoo's Museums and Exhibits page. You'll return to that page directly. Click the Cancel button to close the History window.
7. Click on the link entitled Planet Ocean. This will retrieve a site at the Smithsonian Institute's Museum of Natural History (`http://seawifs.gsfc.nasa.gov/ocean_planet.html`).
8. Click on the all-caps link, ENTER THE EXHIBITION HERE. Your screen will now look like Figure 10.8.

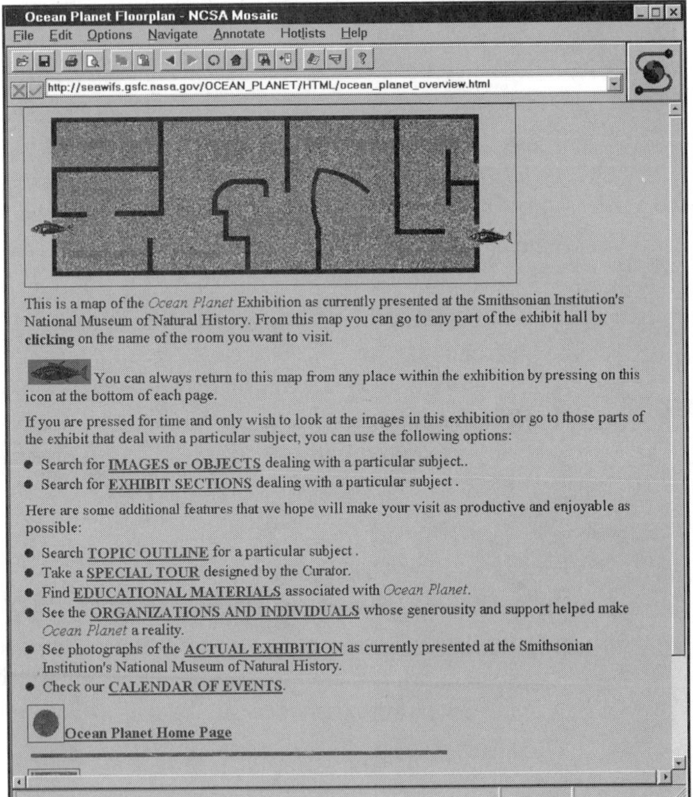

Figure 10.8.
Map page for Planet Ocean exhibit.

9. From this page, you can search for exhibits or items by clicking on the Search links. Or you can click directly on the imagemap of the floor plan to move to that particular exhibit. Here, click on the Sea Peoples area of the floor plan. You'll receive a picture of a Sri Lankan fishing, and you can get a great deal more information by clicking on the Community, Knowledge, and Risk links.

The remainder of this exhibit is similarly rich and is highly recommended for Web newcomers, or for anyone interested in the topic. If you know someone doing a school project in this area, think of the resources suddenly at their command!

Task 10.8: Use Mosaic's right mouse button features.

1. From the current Sea Peoples page, right-click on the picture of the Sri Lankan. Mosaic will display a small menu with two choices.
2. Click on Image Information. The resulting window will give you the URL of the image, the type of file (.GIF graphics file, in this case), and the size of the graphic (90944 bytes, for this image). Click Cancel to get rid of the box.
3. Right-click on the image again. Select Save Image. A cascading menu leads to two choices: Windows BMP Format or Remote Site Format. Both allow you to save the image to your hard disk for your own use. The first gives you Windows' standard .BMP format, and among other things, you can then use the image as your new wallpaper. The second saves the file in the same format as it exists on the host computer (in this case, .GIF). Save the file if you want at this time.
4. Now, right-click on the paragraph in the middle of the page (`Seafaring, whether a...`). Several other options area available, all referring to the currently loaded page. You can save the page to your hard disk, or you can create a shortcut to the page which you can later select via the File/Open Local File command. You can also "spawn" a second instance of Mosaic that will use this page as its starting point; very useful if you want two or more Mosaic windows for browsing in different directions. Or you can change the font for that type of text (here, `Normal`).

Task 10.9: Send e-mail from Mosaic.

Mosaic isn't capable of receving your e-mail, but you can send an e-mail message directly from the program. Mosaic will also handle newsgroups, but not as capably as Netscape, so we'll examine newsgroups there instead. To send e-mail from Mosaic, follow these steps:

1. Configure Mosaic to send e-mail by selecting Preferences from the Options menu, and then clicking on the Services tab.
2. Type your name and e-mail address in the appropriate fields, and tell Mosaic the name of your SMTP server. Usually, this is the same as the domain name of your e-mail address, but it's best to check with your Internet provider to be sure. If you know the information for news and telnet, fill it in here as well. Click OK to close the dialog box.
3. Select Send E-Mail from the File menu. You'll receive the window shown in Figure 10.9, although with your own e-mail address showing.

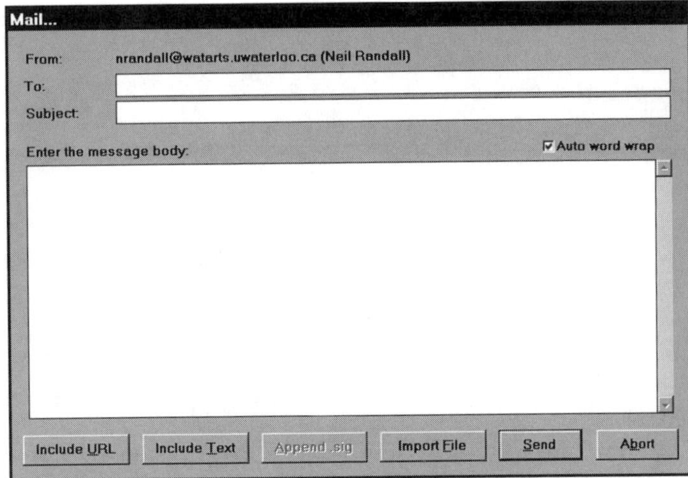

Figure 10.9.
Mosaic's e-mail window.

4. Fill in the To: and Subject: lines, and then type your message.
5. If you want to send your recipient the URL of the Web page you're currently visiting, click on Include URL. If you want to include the text of the page, click on Include Text. You can import a text file into your message by clicking Import File, and if you have a signature file you can include it as well. Click Send to send the message.

Task 10.10: Save pages in Mosaic's Hotlist feature.

As you explore the Web, you'll want to bookmark sites so you can return to them easily. Mosaic's bookmarking feature is called the Hotlist, and it's extremely easy to use. To save pages in Mosaic's Hotlist feature, follow these steps:

1. Select Hotlist Manager from the Navigate menu. You'll see the window shown in Figure 10.10, with the Starting Points Hotlist that came with the program already ready for use (if the Hotlist isn't open, double-click on the Starting Points folder).
2. To begin your own folder of sites, Select Insert New Hotlist from the Edit menu of the Hotlist Manager and type **`My World Wide Web Sites`** (or whatever you want to call it).
3. Click on your new hotlist to highlight it, and then select Add Current at Selection Point from the Edit menu.
4. Double-click on the new Hotlist to open it. You'll see the Ocean Planet: Sea People page added as a hotlist.

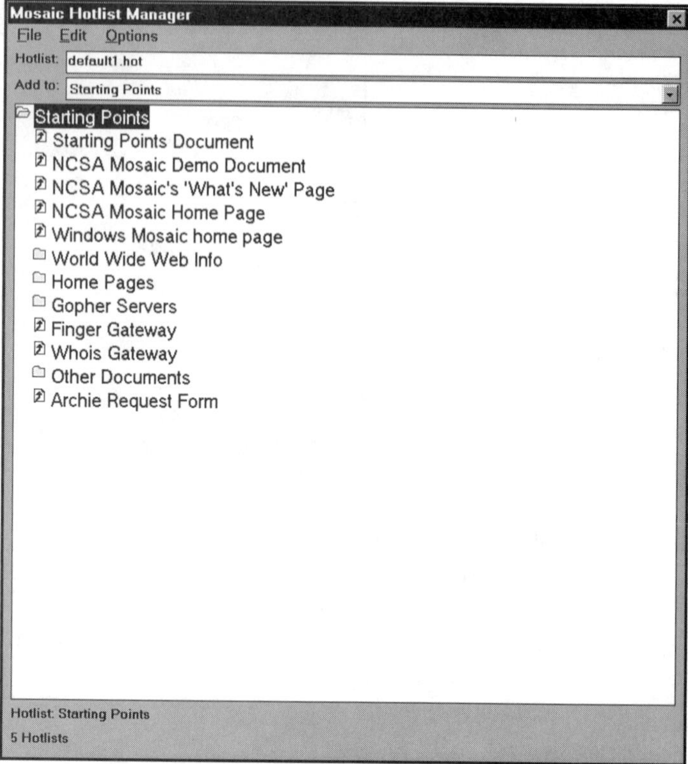

Figure 10.10.
The Hotlist Manager window in Mosaic for Windows.

5. Save the Hotlist (File/Save), and then close the window.
6. Click on the Hotlists menu in Mosaic. You'll see two items: Starting Points, and your new Hotlist. A cascading menu in your new hotlist will point to the Ocean Planet site. From now on, whenever you want, you can return to that site by using the Hotlists menu.

Tip: The Hotlist Manager in Mosaic and the Bookmarks feature in Netscape are probably the most powerful browser features at your disposal. By creating a series of well-defined folders, and storing pages inside those folders (and even subfolders), you can make your Web browsing increasingly efficient. It's worth doing right the first time, because cleaning up a disorganized list of bookmarks is time-consuming and frustrating.

Accessing the Web Through Netscape

First off, Netscape is the name of the company, while Netscape Navigator is the official name of the browser. But everybody calls the browser *Netscape* (which is what it was originally called), so we'll continue that tradition.

Released in late 1994, Netscape quickly became the browser of choice for many Web users. By spring of 1995, it was in use all over, and some sources claimed it had gained almost 70 percent of the Web browser "market" (it's free over the Net, so "market" seems a strange term). Its popularity was due to two main features.

First, Netscape is modem-friendly. It was the first to let you act on text and hyperlinks while the graphics were still downloading, which meant no more horrendous waits (all browsers have since picked up this feature). It also introduced page caching to the modem user, which meant frequently visited pages loaded more quickly.

10

Second, Netscape is graphically very appealing. The browser supports advanced design codes (called *HTML tags*) such as line justification, horizontal line thickness, and page backgrounds. The result is pages that look much more like magazine pages, and as a result are more pleasant to work with. Many Web developers have denounced these capabilities because they are non-standard—the Web is built on the idea of pages that are *not* browser-dependent—but their popularity is extremely high.

Like Mosaic, Netscape is available for the three major platforms—UNIX, the Macintosh, and Microsoft Windows. Unlike Mosaic, however, all three Netscape versions work almost identically. Use one, and you've used the other. Updates to the three versions are released simultaneously, and installation of all three is easy.

In the next several tasks, you'll work with Netscape. At that point, you can decide whether you like Netscape or Mosaic better. Or you can just keep them both, using them as you wish. At these prices, what's the difference?

Task 10.11: Acquire and install Netscape.

To acquire and install Netscape, just follow these steps:

1. Anonymous FTP to **`ftp.netscape.com`** (see Chapter 7 for details on FTP). Enter the directory `/netscape/windows`, or (`/netscape/mac`) if you're a Mac user.
2. Get the file called `n16e11n.exe`, (or `n32e11n.exe` if you have the Windows 32-bit extensions loaded, or if you're running Windows 95 or NT).
3. Mac users have pretty much a free ride from here. If you're a Windows user, move the file to a new directory, and then use a DOS window to enter that directory and type **`n16e11n`**. The file will decompress into several separate files.

4. Use the Run command from Program Manager or File Manager to launch the Setup program from the new directory. Follow the instructions to install Netscape.
5. Create an icon for Netscape in a Program Manager group. Mac users will already have an icon.

Task 10.12: Launch Netscape and move to the Netscape home page.

To launch Netscape and move to the Netscape home page, just follow these steps:

1. Double-click on the Netscape icon to launch the program.
2. Choose Open Location from the File menu. In the resulting box, type **`http://www.netscape.com/`** to move to the Netscape Communications home page. Click OK. Your screen will now look like Figure 10.11.

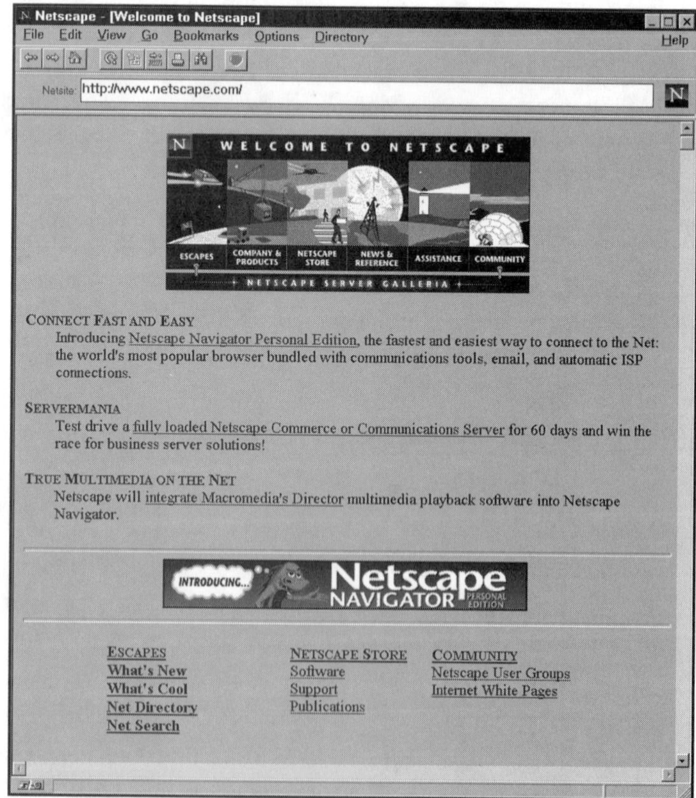

Figure 10.11.
The Netscape Communications home page through Netscape Navigator.

Task 10.13: View the advanced graphical display features of Netscape.

To see the advanced design features available with Netscape, follow these steps:

1. Select What's Cool from the Directory menu. From the resulting page, select The Enhanced for Netscape Hall of Shame. If it's not on the What's Cool page, go directly to the page by choosing File/Open Location and typing the following URL:

   `http://www.europa.com/~yyz/netbin/netscape_hos.html`

2. The resulting page, partially displayed in Figure 10.12, uses several Netscape enhancements—centering (which was first available in Netscape), blinking, differing font sizes within headings, and a background (albeit a subtle one). More interestingly, however, it offers links to home pages that have been designed expressly with the enhanced Netscape tags. Click on the Dave link to see an example, or move there directly via URL `http://pubweb.acns.nwu.edu/~dsimons/`. The result is a colorful page with a very nice background, plus right-aligned graphics and other enhancements.

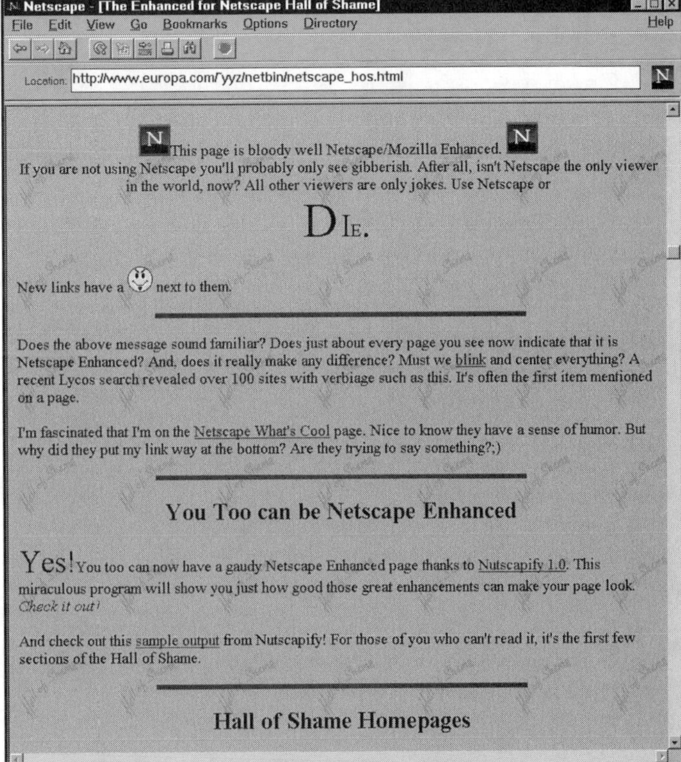

Figure 10.12.
Enhanced for Netscape Hall of Shame home page.

3. Select Netscape Galleria from the Directory menu. Scroll the list until you come to the MCI link. Click there. The results will be a small window telling you that you're moving into a *secured site.*

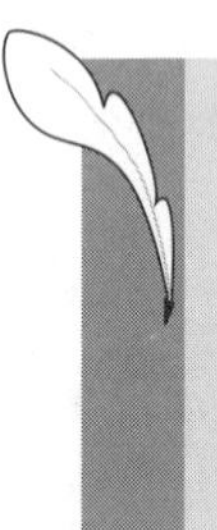

Tip: What's a secured site? One of Netscape's features (and increasingly a common Internet feature) is document security. Security is necessary for activities such as credit card transactions, and Netscape Communications was the first to offer a commercially available Web server that offered a reasonable degree of security. When the Netscape browser accesses a page at a secured site, you see this notice. When you're about to transmit information into an unsecured site, you'll be warned about this as well. Never, ever give out your credit card number to an unsecured site, and think twice about doing so to a secured site. Check it out first by phoning the company who set up the page.

4. Click on the imagemap button labeled `marketplaceMCI`.

Task 10.14: Begin to purchase an item through fill-in forms.

One of the most powerful features on the World Wide Web is the fill-in form. When you see a form on a Web page, you can fill in the blanks and send the data to the owners of that site. Increasingly, these forms are used for shopping; fill in the form, including how you intend to pay, and a few days later, your package will arrive by mail or courier (see Chapter 16 for much more on Web-based shopping).

1. Click on the link named The PC Zone and the Mac Zone. Your screen will look like Figure 10.13.
2. Click on the PC Zone side of the resulting imagemap, and then on the Hardware button. Click on one of the resulting products. At the time this was written, one product was a 17-inch monitor, as shown in Figure 10.14.

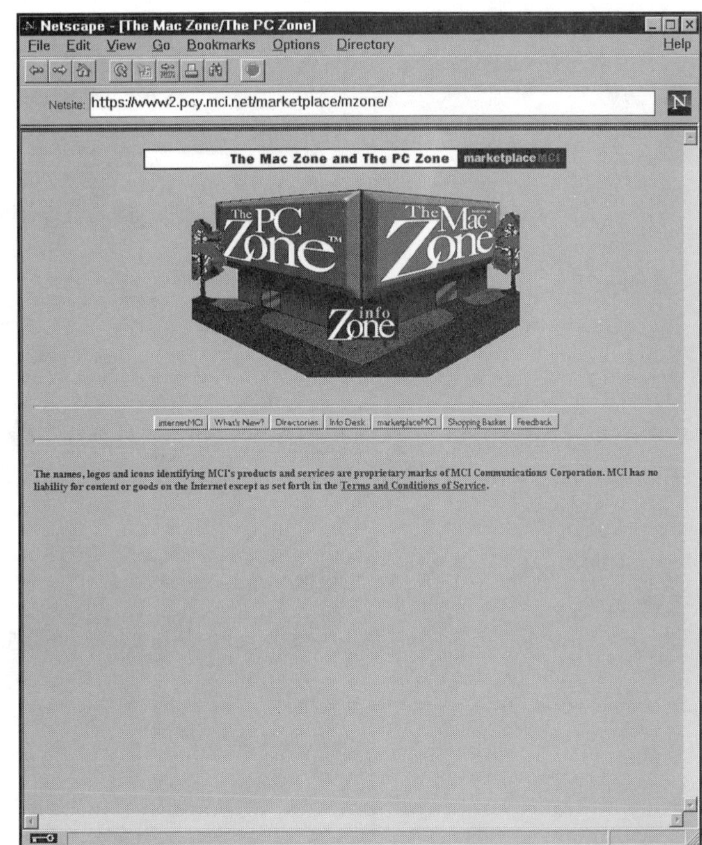

Figure 10.13.
The PC Zone and Mac Zone home page from Netscape.

3. Change the quantity from 1 to 2 by clicking in the Quantity field and typing **2**.
4. Click the Add to Basket button. The screen will now look like that displayed in Figure 10.15.

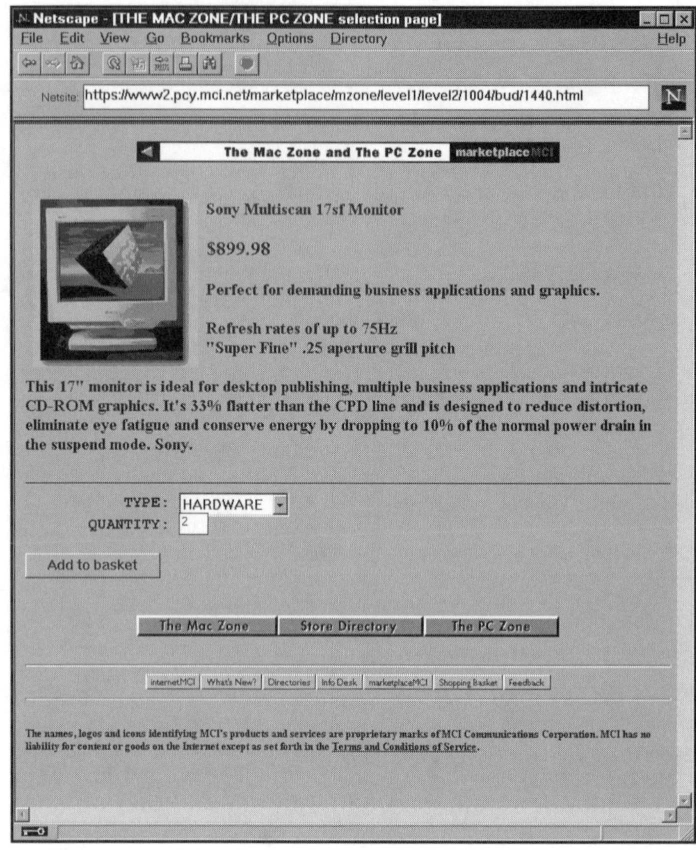

Figure 10.14.
Hardware special from the PC Zone, with selection form.

The "shopping basket" is an interesting feature on the Web. The idea, obviously, is the real-world shopping basket, in which you place goods as you shop. The marketplaceMCI site (like several others on the Web) keeps track of what's in your shopping basket, totaling prices and displaying quantities. Here, you can keep shopping or head for the check-out stand. Notice that the shopping basket will remain as is for up to twelve hours; you can return to this site and keep shopping or check out at that time.

5. Click the Checkout button. Don't worry; you won't actually buy anything yet. You'll be presented with a complete list of what's in your shopping basket, separately, for each store in marketplaceMCI you've visited.
6. Click on Continue Checkout. You'll see the screen shown in Figure 10.16.

Figure 10.15.
The Shopping Basket screen from marketplaceMCI.

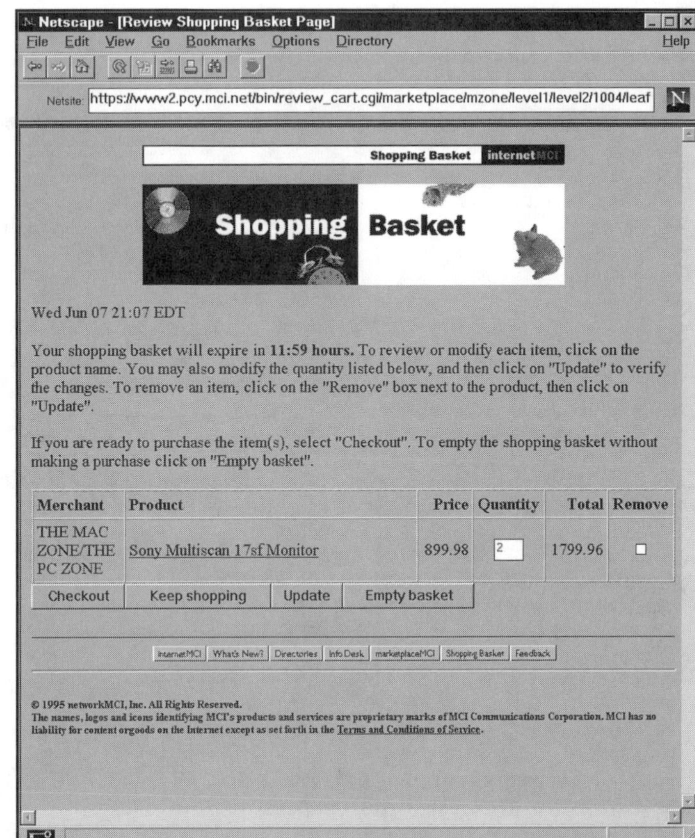

This is an example of a fill-in form. Click in each field (or tab from one to the next), filling in the details as you go. At the bottom of the form, you can select from four different credit cards, filling in your number and expiration date. If you actually want to purchase the item, click on Continue Checkout. If you make a mistake in several fields, click on Clear This Form.

7. Since the idea here isn't to buy anything, exit marketplaceMCI by selecting the Go menu and then Welcome to Netscape. You'll be back to where you started.

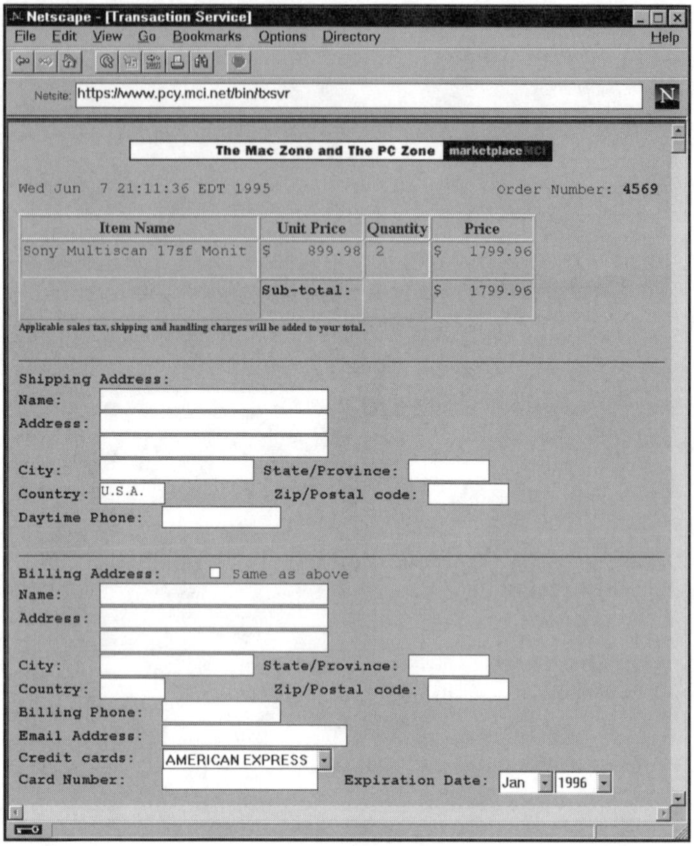

Figure 10.16.
The fill-in form to pay for items from marketplaceMCI.

Task 10.15: Send e-mail from Netscape.

While neither Netscape nor any other Web browser can receive e-mail directly, most enable you to send e-mail messages through a separate mail feature. Netscape's is shown here, although Windows 95 users can tell Netscape to use the Microsoft Exchange program instead.

1. First, configure Netscape to accept your e-mail. Select Preferences from the Options menu. In the Set Preference On field, click the arrow to the right of the field and select Mail and News. You'll see the Mail and News dialog box, shown in Figure 10.17.

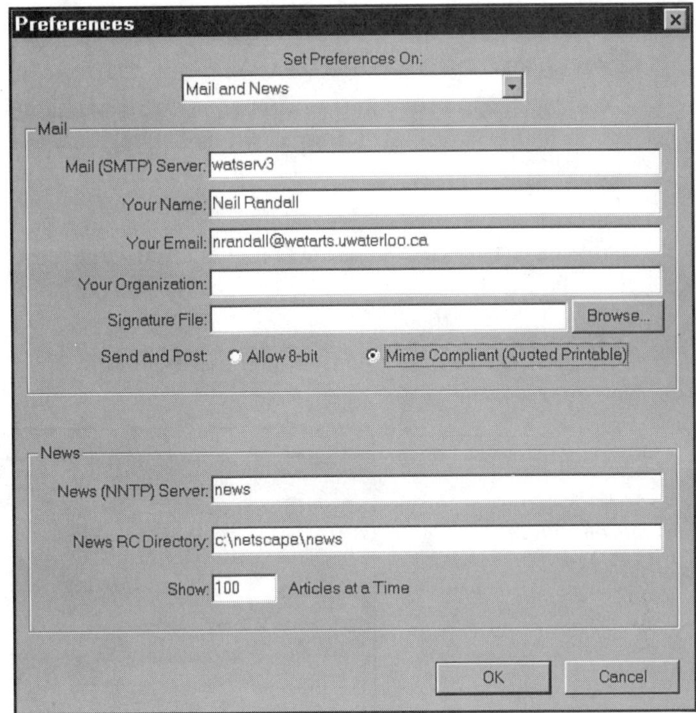

Figure 10.17.
Mail and News dialog box in Netscape.

2. Fill in details about your mail server (check with your Internet provider), your real name, and your e-mail address. Fill in your organization's name if you want, and if you have a signature file to attach you can browse for it on your hard drive. If you know the information about your newsgroup server, fill these in now as well.
3. Click OK to close the window.
4. Select Mail Document from the File menu.
5. Fill in the Mail To: field. You can also post this message to a newsgroup if you want to include a newsgroup name. The subject line shows the current URL by default, but you can change this. If you want to include the text from the current Web page, click on Quote Document. Finally, if you want to attach an entire file to your e-mail message (refer to Chapter 4 for details on attaching files), click the Attach button and choose the file from your hard drive.

Task 10.16: Work with Netscape's bookmarks feature.

Netscape offers an extremely rich bookmarking feature, but it's far from easy to use. In fact, it's the least user-friendly feature of the entire program. But you'll need it, so here's a quick tutorial.

1. Select Open Location from the File menu and type the URL **`http://wings.buffalo.edu/world`**. This will display the Virtual Tourist site you saw in the Prerequsite.
2. Select View Bookmarks from the Bookmarks menu. When the window appears, click the Edit button to show the right half of the full dialog box. The window will appear similar to Figure 10.18, although unlike mine, yours will be empty.

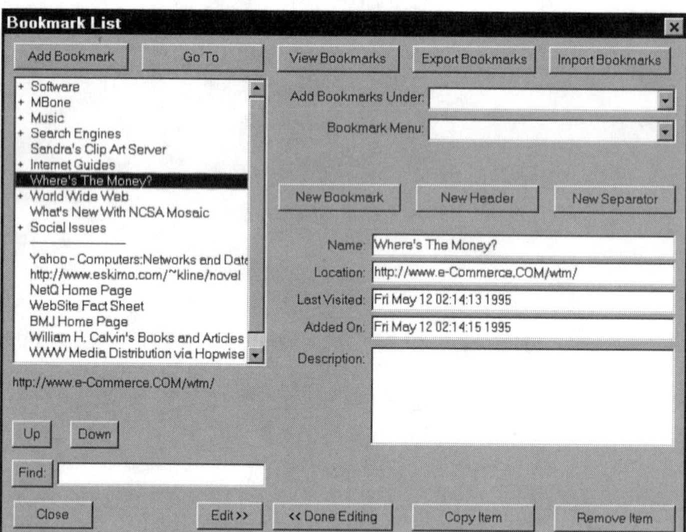

Figure 10.18. *The Bookmark List dialog box from Netscape.*

3. Begin a new bookmarks folder by clicking on New Header. Type **`My World Wide Web Bookmarks`** in the Name field. Click on the new header in the bookmark list to highlight it.
4. Click the Add Bookmark button to add the Virtual Tourist site to the bookmark list. The right side of the dialog box will fill in with URL, name, and dates. You can change the title and add a description.
5. Now, move the Virtual Tourist bookmark into the new folder. Click on the Virtual Tourist bookmark in the bookmark list to highlight it. Click the Up button to move it just beneath the My World Wide Web Bookmarks header, and indented to

the right. A plus sign will appear beside the header, meaning the bookmark is inside that header. Double-click on the plus sign to close the header, and then again to reopen it.

6. To add all new bookmarks to the new folder, click on the arrow following the Add Bookmarks Under: field at top right. Select your new header. Click the Close button.
7. Move to the White House site by selecting Open Location from the File menu and typing **`http://www.whitehouse.gov`**. When the page appears, select Add Bookmark from the Bookmarks menu. This bookmark will be stored in your new bookmarks header.

Task 10.17: Access newsgroups from Netscape.

Netscape is a very capable newsgroup program. You can post, follow up, and reply to messages (refer to Chapter 5 for details about newsgroups). Furthermore, Netscape offers an easy to understand graphical tree of the newsgroups, letting you know instantly which messages belong to which topic.

1. Select Preferences from the Options menu, and select the Mail and News category.
2. Fill in the news server information.
3. In the fill-in field, type **`alt.architecture`** (or another newsgroup, if you prefer). (If you don't know of any groups, click on the View All Newsgroups button, and then wait until they appear.) The new group will appear on the Netscape newsgroups page.
4. Click on the `alt.architecture` newsgroup. The articles will load, and you'll see a page resembling Figure 10.19.

   Notice the well-organized appearance of the page, with topics and sub-topics easily seen. At the top of the page (and the bottom as well if you scroll to it) are buttons for posting, catching up, showing old articles, unsubscribing from the newsgroup, and going back to the subscribed newsgroups page from which you started.
5. Click on one of the articles to read it. When you've finished, click the Post Reply button to respond to the message. You'll see Netscape's e-mail window, with the Post field already filled in.
6. Experiment with the other newsgroup buttons. The arrow buttons send you to the next message in the thread or to the next thread (or previous ones), the Post and Reply button includes the sender's e-mail address in the mail message, and so on. All in all, this is a very good newsreader, but it lacks some of the features of dedicated newsreaders.

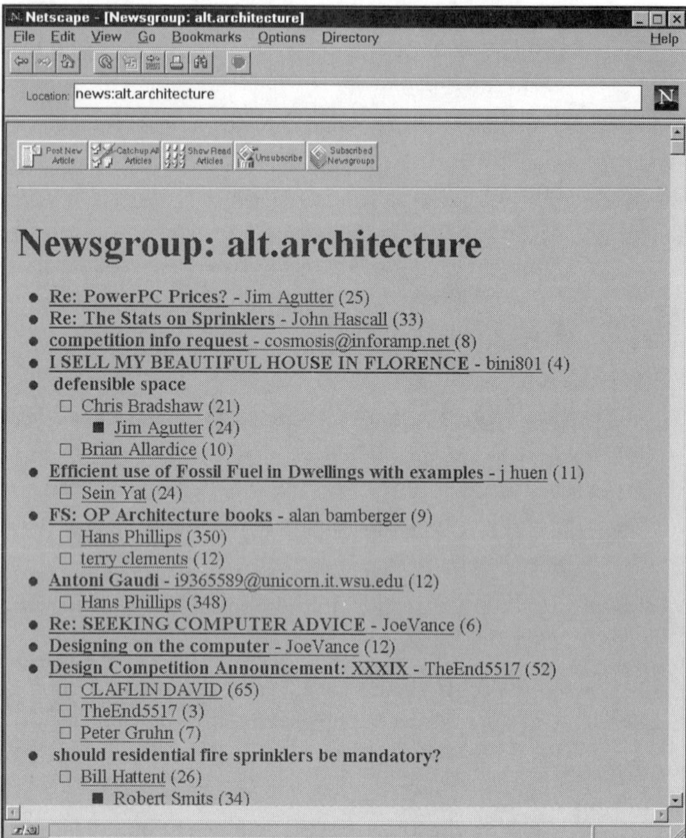

Figure 10.19.
Newsgroup articles through Netscape's newsreader.

Summary

The World Wide Web is growing swiftly, and it shows no signs of slowing down. Pages and sites are being added daily, and keeping track of all of it is impossible. But it's the most important resource on the Internet today, so it's necessary to acquire a browser and learn your way around. That's what this chapter has been all about.

Your choice of a World Wide Web browser is almost as important as your decision to get on the Internet in the first place. NCSA Mosaic was the first widespread browser, but it has been largely supplanted by Netscape, which now commands between 40 and 80 percent marketshare (depending on whom you talk to). Better yet, why not try these two and any others that become available. Since they can be had for the price of a download (in other words, free), all you need is disk space and an open mind.

Task Summary

In this chapter, you performed the following tasks:

- Used Mosaic to discover the benefits of multimedia
- Examined the Web design advantages available through Netscape
- Decided on the best Web browser for you
- Entered the Web via the subject-oriented meta-lists

Key Terms

10

With the Web's popularity has come an entire set of related terms. After a while, you'll know these by heart, but for now, here's a few to get you started. When you see a term you don't know, check here first; these are the most common.

World Wide Web—A hypertext system allowing easy access to formatted documents across the Internet

Mosaic—The first graphical Web browser, and still important today

Netscape—The most popular Web browser, officially known as Netscape Navigator

Netscape Communications—The company who produces the Netscape Navigator, and where Mosaic designer Marc Andreesen finally found a paying job

NCSA—The National Center for Supercomputing Applications at the University of Illinois at Champaign-Urbana, the home of the Mosaic Web browser

Enhanced Mosaic—The supported and secure version of Mosaic, as licensed by Spyglass

URL—Uniform Resource Locator, the "address" for a World Wide Web page (but also for Gopher and FTP pages as well)

Browser—World Wide Web client program, designed to retrieve and display HTML documents

HTML—HyperText Markup Language, the coding system with which Web pages are designed

Meta-list—Web site that organizes World Wide Web pages into subject categories

Home page—World Wide Web page, usually the first page of an organization's or a person's Web site

Q&A

Q Why do I get so many messages telling me the hypertext link couldn't be opened?

A Keep in mind that a link in the World Wide Web usually hooks you up to another computer in another place. Not every computer is available at all times. Some of them shut down for periods of time, usually because of maintenance or (more recently) cost issues. Most of them are busy at certain times of the day handling extensive local computing issues, and in the case of universities, they may well be overloaded late in the term when assignments are due. Always consider the time of day where the physical machine actually resides. If you stick to Webbing in after-hours (for the destination computer, not for you), you'll run into very few problems. There's always the chance, however, that the systems people have simply cut off outside access.

Q Can I access Gophers through Web browsers?

A You sure can. In fact, the Gophers look better this way than they do in character-based Gopher software. But Web browsers aren't as strong as dedicated Gopher browsers, so if you're serious about Gophering you should get software designed to handle it specially. However, you can FTP, telnet, and newsgroups through the Web as well, so it's practically an all-purpose tool.

Q Does anybody really know how to read URLs?

A Apparently, yes. If you think about a URL as a kind of extended directory path, it might be easier. In fact, that's more or less what it is. DOS users have little trouble with a command like `copy c:\wp51\docs\memos\october\project.rpt`, and one glance at a URL will tell you it isn't much different. The problem is that there's no easy equivalent to a `DIR` command to find out which URLs are available. You just have to start clicking around and bookmarking the pages (which means storing their URLs) you find most intriguing.

Q I access the Web through a modem, and the graphics take forever to appear. Anything I can do about this?

A Yes. The graphics that appear automatically with Web pages are called *inline* graphics. Graphical browsers enable you to turn off this feature. Check the Options or View menu or your browser to turn off images.

Q Can I create my own World Wide Web pages?

A Sure. You need to learn HyperText Markup Language (HTML), although HTML editors are now available for Word for Windows and WordPerfect for Windows, and many third-party add-ons perform this function as well. You can even store the pages on sites created specially by some Internet providers, and this is a good way to get your stuff out there. If you're interested in doing it properly, pick up one of several good books on the topic.

Q I use Mosaic. Why do so many Web pages tell me that I would be better off downloading Netscape?

A Netscape's specialized "tags" allow such page design features as placement of graphics, differently colored and textured backgrounds, and variations in fonts and lists. Because these tags are considered "cool" by many, and simply better (from a document design standpoint) by others, an increasing number of Web publishers design principally for Netscape. In a few cases—and thankfully only a very few—a page will barely even display without Netscape. If you're considering designing a Web site, make sure non-Netscape users will be able to access it and use it to full advantage. Otherwise, you're simply being unresponsive to the many people in the world who don't use Netscape for whatever reason.

11

DAY 4

Choosing a Web Browser

One thing about the popularity of the Web is that there seems no end to the number of Web browsers hitting the market. Some are as strong, in their own ways, as Netscape and Mosaic, while others are older and much less capable. Some are included in collections of Internet software, others as part of a commercial online service. There are many to choose from, and which one you decide on will go a long way toward determining how much you get out of the Web.

Task List

In this chapter, you'll learn how to do the following tasks:

- ☐ Use UNIX's Lynx program to access the World Wide Web home page
- ☐ Use WinWeb to download a copy of the *New York Times*
- ☐ Explore the Internet Movie Database with I-Comm, the graphical browser that does not require SLIP/PPP connections
- ☐ Learn of other World Wide Web browsers

Mosaic and Netscape Aren't the Only Game in Town

In Chapter 10, you learned all about Mosaic and Netscape, by far the most popular World Wide Web browsers. But you can navigate the Web with any number of programs, and the number of browsers keeps increasing despite the apparent lock the big two have on the market. And even if you *do* use Mosaic or Netscape, there's very little reason not to try some of the others, as long as they operate over your SLIP or PPP connection, or through your UNIX shell account.

Web browsers can be divided into three essential categories. The first are the non-graphical UNIX browsers, of which the CERN line-mode browser was the first and Lynx the most common (only Lynx is examined here). Next are the browsers that require SLIP, PPP, or other direct access, and this category is the most common. This chapter looks at Quarterdeck Mosaic, AIR Mosaic, WebSurfer, and WebExplorer. Finally, several browsers are available that work without SLIP/PPP access, and these are growing in number. The browsers available through America Online and Prodigy fall into this category, as do browsers such as I-Comm and SlipKnot, which offer graphical browsing through your UNIX shell account.

In this chapter, you'll work with only a representative sample of browsers from each category.

Accessing the Web Through Lynx

The World Wide Web makes multimedia possible, but multimedia isn't necessary. Originally, the Web was proposed as simply a hypertext project, with multimedia a sideline. The

first Web browsers weren't multimedia-capable at all, and one of these continues in relatively strong general use. That browser's name is *Lynx.*

Lynx is found on many UNIX servers. If you have a UNIX shell account, chances are Lynx is available to you. The following tasks introduce you to the Web through the Lynx browser. It remains the fastest of all browsers, primarily because it doesn't have to transfer the Web's extensive graphics.

Task 11.1: Use Lynx to access the W3 home page.

The World Wide Web project is overseen by the W3 Consortium. In this task, you'll go to its home page.

1. Log into your UNIX shell account.
2. Type **`lynx`** at the UNIX prompt. If you're told that you don't have lynx (`command not found` message), telnet to **`fatty.law.cornell.edu`**, and type **`www`** at the `login:` prompt.

Note: The remainder of these Lynx tasks will assume that you have telnetted to that site; if you're running Lynx locally, you can follow along as long as the Go command works (press **`g`** to find out).

3. Move directly to the W3 home page by typing **`g`** and then, at the prompt, **`http://www.w3.org`**. Before pressing Enter, your screen should look like Figure 11.1.

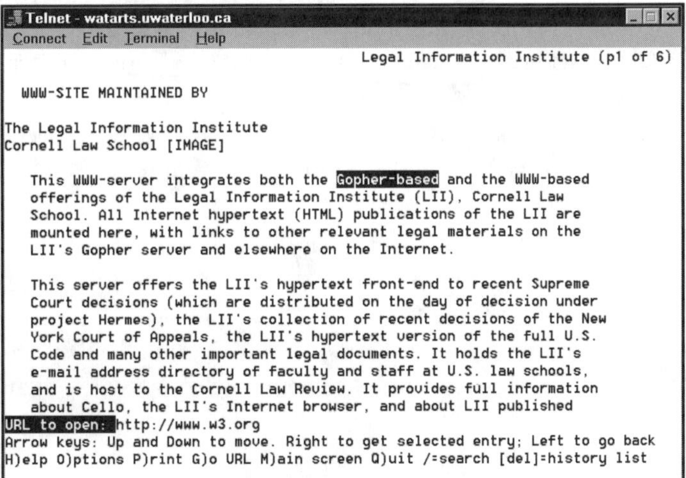

Figure 11.1.
Lynx screen showing filled-in URL to open field.

4. Press Enter to connect to the new site, which appears in Figure 11.2.

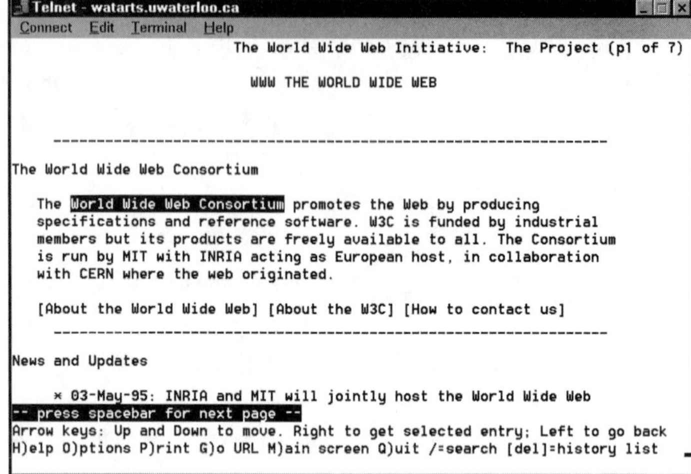

Figure 11.2.
The home page of the W3 Project, in Lynx.

Note the highlighted phrase. This is a hypertext link, which you select in order to move to another Web page. When you open a new page, your cursor is placed on the first available hyperlink, which in this case is entitled World Wide Web Consortium.

5. Move to the next hyperlink, press the down arrow (*not* the right arrow—if you press the right arrow by mistake, immediately press the left arrow to take you back). The word `specifications` should now be highlighted. Continue pressing the down arrow until the phrase `INRIA` is highlighted.
6. With `INRIA` highlighted, press Enter *or* the right arrow key. You'll be taken to a new page, this time on a machine in France, at the Institut national de recherche en Informatique et en automatique. INRIA is a partner of MIT in the development of the World Wide Web.
7. To move down to the next screen (most Web pages are longer than one screen), press the spacebar. At this point, your screen will look like the one shown in Figure 11.3.

   Notice the list of tags labeled `[IMAGE]`. Here you see Lynx's primary disadvantage. These `IMAGE` tags are actually graphics images, but Lynx cannot display them.
8. If you know French, you'll be in heaven here. Assuming that you don't, however, press the hypen key (-) to move back to the first screen of this document. Press the down arrow until the phrase English Version is highlighted, and then press Enter or the right arrow.

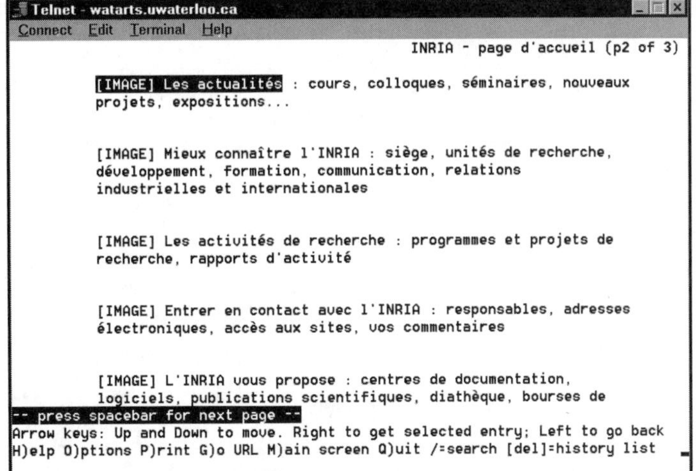

Figure 11.3. *Second page of INRIA site, showing place markers for images.*

9. Press the spacebar to move to the second screen of the site. You'll see the same hyperlinks as in Figure 11.3, except that now they're in English. Figure 11.4 shows these.

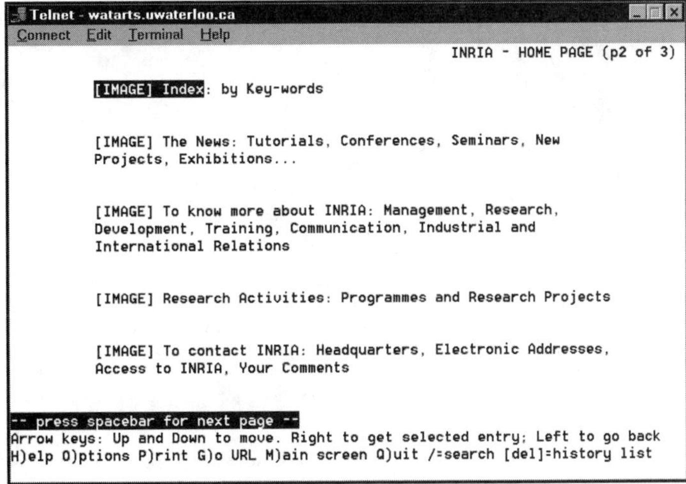

Figure 11.4. *Second page of INRIA site, with links in English.*

10. Maneuver around the INRIA site, selecting the links you want. Of particular interest is the Other servers link, which offers hyperlinks to a wide variety of additional Web sites. Most World Wide Web pages contain a similar kind of link.
11. After selecting several sites, press the Delete key. This will show you a "history" list, telling you where you've been on the Web so far. It will look something like Figure 11.5.

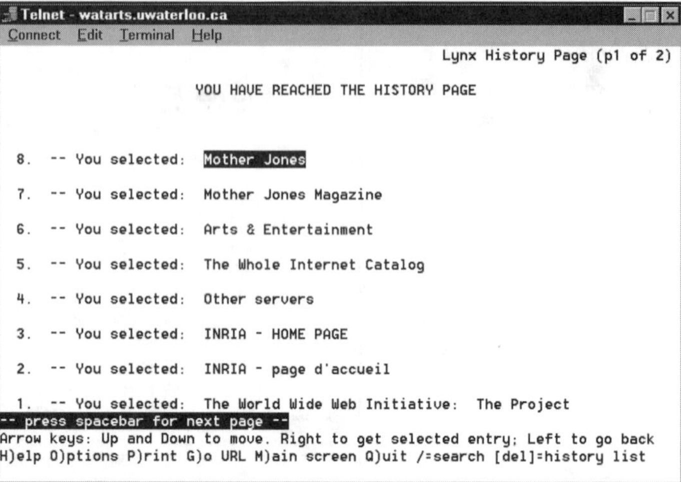

Figure 11.5.
History list in Lynx.

You can maneuver through this page in the same manner as the rest, selecting a site and then pressing Enter (or the right arrow key) to move back to it.

12. Press `h` to get Lynx's help screen. From here, you can access Lynx's user manual and learn about all the possible commands.

Note: Although Lynx does not handle graphics, it handles forms extremely well. To try a form, type `g` and `http://www.whitehouse.gov`, and then cursor to Comments to access the White House comment form. Choose either President Clinton or Vice-President Gore, and then fill in the form as you want.

Congratulations. You know Lynx, and you have a sense of the World Wide Web. Now it's on to other graphical browsers.

Accessing the Web through WinWeb

Although WinWeb is in urgent need of an upgrade (late 1994 was its most recent at the time of this writing), it's not a bad little Web browser to have available if you're a Microsoft Windows user. It's not as capable as its Macintosh counterpart MacWeb (see below), but it's fast and it's easy on your PC's systems resources. The program runs well on a 4-megabyte Windows platform, and takes up only about a megabyte of hard disk space. It handles forms and imagemaps just fine, but it stumbles when trying to display documents filled with advanced HTML tags. Still, it's worth having.

Task 11.2: Get a daily copy of the *New York Times* through WinWeb.

WinWeb is tied directly to the EINet Galaxy. As a result, when you first load it, it takes you directly to the Galaxy, where you can perform a search. This task takes you step by step through downloading WinWeb and using it for a specific search.

1. Obtain WinWeb through FTP by launching an FTP session to **`ftp.einet.net`** and moving into the directory **`/einet/pc`**. Get the file named `winweb.zip`.
2. Using pkunzip.exe, unzip the file into a new directory such as `c:\winweb`.
3. Create an icon in Program Manager for WinWeb, and then double-click on the icon to launch the program. When it launches, it will look like Figure 11.6.

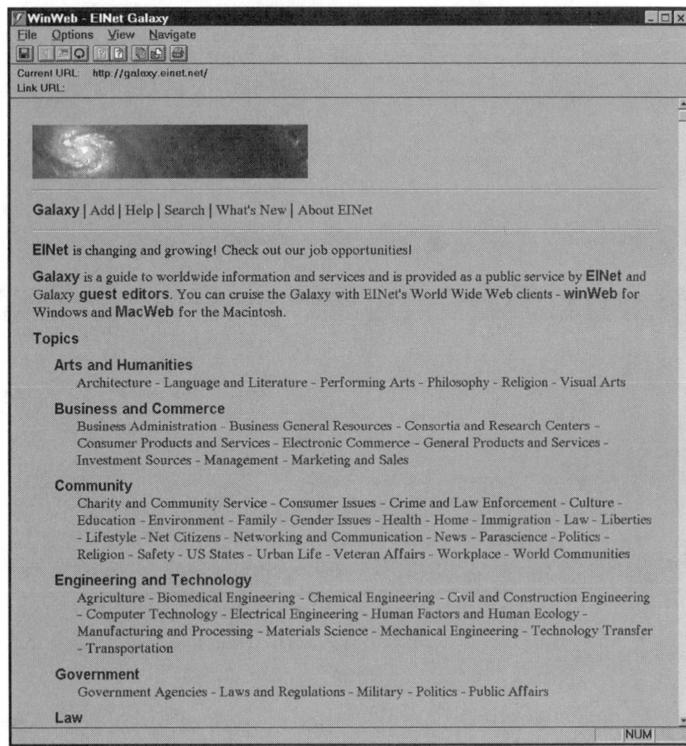

Figure 11.6.
WinWeb on first launch, showing the EINet Galaxy.

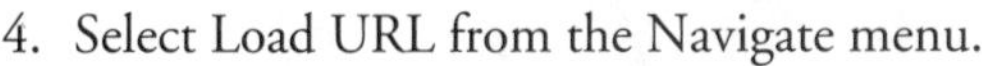

4. Select Load URL from the Navigate menu.
5. In the Load URL box, type **`http://nytimesfax.com/`**. The resulting page will be the home page for the *New York Times*, with an offer to receive a "fax" version. This version is available directly over the Web. You need Adobe Acrobat software to read it, and it, too, is available from this site.

6. Click on the graphics on the New York Times Fax page. This will take you to `http://nytimesfax.com/cgi-bin/tmp/login`, complete with the form shown in Figure 11.7.

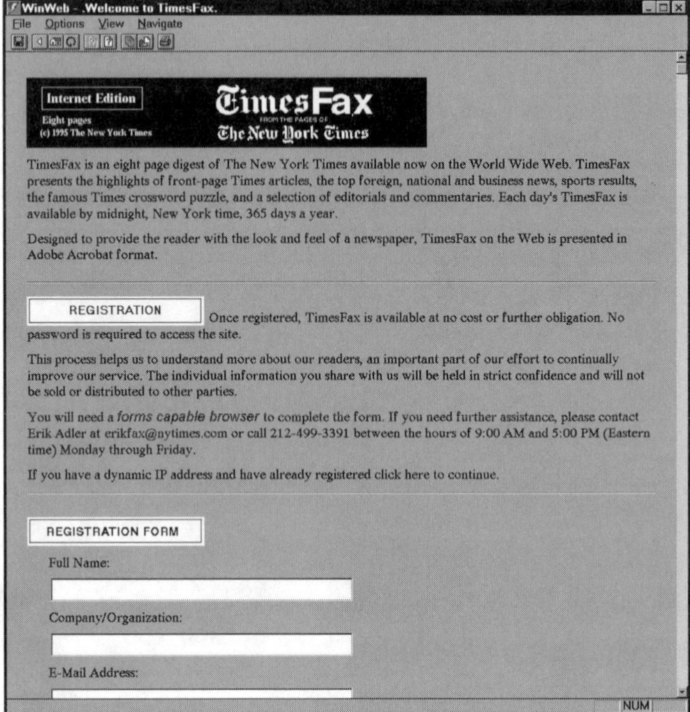

Figure 11.7.
The subscription form for the New York Times fax edition.

7. Fill in the Registration form. There's no charge to get the fax edition, and you don't need to include your credit card number.
8. On the resulting page, you'll see a hyperlink named TimesFax and another named Adobe Acrobat. If you don't have Adobe Acrobat already, click on that link to download it. If you do have it, click on TimesFax and download the file. When you have it, load it into Adobe Acrobat to read or print it.

WinWeb has none of the sophistication of Mosaic or Netscape, or any of the commercial browsers such as Quarterdeck Mosaic or GNN Works, when it comes to configurations such as helper applications. It's a bare bones browser, in fact, but it works and works well.

Accessing the Web Through I-Comm

I-Comm is one of two graphical browsers available for Microsoft Windows users that don't require SLIP or PPP access. All you need, in fact, is your UNIX shell account. The other such

browser is *SlipKnot.* This chapter looks at I-Comm because, while slightly less capable than SlipKnot, it's easier to set up.

Task 11.3: Explore the Internet Movie Database through I-Comm.

If you're a movie buff, you'll want to spend a great deal of time at the well known Internet Movie Database. Here you'll see how the site looks by using I-Comm, although you'll want to try other browsers as well.

1. Acquire I-Comm through FTP from **`ftp://ftp.best.com`**, in the directory **`/pub/icomm/`**. Get the file named `icomm103.zip` (or whatever number it's up to by the time you try this).
2. Using pkunzip.exe, unzip the file into a temporary directory.
3. Using File Manager (or the Run command in Program Manager), run the setup.exe program from that temporary directory. I-Comm will install by default into a `c:\i-comm` directory.
4. Create an icon in Program Manager for the i-comm.exe program, found in the `c:\i-comm\bin` directory.
5. Double-click on the new I-Comm icon to run the program. Your screen will look like the one shown Figure 11.8.

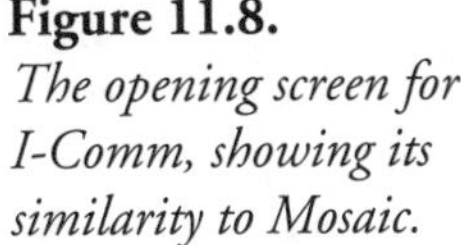

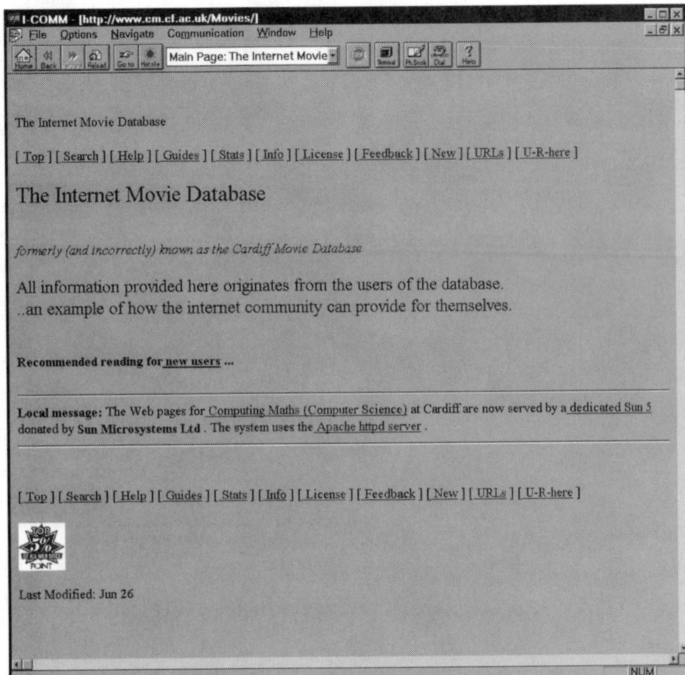

Figure 11.8.
The opening screen for I-Comm, showing its similarity to Mosaic.

6. Select Phone Book from the Communication menu. In the resulting Phone Book dialog box, select Edit to create a new phone entry. Fill in the phone number and the details about your modem and port. Click OK when finished.

   In order to use I-Comm at all, your shell account must have a `zmodem` command and either the Lynx or WWW text browsers (most have one or the other). You can set these features in the Communication menu, although for most shell accounts I-Comm will work as installed.
7. Click Dial to start the connection.
8. When I-Comm connects, fill in your username and password exactly as if logging into your UNIX shell account. Do *not* type SLIP or PPP at the prompt.
9. When you've completely logged in, click on the Browser icon in the toolbar. You will be returned to the screen shown in Figure 11.8.
10. Click on the hyperlink named Art & Entertainment.
11. Click on the hyperlink named Internet Movie Database. Your screen will resemble Figure 11.9.

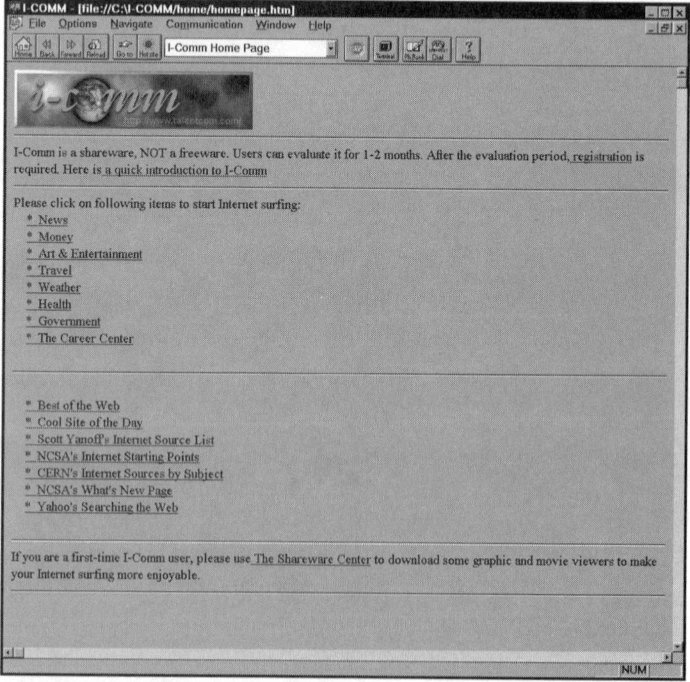

Figure 11.9.
The Internet Movie Database as seen in the I-Comm browser.

From here, you can use I-Comm exactly as you would any other browser. Notice that you haven't established a SLIP or PPP connection at all, yet the browser still works. If you like it, register it and pay for it. It's shareware, not freeware.

Other Web Browsers

So far, you've looked at five World Wide Web browsers—Mosaic, Netscape, Lynx, WinWeb, and I-Comm. If your goal is to find the perfect browser for your needs, you still have a long way to go. Many more browsers await your evaluation, although from this point on, most (but not all) will cost you money. Several, in addition, are part of an entire suite of Internet tools, and that might affect your decision. The one certain thing, if you're anything like me, is that trying out all the new software will be more than half the fun.

SlipKnot

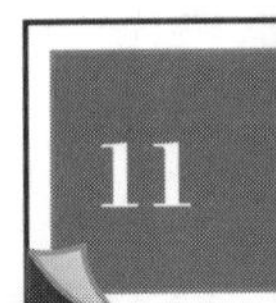

Like I-Comm, *SlipKnot* offers you a graphical browser without the need for a SLIP or PPP connection. SlipKnot uses the Xmodem or Zmodem capabilities of your UNIX shell account (or other downloading protocols) as well as the popular Lynx browser for UNIX to give you full graphical capabilities. It's a bit harder to set up than I-Comm, but it offers more features. Because both are shareware, you might as well try the two of them. Truly worthwhile.

Information about SlipKnot is available on the Web at `http://www.interport.net/slipknot/slipknot.html`.

SPRY Mosaic

Available as part of the Internet in a Box suite, and alone in the Mosaic in a Box package, *SPRY Mosaic* is an extremely strong implementation of Enhanced Mosaic. It features many advanced features, excellent setup and configuration, and as an offering of the CompuServe organization it will almost certainly be well supported. SPRY Mosaic is the browser offered with CompuServe's Internet access package.

For information, see `http://www.spry.com/`.

GNNWorks

An exciting software package that's been available in beta form for months under the name InternetWorks, *GNNWorks* is a MegaWeb network and is owned by America Online. GNNWorks uses a Web browser as the front end for the entire Internet, and the finished product promises a full-featured e-mail and newsgroup program as well. The program is fully multithreaded, allowing you to have any number of activities happening simultaneously (several Web page retrievals, for example), and an excellent bookmarking/organizing system.

The full GNNWorks package includes e-mail and newsgroup programs, and requires access via a separate monthly account.

For information, see `http://www.megaweb.com/`.

WebSurfer

The Web browser in Netmanage's Chameleon software suite is called *WebSurfer*, and it's a good if unspectacular program. It doesn't load text and graphics separately (you have to wait for the whole page to download before continuing), but its bookmarking is strong and it's faster than some other browsers. If you want to use the program, WebSurfer is available in selected Internet books, including my own *Plug 'n' Play Internet for Windows.*

For information, see `http://www.netmanage.com/`.

Emissary

Long under development, the Wollongong Group's suite of Internet tools is now called *Emissary* and is available in beta format. The secret here is that everything happens in one main window, with access to e-mail, newsgroups, FTP, telnet, and the World Wide Web, in a kind of File Manager-like setup on the left side of the screen. Although no single one of the modules is as full-featured as a dedicated program might be, together, the Emissary package is formidable, and for many users might be all they need. This one's worth following, to show how all these essential tools can merge.

For details, see `http://www.twg.com/`.

The Prodigy Web Browser

If you're a member of the Prodigy service, you already have World Wide Web access. The browser is fully capable of handling graphics, fill-in forms, and Gopher and FTP sites, and its caching system is strong. More importantly, access is effortless; as long as you're in your Prodigy account, you have access to it, with no need for SLIP or PPP connections.

For information, click on the Browse the Web button in Prodigy itself.

The America Online Web Browser

America Online subscribers have full access to the Web, as well. AOL's Mac and Windows software includes a Web browser, which is accessible from within the AOL network. No SLIP or PPP connections to worry about, and the browser fits perfectly with the larger AOL interface. Furthermore, because AOL offers 28.8 kbps access in many areas, as well as strong page caching, Web browsing through AOL is fast as well.

For information, enter your AOL account and click Internet Connection.

MacWeb

Besides Netscape and Mosaic, Microsoft Windows users have no truly worthwhile free Web browsers to choose from. Mac users have one, however—*MacWeb.* Much stronger than its Windows counterpart, WinWeb (available from the same designers), MacWeb is smaller and less resource-hungry than the big two Mac browsers. And fast, too.

For information, see `http://www.einet.net/EINet/MacWeb/MacWebHome.html`.

WebExplorer

If you're runningIBM's OS/2 Warp operating system (or later), you already have access to *WebExplorer.* A strong browser, and under continual development, WebExplorer is the only OS/2 browser to date. You can use it via an IBMNet account or through your existing account (connection software is part of the OS/2 suite as well), and its capabilities are worthwhile. Especially strong is its history feature, which creates a new Web page rather than having you sift through lists.

For information, see `http://www.austin.ibm.com/pspinfo/bonuspak.html`.

Summary

Following the world of Web browsers is exciting. Although Netscape has become the unquestioned leader, and Mosaic is the most licensed browser, there's always a new company or programmer willing to offer their own vision of what a browser should be. That's good for all of us, because it means a continual upgrading of browser features. If you're satisfied with one particular browser, by all means stick with it, but as you continue to use the Web, you'll probably find yourself wishing for more and more features. Sometimes the only way to get them is to use two or more browsers simultaneously.

Task Review

In this chapter, you learned how to do the following:

- ☐ Use UNIX's Lynx program to access the World Wide Web home page
- ☐ Use WinWeb to download a copy of the *New York Times*
- ☐ Explore the Internet Movie Database with I-Comm, the graphical browser that does not require SLIP/PPP connections
- ☐ Find out more about other World Wide Web browsers

Q&A

Q If I already have Netscape or NCSA Mosaic up and running, why would I want to bother with any of these other browsers?

A Many people won't. For others, however, trying out new software is always a pleasurable experience (I'm one of them), partly because they keep searching for the absolutely perfect program, and partly because downloading and installing a new program is just plain fun. More seriously, however, different browsers have different advantages. If you're not running the Win32 extensions, for example, you can't use the latest NCSA Mosaic versions, and Netscape is something of a resource hog itself. WinWeb, while less capable than either, runs in less memory and uses less hard disk space, so for users with less powerful machines, it might be the perfect answer. I-Comm provides an answer for users who don't have SLIP or PPP connections, while Lynx is worth learning simply for those times you want to connect with your shell account only (and when you want a full-speed browser). And keep in mind that friends might ask you to help them select a browser, and you'll save yourself a lot of time by knowing their needs and their equipment, hence the browser that's right for them.

Q Where can I find out about new browsers as they become available?

A A number of sites on the Internet store new software for download. On the Web itself, several sites are of interest. Windows users will want to check out The Ultimate Collection of Winsock Compliant Software (TUCOWS) at `http://gfecnet.gmi.edu/Software/`, and Stroud's Consummate Winsock Apps List at `http://uts.cc.utexas.edu/~neuroses/cwsapps.html`. OS/2 users have The OS/2 Shareware BBS at their disposal (`http://www.os2bbs.com/`), while Macintosh users can start by turning to Macintosh Software on the Net at `http://www.macfaq.com/software.html`.

12

DAY 4

WWW Search Tools: Finding What You Need

Using the World Wide Web is easy: call up a page, click on the hyperlinks, and wait until the subsequent page is loaded. That's great if you have time to browse from site to site, but not very useful if you're looking for something in particular. In your explorations of the Web so far, you've been primarily concerned with learning to use the browsers, and "surfing" your way from Web site to Web site. When it comes to finding information about a specific topic, things change considerably.

Fortunately, a number of people have recognized the problem and have set about trying to solve it. They've done so by providing two kinds of tools: meta-lists and search engines. In this chapter, you'll make use of both, and in all likelihood, they'll quickly become the starting point for most of your Web activity. They're extremely important if you intend to use the Web as an information resource rather than simply a nice place to visit.

Task List

In this chapter, you learn how to perform the following tasks:

- Find information through the Web meta-lists Yahoo, the EINet Galaxy, the Whole Internet Catalog, the World Wide Web Virtual Library, and the Commercial Sites Index
- Search for sites on the World Wide Web by using Web search engines such as the CUI WWW Catalog, AliWeb, the World Wide Web Worm, Lycos, OpenText, CUSI, and the Search Engine Room

The World Wide Web Search Tools

The World Wide Web is hot for two reasons: it's easy to navigate, and everybody on the planet seems to be supplying information for it. Of course, the Web's popularity level has created its own set of problems as well. In particular, all that information is extremely hard to track down. Fortunately, a number of enterprising (and kind) individuals have provided search tools with the kind of versatility and power never before seen on the Internet, and finding files and sites is less difficult all the time.

Less difficult, however, does not mean easy. The Web remains a largely chaotic resource, nothing at all like the organized splendor of America Online or CompuServe. For many people, this is a problem, and article after magazine article harps on the need for indexing, editing, and organizing.

To be honest, I don't buy all that. I believe that bringing in the editors and the catalogers will make the Web far more efficient to search, but also will result in an information base controlled in the same way that the production of books is controlled today. The Web might well be the only chance most people will have at global publishing, and to see it operating at the whims of "official" publishers would be a true shame.

So I present these search tools in the spirit I believe they should always exist: helpful but not determining. I recommend them, but I recommend just-plain-surfing as well. End of soapbox, and on to the tools.

Note: For the remainder of this chapter, you'll need your World Wide Web browser up and running.

Using the World Wide Web Meta-Lists

The best way to find your way around the World Wide Web (and the rest of the Net, for that matter) is through the meta-lists. This is a short introduction to the major ones, although the best way to find out which you like best is to explore them in depth on your own. What's guaranteed is that you'll use these resources frequently, perhaps even daily.

Task 12.1: Browse the Society and Culture category in Yahoo.

Yahoo stands for *Yet Another Hierarchically Organized O...* (the last *O* is up to you), but the main point is that this is probably the most popular list on the Web. It's an excellent, constantly changing resource, with a major set of topics giving way to a seemingly endless set of sub-topics. Highly, highly useful. To browse the Society and Culture category in Yahoo, follow these steps:

12

1. Enter Yahoo at the following address:

   `http://www.yahoo.com/`

   You'll see a listing of categories.
2. Click on the hyperlink named Society and Culture. Your screen will look like the one shown in Figure 12.1.
3. Notice the numbers in parentheses next to the individual hyperlinks. These numbers tell you how many links are available within that particular subcategory. Abortion Issues has over two dozen available, while Religion has several hundred. To see where the Religion link takes you, click on it now.
4. Clicking on a bold-faced link on a Yahoo page takes you to another Yahoo page with further subcategories. Non-bolded links take you directly to the site. From the page you're currently viewing (`http://www.yahoo.com/Society_and_Culture/Religion/`), for example, click on the link named Dead Sea Scrolls Exhibit. You'll find yourself looking at the screen shown in Figure 12.2.

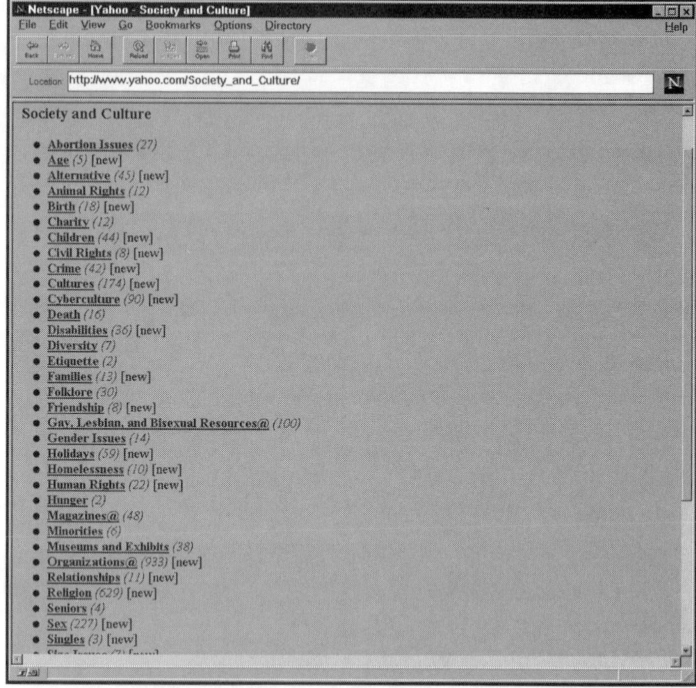

Figure 12.1.
The Society and Culture category in Yahoo.

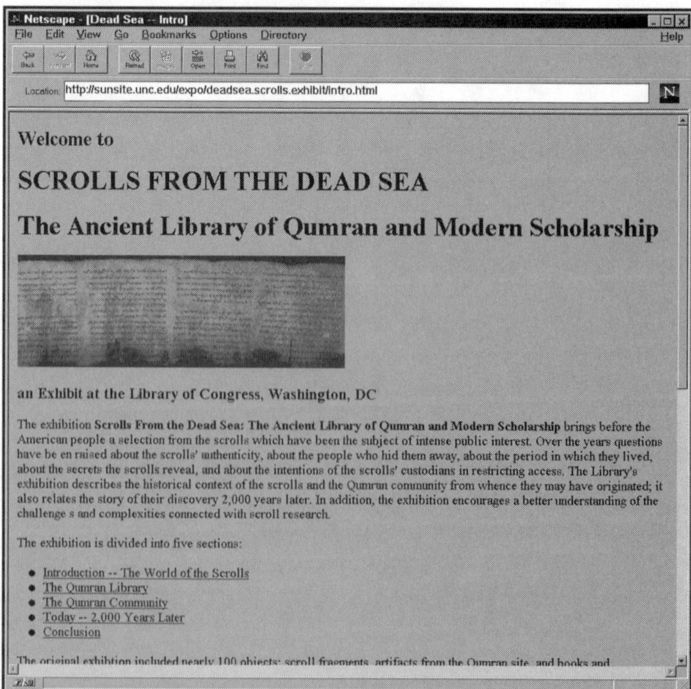

Figure 12.2.
The result of clicking on Dead Sea Scrolls Exhibit in Yahoo.

Task 12.2: Browse the Religion pages in the EINet Galaxy.

The EINet Galaxy has been the most popular meta-list for many months, only recently supplanted by Yahoo. EINet's strengths lie in its large number of subtopics and its organization into collections and organizations that offer resources in the specied topic area. It is a strong search engine, as well. The Galaxy has recently become a commercial site, and it will be interesting to watch its development from this point on. To browse the Religion pages in the EINet Galaxy, follow these steps:

1. Enter the Galaxy at the following address:

   `http://www.einet.net/`

2. You'll see that the topics are organized quite differently from Yahoo's. Here there are two Religion subcategories, one under Arts and Humanities and the other under Community. Both are interesting, but for now, click on the link under Community. Your screen will look like Figure 12.3.

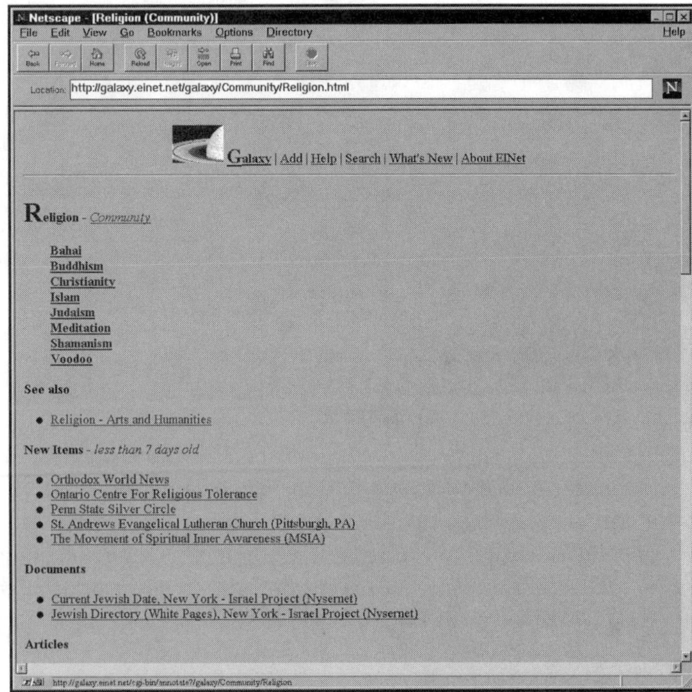

Figure 12.3.
The Community/Religion main page from the EINet Galaxy.

3. Scroll down the page to see how the Galaxy organizes its material. You'll find links to directories, organizations, articles, collections, and documents. Scroll back to the top and click on Buddhism.

4. From the Buddhism page (`http://galaxy.einet.net/galaxy/Community/Religion/Buddhism.html`), click on the link called Global Buddhist Resources. This will take you out of the Galaxy to the page shown in Figure 12.4, located at `http://www.psu.edu:80/jbe/resource.html`.

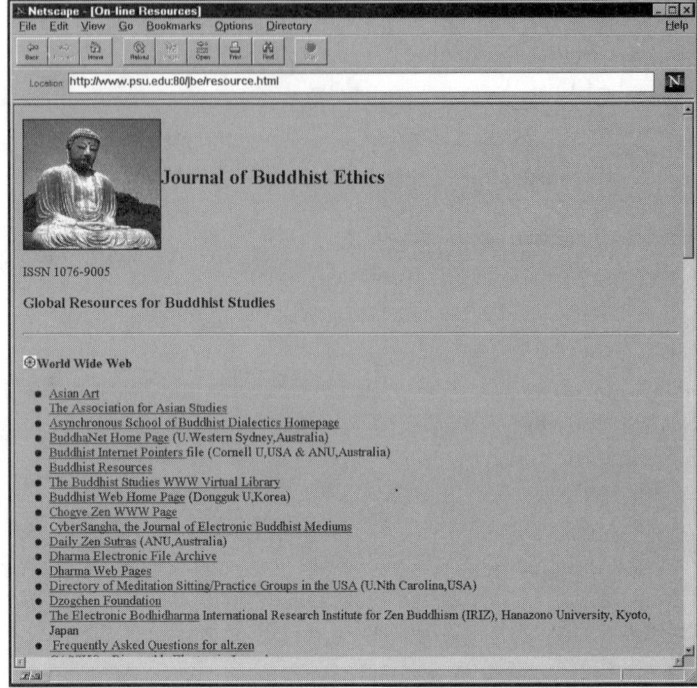

Figure 12.4.
The Global Resources for Buddhist Studies page from the EINet Galaxy.

Task 12.3: Explore newspapers in The Whole Internet Catalog.

Part of the generally superb Global Network Navigator (GNN) site, The Whole Internet Catalog is well organized into its major topics and sub-topic areas. Its only problem is the difficulty in accessing GNN, many of whose mirror sites are also frequently busy. One very good idea is that the WIC acts as a buffer between you and the rest of the Net. When you click on a topic's site, you usually move to a page introducing that site, then onto the site itself. This prevents many unresolved links. To explore newspapers in The Whole Internet Catalog, follow these steps:

1. Enter the Catalog at the following address:

   `http://www.gnn.com/wic/newrescat.toc.html`

2. Scroll down the page until you come to the Daily News major heading. Click there. Your screen will look like the one shown in Figure 12.5.

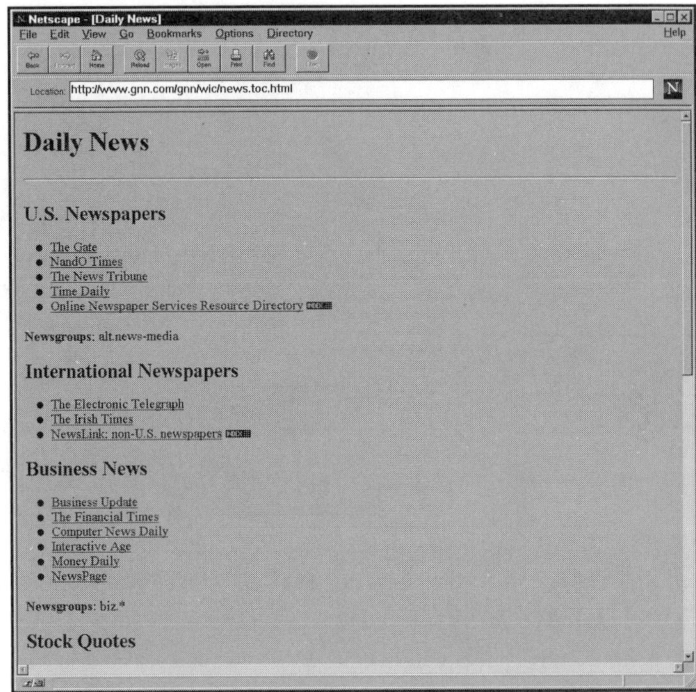

Figure 12.5.
Daily News page from the Whole Internet Catalog.

3. Click on the hyperlink named Time Daily. This will take you to `http://www.gnn.com/gnn/wic/news.25.html`, from which you can return to the WIC or move on to the Time Daily site. Click the Go button to move to Time Daily.

4. You have now reached *Time* magazine's daily news update site. Your screen will look similar to Figure 12.6, except for the date and the new items themselves.

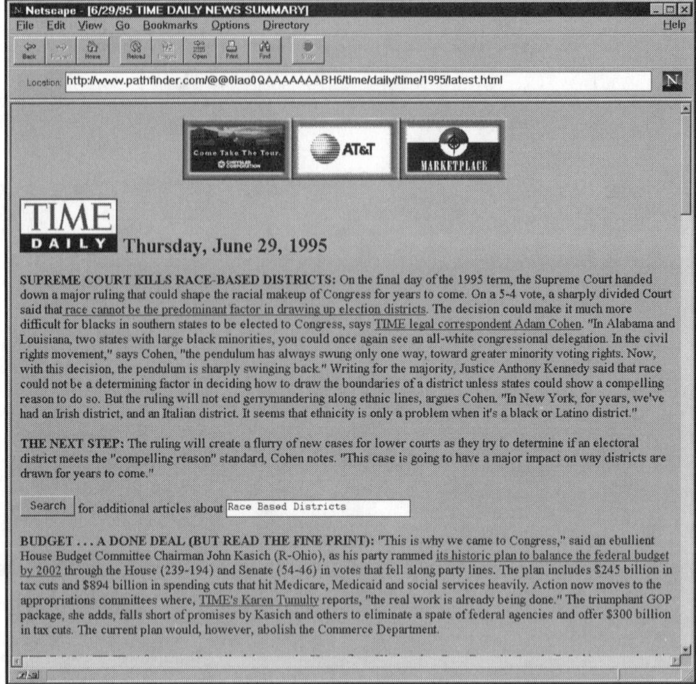

Figure 12.6.
The Time Daily news page accessed from the Whole Internet Catalog.

Task 12.4: Find information about *Beowulf* in the WWW Virtual Library.

The oldest of the meta-lists, the Virtual Library is neither as attractive nor as seemingly well organized as the rest. But it is a very good source of a wide range of Internet material, and it offers a Library of Congress organization as a separate listing, immensely useful for anyone whose research revolves around real libraries. The library links to many other institutions for its sub-lists, which sometimes creates an access problem. To find information about *Beowulf* in the WWW Virtual Library, follow these steps:

1. Enter the Virtual Library at the following address:

   `http://www.w3.org/hypertext/DataSources/bySubject/Overview.html`

2. *Beowulf* is an Old English poem and will probably be found in medieval studies. Although you could scroll to the Medieval Studies link directly from this page, take a look at one of the Virtual Library's more interesting features. Click on the hyperlink named Library of Congress Classification in the first line of text. Your screen will resemble Figure 12.7.

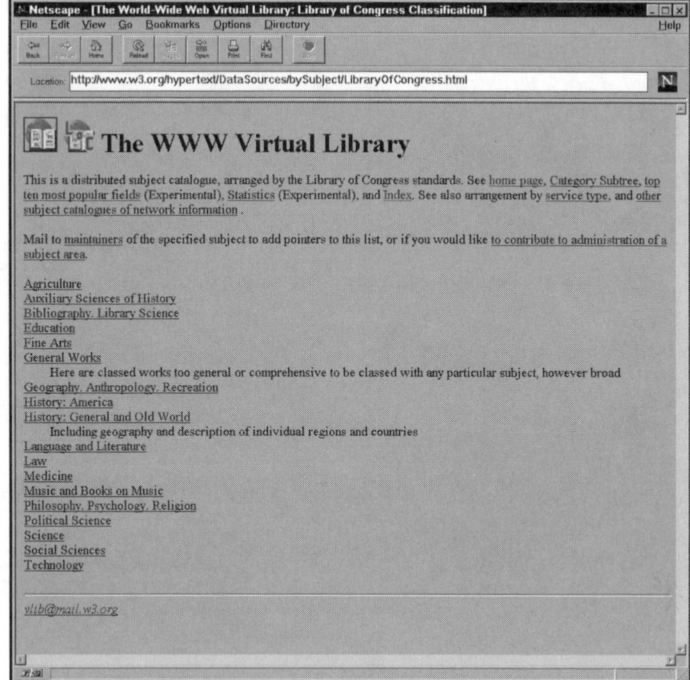

Figure 12.7.
The Library of Congress page in the Virtual Library.

3. This page gives you access to the Virtual Library as if you were searching the card catalogs in a library, organized according to the Library of Congress classifications. This is extremely useful, especially for students and researchers. For this task, click on the link called History: General and Old World.
4. On the subsequent page (`http://www.w3.org/hypertext/DataSources/bySubject/LibraryOfCongress/hisgo.html`), click on the Medieval Studies link.
5. Scroll to the link named Digital Beowulf Project and click. This takes you to the page shown in Figure 12.8, a truly fascinating site to explore.

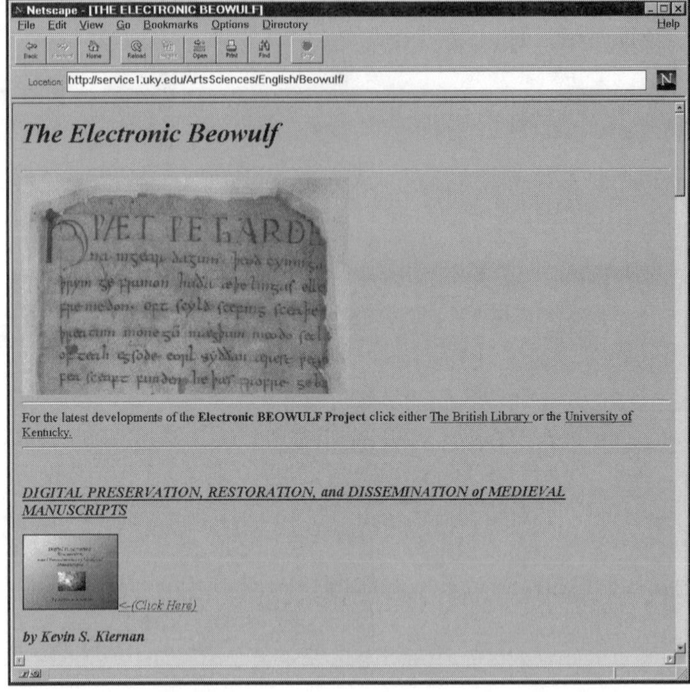

Figure 12.8.
The Electronic Beowulf home page, with clickable images.

Task 12.5: Find business sites dealing with management in Open Market's Commercial Sites Index.

If it's business information you want, Open Market maintains an extremely useful meta-list of commercial Internet sites. The list is organized alphabetically, but you can search for specific products or locations (or anything else) as well. The index has grown by leaps and bounds over the past year, and will continue to do so as the months go by. To find business sites dealing with management in Open Market's Commercial Sites Index, follow these steps:

1. Enter the Commercial Sites Index at the following address:

   `http://www.directory.net/`

2. In the search box, type the word `management`.
3. Click on the Search button. The result will be a page much like Figure 12.9, although with different entries.
4. Click on an entry that looks interesting.

Notice that you can also browse the Commercial Sites Index alphabetically, searching for hyperlinks to companies that interest you. To find the Rockefeller Center, for example, click on the link named alphabetical listings from the main page, and then click on the letter `R` at the top of the page. On the resulting screen, scroll to the link named Rockefeller Center.

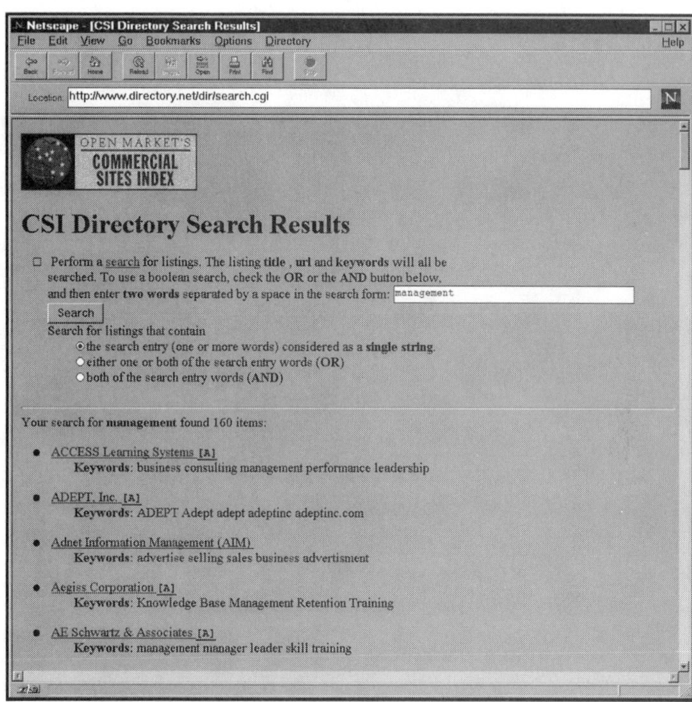

Figure 12.9.
The results of a search for sites dealing with management in the Commercial Sites Index.

Using the World Wide Web Search Engines

In Chapter 5, you accessed the World Wide Web's popular meta-lists—Yahoo, The EINet Galaxy, The Whole Internet Catalog, and The Virtual Library. Each of these sites offers its own search mechanisms. This does not revisit them, however. Instead, this chapter explores Web sites that are designed exclusively for searching purposes.

Task 12.6: Find information about baseball through the CUI W3 Catalog.

One of the oldest search pages on the Web, the *W3 Catalog* selects its information from a variety of sources on the Internet. The main CUI home page resides on a Swiss machine (`http://cuiwww.unige.ch/w3catalog`), but several other sites are available. A U.S. mirror exists at `http://www.winc.com/W3Catalog.html`, and this is shown in Figure 12.10. To find information about baseball through the CUI W3 Catalog, follow these steps:

1. Enter the CUI mirror site at **`http://www.smartpages.com`**.
2. In the search box, type the word **`baseball`**.
3. Click on the Submit button.

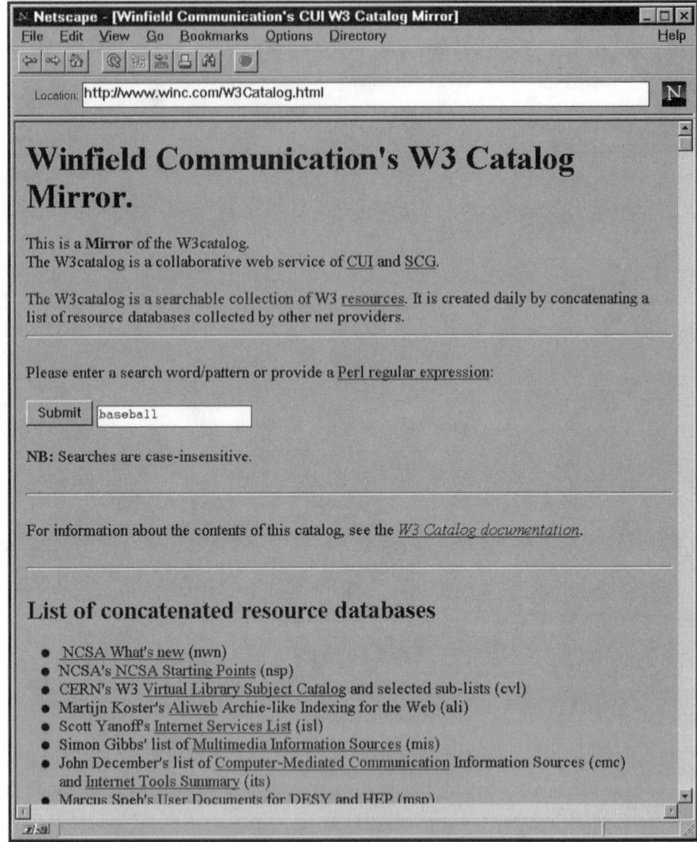

Figure 12.10.
U.S. mirror site for Winfield Communications' W3 Catalog.

The result of your search will appear in a few minutes. The lower portion of a typical results page appears in Figure 12.11.

Figure 12.11.
Result of the search for baseball information through W3 Catalog.

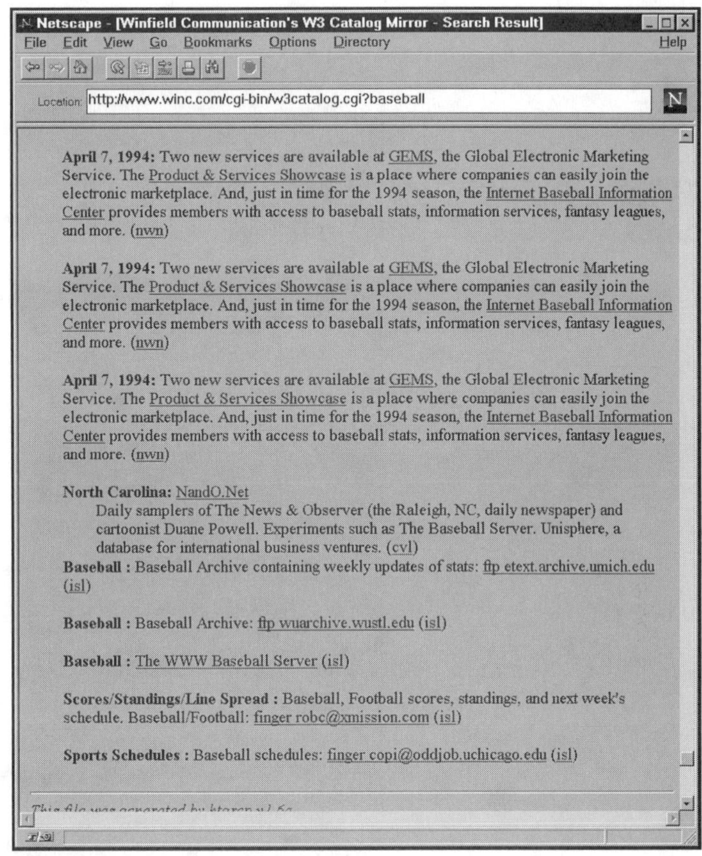

Notice the bracketed initials at the end of each entry; this tells you where the information originally came from. The sites in Figure 12.11 include `nwn` (NCSA's What's New page), `cvl` (Cern's Virtual Library), and `isl` (Internet-services mailing list). You can click on the initials to go directly to these information sites.

Task 12.7: Search for information about constitutions through ALIWEB.

ALIWEB is an acronym for *Archie-like Indexing for the Web.* ALIWEB goes a bit further than plain Archie, however, enabling you to select the fields and document types you want to search. To search for information about constitutions through ALIWEB, follow these steps:

1. Enter the ALIWEB search form at the following address:

   `http://www.cs.indiana.edu/aliweb/form.html`

   Several mirror sites are also available. Figure 12.12 shows this page.

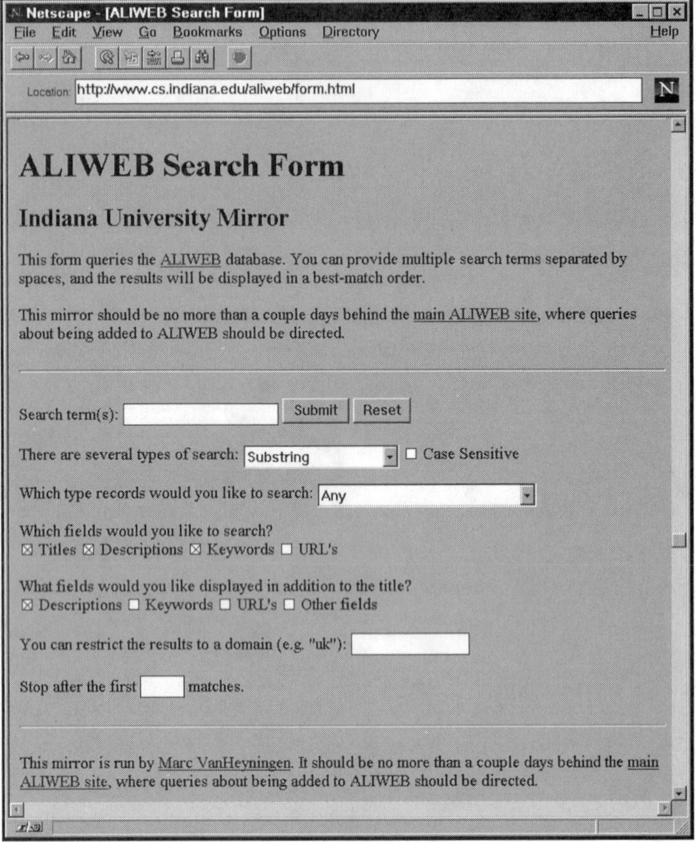
Netscape - [ALIWEB Search Form]
File Edit View Go Bookmarks Options Directory Help
Location: http://www.cs.indiana.edu/aliweb/form.html

ALIWEB Search Form

Indiana University Mirror

This form queries the ALIWEB database. You can provide multiple search terms separated by spaces, and the results will be displayed in a best-match order.

This mirror should be no more than a couple days behind the main ALIWEB site, where queries about being added to ALIWEB should be directed.

Search term(s): Submit Reset

There are several types of search: Substring Case Sensitive

Which type records would you like to search: Any

Which fields would you like to search?
Titles Descriptions Keywords URL's

What fields would you like displayed in addition to the title?
Descriptions Keywords URL's Other fields

You can restrict the results to a domain (e.g. "uk"):

Stop after the first matches.

This mirror is run by Marc VanHeyningen. It should be no more than a couple days behind the main ALIWEB site, where queries about being added to ALIWEB should be directed.

Figure 12.12.
ALIWEB search page with several selectable items.

2. In the search box, type **`constitution`**. Click on the keywords item in Which fields would you like to search? and click on URL's in the following set of choices. Tell ALIWEB to stop after the first 30 matches.
3. Click on the Submit button. The results appear as shown in Figure 12.13.

Among other things, there are locations for the U.S. Constitution (and amendments), the Consitution for Pennsylvania, and the German Constitution. Sounds like interesting reading.

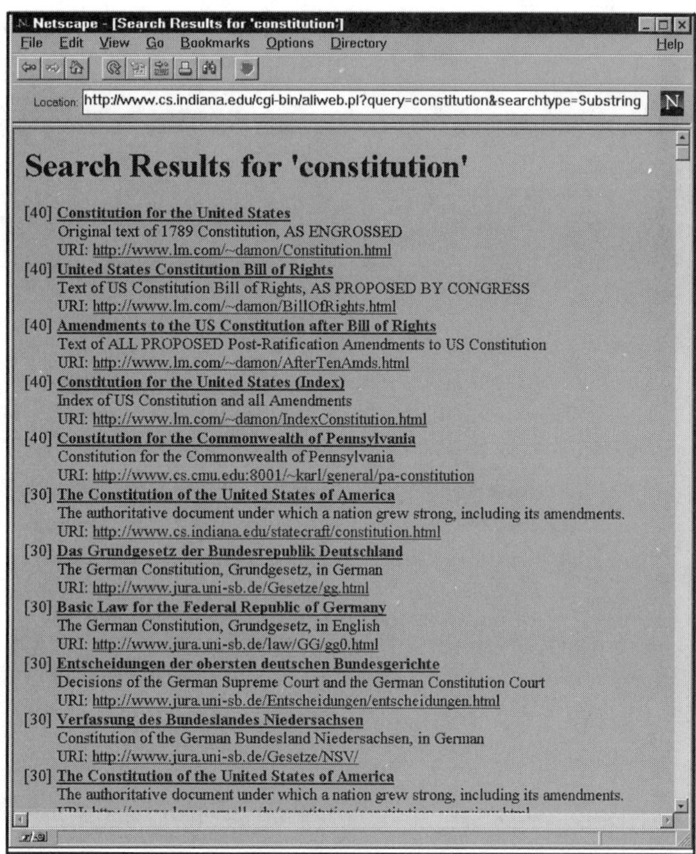

Figure 12.13.
Results of ALIWEB search for "constitution."

Task 12.8: Find information about the European Community through the World Wide Web Worm.

The Worm, or WWWW as it's called, offers an extremely simple search form and some very complete results. To find information about the European Community through the World Wide Web Worm, follow these steps:

1. Enter the WWWW site at the following address:

   `http://www.cs.colorado.edu/home/mcbryan/WWWW.html`

2. In the top box, select Search all URL references.
3. In the second box, select AND-match all keywords.
4. In the number of matches box, select 500 matches (why not make it extensive?).
5. In the keywords box, type **`european community`**. Note that the AND options selected previously demands that WWWW finds documents that contain *both* of the two words, not just one or the other.

6. Click the Start Search button. The result will look much like Figure 12.14, including sites from Hungary, Germany, Belgium, and other nations.

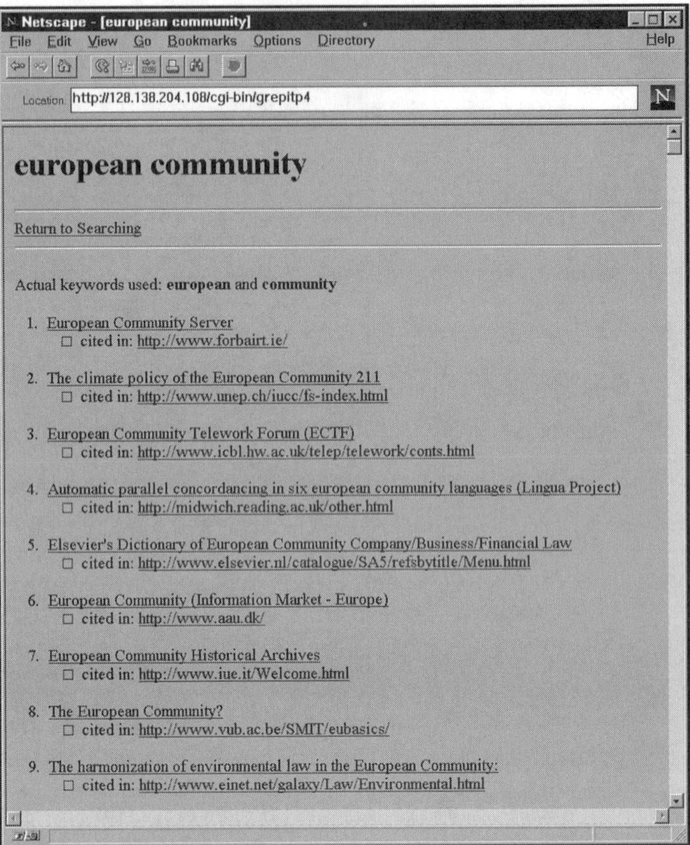

Figure 12.14.
Result of search for European Community in the World Wide Web Worm.

Task 12.9: Search for information about the U.S. Constitution through Lycos.

Lycos has become an important search tool for frequent Web users, because it returns more information than most, although not necessarily more links. To search for information about the U.S. Constitution through Lycos, follow these steps:

1. Enter the Lycos search page at the following address:

   `http://lycos11.lycos.cs.cmu.edu/lycos-form.html`

2. In the Query field, type **`united states constitution`**.

3. In the Max-hits field, type **30** (or any other number you want).
4. In the Min-terms box, type **2**. This tells Lycos that the results you want must include two of the three terms.
5. Leave Min-score as it is, unless you want to guarantee a closer match (see the instructions in the Search language help link). The filled-in form is shown in Figure 12.15.

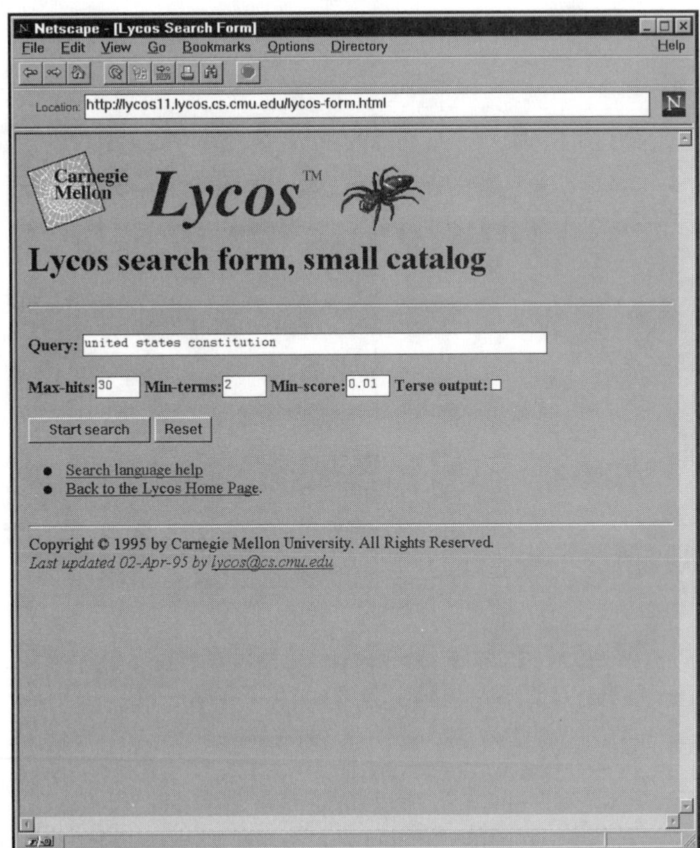

Figure 12.15.
Lycos search form with all fields filled in.

6. Click on the Start search button. You'll receive a listing that looks like Figure 12.16.

The actual results are in the lower half of Figure 12.16 (and the page scrolls considerably). Next to each result is both a score and the number of terms matched. At the top of the page are more potential results.

12

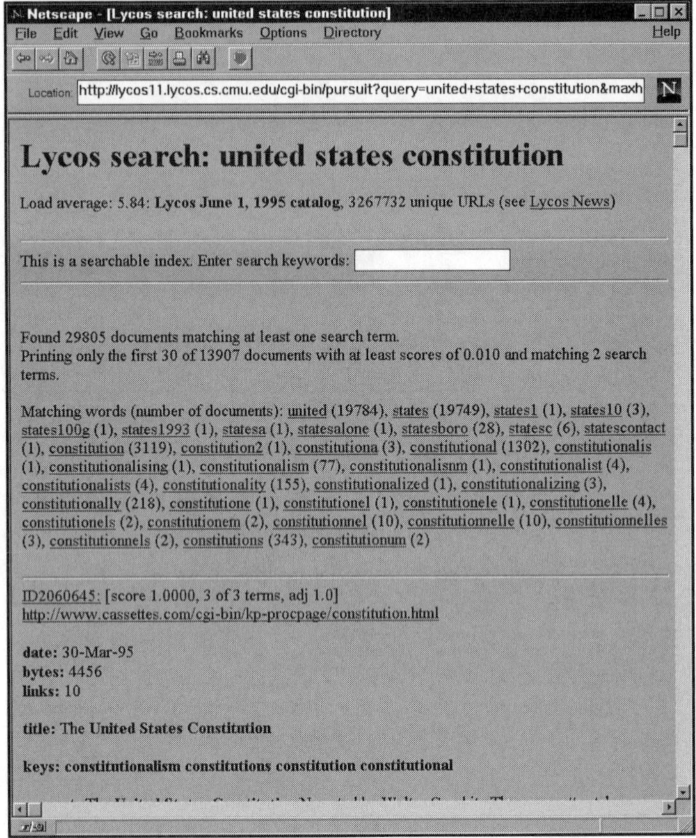

Figure 12.16.
The results of a Lycos search for information about the U.S. Constitution.

Task 12.10: Search for a specific text string in the Open Text Web index.

The *Open Text Web* search is an offering of Open Text Corporation, and it is unique in that it maintains an enormous database of Web-based files in which it searches. When you enter a word or phrase, it finds the matching instances across the Web pages it stores. To search for a specific text string in the Open Text Web index, follow these steps:

1. Enter the Open Text Web Index at the following address:

   `http://www.opentext.com:8080/`

2. In the Quick Search box, type **`to be or not to be`**. Let's see if there is some Shakespeare out there on the Web.
3. Click the Search button. The results will appear as they do in Figure 12.17.

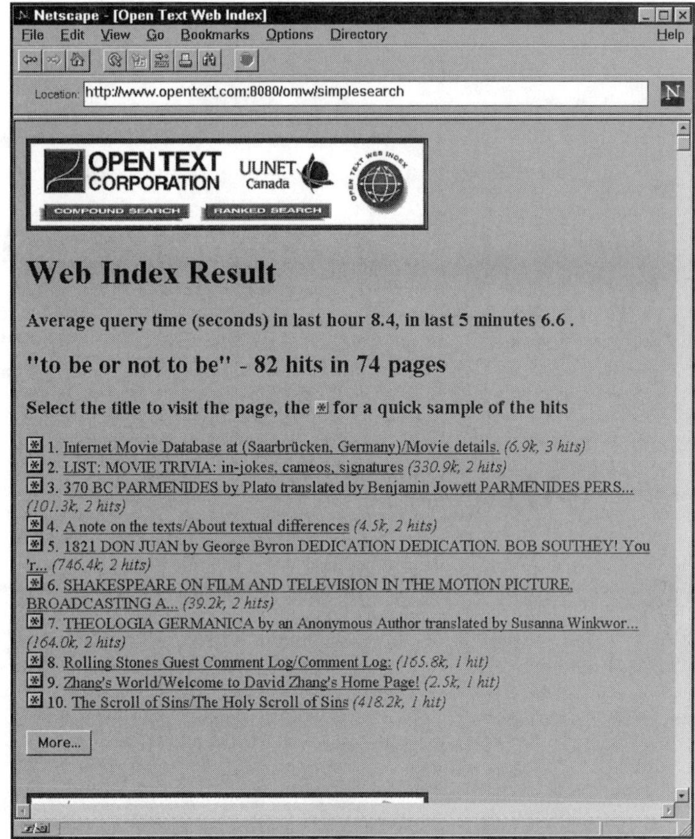

Figure 12.17.
Results of search for `to be or not to be` *in Open Text Web Index.*

4. Click the More button if you want to see more.

You can perform a compound search through the Open Text index as well, by clicking on Compound Search in the company logo box. A ranked search is possible as well. This is a fast, well-designed search site.

Combined Search Sites

Now that you know so many ways to search the Web for information, you'll be pleased to know that other helpful individuals have combined the various search tools so you don't have to access them separately. Here, you'll access three of them, each with its own characteristics.

CUSI

The *CUSI* page combines all major Web-based search engines. Mirrored at several sites, one of which is shown in Figure 12.18, this page enables you to search via CUI, ALIWEB, Yahoo, the EINet Galaxy, Lycos, and others. You also can access Archie and Veronica, and you can even use Netfind and a number of online dictionaries. This page is highly useful.

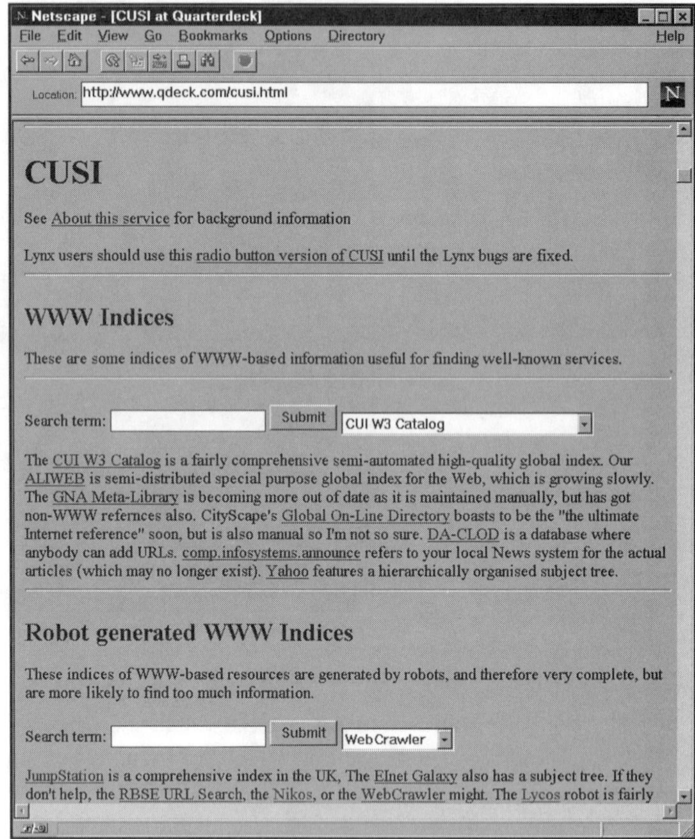

Figure 12.18.
The CUSI combined search page at `http://www.qdeck.com/cusi.html`.

W3 Search Engines

Located at `http://cuiwww.unige.ch/meta-index.html`, the *W3 Search Engines* page, like CUSI, combines all the major Web search tools. The home page encourages you to download a copy for your own site (including your PC), since it does nothing but point to other sites and can thus be used locally (that is, you don't have to be at the Swiss computer to conduct a search). Figure 12.19 shows the search boxes and submit buttons for several of the search engines.

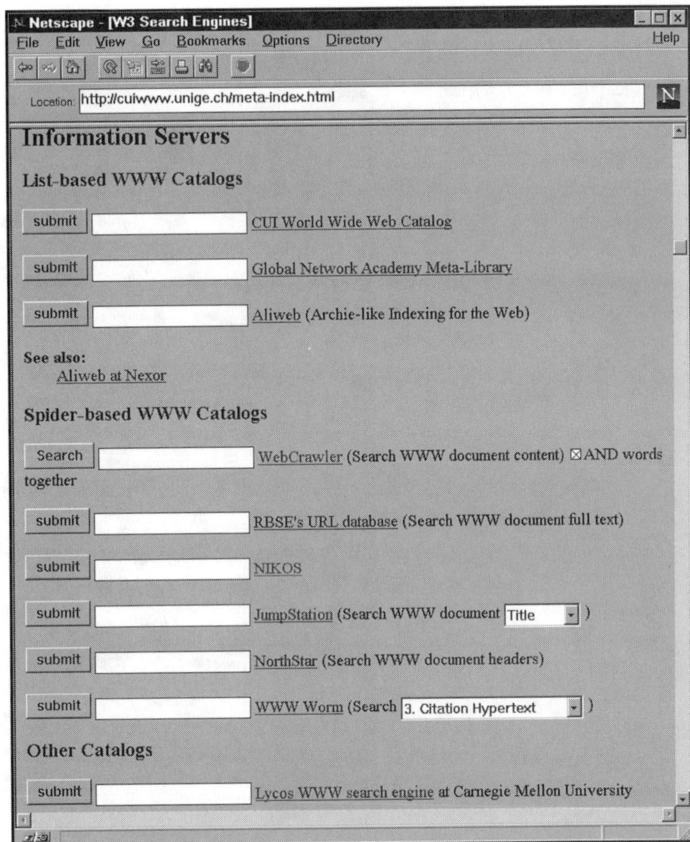

Figure 12.19.
Searches are available directly from the W3 Search Engines page.

12

Search Engine Room

You can't actually do searches from the *Search Engine Room*, but you can access any search engine on the Web from this useful imagemap. Available at `http://www.nosc.mil:80/plant_earth/library.html`, this page is shown in Figure 12.20, and new items are added as they come into being.

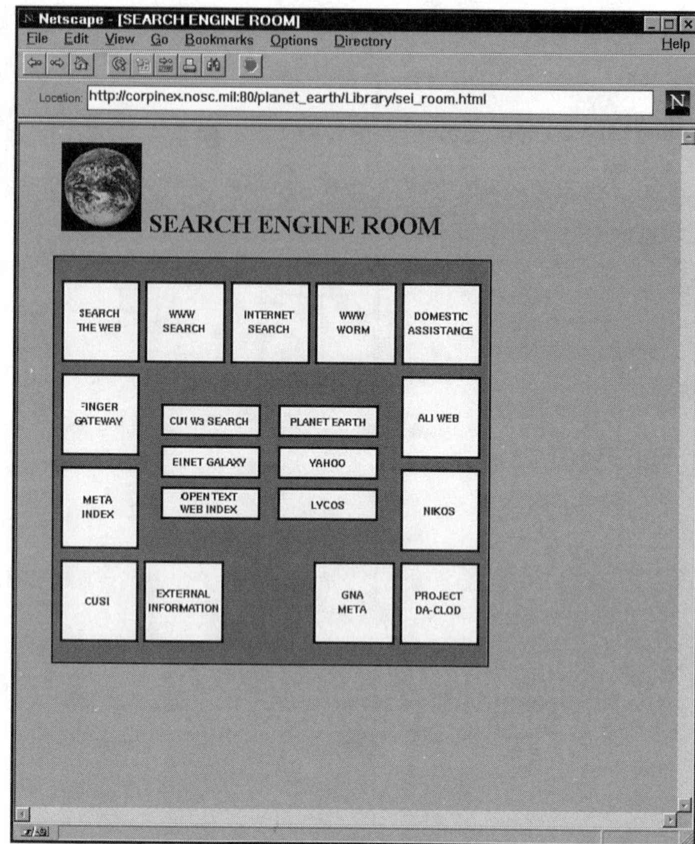

Figure 12.20.
The Search Engine Room gives you all the search engines on one easily used imagemap.

Summary

You'll never find everything you want on the World Wide Web, not without hour upon countless hour of browsing, searching, and cataloging. But it's no longer as hopeless as it once was, because a number of enterprising (and kind-hearted) programmers have developed subject lists and search tools to help you find your way around. As you become more accustomed to the Web and its many resources, you'll find these catalog and search tools increasingly valuable, and very quickly you'll wonder how you ever got along without them. They can be frustrating, and they can lead you widely astray, but for the most part they're indispensable.

Task Review

In this chapter, you were shown how to accomplish the following tasks:

- ☐ Use the World Wide Web meta-lists to find information about specific topics
- ☐ Use the major World Wide Web search engines to search the Web for information you might be interested in
- ☐ Learn of the whereabouts and functions of the combined search engine pages

Key Terms

The number of new terms you'll have to learn to master the Web's search tools is quite small. Within specific search engines, you'll find words and phrases peculiar to that particular type of search, but they're usually explained somewhere on the engine's pages. Here are a few, as a means of getting you started.

Combined Search Engines—Recent search pages offer access to several search facilities through one standard interface. The most sophisticated are multi-threaded, meaning you can search for one topic or phrase across several different search tools simultaneously. Look for more such sites in the future.

Meta-list—Also known as meta-index or meta-directory, these listings offer links to a wide variety of Web resources, and are usually sorted by topic.

Search Engine—An Internet search engine is a program (or set of programs) that enables you to search for specific words, phrases, or other items in a variety of ways. Most meta-lists include search engines, but many search engines are not meta-lists.

Q&A

Q Often when I try a search, I get link after link with unrelated information. What am I doing wrong?

A Maybe nothing. Maybe everything. Sorry to be so vague, but it's often extremely hard to tell if you're using a search engine correctly (or at least efficiently). Be sure to read the instructions on the search engine's page, if any exist. And be sure to understand how your search engine treats multi-word phrases.

For example, searching for an item such as `Academy Awards nominations` will give you different results in different search engines. Some will give you links to all pages it found that contain *any* of the three words, so you'll get some with `academy`, some with `awards`, and some with `nominations`. In these sites, you might need to specify that you want them all searched as one, and you might require the word `and` between all terms. `Academy AND Awards AND nominations` is known as a Boolean `AND` search, and it tells the engine to look for pages that contain *all* the links. These types of searches can become quite complex, and some search pages have basic and advanced interfaces to enable you to narrow your searches as you wish. Learning complex searches is anything but easy, however, so be prepared to spend some time with them.

Q If the Web is so big, how do the search engines do their job?

A The flippant answer is, "with a great deal of difficulty." And it's true. Search engine designers create programs that go out onto the Net and search for Web pages, Gopher sites, FTP sites, and other locations, and then download the text of these sites to feed into searchable databases. In addition to these tools, Net users spend hours going through new sites and feeding them into databases. The Web is changing constantly, so don't expect your searches to be absolutely up-to-date. On the other hand, even a slightly outdated search is better than doing all this work yourself.

DAY

5

The Internet at Home

13

DAY 5

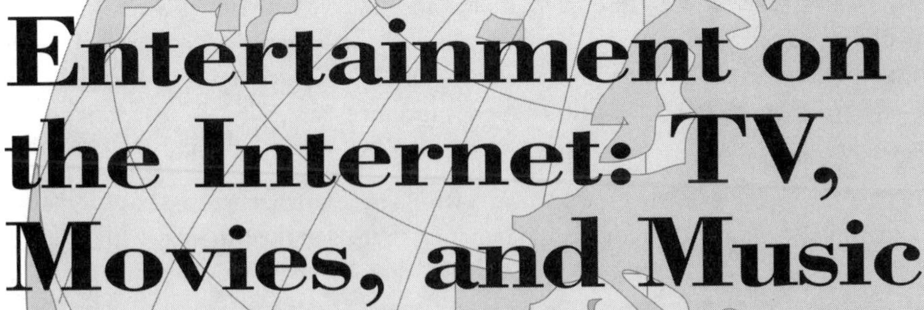

Entertainment on the Internet: TV, Movies, and Music

Television, movies, and music are such popular forms of entertainment that it's hardly surprising they've made their way onto the Internet. The Net allows the marketing of these entertainment forms, as well as discussion and exchange of ideas from fans and critics alike. While you can't actually watch a movie or a TV show on the World Wide Web, you can retrieve still photos, actor biographies, and all kinds of fan information. The music scene is the same, although here you can actually get entire songs for the asking. This is a quickly growing area.

Task List

In this chapter, you'll learn to perform the following tasks:

- ☐ Join television-oriented newsgroups
- ☐ Explore television-oriented Web sites
- ☐ Examine a TV network available online
- ☐ Maneuver through the Internet Movie Database
- ☐ Examine other motion picture resources online
- ☐ Discover the riches of the Internet Underground Music Archive

Entertainment on the Internet

The three major forms of entertainment today are television, movies, and music. People—many people, in fact—enjoy them. And these people don't just sit back and enjoy these entertainments passively; they discuss their likes and dislikes with others (often vigorously), they read reviews and critiques, and they watch awards shows in the hopes that their favorites will be given the acknowledgment they deserve. Some people go so far as to write letters and, yes, e-mail messages to the entertainment stars, and for (thankfully) a very few it goes even further than that.

In other words, and despite what the TV critics would have you believe, media entertainment is already active, already *inter*active. Small wonder, then, that the Internet, with its inherent interactivity, would have so much to offer. On the Net today are discussions and sites dealing with just about any entertainment issue you could want, and if you don't find what interests you, you can even establish a site or newsgroup of your own. In this chapter, Stephanie Wunder takes you on a small tour of the Net's entertainment archives, but let me caution you in advance that this is barely the tiniest tip of the entertainment iceberg.

Television and the Net: A Growing Partnership

by Stephanie Wunder

Although the pair may seem slightly ironic at first glance, television and the Internet have developed an addictive relationship that will entice even the most reluctant viewers. Intrinsic to this coupling is the fact that television and the Net operate on many of the same basic principles. Users flip from site to site or channel to channel, pluck what interesting details catch the eye, and move on. Both networks possess an enormous addictive power and neither lets us get our work done on time. Inevitably, television, the electronic wave of the century, must merge with the Internet, the electronic wave of the future.

In an effort to maintain its highly utilitarian function, the Internet has taken a fundamentally different approach to entertainment than television. Rather than constructing sites with plots and story lines intending solely to please or amuse (although these do exist), Web users have created a larger number of sites devoted to discussion, updates, trivia, and news about your favorite programs. In this way, the Internet does not threaten to replace or diminish television audiences, but assists in their viewing enjoyment.

The two Internet areas most strongly affected by the computerized activity of television networks are newsgroups and the World Wide Web. This chapter explores both forums to attain an adequate understanding of the presence and potential for what I will call, *TVNet.*

Task 13.1: Subscribe to and explore some TV-oriented newsgroups.

Your experience with newsgroups up to this point in your Internet education has probably indicated that if you can think of a topic, a discussion group dealing with that topic usually exists. Newsgroups host a variety of such television-oriented sites or discussion groups, ranging from fan clubs that focus on famous TV celebrities, to sitcom updates, to ethical debates on program content, and more. To sample some of these groups, let's explore Usenet's more popular TV-related entries using Free Agent, a Windows-based newsreader.

1. Fire up the newsreader by double-clicking on the Free Agent icon in your program directory.

> **Tip:** If you haven't used your particular newsreader for a prolonged period of time and the program does not refresh groups automatically, it is a good idea to update existing groups and scan all New Usenet Groups. New television-oriented groups are being constructed continually and you wouldn't want to miss out on any additions.

2. Select the Show All Groups option from the Group menu at the top of your screen or click on the All Groups icon featured in the toolbar.
3. Choose the Find command from the Edit menu or click the Find icon displayed in the toolbar. In the search box, type **`alt.tv`** and then click the Find First button. If you want to save yourself this trouble and have a little time on your hands, this process can be completed by simply scrolling down the full list of group entries until you reach the `alt.tv` listings.

   Now you have reached the largest and most popular newsgroup resource for television sites. Most `alt.tv` listings are categorized by the individual television program or by celebrity name, and you have over 60 entries to choose from just in this section of the All Groups list! Some of the most famous groups are the `90210` sequence. Let's explore these sites as examples of a more active television presence on the Net.
4. Scroll down the alt.tv list until you reach `alt.tv.90210`. To subscribe to this newsgroup, click the Subscribe icon in the toolbar or select the Subscribe command from the Group menu. Your subscription is acknowledged by the newsreader if a small icon appears next to the group name in the All Group list.
5. To read some of the articles in `alt.tv.90210`, double-click on the group name and Free Agent will display the message shown in Figure 13.1.
6. Because the `90210` groups are so active and you just want to browse the entries, select the first option, `Sample 50 Article Headers`.
7. To read any of the sample postings, double-click on the header title and Free Agent will display the full article and any posted replies at the bottom of your screen.

   When I accessed this group, topics included simple gossip about who's cute and who's not, complaints about reruns and program content, and character status on the program. In essence, the `90210` groups consist of the same types of conversations you may have with a friend about a particular episode or character. In this respect, newsgroups are probably the most informal venue on the Net, but some participants take their membership very seriously, so remember to post according to the rules of netiquette.
8. Read through a sample of articles contained in this group to decide if you want to remain subscribed and access the entire list of article headers. If you want to

unsubscribe from the group, simply highlight the Newsgroup name and click the Subscribe button once again.

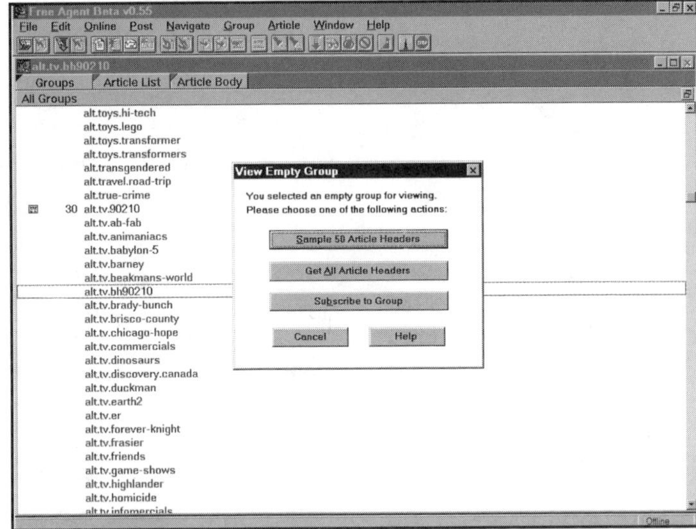

Figure 13.1.
Reading articles using Free Agent.

9. The other main 90210 newsgroup is located at `alt.tv.bh90210`. If you are interested, scroll down and repeat the preceding steps to view some additional postings. Otherwise, browse the alternate `alt.tv` groups to find one that suits your tastes. Figure 13.2 shows a sample of the type of headers you are likely to see in the `alt.tv.bh90210` newsgroup.

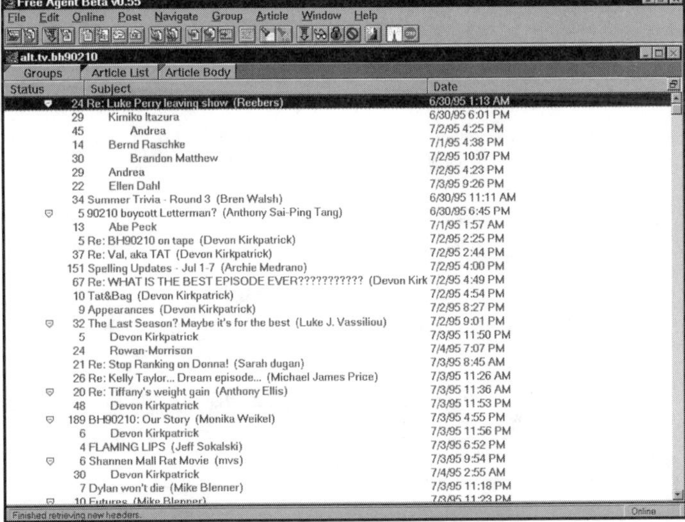

Figure 13.2.
Sample headers from `alt.tv.bh90210`*.*

The second main selection of television-oriented newsgroups is located much further down on the All Groups list and begins with `rec.arts.tv`.

10. Select the Find command from the Edit menu and type **`rec.arts.tv`** in the search box. Click the Find first button.
11. The first entry that Free Agent will take you to is `rec.arts.tv`, a miscellaneous television site that deals with virtually any issue on any television show you want to discuss. Double-click on the title and retrieve a sample of this group's article headers or subscribe to the group by choosing the Subscribe icon at the top of your screen.
12. The `rec.arts.tv` listings also contain a series of more generalized soap opera sites, including `rec.arts.tv.soaps`, `rec.arts.tv.soaps.abc`, `rec.arts.tv.soaps.cbs`, and `rec.arts.tv.soaps.misc`. Soap operas are famous for their capability to incorporate an audience directly into the plot as quasi-participants in their characters' lives. Newsgroups offer a venue for discussion among these participants and assist viewers with updates and answers to questions that members may have about their favorite daytime shows.
13. To find those television newsgroups that may be of interest to you, simply conduct a Find search or spend some time scrolling through the All Groups list at random.

The profound impact that television has had on the Internet is most evident with the development of international TV sites, such as `chile.tv`, `aus.tv`, or `zer.z-netz.freizeit.tv`. Even local TV networks and sponsors have established Net sites for audience information updates, but most of this activity takes place on the World Wide Web itself, so we now move to the heart of the Internet.

Task 13.2: Find and explore some television-oriented Web sites.

Because Yahoo offers one of the most diverse and accurate resource pages on the Net, it seems to be the obvious starting point for a thorough television exploration. Yahoo's home page offers users the capability to locate data by subject or to find sites by conducting a keyword search within the Yahoo entries.

1. Locate the Yahoo home page by typing **`http://www.yahoo.com/`** in the URL box and then pressing Enter. You will receive the Yahoo screen shown in Figure 13.3.
2. Because you are dealing primarily with the entertainment industry, select the Entertainment entry from the main directory. Yahoo will display another directory of more specific entertainment categories.
3. From this directory, select Television by clicking once on the title. You will receive the list of possible sites shown in Figure 13.4.

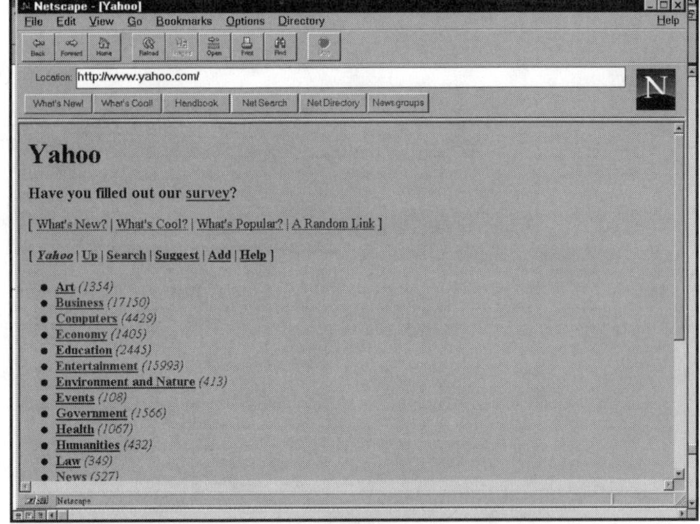

Figure 13.3.
The Yahoo home page with menu listings.

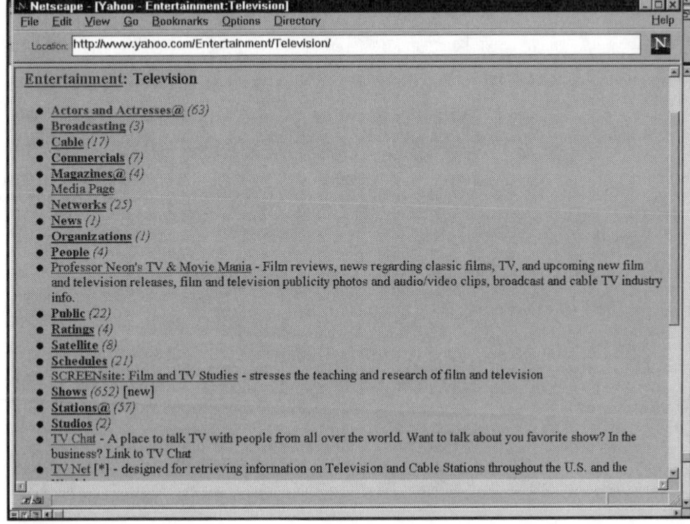

Figure 13.4.
Yahoo's television directory.

Yahoo's television archives provide users with an extensive range of TV sites, incorporating networks, satellites, cable connections, and daily programming into their WWW links. Surf through some of these sites to see what the Web can really do for you.

4. First, access a discussion site similar to those you browsed with Free Agent. Select the TVChat link located near the bottom of Yahoo's television menu. Yahoo should present you with a screen of directions, as shown in Figure 13.5.

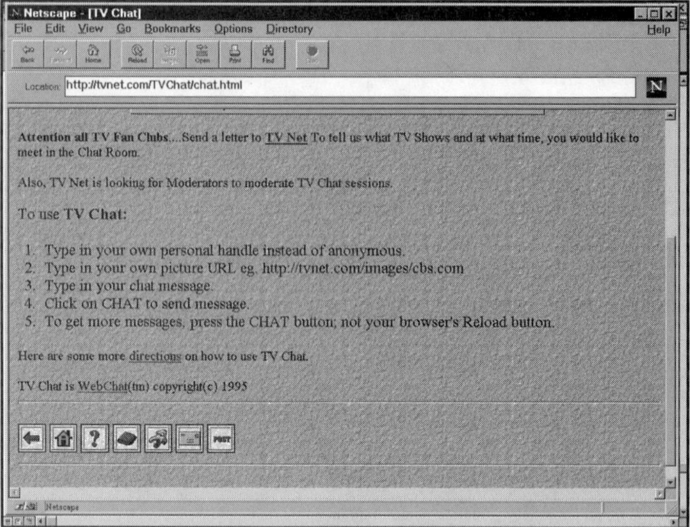

Figure 13.5.
TVChat's introductory directions.

TVChat functions on the same basic principles as a newsgroup, allowing users to post and read each others' messages concerning almost any related topic. When I accessed TVChat, the site was under construction, but the startup directions were clear and concise. Basically, users may construct messages and/or pictures to send to various chat sessions that are categorized by TV show or topic. By reading and posting articles, members may chat back and forth on the Net, just as they would in person. One significant benefit of TVChat is that many chat rooms have moderators who monitor the discussion's content and filter any inappropriate messages, saving users' time and effort.

5. If TVChat is up and running when you access the site, read some of the posted articles—you may even decide to post some of your own. Follow the directions provided by the site's help index and chat away!
6. Now return to Yahoo's main television directory (`http://www.yahoo.com/Entertainment/Television/`) and select the TVNet entry directly below TVChat. You will receive a list of options similar to the screen shown in Figure 13.6.
7. Click on the New TV Links icon to receive a list of recent network additions and their geographical locations. Direct links are provided to these sites so that you can double-click on a station name and travel immediately to the desired site. Updated information is also provided for some of the larger television networks on the Net.
8. Select New TV Shows and you will see the screen shown in Figure 13.7.

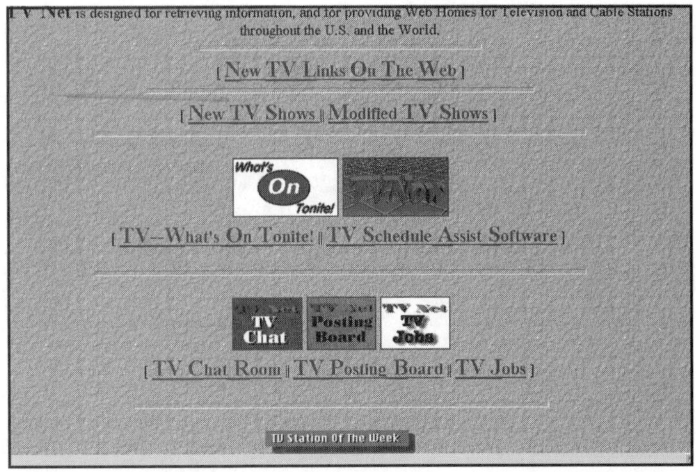

Figure 13.6.
TVNet's home page via Yahoo's Entertainment directory.

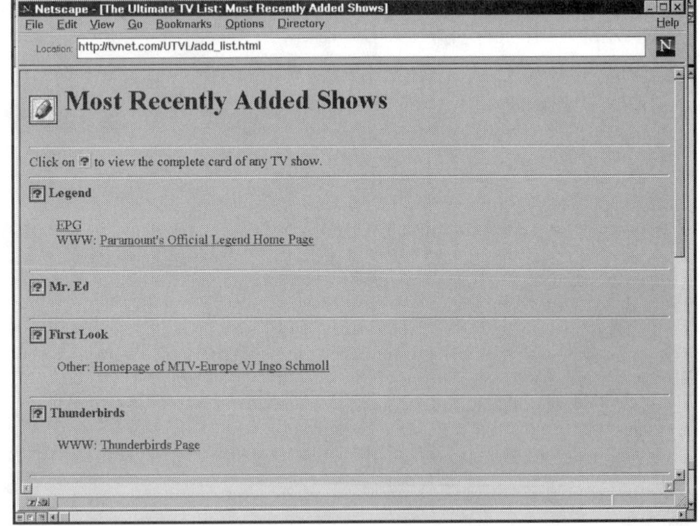

Figure 13.7.
Yahoo's link to New TV Shows on the Net.

This menu provides links to shows, such as *ER*, *A Pup Named Scooby Doo*, or *Robin of Sherwood*. More importantly, the menu contains a link to The Ultimate TV List, a directory of topics that leads to 367 WWW pages and 319 television shows, including *The Simpsons* and *Married with Children*. Figure 13.8 shows an example of the *The Simpsons*' home page and Figure 13.9 shows an example of *Married with Children*'s WWW home page.

Figure 13.8.
The Simpsons' *home page via The Ultimate TV List.*

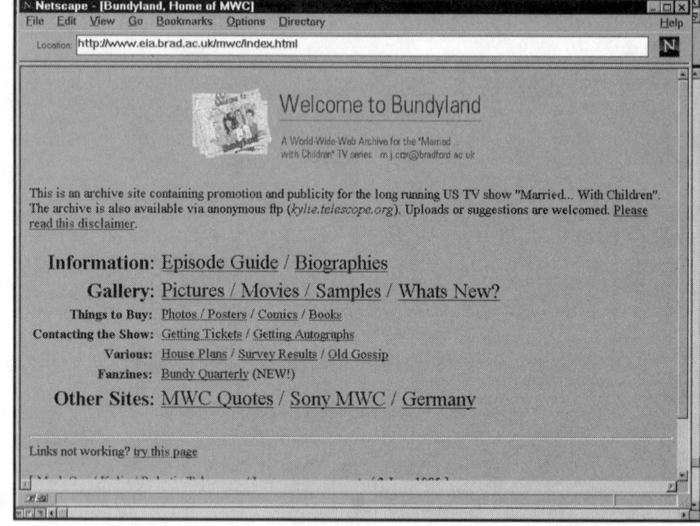

Figure 13.9.
Welcome to Bundyland: a Married with Children *WWW page.*

9. If you are a resident of the United States and want to check the 24-hour weekly television listings in your area, click on the TV-What's on tonite? option and choose your geographical location. Yahoo will provide you with links that produce your own personal *TV Guide* online.
10. Now return to Yahoo's main television directory one last time and browse any other areas of interest to you.

    The first link (Actors and Actresses) provides an alphabetical list of celebrity names that you can select to link you to related home pages, newsgroups, and mailing

lists. You also can access television commercial sites, cable system information, or film and magazine reviews. The most important thing to note about this site is that its information directories provide links that span the full Internet boundaries from Web pages, to Usenet, to mailing lists. Yahoo ensures that your television exploration is thorough and enjoyable. It is impossible, however, for Yahoo to collect *all* television sites that exist on the Net, and I'm interested in seeing what a Web search will produce.

11. Click the Net Search button located on the toolbar at the top of your Netscape screen, or access the search page directly by typing **`http://home.netscape.com/home/internet-search`**.
12. Select the Webcrawler search engine from the listed options and enter **`television`** as your keyword sequence. Because you are looking for a large variety of related archives and not one specific site, set your search result setting at **`100`** and click the Search button. Webcrawler will produce the results shown in Figure 13.10.

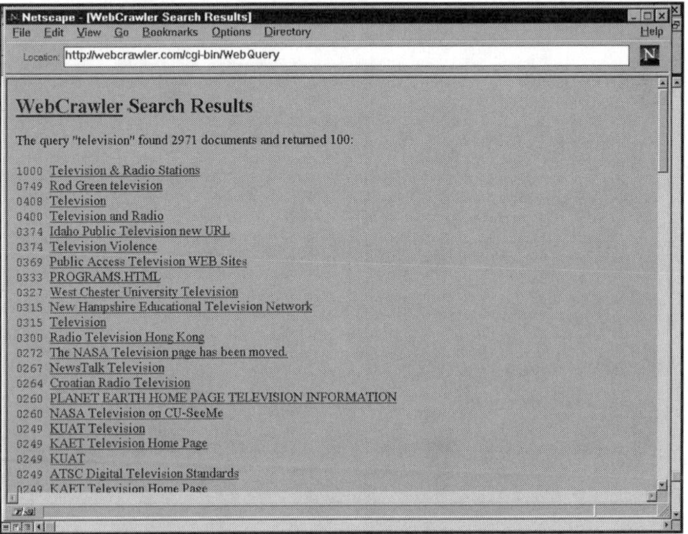

Figure 13.10.
A portion of Webcrawler's television search results.

This search has produced a number of sites that were not featured in Yahoo's directory and that are more news- and radio-oriented. The list contains local television station home pages and information, as well as some more interesting and creative sites. You can access an *Australian TV Guide* or your local networks' news broadcasts, links to specific television show home pages, or cable networks. Figures 13.11, 13.12, 13.13, and 13.14 show examples of the pages you might find in your exploration of these results.

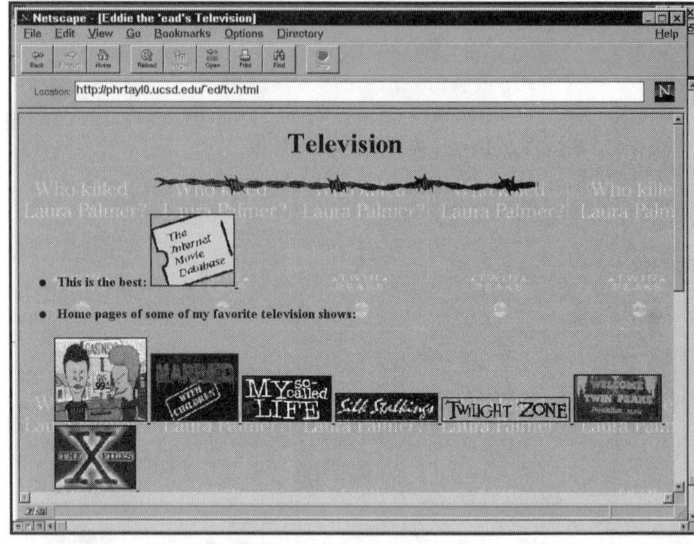

Figure 13.11. *Eddie the 'ead's television site.*

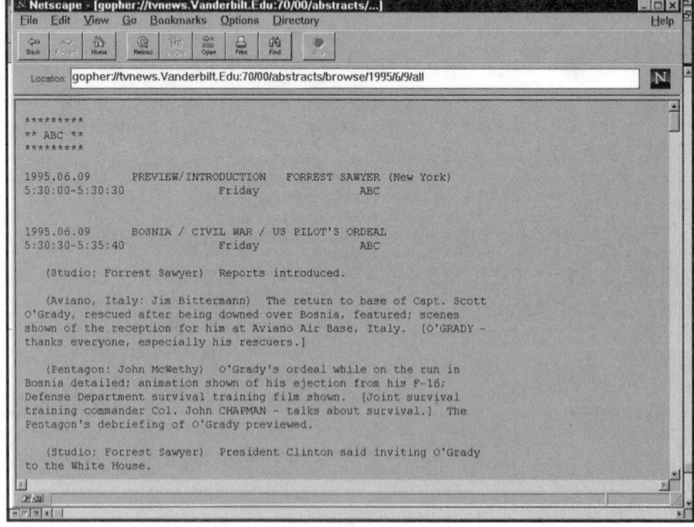

Figure 13.12. *Evening news archives for June 9, 1995, from Vanderbilt University television—not very pretty, but informative.*

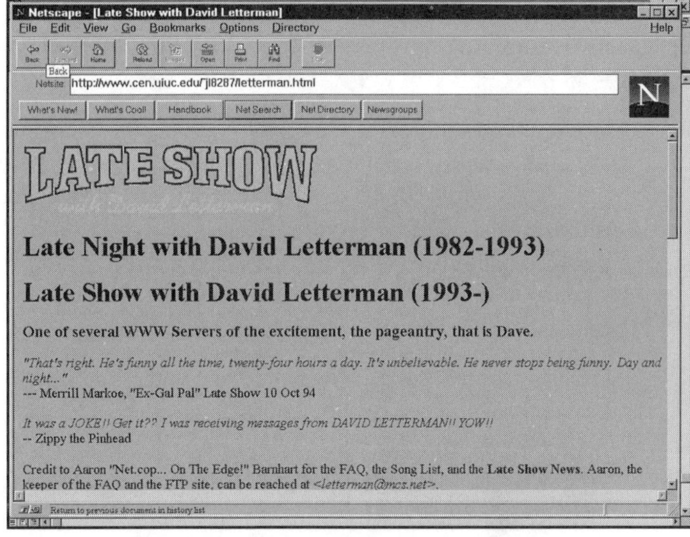

Figure 13.13.
The Late Show with David Letterman page from Links-o-Rama: Television.

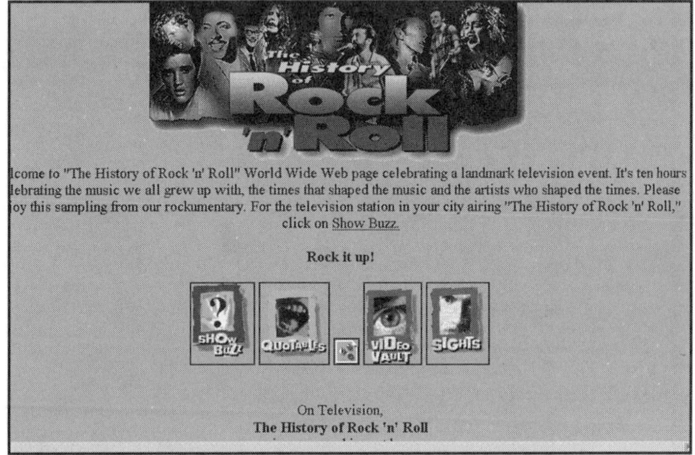

Figure 13.14.
The History of Rock 'n' Roll on the Net.

Task 13.3: Explore a television network on the Net.

So far, you've examined a range of individual television programs and information sites that are located on the World Wide Web, just to give yourself some background on what is actually out there. But what if you want some thorough information on a specific television network, not just on the entertaining shows that network may provide? The Net can assist you in this research as well.

More and more cable networks across the world are picking up on the Net as the technological wave of the future, and are including themselves as part of its development. Newsgroups, mailing lists, and Web sites devoted to specific television broadcasters bombard the Internet with constant updates and additions that add to the more professional aspect of the television entertainment industry. Browse one such network to sample the type of information that is becoming available and to familiarize yourself with the steps involved in attaining this data. Begin with CBS, by following these steps:

1. Browse your current list of television search results. The previous task has given you a range of television-oriented sites to work with, and you know that approximately 2,000 more are available to you, so make use of the results you've already got.
2. Select the PLANET EARTH HOME PAGE TELEVISION INFORMATION link from the search directory. You should receive the list of options shown in Figure 13.15.

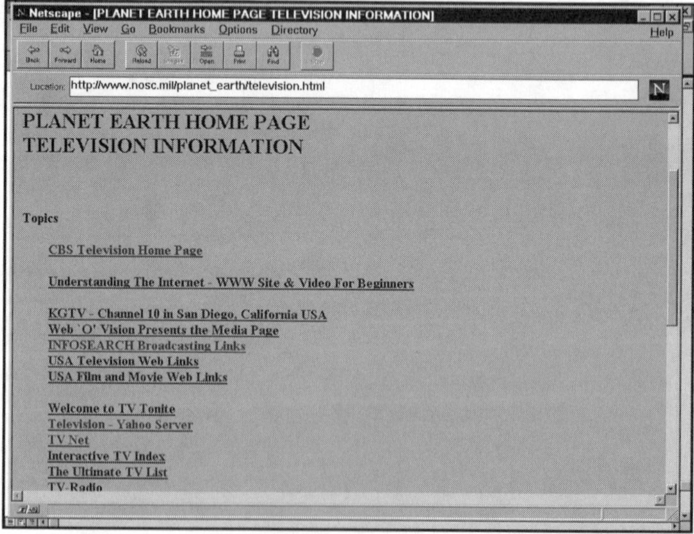

Figure 13.15.
The Planet Earth home page directory of television links.

I was prepared to direct you to the INFOSEARCH Broadcasting Links, but already you have a direct link to the CBS home page. This may seem like an unbelievable coincidence but often that's exactly how the Net works…by chance.

3. Click on the CBS link and you will see the screen shown in Figure 13.16.

   The CBS home page gives us direct links to specific shows that it hosts as well as to more technical considerations, such as weekly programming and preview schedules or information on actors, actresses, and producers.

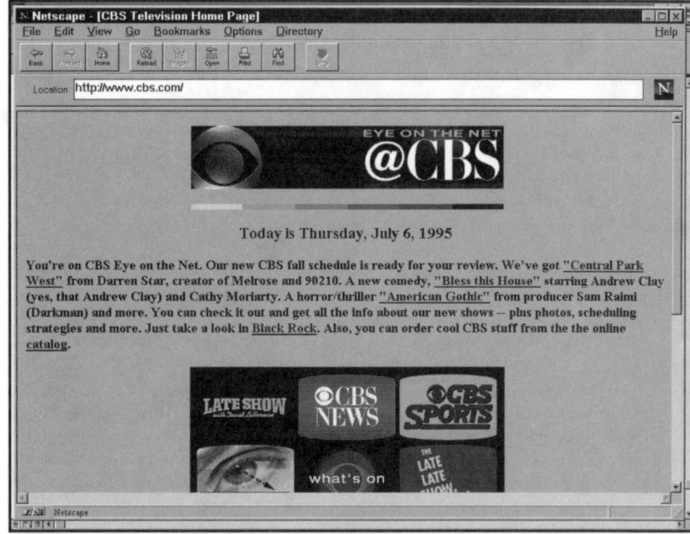

Figure 13.16.
The CBS home page from Planet Earth's directory.

Tip: If you want to explore the CBS archive at a quicker pace, select the "text only" link at the bottom of the home page and all graphics will be removed. This makes surfing much faster but you lose aesthetic appeal.

4. Click the CBS News icon from the graphical directory and you will be given access to the types of pages shown in Figures 13.17 and 13.18.

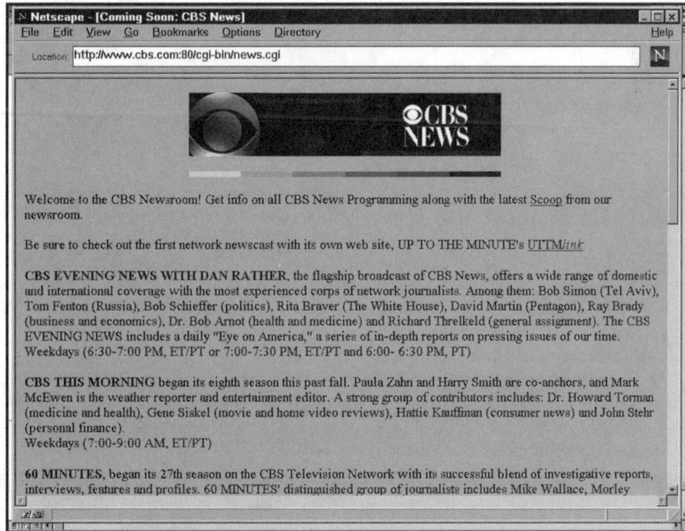

Figure 13.17.
A description of all available CBS News programs and their features.

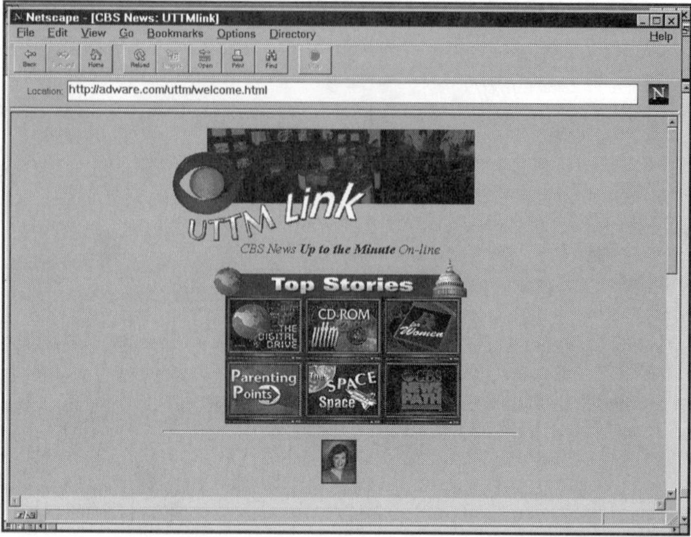

Figure 13.18.
CBS's UTTM link: Up to the Minute online.

The last link provides another directory of issues and shows to choose from and could lead you to more extensive pages. Remember that you are still in the CBS News link that you accessed from the CBS home page and seven other options still await.

5. Browse this area as much as you want and then to return to the CBS home page, type **`http://www.cbs.com/`** in the Location box and press Enter.
6. Now select the CBS Sports link from the top right corner of the graphical icon box and you will see the screen shown in Figure 13.19.

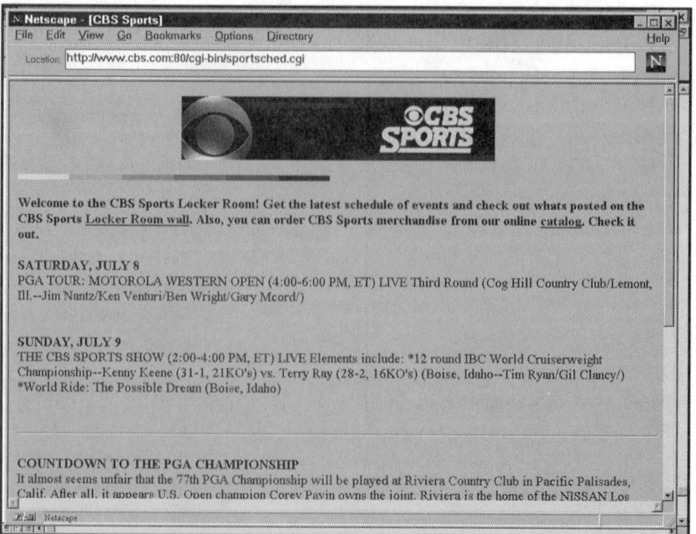

Figure 13.19.
The CBS Sports home page directory.

The CBS Sports page gives a list of upcoming sporting events, as well as access to two main links. The first is the Locker Room wall page and the second is a catalog of sporting merchandise that is available to you for purchase directly on the Net, as shown in Figure 13.20. For more information on purchasing these products see Chapter 19, "Shopping on the Net."

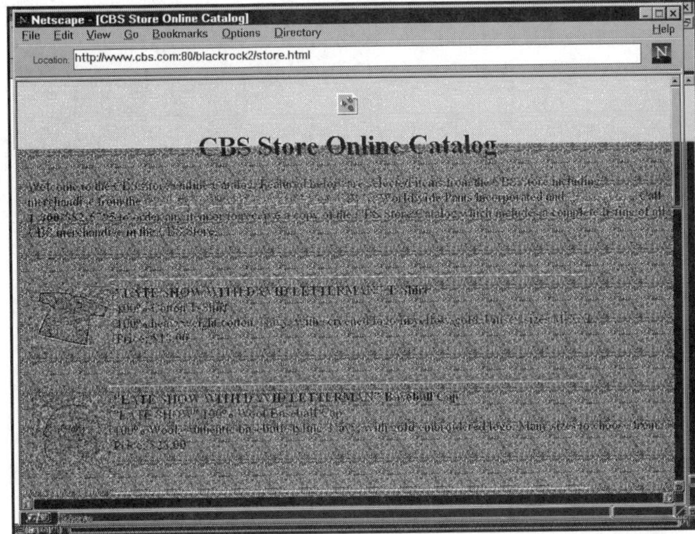

Figure 13.20.
CBS merchandise available for purchase.

7. Move on to the next CBS site by returning to the home page and selecting Black Rock. This site provides the current CBS fall schedule and marketing information links. Figure 13.21 shows an example of what the page might look like.

   The Eye on Club link from the CBS home page leads to a club entry form. If you want to join the Eye on Club and maintain an active participation in the CBS archives, fill out the form and follow the membership directions.

8. Continue to surf the CBS links as long as you want and remember that the pages are updated daily so that you can start all over again tomorrow. Also remember that this entire archive of information came from one search result in your Webcrawler television search. To conduct an even more thorough exploration of CBS, continue surfing the Webcrawler list to see what you can find.

   You have gained extensive knowledge of the CBS home page and related links, but how do you know if there is anything else on the Net concerning the CBS network? And what about newsgroups or mailing lists? Finding the answers to these questions is simple, thanks to the Web's Search materials.

9. To begin a Web Search click the NetSearch icon on the toolbar at the top of your Netscape Screen and choose a search engine.

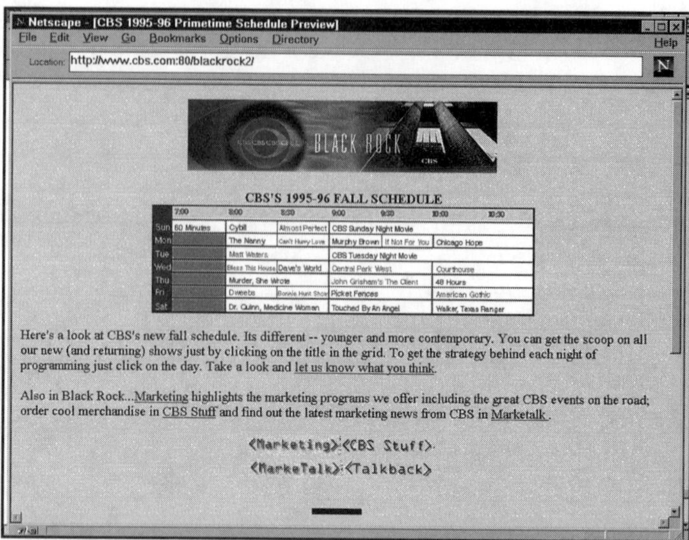

Figure 13.21.
CBS's fall schedule 1995.

10. Type `CBS Network` as your key search words and activate the search. Surf through your results to see if you can locate any additional information.
11. Finally, you move on to newsgroups. Start up your newsreader and display all the active Usenet groups.
12. The easiest way to locate any CBS related newsgroups is to conduct a search (again!). Click the Find... icon at the top of the screen and type **`CBS`** in the search box.

    The only newsgroup you will receive is called `rec.arts.tv.cbs`, but now that you have become more familiar with the programming and content of most CBS broadcasts, you can conduct a more specific search. For example, typing **`letterman`** in the search box yields two additional CBS-related newsgroups.
13. Browse the posted articles at your leisure and remember that newsgroups are where you will find any CBS mailing lists, so keep your eyes open for subscription details.

Although your network study centered on CBS, the same applications will produce similar results with any other network or television show on the Net. As time passes, the archives will grow and improve and more broadcasters will begin to realize the awesome potential that the Internet possesses as both a marketing and advertising tool. More importantly, these sites increase viewer interest and may even boost their ever-important ratings by embracing another technological resource.

Movies

One of the largest money-making businesses in the world today is the motion picture industry. Each week, new features call millions of avid moviegoers to local cinemas where the glitz and glamour of Hollywood becomes momentarily real.

Motion pictures have the intense and powerful capability to capture our hearts and minds, to incorporate a distant audience into a fictional plot, and to leave viewers with an imagined participation. Think of the last time you walked out of a theater with tears in your eyes or a happy smile on your face, and you'll recognize the profound emotional and psychological effect that movies can have on us.

But motion picture mania doesn't stop when the reel is empty. Instead, stores cram their shelves, for weeks and even years, with movie garb—hats, shirts, posters, lunch boxes, and just about anything else you can imagine that would appeal to the movie's prime audience. With hits like *The Lion King* and *Pocahantas* for the children, and *Pulp Fiction* or *Natural Born Killers* for the more adventurous, it became only a matter of time before the movie craze would bombard the Internet...and so it has.

Task 13.4: Locate and explore the Internet Movie Database.

As you may already have suspected, one of the easiest and most organized means of locating movie archives is by accessing Yahoo's Entertainment directory and browsing the available subject headings or conducting a localized search.

Among the many thousands of links displayed, you will find the Internet Movie Database connection, an archive of essential data for avid motion picture fans. To go there now to see just what this database has to offer, follow these steps:

13

1. Access your Web browser and enter **`http://www.yahoo.com/`** in the URL box. Press Enter to submit Yahoo's URL address.
2. From Yahoo's home page, choose the `Entertainment` directory.
3. Now select the Movies and Films heading to take you to a list of directly linked motion picture archives. The screen in Figure 13.22 displays only a portion of the resulting list.
4. Scroll down this list and select The Internet Movie Database. You will see the screen shown in Figure 13.23.

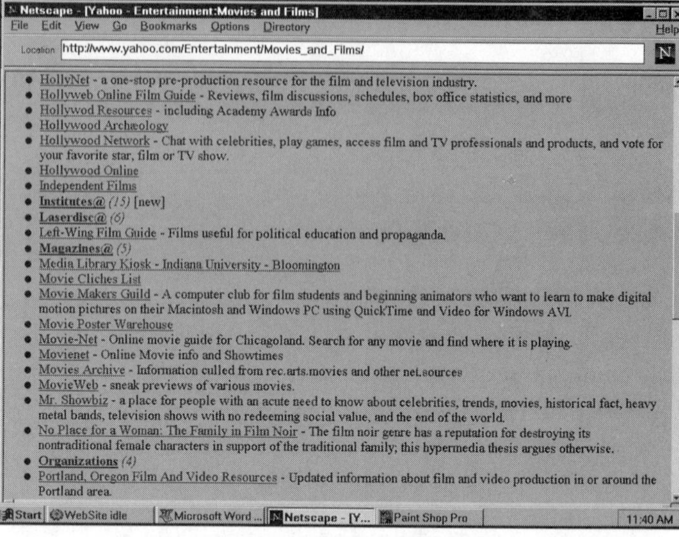

Figure 13.22.
The Yahoo Movie and Film directory.

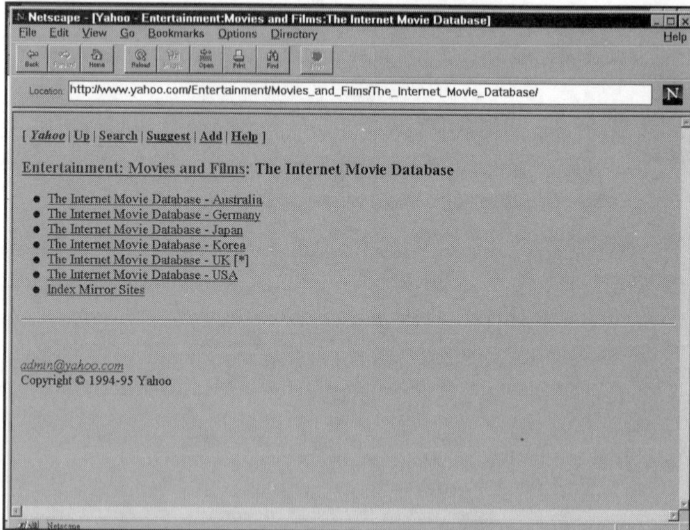

Figure 13.23.
The Internet Movie Database menu.

5. Next, select the Internet Movie Database server that is closest to your geographical location (for most of you, this will be The Internet Movie Database US). All database information is the same, regardless of the site's location, so it makes sense to choose the one closest to you. However, if a particular database is downloading slowly, you do have other options. After accessing a database, you will be given a list of command links and recommended reading for new users.

The Internet Movie Database is host to thousands of movies and their related sites, as well as biographies, reviews, ratings, and trivia. It would be impossible for the site to compile an alphabetical list of entries (as you've seen with the television sites) due to the enormity of the task. Instead, the database offers a search mechanism and guides for touring the WWW links. So choose a particular movie and browse through some of the suggested links.

Because the Batman series has taken the world by storm, conduct a search for any Batman links.

6. Click the Search button from the available commands. You will receive a list of all available types of searches, but for the purpose of this task, click on the Movie title option.
7. Type **`Batman`** in the title search box and click the `Start Title Search` button to activate the process. You should receive a screen of Batman-related links that looks something like Figure 13.24.

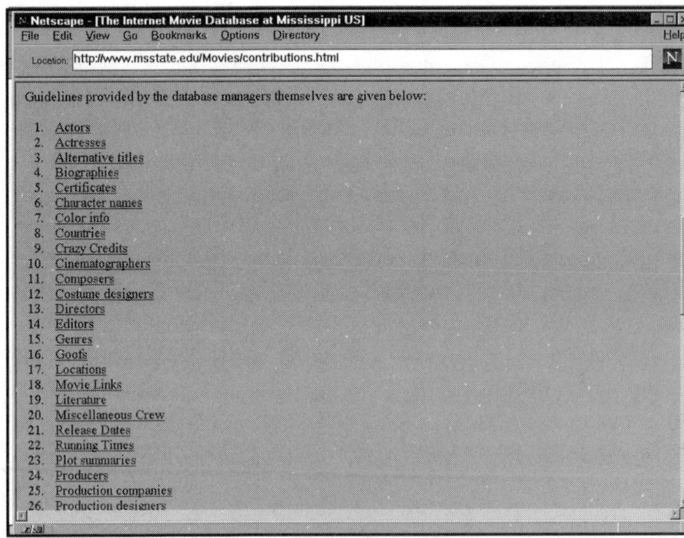

Figure 13.24.
Some suggested guides to the Internet Movie Database.

8. Browse through some of these entries to see what the database contains. The screens in the following three parts of this task are some of the screens that will be accessible from your search. Some may appear the same in your searches, but the site updates regularly and links may change.
9. Click on the Batman Forever link to access the technical data shown in Figure 13.25.

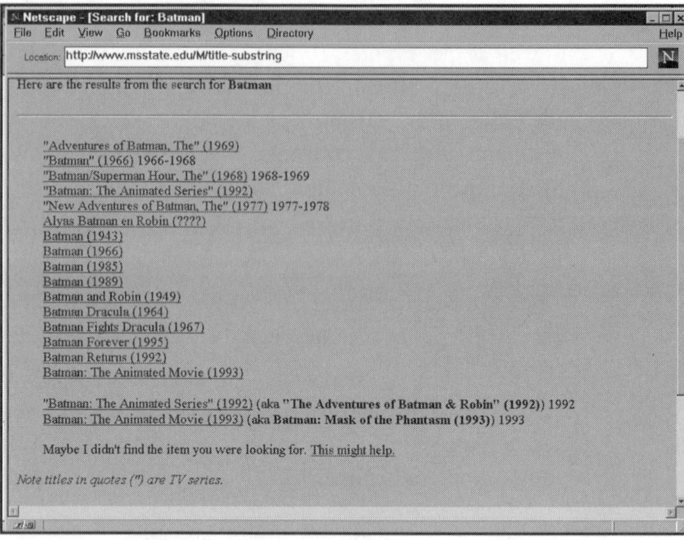

Figure 13.25.
The Internet Movie Database Batman search results.

10. Scroll down this page to view the cast list and rating chart provided with each movie link. If you want, rate the movie by clicking on a number from 1–10.
11. To further explore the Batman Forever archive, click on the additional information icon called Disney MGM 20th C Tristar that appears at the bottom of the screen. This link gives you a screen shot of the *Batman Forever* logo.
12. The additional information icon entitled 4 will display the release dates for the film in a list similar to that shown in Figure 13.26.

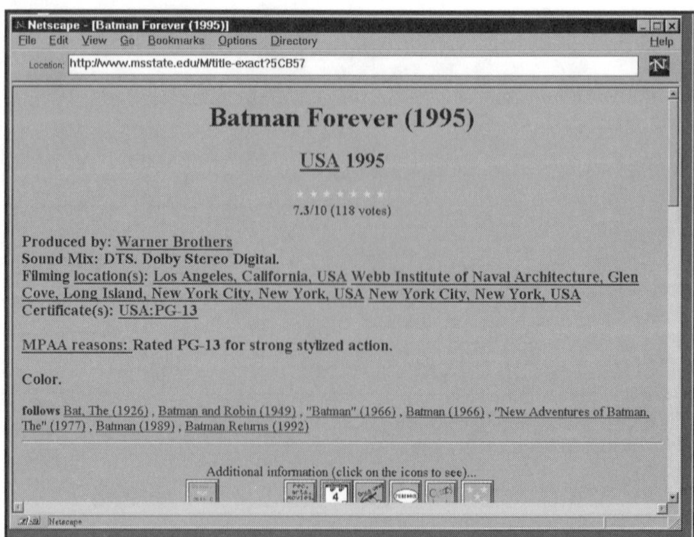

Figure 13.26.
Batman Forever *technical information and rating page.*

13. The other additional information icons give access to sound files of memorable movie quotes, newsgroup discussions, and the results of the Internet audiences rating for the movie. Browse through some of these areas to explore the Internet Movie Database's many possibilities.
14. Now return to the initial search results and select another heading to view. Under *Batman: The Animated Movie* (1993) I found the piece of trivia shown in Figure 13.27.

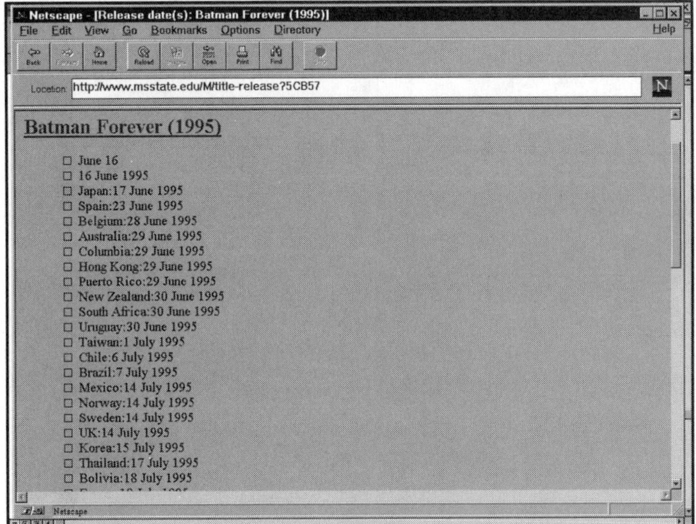

Figure 13.27.
Batman Forever *release dates from the Internet Movie Database.*

15. Scroll down the Search options page of the Internet Movie Database and you will find a resource of additional WWW links concerning more general information (see Figure 13.28).

Now that you have had a brief introduction to the Internet Movie Database, explore the archive by conducting other types of searches on your favorite movies. The sites and search functions operate essentially on the same principles as those you have sampled, and all eventually will lead to a massive storehouse of motion picture information. The truly astounding fact is that you have, up to this point, only explored one link on the Yahoo Movies and Films directory. So move on—much more awaits you.

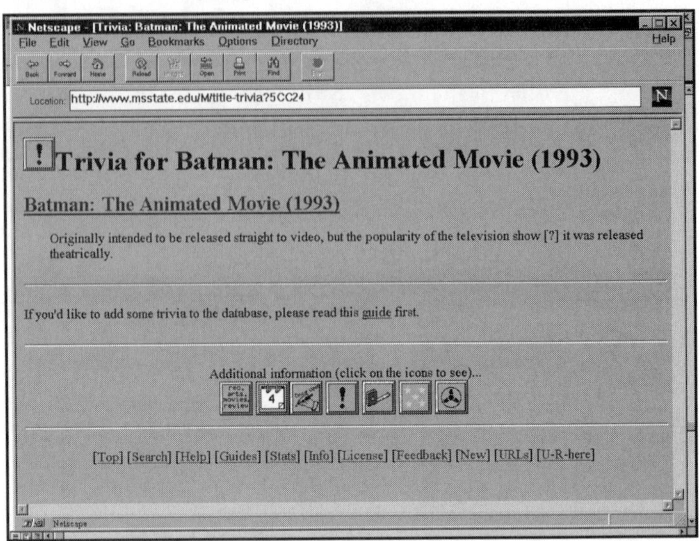

Figure 13.28.
Batman: The Animated Movie *trivia tidbit.*

Task 13.5: Find more motion picture sites on the Net using Yahoo's directory.

Returning to the Yahoo directory gives a sense of the huge span of movie material available electronically. Consider the fact that you may already have spent hours just surfing through the Internet Movie Database, if you were to do this with all the possible sites…well, you get the picture. But there's always time for a few more simple excursions.

1. Select the Awards link at the top of the Yahoo Movie and Film directory and click on the Academy Awards link.
2. Choose the Academy Awards link once again and you will see the screen shown in Figure 13.29.

   This page gives users access to nominee and winner information dating from the 1920s. Clicking on a date will produce a list of actor/actress names and their status at the awards ceremony. Click again on the actor/actress's name and you will receive a full screen of biographical information along with the film's technical data.
3. Access the Flash: Oscar Mania link and you will be presented with links to produce the screens shown in Figures 13.30 and 13.31.

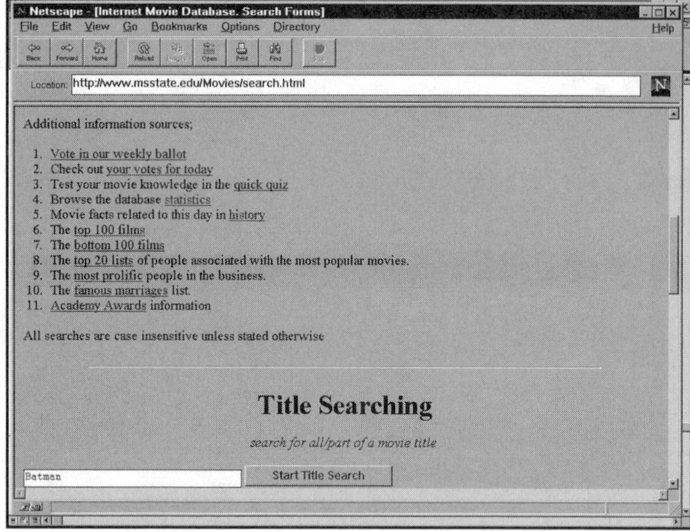

Figure 13.29.
Other links offered with access to the Search command.

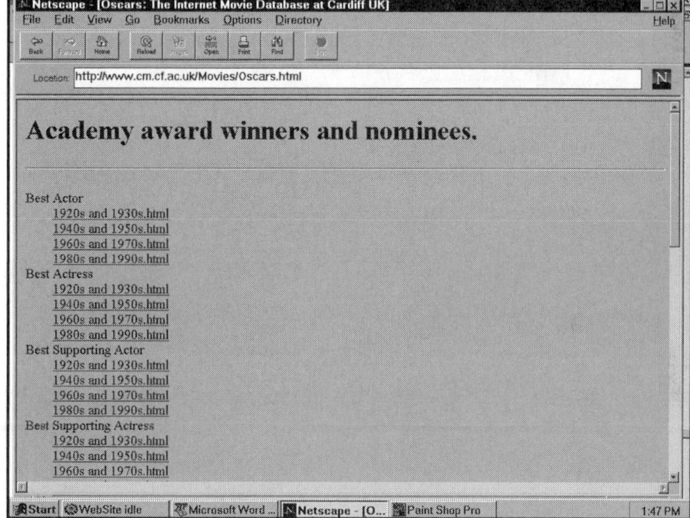

Figure 13.30.
The Academy Awards history page using Yahoo's Movie directory.

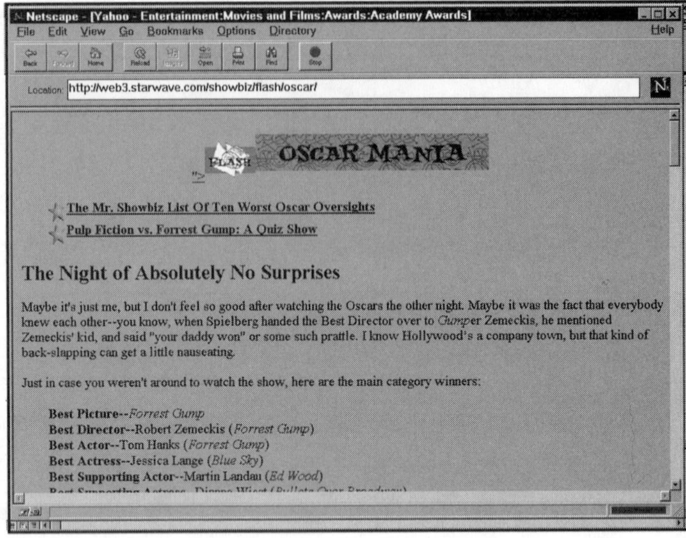

Figure 13.31.
The Oscar Mania home page.

4. Enough Oscars for now. Return to the Yahoo Movie and Film directory and browse some of the available sites. First select The Entertainment Center and explore the link to locate some of pages shown in Figures 13.32, 13.33, 13.34, and 13.35.

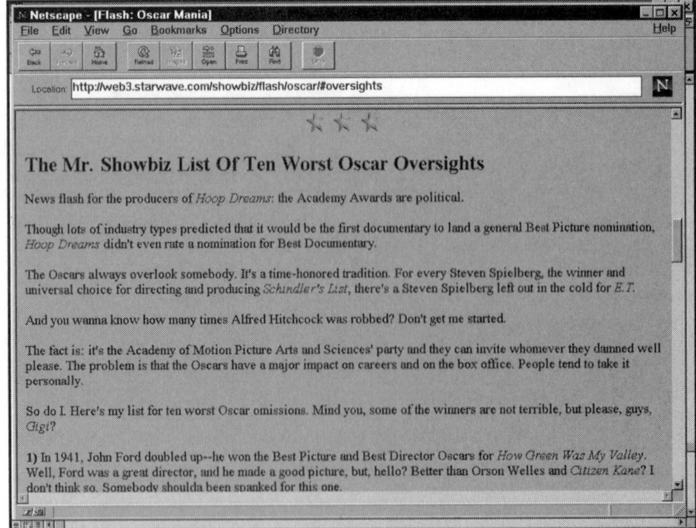

Figure 13.32.
Mr. Showbiz's Top Ten Oscar Oversights.

Figure 13.33. *The Hollywood Online home page.*

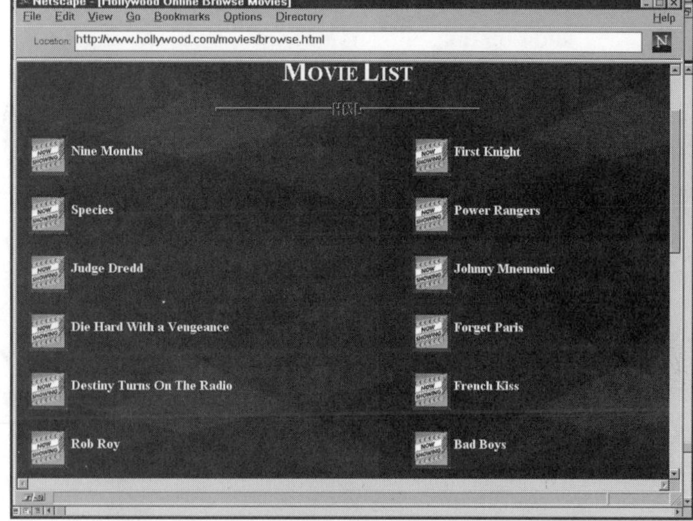

Figure 13.34. *Hollywood Online's Movie List.*

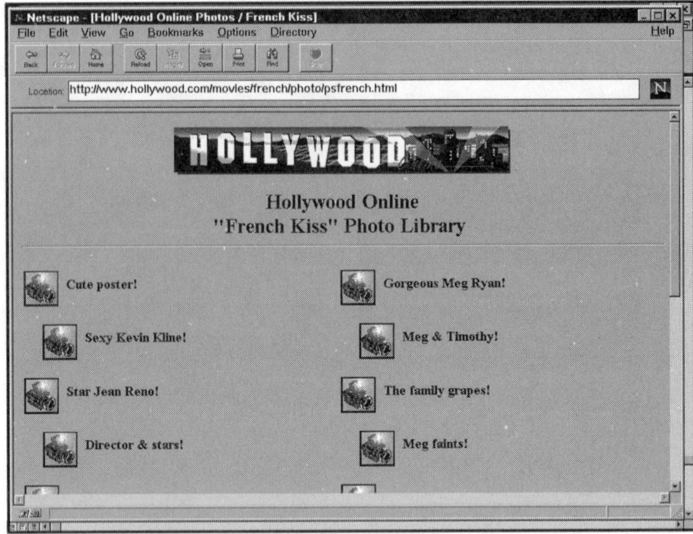

Figure 13.35.
The "French Kiss" Photo Library from Hollywood Online.

Choose Guides from the listed commands and you should receive the list of movie and film links shown in Figure 13.36.

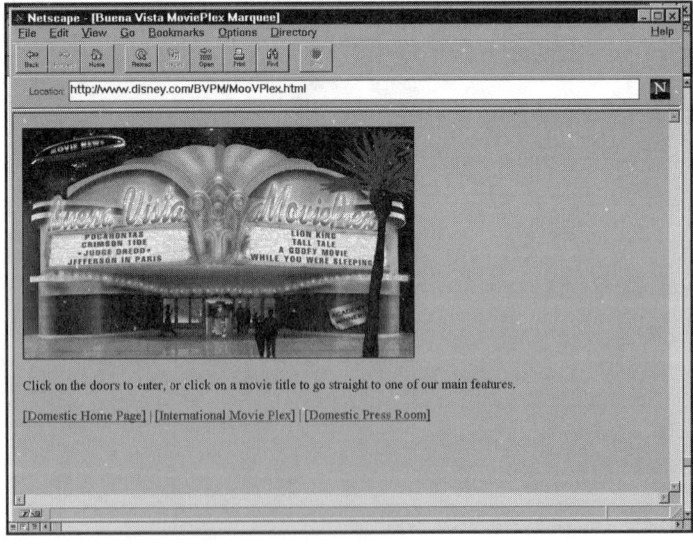

Figure 13.36.
The Buena Vista Movieplex from www.disney.com/.

7. The obvious choice seems to be Movie Links, so click on the title and see what you get.

From here, it's simply a matter of working your way around this spectactular resource, examining movie details, voting on your favorites, and just generally soaking up everything you can about the cinema.

Music

Musicians already have one medium under their control—radio. But radio has one major downside: it's utterly predictable. Work your way through the stations on any given day, and you'll hear a very typical combination of classic rock, somewhat modern rock, country, new country, and talk shows. If you live in a good radio area, you might get classical and contemporary pop, dance, and rap, but that's hardly for certain. And if you're looking for the alternative and underground scenes, for the most part you might as well forget it.

There's a great deal of musical information on the Internet, but this section examines only one source, the Internet Underground Music Archive on the Web. By all means, check out the newsgroups devoted to musicians and bands (as with television, there's a newsgroup for every conceivable topic or artist), but the real interest today lies in the Web. Whether your interests are in mainstream musicians or the most unknown of the unknown, you'll find them working their wares on the World Wide Web.

Task 13.6: Enter the fascinating world of IUMA.

The Internet Underground Music Archive has been written up just about everywhere, but here, you're going to take a long, leisurely stroll through its offerings. Without question, IUMA is the best music site on the Internet; in fact, it's one of the best Web sites in any category. If you're a music fan, you'll want to visit here often.

1. Go to the IUMA home page by setting your Web browser for **`http://www.iuma.com/`**. You'll see Figure 13.37.
2. Because you're a new user, click on the link called New Users, Please.
3. Fill out the registration form with as much information as you care to give. Note that this won't cost you any money, although you might receive a bit of advertising mail (it's junk only if you don't want it).
4. After your registration has been accepted, return to the IUMA home page and click on the colorful link named Bitblasting Color (actually, finding this the first time is a bit unnecessarily confusing). Your screen will now look like Figure 13.38.

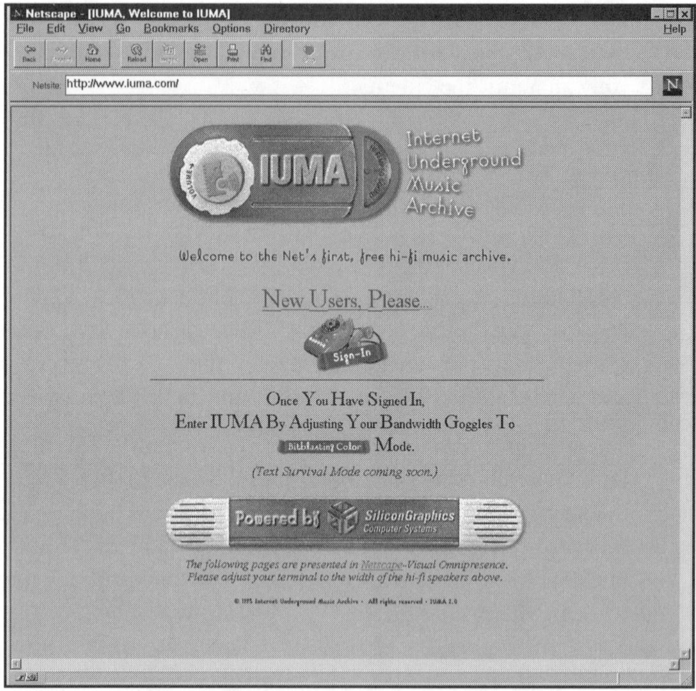

Figure 13.37.
The home page for the Internet Underground Music Archive.

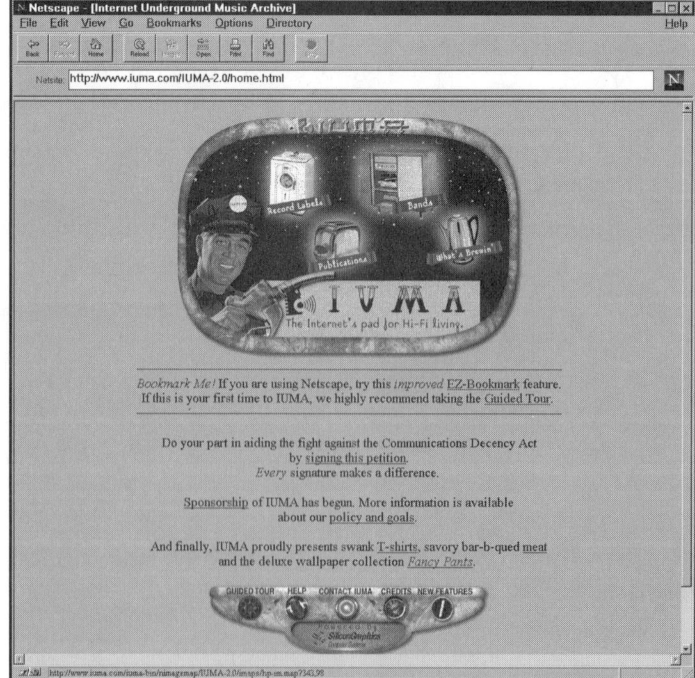

Figure 13.38.
The entry point for IUMA.

5. Since you're just learning about IUMA, why not take their guided tour? To do so, click on Guided Tour in the graphic at the bottom of the screen, and then read each subsequent screen, clicking on Continue as you finish the page. After you finish the tour, return to this entry point page.
6. From the large graphic at the top of the screen, click on Bands. You'll see the screen shown in Figure 13.39.

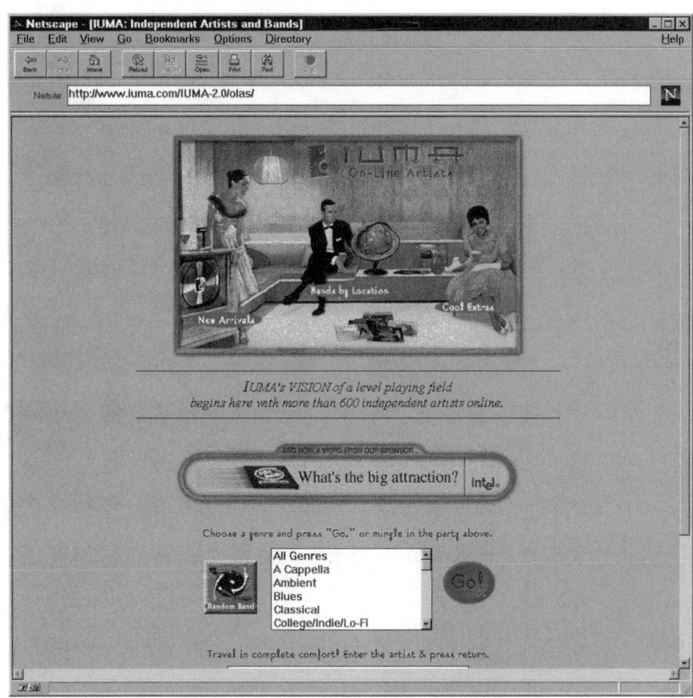

Figure 13.39.
The Bands entry page from IUMA.

This page is the heart of IUMA. From here, you can access information for a large number of bands, some well-known, but many you've not likely heard of. If you're a fan of new music, you'll spend hour upon hour poring through the information and the downloads from these pages, all of it very enjoyably.

7. Scroll through the list of musical genres at the bottom of the screen, and then return near the top and select College/Indie/Lo-Fi by clicking on it. Click the Go button. You'll find yourself looking at a screen that looks like that shown in Figure 13.40.

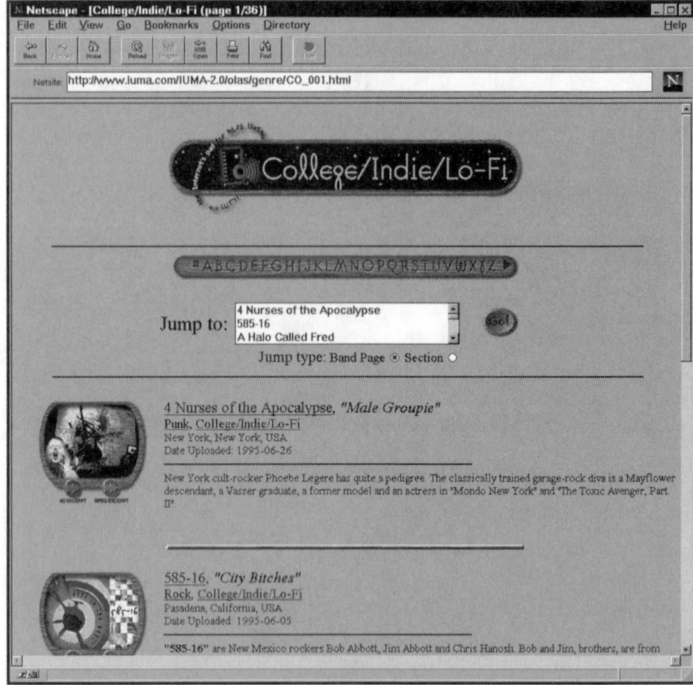

Figure 13.40.
The College/Indie/Lo-Fi page from the IUMA Bands list.

8. The wooden-looking graphic near the top of the page enables you to select which letter of the alphabet you want to move to. For now, click on the letter T. This will take you to the list of College/Indie/Lo-Fi bands whose names begin with T.
9. Scroll down to the band named Tone Deaf Teens (it might not be there by the time you read this, but it should be), and click on the link. You'll see the screen shown in Figure 13.41.
10. Read through the bio, and then look at the top of the screen. Here you'll see several buttons that look like little circles with arrows in them. Beneath the row of buttons is some information that reads (Excerpt 146K 220k / Full song 4 mins, 2.92M, 5.85M). This interface enables you to download either the full-featured song from that band, or an excerpt from that song. One of the buttons enables you to download in .AU format (the most common), and the excerpt is also available in MPEG format. If you prefer, you can download the entire song in either MPEG mono or MPEG stereo (look for RealAudio format in the future). The .AU excerpt in this case is 146K long, while the full MPEG stereo version is 5.85 megabytes. If you have a modem slower than 28.8 kpbs, and you decide to download the full MPEG stereo version, you can safely go for dinner while the song is downloading. Once you have it, however, you have a new piece of music to listen to.

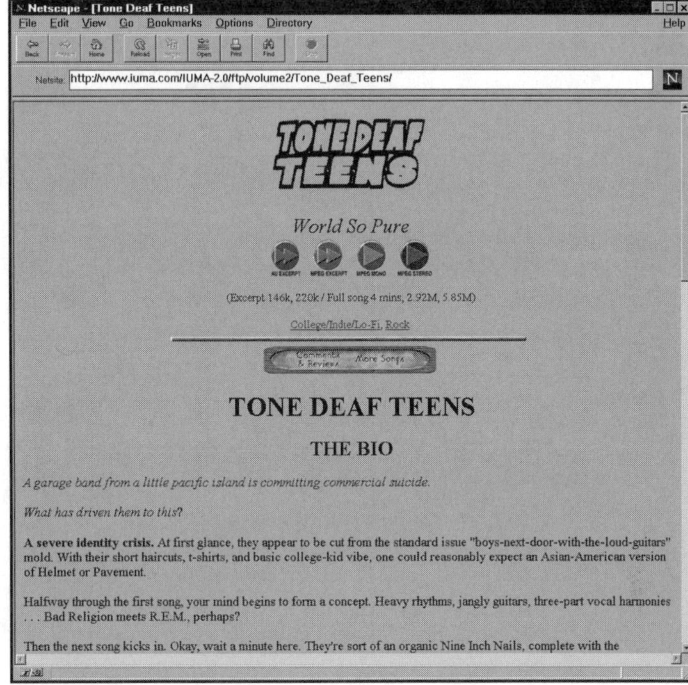

Figure 13.41.
The Tone Deaf Teens page from IUMA.

11. Scroll to the bottom of the page and click on the IUMA Home graphic.
12. Click in the graphic on the Record Labels icon. You'll see the screen shown in Figure 13.42.
13. To see how a relatively major label handles its presence in IUMA, scroll to the bottom of the screen (or select from the scrolling list at top), and click on the Windham Hill icon. You'll be taken to `http://www.windham.com/`.
14. Click on the Our Music link and select the link for Jon Anderson. This is Jon Anderson from former progressive (okay, pretentious) rockers Yes, and a sample of his work resides in this site. Click on the Deseo link and then on the song title listed next to the musical note icon.

And that's it—a quick tour through one of the best Web sites of all. There's more to IUMA that what you've seen, but the important point is that it's easy to move through and endlessly entertaining. Enjoy.

Figure 13.42.
The Record Labels page in IUMA.

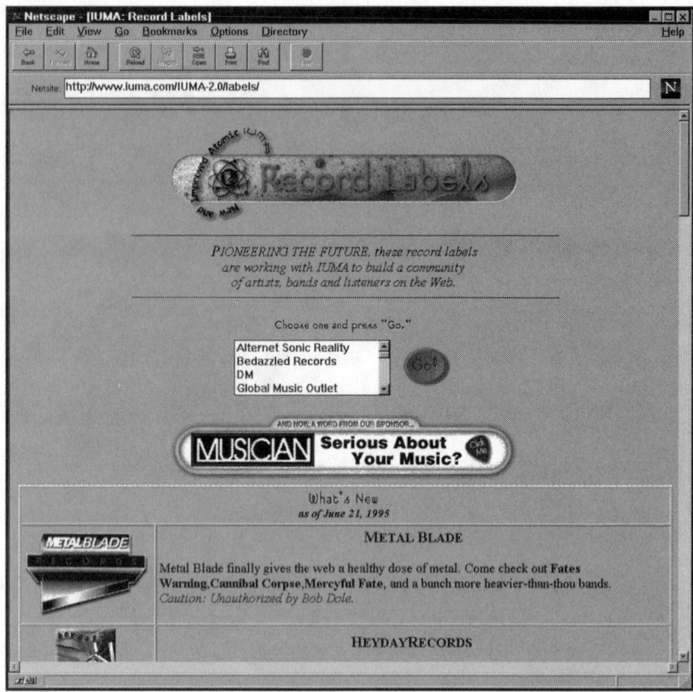

Summary

Entertainment on the Internet continues to grow. Whether you're interested in television, movies, music, or any other form of entertainment, you'll find it on the Net, particularly in newsgroups and on the Web. As the Web grows in multimedia capabilities, the entertainment focus will increase even further, to the extent that the Net might well become the major focus of entertainment for many people. This should hardly be surprising: television followed this route, too, from educational medium to entertainment medium, as in fact have most twentieth-century media technologies.

Task List

In this chapter, you learned how to perform the following tasks:

- ☐ Join television-oriented newsgroups
- ☐ Explore television-oriented Web sites
- ☐ Examine a TV network available online
- ☐ Maneuver through the Internet Movie Database
- ☐ Examine other motion picture resources online
- ☐ Discover the riches of the Internet Underground Music Archive

Q&A

Q So when can we watch TV over the Net?

A Either soon, or never, depending on your point of view. On the one hand, cable companies are beginning to offer Internet access at significantly higher speeds than today's fastest modems. But the current system of distributing video signals is firmly in place, and unlikely to be supplanted by an Internet-based system in the near future, or possibly ever. But that's only if you mean watching TV as we know it today. Much more likely is the possibility of a convergence of TV and the Net, in which you watch your television set (or a TV card in your computer), and then interact with the show in some way or another. The obvious possibilities are game shows and talk shows, but even here there's no hard evidence that home viewers actually *want* to participate. Still, the possibilities are certainly there.

Q Don't musicians lose money by making their material available over the Internet?

A Probably the opposite, in fact. Look at two possibilities—the famous musician with international distribution, and the unknown band without a recording deal. How can the Net serve either? First, the famous musician has one major need: to stay in the public eye. To that end, *any* medium must be addressed, from newspapers to television, to radio, to CompuServe, to airplane magazines, to the Net itself. Popular musicians must be seen to be reaching out to their audiences at all times, and to this end, the Net becomes important. Equally important is the trend for fans to place materials on the Net, essentially replacing the fan club idea. Exposure is all. In the case of the unknown band, their goal is to get recognized and appreciated to the point where a recording deal becomes possible. They don't have a fan base, so they tour extensively to build one. As of now, however, they can consider the Net a form of touring. They can put up a Web site that offers pictures, sound samples, maybe even their first EP in its entirety. They can announce gigs so that people from different geographical areas will hear about them, and they can even use the Net as a means of trying to get new gigs (that is, through local fan interest). And besides, the Web offers a new mode of creativity, and that, too, can help a new band.

14

DAY 5

Traveling with the Net

This chapter focuses on travel information available on the Net. In this chapter, you'll examine newsgroups and mailing lists devoted to travel, and you'll explore FTP, Gopher, and World Wide Web sites in search of the perfect destination. Eventually, you'll want to turn off the machine and actually visit some of these places, but the Net is cheaper; unless, of course, you win the big prize on *The Price is Right.*

Task List

In this chapter, you'll perform the following tasks:

- ☐ Subscribe to mailing lists that focus on travel issues
- ☐ Join newsgroups that deal with travel destinations and concerns
- ☐ Retrieve information about travel from FTP sites
- ☐ Explore Gopher sites for details about travel destinations and issues
- ☐ Browse the World Wide Web for multimedia presentations of travel destinations

Note: This chapter is in a slightly different format from most of the others. Here, you'll follow Marion as she makes her way around the Web, joining in by performing the tasks as she does them. This is a less prescriptive approach than most chapters, and I'm interested in which you think is more useful. E-mail me at `nrandall@watarts.uwaterloo.ca` to let me know, okay?

Traveling with the Net

This one, you'd think, should be the easiest surfing there is. The Internet is all about different destinations, after all, and although most of those destinations are computers, you'd expect to find an almost infinite amount of information about the geographical sites in which those computers reside. Everybody's putting that material online, aren't they?

Some are, yes. But finding travel and tourism information isn't the cakewalk it might seem to be. And, on reflection, this may not be so hard to understand. The Internet was originally a collection of research sites, and putting details about local bed-and-breakfast establishments in FTP sites was quite naturally frowned upon. In all likelihood, there was a feeling that making this kind of information readily available would actually detract from the Internet's purpose, so it took a while for the resources to build up. Then there's the other major point: the Net is supposed to overcome the notion that people are actually *located* somewhere. Virtual worlds and all that.

When Marion Muirhead expressed an interest in locating travel information, I figured she'd spend 8 to 10 hours collecting archive after archive with details about places to visit, tourist traps, restaurants and theaters, prices of all kinds, customs and immigration assistance, and everything else associated with travel and tourism.

A few weeks later, she was clearly dissatisfied. There was no problem with the messages from other Internetters—one newsgroup and one mailing list had provided hundreds of travel anecdotes and words of advice—but the rest didn't seem to be falling into place. Gopher and FTP sites proved useful, but primarily for collecting travel stories from other Net users—valuable, to be sure, but still not enough for a strong collection.

A breakthrough of sorts came with access to the World Wide Web. While newsgroups, mailing lists, and Gopher/FTP sites provided travel *stories*, the Web offered travel *details* (and some stories as well), taking good advantage of the graphical capabilities. Virtual touring on the Web is addictive, informative, and more than a little entertaining. But after hours upon hours of WWW exploration, I'm about to concede that the travel stories from the other sources are every bit as—maybe even more—valuable. The Web lends itself to Fodor-like travel guide material, while the trials and tribulations of real travelers appear on the less glamorous newsgroups and mailing lists.

The Web's potential as a repository of travel and tourism information is enormous, but it hasn't even begun to be realized. When I can use the Web as my personal travel agent, making aircraft and hotel reservations and checking out local attractions, restaurants, theaters, and shopping in a fully interactive way, then I'll know it's working. Until then, the Internet offers a good—but not superb—set of travel resources, and here we outline the best of them.

Searching for Travel Resources on the Internet

By Marion Muirhead

I began with no particular destination in mind; I just wanted to find out what information was available on destinations all over the world. It seemed like a good idea to get as much specific information as possible before making a decision about where to go, and then I wanted to know exactly what to expect.

14

Chances are, your travel agent won't give you the most honest evaluation of destinations or hotels, or give you warnings that might frighten you off, but people compiling travel archives or subscribing to mailing lists usually have no reason to lie (although they may embroider the truth a bit now and then). I like to know what I'm getting into before I leave—I've had some fairly arduous adventures in the world already! One of the wonderful things about the Net is that it tends to be devoid of commercial motives; knowledge and information exchange are the prime values here.

The TRAVEL-L Mailing List

First, I subscribed to a mailing list—*TRAVEL-L*—that discusses all aspects of travel: transportation, accommodations, tours, agents, food, everything. You can lurk and learn from discussions other subscribers are having.

Task 14.1: Subscribe to and maintain TRAVEL-L.

Subscribing to the TRAVEL-L electronic mailing list involves sending an e-mail message to the following address:

```
listserv@trearn.bitnet
```

1. Fire up your e-mail program of choice and insert the mailing list's address on the `To:` line.
2. In the message text area, type the following brief instruction:

   `subscribe travel-l` ***`firstname lastname`***

Warning: As always, when subscribing to a mailing list, be sure to leave the subject line blank, and remember to erase your signature.

3. Send the message. You will receive a message within a short while confirming your subscription. To respond, type the following message:

   `confirm travel-l`

Every so often, you will be required to renew your subscription to the mailing list. The system will prompt you with an announcement sent to all subscribers when renewal is necessary; you will receive a message that can simply be forwarded back to the list without having to compose anything, if you prefer.

Note: Confirming a subscription isn't usual with mailing lists, but it's possible with an unusually high-volume list. If you join TRAVEL-L, or any other list with required confirmation, simply follow the instructions. One advantage of this procedure is that if you *don't* want to continue with the list but you forget how to unsubscribe, you'll be spared the necessity.

If you plan to be away from your computer for some time, you can sign off from the list to avoid being swamped by an accumulation of mail when you return.

4. To sign off from the mailing list, type

```
signoff travel-l
```

You may resubscribe whenever you want.

Tip: Again, with a high-volume list of this type, the `signoff` message can be invaluable. It's not unusual for TRAVEL-L to send 50 or more messages in a day.

5. To mail a message to all subscribers—if perhaps you had a request for specific information about some aspect of a destination—send an e-mail message to the following address:

```
travel-l@trearn.bitnet
```

If you're after information about a specific travel location, TRAVEL-L maintains an archive of past discussions you can access.

6. Send the message

```
index travel-l
```

to the following address:

```
listserv@trearn.bitnet
```

Warning: Be sure to send this type of message to the `listserv@trearn.bitnet` address, and not to the mailing list at `travell@trearn.bitnet`. Some people get cranky about the volume of material from this mailing list, so remember: if you send this or any other maintenance message to all subscribers, you may quickly become disliked.

7. When you have decided what files you want, send the message

```
get travel-l log file_number
```

to receive files, replacing *`file_number`* with the correct numbers for the file.

What TRAVEL-L Offers

One of the advantages of the mailing list is that you get different opinions. Sometimes people disagree (sometimes violently—or, at least, as violently as one can be with only a keyboard as a weapon) on what is good or bad about a destination, so you can make up your own mind from the information you find in a discussion.

For example, someone recently posted a message requesting suggestions as to what to see in New York. Someone else wrote back with all the usual tourist attractions and directions for the easiest way to get to them. At this point another subscriber, presumably someone from New York or at least very familiar with the city, asserted that the first respondent's suggestions were overly "touristy" and proceeded to list out-of-the-way places, including ethnic restaurants that were her favorites. The first respondent rejoined, commenting that the second respondent's suggestions were "the most Bohemian places he'd ever heard of." They flamed each other, but it really was perfectly instructive on the whole, despite the insults, for anyone interested in going to New York.

Usually the discussions are pretty amicable, but occasionally something untoward is suggested, someone reacts, and subscribers get sarcastic. If you don't find it entertaining or at least instructive, you can just tune in to a more sedate discussion. Often people just want to be helpful and share the useful things they've found. Look at the following example (the names and numbers are altered for privacy's sake):

```
From: "Walcott P. Thompson" <WPTHOMPSO%CCVAX.BITNET@vm.hhh.de>
Subject:      Toll-free line, British Tourist Authority
Comments: To: travel-l@trearn.bitnet
To: Multiple recipients of list TRAVEL-L <TRAVEL-L%TREARN.BITNET@vm.gmd.de>

This was in my Sunday paper yesterday. Thought it might be of interest.

"The British Tourist Authority is introducing a new nationwide toll-free
telephone number, (800) 462-2748, for prospective travelers seeking
information. Their service, scheduled to begin tomorrow, (Monday April 4) will
be available from 9:30 a.m. to 7 p.m. Monday to Friday. In Manhattan, callers
should dial 555-2200."
```

TRAVEL-L is a hugely active list, with messages coming in constantly. You really have to keep up with it, or else deal with going through the hundreds of messages that will accumulate. This can take hours. Assuming that your mail reader gives you a subject line for each message, you can delete any that don't interest you without having to read them. Or you can receive all the messages from TRAVEL-L under one heading with a subdirectory, so that your other mail messages don't get swallowed up in the deluge.

Tip: If you're serious about maintaining travel information, set up a series of appropriate folders in your mailer. I saved useful messages in my Pine mail folder (organized by country, area, or topic) using the s (save) command. You can do so with other mailers as well.

The Internet tends to cater to a wide range of lifestyles, so quite often information that would be hard to find elsewhere will be highlighted here.

Tip: On the TRAVEL-L mailing list, postings frequently appear detailing other sources of information. These may be other Internet sites, regular snailmail lists and newsletters, or books and travel guides recommended by subscribers. Also, people may be advertising accommodations for rent at a travel destination. And, of course, there are always a number of discussions going on about things to see and do and places to stay and eat at various travel destinations by people who have spent time there. A lot of these people have traveled extensively and have good advice to give.

If you require any specific information, you can post a message to all or one of the list subscribers. People in the list suggest that very general questions should be avoided. Decide exactly what you need to know. You might want to e-mail someone who is active in the list and seems knowledgeable in your area of interest.

If you are new to the list, it is best to read messages for a few days to get a feel for appropriate topics. People get quite upset if they read something unrelated to the topic. Also, if you are looking for other sources of Internet information, it won't likely help to make a request here. Many subscribers have e-mail capabilities only, so they have no interest in Gopher, FTP, or WWW sites, and they even seem to resent those who do. They may be so blunt as to tell you to buy a book.

Travel-Oriented Newsgroups

As always, newsgroups provide the most interesting discussions on the Net. As you might expect, people are more than willing to share their travel experiences. Here are a couple newsgroups worth looking into, although there are certainly others.

Task 14.2: Browse some recreational groups.

Newsgroups that focus on air fares, accommodations, and a variety of general advice can be accessed through rn or any other newsreader. The first such group I tried was the popular `rec.travel`. To access this newsgroup, follow these steps:

1. Type the command **`rn`**. Your newsreader will start the rn and present a standard command prompt (refer to Chapter 5 for other newsreader commands).
2. At the prompt issue the following command:

```
get rec.travel
```

3. If you want to view articles using subject threads, press **`y`** to go to the first article, and then type **`_t`** to thread the group.
4. To view a particular thread, press the letter preceding it, or move the cursor down to it using the arrow keys and press +.
5. To select specific articles for viewing, type the appropriate letter.

   Following are a few sections from the advice of a seasoned traveler:

   ```
   What to take when traveling abroad? There's an old saying that aptly
   applies:
   Take half as many clothes and twice as much money.

   lomotil for diarrhea
   anti-histamine dalmane or halcion to sleep on the plane
   combid spansules (prochlorperazine & isopropamide) for nausea & diarrhea
   ```

   When you have finished reading all selected articles, you will be returned to the list of threads.

   A few other newsgroups you might want to try are `travel.air` and `travel.marketplace`.
6. To select a new group simply type g newsgroup name. To access the `rec.vacation` group, for example, type **`g rec.vacation`**.

The `rec.vacation` group has information on cheap fares, meals, airline 1-800 numbers, frequent-flier deals, service records for various airlines, and instructions on how to complain effectively if you've had a bad flight. Some suggest that complaining doesn't help unless you suggest some remedy or compensation the airline could make for you. Mere complaining tends to be ignored.

Following are three examples of postings from the various newsgroups to give you an idea of what to expect. The last of these is fairly rare, an announcement of a World Wide Web site devoted to travel. You don't usually see postings informing you of other Internet sites, at least not on the travel newsgroups.

```
-------------------------------------
We arranged a 1 week package that included r/t air from Riga, Latvia to
Larnaca, Cyprus, hotel transfers, and 7 nights in a 3 star hotel in Agia
Napa (or Ayia Napa). The hotel was $28.00 /night per person in a double
 (so essentially $56.00 per night). The hotel (Napa Mermaid) was right
across the street from a beautiful white sand beach. There are also hostels
in the main areas that are around $10.00 per night. We had no idea what to
expect so we booked a hotel ahead of time but would do the hostel route next
time since so little time is spent indoors.
```

```
Since Cyprus is mainly Greek, it feels and looks much like Greece. It has
all the charm, but since it is so small you don't have to go far to get a
completely different "hit".
------------------------------------
Could someone tell me more about the Eurail Youth Flexipass, I'd like to buy
the 5 travel days in 2 months pass. My specific questions:
1) do you need a youth i.d. card?
2) should we make reservations for the specific trains?
3) what kind of trains can we take?

At this late date, what is the cheapest (and available) fare I can get for
flying from Nashville to Paris (16 Sept) and returning via Madrid (4 Oct)?
Right now, I was quoted a price of $925.95.

------------------------------------

**The Avid Explorer** - A World Wide Web server providing a variety of
information on travel destinations around the world is now available. In
addition to providing convenient links to the wealth of travel information
on the Internet, The Avid Explorer presents specific and up-to-date
information of interest to special groups of travelers. Current areas under
development include *scuba* and *skiing/snowboarding*; other areas will be
developed based on user feedback. In addition, we offer the *Travel Bazaar*,
a growing forum where you may find information on a variety of travel
product and service providers.

The Avid Explorer also features the latest information on cruises, tours,
FIT's, and domestic vacation alternatives. Special value packages will be
presented and updated frequently. Our goal is to provide a fun place on the
Web for exploring the incredible diversity of travel options now available.
Connect with Mosaic or other graphical or character-based browser via:

URL = http://www.explore.com
```

Like the mailing lists, travel-oriented newsgroups abound with hints, tips, and stories. For anyone trying to determine where to vacation or travel, these mailing lists can be invaluable.

Gopher Sites

Gopher remains a valid resource for Internauts interested in travel issues. Although the Web is taking precedence, Gopher sites provide an excellent means of accessing sorted information, especially archived files.

Task 14.3: Locate Internet Express Gopher and begin digging.

As always, Gopher sites are among the easiest to access and use. They also contain a variety of information, ranging from travelogues to country and regional information. But they take some digging, and the resources tend to be a bit disappointing. Still…

Internet Express, an Internet provider in Colorado, has developed a strong Gopher site. Included are some very useful travel items. You begin your exploration there.

1. Type **`gopher earth.usa.net`** to connect to the Internet provider.
2. To access the available ski information on facilities, locations, rates, classes, addresses, and phone numbers, as well as other subjects, scroll down to the appropriate menu location and press Enter. You may reach the site quicker by entering the site number (if it is a numbered list) and pressing Enter.
3. To access the electronic version of the *CIA World Fact Book*, enter the Internet Express Gopher through the item path, and then `Reference - The CIA World Fact Book`. This will give you geographical information as well as cultural facts about different countries.

Tip: Cultural information can be extremely useful for planning a trip. A strong source of cultural information exists at `ukoln.bath.ac.uk`.

4. Gopher to the `ukoln.bath.ac.uk` site through the following directory lists:

   ```
   BUBL Information Service/ BUBL Subject Tree
   Links to Resources in Gopherspace
   BUBL/ 008 - Cultures and Civilizations.
   ```

   From this Gopher, you can access a range of cultural and ethnic information, including details on Israel, Scandinavia, Greece, and Romania. You also can find information on Edinburgh in this directory. There are also files on French, Polish, Indian, Native American, and Tibetan cultures.

   While at the Bath Gopher, it might be a good time to conduct a Veronica search. The University of Cologne (Germany) is one option for this type of search.
5. Select the Veronica search menu from the presented list. You will receive a standard Gopher search screen and will be prompted to insert a topic or keyword.
6. Type the keyword **`travel`** in the search box and press Enter. Your search will take some time, resulting in a huge list with 200 items, plus a closing reference to about 6,000 additional items. However, this material is not organized hierarchically (or in any other way, for that matter). Some items are only very small blurbs on some book or a message from a discussion group. Only a great deal of browsing work can determine which items are worthwhile.
7. Pennsylvania State University maintains a large archive that can be accessed through Gopher at `genesis.ait.psu.edu`.

   Access the Pennsylvania State University site. This leads to a telnet site (you can also simply telnet to `psupen.psu.edu` if you want to access it directly) that contains travel information, including advisories.

8. Log in as **PENPAGES** (if you're in the U.S.) or **WORLD** (if you're anywhere else) and follow the prompts to the keyword search.
9. In the search box, type **travel** and choose L to list the files. Following is a sample of those available:

```
TRAVEL
33 documents found
------------------------------------
 (L) List Titles     (R) Reduce Selection     (S) Search Again     (?) Help
(E) Expand Selection     (D) Display Options  (@) Exit
------------------------------------
Enter choice: <L>
List of Titles
------------------------------------
TRAVEL

From: 26-APR-1994     To: 21-DEC-1988          TOTAL DOCUMENTS: 33

#              TITLE                                     DATE
1     Sources on Mexican Americans/ Chicanos (NLS3a)    26-APR-1994
2     Sources on Mexican Americans/ Chicanos (NLS3b)    26-APR-1994
3     Traveler's Tips                                   30-JAN-1994
4     What Does the Peace Corps Offer?                  30-JAN-1994
5     American Express Billing Inquiries                15-DEC-1993
6     Club Discounts                                    15-DEC-1993
7     Contracted Travel Agencies                        15-DEC-1993
8     Corporate Hotel Discounts                         15-DEC-1993
9     Insurance Coverage                                15-DEC-1993
10    Rental Car Discounts                              15-DEC-1993
11    Research on Needs of Female Business Travelers    22-AUG-1993
12    Ideas for Better Living (July 1993)               12-JUL-1993
---------------------------------------------------------------------------
 (N) Next Titles     (R) Reduce Selection     (S) Search Again     (?) Help
 (P) Previous Titles (E) Expand Selection     (D) Display Options  (@) Exit
------------------------------------
```

While the advisories are intended for American citizens, much of the information is useful for other travelers. Information on most countries includes the political situation, crime rate, and penalties for breaking laws, among other things. The archive has a directory on Africa that includes information on biking in Africa as well as African art.

If you are interested in museums or botanical gardens, information can be found that includes exhibits, their locations, and hours, through the Internet. The Bishop Museum in Honolulu maintains a Gopher that can be accessed by the following command:

```
gopher bishop.bishop.hawaii.org
```

Other Museum Information and Services contains information on exhibits, hours, admission prices, and other pertinent data at major museums around the world. You can browse the frog and toad collection at the Museum of Natural History at UGA, but it's not quite the same as being there. If you want to preview exhibits where you are headed, this is definitely one way to check them out.

Other link possibilities from this Gopher abound. If you have audio capabilities on your computer, you can enjoy whale sounds at the Museum of Paleontology in UC Berkeley in Sun Audio (.AU) Format, a directory in Remote Nature Exhibits. If you have graphics capabilities, you can download images of birds, plants, and environments, also from Remote Nature Exhibits file. A new spot for museum info can be found in Greece by Gopher. The address is `ithaki.servicenet.ariadne-t.gr`.

The directory includes Hellenic Civilization, with sculpture, painting, music, literature, and theater. At the time of writing, some files were still unavailable. In fact, the Internet has no shortage of museum exhibits to visit; the only problem being that all such visits are virtual. Still, if you're interested in planning a trip with visits to museums, Gophers such as these can be an excellent starting point.

If you want to search for books or articles on travel, you can telnet to the Electronic Newsstand at `gopher.internet.com` and log in as `enews`. I searched `travel travelogue` and came up with articles and books that contained the keywords. I did find a magazine of interest, but it was not an electronic journal. `Enews` has samples of contents from magazines and subscription information. I found an ad for *Today's Traveler Magazine*, a magazine that focuses on travel as a learning experience rather than the bargain-hunter perspective of some mailing lists.

Learn Your FTPs

FTP is one of the Net's oldest programs, but it's an important one to learn. For travel afficionadoes, FTP offers access to huge archives of files, many of which provide invaluable information about destinations and details.

Task 14.4: Access and manipulate travel archives.

One good source of travel information is the `rec.travel` archive at the University of Manitoba. The archive is organized according to regions of the world (and a few other topics), and has information on most countries, including the travelogues from people who have been to them. Access to this archive may be attained through anonymous FTP. To access a travel archive, follow these steps:

1. Enter your Internet account, exit all Gopher or Mail programs, and type the following command:

   `ftp.cc.manitoba.ca`

2. At the `login:` prompt, type **`anonymous`**. Now you will be asked for a password, just as if you were logging on to your Internet account. Rather than typing your regular password, type your full Internet address, as in the following:

   `password: nrandall@watserv1.uwaterloo.ca`

Manitoba's server will present a message telling you that you're in, and an `ftp>` prompt will appear.

3. Change the directory using the `cd` command followed by the directory name. Type **`cd rec-travel`** for best results.
4. When you have chosen a file to view, type **`get`** ***`filename`***. The file will be transferred to your account.

   At this site you will find a directory of information on most countries, as well as airline, restaurant and cultural information, rates, pen-pal clubs, and online ski information. The following is an example of the files found at `umanitoba` in `/rec-travel/north_america/mexico/`:

```
-rw-r—r—   1 1000     104            29 Feb 13 06:43 0
-rw-r—r—   1 1000     104          1271 Apr 18 08:01 README.html
-rw-r—r—   1 1000     104          2167 Feb 13 06:57 baja-california
-rw-r—r—   1 1000     104         10384 Feb 13 06:59 cancun.misc
-rw-r—r—   1 1000     104         73216 Apr 17 07:19 cozumel.trip
-rw-r—r—   1 1000     104         10451 Feb 13 07:01 kailuum.trip.sopelak
-rw-r—r—   1 1000     104         13155 Feb 13 07:02 mazatlan.trip
-rw-r—r—   1 1000     104           892 Feb 20 20:34 mexico-faq
-rw-r—r—   1 1000     104         18624 Feb 13 07:05 oaxaca.trip.cisler
```

   Another strong archive of travel and recreation information at MIT can be accessed by FTP at `rtfm.mit.edu`. This archive contains a file on travel "frequently asked questions," or FAQs. You also can find socio-cultural FAQs and files on vegetarian restaurants in various places in the world. This archive is organized conveniently for easy access to information.

5. Once you are connected through anonymous FTP, type **`cd pub/usenet`**.
6. At the next prompt, type **`dir`** and you will gain access to the archive.
7. Following a similar procedure, browse this next travel related site:

   The Omni-Cultural Academic Resource (OCAR) archive contains a variety of interesting files, including photographs with captions, taken in Africa. You can reach it by FTP at `ftp.stolaf.edu`. Or, you can access it by Gopher at `gopher.stolaf.edu`, through the path `Internet Resources`, `St. Olaf Sponsored Mailing Lists`, `Omni-Cultural Academic Resource`, and finally `Going Places`. The following is an abbreviated list of the archive's files:

```
Following this index, I'm going to post Egypt 256-color pics
taken in my trip in Cairo, Luxor and Sharm el Shaykh in April.
Enjoy

Egypt03.jpg ---- Evening in Street of Cairo, 799x556
Shopping after sunset is enjoyable in Cairo.

Egypt13.jpg ---- Church of Al Muallaqa (Coptic), 521x800
One of the oldest Christian places in Egypt.
The Coptic Christianity came to Egypt in the
1st century AD.
```

```
Egypt14.jpg ---- Dawn in Luxor, 700x482,
Luxor started 4000 years ago on the site of
ancient Thebes. Its excellent preservation of
historical sites makes it as the most
attractive center for tourists.

Egypt16.jpg ---- The west bank of the Nile in Luxor, 800x504
It is the necropolis of the ancient Thebes
(present Luxor), including tombs for the Kings
and even ordinary workers. It seems a museum
of technology for construction, decoration and
concealment of tombs.
```

These locations (FTP and Gopher) offer files dealing with travel advice, airline info, maps, slides, travel agent recommendations, travelogues, and information on an info-line in Japan. OCAR also contains a file with addresses of YMCAs in Asia and Australia. One file in the directory is called `Share the World`, a program for adult cultural exchange. You can find people who live in places you want to visit who share your interests, and then arrange to visit one another.

Telnet

Less and less use is being made of telnet every day, at least as a means of accessing Internet resources and archives. Here's one useful idea, although it too is being supplanted by the Web.

Task 14.5: Find and use *subway navigator.*

Because telnet is the most direct means of getting onto machines around the world, it seems the obvious choice for any extensive Internet search. *subway navigator* is an interactive map containing detailed navigations for subway systems around the world. To access subway navigator, begin by telnetting to France.

1. To connect to a remote machine, type **open** followed by the desired host name. In this case, the command is **`telnet' metro.jussieu.fr 10000.`**

   When you access the site, you receive instructions for logging on. The following is a sample opening session:

```
Quelle langue desirez-vous ?          ¦ Which language do you want to use?
Votre choix ? (Francais/Anglais)      ¦ Your choice ? (French/English)
Choix/Choice [Francais] : English

Do you want to use the X Window System [No] :

Choose a city among these ones:
canada/montreal         hong-kong/hong-kong
canada/toronto          nederland/amsterdam
france/lille            spain/madrid
france/lyon             united-kingdom/london
france/marseille        usa/boston
france/paris            usa/new-york
```

```
france/toulouse         usa/san-francisco
germany/frankfurt       usa/washington
germany/muenchen

Your choice [france/paris] : nederland/amsterdam

The network includes all Amsterdam subway and train stations.

Times are estimates for a "normal" day (outside off hours).
Note:
GVB = "Gemeentelijk Vervoerbedrijf Amsterdam" (Municipal Transport Company)
NS = "Nederlandse Spoorwegen" (Dutch Railways)
Source : From a september 1993 map supplied by Gerben Vos.
All electronic data supplied by Gerben Vos.

Departure station [no default answer] :
```

2. For information on skiing in British Columbia, telnet to **CIAO.trail.BC.ca** and log in as **guest**, and then follow the menus to Health and Recreation.

The World Wide Web

Hardly surprisingly, the Web is making huge waves in the travel area of the Net. The reasons are obvious: Web pages can be designed to look like maps, brochures, and travel guides, and they provide interactive walk-throughs and add-ons as well. Popular as it is, however, the Web has barely begun to be explored as a travel resource. Keep watching; over the next several months we'll see much, much more.

Task 14.6: Tour the Web's travel sites.

With a WWW browser at your disposal, you can access a wealth of travel information by clicking the hypertext links highlighted on your screen. Some of the best travel information (some of it nearly in travel brochure form) is accessible this way.

Canadian Airlines operates a WWW site that promises departure information in the near future. At the time of this writing, these features have yet to be fully implemented for all locations, but departure and arrival times are available for most major cities. Soon this site should enable you to type in your preferred days of departure and arrival in cities of your choice, and in return give you a response that enables you to choose flight times.

1. Access the Canadian Airlines International WWW Page at **http://www.cdnair.ca/** (see Figure 14.1). The page lists Weather/Leisure, Travel, and Accessories as options.
2. Choose the Weather/Leisure menu item.

   Here, you'll find several weather information maps. The site also contains ski information from British Columbia and includes current slope conditions. The Weather/Leisure menu contains descriptions of accommodations, restaurants, bars, and tourist attractions so that you may plan your entire trip from your keyboard.

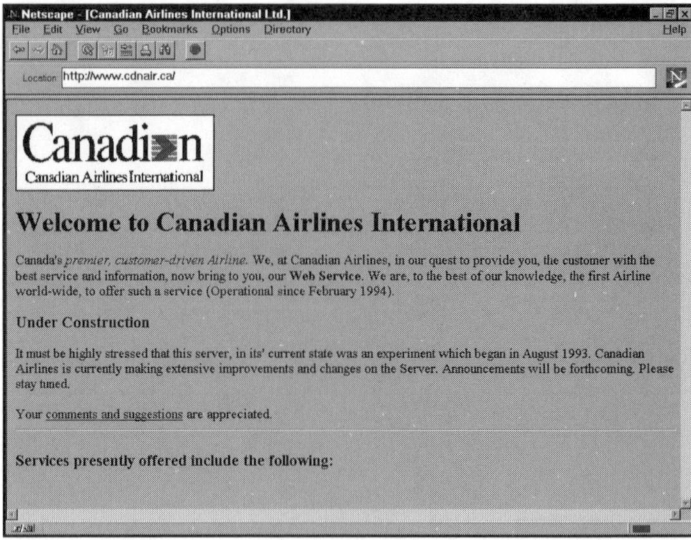

Figure 14.1.
The Canadian Airlines International home page.

3. Time for a site change. This time, browse The Singapore Online Guide, issued by Singapore's tourist board, by typing **`http://www.ncb.gov.sg/sog/sog.html`** in the location box (see Figure 14.2).

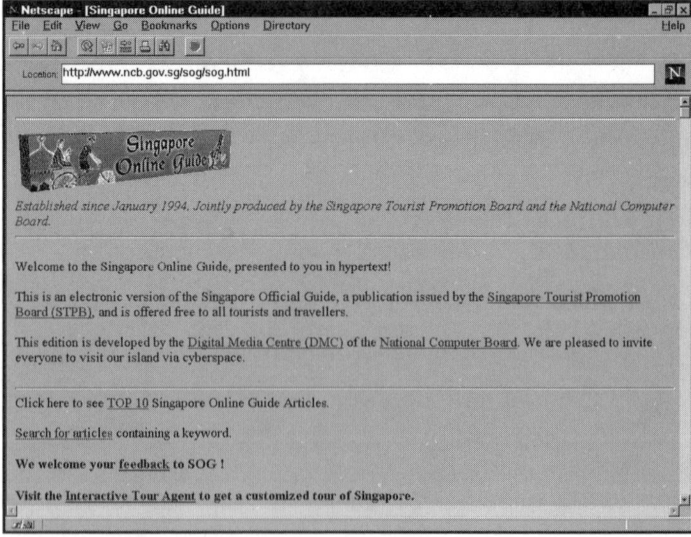

Figure 14.2.
The Singapore Online Guide.

4. These people have put together quite an extensive sampling of information, but because we don't know what to expect, select What to Expect in Singapore (see Figure 14.3).

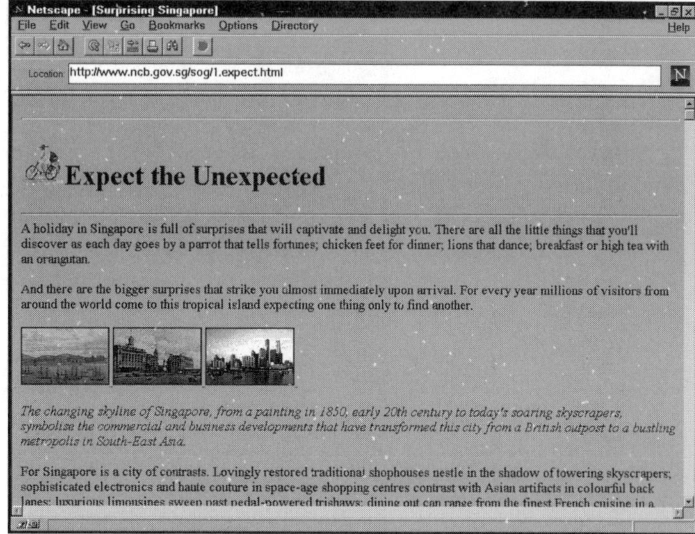

Figure 14.3.
Expect the unexpected, from The Singapore Online Guide.

Other selections include history, culture, etiquette, food, sight-seeing, and geographical details, to mention but a few. It's a pretty thorough guide and worth checking out if you're planning a trip to Singapore (or just want to do some traveling from your computer).

Another nice WWW site for travel to New Zealand is the Akiko International home page. Akiko International has information on travel discounts, tourism, trade and business and virtual tours.

5. Type **`http://www.akiko.lm.com`** in the location box to access Akiko International's home page.
6. Through Akiko's home page, you can access the Other Information on New Zealand link. See Figure 14.4 for the New Zealand/Aotearoa submission (`http://www.akiko.lm.com/nz/`).
7. From the Travel and Tourist Information item, choose the first option, An Illustrated Tour of the Country, which will produce a map of New Zealand (see Figure 14.5).

   By clicking the island of your choice, you start a guided tour complete with photographs, history, places to see, and information about the area.

   Another interesting stop on my Web travel was the GNN Travelers' Center (see Figure 14.6). This site is among the best sources of travel information on the Web. The GNN Home Page includes direct links to featured articles and information as well as a subdirectory called Special GNN Publications. This directory includes sports, education, book, finance, movie, and magazine sections as well as a travel icon.

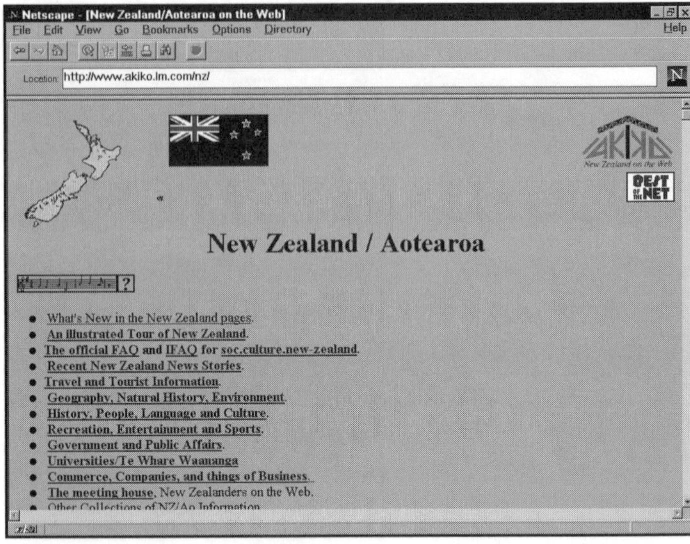

Figure 14.4.
New Zealand/Aotearoa.

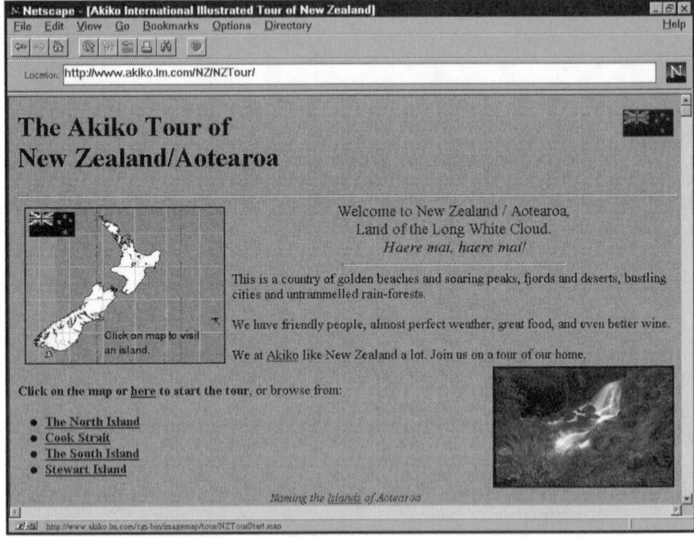

Figure 14.5.
An illustrated tour of New Zealand.

GNN's travel section includes links to worldwide travel advisories, travel book features, region, country, state, and city guides, and even a water sport directory called Cyber Wharf. In addition, an interactive forum in which you will be able to chat with travel authorities is planned for GNN.

8. Access the GNN Home Page by typing **`http://gnn.com/gnn/GNNhome.html`** in the location box at the top of the screen.

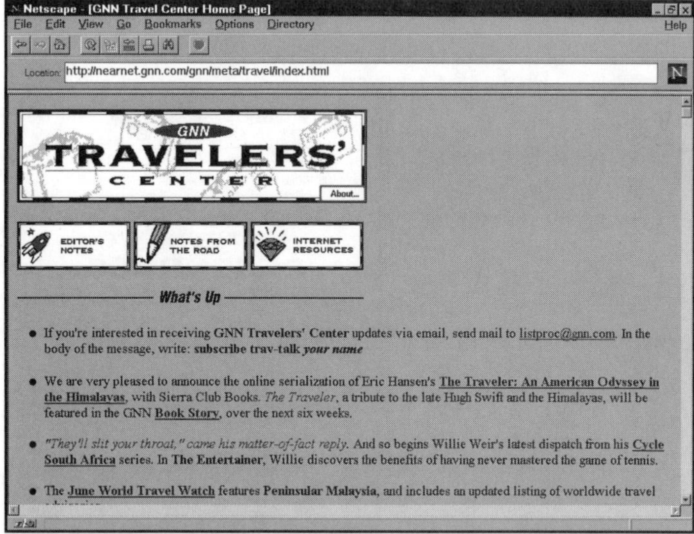

Figure 14.6.
The GNN Travelers' Center.

9. Move to the GNN Travelers' Center by selecting the Travel icon from the Special GNN Publications directory.
10. Select Travelers' Tales from the GNN Resource directory (see Figure 14.7).

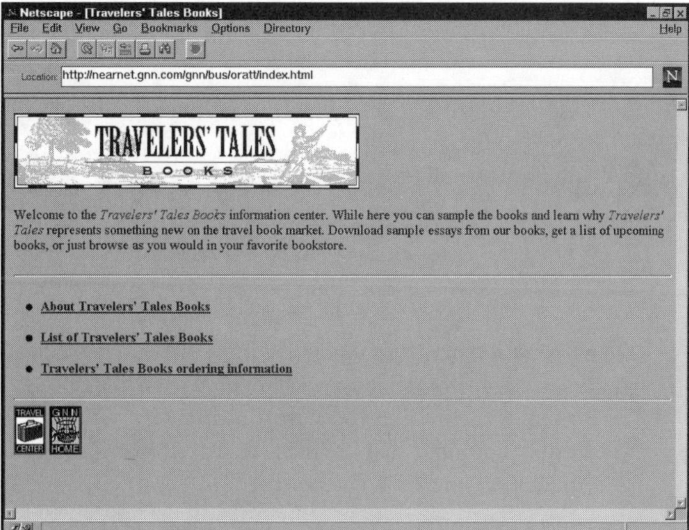

Figure 14.7.
Travelers' Tales Books, from GNN Travelers' Center.

One of the best features in the Travelers' Center is Internet Resources (see Figure 14.8). From here, you can access a range of travel-related sites, but before doing anything else be absolutely sure to click Net Travel - Using the Internet to Prepare for a Trip. It's excellent supplementary reading for this chapter.

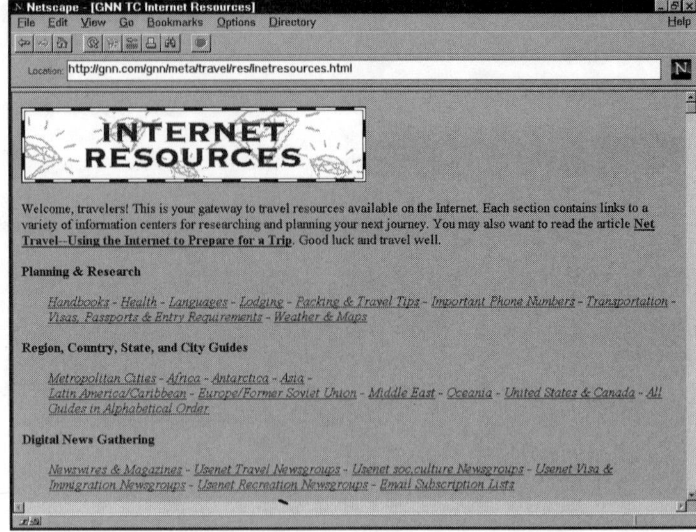

Figure 14.8.
The Internet Resources page from the Travelers' Center.

11. Click this page's Recreation item listed under Things to do, and you should receive a number of links to a variety of pages.

Warning: To view any videos contained in these links, you must set up your WWW browser properly. Because some files may be in Microsoft Video for Windows (VFW) format, that means pointing the .AVI extension in your `MOSAIC.INI` or `CELLO.INI` file to `MPLAYER.EXE`, which will display VFW files. Note, however, that you can substitute Cello for Mosaic if you use Cello instead.

The Recreation item menu contains links to a variety of sport and leisure entertainment links on the Web. There are options for all kinds of different tastes, including a list of restaurants in Boston, and climbing and skiing information sources. I wanted to check out restaurants in Boston and found that the file focused on moderately priced fare, brew pubs, and places to drink cider, interestingly enough.

Some of these ideas should help get you into travel on the Web. You will, no doubt, find other resources that fit your interests as you surf around with your browser. The Web is expanding rapidly, so more exciting sites are on the horizon!

If you have a particular interest that leads you to travel—such as art and architecture—you might want to focus your search for information that way. Perform searches on art exhibits and note the locations where the most interesting art can be found. This approach should narrow down the destinations you have to read up on in the mailing lists and archives.

However you approach your search for travel information, you are sure to discover much more than you anticipated on the Internet. It's a great trip in itself!

Summary

This chapter has explored the variety of travel resources on the Internet. Mailing lists and newsgroups demonstrate the Net's capacity for letting travelers and would-be travelers correspond and share stories and details, while FTP and Gopher sites provide access to graphics and (predominantly) text files that can help you determine your next travel locations. Finally, an extensive travel tour on the World Wide Web showed both the benefits and the potential drawbacks of multimedia travel planning, with information about a variety of different locations.

Task Review

In this chapter, you learned how to perform the following tasks:

- ☐ Subscribe to a mailing list that focuses on travel details and stories
- ☐ Find and join newsgroups that deal with travel destinations and concerns
- ☐ Retrieve information about travel from FTP sites
- ☐ Explore Gopher sites for details about travel destinations and issues
- ☐ Browse the World Wide Web for multimedia presentations of travel destinations

Q&A

Q Will I ever be able to use the Internet exclusively for making travel arrangements?

A Probably. In the works as of this writing is a "secure" version of NCSA Mosaic, designed expressly so that organizations can accept such items as credit card information over the WWW (right now, the Net is too open for this to be completely safe). Once that's in place, you'll begin to see a range of commercial sites that will enable you to place orders. Combined with the Web's forms capabilities (which Mosaic now offers and which Cello will offer in its next release), there's no reason whatsoever why you won't be able to access tour and travel information, figure out via a series of multimedia presentations where you want to go, and then

make transportation and accommodation arrangements by filling in the appropriate forms. Of course, it will likely be a long while before the less traveled parts of the world make their debut this way, so if you're interested in unusual locations, you may not find the Net of as much use, except through newsgroups and mailing lists.

Q Will the degree of detail about individual locations improve significantly?

A Yes, I definitely think so. There's every reason in the world for individual towns and cities (and countries, for that matter) to provide extensive information over the Internet, through both Gopher and Web sites. Cities are in competition for tourism dollars, but they're also fiercely competitive about corporate relocations. As corporations and other organizations move onto the Net, they'll want to use it as a research tool for this kind of information. What could be more immediately attractive, from the standpoint of a technologically savvy corporation, than to see an equally savvy community demonstrating itself in multimedia fashion on the World Wide Web? If you're currently working for a town or city, think about starting the process.

Extra Credit: Travel Excursions

Marion's search has yielded an extensive amount of information, including resources for searching the Net even further. I'd like to spend the rest of this chapter exploring the Web a bit further, to let you see some of the other resources available and the way in which these resources are growing. Follow along with your Web browser, and see what's out there. I guarantee you'll be amazed.

Excursion 14.1: The Virtual Tourist and Beyond.

An extremely worthwhile stop on your travel search is the Virtual Tourist (`http://wings.buffalo.edu/world`), which provides a clickable map of the world (see Figure 14.9).

By clicking one of the inset sections, you call up a more detailed map of that region. Figure 14.10, for example, shows the detail map of Europe.

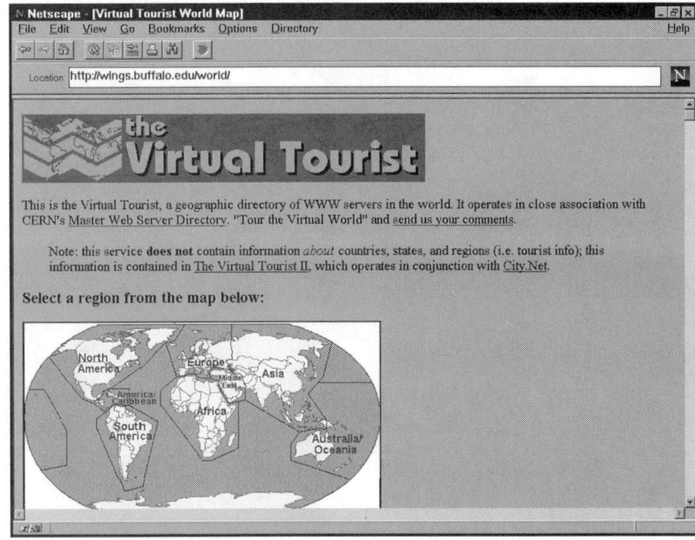

Figure 14.9.
The Virtual Tourist's clickable world map.

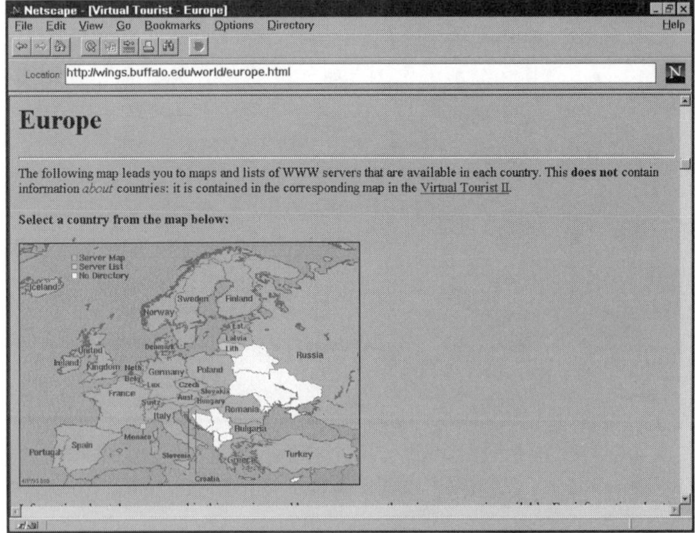

Figure 14.10.
The Virtual Tourist European map.

Nor is this the end of the interactive map chain. Several of the sites in the Virtual Tourist display lead to other clickable maps, such as the UK map displayed in Figure 14.11.

Figure 14.11.
The clickable map of the UK and Ireland.

Warning: When using a clickable (interactive) map, be sure to check the map's key before making your choice. Some of the locations point to WWW sites (including other maps), while others lead to Gophers or even text files. Furthermore, don't expect most sites to be travel-oriented. The vast majority of these links are to universities or governmental institutions, not to travel destinations. Still, some of the educational sites offer links to sites dealing with the local area and to other informative sites within the same country.

The UK and Ireland are nice places, to be sure, but we have more exotic fish to fry (or whatever the metaphor is). So let's head eastward from the enchanted isle and get a smattering of what else is available.

First stop, Paris. Oh, why not? There are other Web sites scattered throughout France, but it's spring as I'm writing this, and Paris and spring form an irresistible cliché.

Figure 14.12 shows a home page for Paris, including a link to some virtual tours. One such tour leads to a historical walk through the city, including an informative and colorful view of Paris's historic river, the Seine.

Skipping an unbelievably large portion of the world, we arrive in Australia. Australia has a number of worthwhile Internet sites to visit, but an excellent starting point is the home page at `http://www.csu.edu.au/education/australia.html`, which offers a variety of travel, government, and education links (see Figure 14.13).

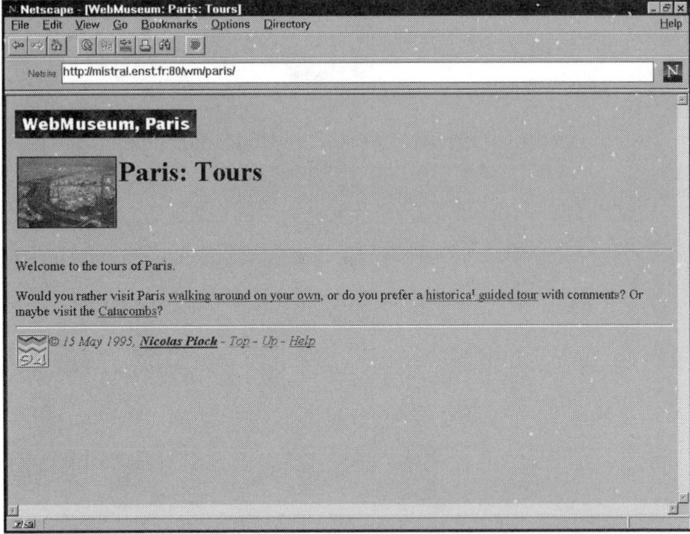

Figure 14.12.
The Paris home page.

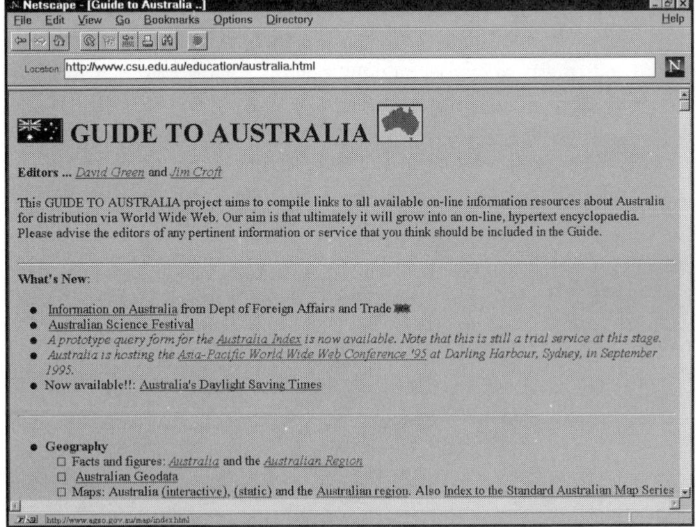

Figure 14.13.
The Australian home page, with travel and other links.

A link to Tasmania found under the Guide to the States and Territories leads us to the Tasmanian home page. Having always been fascinated by this island state (and what Bugs Bunny fan hasn't?), it's only natural that I would want to travel there, even if only virtually (see Figure 14.14).

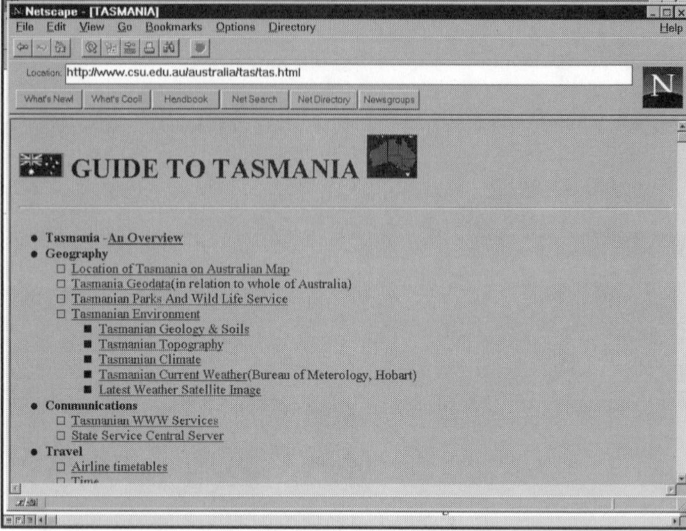

Figure 14.14.
The Tasmanian home page.

Last stop, Japan. While the Japanese have only begun building their presence on the Internet, it's clear from their earliest efforts that when the construction begins in earnest, it's going to be little short of spectacular. Here is a source of information particularly valuable to anyone wishing to visit the islands.

Figure 14.15 is part of the growing Japan information section of Stanford University's Japanese WWW initiative. From here are several obvious links to Japanese travel and tourism.

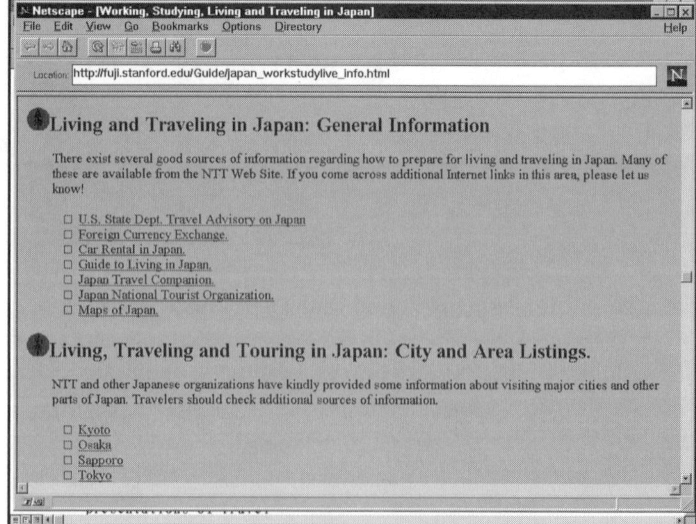

Figure 14.15.
Stanford's Living and Traveling in Japan.

The Japan Travel Companion link takes us to Figure 14.16 (residing, as the URL address shows, on a computer in Japan itself), which not only gives us travel information, but also promises details on how to travel cheaply. Since we've all probably heard that Japan is an extremely expensive country to visit, this will surely be of interest.

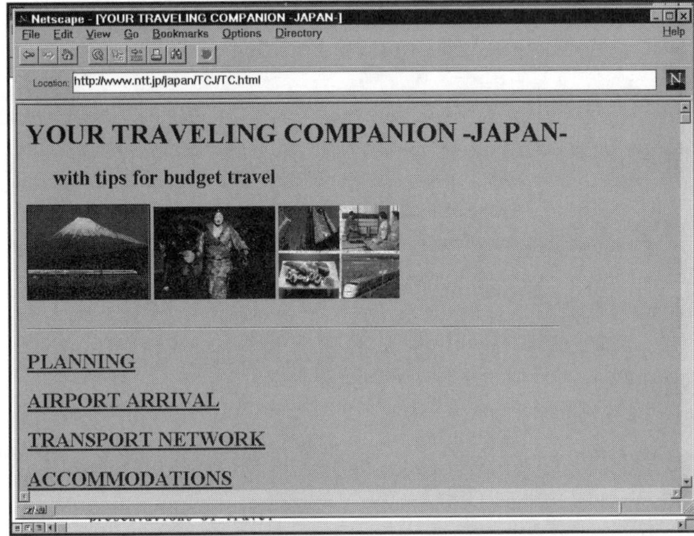

Figure 14.16.
The Japan Travel Companion.

Travel and the Web: Made for Each Other?

Is the World Wide Web the best Internet site for travel information? In one way, yes, because it points to practically all other resources. In another way, however, the Web seems to be establishing itself as a source for appealing but undetailed information, along the lines of a published travel guide or (perhaps at best) an encyclopedia entry.

After more common Web access is available, however, this will likely change, if the history of Internet usage is any indication. Before long, we should see travel journals and collections of travel stories (both the wonderful and the horrific) make their way in numbers onto the Web, counterbalancing the tame multimedia efforts so far established. In addition, we'll start to see in-depth guided tours that will enable you to learn about these places in much greater detail.

A very tiny percentage of us will visit more than 10 percent of the nations of the world, so multimedia traveling via the Web can, if it's done right, make a big difference in our appreciation of other lands—as long as it becomes a technology for virtual *travel,* not just virtual tourism.

15

DAY
5

Art on the Net

With all the files available through Gopher, FTP, and World Wide Web sites, it's hardly surprising that some of them are digital reproductions of works of art. Digitized art has been available ever since someone first designed a computer monitor capable of displaying it, and today's graphics-capable monitors have made downloading reproductions more appealing than ever. Your favorite Michelangelo or Picasso in .GIF or .JPG form, after all, can be displayed when your computer boots up, and if you have enough of these on your hard drive you can assign them to appear randomly as wallpaper or screen savers. Chapter 15 offers a glimpse at the horde of artwork the Internet holds.

In this chapter, you will learn how to perform the following tasks:

- Use e-mail to contact other art enthusiasts
- Subscribe to newsgroups that contain information about digitized art
- Explore for art files using the resources of Gopher
- Find and retrieve reproductions from the World Wide Web
- Search for art using Veronica
- Use the World Wide Web to learn of artist activities on the Internet

Art and the Internet

The goal of art is human expression. To attain that goal, artists have always been eager to explore new media. A wall in a cave, a ceiling in a church, a slab of marble, a square of canvas: these have been only some of the artistic media used in the past, and it takes little knowledge of the fine arts to list a dozen more. Far from being frightened by the new media offered through high technology, artists have in fact consistently been among the first to embrace it. Artists dipped their brushes into computer pixelization almost the moment the technology existed, and computer art has been expanding into a new set of genres over the past quarter-century. Small wonder, then, that the Internet should attract artists now.

Most artwork on the Internet consists of graphics files. Find one, and you can download it or (in some cases) view it online. Increasingly, though, we're starting to see Internet-specific experimental art work its way onto, primarily, the World Wide Web. Within a year and a half, artists will undoubtedly have found a way to parlay the power of this new global interactive medium into yet another method for articulating their vision. That's the way it's always been, and thankfully it's not about to change now. The problem, of course, is that the Internet relies exclusively on flat-image, nontactile materials, but maybe that too will eventually change.

In the meantime, there's lots to explore. Whether your choice is modern or ancient, you have a significant amount of material available to you. And because traveling around the world building a collection of great art is something most of us have at least thought about,

navigating the Internet in search of the images you want seems merely a natural (or is that virtual?) progression.

One such searcher is Internet author Celine Latulipe, who takes you on an artistic odyssey for the major part of this chapter. After that, we'll take a look at the explosion of artistic activity that has been taking place on the World Wide Web over the past year and a half or so.

Art on the Net

by Celine Latulipe

Art has always been a hobby of mine, but since high school, my time constraints have doubled and my watercolor painting has practically become a thing of the past. I've always wanted to be a collector of great art, but being a university student, it seemed completely out of the question. Buying art, even in print form, is far too expensive, and I've never liked buying books containing plates because you often end up paying for pictures you don't even like. All I really wanted was to be able to find paintings that I enjoy looking at and have them at my disposal to appreciate when I please.

I thought I was asking for the world until I realized the resources available over the Internet. Since I began my search, I've collected many masterpieces, by the masters as well as currently working artists. The great thing is that the search is never-ending, and whenever I have a few minutes, I go hunting for more specimens for my collection. It has become something of an obsession (always a danger for Netters) and a very private, self-centered obsession at that.

My first thought was that I would be doing a million keyword searches, so in anticipation, I scribbled out a bunch of subjects and names on a Post-it and stuck it to the side of my screen. Being an eclectic sort of art collector, there was no specific artist or group of artists I was looking for; all I knew was that I liked paintings and pen and ink sketches, but I didn't really appreciate sculpture, photography, and a few other media. So my list included a few of my favorite painters—Leonardo Da Vinci, Vincent Van Gogh, Georges Seurat, and Lauren Harris—as well as some general subject titles: fine art, art, paintings, pictures, and gallery. I later realized that, in the art subject at least, keyword searches are necessary only a fraction of the time, especially when you don't know exactly what you're looking for.

Note: This chapter is in a slightly different format from most of the others. Here, you'll follow Celine as she makes her way around the Web, joining in by performing the tasks as she does them. This is a less prescriptive approach than most chapters, and I'm interested in which you think is more useful. E-mail me at `nrandall@watarts.uwaterloo.ca` to let me know, okay?

Newsgroups

Like all special interest areas, art has a solid share of newsgroups. Activity on these groups varies widely and sporadically, but if you have an interest in a particular artist, art form, technique, or general topic, you're almost sure to find someone willing to talk to you about it.

Task 15.1: Conduct a newsgroup search.

Newsgroups are something I had trouble with from the beginning; user-friendly is a concept that newsgroup reader programs such as trn (which I used) have managed to evade. I could get in, and I learned fairly quickly that pressing s subscribes and u unsubscribes, but useful things such as typing h for help isn't found on the screen. Fumbling through the reading of messages was easy, but I couldn't figure out how to respond to any particular message. It took awhile, but with the aid of the help menu, I finally was able to search for newsgroups, and at this point my list of keywords was put to use. To conduct a newsgroup search, follow these steps:

1. At the command prompt, type **trn** to start your newsreader.
2. Rather than scrolling through thousands of groups, trn offers users a way to search for specific topic related entries. Use `fineart` as your keyword and at the newsgroup prompt, type **1 fineart**. This command tells the newsreader to locate all groups with a title containing the word sequence `fineart`.

   This search demonstrates some of the confusion with using trn. The following screen displays the product of my first attempt (boldfaced text represents what I typed):

```
****** End of newsgroups — what next? [npq] l fineart
Completely unsubscribed newsgroups:
 [Type Return to continue]

Unsubscribed but mentioned in /home/clatulip/.newsrc:

****** End of newsgroups — what next? [Npq] l art
Completely unsubscribed newsgroups:
alt.artcom
alt.arts.nomad
alt.ascii-art
alt.ascii-art.animation
alt.autos.karting
alt.binaries.clip-art
alt.binaries.pictures.cartoons
alt.binaries.pictures.fine-art.graphics
alt.destroy.the.earth
alt.fan.kali.astarte.inanna
alt.party
```

```
alt.pave.the.earth
alt.save.the.earth
alt.sport.darts
alt.startrek.creative
alt.startrek.klingon
alt.support.abuse-partners
alt.support.arthritis
```

Obviously, there are no newsgroups that matched the fineart category. So, try a broader category—`art`. What is shown in the previous screen is only the very first part of the list, but notice that many of the items listed are not at all what we are looking for.

3. To search for newsgroups containing the word art, type **`1 art`** at the command prompt and press Enter.

Note: When you search newsgroups, you'll almost always get more than you bargained for. trn pulls out anything with the successive letters `a`, `r`, and `t`, in that order, so I ended up with newsgroups such as `alt.support.abuse-partners` and `alt.party`. Cool (well, the last one anyway), but not what I wanted.

The first two newsgroups I came up with were `alt.binaries.pictures.fine-art.graphics` and `rec.arts.fine`. The first, which looked like the most interesting and applicable to my interests, turned out to be very inactive; I didn't see a single message posted there in a span of two weeks. Undaunted, I pursued the second group, and found some interesting (and some uninteresting) conversations going on.

4. To `access rec.arts.fine`, type **`g rec.arts.fine`** at the prompt and press Enter.
5. You can browse the postings for any valuable or exciting information by entering the letter that appears at the beginning of each post.

When I opened this group, I gained access to a variety of art related conversations. A discussion of the use, supply, and pros and cons of using masonite as a base for oil paintings was probably great for anybody actually involved in the activity, but having tried oils only twice (and never having had any success), I ignored that thread. There was, however, a somewhat controversial discussion going on concerning the impact of (homo)sexuality on the works of different artists. I learned a lot about a few different artists and felt as though I got to personally know some of the group contributors. It was an experience that made me realize how small the world can quickly seem to someone who uses the Internet regularly. I read a message typed probably a minute earlier by someone on the other side of the ocean, in reply to someone else on the other side of the continent.

So far, however, I wasn't much closer to finding what I'd set out to find. That began to change, however, as soon as I saw the following posting (I've only reproduced a portion of it here):

```
This is intended to be the same sort of information that would be
included in an art book.

A long-term goal would be to assemble an art book and/or a CD-ROM
based on the work submitted. (Of course, we would request the consent
of each poster prior to including their work.) This would include
the possible non-profit distribution to art departments worldwide.

People wishing to discuss the use of computer graphics in fine arts
may submit their postings to alt.pictures.fine-art.d

archives can be found in the file
/pub/fine-art
on uxa.ecn.bgu.edu
by anonymous ftp.

The file "list" will contain a list of what we have.

 (Remember to set binary — most everything is binary or compressed
```

Taken from the `alt.binaries.pictures` newsgroup, this message states that the pictures that had been posted to the newsgroup were available for downloading at an FTP site. Most newsgroups have this type of thing in operation: the sites are known as *archives.* There are even search tools designed specifically for searching archive sites. The sites can hold a lot of completely unimportant stuff, especially if the unnecessary messages aren't weeded out before being archived. However, tons of information is available at these sites, and I checked out the one recommended in this posting.

Gopher

Gophers are falling out of favor with the artistic community, because of their inability to display graphics. For that reason, the Web is taking over (as it is with just about everything else, as well). But Gopher sites remain valid as archives of existing image files and published information, so it's well worth spending some time checking them out.

Task 15.2: Use Gopher to locate art on the Net.

My first Internet account was through Carleton University in Ottawa, and my Gopher search therefore began at the Carleton University Gopher. The Carleton Gopher itself didn't provide much in terms of art, but it did enable me to access Gopher Jewels (`cwis.usc.edu`), a Gopher site with, in my opinion, an extremely appropriate name. You can access Gopher Jewels from almost any Home Gopher.

1. Start your Gopher program and select Gopher Jewels from the menu lists.

Tip: One sure fire way to locate Gopher Jewels is to start your gopher program by typing **`gopher uic.edu`**. This command will present the University of Chicago Home Gopher Server. Select item **`11`** (The World) and press Enter once. Gopher will now present another directory of menus with Gopher Jewels listed as item `9`.

From Gopher Jewels, you can search many different directories, including Arts and Humanities; Museums, Exhibits and Special Collections; and a few others for good measure. These directories all have great stuff in them, but they aren't specifically what I was looking for. Then I chose a directory called Gophers With Subject Trees, which led me to a number of hot spots.

2. To find the Gophers With Subject Trees directory, choose the Education, Social Sciences, Arts and Humanities directory from the Gopher Jewels menu.
3. Select the last menu on the Education, Social Sciences, Arts and Humanities list (item `11`), which offers a search option. Press Enter.
4. Enter the words **`Gophers With Subject Trees`** in the search box and press Enter. Gopher will present you with the desired directory.
5. Browse this directory at your leisure to locate a wealth of available arts directories and pictures. Don't forget to bookmark your favorites for future reference.

   My search led me to the University of Texas, where I found an arts directory, bringing me back to Canada to the Victoria Freenet and a set of numbered (but unnamed) picture files. There I found a Dali picture I wanted, so I used Gopher to save it in my home account. I bookmarked the Gophers With Subject Trees menu, for future reference.

   Figure 15.1 demonstrates one of the problems with searching for files across the Net. This screen shows a portion of a list of pictures available from Victoria Freenet. The one I chose was obviously a Botticelli print, but the filename `Botticelli-03.jpg` did nothing to help me figure out which Dali I was getting. This is one of the main problems with downloading files from directories such as this one; the filenames aren't often the most descriptive.
6. From the Gophers With Subject Trees menu, select item `1`, the `AMI` subject tree (available directly by Gophering to `gopher.mountain.net`).

Figure 15.1.
Gopher menu showing pictures from Victoria Freenet.

```
                 Internet Gopher Information Client 2.0 pl3

                       Pictures from Victoria Freenet

      19. Botticelli-03.jpg.
      20. Botticelli-04.jpg.
      21. ByAnyOther.gif <Picture>
      22. Chagall_selfportrait.jpg.
lqqqqqqqqqqqqqqqqqqqqqqqqqqqqqqqqqqqqqqqqqqqqqqqqqqqqqqqqqqqqqqqqqqqqqqqqqqk
x                                                                          x
x Save in file:   dali1.gif                                                x
x                                                                          x
x                                        [Cancel ^G] [Accept - Enter]      x
x                                                                          x
mqqqqqqqqqqqqqqqqqqqqqqqqqqqqqqqqqqqqqqqqqqqqqqqqqqqqqqqqqqqqqqqqqqqqqqqqqqj
      30. Edouard_Manet-A_Bar_at_the_Folies-Bergere.gif <Picture>
      31. Edouard_Manet-Le_Dejeuner_sur_l'herbe.gif <Picture>
      32. Edouard_Manet-Le_Repos.gif <Picture>
      33. Edouard_Manet-The_Fifer.gif <Picture>
      34. Edouard_Manet-The_Railroad.gif <Picture>
      35. Einstein-01.gif <Picture>
      36. Einstein-02.gif <Picture>

ress █ for Help, █ to Quit, █ to go up a menu                   Page: 2/11
```

7. Under the AMI Gopher, you will find two great directories: the `Art, Music, Sound, and Humanities` directory, and the `Images and Pictures` directory. Open the `Art, Music, Sound, and Humanities` directory and select the RiceInfo (Rice University Arts) Gopher (see Figure 15.2). Press Enter.

Figure 15.2.
Rice University Arts Gopher menu.

```
                 Internet Gopher Information Client 2.0 pl3

                   RiceInfo (Rice University CWIS) (Arts)

-->█ 1.  About this directory.
     2.  Art Com Magazine/
     3.  ArtFBI ArtFax.
     4.  Arts Wire Artist's Network Gopher/
     5.  Australian National University Art History
     6.  Bay Area Bookstore Events/
     7.  Cal Performances/
     8.  California Museum of Photography: Network Exhibitions/
     9.  Contest: New Voices and New Visions in MultiMedia, $5,000 prizes.
     10. Dallas Museum of Art - Information & Images/
     11. FineArt Forum/
     12. FineArt Forum (e-journal and resource directory)/
     13. FineArt Forum Online/
     14. Fourth Int'l Symposium on Electronic Arts (Nov 4-7, 93, Minneapoli../
     15. Grateful Dead/
     16. Leonardo/
     17. Manifestos/
     18. Minneapolis College of Art and Design Gopher/

ress █ for Help, █ to Quit, █ to go up a menu                   Page: 1/2
```

8. From Rice, Gopher to the `Dallas Museum of Art` and a directory called `Museum Galleries (images)`.

   In the `Museum Galleries` directory, you will find subdirectories dividing the available online art into `Europe`, `Americas`, `Asia`, and `Contemporary` art. Some directories may not have files in them, but most will have a few.

9. After bookmarking the `Museum Galleries`, move back to the `AMI` home directory by pressing **`u`** to return to the previous menus or by locating it via bookmark.

10. Select the **`Art and Images`** directory, item **`16`** on the list.

I checked out several of these directories, but I was most impressed by the `Art & Images` directory, which contained a plethora of art sources. My two favorites were Impressionist Art from University of Vermont and Postcard Collection from University of Vermont. From these sources, I downloaded a bunch of .JPG files.

Figure 15.3 shows one of the pictures I found. The shot shows the graphics file itself, displayed in PaintShop Pro, and Winsock Gopher in the background. As the Gopher windows appeared, I started in the AMI Gopher. From AMI, I chose Images and Pictures, and then chose Art and Images. I finally ended up at Impressionist Images From the University of Vermont, where I chose the Renoir picture, "Young Women Talking." I downloaded it to my hard drive. Notice the title bar in the Paint Shop Pro screen: The computer renamed it *RENOIR.GIF.* It sometimes can be a problem when the computer shortens a UNIX name to fit DOS's filename format; the new names are often even more ambiguous than the UNIX names.

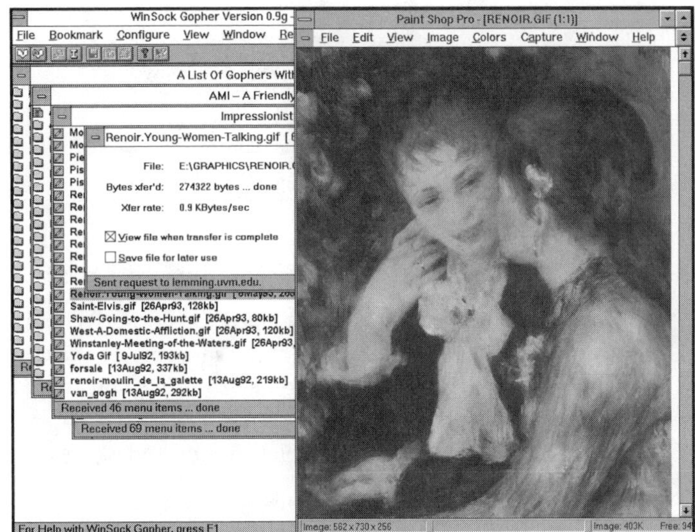

Figure 15.3.
Renoir's "Young Women Talking" from the University of Vermont.

At this point, I decided to turn to the World Wide Web browser, Mosaic. Although Mosaic is a World Wide Web browser, it handles Gophering extremely well. Figure 15.4 shows an art directory I located in the Netherlands after clicking on several Gopher items. Here, I have found a site offering numerous picture files in .GIF or .JPG format. I can't remember how I found the site (I could have used Mosaic's history feature, but only while engaged in the same session), or what it's called, but it really doesn't matter. Below the menus is the Document URL box, showing which Gopher or FTP site is being visited; all I have to do is use Mosaic's Open URL feature to return there.

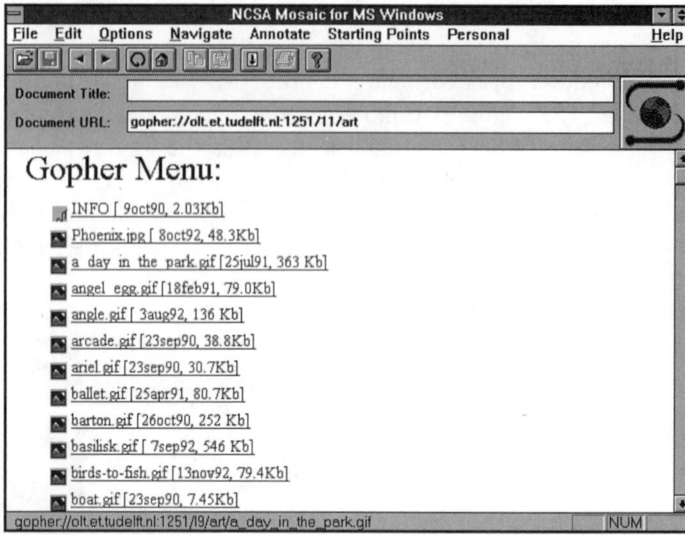

Figure 15.4.
Netherlands Gopher site with downloadable art.

When Searching Fails, Ask

Most of us, it seems, are reluctant to ask directions. Whether out of embarrassment or sheer pride, we'll drive around for an hour or more rather than stop at a service station and ask for help finding a building or a street, and the same reluctance appears to hold true on the Net. In both cases—the service station and the Net—you'll find someone willing to help you in your search, so why not stop by a newsgroup and locate what you want much more quickly?

Task 15.3: Post a request to a newsgroup.

I was pleased with my searching so far, but I felt I should be finding much more. So I turned back to the newsgroups to see what I could come up with. Having joined the `rec.arts.fine` Usenet newsgroup, I decided to get aggressive and just ask for what I wanted. So I posted a message asking for information on online galleries. When you decide to post to a newsgroup, make sure that you are familiar with the group itself in terms of content, members and their use of netiquette, to avoid repetitive or misplaced questions (also check the FAQs).

1. To post a message to the entire newsgroup, as I wished to do in this case, start your newsreader and open the appropriate group.
2. Select the `post` command (under Article in NewsX2 or type **`postnews`** in UNIX). A UNIX-based newsreader will ask whether you are responding to a previous article or if you are starting a new thread. To post to the entire group on a new topic, indicate that you are starting a new thread.

3. At the next prompt, indicate which group to post the message to. In my case, it would be **rec.arts.fine**. You will now be taken into vi to compose your article.
4. Type a complete and concise request that is well tagged so that readers will be able to judge the message's applicability from the subject line.
5. When your message is complete, press **z** twice and you will be returned to the UNIX prompt.

Within a day of my own request I had received four responses, offering more sources. One of them pointed me to another Usenet group called `alt.binaries.pictures`, where pictures are sometimes posted. Another person sent me the names and e-mail addresses of three people involved in the area. I promptly thanked the people who had sent me information, and then wrote e-mails to the new sources. The last e-mail I received gave me a direct source: an FTP site in Sweden that apparently had a huge number of masterpieces online. With David's permission, here's the first part of the message:

```
Date: Mon, 7 Mar 1994 10:23:30 - 0600 (CST)
From: david furstenau <df@unlinfo.unl.edu>
To: clatulip@ccs.carleton.ca
Subject: ONLINE ART

Dear Celine ...

Though I paint and draw with traditional tools, I'm
primarily an airbrusher. Whilst surfing the Net to see if I could
find anything of value for like-minded individuals, I fell into the
most impressive art collection I've seen on the Net. Mostly .gifs and
jpegs, but they are images from most any significant artist you can
name: Dega, Van Gogh, Monet, etc. Even modern people like
Geiger, Escher, and Patrick Nagel.
Being an airbrusher, I was especially drawn to the
impressive works of: Hajime.Sorayama, and Boris.Vallejo. Simply:
ftp ftp.sunet.se (ANONYMOUS)
It's at the University of Sweden, so keep in mind the time
difference.
```

This reply was among several I received, but it was by far the most helpful. In fact, it was the first reply I got after posting, and it was on my computer when I logged on the very next morning. That's one of the beauties of the Internet, especially in contrast to snailmail: responses can be instantaneous. The message came from an Internet user who is obviously very happy about what he's found, but who is also clearly very guarded. In it, David basically warns me that I should remember my Netiquette and keep in mind the time difference between here and Sweden, so as not to force them to restrict access and therefore, ruin the source for the rest of the Internet world.

Warning: Many FTP sites are not designed exclusively for public use; in most cases, that is the last purpose. In other words, many sites are corporation or government department computers that are already heavily utilized during the day, and public users may not be completely welcome during work hours. For this reason it is always a good idea to consider the time difference and FTP only during off-hours.

6. To locate this site, type **`ftp ftp.sunet.se`**, and then log in anonymously (**login: `anonymous`**).
7. Under password, insert your full Internet address. In a few seconds you will be in the system and an `ftp>` prompt will appear.
8. Change the directory to the appropriate path by entering **`cd pub/pictures/art`**.
9. Next, type the `list` command (`ls`) to see what's there. Part of my initial result was as follows:

```
Michelangelo
George.Ouanounou
Eric.Jordan
Leonardo.da.Vinci
William.Blake
Ken.Kelly
Dennis.Lu
Thomas.Cole
Camille.Pissarro
Ken.Foote
Berthe.Morisot
Gustave.Caillebotte
Alan.Lee
Edgar.Degas
H.R.Giger
Zhou.Jun
Stephen.Whealton
Stefan.Torreiter
Boris.Vallejo
Limbourg brothers
Mihaly.Zichy
226 Transfer complete.
631 bytes received in 0.51 seconds (1.2 Kbytes/s)
ftp>quit
```

David was right; a great selection was available. Within the art directory, there were directories for a number of different artists, including Degas, Da Vinci, Monet, Blake, Van Gogh, and many others. I left my university account and fired up my commercial one, and then used Cello to FTP to the site and downloaded straight to my hard drive (a bonus with this account) and checked out my findings in PaintShop Pro. At this site, I found my favorite Escher print, and then downloaded it to my hard drive.

15

The ANIMA Project

There are many art archives worth exploring, but as you'll discover here, ANIMA is perhaps the best single place to begin.

Task 15.5: Explore Artworld from ANIMA.

I'm a firm believer in Murphy's Law. Maybe that's why, after spending a large number of hours browsing the Net looking for masterpieces online, I got another response to my Usenet request for online images information that seemed to be the answer to all my problems. It seemed that almost all of the time I had spent in searching could have been saved had I known about one single resource—ANIMA—right from the start. Actually, that's an exaggeration; some of the parts of the resource were accessed more easily by direct Gopher or FTP, but in many instances, ANIMA was the perfect Internet resource for artists. Following is a portion of the e-mail message I received; I reproduce it here because it also demonstrates the friendliness and goodwill on the Internet, which never fails to amaze me.

```
Date: Wed, 9 Mar 94 02:18 PST
From: Derek Dowden <ddowden@wimsey.bc.ca>
To: Celine Latulipe <clatulip@ccs.carleton.ca>
Cc: ddowden@wimsey.bc.ca
Subject: Re: Online Masterpieces

Hi Celine,

As a Carleton graduate myself, I thought you might be interested in my
current online art project ANIMA. (I have been running art networks online
since 1984 with ArtNet out of Toronto). It is really useful to somehow get
Mosaic access to the Net, there is a lot of art now available
only through the World Wide Web. Good luck with your book on the Internet.
Please let me know if you find any art resources on the Net we don't have
in ANIMA.

Here is my current release blurb:
ANIMA - Arts Network for Integrated Media Applications

The WebWeavers presents the premiere of the public version of 'ANIMA -
Arts Network for Integrated Media Applications'. The ANIMA information
service provides a network source for information focusing on the
intersection of arts, technology, and media.

ANIMA is a newly available multimedia cultural information service now
distributed over the World Wide Web global hypertext network. ANIMA
provides online access to cultural theory and expression, ideas, and
research.

ANIMA explores the possibilities of networking as an information resource
and tool for research in art and technology, the development of virtual
communities for creative collaboration, and the network as a medium for
artistic exploration and expression.
```

```
Currently available ANIMA features includes
ArtWorld: a service center for the arts online;
Spectrum, a selection of electronic publications,
NEXUS: an online gallery space for artists projects;
ATLAS a reference library on art and technology,
Sphere: a journal for communications theory;
Techne: research on media tools and techniques;
Virtuality: the impact on the interface of interactivity and immersion; and
Persona: a community forum for empowering voice and vision on the N.
Many new features will be released over the upcoming weeks on a regular
basis.

ANIMA can be now be accessed with a direct connection to the Internet
using Mosaic software available for Macintosh or Windows. The URL for ANIMA
is - http://wimsey.com/anima/ANIMAhome.html.

For further information on how to connect, contribute, or participate in
ANIMA please email anima@wimsey.bc.ca.

- - - - - - - - - - - - - - - - - - - - - - - - - - - - - - - - - - - -
Derek J. Dowden,
The WebWeavers, anima@wimsey.bc.ca
ANIMA - Arts Network for Integrated Media Applications
URL http://wimsey.com/anima/ANIMAhome.html
```

I checked out this ANIMA network, specifically the ArtWorld section. Figure 15.5 shows the ArtWorld home page, one page below the ANIMA home page.

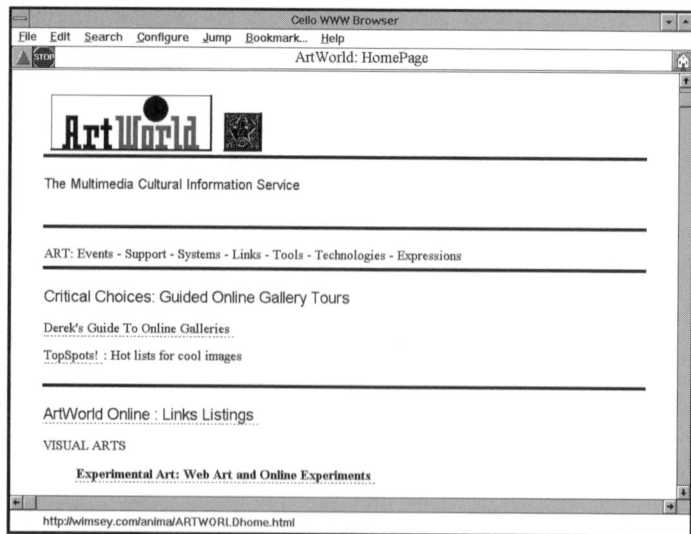

Figure 15.5.
ArtWorld home page, from ANIMA.

The title `ArtWorld` was underlined, indicating that it is a hypertext link. Clicking it brought up the linked screen. On this page, I found items such as Derek's Guide to Online Galleries, and Traditional and Fine Arts. Under this last item, I found a lengthy list of online art, with the title *Experimental Art: Web Art.* The list included the OTIS project, a Random Portrait Gallery, Off the Wall Gallery, the Marius Wate Home Page, Underworld Industries, Playground Gallery, and a whole host of other directories. The great thing about ANIMA is that in many instances, the creators have given a description and critique of the sites, galleries, and so on, which make up the user's options. This is a nice feature; most other art browsing sites don't offer it.

Anything with a title like "Off the Wall Gallery" simply has to be checked out, so I did. Figure 15.6 shows two pages deeper in the ANIMA directory, and demonstrates one of the nicer aspects of ANIMA—relatively thorough descriptions.

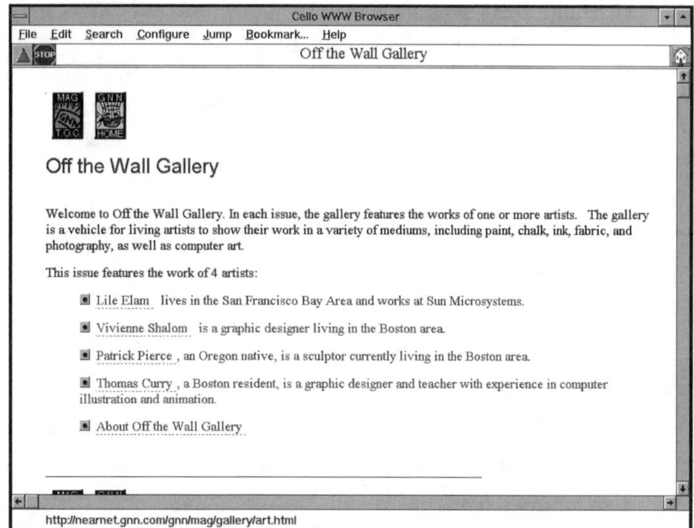

Figure 15.6.
Off the Wall Gallery page.

Artists' names are in hypertext, and when I clicked them, I got directories that let me see their work. I downloaded some files and discovered (although I wasn't really surprised) that some really interesting stuff was in there. The fact that this collection changes monthly also is nice; it's like having a neighborhood gallery featuring different exhibits and free admission.

The part of ANIMA I checked out was minimal—the service is obviously very extensive, and not limited to my specific topic of painting. Like many other of the sites mentioned in this chapter, the arts in general are represented extensively on the Internet. I came across directories for dance, theater, literature, sculpture, television, graphic design, architecture, and numerous other subjects. Any of the main directories that have been mentioned are good starting places for searches on any of these or related topics.

Of course, there also are many directories, newsgroups, FTP sites, and so on, for computer art of all sorts. Simply start searching, and I guarantee you'll find more than you thought you were asking for.

Note: The image (.GIF, .JPG, and so on) files that I have mentioned also are not exclusively for paintings, and there are .GIFs of photographs all over the Net, as well as .GIFs of photographs of other arts (architecture, sculpture, design).

For me, the search for art is never-ending, and even if my monitor gives me only 16 colors and mediocre resolution, I'm not about to stop. Half of the fun, after all, has been the challenge of finding the masterpieces to which I want ready access. If I really want to have a good copy of them, I can take the file to a store that does laser printing, and get my "print" there, or have them turn my files into slides. And the great masterpieces aren't the only material I ended up with. For example, I even went out and found a .GIF file of a photograph of my roommate's favorite: penguins. Of course, I have no idea where I downloaded it to or what it got named when it was downloaded, so I haven't looked at it yet, but I know it's on my hard drive somewhere.

I now know how to navigate the Internet. Now, if only I could figure out how to use my own computer.

Summary

As Celine has demonstrated, the Internet is a rich and intriguing resource for starting your own art collection. In fact, it's equally rich for establishing an archive of photographs or related documents. Despite the wide range of searching and downloading Celine went through, she readily admits that she hasn't even begun to explore the Net's wealth of information about art, art history, and other art-related issues. What she has done, however, is make an excellent start.

The combination of tools demonstrates the multimedia nature of art. Not only are newsgroups and e-mail extremely useful, but Gophers and FTPs also are essential to make the collection happen at all. Then, too, there's the issue of actually viewing what you've downloaded, and here a knowledge of your own computer's software is needed. I have a feeling that the World Wide Web will soon receive the majority of attention from Internet artists, but so far that hasn't happened. Still, if resources like ANIMA are any indication, that day can't be far off.

Task Review

In this chapter, you learned how to perform the following tasks:

- ☐ Use e-mail to contact other art enthusiasts
- ☐ Subscribe to newsgroups that contain information about digitized art
- ☐ Explore for art files using the resources of Gopher
- ☐ Find and retrieve reproductions from the World Wide Web
- ☐ Search for art using Veronica
- ☐ Explore a few of the Web's art exhibitions

Q&A

Q Now that I've downloaded some pictures, how do I go about looking at them?

A As mentioned throughout the chapter, you need viewers. This isn't a special Internet problem; it's endemic to all computing activity. If you have a certain kind of file on your hard drive, you need a program that will let you work with it. In the case of graphics files, you'll find, for the most part, two major types. The first has the extension .GIF, the second the extension .JPG. Many graphics or paint programs enable you to view .GIFs; in fact, it's likely your system shipped with some kind of .GIF-capable program or another. To view .JPG files, however, you might need a separate program. Fortunately, shareware and freeware packages abound, and they're available on the Net, on commercial services such as CompuServe or America Online, or on shareware floppies or CD-ROMs.

A more difficult issue is setting up your Gopher or Web program to let you view pictures automatically. In all cases, the installation instructions will guide you through the procedure of associating various types of files with specific programs, but don't expect it to be easy. Windows Mosaic, for example, is hopelessly convoluted in this regard, and even the friendlier Cello could use some help here. Gopher programs range in ease this way, and you can expect most programs to assume that you have more knowledge about this kind of thing than you may well have. Fortunately, it's not easy to botch things up completely, so do some experimenting.

The general principle is this: if you want to automatically view a file as soon as it downloads, you have to associate that type of file with a specific viewer program. In other words, if you plan to use PaintShop Pro for Windows (as Celine has done throughout her exploration) to view .JPG files in Mosaic, you have to specify somewhere in the program's configuration file that .JPG extensions will be associated with `c:\pshop\psp.exe` or whatever your path and filename may be for the program. Next time you download a .GIF file in Mosaic, PaintShop Pro will automatically load and display your picture.

Having said all this, it's important to note that the new Web browsers will display graphics files directly. The first to do this was Netscape, which shows GIF and JPEG files (the most common types) in the browser window itself. Others are following suit, and this is a particularly important capability for anyone following art on the Internet.

Q I've just found an archive of experimental computer art, and I've downloaded some of the best. Am I allowed to use them in my business presentations?

A In a word, no. Several online galleries contain a README file of some sort that states quite clearly the conditions surrounding the use of downloaded files. Usually it goes something like this:

> You may use the files for personal or noncommercial use, but any commercial use is strictly off-limits. A business presentation is a commercial use, even if you're a member of the firm's nonprofit R&D facility.

There's an easy way around this problem, although it takes a bit of planning. There's almost always an information area for galleries, containing the names of the people involved in setting it up. E-mail them and ask permission. If the permission isn't theirs to give, they'll let you know who can do so. This is a good idea for noncommercial use of the material as well, even though it might not strictly be necessary.

Q Is there anything I can do to speed up the downloading of these pictures?

A Yes. Either buy a new modem or establish a high-speed direct line. Buying a new modem requires a knowledge of your service provider's options: if you nip out and get a spanking new 28.8 kbps model, for example, it won't do you any good if your service provider is using only 14.4 kbps modems. As for the direct line approach, it's a great idea, but it's extremely expensive (possibly a few hundred dollars a month).

There are two ways around the cost. First, your company might already provide a high-speed Internet connection; check with your systems people. For the home user, keep tabs on the developments at your local cable-TV company. As I write this, for example, I've just learned that a cable-TV provider in Massachusetts is beginning a high-speed Internet service through the cable system. It's quite expensive, but it's very fast.

Extra Credit: Art Exhibits on the World Wide Web

Over the past twelve months, the amount of art appearing on the World Wide Web has practically exploded. This section briefly examines a few sites that are referenced in the Yahoo listing. So let's head for Yahoo one more time, at the risk of wearing out our welcome.

Excursion 15.1: Establish Yahoo's Art listing as a base of operations, and enter the Exhibits listing.

1. Enter Yahoo at **`http://www.yahoo.com`**.
2. Click on the first link, Art. From here, you have access to well over 1000 hyperlinks.
3. Click on the link named Exhibits (notice that there are over 250 sites available from this link). Your screen will look like Figure 15.7.

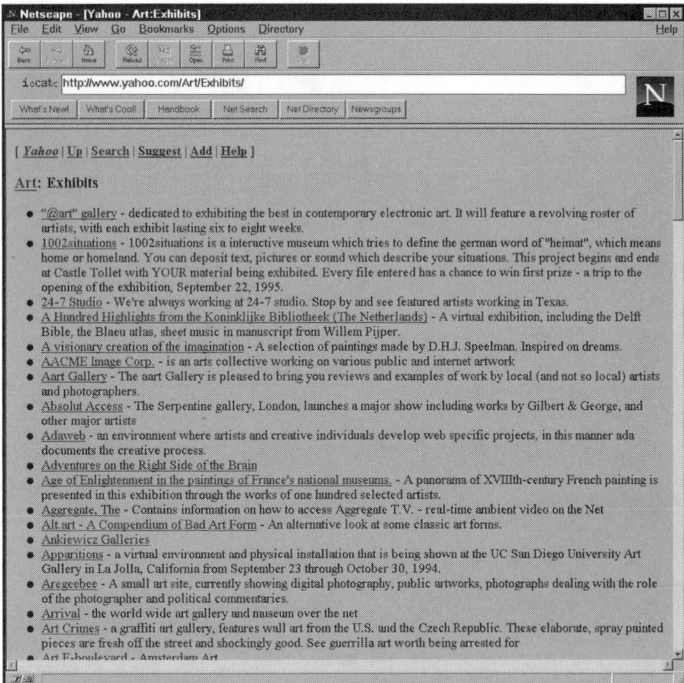

Figure 15.7.
A small portion of the Exhibits page from Yahoo's Art listing.

Excursion 15.2: Enter three small online galleries.

One of the Net's great benefits is that it offers a world-wide audience to lesser-known businesses, writers, and artists. Many of the exhibits available through Yahoo feature new or experimental artists, of the kind you're not likely to see in the larger, (and more popular) actual galleries. The following steps take you to three exhibits:

1. Scroll down the Exhibits list to The Gallery of Functional Art and click. You'll arrive at **`http://sigmar.artdirect.com/gfa/`** (see Figure 15.8).

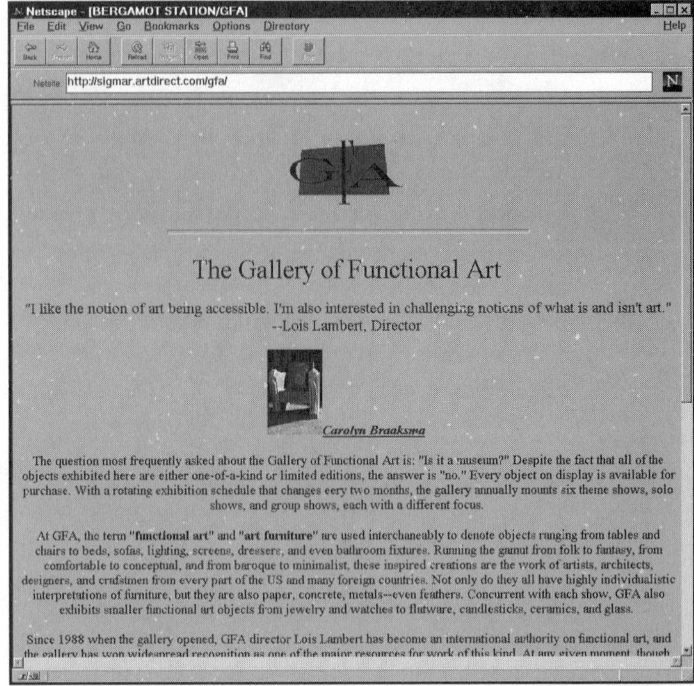

Figure 15.8.
The Gallery of Functional Art home page.

2. Click on the link named Carolyn Braaksma. This will take you to a graphic and a text explanation of one of this artist's works. The page isn't elaborate, but it gives an idea of what she's done.
3. Return to the Yahoo Exhibits page and scroll to the link named The Old Schoolhouse Virtual Art Gallery. Clicking here will take you to `http://www.cuug.ab.ca:8001/~dicka/gallery.html`, an Alberta site featuring the works of a few selected artists.
4. Scroll down until you see the gallery of paintings by artist Ellen Dick. Your screen will resemble Figure 15.9.
5. Click on one of the pieces to get a larger view of the same work.
6. Scroll to the bottom of the page and click on the link labeled A List of Art Galleries and Resources on the Web. Many online galleries have similar links. Explore some of these if you want.
7. Now, return to the Yahoo Exhibits page.
8. Scroll near the bottom of this listing and click on The Wingspread Collectors Guide to Southwest, Art. This will take you to a fascinating site dealing exclusively with the art of New Mexico and the American Southwest (see Figure 15.10).

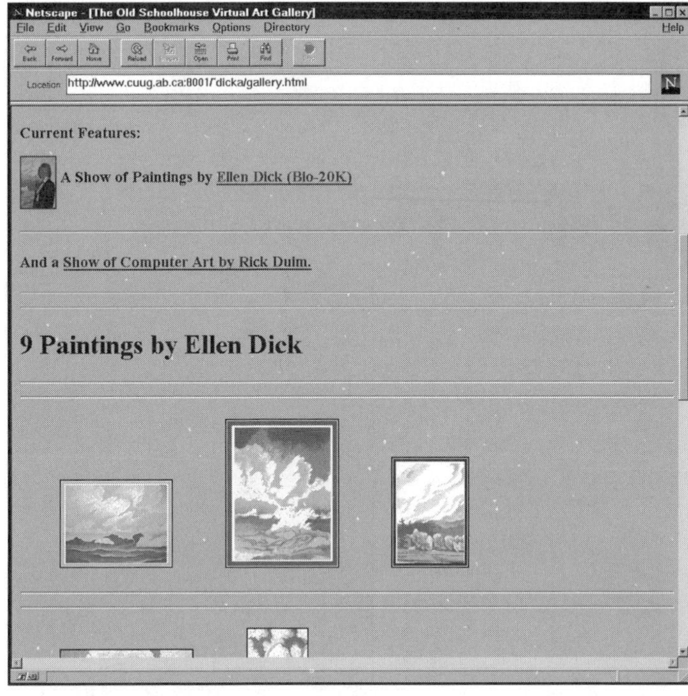

Figure 15.9.
A few of the works shown in The Old Schoolhouse Virtual Art Gallery.

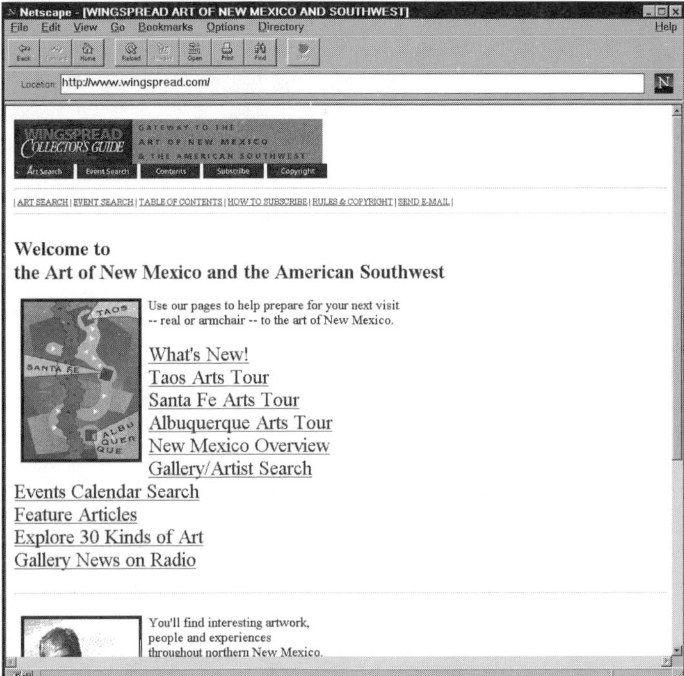

Figure 15.10.
The home page for the Wingspread Collector's Guide.

9. Click on The Santa Fe Arts Tour. Next, click on the link called Explore 30 Kinds of Art, then on Art on the Wall: Two Dimensional, and finally on Western Paintings.
10. This page offers links to several art galleries in the Santa Fe area. As an example, click on The Bardean Gallery. This will take you to a kind of online brochure about this gallery, including visiting hours and pictures of a few sample works. Figure 15.11 shows a portion of this page.

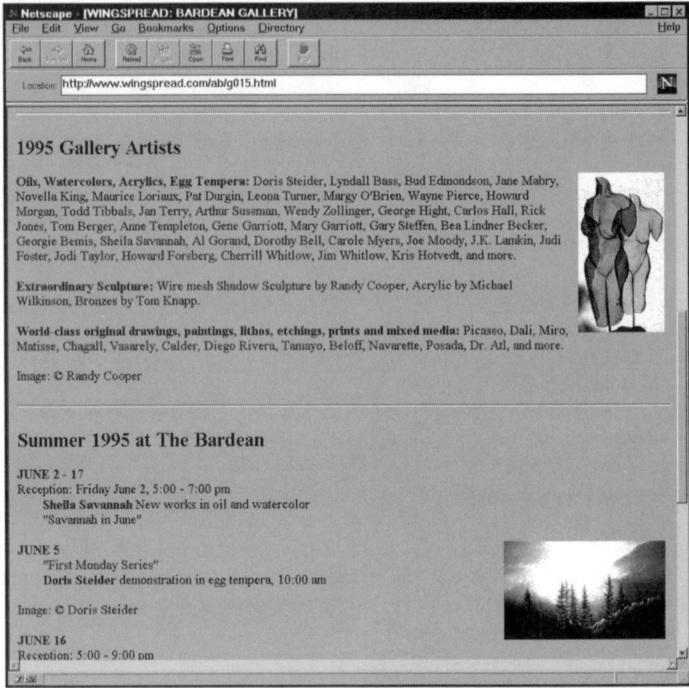

Figure 15.11.
Part of the Bardean Gallery page from Wingspread.

As you can tell, you've barely begun to explore the huge number of Web based galleries. In your next task, you'll see one of the most extensive art sites of all.

Excursion 15.3: Explore the pages of the WebMuseum.

Nicolas Pioch has been creating Web extravaganzas for quite a while now, and his WebMuseum site is something to behold. The site is mirrored on several different computers around the world, and your first task is to enter the site and find the mirror nearest to you. This will speed your access to the site, and hence your enjoyment.

1. Enter the WebMuseum at `http://www.emf.net/louvre/` (you can get there through Yahoo by selecting Museums from the Art listing, Le Louvre, and finally WebMuseum California).
2. Scroll down the list until you find a mirror site close to you. In my case, that's Atkinson College, York University, but in your case, it might very well be Chile or Singapore.
3. Click on the Mona Lisa image to get a full screen view. You don't actually have to do this, but it's fun. If you want, you can save the image to your hard disk, and you can even use it as your background (wallpaper) for your display. Leonardo would likely be proud.
4. Scroll to the bottom of the page and click on the Famous Paintings link.
5. From here, click on the link called The Italian Renaissance, and then click on The High Renaissance. You'll get a short explanation of what the High Renaissance was.
6. Click on the Michelangelo link (see Figure 15.12).

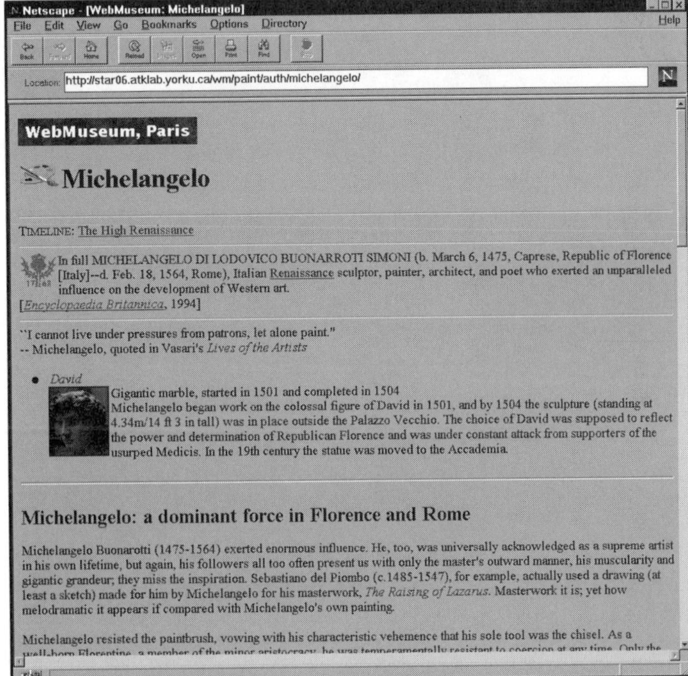

Figure 15.12.
The Michelangelo page in the Famous Paintings collection.

7. Read through the page to get a sense of the depth of detail covered here. Click on any of the images to see larger versions of them. Notice the details available about the Sistine Chapel. Explore to your heart's (and mind's) content.
8. Return to the WebMuseum home page and select Auditorium or the tour of Paris. Enjoy.

The Internet at the Office

16

DAY 6

Electronic Commerce: Shopping on the Internet

This chapter focuses on something that most of us love to do—shop. In this chapter, you will locate and explore some key Internet shopping sites, master the four primary purchasing methods, and perhaps even pick up some souvenirs from Japan, Mexico, Hawaii, or Ireland. You will browse the largest array of stores you could ever want to visit, so get your credit cards ready and let's begin.

In this chapter, you will learn how to perform the following tasks:

- ☐ Locate the primary shopping networks using Netscape's guide to the World Wide Web, including Yahoo's Internet Shopping Network and marketplaceMCI, a virtual mall, and a variety of other commercial services
- ☐ Learn to purchase items in secure and insecure areas
- ☐ Discover the benefits of a shopping basket
- ☐ Set up accounts with companies or contolling companies
- ☐ Explore a range of international shopping networks
- ☐ Get a taste of the Net's more eclectic shopping possibilities

Shopping on the Net

by Stephanie Wunder

Attention shoppers! The advanced ease of bank machines and Interact services at your local malls has recently become fundamentally easier. Now you can fulfill virtually all your purchasing needs from the comfort of your computer terminal. Essentially, the malls have moved into your homes.

The Internet offers users access to shopping malls, custom boutiques, and consumer services, enabling you to not only to browse store contents but to actually select items, pay for them, and even have them delivered to your home, all within the span of a few days. Products range from software and modems to microwaves, clothing, and jewelry. In fact, almost any item you can think of may be purchased on the Net, if you know where to look. Sound too simple? It very well may be.

Financial endeavours of this sort raise the cynic in even the most accepting of individuals. Questions like "How do I pay?", "How much more do I pay?", "How do I know what I will actually receive?", and "How safe is the transaction?" create doubt and superstition among potential shoppers. But the lure of the malls remains more powerful and a tour of the commercial possibilities that the Net offers will inevitably leave you confident...and hooked.

The Web's potential as a consumer-oriented network is enormous, but the possibilities have only begun to be realized. Shopping—the idea itself of trading money for products—is an addictive venture, and as you must have discovered by now, the resources of the Internet lend themselves to such behavior. Shopping on the Net requires informed choices and the following tour of retail sites will give you the introduction you need to become a buying expert.

Task 16.1: Locate Yahoo's Internet Shopping Network.

As you've already discovered in this book, Yahoo is one of the most informative and expansive guides to millions of destinations located on the Net. The famous site offers a list of subject-oriented links that branch out to cover thousands of related pages. Among these pages exists a large selection of shopping links that enable users to purchase items from all over the world by exploring sites that connect to one central menu.

One link available through Yahoo is the *Internet Shopping Network*. You don't have to use Yahoo to get to it (you can go directly to `http://www.isn.com`), but because Yahoo offers a great many resources, it's a good place to start, if only to come to grips with the sheer number of shopping resources out there. The Internet Shopping Network itself is one of the Net's more advanced shopping links, presenting a range of products and purchasing methods constructed with aesthetic appeal.

1. To enter the Yahoo site, type **`http://www.yahoo.com/`** in the URL box of your browser. You'll soon see Yahoo's alphabetical list of subjects.
2. Select the Business heading by clicking once on the hypertext link.
3. Choose the Products and Services link from the presented list and scroll down to the Shopping Centers entry. Access to this link can serve as a base for your future shopping endeavours. Yahoo's collection of shopping sites is by far the most diverse, extensive list that I discovered in my search, and this menu gives an idea of the enormous commercial activity already present on the Web. The screen shown in Figure 16.1 displays only a segment of Yahoo's Shopping Centers list.

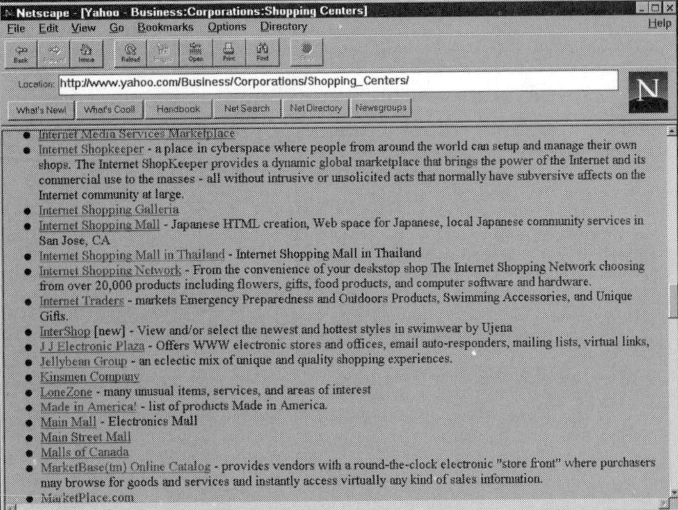

Figure 16.1.
Yahoo's Shopping Center listing.

4. Now select the Internet Shopping Network link from Yahoo's directory.

   The Internet Shopping Network provides descriptions, pricing, and advertisements for products ranging from cars, to flowers, even including a hard drive bargain for your computer. Nearly all ISN pages are graphically oriented in realization of the importance of aesthetics to shoppers (and those with graphical browsers), but for those purchases you need on the run, a text-only mode is available by clicking on the text icon at the bottom of all ISN screens.

   The most important aspect of this shopping network is that it presents a detailed overview of its products to compensate for the physical immateriality of the images themselves. The ISN's home page is shown in Figure 16.2.

Figure 16.2.
The ISN home page as seen in Netscape.

5. Click the Hot Deals icon from ISN's home page for a sample of available products and services. The following screen presents more links, this time a Global Plaza and a Netshop Hot Deals connection.
6. The Global Plaza contains a list of hot buys, including photos and descriptions of the advertised products. Click on the small images to receive a larger photo and full item checklist as well, to access ordering information (see Tasks 16.5 through 16.8 for purchasing methods). When I called up this information, one of the available products included The World Atlas of Wine. Surf through any additional products of interest.
7. Now return to the Hot Deals menu and click the Netshop Hot Deals icon. This link provides a longer list of computer accessories with photos and pricing, as well as a directory of key feature components. These product lists are changed every Tuesday and Friday to provide up-to-date, accurate postings. Figure 16.3 is a sample screen taken from Netshop Hot Deals.

16

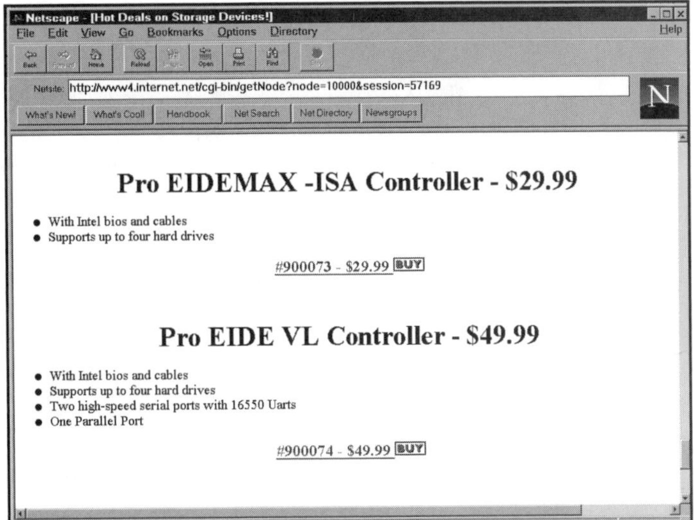

Figure 16.3.
Netshop Hot Deals list.

8. Return to the ISN home page and select Gifts and Flowers. At the bottom of the following screen, an advertisement for the Chrysler Corporation will appear. Click on the Chrysler icon. At first glance, this site resembles an ad that you may normally skip over in a magazine. However, further exploration grants you the capability to tour the Chrysler plant and view individual cars. Figure 16.4 shows a sample of some of the information available in the Chrysler advertisement.

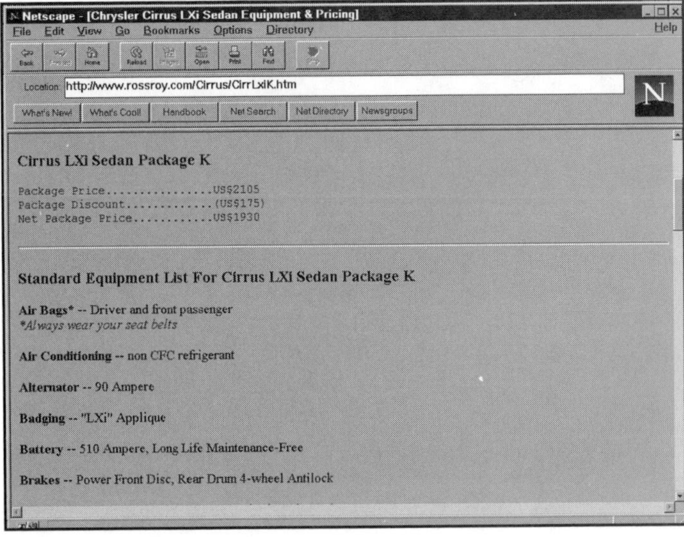

Figure 16.4.
Sales information on the Chrysler Cirrus.

9. Now return to the ISN home page and continue browsing.

Over 20,000 additional items are categorized according to use and can by accessed by the appropriate icons.

As you can see, the ISN is a concise and versatile host to a variety of products, fulfilling the many needs of today's consumer. But remember, this is just one link on Yahoo's enormous list of shopping centers. Now return to Yahoo and explore another. This time it's marketplaceMCI.

Task 16.2: Locate marketplaceMCI.

marketplaceMCI is a shopping center organized by the merchant or company's name. Again, products range from art, to clothing, to global networking, indicating the great diversity of this particular site. The key to finding useful products in this archive is to dig deeper into the connected links. You will discover innumerable options.

1. To return to Yahoo's list of shopping centers, type **`http://www.yahoo.com/Business/Corporations/Shopping_Centers/`**.
2. Scroll down the list of sites until you reach the marketplaceMCI heading. Click on this link to connect to the marketplace's directory of stores, as shown in Figure 16.5. (If you prefer, you can get to this site directory through `http://www.internetmci.com/`.)

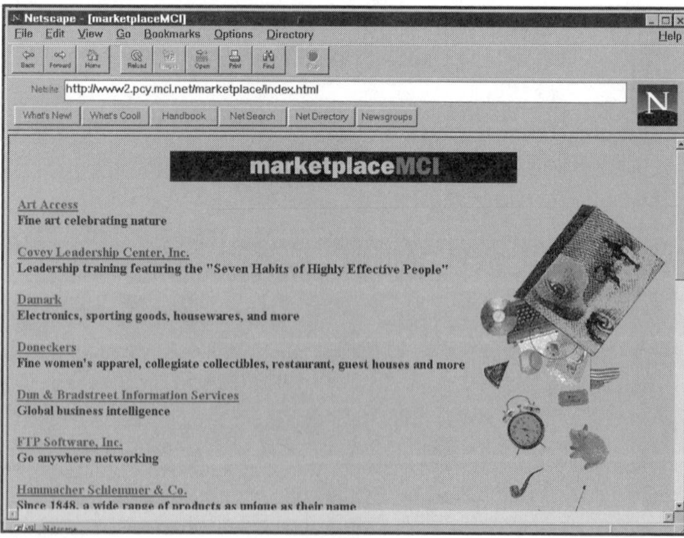

Figure 16.5.
The marketplaceMCI home page menu.

3. To begin browsing, select the first store: Art Access. This location depends heavily on graphics, but provides a fairly simple and efficient path for exploring the site's contents (the page is shown in Figure 16.6). Click on the storefront door to begin

and then select categories of Art to View. The arrows at the top of all marketplaceMCI screens move you forward and backward among pages of the catalog type entries.

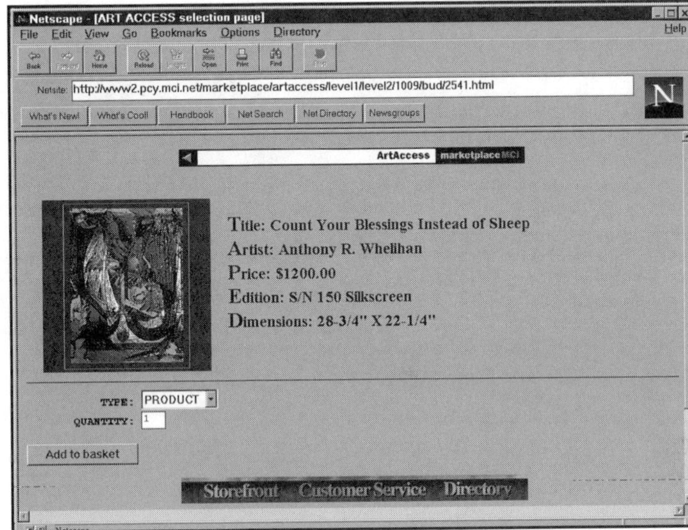

Figure 16.6.
A selection from Art Access in marketplaceMCI.

4. Select the Dun and Bradstreet store from the marketplaceMCI listing and surf through their product directory. Dun and Bradstreet is a famous information firm that provides customers with business and financial advice. Choose one area of interest from the product directory and Dun and Bradstreet will present you with two minute strategy and solution icons. Most product solutions consist of high-priced books or CDs that offer literature and verbal assistance from financial experts. Choose the solution listed under See the Big Picture (Purchasing) and you will see the screen shown in Figure 16.7.
5. Now that you have an idea of how marketplaceMCI functions, continue surfing through the stores and products. Some exceptional sites include the following:
   - Shocker T-Shirt and Apparel Company, Inc.
   - Hammacher Schlemmer & Co.

One benefit of marketplaceMCI's shopping system is the use of the shopping basket. When ordering items from the product directory, marketplaceMCI allows you to place the items in an imaginary shopping cart until you have finished browsing and are ready to pay. This feature more clearly simulates the actual shopping procedure and saves you the hassle of buying products individually. Although other shopping networks also employ this standard feature, the marketplaceMCI basket option immediately follows each product, simplifying the process.

Figure 16.7.
Product description from Dun and Bradstreet.

You've only brushed the surface of these two links, but extensive shopping opportunities exist beyond Yahoo's directory. The next task shows you how to conduct your own search to see what you can find.

Task 16.3: Search for and access a virtual mall.

By now, you've probably heard of virtual libraries and all other types of virtual exploration sites. Add to that list virtual shopping malls—electronic centers that make up hundreds of sales-oriented sites and nicely supplement your ShopNet experience. The best way to locate these virtual malls and any other shopping sites is to conduct your own Internet search.

1. To begin your shopping search, click the Internet Search button in Netscape, or head for the All-in-One Search page at **`http://www.albany.net/`**.
2. Choose WebCrawler from the list of search tools and enter **`virtual mall`** as your key words or search string. Because you already have an idea of the enormity of the shopping index on the Net, set your number of results at **`100`** and get ready to surf.
3. Click Search to submit your inquiry and receive results. You should be presented with a screen very similar to Figure 16.8.
4. Choose from among these 100 links to explore the world of virtual shopping malls. One interesting site is I 2020, which isn't actually a virtual mall at all, but rather an Internet provider in central Virginia. Scroll down to the heading Welcome to I 2020! and enter the site.
5. At the I 2020 home page, select the virtual mall hypertext link and a screen similar to Figure 16.9 should appear.

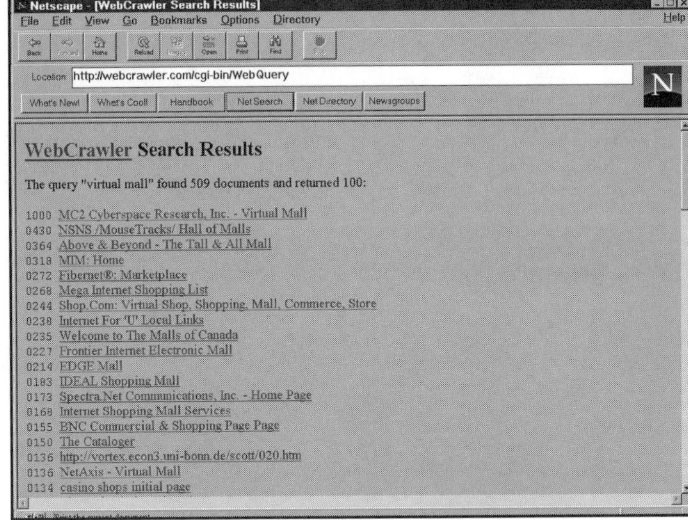

Figure 16.8.
The results of WebCrawler's virtual mall search.

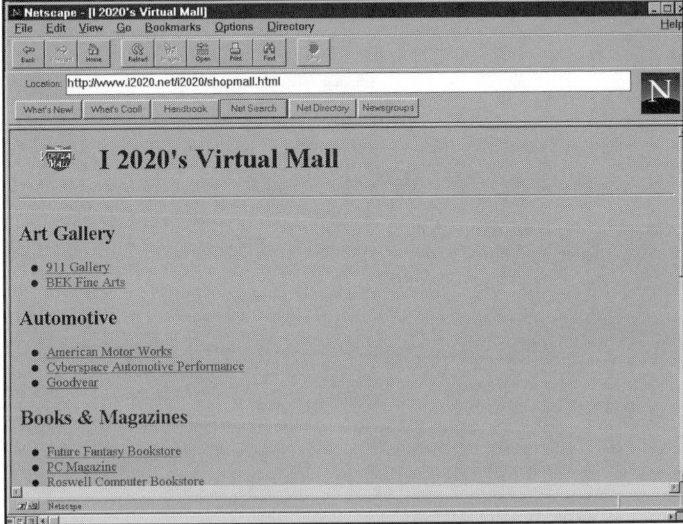

Figure 16.9.
I 2020's Virtual Mall home page.

6. This mall, in itself, contains a variety of resources that can be accessed with a simple click of your mouse. Topics range from art to automobiles, with product photos and pricing displayed for consumer interest. Surf through these stores to see what is available and of interest to you.
7. The link I found most interesting when I explored the I 2020 Virtual Mall was a different mall entirely—the Branch Mall (its link is found at the bottom of the I 2020 Virtual Mall home page). This is another example of getting to a site from a

number of different sites on the Net; the Branch Mall is available from several different locations. Click on this item (or go directly via **`http://www.branch.com`**) and you will see the screen shown in Figure 16.10.

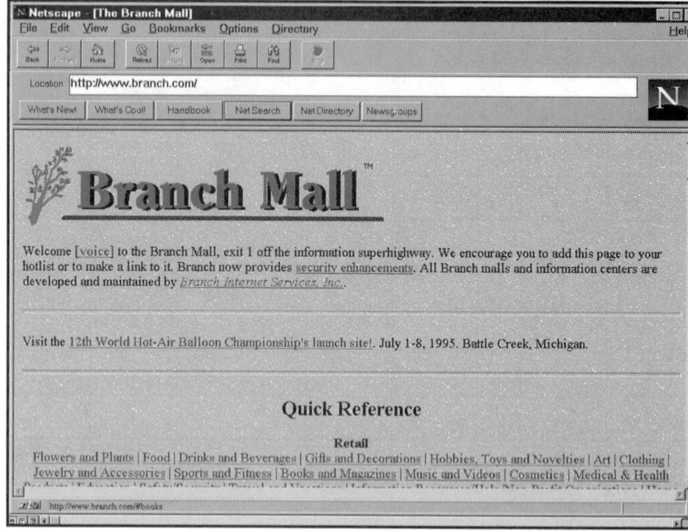

Figure 16.10.
The Branch Mall home page.

Although this home page is much less dependent on graphical appeal than either ISN or marketplaceMCI, the Branch Mall site contains such a large number of stores and products, so that a little shopping cannot be passed up. Browse through the mall at your leisure and you will find an enormous selection of products to choose from. It's definitely not just your average trip to the mall!

Task 16.4: Find the Emall and browse its contents.

During my Shopnet excursions, I came across one additional site of interest to those who love to buy. The *Emall* is located at `http://emall.com/` and provides an example of a more advanced and complete virtual mall.

1. To locate Emall, type **`http://emall.com/`** in the URL location box of your browser and press Enter.

Note: Because the Emall contains a large number of inline images, access may take a while, especially with slower modems (or jammed networks). However, the Emall is one of the better constructed shopping networks and is well worth checking out.

2. Navigate among the various stores and locate any products you may want to purchase (or at least think about purchasing). The following figures are samples of the pages you may see in the Emall directories. Figure 16.11 shows CCI World, Figure 16.12 is taken from the Fine Food home page, Figure 16.13 displays LEASCO's site from the BizLink, and Figure 16.4 shows the American Horticultural Society.

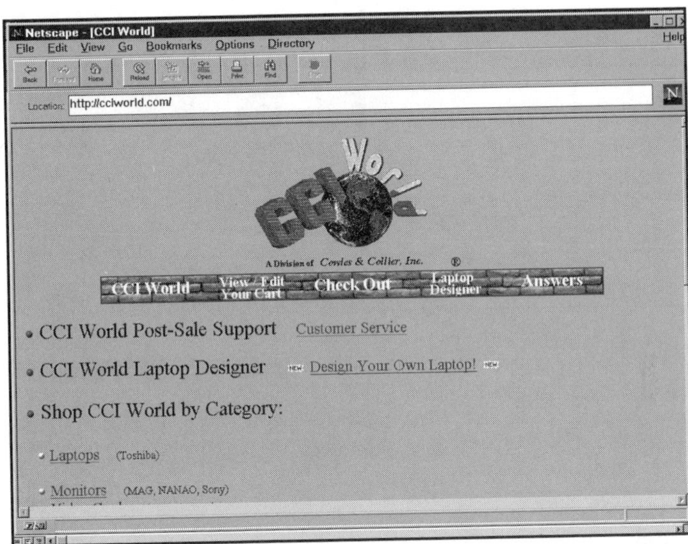

Figure 16.11.
CCI World from Emall's General Store.

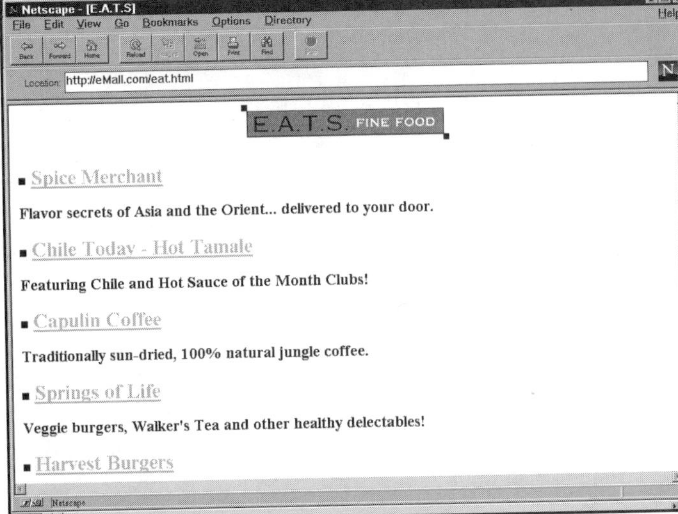

Figure 16.12.
E.A.T.S. Fine Food home page from Emall.

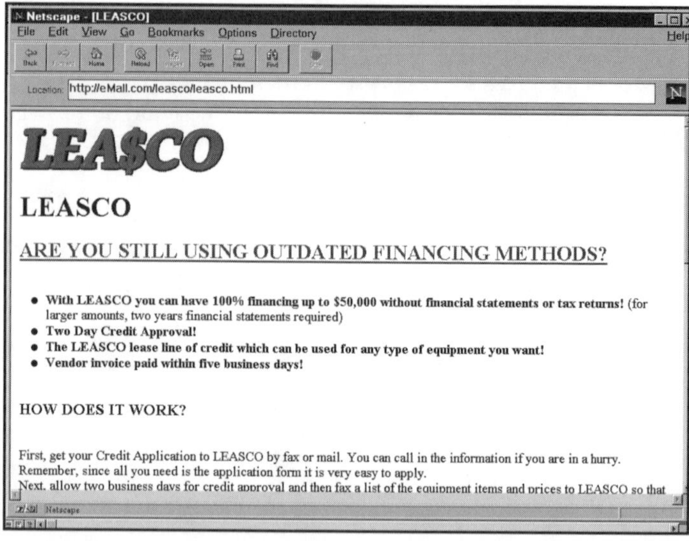

Figure 16.13. *LEASCO's home page from Emall's BizLink.*

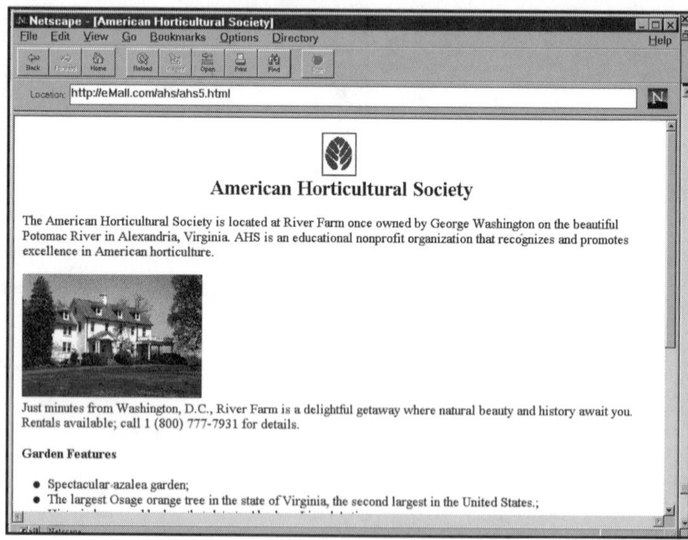

Figure 16.14. *The American Horticultural Society from Emall's Garden Marketplace.*

This brief overview of the Net's commercial capabilities has given you the resources you need to search and browse the thousands of shopping sites and malls that the Internet has to offer. You still haven't actually bought anything, however, and you're probably wondering if, from the standpoint of security, it's even a good idea. On the premise that buying is a lot more fun than just shopping, however, take a look at what buying entails.

Charge It! Buying Stuff on the Internet

16

Once you realize that entire companies have found a venue for retail sales in the Internet, it becomes tempting to participate. Whether you choose to shop on the Net or to construct a shopping network for your individual company, the Internet succeeds in making your life significantly simpler by catering to individual consumer needs.

But how do you buy? And is the Net a safe medium for conducting transactions? Rest assured that all of the security questions and hesitations that you have considered have also been considered by the various retail merchants on the Net, and they have come up with four main shopping techniques to satisfy customer concerns.

The original Internet purchasing method involved placing a call to a 1-800 telephone number that was posted with the item's Internet advertisement and ordering by phone. Then stores began to provide links to online order forms to be completed and submitted to the company via electronic mail. Finally, Net-based merchants created secure access, allowing users to complete a registration form and charge items directly to their credit cards. Although this secure method remains the most popular shopping technique on the Net, presently, some stores offer users the capability to set up accounts with banks or other controlling companies. You will practice each of these methods in the next four tasks.

Task 16.5: Order an Internet product by phone.

Because phone order was the original purchasing technique offered to electronic shoppers, many sites continue to provide phone or fax numbers in their Net stores. However, this method does not allow users to exploit the Net's full commercial potential. In this case, the Web-based stores act much like a catalog, reverting back to the days of mail order…and we know the WWW is much more than that.

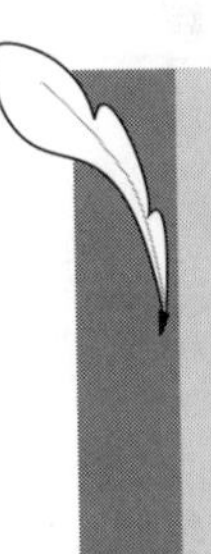

Note: Throughout the following section, you will be traveling between insecure and secure sites. An *insecure site* is one in which an intermediary may be able to access information that you are transmitting, and thus, is fundamentally unsafe for credit card transactions (not that it's stopped many people). In Netscape, these sites are indicated by a broken key on a gray background in the bottom left hand corner of the screen (no other browsers currently differentiate secure and insecure sites this way). A *secure site* is one in which information is transmitted to a Secure Netscape Server (notice that the browser is tied to Netscape's server software directly for this purpose) without the risk of an intermediary obtaining the document. A secure site is indicated by a solid key on a blue background in the bottom left corner of your Netscape screen or by the site's URL address, which will begin with `https://`.

Transmitting secure information on the Net is somewhat analogous to giving the same information over the phone lines. You must place an initial amount of trust in the server and the company but you may be sure no one else is "listening in."

1. To locate a phone order site, simply browse the shopping malls and boutiques and look for a phone or fax number under the ordering information. If you cannot locate one, conduct another virtual mall search through WebCrawler (refer to Task 16.3 for search directions).
2. From the search results, select The WebWinder: Shopping.
3. Now choose the FutureMall link in the `WebWinder` directory and enter the Consumer Products and Services section. You will see the screen shown in Figure 16.15.

Figure 16.15.
The FutureMall's Consumer Products and Services page.

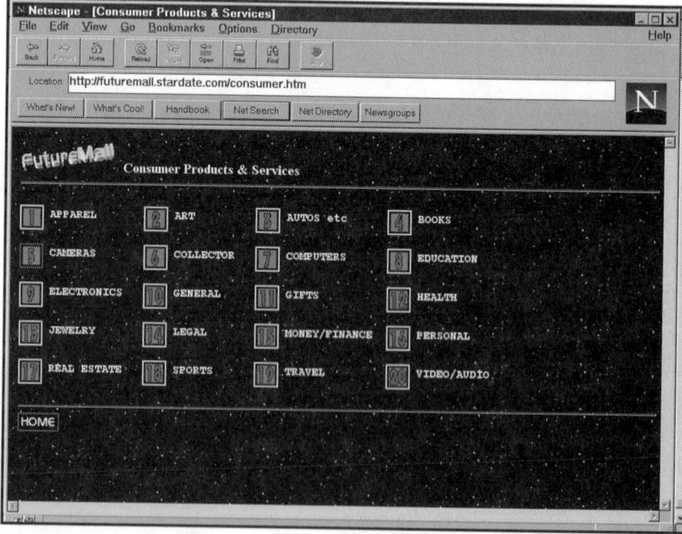

4. Select category `5-Cameras` and the FutureMall will display a list of photography products available for purchase. I chose the `4 in 1 Camera` and came up with an image and product description similar to those you viewed previously in other

malls. At the end of the product identification segment, you will find a FuturePhone number and Fax form link followed by the company's mailing address (see Figure 16.16).

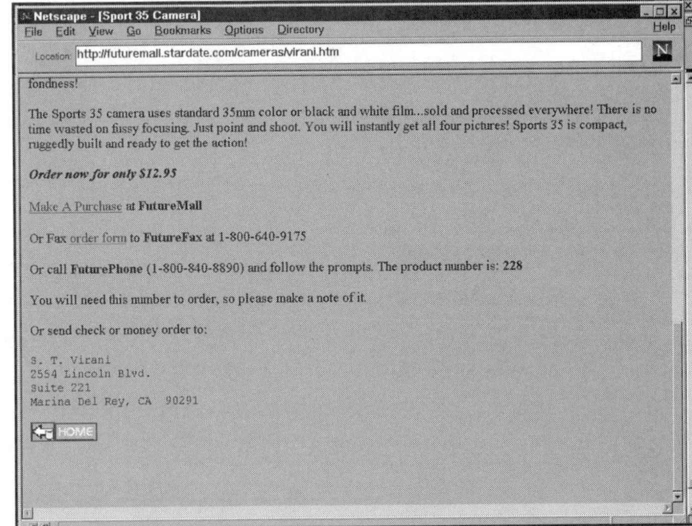

Figure 16.16.
FutureMall's ordering information.

5. To order this particular camera by phone, simply copy down the product number (228) and call the 1-800 number listed. An attendant will prompt you further.
6. To mail in your order, send a check or money order to the posted address at the bottom of the screen. This method follows the same procedure as television sales.
7. If you prefer to Fax the company, click on the orderform link and fill out the required information. It's that simple.

Tip: Whenever you find yourself in a situation that requires you to transmit confidential information, check the screen to see if you are working with a secure server. In the preceding example, you are required to transmit your credit card number and expiration date by fax and the site is insecure. A safer option may be to call or mail the order form to the company. However, if you choose to submit the information by fax, Netscape would present a warning screen informing you of the site's security status and allowing you the option to cancel your entry.

Task 16.6: Order an item by completing an order form and sending your request via electronic mail.

You can order an item using an order form and then send the form via e-mail. To do this, just follow these steps:

1. Return to the WebWinder home page and select the World Mall location from the directory of stores.
2. From the World Mall home page, visit the Retail Center and from there, go to the Mall Directory. Notice that the Retail Center has a link to Mall Security. It is always good practice, when shopping in a variety of areas, to review the individual mall procedures.
3. The Mall Directory gives you a list of stores located in the mall followed by a brief description of the contents. Select the first store, named Bob Reeder and Blackthorn Records, and scroll through the entries.
4. Click the How to Order link located at the end of the product listings and you should see a screen similar to the one shown in Figure 16.17.

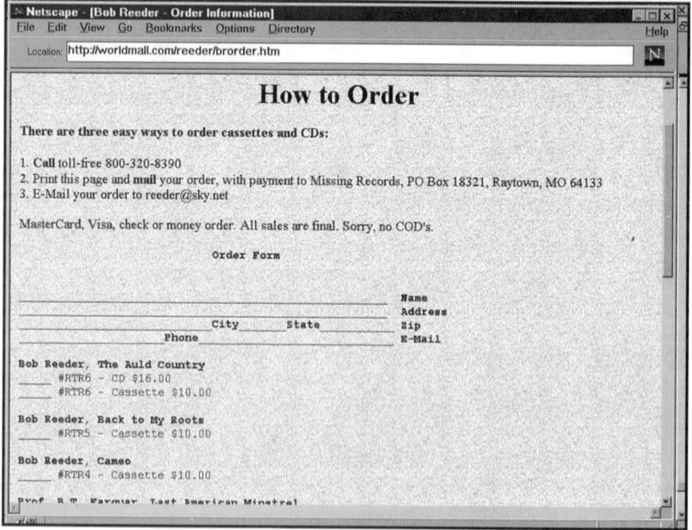

Figure 16.17.
Bob Reeder and Blackthorn Records' How to Order information-e-mail form.

5. To order cassettes or CDs via an electronic mail order form, copy the required information into your e-mail message text and send it to **`reeder@sky.net`**.

If you choose to use this particular order form, you must print out a copy of the electronic message to sign it. Other companies allow consumers to fill the form out directly at the site and submit the message for verification with the click of a Send button located directly below

the form. Because most of these retailers offer secure access, you will examine some of these sites in the following task.

Task 16.7: Purchase items on the Net using secure access ordering.

Because of the Internet Shopping Network's advanced development and secure access, you will now return to that location to purchase some of the items that might have caught your eye earlier in your explorations.

1. To access the Internet Shopping Network directly, type **`http://www4.internet.net/cgi-bin/getNode?node=1`** in the Netsite location box and press Enter.
2. Click the Hammacher Schlemmer icon that I told you about earlier and browse through some of the available products.
3. Pamper yourself and choose the Turkish Bathrobe from the product directory. You should see a screen that displays the robe and a brief description of the product. At the end of this page, you are given the option to buy the robe for $99.99. Click on the Buy icon and you will be presented with the security information shown in Figure 16.18.

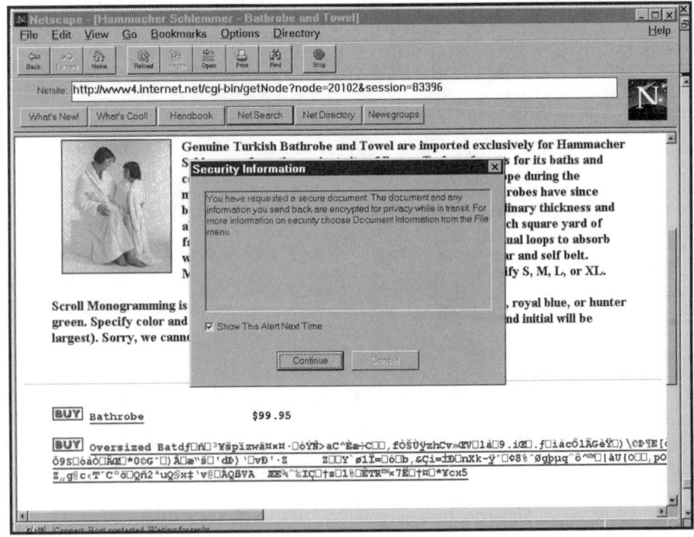

Figure 16.18.
Internet Shopping Network's security warning.

4. Click the OK button at the end of the warning and the next location's URL becomes `https://`.

5. Now select the Click Here link to fill out the secure online form. You will see the screen shown in Figure 16.19.

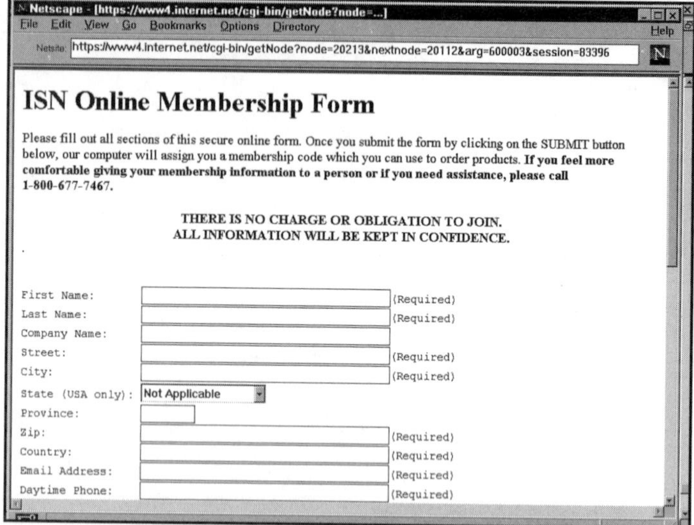

Figure 16.19. *Internet Shopping Network's secure ordering page.*

6. To become a Hammacher Schlemmer consumer, fill out the membership form on your screen and click Submit. This will send the information to the Hammacher Schlemmer company, where they can perform the required credit checks and verifications before accepting you as a client.

   Upon verification of your credit information, Hammacher Schlemmer will return a membership number to you via e-mail. Type this number in the membership box to sign in when shopping in the electronic stores.

7. After you have signed in, enter the number of items you want and click the Send key. Your purchases will be registered immediately and delivery information will follow.

Task 16.8: Set up an account with a company to purchase the items they advertise.

As with most secure access sites, the Internet Shopping Network requires shoppers to complete a membership form prior to purchasing store items. By assigning each client an account number, system operators limit the amount of data that must be processed when repeat customers access the site. *Megamart* is a business on the Net that designs and markets

ordering systems or web pages for small businesses who want to set up shop on the Internet. Many of the purchasing pages you will come across in your shopping searches will incorporate the same basic principles as the examples displayed at this site.

1. To access the megamart, type **`http://www.megamart.com/`** in the Netsite or Location box and press Enter. You will receive the MegaWeb Business Mart home page to browse, as shown in Figure 16.20.

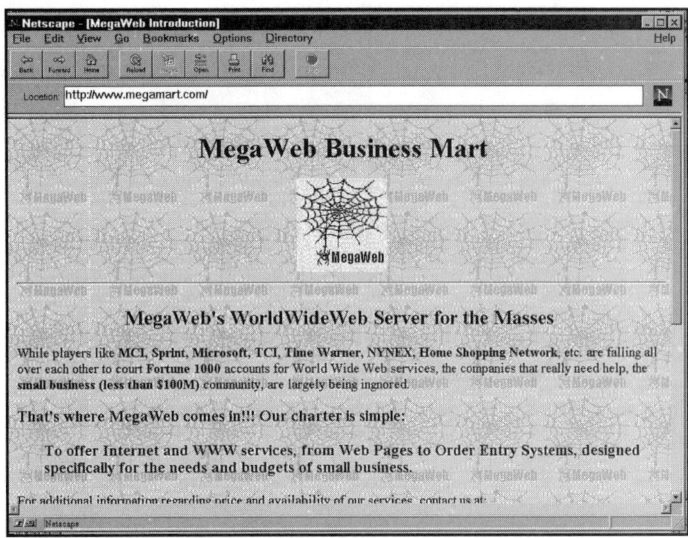

Figure 16.20.
The MegaWeb Business Mart home page.

2. Scroll down the page and click on the What's New at MegaWeb link to access ordering information.
3. Select the Internet Ordering System™ demonstration link to view some of the system designs this company has created.
4. Because you are interested in shopping sites that require you to set up accounts on the Net, choose the first option, Setting up an account. Figures 16.21 and 16.22 display the types of forms you might receive when setting up an account at a specific shopping mall on the Net.
5. After filling out the required information, to set up an account, click on Set Up Account and follow the prompts that the system gives you for ordering and shipping actual merchandise.

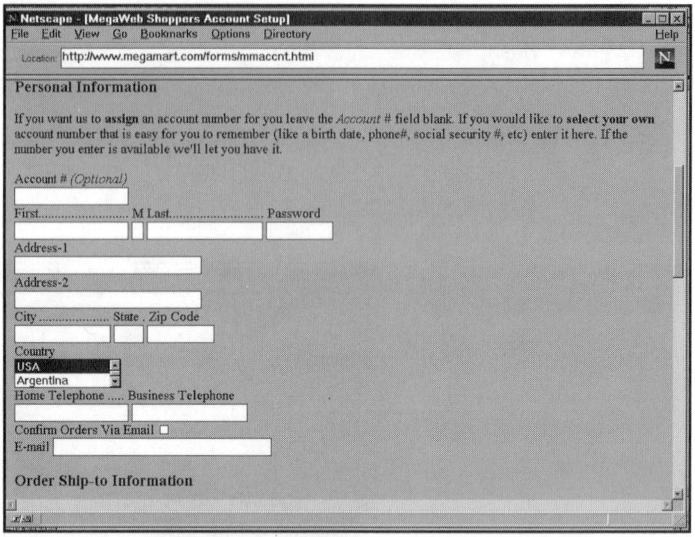

Figure 16.21.
A Personal Information form from MegaWeb (setting up an account).

Netscape - [MegaWeb Shoppers Account Setup]
File Edit View Go Bookmarks Options Directory Help
Location: http://www.megamart.com/forms/mmaccnt.html

Personal Information

If you want us to **assign** an account number for you leave the *Account* # field blank. If you would like to **select your own** account number that is easy for you to remember (like a birth date, phone#, social security #, etc) enter it here. If the number you enter is available we'll let you have it.

Account # *(Optional)*
First.......................... M Last........................... Password
Address-1
Address-2
City..................... State . Zip Code
Country
USA
Argentina
Home Telephone ..... Business Telephone
Confirm Orders Via Email
E-mail

Order Ship-to Information

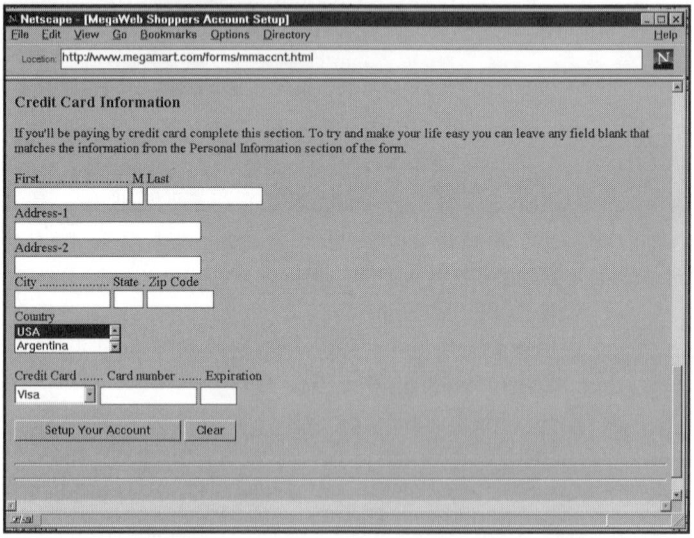

Figure 16.22.
A Card Information form from MegaWeb (setting up an account).

Netscape - [MegaWeb Shoppers Account Setup]
File Edit View Go Bookmarks Options Directory Help
Location: http://www.megamart.com/forms/mmaccnt.html

Credit Card Information

If you'll be paying by credit card complete this section. To try and make your life easy you can leave any field blank that matches the information from the Personal Information section of the form.

First.......................... M Last
Address-1
Address-2
City..................... State . Zip Code
Country
USA
Argentina
Credit Card .... Card number .... Expiration
Visa
Setup Your Account | Clear

Task 16.9: Set up an account with First Virtual.

Now you've seen various sample order forms that move to the actual sites that employ them. The *MegaMall* is a virtual mall with a vast resource of products and services offered online for users to browse. Purchasing at this mall is filtered through an accounting company called

First Virtual-Banking Merchant of the Internet. To order any products you must first register with First Virtual to set up an account, by following these steps:

1. To locate the MegaMall type **`http://infotique.lm.com/cgi-bin/phpl.cgi?megamain.html`** in the Netsite or Location box and press Enter.
2. From the MegaMall home page that you receive, select the Shop or Shop at the Mall links and the MegaMall will display the screen of options shown in Figure 16.23.

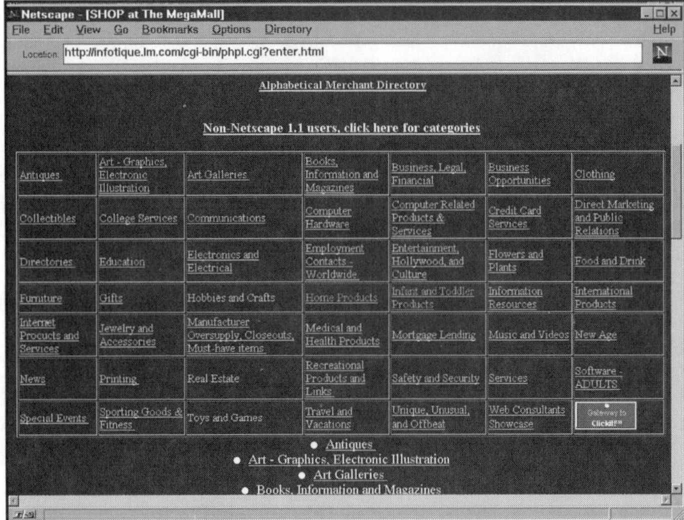

Figure 16.23.
The MegaMall store directory.

3. Click on any of the boxed categories or text directory entries and browse the products available from the merchants listed.

   With such a large range of products and stores to choose from, it is likely that you will find some items of interest that you may want to select for purchase. At this point, you must register with First Virtual and set up an account.
4. Click the First Virtual Accepted button from the product directory and click on the First Virtual Holdings logo for application information. Your screen will look like the one shown in Figure 16.24.
5. Click the Apply button or icon to receive the application form shown in Figure 16.25.

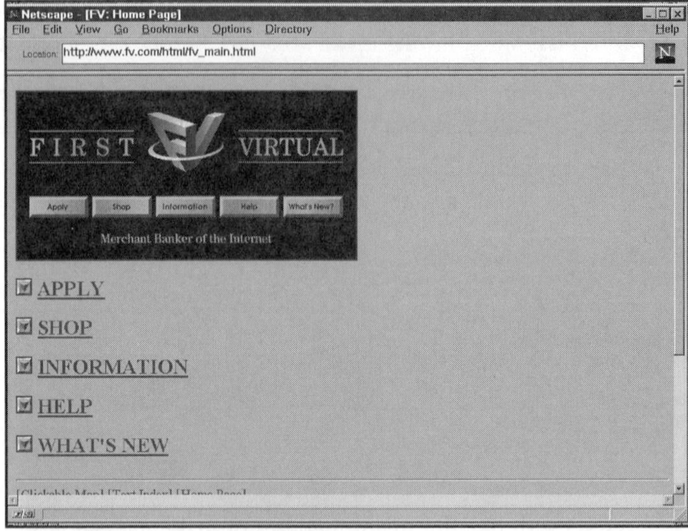

Figure 16.24.
The First Virtual home page.

Figure 16.25.
Setting up an account with First Virtual Holdings through the MegaMall.

6. Simply fill out this form and click the Set up Account and Request Free Gift button at the bottom of the screen.

First Virtual Holdings is one of the few banking merchants who does not request credit card information and other sensitive data over the Internet. After you fill in this application, all further correspondance will take place via electronic mail. When these formal transactions are complete, you will be able to purchase any items advertised within the MegaMall simply by entering your identification number. That's what I call spending made easy!

16

Summary

Shopping on the Internet is still in its infancy. However, so many companies have committed resources to the possibility that you increasingly will be able to spend real money for real goods over the Net in the next few years. Furthermore, you'll be able to do your banking, reserve rental cars and hotel rooms, and conduct many other types of business, as well. Commerce has been one of the Net's big sales pitches over the past several months, and it remains one of the most exciting promises for the future.

Task Review

In this chapter, you learned how to perform the following tasks:

- Locate and explore shopping malls and stores on the Internet, including the Internet Shopping Network, marketplaceMCI, the Branch Mall, and other shops and malls
- Learn the four major methods of making purchases over the Internet
- Use forms to make secure transactions and to establish accounts with virtual banking firms for the sake of making purchases

Key Terms

Secure Transaction—A transaction of data on the Internet that takes place through one of several major online security systems. The Netscape browser is linked directly to Netscape server software to allow for secure transactions, but it's not the only security system available. Secure transactions are essential for the growth of Internet commerce.

Virtual Mall—A collection of stores, services, and other sales-oriented companies on the Internet, all run from the same server and sometimes using the same shopping interface and payment systems

Unsecure Transactions—The opposite of secure transactions, unsecure transactions are any normal exchange of information over the Net. Your e-mail typically is unsecure (although no one would likely care), and so are fill-in forms in Web browsers. They're dangerous because the data can be intercepted, something no one wants when it comes to credit card transactions (except the thieves, of course).

Extra Credit: Shopping in Thailand

Although you've sampled a variety of sites and shopping techniques, you can never truly understand the enormity of the shopping experience until you find some of the offbeat, trivial sites that show you how advanced buying and spending has really become. Because I came

across these sites as I was surfing randomly through shopping networks, I will spare you the trouble of retracing my erratic steps. Access to any of the following sites may be obtained by copying the URL and inserting the address in the Netsite or Location box of your Web browser. Begin by shopping at the Internet Shopping Network again…this time Thai-style. Thailand's Internet Shopping Network home page is shown in Figure 16.26.

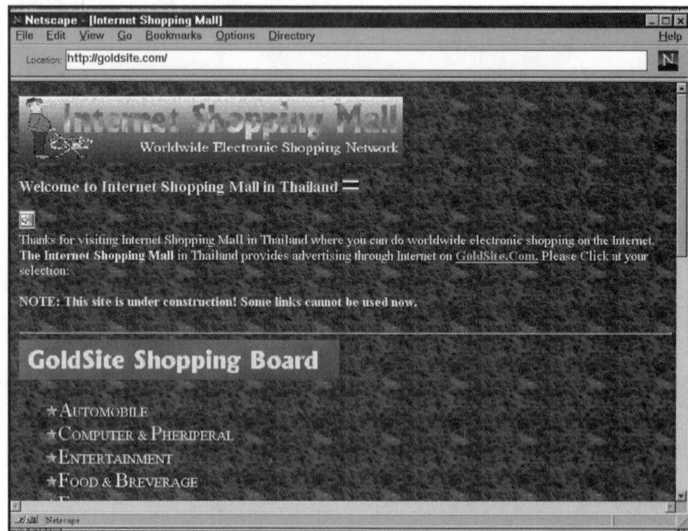

Figure 16.26.
Thailand's Internet Shopping Network home page.

From this page, you'll get a taste of true Thai culture including music, travel, automobiles, and much more. Another international shopping center currently thriving on the Net, and shown in Figure 16.27, resides in Japan and provides a range of Japanese products for consumer purchase in both English and Japanese.

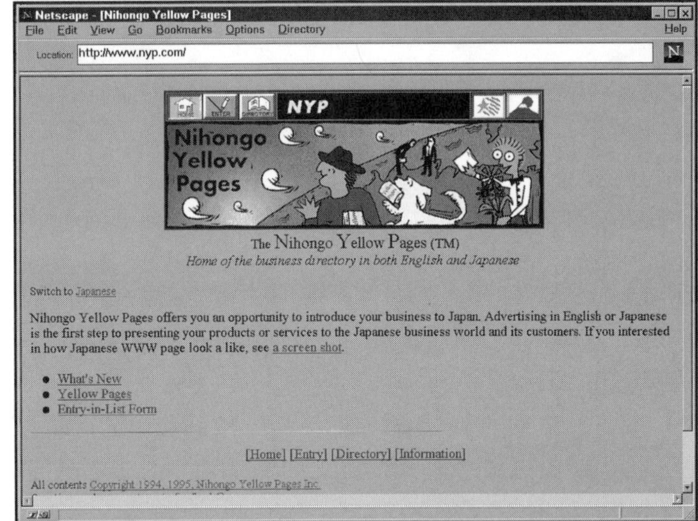

Figure 16.27.
The Nihongo Yellow Pages home page.

17

DAY 6

Doing Business on the Internet

In 1995, the number of Internet addresses in the commercial domain (.com) finally exceeded those in the historically more populous educational domain (.edu). Businesses are moving onto the Internet quickly, developing ways of using the Net for a variety of corporate functions. But the corporate world has a great many questions about what it means to do business on the Internet, and this chapter explores some of the possible answers.

Task List

In this chapter, you'll learn how to perform the following tasks:

- Examine newsgroups dealing with business issues
- Determine which mailing lists might be helpful for your business
- Work through Gophers dealing with business concerns
- Examine how businesses have developed the World Wide Web for corporate purposes

Business and the Internet

With the changes surrounding the NSF's Acceptable Use Policy discussed in Chapter 1, the Internet took on new potential as a place to do business. But what exactly does this mean? Following are some of the questions that are now being asked and others that will be asked in the near future:

- Will the Net become just a different version of television's home shopping phenomenon?
- Will it offer a more interactive form of infomercial?
- Will you be able to publish a product catalog with interactive feedback and ordering systems?
- Can buyers custom-order a computer or a car by filling in World Wide Web forms?
- Does the Web have potential as a videoconferencing medium for business meetings?
- Can it assist product groups with market research and analysis?
- Will deals be struck without two parties ever physically meeting?
- Will the Net allow consortiums and alliances to collaborate on research and development, public relations, and even financial details?
- Can transportation complexities be resolved by tapping Net resources?
- Is it possible to use the Net to establish and implement distribution systems throughout the world?

- Will the Net enhance customer- and technical-service capabilities?
- Can it be set up as a legal and financial consulting medium?

You can undoubtedly add to this list. Just think of the potential of a truly global network with increasingly easy access to businesses and potential customers alike. Questions about your particular business or business interest should immediately spring to mind.

The Internet as Marketplace

The Internet represents a potentially large market, accessed by users who are open to any number of possibilities. It's even open to advertising, albeit a far different kind of advertising than that found in radio, television, or the print media. If you send promotional material via e-mail to an entire list or newsgroup, you'll be inundated with responses indicating contempt, disgust, and even hatred. Unlike junk mail, blanket postings can be responded to, and usually they will be. It's not inconceivable that some particularly irate users will program their computers to respond to such postings by returning them to their senders ten, twenty, even a thousand times over, thus clogging up the offenders' accounts.

17

Until recently, the Internet population was quite committed to an open and essentially noncommercial network. In a way, it still is. That doesn't mean businesses aren't welcome (although many users still abhor the possibilities); what it means is that advertising over the Net is acceptable as long as participation is voluntary. If you put your product catalog on the Net as a Gopher and WWW site, for example, you should let people know it's there, but don't force it on anybody. The same goes for any other kind of service.

Over the past year, business activity on the Internet has increased dramatically. Almost all of this activity has taken place on the World Wide Web, for obvious reasons. Businesses spend a great deal of money on their *image*, and while "image" means public image in some respects it also means *visual* image. You recognize McDonald's "golden arches" as soon as you see them, and the same holds true for any number of other logos, trademarks, and other emblems. The Web is the first technology on the Internet that allows businesses to focus user attention on the visual aspect of their corporate design, a crucial point.

One important point about the Internet, even at this stage in its development, is that its users are already segregated by area of interest. From a marketing standpoint, this means there is a need to develop specialized promotional materials rather than the one-size-fits-all model of broadcast advertising. In fact, the Internet may be the first real example of a technology that not only allows but *requires* narrowcast marketing, with all the attendant pluses and minuses. It's doubtful that the Net will ever be the right place for marketing bathroom tissue, but it may already be precisely the right place to develop awareness of niche market items.

The goal, of course, is transforming product awareness (and I use the term "product" in its broadest sense here) into actual sales or contracts. Right now, the only direct possibility lies with the World Wide Web and its interactive forms (which are discussed later in this chapter).

But you can place phone numbers and e-mail addresses on Gopher servers, in newsgroups or mailing list messages, and in files in FTP sites, specifying full contact information. And keep in mind that any magazine ad carrying an e-mail, Gopher, or WWW address is certain to catch the attention of Internet users, who may well check it out the next time they log on. It's probably a temporary advantage (the way fax numbers were at first), but it's well worth paying attention to.

The Internet as Communications Technology

Businesses have been using the Internet as a communications tool for years. In this context, think of the Net not as a LAN (local-area network), not even as a WAN (wide-area network), but rather as a SWAN (super-wide-area network). (I just made this one up.) It doesn't get any wider than this. Anyone with an Internet account can be contacted through e-mail, and you can establish newsgroups and mailing lists as well. Like any e-mail system, you can use the Net to have your personnel keep in touch with you—and they can do so easily (and cheaply) from anywhere in the world. Clients and associates can also communicate easily with you, to the extent that face-to-face meetings may well be minimized.

E-mail is fast, relatively inexpensive, and often more effective than telephone contact (especially since voice mail has made actual contact nearly impossible). But there's no reason to restrict your communications to e-mail. Mailing lists and newsgroups can work, but you probably don't want to commit sensitive information to them. Telnet and FTP sites, on the other hand, can be password-protected, as can Gopher sites. Security is always a concern, but a well-considered security scheme can make it possible to do *most* global-wide communication on the Net. (The truly sensitive data and communications you will want to restrict to other technologies.)

The Internet as Collaboration Tool

Research groups have been using the Internet as a collaboration medium since its inception. Through e-mail, FTP, and other tools, scientists working on collaborative projects have exchanged data and communicated findings, and more recently they have utilized Gopher and the World Wide Web to make their results public.

It takes only a short stretch of the imagination to see corporate collaboration occurring in much the same fashion. In an era of alliances, industry task forces, and the sharing of resources, collaboration over the Net makes sense. Design work could be handled over the World Wide Web (see Chapter 15 for examples of collaborative art being developed this way), as could frequent presentations of project milestones. In fact, project planning and (to a degree) project management could be covered on the Web as well, through a series of interactive flowcharts, diagrams, and graphs. And as full-motion video becomes more fully

implemented on the Web (requiring top-speed access), other possibilities will be created for collaborative meetings and ventures.

The Internet as Service Bureau

Customer service and product support are always important considerations, and they're not about to go away, especially in a competitive business climate. It makes sense, therefore, to utilize all available means of serving clients and customers and to demonstrate a commitment to satisfying their needs. The Internet is one of those means.

While you may not like the idea of conducting private communications on a massively public network (even with full internal security in place), service is, by its very nature, a public activity. Why not establish an Internet presence in addition to the usual service features, such as toll-free numbers, fax feedback, and whatever else your firm offers? E-mail alone is a possibility, although it absolutely must be staffed. People who send e-mail expect faster responses than those who send faxes.

As the World Wide Web examples in the last part of this chapter demonstrate, several companies have already begun turning to the Net as a service feature. Clients can read and/ or download frequently-asked questions or technical documents from FTP, Gopher, or Web sites, and through mailing lists and newsgroups they can communicate with other customers as well. (This can be dangerous, of course, if complaint becomes the chief mode of expression.) Fax services are already in place for this type of material, and adding Net service is, from a client's standpoint, another positive step.

You also can develop interactive feedback or upgrade forms to be handled on the WWW, and there's no reason not to design Web-based tutorials for specific problem areas or improved performance or installation techniques. Start thinking of the Net as a 24-hour support representative, and you'll start getting a sense of the possibilities.

Business Resources on the Internet

The following section looks at newsgroups, mailing lists, and Gophers of interest to business people. In most cases, the material here represents either information about businesses, or communication among people interested in specific business issues. The subsequent sections of this chapter turn to businesses with an existing presence on the Net.

Note: This chapter is in a slightly different format from most of the others. This chapter explains what to do rather than taking you step-by-step through the tasks. I'll assume that you're already familiar with the tool of the Internet, and that you'll need very little help getting from one task to the next. This is a less

prescriptive approach than most chapters, and I'm interested in which you think is more useful. E-mail me at `nrandall@watarts.uwaterloo.ca` to let me know, okay?

Task 17.1: Explore business-oriented newsgroups.

The Usenet offers two major kinds of business-oriented newsgroups. The first, under the `biz` hierarchy, represents newsgroups dealing with specific businesses, some of which were started by those businesses. The second are more wide-ranging discussions about business issues in general and often attract owners or would-be owners of small businesses.

To access these newsgroups, fire up your newsreader and use the search feature. You'll have no trouble locating them.

Newsgroups in the Biz Hierarchy

One of the Usenet hierarchies (`biz`) is devoted to discussions about business and businesses. The following is an abbreviated list of these groups:

```
biz.americast
biz.americast.samples
biz.books.technical
biz.clarinet
biz.clarinet.sample
biz.comp.hardware
biz.comp.mcs
biz.comp.services
biz.comp.software
biz.comp.software.demos
biz.comp.telebit
biz.config
biz.control
biz.dec.decathena
biz.dec.decnews
biz.dec.ip
biz.digital.announce
biz.digital.articles
biz.jobs.offered
biz.misc
biz.newgroup
biz.next.newprod
biz.oreilly.announce
biz.pagesat
biz.pagesat.weather
```

```
biz.sco.announce
biz.sco.general
biz.sco.magazine
biz.sco.opendesktop
biz.sco.sources
biz.sco.wserver
biz.test
biz.univel.misc
biz.zeos.announce
```

Some of the groups here have been started by the companies themselves, while others are concerned with the products of those companies. The SCO and DEC groups, for example, deal with issues regarding the Santa Cruz Operation and Digital Equipment Corporation, respectively, and are read and responded to by personnel from within those organizations. The following message shows a question from a subscriber (preceded by the > markers) and part of the response from an SCO support representative:

17

```
>Is there a way to get the screenblanker, one might activate by setting
>TBLNK to an other value than 0, to blank *both* displays - the VGA *and*
>the HERCULES? If not, does anybody know of a pd piece of code that could
>be used for this?

Currently, the screen blanker will only blank a VGA screen, and will not work
on CGA, EGA, or Mono video cards.

Since the individual screen driver is what handles the screen blanking,
some work would have to be done in the drivers to support the
correct adapter calls, AC_ONSCREEN and AC_OFFSCREEN as defined in
/usr/include/sys/vid.h.
```

Other questions may be answered by individual subscribers to the group. From the same SCO group comes the following, this time with a very direct and perhaps cryptic answer from a subscriber rather than a company representative (who presumably would have elaborated a bit):

```
>Can Anyone explain to me how I would go about doing either a full screen
>capture under opendesktop 3.0? I need the information then placed into a
>word processor file so I can put together a manual describing how my
>system works and actual usages helps to expain to new users.

man xwd
man xpr
```

One of the major points here is that setting up a `biz` hierarchy newsgroup enables you to respond quickly to specific questions from users, and through those answers to compile lists of questions to be used for product redesign or distribution to other support people. As with any such venture, however, be sure that if you set the newsgroup up, you staff it accordingly. Once it's in place, Internetters will use it, and they expect responses.

General Business Newsgroups

You can find several newsgroups dealing with business issues in general. Among the more interesting are `alt.business.misc` and `misc.entrepreneurs`. The discussion is far-reaching in both of these groups, and subscribers tend to be owners of small or one-person businesses.

Note: Here, as elsewhere in the book, I've changed names and addresses in the messages, as a matter of courtesy. (I don't give out phone numbers, either.) If you want to contact these people, join the newsgroup.

The following are some discussions from `alt.business.misc`:

```
-----------
I am working in economic development in Claremont CA and work with small
businesses. I am working right now with a company that has a coffee and
gift shop. He buys chocolate from a local chocolate shop and packages it
to sell. One product that he buys costs him $.45 and the packaging costs
$.65. He wants to find a way to buy cheaper packaging.

He needs a box that is 2 1/4" wide, 4 1/2" long and 3/4" high. It must be
a see through box. Right now he is using a molded plastic but he could
also use a cardboard box with a window covered with a clear plastic. The
important thing is that it is the right size. There are jewelry boxes
like that but it has to be designed for candy. Does anyone know of a
company that produces that type of packaging?
```

At last count, the poster had received about eight responses, including one that apparently worked things out.

```
----------------
NAFTA for Windows!


Ideal for the business person exploring new North American import/export
opportunities for the first time, or for the experienced professional
```

```
who needs easy access to all the detailed NAFTA terms....quickly! The
complete text of the North American Free Trade Agreement is now available
as a user-friendly Windows 3.1 HELP File! Powered by the standard Windows
WINHELP.EXE program, this is one megabyte of invaluable information for
companies who want to improve their bottom line!

+  Hypertext format, infinitely more readable than the
1000 page printed document!

+  Access topics through Menus, by Key Word Search, or
sequential browsing forward and back.

+  Comprehensive, but concise Synopsis of all key points
instantly available in a second Window!

+  Direct cross-referencing to all related Chapters, Articles,
Schedules and Annexes.

+  Includes Specific Rules of Origin!

+  All "specially-defined" NAFTA phrases and words keyed
as pop-up definitions!
```

This, clearly, is an ad, and they appear fairly regularly in business newsgroups. Although they're generally welcome, there is still a fairly rigid protocol about them. Some ads have become the center of subdiscussions, especially those that prove to be suspect or even fraudulent.

```
- - - - - - - - - - - - - - - - -

Business Opportunity:   (Non-MLM)

South Carolina based manufacturer's rep firm looking for an additional
associate.

Our specialty is providing solutions to indoor air quality problems for
industrial customers. These solutions often include a combination air
handling systems, scrubbers, and close-capture exhaust systems.

We work primarily with industrial end-users, mechanical contractors, and
design/build general contractors who specialize in value engineering.

The person we're looking for has a good grasp of mechanical concepts, has
a broad-base understanding of various manufacturing processes, and is people
oriented. We will provide all necessary training to the right person.

We are not as concerned about what's on your resume as we are about who you
are and what you're looking for in a business opportunity. There is no
limit to what you can earn as this is a commission-on-sales situation.
```

```
If you're looking for a salary, expense account, and company car, this is
not for you. If you're looking for an opportunity to function as an
independent contractor, be your own boss, and control your own income, leave
me an e-mail message.
```

This is yet another kind of ad, this time for help wanted. The last paragraph alone should attract a few people, although no response was noted on the newsgroup itself. At the bottom of this ad was a personal e-mail address, along with instructions to respond there instead.

```
---------

ALO Energy, Eastern Europe's largest space organization, is seeking professional
distributors for its space souvenir items. T-shirts, hats, posters, mugs,
photographs and pins commemorating Russian space programs. Upcoming joint
Russian-US space flights are already heightening interest. Licensing
arrangements also possible.

---------

Entrepreneurial Solutions, a West Virginia company seeks working partner with
capital. Just completed one and a half years of research and develop-
ment. Complete business plan available after signing a non disclosure.
Our companies main activities are customized PC based online systems.
For serious inquires, you may call 1-800-Online-5. From the main voice
menu, select online system sales. For E-Mail; carlucci@ins.infonet.net
```

These, too, are fairly common: ads searching for licensing or business partners. Again, personal e-mail addresses are included, so responses weren't posted to the group.

```
----------

Hi everyone!

I have compiled a book containing 5 reports that will show you how to do
the following:

Report #1
HOW TO GET FREE ADVERTISING

I will show you who to contact, where to go to, and exactly what to do.
Use these secrets to help advertise your business or event. This
information can translate into HUGE SAVINGS to you as a business or an
individual.

Report #2
GETTING FREE PUBLICITY
```

```
I will show you this little known method in getting FREE PUBLICITY. How
to approach these people giving away the publicity. And give you actual
examples of successful methods of gaining free publicity.

Report #3
THE SECRETS TO MAKING MONEY IN MAIL ORDER
```

As always, the get-something-free message is intriguing. Presumably, this idea will eventually mean spending some money, but the advertiser certainly makes it easy.

What becomes clear after reading only a few messages on these newsgroups is that if you ask a sensible question you will more often than not get at least one response, and usually several. Keep your questions short, don't flaunt advertising, and you'll be helped by people who've been there and who know the ins and outs. All for the measly price of a Usenet connection.

Task 17.2: Subscribe to business-oriented mailing lists.

The differences between mailing lists and newsgroups on business topics are much the same as for any other topic. Newsgroups are less formal, a bit more difficult to work with, and more open to a wide-ranging discussion. They're also at least somewhat open to advertising, which few mailing lists are. Some companies have established newsgroups and mailing lists to serve essentially the same function, but the lists shown below are more serious research-based lists.

Here are several worthwhile lists, each with a different topic, and complete with a portion of their "official" descriptions. The author followed six of them for a month. It became clear that they do what they were designed to do, and the messages, while ranging freely within the topic, stick precisely to that topic in almost all cases. That, too, distinguishes mailing lists from newsgroups on the whole.

This is just a selection, but from them you'll learn of other lists as well. See Chapter 4 for information on joining a mailing list.

`AJBS-L@NCSUVM.BITNET`: The Association of Japanese Business Studies, devoted to research and discussion of Japanese business and economics

`HHI-RES@UTARLVM1.BITNET`: HHI Research Findings, dealing with issues of general interest to real-estate researchers

`E-EUROPE@NCSUVM.BITNET`: Eastern European Business Network, on doing business in Eastern Europe countries, with a goal toward helping these countries in their transition to market economies

`IBJ-L@PONIECKI.BERKELEY.EDU`: Internet Business Journal, distribution list for this FTP-retrievable journal dealing with business on the Internet

ICEN-L@IUBVM.BITNET: International Career and Employment Network, self-explanatory

JMBA-L@ISRAEL.NYSERNET.ORG: Jewish MBA List, dealing with issues of being Jewish and in business or in an MBA program

LATCO@PSG.COM: Latin American Trade Council of Oregon list, devoted to information and ideas regarding business and trade with Latin America

MARKET-L@UCF1VM.BITNET: Marketing List, for academic and day-to-day discussions of issues related to marketing

MBA-L@MARIST.BITNET: MBA List, with information and discussion about MBA programs

ORCS-L@OSUVM1.BITNET: Operations Research and Computer Science, for researchers and practitioners alike

PA_NET@SUVM.BITNET: Public Administration Network, on public administration issues

FLEXWORK@PSUHMC.BITNET: Flexible Work Environment, discussions on how people handle flexible work situations

TRDEV-L@PSUVM.BITNET: Training and Development Discussions List, about the development of human resources

SPACE-INVESTORS@CS.CMU.EDU: Investing in space-related companies, including new products, contracts, venture capital, etc.

HTMARCOM@cscns.com: Discussion of high-tech marketing communications related to computer and electronic products – also LISTSERV@cscns.com

INET-MARKETING@EINET.NET: One of the best mailing lists on the Internet (for *any* subject), INET-MARKETING offers detailed and energetic discussions of marketing on the Internet. Also LISTPROC@EINET.NET

RITIM-L@URIACC.URI.EDU: Topics on this thoughtful list range from marketing to technological advances in the cable, telecommunications, and public policy areas

AETHICS-L: Here's a list devoted to a discussion about ethics in accounting. And you thought accountants only worried about the bottom line. Also LISTPROC@SCU.EDU.AU

COMMERCIAL-REALESTATE@SYNCOMM.COM: Devoted to real estate professionals, this list discusses sales, management, acquisitions, and development of commercial property. Also LISTSERV@SYNCOMM.COM

BIZBOT@TELETRON.COM: BizOpList is a useful, low-volume list devoted to business opportunities, including announcements about new businesses and self-employment possibilities

WALLSTREET ON MAJORDOMO@SHORE.NET: A discussion of trading and investing services and products, both on and off the Internet, concentrating of course on Wall Street activities themselves

Note: For a more thorough examination of business-related lists (or any other mailing lists for that matter), use your Web browser to move to `http://www.nova.edu/Inter-Links/listserv.html` and search for the subject areas you want.

Task 17.3: Examine business-related Gophers.

As ever, Gophers are easy to browse, and hidden beneath their menus is a wealth of information. Several businesses have established Gophers on the Net, complete with FAQs and downloadable technical and marketing information (including such items as press releases and product announcements). These are on the increase. For now, let's look at Gophers featuring information about business in general, rather than specific companies or industry details.

17

A good starting point is Gopher Jewels, at `cwis.usc.edu` (and mirrored on several other sites). The Economics and Business item yields the following menu:

```
Economics and Business

1.  Bureau of Labor Statistics, US Dept of Labor - Sam Houston State U../
2.  Business - Go M-Link/
3.  Business - Texas A&M/
4.  Business - The Management Archive/
5.  Business - Univ of California, Berkeley, Library (InfoLib)/
6.  Business, Economics, Marketing - University of Missouri-St. Louis/
7.  Commerce Business Daily - Vai CNS, Inc Gopher/
8.  Economics - Resources for Economists - Washington Univ., St. Loui../
9.  Economics - Berkeley Roundtable on the International Economy (BRIE../
10. Economics - Budget of the United States Government, Fiscal Year 19../
11. Economics - Computing Centre for Economics & Social Sciences (WSR)/
12. Economics - Economic Democracy Information Network (EDIN)/
```

The M-Link Gopher (directly accessible through `vienna.hh.lib.umich.edu`) offers another very healthy source of material.

```
1.  Business Gophers/
2.  Business Journals from CICNet/
3.  Business Sources on the Net /
4.  Business Statistics/
5.  Catalog of Federal Domestic Assistance/
6.  Commerce Business Daily/
7.  Current Stock Market Reports <TEL>
```

```
8.  Defense Conversion and Reinvestment (SPARC)/
9.  Employment/
10. Industry/
11. International Business & Exports/
12. Michigan Business/
13. NASA Shuutle Small Payloads Info/
14. Occupational Safety and Health (OSHA) Regulations/
15. Querri Database (Community Resource Development) <TEL>
16. Safety Information Resources on the InterNet/
17. Small Business/
18. TQM/
```

There is a lot to work with here, but let's start somewhere. Near the bottom is a directory for `Small Business`, which obviously will be of interest to anyone in that category. After you select it, you will see the following short menu:

```
1.  Basic Guide to Exporting (NTDB) /
2.  Catalog of Federal Domestic Assistance/
3.  Newbiz <TEL>
4.  Overseas Business Reports  (NTDB) /
5.  Small Business Administration Industry Profiles /
6.  Small Business Administration State Profiles /
```

Assume an interest in overseas markets. Selecting item `4` takes you to the following (partial) menu, which presents reports on a variety of nations outside the U.S. (whether technically "overseas" or not).

```
Overseas Business Reports  (NTDB)

1.  ***** Via the University of Missouri-St. Louis *****  .
2.  ARGENTINA      - OVERSEAS BUSINESS REPORT - OBR9211    .
3.  AUSTRIA        - OVERSEAS BUSINESS REPORT - OBR910903 .
4.  BAHAMAS        - OVERSEAS BUSINESS REPORT - OBR9208    .
5.  BOLIVIA        - OVERSEAS BUSINESS REPORT - OBR9212    .
6.  BRAZIL         - OVERSEAS BUSINESS REPORT - OBR9205    .
7.  CANADA         - BUSINESS GUIDE           - OBR9304    .
8.  CHILE          - OVERSEAS BUSINESS REPORT - OBR9210    .
9.  GABON          - OVERSEAS BUSINESS REPORT - OBR9109    .
10. GERMANY,-W.    - OVERSEAS-BUSINESS REPORT - OBR9102    .
```

The following is a tiny portion of the Brazil business report. Included in the full report are statistics for each Brazilian industry, methods for exporting, trade policy and role of government, and so on. This is useful for every company, not just a small business, with designs on the Brazilian marketplace.

```
Introduction

This report is designed to acquaint the U.S. business community with
Brazil's economic and commercial environment and provide guidance on
exporting to Brazil. Brazil's rules and regulations affecting trade and
investment are in a state of rapid change as the Brazilian government
implements various programs intended to stimulate economic competitiveness
through opening its traditionally restricted and protected markets to
greater foreign and domestic competition.

Considerable attention has been given to the details of Brazil's import
system because it is important to understand how the system operates.
Exporters must be familiar with Brazil's import procedures and documentation
requirements, which are stringently applied. Non-compliance inevitably
results in delays and financial penalties. Information is also provided on
Brazilian regulations affecting foreign investment.
```


Also from this `Small Business` item comes the Catalog of Federal Domestic Assistance Gopher, which features only two items, as follows:

```
1.  Introduction to the Catalog of Federal Domestic Assistance .
2.  Search the CFDA.src <?>
```

A quick search using the keyword `loans`, however, reveals how extensive the information is. Following is the first portion of a five-page menu containing files dealing with loans:

```
Search the CFDA.src: loans

1.  84.032 Federal Family Education Loans.
2.  10.410 Very Low to Moderate Income Housing Loans.
3.  10.406 Farm Operating Loans.
4.  64.114 Veterans Housing_Guaranteed and Insured Loans.
5.  10.051 Commodity Loans and Purchases.
6.  10.404 Emergency Loans.
7.  59.008 Physical Disaster Loans.
8.  59.041 Certified Development Company Loans (504 Loans).
9.  10.416 Soil and Water Loans.
10. 10.407 Farm Ownership Loans.
11. 10.768 Business and Industrial Loans.
12. 59.012 Small Business Loans.
13. 10.766 Community Facilities Loans.
```

Because you're in the Small Business Gopher, why not check out the information on `Small Business Loans`, item `12`. The following is part of the Application and Award section of the resulting (fairly short) document:

```
APPLICATION AND AWARD PROCESS:

Preapplication Coordination: None. This program is excluded
from coverage under E.O. 12372.

Application Procedure: Applications are filed by the
participating lender in the field office serving the territory in
which the applicant's business is located. Where the participating
lender is in another territory, applications may be accepted and
processed by the field office serving that territory, provided
there is mutual agreement between the two field offices involved.
 (See listing of field offices in Appendix IV of the Catalog.)

Award Procedure: Applicant is notified by authorization
letter from district SBA office, or participating bank.

Range of Approval/Disapproval Time: From 1 to 20 days from
date of application acceptance, depending on type of loan and type
of lender program.
```

Similarly, the Gopher menu at Texas A&M (`gopher.tamu.edu`) contains a wealth of business-related material, much of which points to international sites.

```
1.  Internet Business Pages/
2.  Singapore's IT2000 Nation-wide Plan for Info Technology/
3.  Trade News/
4.  Arizona State Economic Development Database (3270) <TEL>
5.  Asia Pacific Business & Marketing Resources/
6.  Automated Trade Library Service at Cal State Fresno (vt100) <TEL>
7.  Business Information Directory from Tucson, Arizona/
8.  College of Business at Florida State University/
9.  Current Business Statistics/
10. Descriptions of Information Products, Office of Business Analysis/
11. East and Southeast Asian Business and Management/
12. Economic Bulletin Board via U Michigan/
13. Finance software (DOS)/
14. Israel_Business_Today/
15. Izviestia/Financial Times Newspaper (Sample Issues - Russian) /
16. Japan Economic Newswire/
17. Pacific Region Forum on Business and Management /
18. Pennsylvania State Economic Development Information Network (.. <TEL>
19. Pragati/
20. Small Business Development (from WiscInfo)/
21. The Internet Business Journal/
22. Travel Information/
```

One example of the kind of material available here is shown in the next menu, yielded by selecting item `11`, `East and Southeast Asian Business and Management`.

```
1.  Communicating to Asia-Pacific Consumers.
2.  Cross-Cultural Face-Negotiation.
3.  Globalization & Human Resource Management.
4.  Government & Business Relations in Indonesia.
5.  Negotiations with the Pacific Rim.
6.  Networking & Business in Southeast Asia.
7.  Political Change & Business Dynamics in Vietnam.
```

All these could be of use to anyone about to conduct business in Southeast Asia. Selecting item `2`, `Cross-Cultural Face-Negotiation`, displays the following essay/report, which elaborates considerably on these four areas. This, once again, is but a small portion of a highly recommended paper.

17

```
3. Uncertainty avoidance. Hofstede found that Canada and the US are low
in uncertainty avoidance, i.e., we like to take risks, take individual
initiative, and enjoy conflict. Whereas cultures like Japan, Hong Kong,
and South Korea are high in uncertainty avoidance, i.e., do not like
conflict, but pursue group harmony; people within these organizations
need clear rules, procedures, and clearly defined job responsibilities.

4. Masculinity versus femininity. This dimension has been controversial
because many people feel it is sexist. Hofstede discovered that Japan
rated high on masculine dimensions (males expect an "in-charge" role).
In contrast, countries like Norway and Sweden have a stronger feminine
dimension, which means that roles are more fluid between males and
females.  Canada rated high on the masculine dimension compared with
many Northern European organizational practices.
```

Finally, examine a Gopher established by a company. In this case, choose `Bell Atlantic`, for no other reason than it has perhaps the most easily remembered Gopher address of all (`ba.com`). Entering this Gopher displays the following menu:

```
1.  +Welcome.
2.  Company_History/
3.  Congressional_Hearings/
4.  Education/
5.  Financial/
6.  Information_Law_Alert/
7.  Media_Contacts.
8.  News_Releases/
9.  Other_Gophers/
10. Speeches/
11. Video/
```

None of these items is, as of this writing, fully fleshed out. The idea, however, is that providing a well-designed shell will offer expansion capacity later. For now, however, Bell Atlantic has posted recent speeches and other media information, as well as public legal and financial details. From the `Financial` item you can get the 1994 reports, including the following portion from first quarter 1994:

```
Reported net income for the first quarter of 1994 was $389.2
million compared with $329.2 million for the first quarter of
1993, an increase of 18.2 percent. Total operating revenues
for the first quarter of 1994 were $3.37 billion, an increase
of 6.6 percent compared with $3.16 billion for the same period
last year. Revenues, excluding financial services,
increased by 7.3 percent over the first quarter of 1993.
Wireless revenues, including cellular and paging, were 42.3
percent higher than the first quarter of 1993.
```

Bell Atlantic's Gopher provides a good model from which to work. Don't worry about getting overly elaborate all at once. Post information that you know people will want, and let their reaction determine much of the rest.

Task 17.4: Explore businesses on the World Wide Web.

In this task, you'll look at some businesses that have already committed to an Internet presence. All the examples shown here are from the World Wide Web. The reason, quite simply, is that the Web enables businesses to appear in the most attractive possible light. However, most businesses with a WWW site also offer Gopher and/or FTP sites. Few have committed exclusively to the Web because far more users have access to Gopher than Mosaic or Cello. Soon, that is almost certain to change.

The Web offers the following advantages:

- **Graphics**: Imagine relying on letters alone to make potential customers aware of your products and services and you will quickly understand why e-mail and downloaded text files have severe limitations. Through Mosaic or Cello, customers can be shown visually striking designs, which is crucial to any marketing or communications strategy.
- **Sound**: Commercials, showrooms, videoconferences, strategy sessions—they all have a sound element. Try to conduct business for one single day without it, and you'll get an idea of why it's so important. Without the Web's sound capabilities,

the Internet is nothing more than a sophisticated print medium; with it, it merges and amplifies several media.

- **Video**: Television is the most popular medium for a very good reason. There is movement, dialogue, and music, all at the same time. Except for the music (and the impossible story lines), it's just like real-life. The still-life media, print, and even radio, rely heavily on the user's imagination. The premise of television is that most people want things imagined *for* them. As the Web develops, it is likely to become more like television.
- **Interactive Forms**: The Web is interactive. That's why its potential as a business tool is even stronger than TV's. Interactive TV, at this point, means that a user sees a phone number on the screen and places a call. But most people don't want to get up from the couch and do that—they might miss part of the show, they can't remember the phone number, they don't want to go get their credit card, they'll do it later. People on the Web, by comparison, are in interactive mode from the minute they log on. Show them a form they can fill out and then send with the click of a mouse, and you have a potentially ideal tool. These forms—currently available only in the UNIX and Microsoft Windows versions of Mosaic but soon to appear in MacMosaic and in Cello—make it possible for customers to order products, to offer feedback, to complete surveys, and even to participate in online meetings. Currently, one major concern is with security, but that may well be addressed by the preparation of a "secure" version of Mosaic, which has recently been announced.
- **Ease of Use**: Let's face it—if the future of business on the Internet depends on your customers, clients, and personnel knowing the intricacies of Telnet and FTP, you can close up shop right now. Gopher is an exceptionally strong interface, but even a graphical Gopher program doesn't provide the Web's ease of use. At this stage in its development, the biggest problem with Mosaic and Cello is setting it up, not using it, and that situation will only improve. Eventually, even complex operations like configuring download directories will be taken care of automatically. These programs let people see something and then click on what they want next. Using the Web eventually will be as easy for your customers and associates as using the most basic features of their TV's remote control. Maybe easier.

An excellent place to start exploring businesses already on the Web is Open Market's List of Commercial Services page at `http://www.directory.net/`. As you can see from Figure 17.1, which displays only the top portion of this page, the list is extensive. Also, as you might expect, a number of high-tech firms appear prominently, but there are others as well.

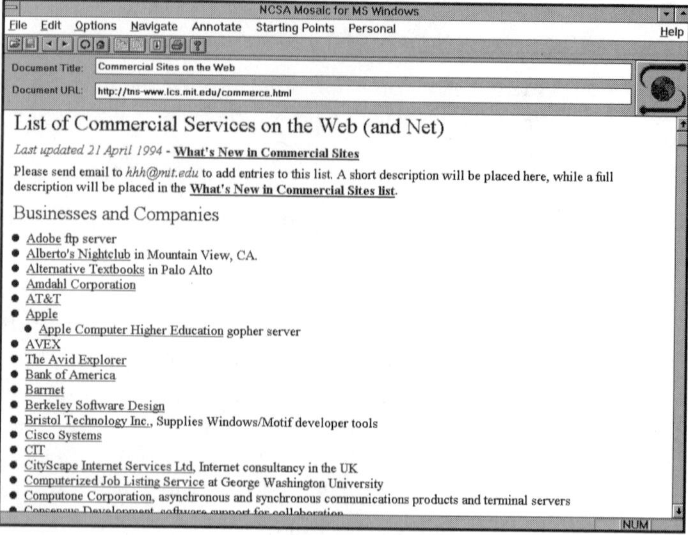

Figure 17.1.
List of Commercial Services on the WWW and the Internet.

Further down this page, the links are divided according to server. CommerceNet, for example, is being coordinated by Enterprise Integration Technologies and represents a consortium of different firms. The links of most of those firms are gathered under one major link, as shown in Figure 17.2.

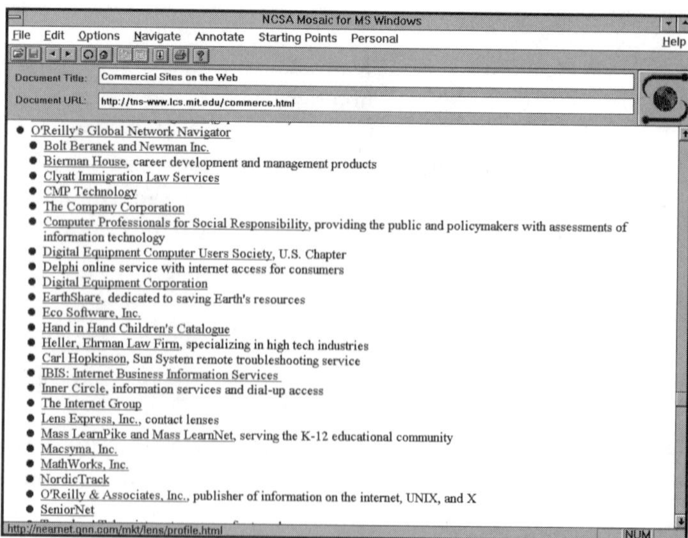

Figure 17.2.
List of Commercial Services: CommerceNet.

The CommerceNet idea looked intriguing, so click on the appropriate link. This takes you to the CommerceNet home page, which offers a selection called Directories. Choosing this brings you to `http://www.commerce.net/directories/directories.html`, the CommerceNet directories page, as displayed in Figure 17.3.

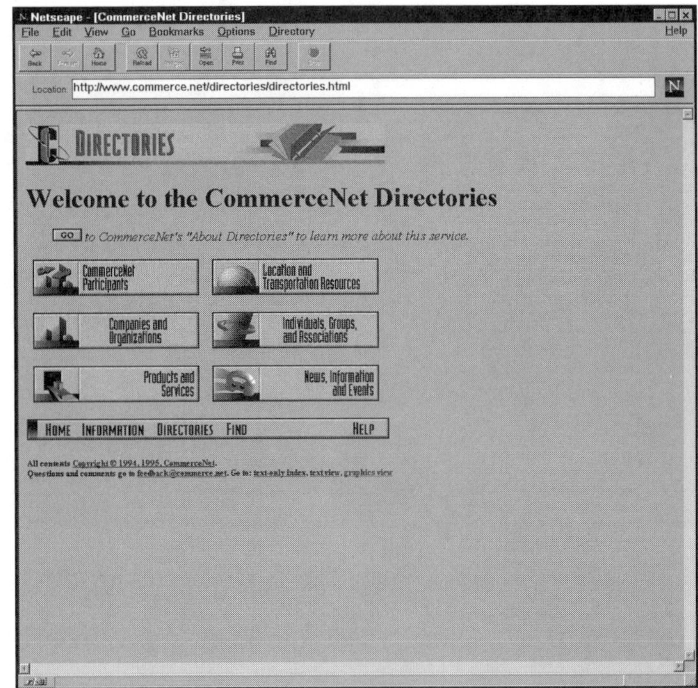

Figure 17.3.
CommerceNet directories Web page.

As of this writing, this site was very much under construction, but already you can see the focus it will take. You also see how corporate interests view the potential of the World Wide Web; the color and easy accessibility of this page are exemplary, even if, with a slow connection, it takes a long time to load. The point is that Internet access will soon be faster, and pages like this will no longer be a problem.

Another intriguing offering from the List of Commercial Services is the Internet Mall (`http://www.mecklerweb.com/imall/`). This is another page listing commercial ventures on the Net, and it includes a number of telnet and FTP sites, in addition to the more obvious Gopher and Web sites. Figure 17.4 shows the Mall's home page.

From the home page it's a matter of clicking on the selections you want. The Mall is organized according to floors, like a real-world department store. Different types of goods appear on different floors. As an example, clicking on Furniture and Household Items, and then subsequently on Furniture, takes you to the screen shown in Figure 17.5.

Figure 17.4.
The Internet Mall home page.

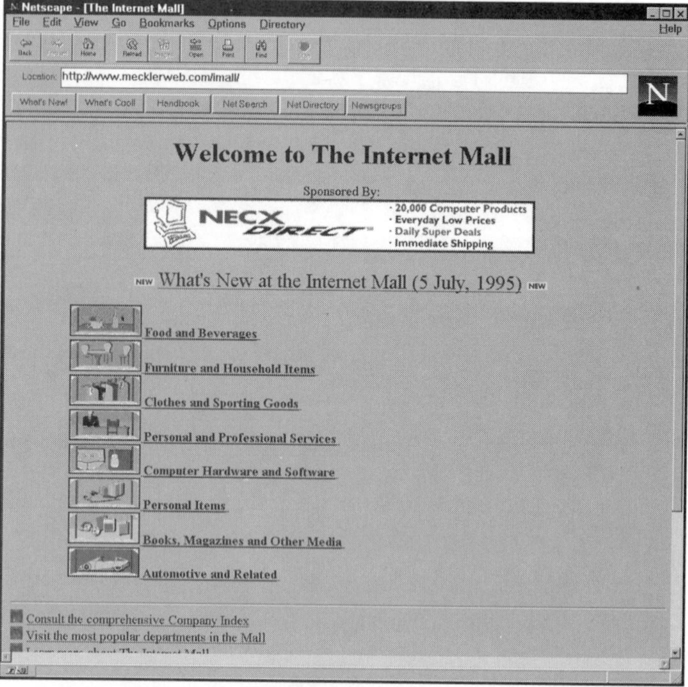

Figure 17.5.
The Internet Mall's Furniture department.

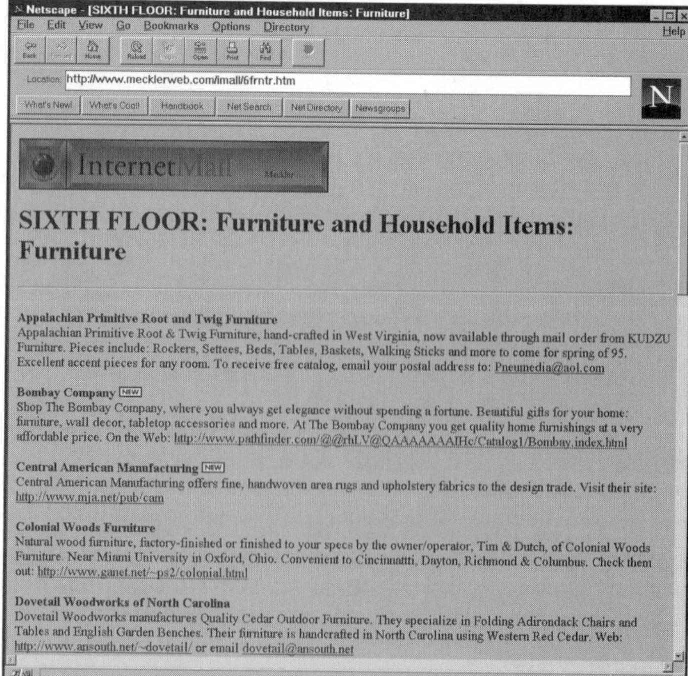

Clicking on any of these links takes you out of the Internet Mall and into the pages referenced by the links. For example, Figure 17.6 shows the results of clicking on the link for Dovetail Woodworks of North Carolina (`http://www.ansouth.net/~dovetail/`). In fact, one of the real benefits of the Internet Mall over other malls is precisely that it links to a wide variety of external sites. You're not just confined to the Mall itself.

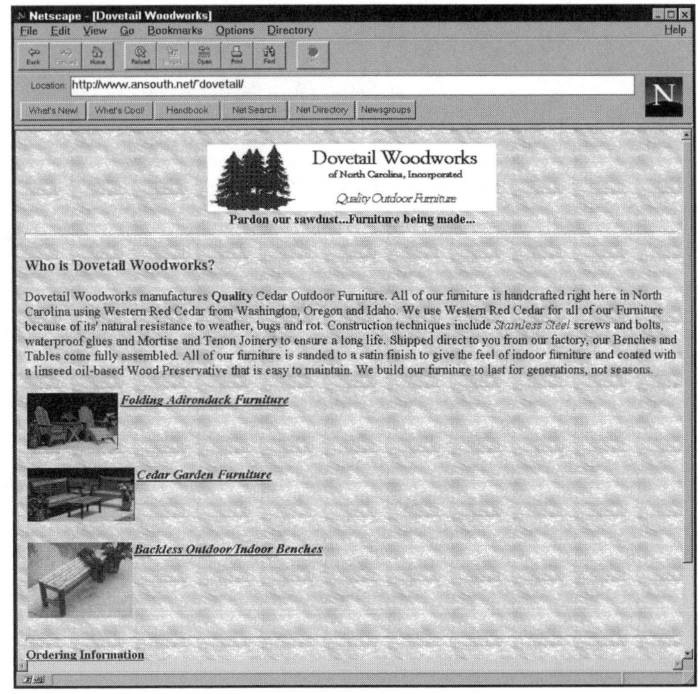

Figure 17.6.
Home page for Dovetail Woodworks from Internet Mall.

One of the most extensive uses of the Web comes from the computer companies: Microsoft, IBM, Digital Equipment, and so on. One of the most impressive Web sites is that of Hewlett-Packard, whose home page (`http://www.hp.com/`) is displayed in Figure 17.7.

This is a well-developed page for a number of reasons. First, all the information is accessible by clicking on named boxes, *or* (and this is important for many users) through text links below the graphic. Second, the page is graphically consistent with the company's well-known packaging designs, and therefore, acts as part of the overall marketing effort.

One of the features in HP's site is their customer service area, SupportLine. To get there, click on the Products link from the home page, and then on Services and Support.

A similar site is the Digital Equipment Web, found at `http://www.dec.com/`. The home page consists primarily of an imagemap with multiple fonts, one of which takes you to the Products and Services page at `http://www.digital.com:80/info/products.html`, shown in Figure 17.8.

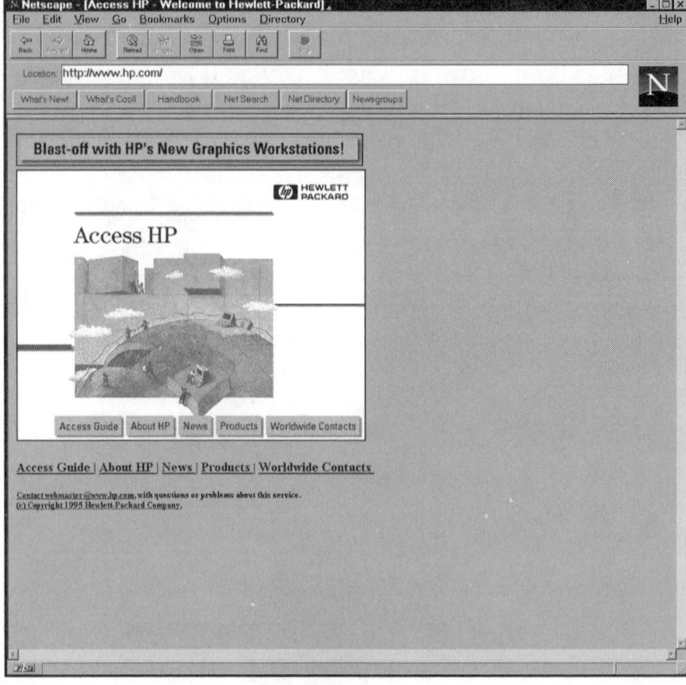

Figure 17.7. *Hewlett-Packard home page.*

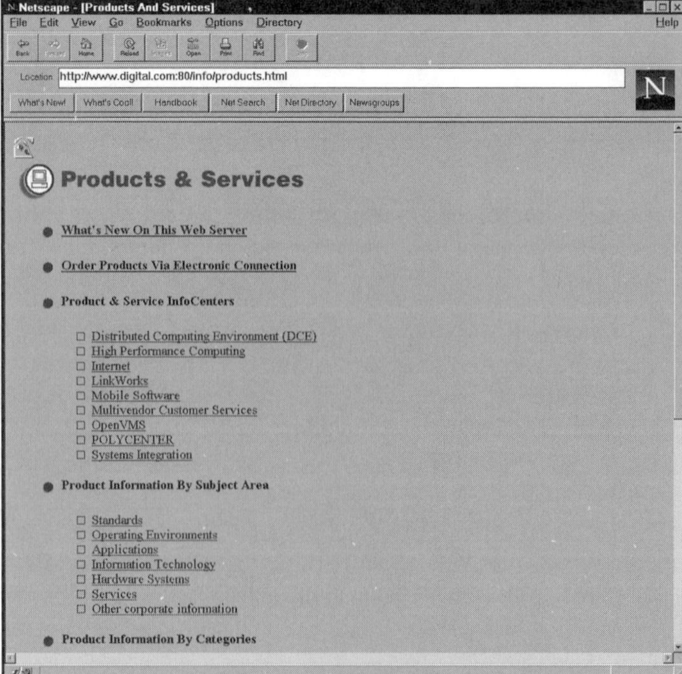

Figure 17.8. *Digital Equipment Corporation's Products and Services page.*

If you're a Digital customer, you can get a great deal of information from these well-defined pages. A typical archive is seen in Figure 17.9, one of the HPC InfoCenters. This one is for High Performance Computing, and offers an extensive series of technical and customer service items.

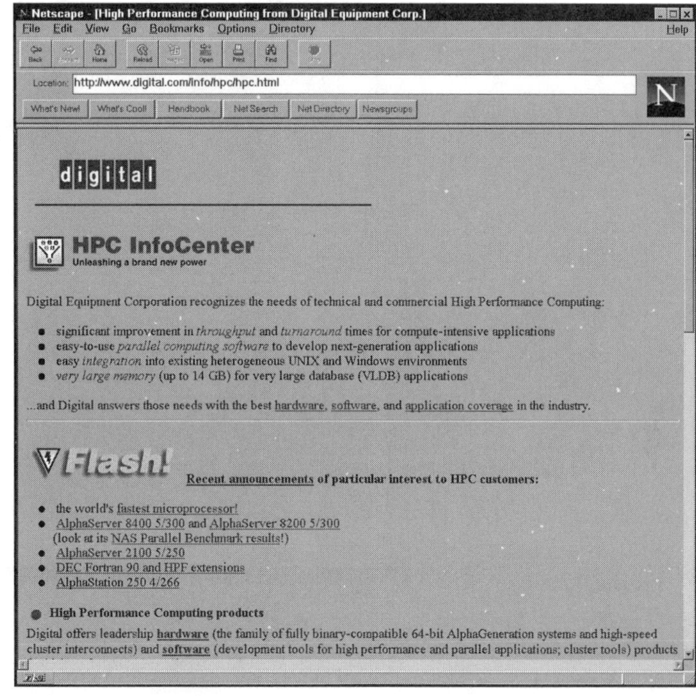

Figure 17.9.
The High Performance Computing InfoCenter from Digital Equipment's site.

Another important area in the Digital web is the area called Reading Rooms (accessible from the home page). From here, you can click on the link to the Research Reading Room (`http://www.digital.com/info/edu/research.htm`), shown in Figure 17.10. Once again, an extensive amount of information is available here for Digital customers, plus links to other related sites.

From here, it's on to British Columbia, Canada. Figure 17.11 shows the home page for the Westcoast Interchange, which offers a link to its Town Centre, and from there to the World Real Estate Listing Service. From here you can click from country to country to see what's being offered on the Net, or proceed to other Internet real estate directories available from the Westcoast pages. Figure 17.12 shows a text-only page regarding a converted 16th century manor house for a mere one million French francs.

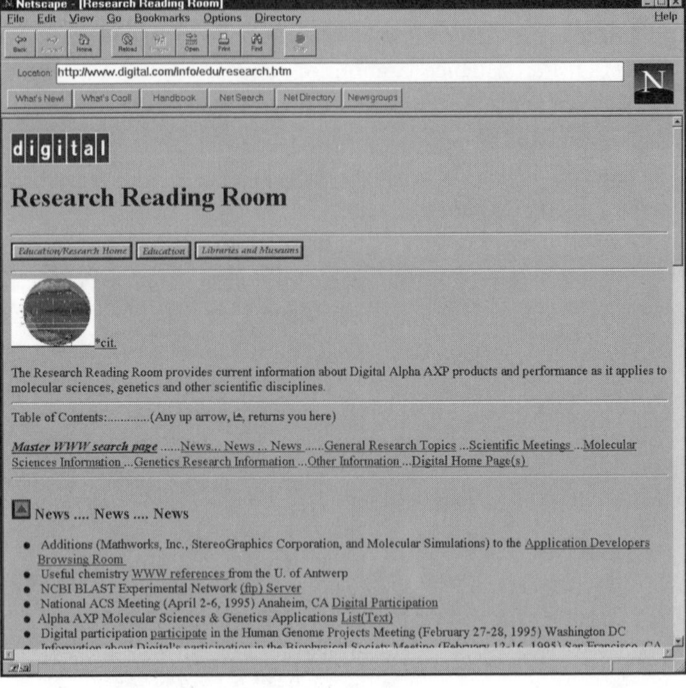

Figure 17.10.
The Research Reading Room from the Digital site.

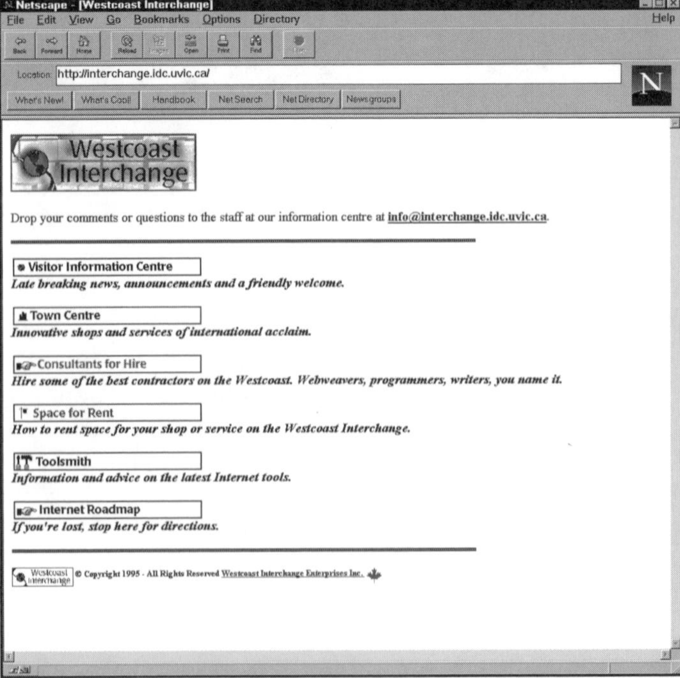

Figure 17.11.
Westcoast Interchange home page, showing link to Town Centre.

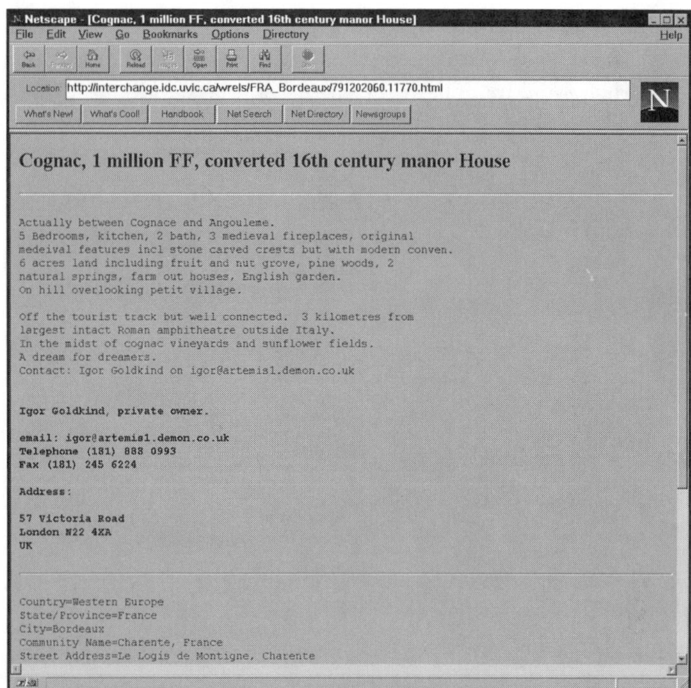

Figure 17.12.
Listing of French manor house in Westcoast real estate directories.

17

Clearly, the Internet—and especially the Web—has excellent applicability for real-estate firms, especially as access to the Net becomes more common. Entire walk-throughs of houses and neighborhoods could easily be part of a company's presentation.

Next you come to Novell, Incorporated, whose home page (`http://www.novell.com`) uses a graphic similar in design to HP's, one that has, in fact, changed several times over the past several months. Novell has been busy, acquiring WordPerfect Corporation as just one example, and the changes have brought a renewed focus on Web-based materials. Figure 17.13 shows the Novell home page.

One of the services offered in the Novell site is user documentation. Clicking on the Manuals button from the home page takes you through a series of pages, one of which tells you that the service might not be there when you check next (then again, it might not be there by the time you read this). Nevertheless, Figure 17.13 shows what happens if you make it through to the collection of manuals for NetWare 4.1, one of Novell's primary products.

Equally important for Novell customers is the searchable database provided from the Web site. Figure 17.15 shows what the database search page looks like, and suffice it to say that the results are quite spectacular from the standpoint of sheer amount of information.

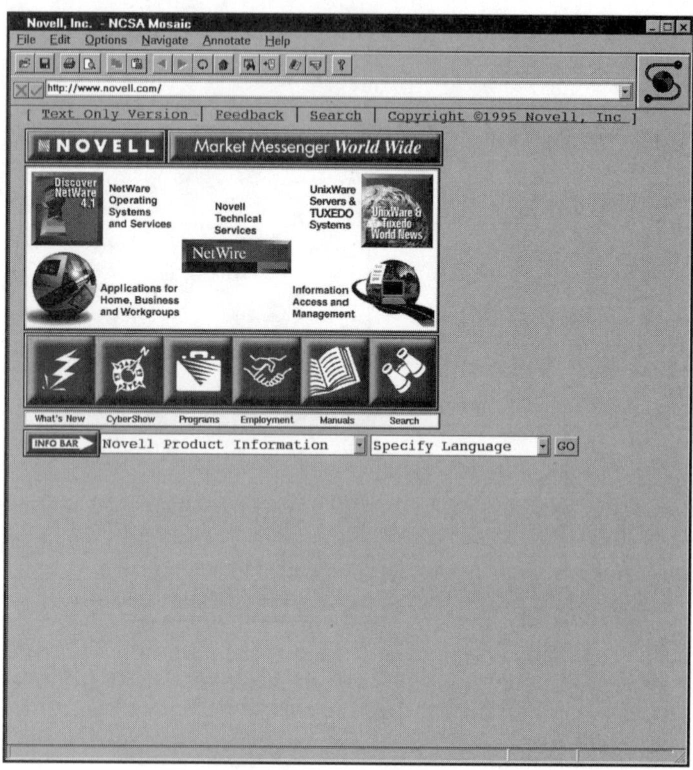

Figure 17.13.
Novell home page, with colorful imagemap.

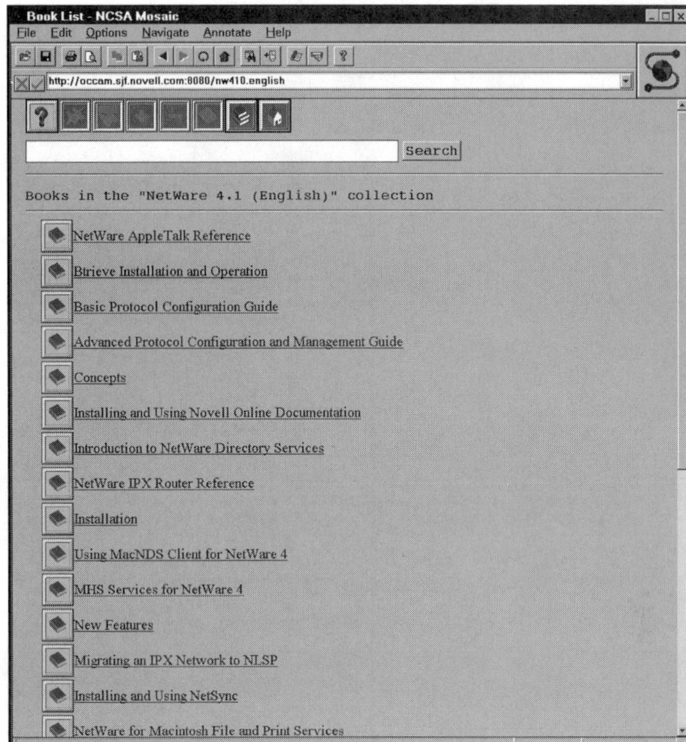

Figure 17.14.
The manuals collection for NetWare 4.1 from the Novell site.

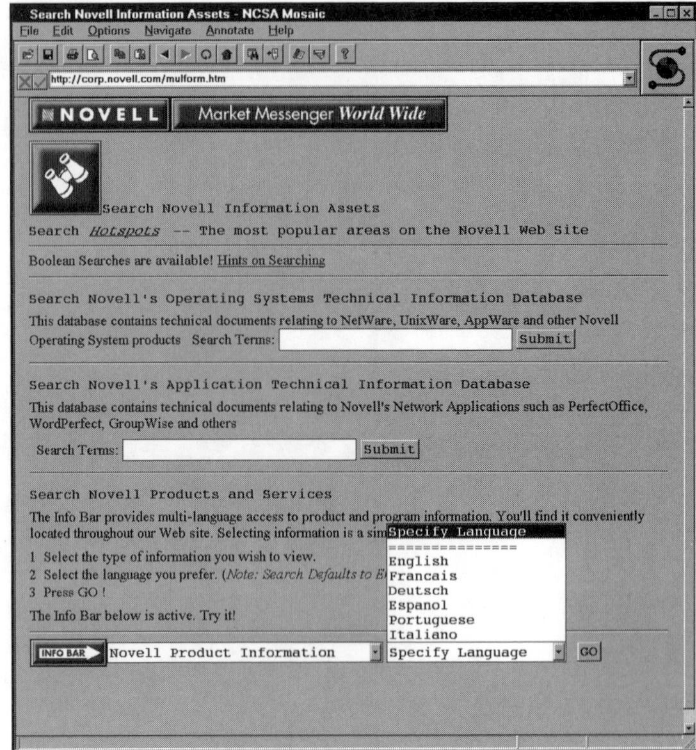

Figure 17.15.
Novell support database-search results for NetWare.

Moving out of high-tech and into finance, you arrive at the Bank of America home page (see Figure 17.16). Here you see very clearly how a major bank plans to offer Internet services. Most of this page is still under construction, but the goal is quick, easy, and reasonably detailed access.

Selecting HomeBanking, for example, leads to the screen shown in Figure 17.17. Among other things, this page describes a developing system for paying bills and performing other financial activities by computer. Interestingly, the Bank of America has changed its tune somewhat from its initial site, when it proposed to offer extensive financial services over the Web, a fact that points to some of the difficulties still being experienced by companies that are attempting fully secure access. Still, this is interesting and potentially useful.

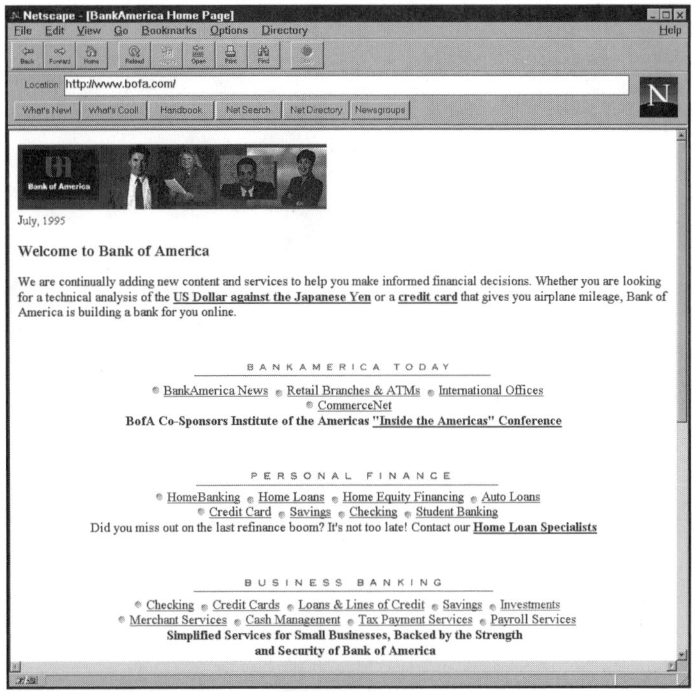

Figure 17.16.
Home page for the Bank of America.

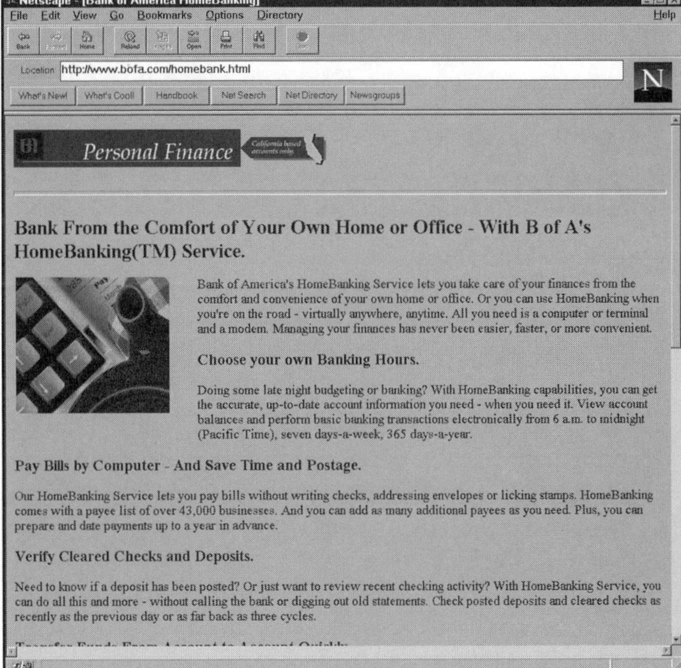

Figure 17.17.
Bank of America HomeBanking page.

Another approach to banking on the Web can be seen by accessing the Wells Fargo Bank home page at `http://wellsfargo.com/index.html`. As shown in Figure 17.18, the bank's home page promises the capability to get account balances on the Internet.

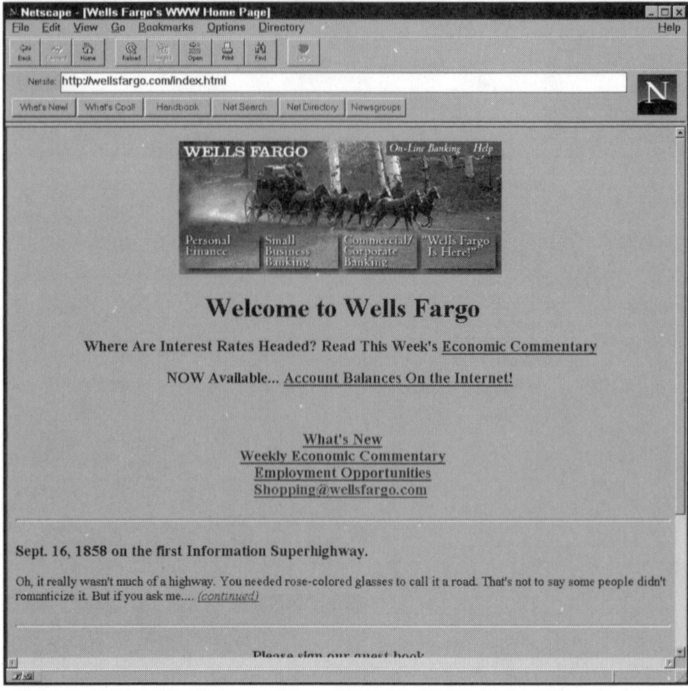

Figure 17.18.
The Wells Fargo Bank home page.

Admittedly, this is hardly financial nirvana, especially since you can get account balances and pay bills directly over the phone these days. In fact, Internet-based banking might not be a particularly notable future for the financial sector. But the involvement of major banks will spur development of Web-based services in general, a fact that can only help with Internet commerce in general.

One especially worthwhile bank site to visit is Canada's Toronto-Dominion Bank at `http://www.tdbank.ca/`. The TD Bank site, whose home page appears in Figure 17.19, has been recognized by several publications as one of the Web's better business sites, gives you access to a widening library of useful information and tools for financial planning and investment, although none of it transpiring over the Internet itself. Of interest to many people is the Today's Numbers link (from the imagemap at the top of the screen, which gives you an up-to-date commentary on money markets, foreign exchange, and bond markets.

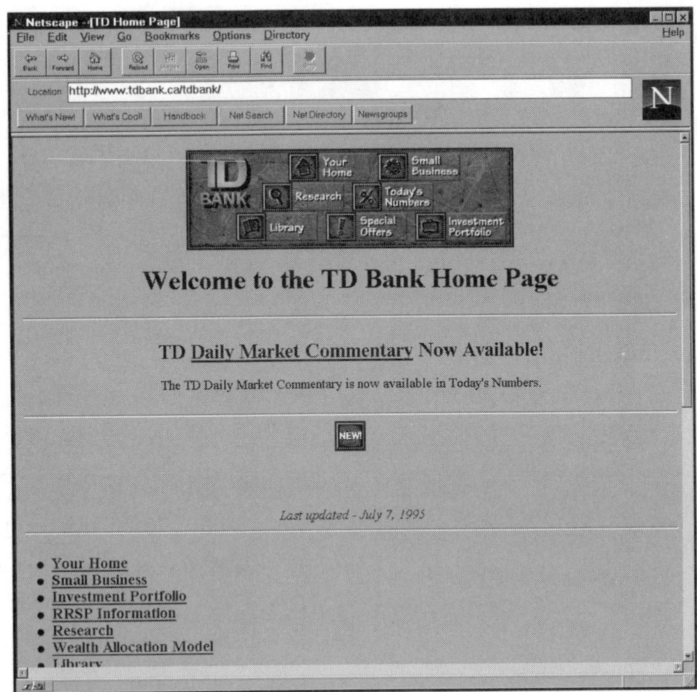

Figure 17.19.
Home page for the Toronto-Dominion Bank.

The next two screens show the Web offerings in the Future Fantasy Bookstore (`http://futfan.com/`). From the home page, you can obtain information about upcoming signings or you can use the store's online catalog (see Figure 17.20). A nicely designed search form appears when you select the catalog, and after a search, you see the screen shown in Figure 17.21, this Web site's coup de grace: a chance to order the book online, an extremely important service for this kind of potential impulse buying. This is an excellent example of making Web forms work for your business.

There are three more items before you finish this chapter. First is the most extensive site for stock quotes and other financial information, Quote.Com. Available at `http://www.quote.com/`, this site permits free limited use, but for extensive quote and portfolio tracking, you must subscribe (beginning at $9.95 US per month). (See Figure 17.22 for the home page.)

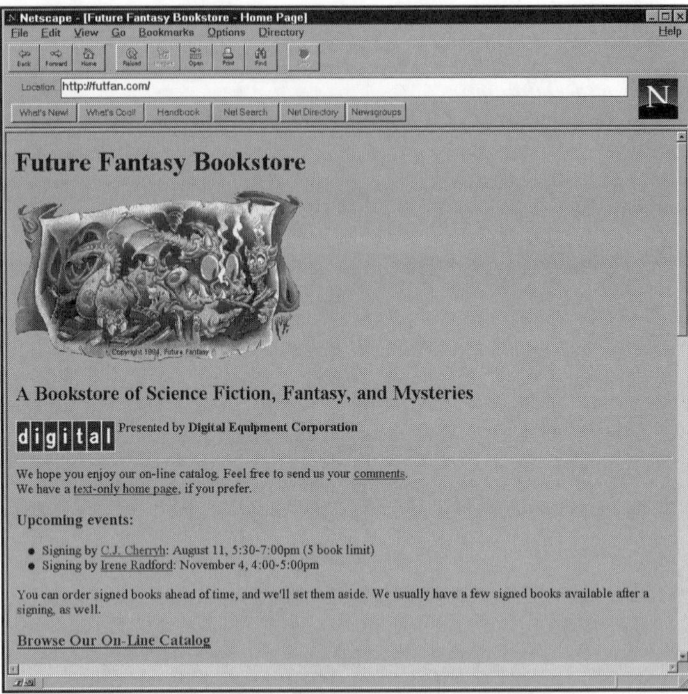

Figure 17.20.
Future Fantasy Bookstore home page.

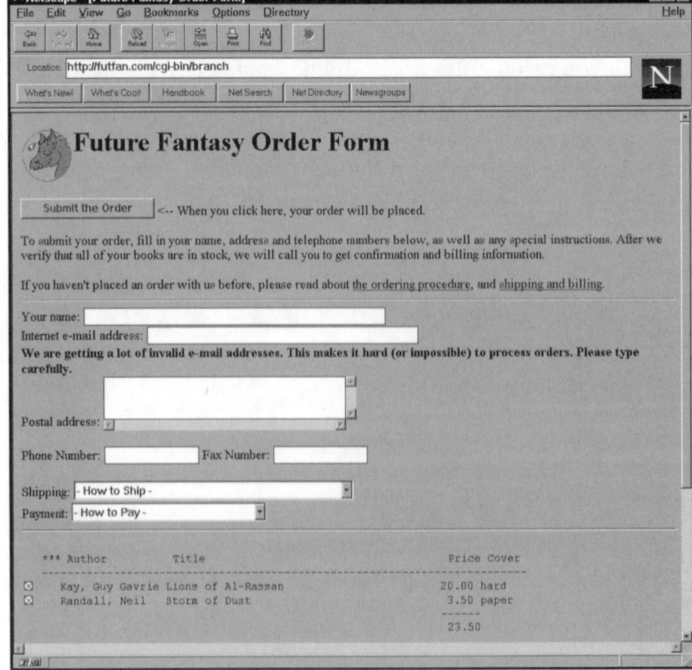

Figure 17.21.
Future Fantasy order form.

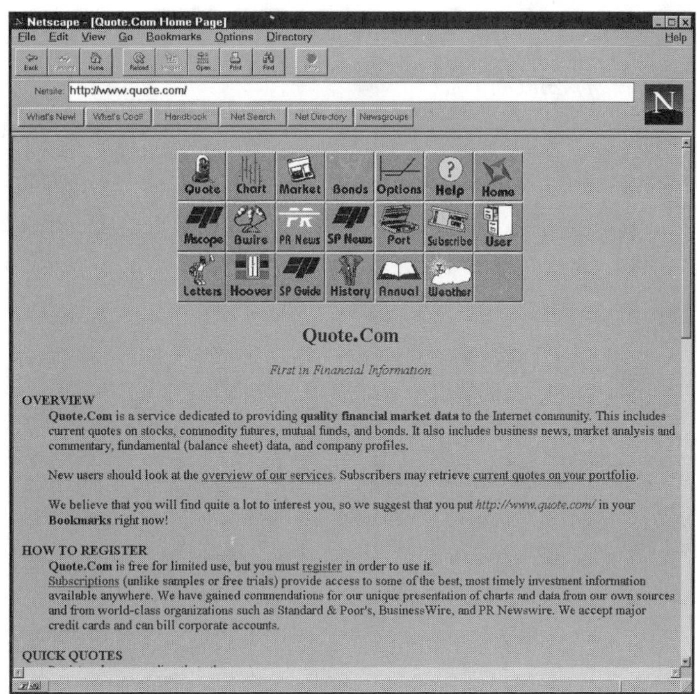

Figure 17.22.
The Quote.Com home page with large imagemap.

17

To get an actual quote, you must conduct a search by ticker symbol. If you don't know the ticker symbol of the company you're looking for, a very good search mechanism is available. Figure 17.23 shows a typical search, this one for Lotus Development Corporation, whose ticker symbol is `LOTS`, and the result of the search, the quote itself.

Quote.Com is a remarkably extensive site, and one that you'll return to repeatedly, as long as you have a financial reason for doing so. A huge amount of financial information is available from this one site.

One of the simplest and most purely useful sites on the Web is the Federal Express site (`http://www.fedex.com/`). As Figure 17.24 shows, there's nothing elaborate about these pages, but their utility makes them worthwhile. Just fill in your airbill tracking number, click on Send Request, and see where it is. Sure beats waiting on the phone to get precisely the same information. As you might expect, United Parcel Service offers the same tracking capability at `http://www.ups.com/`.

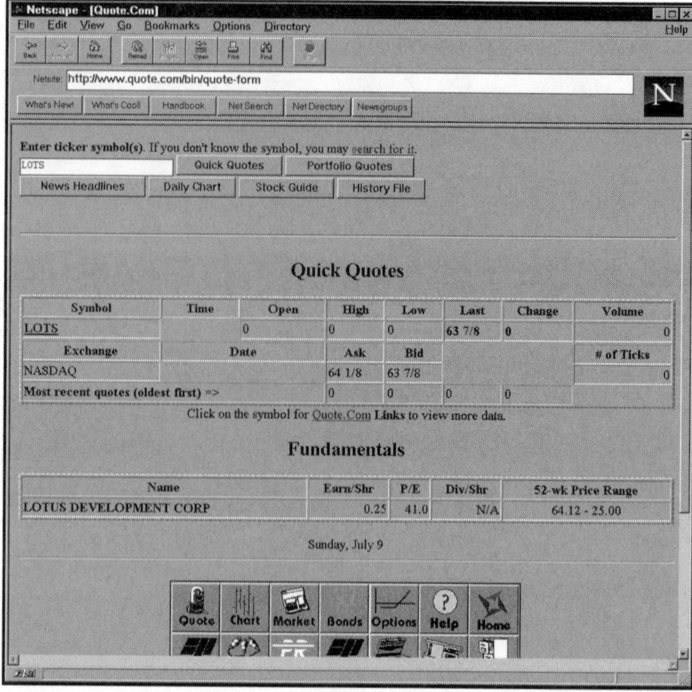

Figure 17.23.
Stock quote for Lotus Development Corporation.

Figure 17.24.
The Federal Express tracking page.

And, finally, for probably the silliest use of the World Wide Web for business, visit the Pizza Hut site at `http://www.pizzahut.com/`. Yep, Pizza Hut. As Figure 17.25 shows, you can actually use your Web browser to order a pizza, choosing from all the toppings and sizes. Why did I call this silly? Because I can't imagine ever using the Web to do this, when it's so easy to pick up the phone (many of the numbers are implanted in our brain cells by now) and order that way, in the process hearing about specials and other deals. The only time it might happen is when you don't want to log off to hang up the line, but that strikes me as rare. But be sure to check next year and find out if I've miscalculated.

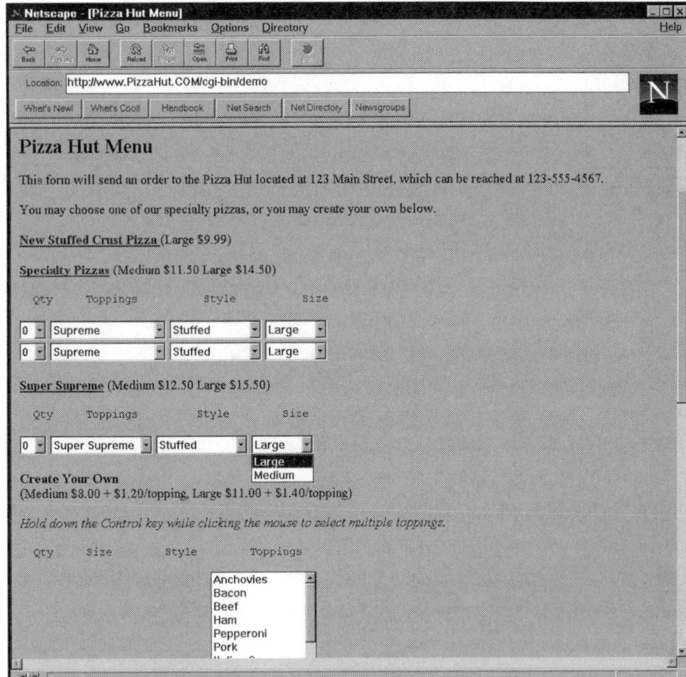

Figure 17.25.
The order form from the Pizza Hut Web site.

Summary

This chapter has provided an introduction to using the Internet to conduct business. There are options for discussing business concerns, for engaging in advertising and product awareness, and for researching business issues through Gopher sites and elsewhere. In addition, you looked extensively at some of the businesses that have established a strong presence on the World Wide Web, looking at what they offer and what they plan for the future.

Task Review

In this chapter, you learned how to perform the following tasks:

- Examine various newsgroups dealing with business issues
- Get an idea of which mailing lists your business might want to participate in
- Work through business-oriented Gophers and examined available documents
- Explore how businesses have developed the World Wide Web for corporate purposes

Q&A

Q How should my company start establishing an Internet presence?

A The first step, of course, is getting an Internet account. This can be done through a service provider, which is recommended until and unless you're planning to go whole-hog. You'll need an Internet account to allow your customers/clients/associates to reach you via e-mail. Next, it's probably a good idea to develop a Gopher, and you'll have to decide whether to maintain it yourself or have it stored on a provider's system. For a while, unless you have someone in your firm technologically capable (and with enough time) to develop and maintain it, the latter is probably a better option. Talk to your provider about this, or look to the Net for companies willing to do this. Third, get the Gopher up and running, make sure that it works properly, and then send a message to your clients and associates telling them it exists. If you want greater publicity, send a notice to the Gopher Jewels or Net-Happenings mailing lists (see Chapter 4 for information about the latter), and post to an appropriate newsgroup or two. Then, determine whether you want to start a news-group or mailing list of your own.

Once all this is in place, decide whether a WWW site would suit your purposes, and how extensive you want that site to be. By this point, you'll want to hook up with an established provider or consultant to give you expertise on developing the site, and to put it on equipment you know will be dependable. Through all of this, start training your own people to use the Internet in a number of ways, and establish a team to maintain your Internet site. At some point, you'll have your own people and equipment devoted to Internet functions, but that can be a year or two down the line.

Q If my Internet pages contain links to other sites, won't I simply lose browsers before they have a chance to explore my information thoroughly?

A This is an excellent question, and it brings up another point. One of the strengths of a Web page or a Gopher list is that it provides instant links to other sites. That means that someone who visits your site can just as easily leave it, never to return.

As a hypothetical example, assume that you've developed a cracker-jack home page that included colorful, appealing links to the home pages of some of your own clients (by cooperative arrangement, and all that). Someone lands on your page, thinks it looks fascinating, but before getting to the order form, they decide to head for your client's page instead. Even if your client has included your firm as a link (you'll make sure of this, of course), there's no guarantee that the browser will *ever* return to you.

A couple of possible solutions present themselves. First, make sure your page is referenced on a wide number of other pages. This can be done through a series of mutually cooperative ventures. Second, and more importantly, design your page so that browsers will stay and visit. How? Nobody knows yet. This is one of the most interesting and potentially rewarding challenges for a design artist in this decade (a similar problem to those faced by TV advertisers who have to deal with channel-surfers). How do you get people to stick around? Hmmm. It sounds like another business opportunity to me.

18

DAY 6

Finding a Job on the Internet

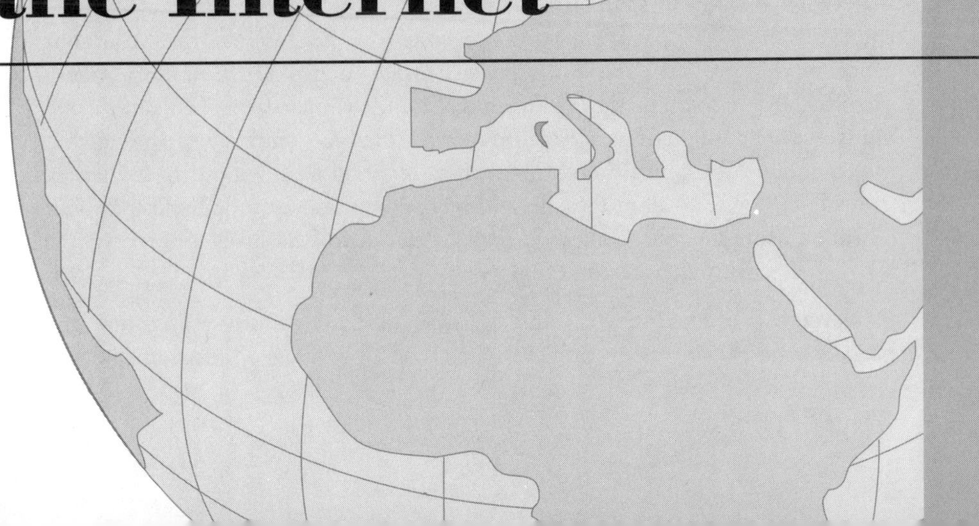

There's no reason the Internet has to be a one-way cash transaction—that is, you pay while somebody else gains. Since you're paying for an account anyway (at least, most of you are), why not see if it can start to pay you back? One way to make this happen is to write books about the Net, of course, but we really don't need any more of those things, do we? (Nudge, nudge...) Another way, and a more serious and perhaps more permanent way, is to use the Net to look for a job. This chapter takes you to this attractive possibility, introducing you to the growing number of resources available to would-be employees.

Task List

In this chapter, to help you become the ultimate job seeker on the Net, you will work through the following tasks:

- ☐ Read newsgroup postings for jobs in a particular geographical area (Usenet)
- ☐ Search a mailing list for job announcements (mailing lists)
- ☐ Post your resume on a Web-based career service (WWW)
- ☐ Look for an entry-level position at an education institution (Gopher)
- ☐ Focus and conduct a job search by the industry in which you want to work (WWW/Gopher)

Each of the preceding tasks not only points you to a specific reference on the Internet, but hones your skills in using particular Internet resources so that you can continue your search on your own.

Finding a Job on the Internet

By Karin Trgovac and Neil Randall

As the use of the Internet in all facets of our lives becomes more ubiquitous, it stands to reason that finding gainful employment will be one of the brightest of those facets. When potential employers first began posting job announcements on the Internet, the job announcements generally were for very specific, high-tech oriented positions. Now, primarily because providing information on the Internet has become so much easier, many more main-stream industries are taking advantage of the international job market available to them on the Internet. Educational institutions, non-profit organizations, publishing houses, even house painting businesses—all of these have developed a presence for advertising their available positions. More and more companies realize that starting the hiring process over the Internet is a cost effective way to recruit employees.

However, this new market isn't only a buyers' one. Several new venues now exist for job hunters to post their resumes and even their own "Job Wanted" ads. Some of these services

are free and others you must pay for. In addition to job ads, some of these sites also offer advice: general advice about resume writing and interviewing as well as specific advice about job hunting on the Internet.

Task 18.1: Read Usenet postings concerning jobs.

There is a hierarchy of newsgroups on Usenet, which contain postings about employment opportunities. This is the `*.jobs` hierarchy and is generally organized by geographical area. The following list shows a partial listing of this hierarchy:

```
austin.jobs
ba.jobs.offered
ba.jobs.resumes
bc.jobs
can.jobs
chi.jobs
dc.jobs
de.markt.jobs
fr.jobs.offres
houston.jobs.offered
```

18

Sometimes these headings can be a little tricky. Most are indicated by country (such as `can.jobs` for jobs in Canada; `de.markt.jobs` for jobs in Germany (Deutschland)); some will be indicated by region (`ba.jobs` is jobs in the San Francisco Bay Area; `tx.jobs` for jobs in Texas) and some are listed by city (`austin.jobs` and `chi.jobs` (Chicago)).

Suppose that you are looking to relocate in the Lone Star State, preferably the Austin Area. So, using your newsreader, select or subscribe to the `austin.jobs` newsgroup. I use trn in UNIX, so I would type at my newsreader prompt `<End of newsgroups-what next? [npq]>:` **`g austin.jobs`**. (`g` is for `go`).

Note: If you are using a graphic interface newsreader such as News Xpress for Windows, there will be a Find command or button. You can click on this command and type the group you are looking for.

After you subscribe to `austin.jobs`, you should list the contents of the newsgroup by heading so that you can search for a particular keyword. In the graphic interface, you can usually just double-click on the group and that will display a listing.

In UNIX, type = at the <55 unread articles in austin.jobs—read now? [+ynq] > prompt to get a list of job headings:

```
2524 TX-Austin Oracle Programmer Position
2525 US-TX-Austin-MGR-Call Center Manager/Help Desk-Recruiter
2526 US-TX-Austin  Design Engineer, Analog and Digital  Recruiter
2527 Software Business Opportunity
2528 3D animator/designer in DC needed
2529 Programmer Seeks Employment
```

You can search through this listing of jobs. In UNIX, type / followed by the word(s) for which you are looking.

Suppose that you are looking for a software position. Type **/software** at the newsreader prompt. In the graphics reader, you can use the same Find command to locate a particular phrase. If the newsreader finds the phrase for which you are looking, it will take you to the first posting or article with that phrase in the subject line. You then can read the article and see whether it is of interest to you. If not, try searching for the keyword again. (For a more detailed discussion of newsgroups, see Chapter 5.)

Warning: If you reply to a Usenet posting about a job, make sure it is going to the right address. Sometimes, the person who posts a job offering is not the address to which your resume should be sent. Check carefully.

Task 18.2: Searching the archives of a mailing list for job postings.

Because the *.jobs hierarchy on Usenet is organized by geographical area, locating a position in your particular field can be somewhat hit and miss. A more targeted approach to job hunting can be accomplished by searching through a mailing list for job postings.

There are thousands of mailing lists on the Internet, and a good percentage of them will enable you to search through their archives without actually being subscribed to the list. But before you learn how to search a mailing list, you have to choose one that is appropriate.

Suppose that you are a marine biologist, fresh out of graduate school and you're looking for your first academic position. You know there are mailing lists on the Internet that focus on marine biology, but how do you find them? Fortunately, Diane Kovacs and the Directory Team have created a listing of Scholarly Electronic Conferences that you can search by subject. (`http://www.mid.net:80/KOVACS/`). Figure 18.1 shows a section of this subject listing. Hmmm...#26, `Genetics, General Biology, Biophysics, Biochemistry`, looks promising.

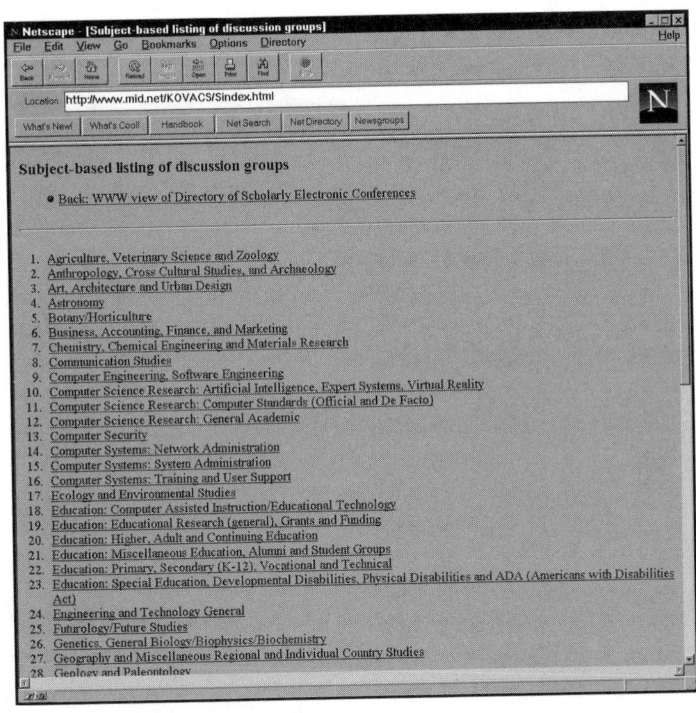

Figure 18.1.
Subject List from the Directory of Scholarly Electronic Conferences.

By clicking on on this link, you get a list of relevant mailing lists. This particular list, at `http://www.mid.net/KOVACS/CD/S0005S.html`, is shown in Figure 18.2.

Some of these list names can be cryptic. They are all hypertext links with full descriptions of the lists attached to each one; however, before you go searching through all 22 of them, take a quick look through the list. `MAR-FACIL Marine Facilities`? Click on it to see if it might be helpful. You'll get the following information:

```
Topic Information:

MAR-FACIL is an electronic mailing list for managers and technical staff at
marine research facilities, aquaculture operations aquaria and other facili-
ties supplying seawater for the support of marine life. The list is intended
as a forum for the discussion of technical and business topics; however
discussion of other matters is welcome and encouraged.
Subscription Information:
Mailserv@ac.dal.ca
```

```
Edited?
No

Archives:
Yes
```

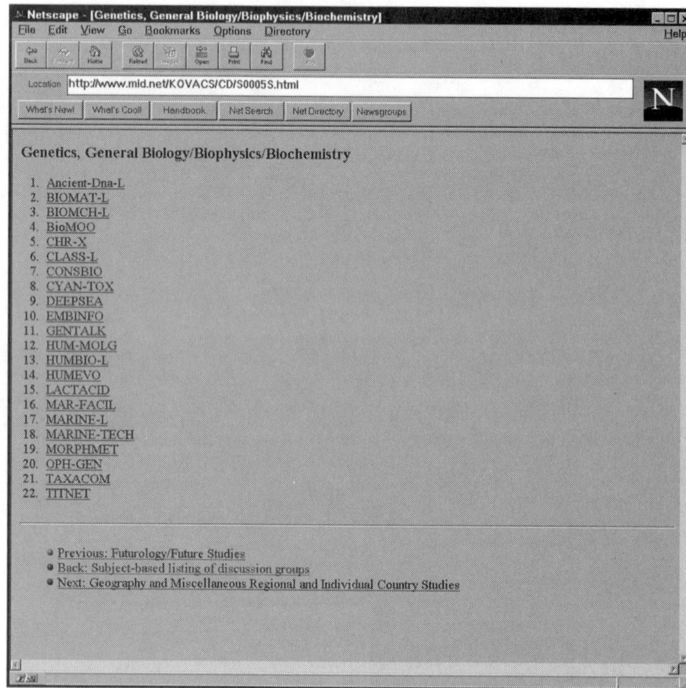

Figure 18.2.
Mailing lists for Genetics, General Biology, Biophysics, Biochemistry.

This looks promising; there might be job ads posted here, and it doesn't say that the archives are private, meaning that you must be a member of the list to search them. This is just what you're looking for. You don't want to have to subscribe to all these lists just to search their archives.

Tip: Several mailing lists are mirrored as newsgroups in the `bit.Listserv.*` hierarchy. If you feel more comfortable using Usenet, this might be a better method for you to search the same information.

This particular mail server (unlike the original Listserv software) doesn't allow for specific term searching. You first must download the archive and then search for it in your own mailbox. Because most mailers have a `search` or `where is` function, this is not a problem.

Note: To get directions from a specific Listserv or mail server on how to search their archives, send an e-mail message to the Listserv containing the line `help`. This will return a set of commands.

You can send e-mail to the mail server, which looks something like this: **`send mar-facil.1995*`** (this tells the mail server to send you all the archives for 1995 from this list). If you only want to retrieve one month at a time, modify your e-mail message to read **`send mar-facil.199506`** (for June 1995). The mail server will return the file to you (usually pretty quickly). Then, in your mailer, open the e-mail and search for the word `job`, `employment`, or `position` (you might have to try a couple of different words). For this particular file, the first hit you see is for a position as a Marine Biologist in Molluscan Culture.

```
Date: Fri, 16 Jun 1995 09:57:59 -0400 (EDT)
From: crusty@clamfarm.com (Jack Crustacean)
Subject: Job Announcements
Marine Biologist/Molluscan Culture
SeaDream's Atlantic ClamFarm is seeking a highly motivated self-starter who can
manage a 6-month growout project in North Carolina. Opportunities for permanent
salaried positions after project completion for the right, production oriented,
hard working individual. Project period: Jul/Aug '95 - Jan/Feb '96. Salary:
$2,000/mo.
```

Perfect! Your major in Marine Biology was Molluscan Culture, wasn't it? For more information on mailing lists, see Chapter 4.

18

Task 18.3: Posting your resume on a Web-based career service.

Searching for a job on theInternet can take some time, especially while you're becoming adept at mastering the tools of the trade. Why not put your resume out there on the Internet while you're hunting for that perfect job? Maybe a recruiter will see it and e-mail you!

The Online Career Center, whose home page (`http://www.occ.com/occ/HomePage.html`) is shown in Figure 18.3, allows you to post your resume in their database at no charge, provided that you e-mail it in yourself. If you don't have access to the Internet and can only snailmail them a paper copy, they will input it into their database for only $10.00 (U.S.). If you are going to mail the OCC (or any other online service for that matter), you should have an ASCII version of your resume available. ASCII is plain text that nearly any word processor or text editor can read. You do not want to send a word processor file via e-mail. The OCC provides some tips on preparing an electronic resume accessible from this home page (`http://www.occ.com/occ/JLK/HowToEResume.html`), as does The Catapult:a Springboard for Career Service Practioners (`http://www.wm.edu/catapult/jsguides.html`).

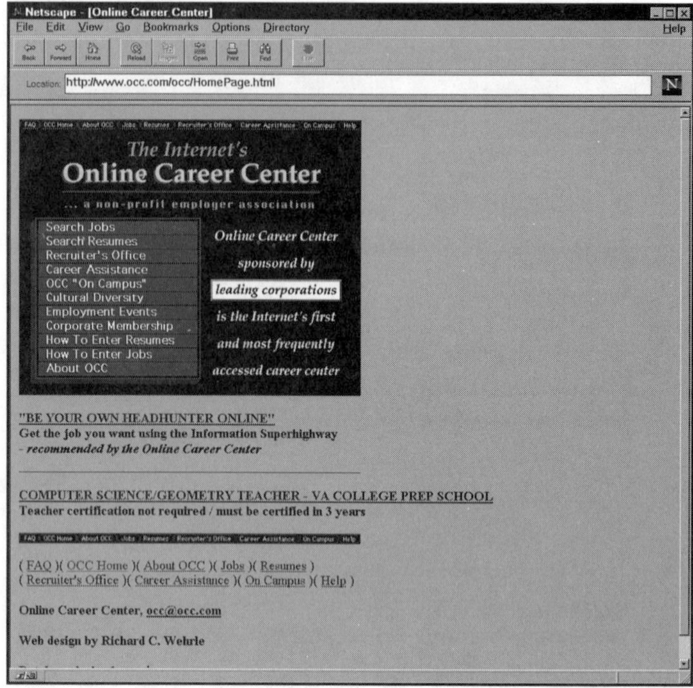

Figure 18.3.
The home page for the Online Career Center.

After you prepare an ASCII version of your resume, you will want to send it into the OCC. They provide their e-mail address in the form of a "mailto" hypertext link on their Web page. Using this link will call up the mailer portion of your browser. You can paste your resume into the space provided by your browser or you enter their e-mail address into your UNIX mailer (Pine, for example) and then send them your resume that way. I recommend the latter method—sometimes the mail feature from the various browsers interprets the end of lines in different ways. You want to make sure your online resume looks as good as it can.

While at the OCC, you should check to see if they have any postings in your area. You can conduct a search by geographical area or by keyword in the job advertisement's text. Your search results are returned as hypertext links and are sorted in reverse chronological order. Figure 18.4, for example, shows the results of a search for `marketing` positions.

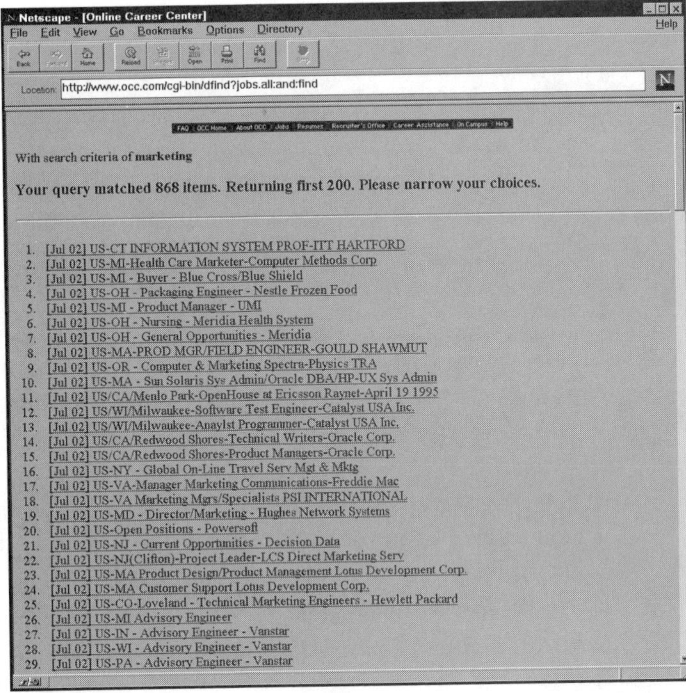

Figure 18.4.
Marketing (or related) positions from job search in OCC.

Task 18.4: Search for an entry-level administrative position at an education institution.

As mentioned in the introduction of this chapter, job postings are available on the Internet for a wide range of skills and levels. More and more universities are putting up announcements about their entry-level administrative and clerical positions. Suppose that your spouse has just been awarded a position in Philadelphia, near the University of Pennsylvania. You have agreed that you will look for a new job in Philadelphia. It might be nice to work near your spouse's location, so why not check and see what positions the university itself has available?

You know that there is a list of Gopher sites sorted by geographical area. On your local system, look for the entry that reads something similar to `Gophers around the World` or `Other Electronic Resources`. As an example, suppose that you start from the University of Illinois Urbana-Champaign, at `gopher.uiuc.edu`. The opening screen looks like the following:

```
Internet Gopher Information Client v2.0.12
Root Gopher server: Gopher.uiuc.edu
1. Welcome to the University of Illinois at Urbana-Champaign Gopher
2. Campus Announcements (last updated 5/19/95)/
3. What's New?/
4. Information about Gopher/
5. Keyword Search of UIUC Gopher Menus <?>
6. Univ. of Illinois at Urbana-Champaign Campus Information/
7. Champaign-Urbana & Regional Information/
8. Computer Documentation, Software, and Information/
9. Libraries and Reference Information/
10. Publications (U of I Press, Newspapers, Newsletters, etc.) & Weath../
11. Other Gopher and Information Servers/
12. Phone Books (ph)/
13. Internet File Server (ftp) Sites/
14. Disability Information and Resources/
```

`#11`, `Other Gopher and Information Servers`, is what you are looking for. If you select `#11` (or a similar heading in your own Gopher) you will find, after a listing of local Gophers, a heading called `USA`, and under it will be headings for each of the 50 states. Choose `Pennsylvania`. This will give you a listing of all the Gophers in Pennsylvania.

Note: You may see the heading `Other CWIS's`. *CWIS* stands for *Campus Wide Information System,* which is an acronym that many colleges and universities use to describe their Gophers.

Under `Pennsylvania`, you will see several pages of all the Gophers. The University of Pennsylvania will probably be near the end (they are listed alphabetically). Select it and you will be in the Gopher system (or PennInfo as they call it) of the University. Because providing information on the Internet is by no means standardized, you will have to do a bit of brainstorming. You can begin in one of two ways:

- Follow likely leads to get to the job listings. This would include looking under topics, such as `Administrative Departments` or `Information for Staff`—anything that looks like it would get you to information about `Human Resources`, the heading under which most universities place job information.
- You can search the Gopher. Most Gophers have a search facility and PennInfo is no exception.

Under PennInfo, there is a choice marked `Search PennInfo`. Choose it. You now want to do a keyword search for something similar to `employment opportunities`.

Tip: Searching for something specific such as `Employment Opportunities` will yield much more tailored results than something like `job`. If the more specific term doesn't work the first time, try gradually broadening it. Try `employ`, for example; the Gopher will pick up all words with that word pattern in it, including `employment` and `employer`.

Hmmm. `employment opportunities` seems to be too specific. Try `employment`. This yields eight screens of headings. These results are all the files or directories in `PennInfo`, which contain the word `employment`.

When looking through them, remember that a `/` behind the entry means that it is a directory. So, in the following list, `#7` will probably be more fruitful than `#8`, which may just be general files about employment.

```
Internet Gopher Information Client v2.0.15
Keyword Search: employment
1. Employment Changes - Jobs & Applications
2. Human Resources
3. Career Development
4. Of Record - Standardized Employment Ad.
5. Verifying Application Info for External Staff Hires
6. Job Listings for Penn Tower Hotel
7. Employment Openings/
8. Employment at Penn
```

18

Sure enough, after choosing `#7`, `Employment Opportunities`, you are presented with a menu of choices about job vacancies. You can look through here to find positions that match your qualifications and then contact Human Resources at the University for an application.

Warning: While some education institutions are faithful about posting their job openings, they are not always as diligent about taking them down. Some job postings may be several weeks, even months old! Always check the closing date of a job posting. Actually, this is now true of all Gopher postings because most institutions are turning to the Web to publish information.

Task 18.5: Conduct a job search based on the industry in which you want to work (WWW/Gopher).

Several employment opportunities available via the Internet are not listed on resources such as the Online Career Center or the Monster Board of Jobs. They are incorporated into the larger picture of the industry to which they belong. The best way to access this larger picture is through the professional societies that make up that industry.

The University of Waterloo's Electronic Library has begun the Scholarly Societies Project, which collects hypertext links to professional societies and organizations in particular fields. Using this listing, at `http://www.lib.uwaterloo.ca/society/subjects_soc.html`, you can visit different organizations (some of which you may already belong to), to see if there are positions available in your area of expertise. Figure 18.5 is the subject listing of the Scholarly Societies Project. It is also available alphabetically as well as for keyword searching.

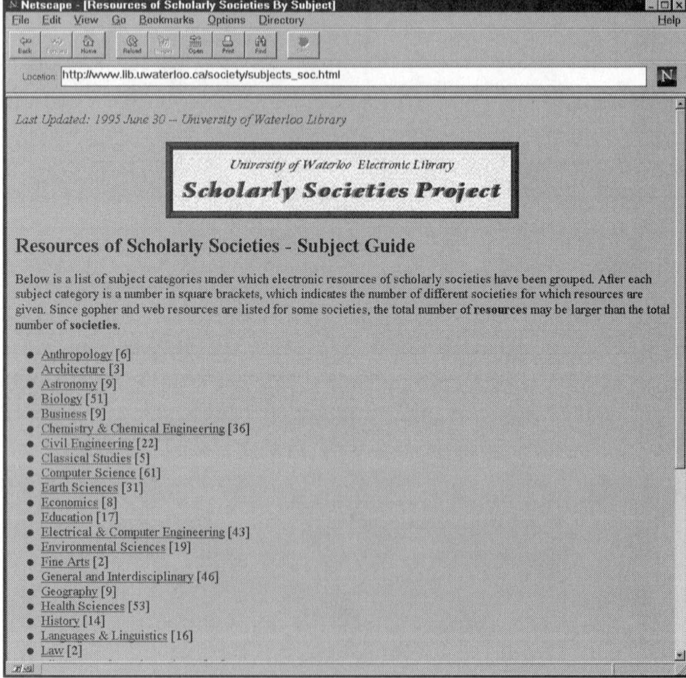

Figure 18.5.
Listing by Subject on the Scholarly Societies Web page.

Suppose that you are a music theorist, looking for a lectureship in composition. You're not all that familiar with the Internet, but you know that the Society for Music Theory has an online presence. Clicking on the Music hyperlink on the Scholarly Societies Project Web page, you see the screen shown in Figure 18.6.

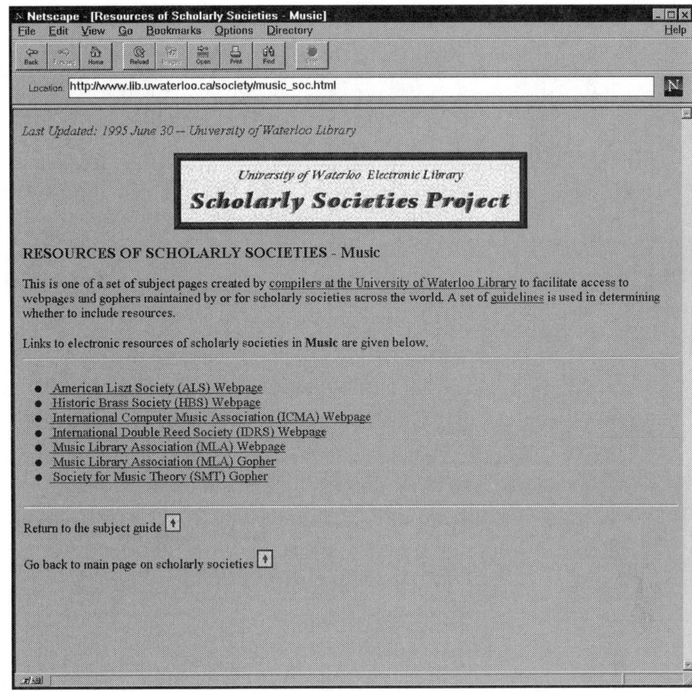

Figure 18.6.
The Music page in the Scholarly Societies page.

The Society for Music Theory's Gopher is listed, so you click on it. The following Gopher menu appears:

```
Gopher Menu
     Music Theory On-Line Archives
     Society for Music Theory Archives
```

There doesn't seem much to go on, but you take a stab at the first one, `Music Theory On-Line Archives`. It sounds like it might be a magazine. After clicking on it, you realize that it is!

```
Gopher Menu
     MTO Documentation, Information
     MTO Software, Information
     MTO Issues
```

You're not really looking for documentation or software, so you choose `MTO Issues` in the hope that this will give you the text of the magazine; there may be advertisements for jobs in there. After choosing `MTO Issues`, you are given a list of issue numbers. Because you are looking for positions that are currently available, you select the most recent issue. Its menu is as follows:

```
Gopher Menu
     Table of Contents
     Announcements
     Articles
     Commentaries
     Dissertations
     Jobs
     Reviews
```

Ah, ha! Your hunch paid off; there is a section on job listings buried in the Society of Music Theory's online magazine. After selecting the jobs link, you get the text of a Lecturer in Composition at the University of Sheffield in England.

Task 18.6. Search for a training job through the Monster list.

Now that you know the basic principles of finding a job on the Net, and the various tools you can use, it's time to move on to the most up-to-date job sites. One of the best is the Monster Board, where you can search for jobs or post your resumes. This is an exciting resource. To search for a training job through the Monster list, follow these steps:

1. Enter the Monster Board at `http://199.94.216.71:81/home.html`. Your screen will look like the one shown Figure 18.7.
2. Click on the Career Search hyperlink or image button.
3. Click on Keyword Search Career.
4. In the Enter search keywords box, type **`training`**. You'll see a page with several jobs that mention the word `training`, even though they might not be training jobs, per se.

You also can receive employer profiles from the Monster Board, and human resources people can visit the resumes section directly. In addition, the Cyberzone enables students and recent graduates to browse through "a virtual world of cybersuites" for information about careers with various companies. All in all, this is an extensive and fascinating job site.

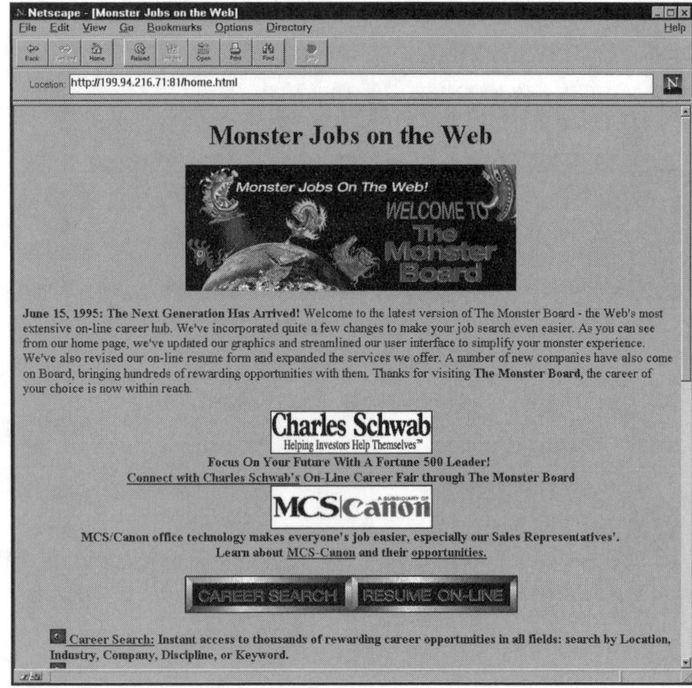

Figure 18.7.
The home page of the Monster Board.

18

Task 18.7: Search for a job through Career Magazine.

Career Magazine offers a site similar to the Monster Board, but it is considerably more understated. Its jobs tend to be computer-related, but increasingly a wider variety is starting to appear. To search for a job through Career Magazine, follow these steps:

1. Enter Career Magazine at **`http://www.careermag.com/careermag/`**. The home page is shown in Figure 18.8.
2. From the imagemap at the top of the page, click on the Job Openings button.
3. Click on the hyperlink named Click here to begin Your Job Search.
4. To show how this search form works, type **`New York`** in the Locations field and **`HTML`** in the skills field. You'll be searching for a job in New York (city or state) writing Web pages. Click on Submit Search and wait for the results.

Career Magazine maintains a large collection of resumes and several useful links to other Internet career resources. There's also a good selection of news stories, and a useful careers discussion area.

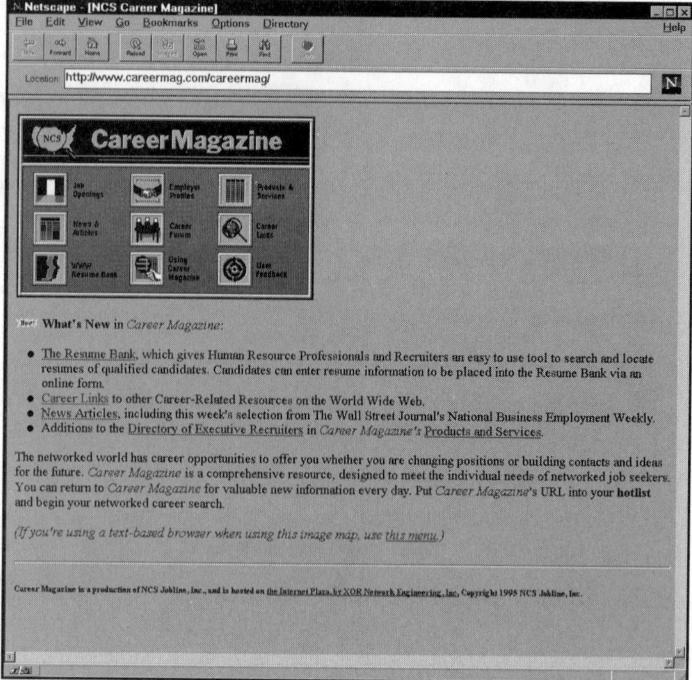

Figure 18.8.
Career Magazine's home page, with a concise imagemap.

Task 18.8: Search for a job through Career Mosaic.

Career Mosaic is one of the oldest job search areas on the Web (in Web terms, "old" means anything over eight months), and it is perhaps the most usefully and attractively designed. The employers tend to be computer firms, but there's no necessary limitation to this. Several firms offer the capability to send your resume directly across the Net. To search for a job through Career Mosaic, follow these steps:

1. Enter Career Mosaic at **`http://www.careermosaic.com/`**. You'll see the screen shown in Figure 18.9.
2. Scroll down the page and click on the Jobs Offered link (also accessible from the opening imagemap).
3. Two search forms are available here. The first is a search of the Career Mosaic database, while the second enables you to search through newsgroup postings. For now, use the first form and type **`analyst and programmer`** in the Description field, clicking on Any Of. Then enter **`CA`** in the State field, to select California. Click the Search button and watch the jobs come up.

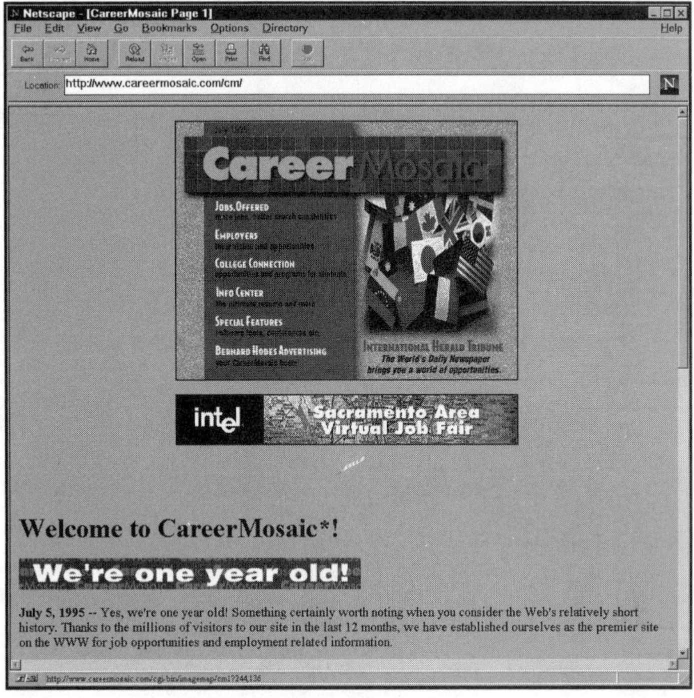

Figure 18.9.
The Career Mosaic home page, with text that scrolls several lines down.

4. Now try the Usenet search form. Type **`accounting`** in the Search for box, and choose North Carolina from the drop-down list box. Click the Submit button and see what you get.

Career Mosaic is a rich site. Be sure to visit the College Collection, and check out the special features (often with career fairs). If you're serious about finding a job, particularly in the high-tech industry, this is a must-visit.

Task 18.9: Search for a job through company home pages.

One of the most important stops in your job search is the Open Market Commercial Sites Index at `http://www.directory.net`. The CSI lists thousands of company Web sites, and many of these offer a link called *Employment Opportunities* (or something similar). You'll examine just one such site, Microsoft Corporation (hey, somebody's gotta work there!). To search for a job through company home pages, follow these steps:

1. Enter the Commercial Sites Index at **`http://www.directory.net/`**.
2. Click on the link named alphabetical listings.
3. Click on the letter M in the middle of the subsequent page.

4. Scroll to the Microsoft link and click. Your screen will look like the one shown in Figure 8.10.

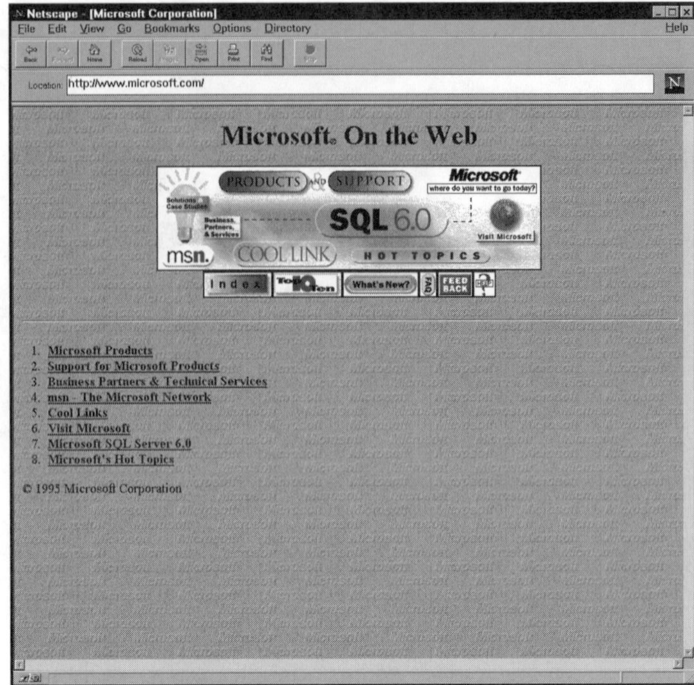

Figure 18.10.
The Microsoft Corporation home page.

5. From the Microsoft home page, click on Visit Microsoft.
6. Click on Employment Opportunities.
7. Gaze wistfully on the inline image of Microsoft's venerable CEO, and then click on Explore the Employment Opportunities.
8. From here, click on the employment area you're interested in.

Many companies—computer and otherwise—are posting positions on the Web. Searching for jobs this way is much faster than visiting libraries for newspapers and magazines, so it makes sense to give it a shot. You might just find something you hadn't even thought of before.

Summary

The phrase "the hidden job market" takes on more meaning when the Internet enters the picture. While hunting for a job on the Internet is still relatively new and the hiring success stories are only beginning to trickle in, the potential for employers to solicit applications, screen candidates, and even conduct interviews is being realized. And the employer is

certainly not the only benefactor. Job hunters find the Internet a useful means for researching companies and obtaining corporate profiles. As with all job hunting, you must be diligent and creative. Information on the Internet is not always organized in the same way.

Task Review

In this chapter, you learned how to perform the following tasks:

- ☐ Read newsgroup postings for jobs in a particular geographical area (Usenet)
- ☐ Search a mailing list for job announcements (mailing lists)
- ☐ Post your resume on a Web-based career information service (WWW)
- ☐ Look for an entry level position at an education institution (Gopher)
- ☐ Focus and conduct a job search by the industry in which you want to work (WWW/Gopher)

Q&A

Q It seems that most of the jobs offered are computer industry positions. Is there anything else?

A The content of the Internet evolves as the community of the Internet evolves. The original community of the Internet was high-tech computer professionals. As more educational institutions came online, we began to see information relevant to that community, including academic job postings. As more mainstream professionals make the Internet a part of their lives, you will see this reflected in the content of the information available. Yes, there are positions available that have little or nothing to do with computers. House painting comes to mind (`http://wanda.pond.com/mall/collegepro/`). Margaret F. Riley, Coordinator of Networked Resources, at Worcester Polytechnic Institute has compiled an extremely useful guide called *Employment Opportunities and Job Resources on the Internet*, which is located at `http://www.wpi.edu/~mfriley/jobguide.html`.

Q Okay, does it really work? Have *you* gotten a job on the Internet?

A Well, I've submitted applications to about ten jobs I've seen advertised on the Internet. Of those, I have had three different telephone interviews and two subsequent "in person" interviews. I'm currently waiting for the outcome of the second in-person interview. Send me an e-mail and I'll let you know how it turned out.

Q Why would employers advertise positions on the Web?

A Although it doesn't seem like it at times, employers are almost always looking for good new employees. The Web gives them access to potential employees from around the globe, rather than restricting them to their local area. Then, too, in the case of high-tech positions, the very fact that you've found the ad means that you know how to use the Internet, which is a good start.

The Internet at School

19

DAY 7

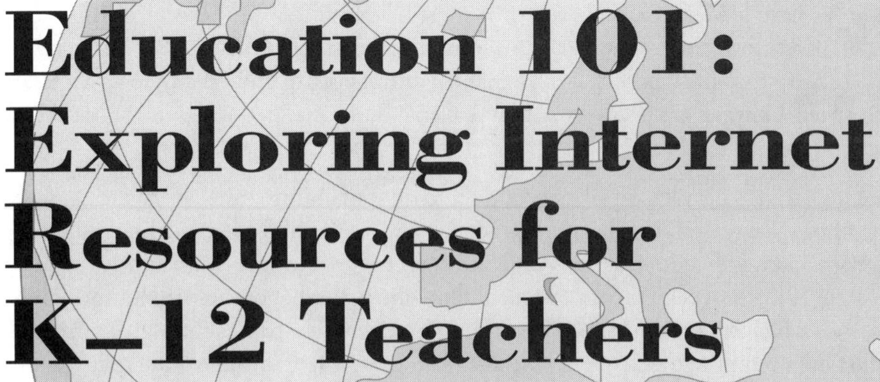

Education 101: Exploring Internet Resources for K–12 Teachers

This chapter focuses on the extensive use of the Internet by K–12 educators. Particularly in the U.S., teachers and curriculum designers are using the Internet to communicate with one another, to make resources available, and to involve their students in a variety of online projects. This chapter illustrates a portion of this explosive activity.

In this chapter, you learn how to perform the following tasks:

- Use Gopher to access the growing number of information servers in the K–12 arena
- Consult WAIS to conduct a search for K–12 documents and information.
- Find mailing lists to keep abreast of new developments in education and educational technology
- Locate educational information on the World Wide Web

Education and the Internet

The Internet may have started as a communications tool, quickly becoming an essential component of research as well, but there's never been any doubt of its potential as a teaching tool. Combine up-to-the-minute research and data with fast, global communications, and you have all the components necessary for an efficient, state-of-the-art education resource with previously unheard-of power and flexibility.

What *has* been in doubt is the degree to which teachers at all levels would have access to the Internet. University professors have been on the Net since its early days, and slowly but surely most universities and colleges in the United States, Canada, the U.K., and a host of other countries have gained access as well. But most of this access has been funded by research organizations to which elementary and secondary institutions have rarely had access. The types of infrastructure grants that have enabled universities to build the systems necessary for high-speed Internet connections simply haven't been available to educators at the lower levels.

Recently, things have changed. Through a variety of means (often very creative), K–12 institutions have established Internet access, and are establishing mailing lists, Gopher servers, and even, in a few cases, World Wide Web sites. Gopher is, far and away, the most common K–12 tool currently in action, and the sheer number of these things springing into existence is almost overwhelming. Everything from working papers through course outlines is showing up on the menus, and teachers from everywhere in the world are invited to see what's going on.

And, in all likelihood, this type of activity has merely begun. With the Clinton administration's push for wider access to telecommunications resources (whether or not the much-touted "universal access" ever comes to pass), schools, school boards, education departments, and

every other related institution will almost certainly strive for complete Internet access. Once in place, and with equipment in the schools themselves (yes, I'm aware of the enormous problems with supplying all of this), it's only a matter of time until the Internet becomes a resource at the classroom level as well. It already is, in a limited number of locations, but this kind of pedagogical activity will expand quickly. In fact, it may be no exaggeration to suggest that K–12 activity will do more than even commercial activity to push the Internet's technologies to their limits.

Internet Resources for K–12 Teachers

by Carol DeVrieze

In the United States and Canada, as well in many other countries, educational reform is occurring on many levels.

Public education faces government cutbacks that naturally force reform of the school system. Educators are faced with the dilemma of providing a high-quality education with less funding, with more students in our classes, with cuts to social programs forcing the schools to provide these services, and so on.

Along with these changes comes the challenge from the business world demanding that its future employees, our students, be educated to keep up with the rapidly changing technological advancements to be competitive in a global economy. Educators also are dealing with the public outcry for accountability. Parents and taxpayers demand quality education; and, in some cases, standardized testing is seen as a way to ensure that learning has occurred.

But educational reform also is coming from educators themselves, who realize that changing the system is necessary to cope with the students we face in our schools every day. Educators are working hard to create new programs to get kids to school at an earlier age—with such programs as junior kindergarten—and to keep them in school instead of dropping out before high school graduation. Programs constantly are being developed to reduce violence in our schools, to help reduce teenage pregnancies, to make students aware of life-threatening diseases such as AIDS, and on and on.

Along with all these programs, teachers are still looking for ideas: new and creative ways to teach literature or science or math to their students; ways to teach and integrate students with learning disabilities within the regular classroom; methods for conflict mediation and resolution strategies with and among students; and techniques to expand the curriculum to be more inclusive of gender, race, and sexuality issues, just to name a few of the current initiatives in education today.

Like many teachers, I'm left questioning whether all of these demands can be satisfied.

With the help of the Internet, I thought I would be able to get a handle on all of the latest information and current ideology. However, I did not find this to be the case. Rather than using the computer to keep me apprised of the prevailing educational trends, I found that there was such a barrage of information related to education that I became even more overwhelmed.

What I discovered is that there is a tremendous quantity of information on the Internet on almost any topic related to education, more information than one person can even hope to assimilate.

I've also learned, however, that the Internet is a potentially valuable tool for educational use. Some of its most worthwhile uses include the following:

- Getting educators in touch with other educators through mailing lists and newsgroups
- Finding educational software
- Keeping informed of daily government decisions and comments on educational issues
- Finding lesson plans on a wide array of curriculum areas
- Locating current articles and educational research for the professional development of teachers
- Determining useful ways students in a classroom can use computers, specifically the Internet, to foster learning
- Linking students with other students from other parts of the country or the world to discuss issues of concern on a personal level, as well as a global level

Because education is becoming one of the most rapidly developed subjects on the Internet, and since I have only a limited amount of space, I will describe only a few of the great places that I have found.

Task 19.1: Explore the New York State Gopher.

One Gopher system with a highly useful educational component is the New York State-developed Gopher. When you connect with this Gopher system, a list of directories is available to you. Remember, these directories frequently are changed and developed, but always maintain an intellectual atmosphere.

1. From your UNIX command prompt, type **`gopher unix5.nysed.gov`** and press Enter. When I last explored the New York State-developed Gopher, I found the items shown in Figure 19.1.
2. Type **`12`** to select `Education News`, a menu which presents a wide range of new items from which to choose. As expected in a Gopher browse, some of these items

may be additional directory names, each with even more items to explore. Remember what I said about being overwhelmed? The first page of the Education News directory included the detail shown in Figure 19.2.

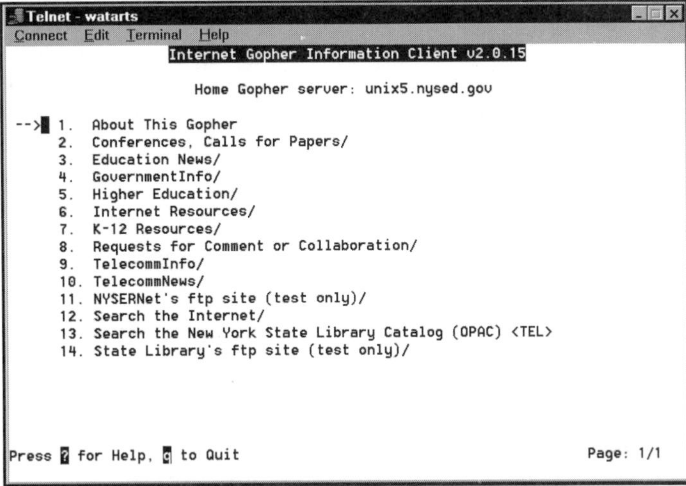

Figure 19.1.
New York State Education Gopher.

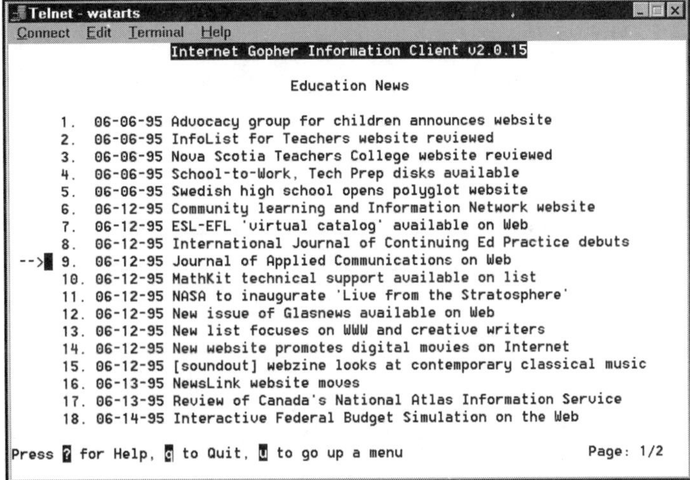

Telnet - watarts
Connect Edit Terminal Help
Internet Gopher Information Client v2.0.15
Education News
1. 06-06-95 Advocacy group for children announces website
2. 06-06-95 InfoList for Teachers website reviewed
3. 06-06-95 Nova Scotia Teachers College website reviewed
4. 06-06-95 School-to-Work, Tech Prep disks available
5. 06-06-95 Swedish high school opens polyglot website
6. 06-12-95 Community learning and Information Network website
7. 06-12-95 ESL-EFL 'virtual catalog' available on Web
8. 06-12-95 International Journal of Continuing Ed Practice debuts
--> 9. 06-12-95 Journal of Applied Communications on Web
10. 06-12-95 MathKit technical support available on list
11. 06-12-95 NASA to inaugurate 'Live from the Stratosphere'
12. 06-12-95 New issue of Glasnews available on Web
13. 06-12-95 New list focuses on WWW and creative writers
14. 06-12-95 New website promotes digital movies on Internet
15. 06-12-95 [soundout] webzine looks at contemporary classical music
16. 06-13-95 NewsLink website moves
17. 06-13-95 Review of Canada's National Atlas Information Service
18. 06-14-95 Interactive Federal Budget Simulation on the Web
Press ? for Help, q to Quit, u to go up a menu
Page: 1/2

Figure 19.2.
The first page of the Education News Gopher directory.

3. Browse those menu items that interest you to locate a vast resource of information. But, when you access this Gopher, remember that some of the menu items might no longer be available. A greater likelihood, however, is that there will be even more to choose from. This Gopher is constantly growing.

All items in this directory are tagged with the date to maintain a current, informative list of educational sources. Most entries are postings that inform browsers of new mailing lists or Web sites that may assist in an educational overhaul of the Internet. Other documents include art reviews, literature analyses, and even advertisements for seminars held on the Web.

It is nearly impossible to explore this site without finding some articles of interest that you may want to save for later use. At the end of each file, the prompt : Press <Return> to continue, <m> to mail, <D> to download, <s> to save, or <p> to print appears.

4. To mail a document to your e-mail account from which you may access it in the future, type **m** followed by your e-mail address. Then send the message. Simple enough to do, and now you'll have a great resource to use at your leisure.
5. To download a file onto your PC's hard drive, type **D** (that is, Shift+D) and choose one of the suggested protocols. Then instruct the software to save the file in whatever directory on your hard drive that you want.
6. To save the document on the machine holding your UNIX account, type **s**. The save feature will suggest an appropriate filename.
7. If you want to return to the directory list, press Enter once. By choosing other options, helpful information is available regarding other places where you can find information such as the InfoList for Teachers, the Nova Scotia Teachers College site, the NASA Live From the Stratosphere event, and many subject oriented mailing lists. It's already easy to feel overwhelmed, and you've barely even started.

   The second directory of precise interest to elementary and secondary school educators is K–12 Resources. This directory has perhaps more practical uses for teachers.
8. At the Education News directory, press **u** to move up one menu. Now, using the arrow keys, scroll down the K-12 Resources directory and press Enter. When this directory is selected, the options shown in Figure 19.3 will appear on-screen.

Tip: Determine your selections by the subjects you teach. Not all of the directories are developed equally, but they all present numerous entry points into your subject area.

9. First, choose Arts and Humanities by scrolling to the appropriate entry and pressing Enter. This directory lists some interesting options such as All Music Guide, Animal Sounds, Art Resources from UT Dallas, Dallas Museum of Art, Art Lessons from Ask ERIC, Student Journalism Gopher, plus many more. I surfed through some of these directories and found interesting files on music and art lessons.

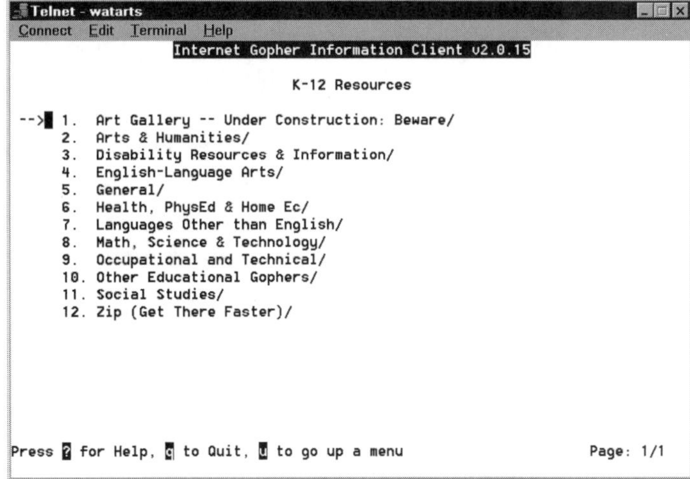

Figure 19.3.
More options from the Education News Gopher.

The most interesting directory from these options for me was the `Student Journalism` Gopher. Although the students at which these files are aimed are college students, having senior high school students access this type of directory would help them become aware of the kinds of writing and projects they can become involved in when they go on to a college or university.

The directory that I was most pleased to discover as an English teacher was English-Language Arts.

10. To access the `English-Language Arts` directory, type **4** or scroll down to the entry and press Enter. This selection provided me with a list shown in Figure 19.4.

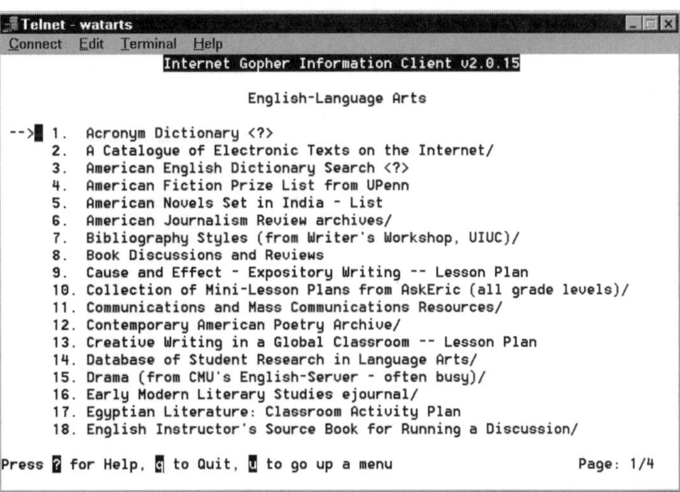

Figure 19.4.
Items in the English-Language Arts section of the Education News Gopher.

11. Select item `60`, `Poetry Readings`, to yield a list of several famous celebrities reading some of the great poetry classics, and even in some cases, the authors reading their own works. These files would be great to access within a classroom. Students could actually listen to T. S. Eliot reading *The Wasteland*, Julie Harris reading some of Emily Dickinson's poetry, or Robert Frost reading *Mending Wall*.
12. Another practical option that I found useful for my classes is contained in the section entitled `Essay Starters`. To access this directory, select either `social studies` or `science` as a main topic area and scroll down to the appropriate menu. These directories provide many great ideas that could be used in the pre-writing process and for discovering writing topics. The following is a partial example of one of them:

```
Problem: Areas of Philadelphia were badly affected with graffiti.
Businesses were disturbed by the resulting atmosphere and by the cost
of continual cleanup.

Proposed Solution: The City developed the Philedelphia Anti-Graffiti
Network (PAGN). This program attacked the problem on several
fronts. On the enforcement front, they worked with police to develop
a program to find offenders, promoted more severe penalties for
violators, and encouraged the passage of a law restricting the sale of
spray paint. As alternative approaches, they helped to develop the amnesty
program to get offenders to pledge not to continue, and they promoted
cleanup as an alternative punishment to incarceration. More importantly,
artists were involved in working with graffiti artists in putting murals.
The murals, located throughout the city, have provided an outlet for the
artistic abilities of the former graffiti painters....

Evaluation: The program has been a success at eliminating much of the
graffiti in the city. The murals have improved the appearance of much of
the city.
```

13. Now select item number **52** from the `English-Language Arts` main directory. This choice gives access to a copy of a new electronic journal called *BooKBraG*. This journal features reviews of children's books that could be used in a classroom setting. It also has articles about many other current issues related to the student reading program along with interviews with authors of children's books.
14. Go back to the first screen of listings under `K-12 Resources`, by pressing **u**, to find the `General directory` (`5`), which is very good for professional development. Figure 19.5 shows the headings.
15. Select item `33`, `Internet Activities`, to receive a list of alternate education-oriented Gophers, as well as detailed lesson plans involving the Internet in the classroom. An example of an exercise designed specifically for teachers and students in grades 6–12, appears in Figure 19.6.

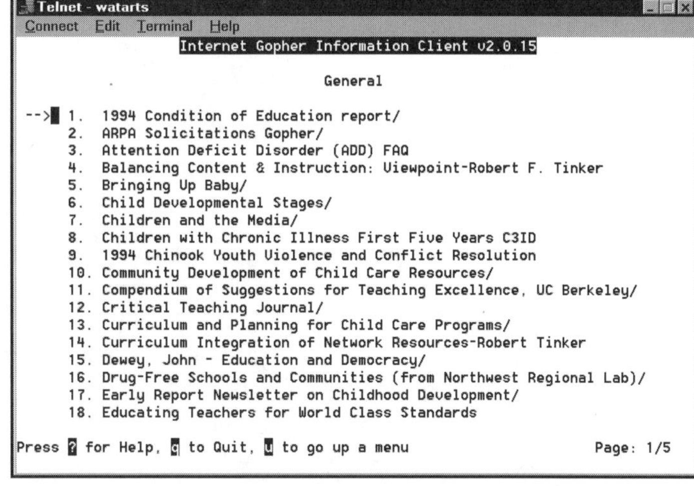

Telnet - watarts
Connect Edit Terminal Help
Internet Gopher Information Client v2.0.15
General
-->1. 1994 Condition of Education report/
2. ARPA Solicitations Gopher/
3. Attention Deficit Disorder (ADD) FAQ
4. Balancing Content & Instruction: Viewpoint-Robert F. Tinker
5. Bringing Up Baby/
6. Child Developmental Stages/
7. Children and the Media/
8. Children with Chronic Illness First Five Years C3ID
9. 1994 Chinook Youth Violence and Conflict Resolution
10. Community Development of Child Care Resources/
11. Compendium of Suggestions for Teaching Excellence, UC Berkeley/
12. Critical Teaching Journal/
13. Curriculum and Planning for Child Care Programs/
14. Curriculum Integration of Network Resources-Robert Tinker
15. Dewey, John - Education and Democracy/
16. Drug-Free Schools and Communities (from Northwest Regional Lab)/
17. Early Report Newsletter on Childhood Development/
18. Educating Teachers for World Class Standards
Press ? for Help, q to Quit, u to go up a menu
Page: 1/5

Figure 19.5.
Professional development resources in K–12 Resources.

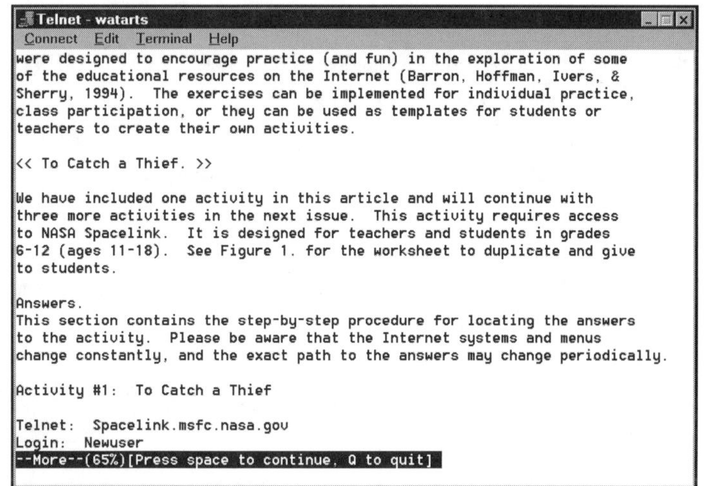

Telnet - watarts
Connect Edit Terminal Help
were designed to encourage practice (and fun) in the exploration of some
of the educational resources on the Internet (Barron, Hoffman, Ivers, &
Sherry, 1994). The exercises can be implemented for individual practice,
class participation, or they can be used as templates for students or
teachers to create their own activities.
<< To Catch a Thief. >>
We have included one activity in this article and will continue with
three more activities in the next issue. This activity requires access
to NASA Spacelink. It is designed for teachers and students in grades
6-12 (ages 11-18). See Figure 1. for the worksheet to duplicate and give
to students.
Answers.
This section contains the step-by-step procedure for locating the answers
to the activity. Please be aware that the Internet systems and menus
change constantly, and the exact path to the answers may change periodically.
Activity #1: To Catch a Thief
Telnet: Spacelink.msfc.nasa.gov
Login: Newuser
--More--(65%)[Press space to continue, Q to quit]

Figure 19.6.
Internet activities for students and teachers.

16. Now select item `65 - Using the Internet in the Classroom`. This directory is another superb resource for both practical ideas and theoretical implications of using the Internet with your students. Again, this list is very long. Some of the options include the following:

```
1. About Classroom Ideas
2. Academe One Project
3. Archaeology Units
4. Ask Dr. Science
5. Ask Prof. Math
------------------
7. At-Risk Students
------------------
```

```
17. The History of Math
------------------
19. Introduction to Computer Science for the 21st Century
------------------
26. Young Kids and Language
```

I accessed the `At-Risk Students` file and mailed myself a copy of this fascinating article on using telecommunications to help teach at-risk students. The following is an excerpt from that article:

```
The number of students that are not graduating from traditional
schools is increasing. We, as educators, need to find a way to make
these students become contributing members of society. As the computer
becomes a vital part of the future job market, we need to make sure that
at-risk students are empowered with the knowledge of computers so that they
may join the next generation of productive thinkers.
```

There seems to be an almost endless source of information that teachers can access in this one Gopher system. I'm not sure I have solved my information-overload problem, but I certainly know what type of information is available and readily accessible using the Internet.

Task 19.2: Explore the California Department of Education Gopher.

Another Gopher system with a wealth of educational material takes you into the California Department of Education system. You can get some excellent information about education in California, but this system enables you to explore many other educational Gopher systems as well.

1. To Gopher directly to this system, type **`gopher goldmine.cde.ca.gov`**. When you connect, you'll see the options shown in Figure 19.7.

Figure 19.7.
The opening screen of the Goldmine gopher.

2. Select item 3, California Department of Education, to receive a lengthy list of options that are mostly related to information about schools in California, finances, charter schools, advisories, calendar of events, and so on.
3. One of the headings I chose to explore was a Curriculum directory. Choose item 7 in the menu, which gives the choices shown in Figure 19.8.

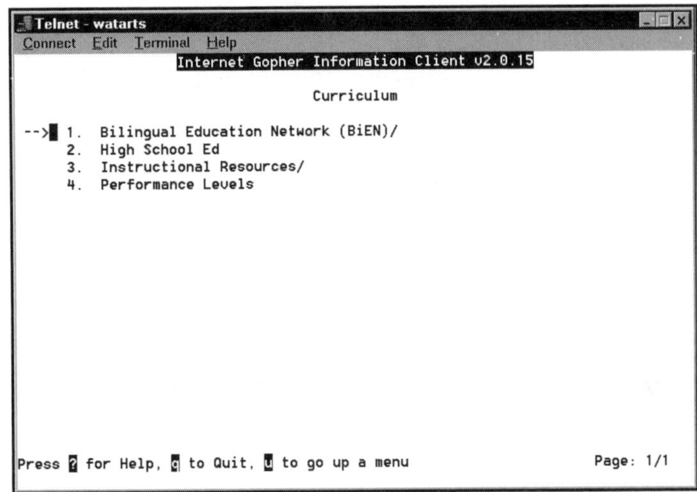

Figure 19.8.
Curriculum directory from the California Department of Education.

19

4. Now select The High School Ed directory (2), which has several entries under the title News, followed by a specific month. These files basically are newsletters coming from the California Department of Education. One of the newsletters that I decided to read had articles about various classroom strategies, performance assessment in the arts, promising approaches to interdisciplinary teaching in the classroom, upcoming conferences, and the like. The following passage provides you with a sample of the type of article you can find here:

```
Promising approaches to Interdisciplinary Teaching in the Classroom
by Twyla Wills Stewart, PhD.
There is no single model of interdisciplinary instruction suitable for
all situations. Approaches to interdiscplinary instruction vary signifi-
cantly by discipline in the range of practical applications use, the
context for teaching and learning, grade level demands and the focus of
inquiry. Consequently, ...
```

5. The next item to explore from the original screen in the Goldmine Gopher is the California School Districts directory. Backtrack to the home Goldmine menu and scroll down to the School Districts listing. Press Enter once.
6. Next move to the San Diego City Schools Gopher server and press Enter. One of the options available here is a directory entitled Lesson Plans.
7. Open the Lesson Plans directory and the following directory entitled UCSD

InterNet Lesson Plans by pressing Enter. I decided to explore, and I received the list shown in Figure 19.9.

8. Select the Biology directory and you may retrieve four directories: Cells, Miscella-

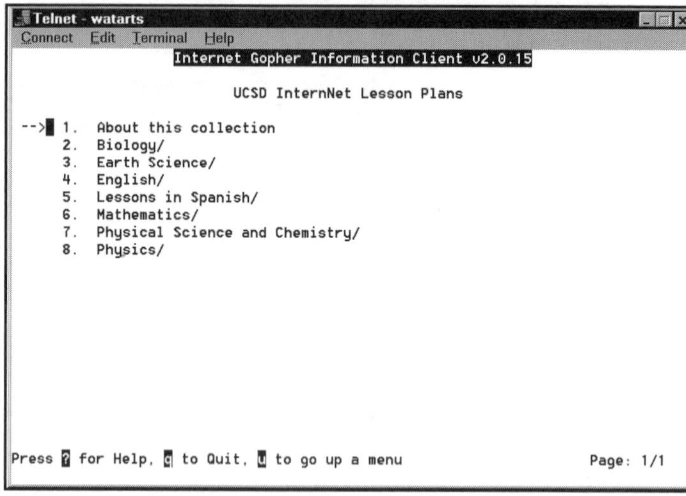

Figure 19.9.
Internet lesson plans from UC San Diego Gopher.

neous Biology Ideas, Physiology, and Plants.

9. Choose the Cells directory and the Gopher gives you two more alternatives: Osmosis with Peas and The Secret Path of Osmosis. Here is an example of a lesson plan teaching the scientific concept of osmosis:

```
Fill a wine glass to overflowing with dried peas, pour in water
up to the brim, and place the glass on a metal lid. The pea heap
becomes slowly higher and then a clatter of falling peas begins,
which goes on for hours.
This is again an osmotic process. Water penetrates into the pea cells
through the skin and dissolves the nutrients in them. The pressure thus
formed makes the peas swell. In the same way the water necessary for life
pentrates the walls of all plant cells, stretching them. If the plant
obtains no more water, its cells become flabby and it wilts.
```

10. Now explore BBN's National School Network Testbed. Go back up four times to move up to the San Diego City Schools directory once again or type **gopher copernicus.bbn.com** for direct access from your UNIX prompt.

    Choosing this directory again provides numerable options for exploring various educational topics, as shown in Figure 19.10.

    Item 1 discusses aims of the BBN project to enable people to construct school- or

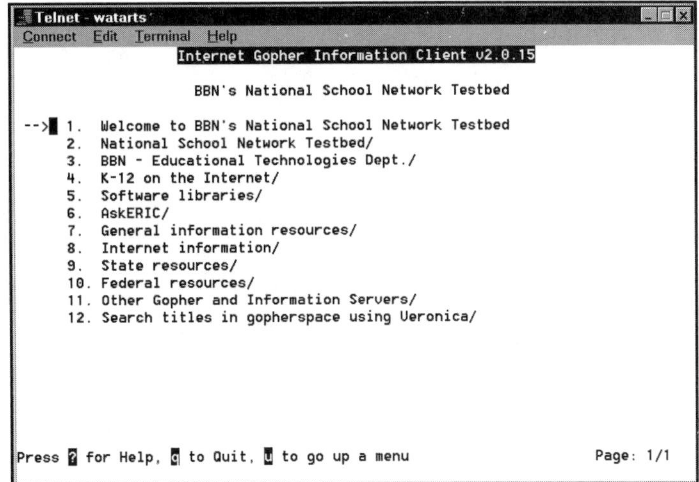

Telnet - watarts
Connect Edit Terminal Help
Internet Gopher Information Client v2.0.15
BBN's National School Network Testbed
--> 1. Welcome to BBN's National School Network Testbed
2. National School Network Testbed/
3. BBN - Educational Technologies Dept./
4. K-12 on the Internet/
5. Software libraries/
6. AskERIC/
7. General information resources/
8. Internet information/
9. State resources/
10. Federal resources/
11. Other Gopher and Information Servers/
12. Search titles in gopherspace using Veronica/
Press ? for Help, q to Quit, u to go up a menu
Page: 1/1

Figure 19.10.
BBNs testbed Gopher.

district-based Internet resources. Choosing item `3`, the `National School Network Testbed` directory, links you to the national network.

Note: *BBN* stands for *Bolt, Beranek, and Newman.* One of the original firms involved in Internet research and development, BBN has been contracted by the National Science Foundation to develop a test site for U.S. K–12 schools. The BBN Gopher demonstrates some of the initial results.

19

11. Now open the `Shadows Science project` directory from the `National School Network Testbed`. This directory links you to an elementary school in New York City. Once connected to this school's Gopher, you can read files about the school and their Internet project.

    I read some interesting articles written by students about current issues in their school (such as the recent science fair, in which many of the school's students were involved). Other menu items contained several files written by the students themselves, their poetry, pictures and their points of view on topics.
12. Go back to the main screen of BBN's National School Network Testbed with its 12 alternatives. Now select item `4`, the directory `K-12 on the Internet`. This choice yields another several directories, as shown in Figure 19.11.
13. Start from the first option, `Best of K-12 on the Internet`, and begin surfing once

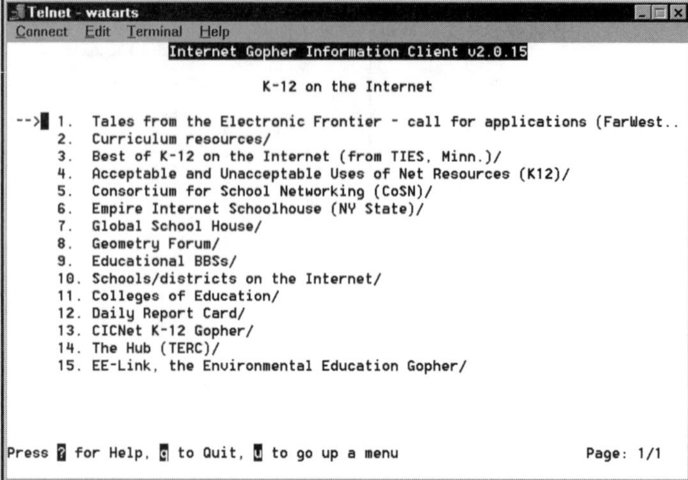

Figure 19.11.
The K–12 on the Internet directory in BBNs Testbed Gopher.

again. Choosing this directory will have amazing results. Forty-six new directories and Gopher links should appear on your screen. I've listed only some of the available selections:

```
1.  Current K-12 Information (postings from select Ed. Listservs)/
2.  Russian Far East Exchange/
3.  The Space Science and Engineering Center (Global Satellite Images)/
4.  WOLF STUDY PROJECT/
5.  Bosnian / Croatian Exchange Project/
- - - - - - - - - - - - - - - - - - - - - - - - - - - -
7.  Selected PICTURES, QUICKTIME MOVIES AND SOUNDS
8.  CNN Newsroom Classroom Guide/
9.  Project Central America/
- - - - - - - - - - - - - - - - - - - - - - - - - - - -
11. Africatrek!/
- - - - - - - - - - - - - - - - - - - - - - - - - - - -
15. Geographic Server <TEL>
- - - - - - - - - - - - - - - - - - - - - - - - - - - -
18. Center for Great Lakes Information Service/
19. NASA/
- - - - - - - - - - - - - - - - - - - - - - - - - - - -
27. TogetherNet, Foundation for Global Unity/
28. K12Net/
29. News From Around the World/
30. Teacher Contacts/
- - - - - - - - - - - - - - - - - - - - - - - - - - - -
32. Canada's SchoolNet/
- - - - - - - - - - - - - - - - - - - - - - - - - - - -
34. Education Gopher at Florida Tech/
35. KIDLINK Gopher/
- - - - - - - - - - - - - - - - - - - - - - - - - - - -
37. StarkNet (Stark County School Disctrict, Canton, Ohio, USA)/
```

38. `TEACHER * PAGES (Pennsylvania Dept. of Ed.) Login: TX <TEL>`

As you can see, there are so many places to explore, too numerous for me to describe them all. Some will be of more interest to you than others. Some that I checked out include `CNN`, `Selected PICTURES...`, `NASA`, `Teacher Contacts`, and Canada's `SchoolNet`. All these have excellent resources for use in classroom assignments and projects.

The `Teacher Contacts` directory lists teachers involved in various projects on the Internet and e-mail addresses where they can be contacted. One of the entries is written by a professor from MIT who is interested in working on computer science projects with high schools. The NASA Gopher is especially excellent for use in a science program.

Canada's SchoolNet Gopher links you to various projects currently in production, such as the Whale Watching Project, the Acid Rain Project, and the Telecommunications Project, as well as a directory of projects soliciting participants.

Two of these eleven other directories include `CICNet K-12 Gopher` and `The Hub (TERC)`. The first connects you to several other directories or searches. One of these, `Education-Related Publications`, is extremely valuable for finding articles useful for teacher professional development or in the classroom with your students. Nine publications are available: `Academe This Week`, `Academy one`, `Equitnews`, `K12ADMIN`, `KIDS`, `KIDS-94`, `KIDSPHERE`, and `Report Card`.

Selecting `The Hub (TERC)` Gopher enables you to find specific topics in education for use in the classroom by grade level, region, and topic. The `By Topic` directory gives you categories such as `Assessment`, `Gender`, `Math`, `Science`, and `Technology`. The `By Grade Level` directory enables you to find classroom information for College (Undergraduate Level), High School Level, and Upper Elementary Grades.

19

Following are some other educational Gopher addresses to explore:

```
garnet.geo.brown.edu
gopher.mde.state.mi.us port 70
gwis.circ.gwu.edu
csd4.csd.uwm.edu
gopher.cic.net
gopher.oise.on.ca
porpoise.oise.on.ca 70
nstn.ns.ca
gopher.ed.gov
gopher.mde.state.mi.us
gopher.cse.ucls.edu
cwis.usc.edu
gopher.briarwood.com port 70
```

Task 19.3: Use Gopher to locate International K–12 activity.

As you might expect, other nations are also actively putting the Internet to its best educational uses. Canada's SchoolNet project has already been mentioned, but the Best of K–12 of the Internet listing (shown previously) can take you to other countries as well.

1. Access the `Best of K-12` Gopher by typing **`tiesnet.ties.k12.mn.us`** at the UNIX command prompt.
2. Once there, select item number `12` of the directory—`InforMNs` Gopher server.
3. Using the arrow keys, scroll down to item `6` of this menu and press Enter to open the `Best of K-12 Internet Resources` line, which yields the menu shown in Figure 19.12.

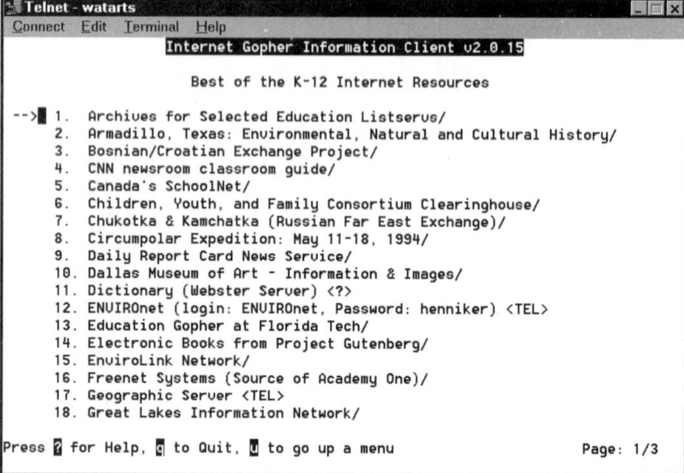

Figure 19.12.
The Best of K–12 Internet Resources listing.

Several internationally-based items present themselves, including the `Russian Far East Exchange`, the `Bosnian/Croatian Exchange Project`, and `Project Central America`. Let's look briefly at each of these.

4. Select line `7`, entitled `Chukotka and Kamchatka (The Russian Far East Exchange)`. This entry yields the menu of items displayed in Figure 19.13.
5. Now choose line `7` again (`Kamchatka Region of the Russian Far East`) to reveal the list of articles and directories shown in Figure 19.14.

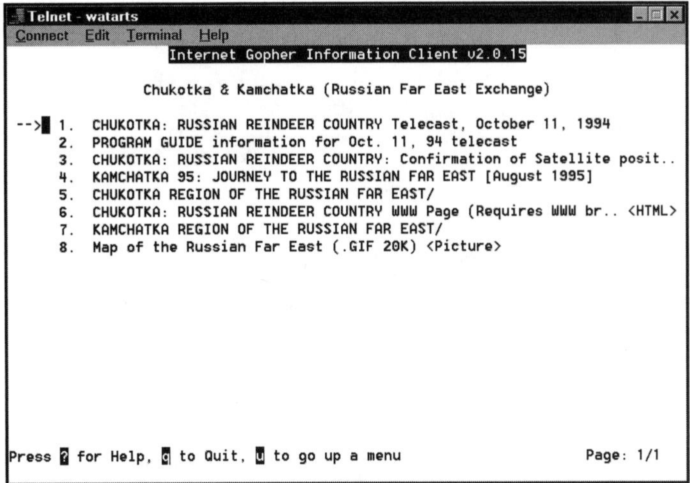

Figure 19.13.
Chukotka and Kamchatka educational details in Gopher.

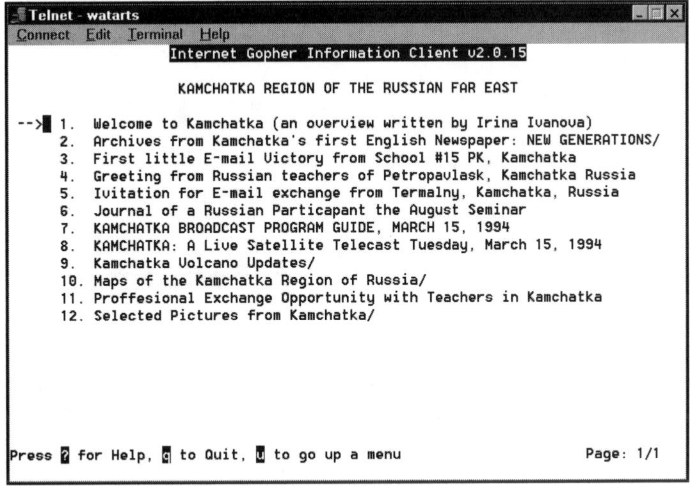

Figure 19.14.
Items and links from the Kamchatka Gopher.

While all are intriguing, we'll look at only two. First, a welcome message from a Kamchatkan teacher, who, in the remainder of this lengthy file, explains the land and the online project.

6. To call up this file, select the first listing in the `Kamchatka Region of the Russian Far East` directory.

```
The following is an overview of Kamchatka written by Irina Ivanova,
English teacher from school #15 in Petropavlask, Kamchatka Russia

* * * * * * * * * * * * * * * * * * * * * * * * * * * * * * * * * * * * * * *
Welcome to Kamchatka!
```

```
Planning to visit Kamchatka?
You are welcome! Any idea why our land is called Kamchatka?
To tell you the truth, we do not know  for  sure ourselves,
though the guides might offer you quite a few versions. One
of them says that our land owes its  name to the Russian
Cossack Ivan Kamchaty, one of the first explorers here.
```

Next, some information about the Kamchatka Professional exchange for teachers or students. This exchange program might well be an idea worth exploring for your own school district.

7. To access this article, scroll down to line `11` and press Enter, where you'll see the information shown in Figure 19.15.

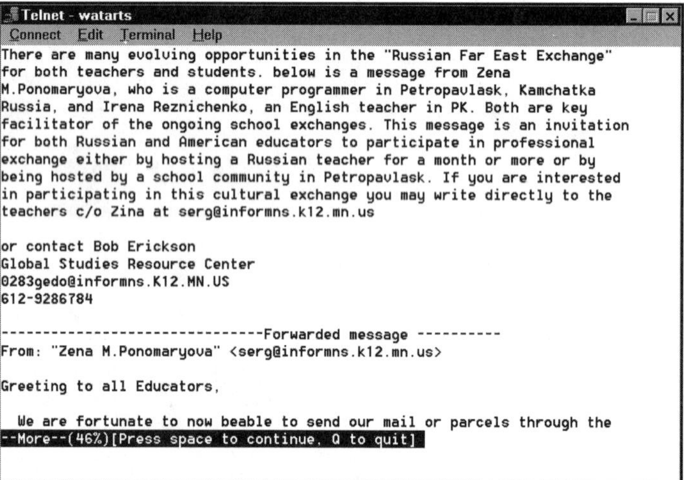

```
There are many evolving opportunities in the "Russian Far East Exchange"
for both teachers and students. below is a message from Zena
M.Ponomaryova, who is a computer programmer in Petropavlask, Kamchatka
Russia, and Irena Reznichenko, an English teacher in PK. Both are key
facilitator of the ongoing school exchanges. This message is an invitation
for both Russian and American educators to participate in professional
exchange either by hosting a Russian teacher for a month or more or by
being hosted by a school community in Petropavlask. If you are interested
in participating in this cultural exchange you may write directly to the
teachers c/o Zina at serg@informns.k12.mn.us

or contact Bob Erickson
Global Studies Resource Center
0283gedo@informns.K12.MN.US
612-9286784

------------------------------Forwarded message ----------
From: "Zena M.Ponomaryova" <serg@informns.k12.mn.us>

Greeting to all Educators,

  We are fortunate to now beable to send our mail or parcels through the
--More--(46%)[Press space to continue, Q to quit]
```

Figure 19.15.
Sample article from Kamchatka Gopher.

8. Return to the main `Best of K-12 Internet Resources` menu by pressing **u** twice and select the `Bosnian/Croation Exchange` listing (item `3`).

From the `Bosnian/Croatian Exchange`, you find a small but fascinating group of items. Among them are letters such as the following, which can't help but demonstrate the need for this kind of collaborative activity:

```
Last May, Aida Bajric, a 16-year-old teenage refugee from Bosnia-
Herzegovina, sent the following message. This message prompted TIES to
work with CARNet (the Croatian Academic and Resaerch Network) to
establish an E-mail vehicle for teens

**************************************************
```

```
Dear lady and gentleman!

First I would like to introduce myself to you. My name
is Aida and I'm 16. 10 month ago because of the war
I had to leave my country Bosnia and Hercegovina and I'm
now spending my time as a refugee in Povlja's hotel "Galeb"
(it is now refugee camp) on the island Brac in Croatia. The
town I come from is Banja Luka (NW Bosnia). My father is
still there (he is doctor of Mechanical Engeneering and has
been lecturing the Computer aided design - CAD). Banja
Luka is the capital of Serbian republic and Serbs don't allow
him to get out. My mother (she is electronic engineer) and
my sister Elma (she is 17) are with me in this hotel. My
sister and me go in the school in Bol which is 31 kilometer
far from Pavlja.
On Saturday 20th of March in hotel "Galeb" came Mr.Ted
Pratt with idea for publishing the news for Bosnian teen
refugees. We have talked a lot about that. He said that
you would be able to finance organization and publishing
and we shall really appreciate if you decide to help us.
```

9. Now select line 32 from the Best of K–12 Internet Resources menu to access `Project Central America`. The first paragraph of Project Central America's description reads as follows:

```
Recent distance learning expeditions have included an educational
component: explorer turned educator.  Project Central America
capitalizes on teacher turned explorer to pull students beyond their
classroom walls and into the world around them.  Project Central America
provides an opportunity to involve and connect learners in an adventure-
driven distance learning project. Teacher-student interaction is an
integral part of the project and not simply a component.  The team of
teachers turned explorers will cycle throughout Central America in the
spring of 1994.
```

The idea is to have the cyclists send back information as they make their way through Central America, and to use these technologies to communicate with schools throughout Central America as well. One journal entry, from Nicaragua, follows:

```
Nicaragua has been hit by so many natural disasters it's incredible. The
capitol city, Managua, is mostly toppled buildings from a massive
earthquake in 1972.  The country's lengthy war has left it with little or
no money to rebuild, therefore hundreds of thousands of people live in the
ruins of Managua.

In 1992, a volcano, Cerro Negro, erupted spewing ash for 50 miles. It was
so heavy in Leon the ash collapsed buildings. Because the ash was hot
every animal covered was killed and whole herds of cattle bones are still
lying in the fields. People had to cover their heads and faces as the ash
would easily burn and choke them.
```

```
As if that wasn't enough, the volcano's eruption caused a shift in the
earth which in turn caused a tidal wave (they think). Anyway, this
country has been hard hit, added are the years of war which really ended
in '92. The country seems to be in a desperate state.
```

Questions from students are filed in the Gopher as well, complete with answers from the touring staff.

Admittedly, these projects demonstrate U.S. applications of Internet resources, but nowhere else has the K–12 community been as focused on making the best use of the technology. Still, these are the types of projects that will bring other nations onto the Net, at which point they will inevitably develop their own internal applications.

Task 19.4: Use WAIS and ERIC to search educational resource databases.

Gopher systems are great; but, as you can see, they are not necessarily very focused. At times you want to be able to find information in a very short period of time.

A relatively quick and simple solution to this problem is the use of WAIS (Wide Area Information Servers) databases available on the Internet. Using WAIS enables you to search through databases of information for a particular topic.

1. Locate WAIS through your Gopher server by accessing a popular Gopher server and selecting the appropriate menu listing. If you have difficulty finding the WAIS directory, type **`gopher uwinfo`** and select item `10` (`Electronic Resources Around the World`). Then choose the final directory in this menu entitled `WAIS databases`. After you select WAIS your screen may look something like the following:

   ```
   1.    About Wide Area Information Servers (WAIS)/
   2.    Subject Sorted WAIS databases from Sweden/
   3.    WAIS (through Think Com) <TEL>
   4.    WAIS (through University of Minnesota)/
   5.    WAIS Sources from Arizona State University/
   ```

   Any one of items `2` through `5` will set you up with databases available for searching. I always start by trying the one closest to my geographical area, although that is no guarantee of an easier, quicker connection. Needless to say, the furthest, Sweden, was the easiest for me to connect to.

2. Choose item `2`, to reveal this screen:

   ```
   1.    About "Experiment with Automatic Classification" (README)
   2.    All WAIS databases in alphabetic (gopher) order/
   3.    Subject tree (based on UDC)/
   ```

3. Select item `2` once again and scroll down through the `A` listings. About 98 items into the list, you come to the `AskERIC Lesson Plans` search heading. Press Enter. You have seen ERIC (Educational Resources Information Center) searches within the two Gopher systems earlier explored. Getting to the ERIC searchers through WAIS, however, is far easier and quicker. After AskERIC Lesson Plans is chosen, you are asked to type in a word that will be searched in this database.

4. In this case, type the word **literature** and press Enter. WAIS will present numerous search results and you may simply surf through the various files.

Some of the lesson plans I found valuable and consequently mailed to my own e-mail address included a teaching lesson (complete with objectives and goals) on preparing students to study for a final exam, a writing process lesson, a media lesson analyzing and deconstructing junk mail, a lesson in improving students' independent listening skills, and a literature lesson on Shakespeare's *Macbeth.* I have listed some excerpts from two of these lesson plan files:

```
Title: The Junk Mail Explosion: Why You Buy and How Ads Persuade
Author: Marcia Nichols, Daly Middle School, Lakeview, OR
Grade Level / Subject: 7-10 / English Mass Media Unit
Overview / Purpose: In 1990, 63.7 billion pieces of the third-class
bulk mail found their way into mailboxes across the nation. This
activity is designed to increase student awareness of persuasion tactics
in "junk mail" advertising.

Objectives: The students will be able to:
1. read direct mail advertising critically
2. identify persuasion techniques
3. employ intellectual defenses against persuasive techniques
4. neatly label and orgainize junk mail into a term paper folder

Resources / Materials...
Activites and Procedures...
Tying It All Together...
The Junk Mail Explosion Project...
Evaluation Scheme...
```

19

Following is another example:

```
Title: Literature Review
Author: Linda Burton, Condon Elementary, OR
Grade Level / Subject: 10-12 (adaptable to 7-9)); language arts.
Overview: This lesson is designed to review a literary work or unit
before an exam. Students should have already read and discussed the
literature. They need to understand in advance that a knowledge question
simply involves recalling a fact from the literature. An interpretation question
involves expanding the facts and offering some insight and / or explanations.
A judgement question calls for an ...
```

As you can surmise, using the WAIS to search an educational resources database is a quick way to find information if you have a specific topic that you want researched. Using any of the other ERIC databases follows the same procedure but enables you to search for other educational topics. If you need information to instruct other teachers in your department or school on a topic such as outcomes-based learning, benchmarks, or any current trend in education, you can use the ERIC archive to search for articles on these topics.

Task 19.5: Join educational mailing lists and subscribe to K–12 newsgroups.

One other area that many teachers find useful is *mailing lists.* Mailing lists can connect you with other educators who are interested in specific topics. You will receive, along with everyone else subscribed to the list, a copy of all mail messages sent by subscribers of the group.

Mailing lists usually are moderated—that is, someone (usually the creator of the list) reads all the messages to make sure they remain professional and focused. In order to receive the mail messages from any of these groups, you need to subscribe to them by sending an e-mail message to their e-mail address.

GS-Net is a relatively new mailing list that connects you with other educators to discuss various concerns. Most of the mail messages contained in this list have been from teachers and classes who are looking for pen pals for their students with other classes from various parts of the world. To subscribe to GS-Net, follow these steps:

1. Fire up your standard electronic mailer (this example uses Pine).
2. In the To: line, type **`GS-Net@earanpe.br`** and press Enter until your cursor reaches the `Message Text` area.
3. Subscribe to the list by typing **`SUBSCRIBE GS-NET`** *`Name`* where *`Name`* is replaced by your first and last name.

Tip: The basic format for subscribing to any mailing list is to type **`subscribe`** *`Listname Yourname`* in the body of a standard e-mail message.

For example, my subscription message looked like this:

```
To: GS-NET@earanpe.br
Cc:
Attachment:
Subject:
Message:
- Message Area -
SUBSCRIBE GS-NET Carol DeVrieze
```

4. Now simply send the e-mail message and you will be added to the list of subscribed members.

The following example is typical of a plea for a class connection:

```
We are a rural elementary school in upstate New York and would
like to communicate with another class anywhere in the country or
worldwide. If you are interested please contact us.
```

Another interesting mailing list is called *APENGLISH.* This list contains teachers who teach Advanced Placement English courses in high school. These teachers share lesson plans, e-texts, curriculum concerns, and approaches to new works of literature. Some teachers send copies of their course outline and summer reading list. The following excerpt is taken from a message sent by a teacher of this special program containing a partial alphabetical list of suggested authors for course readings in Advanced Placement English:

```
Suggested New Titles
Achebe, Chinua. Things Fall Apart is probably taught world wide now. It's a
Nigerian novel about change and adjustment to change from a tribal culture
to conquest.
Allende, Isabelle.
Atwood, Margaret. Handmaid's Tale is a book I strongly advocate that
every person read although I'm not sure that it could be assigned or required
because of its content.
```

Two other mailing lists I became involved in are entitled *Literacy* and *Learner.* These groups have some really interesting discussions on many topics related to new learners of reading and to literacy issues. Bibliographies on research in this field are traded, comments on software for use with new readers is discussed, pen pal requests by new readers and writers are submitted, among many other discussion topics.

Following are some additional list addresses you might want to explore:

19

```
LITERACY@nysernet.ORG
LEARNER@nysernet.ORG
GS-NET@ear.anpe.br
APENGLISH-L-REQUEST@adler.nec.mass.edu
```

Tip: To locate mailing lists of interest to K–12 educators, Gopher to **`rain.psg.com`** and select the item `School Computing` (mostly K–12). Here you'll find four extremely helpful files, one dealing with mailing lists and the others with FTP and telnet sites, among other issues. Mail these to yourself and peruse them at your leisure.

There also are any number of Usenet newsgroups, as might be expected. In fact, there is an entire newsgroup hierarchy devoted to K–12 users! These range from `k12.chat.teacher` through `k12.ed.math`, as you can determine by activating a search in your newsgroup software. Some of these groups are worthwhile, but because most are unmoderated they tend

to be overly informal and rambling (which is typical for newsgroups, of course). My best advice is to search for and subscribe to a few of them, and then decide after a week or so which you want to keep. You may even decide to start one of your own, if the subject matter warrants.

Although using the Internet has not made me feel less overwhelmed by all of the information being written about education today, I know that I have benefited greatly in many ways by making the connection. I know where I can go to search for information related to things that are important to me as an educator, whether they be new lesson-plan ideas, recent articles on educational research and trends, new ways to involve my students so that they become more responsible for their own learning, or just keeping in touch with other educators who are facing the same issues and concerns that I face as a teacher every day in my classroom.

K–12 Information on the World Wide Web

By Neil Randall

Quite appropriately, Carol restricted her searches for K–12 information primarily to Gophers. I say quite appropriately because that's where the bulk of the action is taking place, even now in the era of the Web. The Web's potential for online education is much stronger than Gophers, but a great many schools have text-only access to the Internet.

Still, much of this educational information has appeared on the World Wide Web by now. Figure 19.16 shows a portion of the Gopher servers that can be accessed through your Web browser, as taken from Brown University's WWW-based Gopher list at the address shown in the figure's Location URL box.

A useful place to begin a search for K–12 Web material (or anything else on the Web, for that matter) is the *CUI W3 Catalog*. This is a search engine for WWW materials, and Figure 19.17 shows one of the results of a search for education.

Another excellent starting point (and one referenced from the CUI page and other sources) is *The Internet Services' Educational Archive*. From this colorful page, you can scroll down the page for access links to a number of other interesting Web and Gopher resources (see Figure 19.18). This site is currently under construction but promises to become an extensive educational resource.

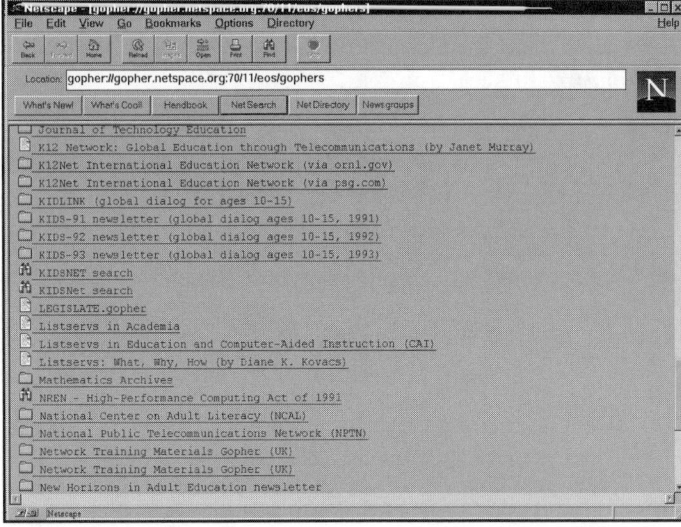

Figure 19.16. *Netscape screen showing education Gopher list.*

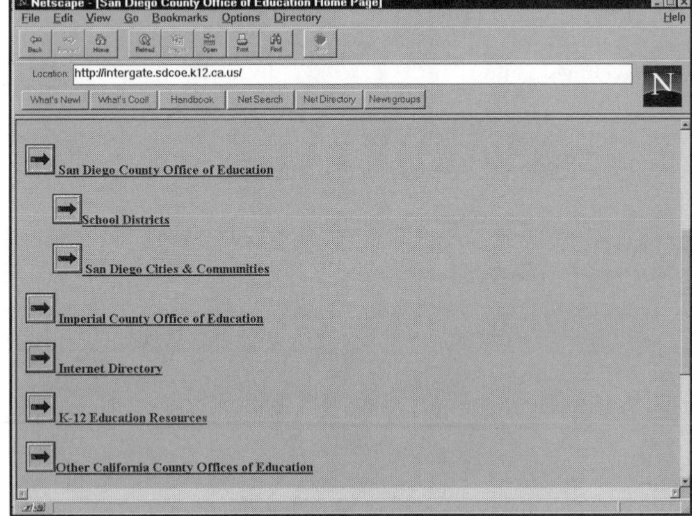

Figure 19.17. *Results of W3 Catalog search.*

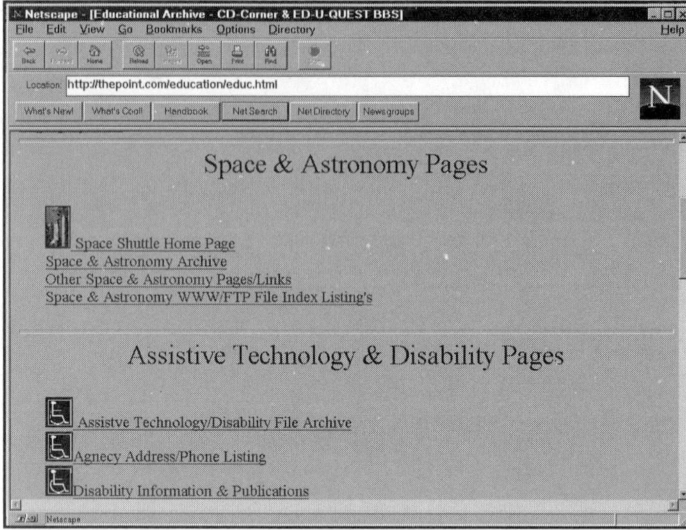

Figure 19.18.
Thepoint Educational Archive screen.

Now one of the most certain ways of realizing how far out of touch you are is to learn that 5th and 6th graders are creating WWW pages with hypertext links, an especially panicky feeling if you're a fifth or sixth grade educator yourself (I'm not but I can easily imagine…). Figure 19.19 displays a sixth-grade page out of Hillside Elementary School in Minnesota. Notice that the site has a page done by third-graders as well, probably as a ploy to make everyone on the planet feel technologically challenged.

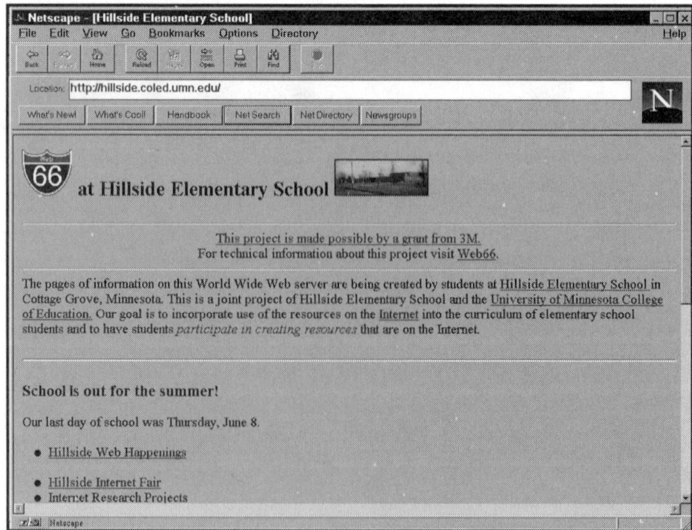

Figure 19.19.
World Wide Web page produced by sixth-graders.

Of course, we should hardly expect the high schools to be outdone by all this grade-school activity. A few secondary schools had made the Web leap as this chapter was being completed, but the most advanced (and probably not surprisingly) was the page sequence from the Illinois Mathematics and Science Academy. Figure 19.20 is the home page for that group, whereas Figure 19.21 shows one of the group's online publications.

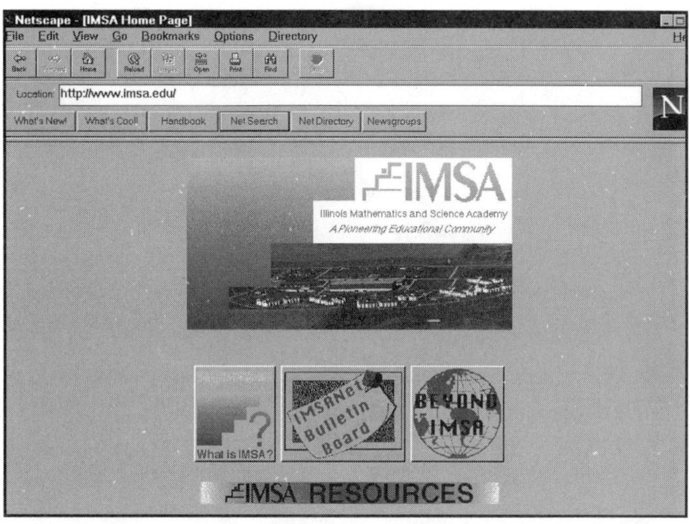

Figure 19.20.
Home page for Illinois Mathematics and Science Academy.

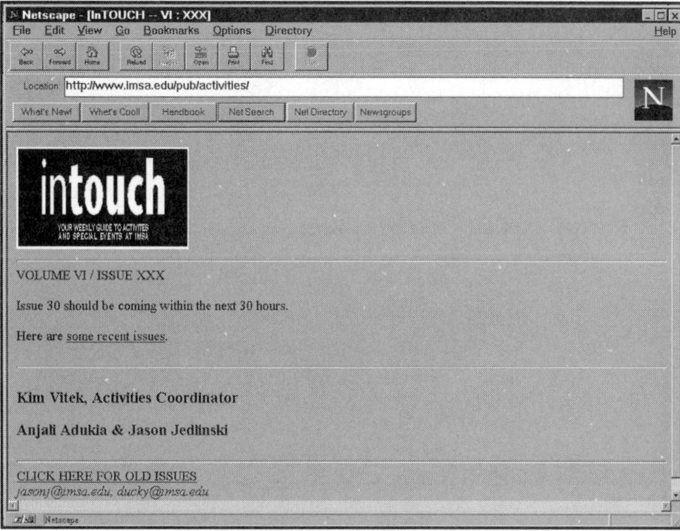

Figure 19.21.
IMSA Activities Newsletter page (Netscape).

If you want to get a good idea of how K–12 education can work over the Web, take a look at the Global Schoolhouse Project (`http://k12.cnidr.org/gsh/gshwelcome.html`). The subtitle is `Linking Kids Around the World`, and the idea is to allow collaborative learning through Internet resources. From the home page of the project, you can access descriptions of ongoing projects, as well as technical support, mailing lists, and information about participating schools.

For continuing information on the efforts of K–12 educators to use the Nets resources, check out GNNs Education Center at `http://gnn.com/edu/`. Here you'll find feature articles about education on the Net, as well as profiles about various educational projects taking place across the Net.

One of the most fascinating projects accessible from GNN is the Creation Stories and Traditional Wisdom project (`http://www.ozemail.com.au/~reed/global/mythdtal.html`). The idea here is to allow kids to read about and actually contribute to a growing set of stories regarding creation, as a means of helping kids from different cultures get to know some of the world's other cultural systems. Suggested classroom activities are listed on this site, as well.

When it comes to online interactive projects on the Web, inevitably you return to NASA. The space agency has worked overtime exploring the Web's potential as a pedagogical tool, and one look at `http://quest.arc.nasa.gov/interactive.html` will show you the results. Coming up in Fall 1995 is *Live From the Stratosphere*, in which students join astronauts—live!—as they conduct their research in space. To see how this project might work, pore through the excellent Live from Antarctica project (`http://quest.arc.nasa.gov/livefrom/livefrom.html`) that took place in late 1994. This page is teacher heaven and could easily be student heaven as well.

And because you need a few good places to find out how other educators are using the Web, and what's happening in education out in cyberspace, check out *Web66: A K12 World Wide Web Project* (`http://web66.coled.umn.edu/`). Here you'll find a large listing of schools on the Web, details on how to set up Web pages and servers for educational use, and a Web66 What's New Page that's modeled after NCSA's famous What's New on the Web page.

Of course, there's always Yahoo, the EINet Galaxy, the Whole Internet Catalog, and a host of additional resources. Plan to spend a weekend or so doing nothing but exploring, then a year or two trying to get things working at your school. You'll be very well rewarded, professionally if not monetarily (budgets, bloody budgets…).

Summary

There's no lack of K–12 educational material on the Internet. Most of it is available through a constantly and quickly growing number of Gopher servers; and because the equipment requirements for Gopher access are less than those for World Wide Web access, this fact is

likely to remain. The amount of information available to educators is staggering in itself, but equally fascinating is the number of pedagogical possibilities that stem from using the Net as a classroom tool. Schools are only beginning to experiment with these ideas, but the next few years will almost certainly demonstrate the natural creativity of educators the world over.

Task Review

In this chapter, you learned the following tasks:

- ☐ How to use Gopher to access the growing number of information servers in the K–12 arena
- ☐ How to consult WAIS to conduct a search for K–12 documents and information
- ☐ Where to start joining mailing lists to keep abreast of new developments in education and educational technology
- ☐ Where to find educational information on the World Wide Web

Q&A

Q Will we ever see K–12 courses conducted over the Internet?

A Yes. Internet-based courses already have been done, albeit primarily by people teaching about the Internet itself. Keep watching the what's-new lists discussed in Chapter 10 to find out about them. Usually, these courses combine Gophers and e-mail, but some have experimented with MUDs and the World Wide Web. The main purpose of such courses for K–12 wouldn't be to improve distance education (as it is for other groups), but rather to take advantage of global connectivity to allow students from different parts of the country or even the world to work together on projects, and to let teachers team-teach where applicable. Anyone with e-mail access can already make this happen, and if you have WWW capabilities, and the time to develop the pages, any number of exciting possibilities present themselves.

Q Are government agencies using some of their resources to help spread Internet use among K–12 classes?

A Apart from funding itself, several government agencies are getting involved. Education faculties in some universities are working with local schools on Internet-based programs, and even if your local university or college doesn't have such a faculty, you'll likely find someone who'd be willing to help with specific projects. Furthermore, as Figure 19.22 shows, the U.S. Department of Education has Gopher and WWW access to a number of documents and activities, and state activity is increasing in this regard as well.

Figure 19.22.
U.S. Department of Education home page.

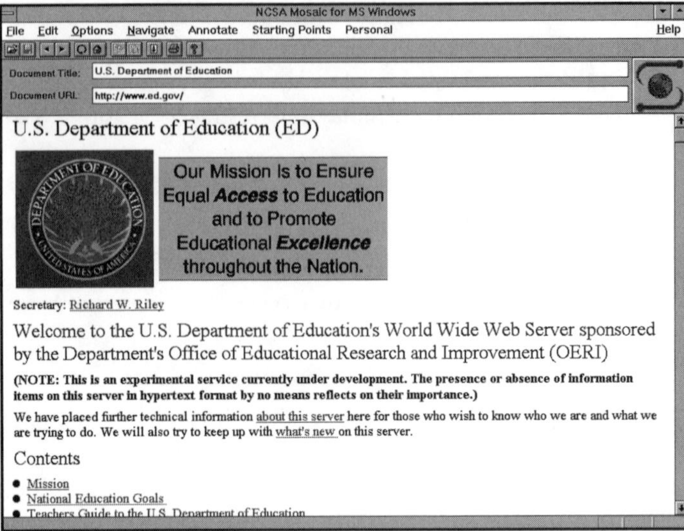

To finish this answer, look at a particularly enticing project undertaken through NASA. Called The JASON Project, it attempts to draw school-aged children into the world of science and technology. Figure 19.23 outlines the mission of the JASON project, and hyperlinks to several stages in the project itself.

Figure 19.23.
The mission of the JASON Project.

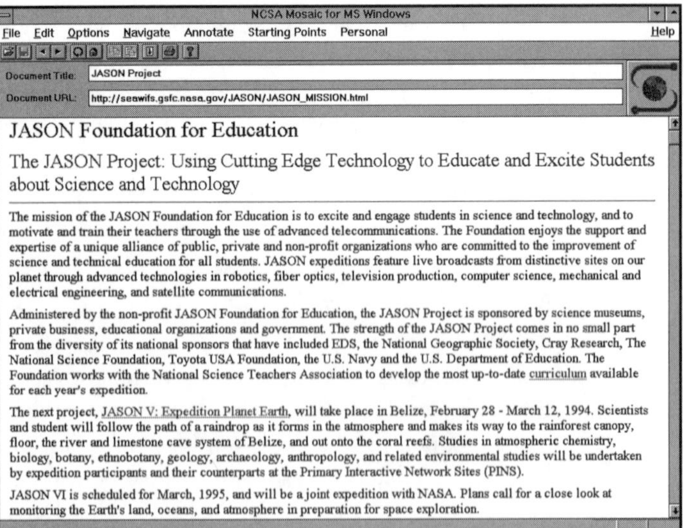

The idea in this particular project was to follow a raindrop through the sky and into the rain forest, and you can click any one of these areas for more information and a look at the results. There's also an intriguing section called Letters from the Rainforest shown elsewhere, but I'll let you find these for yourself.

As a final note, the Greek Jason was, of course, an Argonaut, and the current buzzword for an Internet explorer just happens to be Internaut. Coincidence? You decide.

Making the Internet Safe for Kids: A Guide for Parents and Teachers

With the phenomenal growth in the Internet's popularity has come concerns about the material it contains, and as parents and teachers, you're genuinely and understandably worried. You've heard about the bad stuff that resides out there on the Net, the pornography, the hate mail, and the harassment. Magazines harp on it, Congress harps on it, and it's a subject on television as well. This Extra Credit section offers guidelines and suggestions for making the Net safe for the children under your care. There are a few software solutions in the works, but as long as you're willing to learn the Net for yourself, there's a fair bit you can do right off the top.

The Problem

19

The Internet is huge. Millions of users, millions of files, millions of messages flying back and forth every day. With an estimated 30 million people posting information daily, it's only to be expected that some of the information will be objectionable. Some of it will be well outside the bounds of what we call common decency, and some of it might be even worse.

Let me make it perfectly clear that, despite what you may have heard or read, Internet is *not* a repository for endless collections of pornography, hate literature, and instructions for making bombs and committing suicide. It just isn't. The vast, vast majority of Internet resources are either educational or commercial, with some being given over to just plain silliness. I'd be surprised to learn that more than one-half of one percent of the stuff on the Net could be considered bad, and so should you.

But—and let me make this perfectly clear as well—all these evils *do* take place on the Net. There *is* pornography, and there *is* hate mail, and there *is* harassment, and there *is* information about bombs and suicide. I'd like to deny this, but I can't.

What I *can* deny is that it's easily accessible. Congress would have you believe—as would much of the media—that your child turns on the computer, fires up the Internet account, and is presented with a big icon in the middle of the screen that says, for child pornography click here. That, quite simply, is idiotic. They'd also have you believe that your child will inevitably run into this stuff, and that they'll do so accidentally, and that eventually they'll be drawn into it. Well, they won't *inevitably* run into it, and doing so purely accidentally is extremely unlikely, but if they ever do then—well, they're kids.

So, yes, the Net can be dangerous. Unlikely, but the possibility exists. So what can be done about it? First, governments can start banning material. That's a popular choice among politicians, because it looks good if they vote for something with as leading a title as the Communications Decency Act (had it been named the Communications Censorship Act, it would have provided a much less easy bandwagon). Another choice is to have someone you trust do this work, and that's increasingly becoming a possibility. A third choice is to do the work yourself, under the assumption that, ultimately, you're responsible for your child's safety, and also your child's education.

There's a particular problem associated with computers. They're mysterious, they have viruses, and to many people, they seem almost alive. And they're also difficult to operate. Controlling porn and hate messages on television isn't difficult, because everybody knows how to operate TVs. But when a child can operate a computer better than the adult whose job it is to supervise (and this often is the case), doing anything at all becomes difficult, even frightening. How many people do *you* know who would be willing to type in URLs in Web browsers, after downloading and FTPing the browsers in the first place? Then ask yourself, how many kids would think almost nothing of it?

As of this writing, the most recent sensationalizing of Internet porn was an article in *Time* magazine's July 3, 1995 issue. I won't run through the details of the article, the study on which it was based, or the immediate and incensed reaction of many people on the Net itself. To access the details, grab your Web browser and head for HotWired at `http://www.hotwired.com/`. Click on the graphic called Update on JournoPorn, and you'll get all the details you want.

The point, however, is that *Time* magazine featured cyberporn in the same issue as *Newsweek*, and because of this coverage, it drew attention in the *New York Times*, the *Washington Post*, the *San Francisco Examiner*, *Rolling Stone*, and the *Economist* (among others), and it was topic of the week on *CNN* and in other news media as well. The Communications Decency Act was then making its way through Congress (with evidence based partly on the same study, which since has been denounced as methodologically unsound among other things), and everybody seemed to have an anti-Internet story to tell. Call it a backlash, but the important point is that everyone became alerted.

Whether the news media are accurate or not, the fact is that parents and teachers can't ignore the warnings, any more than they could ignore the distribution of pornography and hate literature at their child's school. They're forced to act, out of concern for their child's safety.

The Extra Credit section offers a few suggestions for keeping the Internet safe, at least on the computer your child customarily uses. There are no guarantees, and the whole thing requires some work, but with what you've learned so far, and with what's at stake, a bit of work certainly won't matter.

The Solutions

There are two major methods of keeping your child away from the Internet's objectionable material—installing software to do the job for you; and learning the Net well enough to do it yourself. Ideally, you'll employ a selection of both.

Note: The idea behind all these solutions is that most users can be stopped or at least hampered from receiving stuff over the Net. If your child is technologically brilliant, there's little you'll be able to do to stop the material from coming in anyway. That's a given, no matter what the problem; if someone really wants something, they'll get it no matter what you do. But for most, some effective countermeasures exist.

Software Solutions (Safeware)

Over the next year, you can expect to see a number of software solutions to the problem of unwanted material on the Net. Their goal is to let you block out whatever material you want, easily and effectively. Obviously, user-friendliness is an issue; you don't want to master computer software, you want to offer some controls to what comes into your child's computer. We'll call this category *safeware,* and maybe we've just invented a new piece of jargon.

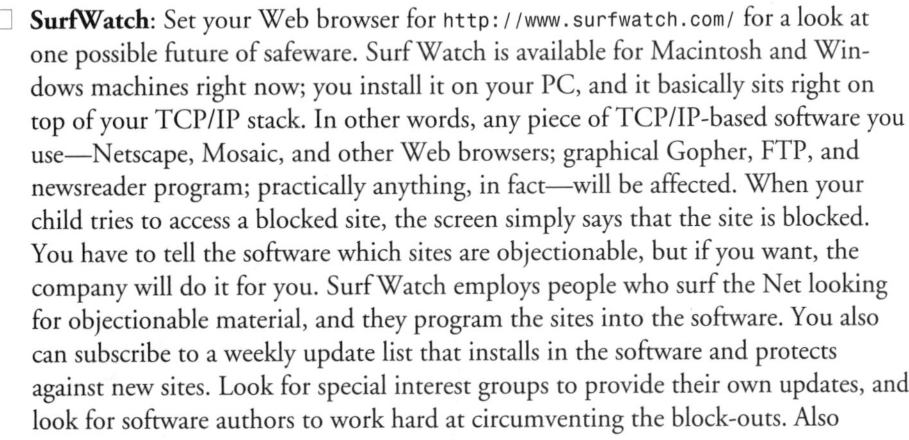

- **SurfWatch**: Set your Web browser for `http://www.surfwatch.com/` for a look at one possible future of safeware. Surf Watch is available for Macintosh and Windows machines right now; you install it on your PC, and it basically sits right on top of your TCP/IP stack. In other words, any piece of TCP/IP-based software you use—Netscape, Mosaic, and other Web browsers; graphical Gopher, FTP, and newsreader program; practically anything, in fact—will be affected. When your child tries to access a blocked site, the screen simply says that the site is blocked. You have to tell the software which sites are objectionable, but if you want, the company will do it for you. Surf Watch employs people who surf the Net looking for objectionable material, and they program the sites into the software. You also can subscribe to a weekly update list that installs in the software and protects against new sites. Look for special interest groups to provide their own updates, and look for software authors to work hard at circumventing the block-outs. Also remember that this works on TCP/IP stacks, which can be end-run by logging into your UNIX shell account without use of TCP/IP. Unless, of course, your service provider uses it on the UNIX machines themselves.

- The Information Highway Parental Empowerment Group. The IHPEG isn't a software solution; instead, it's a consortium of companies whose goal is to place safeware inside Internet software. The idea here is that the software will work as a filter, and that all World Wide Web sites (and newsgroups through them) will be filtered according to a ratings system. The ratings system will be similar to those in existence for the motion picture and videogame industries (and will be voluntary), and again the notion is that the industry and the users can better police the objectionable material than can governments. This solution will be in place late in 1995, according to the companies concerned. These companies, by the way, include IBM, Microsoft, and Netscape, along with Progressive Networks, who bring you the RealAudio sound players for Web browsers. You can access the IHPEG at `http://www.realaudio.com/`.
- **America Online Parental Controls**: Exactly why no one seems to have written about this in the media is beyond me, but America Online has already done its bit for allowing parental control over Internet newsgroups. Through their Parental Controls option in the newsgroups area of the Internet Connection, you can block newsgroups according to a variety of options. For example, you can block specific newsgroups, or newsgroups whose names include particular words. You can set users options for the AOL newsgroup list only, which already blocks objectionable groups, and you can block the user's capacity to download from newsgroups (thereby eliminating the capability to look at graphics or video files). You can even block *all* newsgroups if you just want to do that while you get more information about what's out there. This is extremely powerful stuff, and available whenever you have a master account and subaccounts. In other words, if you get an AOL account and sign up your child under your name, you can do all this blocking and they can't do a thing about it, unless, of course, you tell them the password to your own account.
- **Your Internet Provider**: Although I don't personally recommend this one (I'm for individual choice about these things), if you don't want certain newsgroups available to your child, phone or e-mail your Internet provider and tell them. Internet providers decide which newsgroups they will carry, and they can stop carrying any or all of them if they wish. My commercial Internet provider, for example, carries over 10,000 newsgroups, while my university account gives me access to only about half that many. You're not likely to make yourself popular with either your provider or other subscribers this way, but if you're concerned, it might be worth a try. Look for Internet providers to start offering differing levels of newsgroup access as well, as a means of enabling you to customize your child's access.

Do-It-Yourself Solutions

When it comes right down to it, you're responsible for what your child sees and does, especially in your own home. To that end, I honestly believe that you should develop your own solutions to making the Internet safe. Take it on yourself to learn the Net well enough that you know what to look for and what to do about it. And by all means, take advantage of whatever software comes available to help you.

But the real solution to teaching someone something is to learn it first, and that's where this book comes in. By this time, you've already worked your way through enough tasks and enough software to have a very good sense of what the Net's about. It's simply a matter from here on out of putting that knowledge—and knowledge of software in general—to good use.

- ☐ Explore newsgroups extensively, learning how to read articles and how to download files (Chapter 5 contains all the details).
- ☐ Once you know how to download binaries and save newsgroup postings, check your computer's hard disk drive to see if your child has been saving pictures or files. Yes, this is snooping, but if you're concerned, you're concerned (and you just might be doing your child some good). Use the Find function in the Mac, Windows 95, or in Windows File Manager, and look for files with the extension .JPG, .JPEG, .GIF, .AVI, .MPG, .MPEG, or .MOV. These are the most common binaries containing objectionable pictures. Once you find them, see if they're the ones you don't want, and then deal with the situation as you would any childhood transgression (I always advocate the firm but loving stance, but obviously this isn't a book about child-rearing).

  Incidentally, this checking of hard drives is your primary method of determining what your child is doing online, especially in newsgroups. It will also help you see if there are objectionable images or files that are *not* from the Internet (from bulletin board systems, CD-ROM, and so on). The Internet is by no means the only source of this stuff. This method will also show you what's appeared from FTP sites, although you won't know that's where they came from.
- ☐ Now that you know all this, you understand how difficult it is to get these graphics and video files in the first place. Admittedly, the newest software makes it easier (as does AOL without the Parental Controls in place), but it still takes some effort. That's why it's important you understand how it's done; no matter how good you get, a techno-wizard child might easily know more.
- ☐ As a last resort to controlling newsgroup access, consider simply erasing the newsgroup software from the hard drive. It usually isn't difficult to figure out where the software is located, and especially on Macs or Win95 machines, erasing is easy. True, your child can download it and set it up again, but the fact that it's gone might mean a hesitation at doing so. If it comes back, erase it again, and so on. If your child starts protecting directories with passwords or, worse, encryption, you know you're up against an expert.

- On the World Wide Web, the browsers are your main source of information. Fire up your child's Web browsers (if they know what they're doing, they'll have several), and follow the global history in the browser or the color of the hyperlinks. In Netscape, for example, the links change color when they're accessed, and you can follow where the user has been. Quarterdeck Mosaic takes care of this in the Global History list. The problem is that any user can change the colors and whether or not they change color or appear in a history list. Still, it's a useful possibility, especially since Web sites are the least likely to contain pornographic or otherwise harmful material. Even the Penthouse, Playboy, and Hustler sites have very little that could be even remotely called objectionable, unless (in Hustler's case) you kick in for a monthly subscription. But the Web is largely commercial, scientific, or entertainment-oriented these days, and almost all of it is very much above board.

Contacting the Author

I don't pretend to be an expert at safeware or making the Internet safe for kids, but if I can help, I will. I personally don't consider the whole thing a huge problem, but I understand if you do. Contact me—`nrandall@watarts.uwaterloo.ca`—and I'll try to steer you in an agreeable direction. But, once again, please don't expect an instant response. I do have a day job!

20

DAY 7

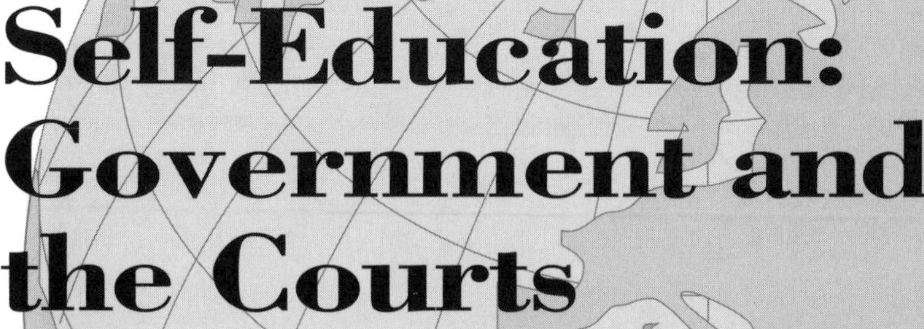

Self-Education: Government and the Courts

In this chapter, you combine all your skills to learn about government and the courts. How? On the Net, of course. While Chapter 19 demonstrated the uses of the Internet by teachers, this chapter shows how you can use the Net to increase your awareness of what's going on in your country and legal system. In fact, the Internet is an endless source of self-education, and that might well be its most exciting promise.

In this chapter, you'll perform the following tasks:

- ☐ Explore U.S. government Gophers
- ☐ Examine the primary Gophers for accessing legal information
- ☐ Explore the growing number of law-related World Wide Web sites
- ☐ Find and read Supreme Court decisions
- ☐ Locate a wide range of other legal information

Government Information on the Internet

If there's been one crucial question surrounding the accessibility of information on the Internet, it's had to do with the willingness of governments to make their own information readily available. It's true, after all (in democratic nations, at least) that governments are public institutions, but it hasn't always been easy or convenient collecting material about their doings. Sometimes the reason has been security; usually, it's because we either don't know where to look, or because getting what we need requires too much effort.

To a significant degree, the Internet has changed all this. Don't expect classified documents to start appearing in your local Gopher site, but do expect to be pleasantly surprised when you discover the wealth of governmental and legal resources available. While the Internet is still no substitute for a well-stocked government bookstore, the indications are that it might be, quite soon. Attribute this change to Vice President Gore's "information superhighway," if you will, but whatever the case, there's never been a time like the present for learning what your government or your Supreme Court is up to (at least, the things they're willing to make public).

This information is especially useful if you're engaged in a project that requires up-to-date research on a specific government or legal topic, or if part of a presentation you're making depends on the timeliness of your institutional data. It's extremely useful material for journalists and teachers as well.

Note: Most of the tasks performed in this chapter are Gopher menu selections. That's because, so far at least, Gopher is the Internet tool most institutions seem to understand best. While it's certainly possible for each government agency to offer an FTP site (many do, in fact), and to build a series of hypertext-linked World Wide Web pages, Gophers have become the early medium of choice. This is for very good reasons: Gophers are easy to access and even easier to move around in, while FTP is still too *computery* for many people. Web pages are beginning to appear, but too few people have access to the necessary connections and software. You can expect to see Gophers proliferating for the next few years.

Task 20.1: Explore the information made available by the White House.

Given President Bush's signing of the High Performance Computing Act in 1991, and the Clinton-Gore pushing of the Internet and the information superhighway, it's not surprising that the White House has been reasonably hard at work developing Internet-based access to documents and files. But that still may not prepare you for the sheer amount of White House information now available. In short, the White House demonstrates quite clearly, to governments the world over, how to use the Internet to make its actions known—not every action, maybe, but certainly a large number and a wide variety. To explore the information made available by the White House, follow these steps:

1. A good first stop for government sources is the same as the first stop for any number of interesting items on the Internet: Gopher Jewels. This exceptionally strong Gopher, highlighted way back in Chapter 8, offers a wide range of information, arranged conveniently by subject. For now, select the item entitled Federal Agency and Related Gopher Sites.

Note: Gopher Jewels is available from many, many Gophers, but you can access it for certain through by typing `gopher cwis.usc.edu` and maneuvering through the Other Gophers and Information Servers menu item.

This will yield the following huge list, presented in detail here to give you an idea of what you're getting into, and how much is available for access:

```
Federal Agency and Related Gopher Sites

Internet Gopher Information Client v2.0.15

                    Federal Agency and Related Gopher Sites (misc)
```

```
       1.  ARPA Computing Systems Technology Office (CSTO)/
       2.  Brookhaven National Laboratory Protein Data Bank/
       3.  Bureau of Labor Statistics, US Dept of Labor - Sam Houston State
➥U../
       4.  Climate and Radiation Server at Goddard Space Flight Center/
       5.  A Collection of US Government Gophers via UC Irvine/
       6.  Commerce Business Daily - Vai CNS, Inc Gopher/
       7.  CPR - Cooperative Programs for Reinvestment/
       8.  Defense Nuclear Facilities Safety Board/
       9.  Defense Technical Information Cntr, Information Analysis Cntrs/
       10. Department of Energy Office of Nuclear Safety (Federal Gov.
➥Info.)/
       11. Department of Housing and Urban Development (HUD)/
       12. Dept. of Labor Occupational Outlook Handbook 1992-93 - U. Minn./
       13. EGIS (Electronic Government Information Service)/
       14. EPA (U.S. Environmental Protection Agency) = Core Server/
       15. EPA (U.S. Environmental Protection Agency) = Future Studies/
       16. EPA (U.S. Environmental Protection Agency) = Great Lakes Nat'l
➥Pgm../
       17. Extension Service USDA Information/
       18. F.B.I. Gopher at NASA Network Applications and Information
➥Center/
       19. FCC Gopher/
       20. Federal Info. Exchange (FEDIX)/
       21. Federal Reserve Board - Internet Town Hall/
       22. FedWorld (NTIS Gateway to Federal Bulletin Boards) VERY BUSY!
➥<TEL>
       23. House of Representatives Gopher/
       24. Lawrence Berkeley Laboratory (LBL)/
       25. Library of Congress (LC MARVEL) (Government Agencies)/
       26. Los Alamos National Lab., NIS-5 Information/
       27. Los Alamos National Laboratory/
       28. Los Alamos National Laboratory, T-2 Nuclear Information Service/
       29. Martin Marietta Energy Systems/
       30. National Center for Atmospheric Research (NCAR)/
       31. National Consumer Week, U.S. Office of Consumer Affairs/
       32. National Coordination Office for HPCC (NCO/HPCC) Gopher/
       33. National Criminal Justice Reference Service (NCJRS)/
       34. National Institute of Allergy and Infectious Disease (NIAID)/
       35. National Institute of Environmental Health Sciences (NIEHS)/
       36. National Institute of Standards and Technology (NIST)/
       37. National Institutes of Health (NIH) Gopher/
       38. National Library of Medicine (National Institutes of Health)/
       39. National Oceanographic Data Center (NODC)/
       40. National Renewable Energy Laboratory (NREL)/
       41. National Telecommunication and Information Administration (NTIA)/
       42. NIST Gopher, Boulder, Colorado/
       43. NOAA High Performance Computing and Communications (HPCC)/
       44. NOAA National Geophysical Data Center (NGDC)/
       45. NSF Center for Biological Timing/
       46. Oak Ridge National Lab, Center for Computational Sciences/
       47. Oak Ridge National Laboratory ESD Gopher/
       48. Occupational Safety and Health, Including OSHA Documents/
       49. Pacific Northwest Laboratory/
       50. U.S. Bureau of Mines Gopher/
       51. U.S. Bureau of the Census Gopher/
       52. U.S. Department of Commerce/
```

```
     53. U.S. Department of Education/
     54. U.S. Department of Energy, Environmental Guidance Memos/
     55. U.S. Department of Energy, Headquarters Gopher/
     56. U.S. Department of Justice Gopher/
     57. U.S. Department of State Gopher/
     58. U.S. Department of Transportation/
     59. U.S. Dept. of Commerce, Economic Conversion Information Exchange
➥(../
     60. U.S. Dept. of Energy, Environment, Safety & Health, Tech. Info.
➥Se../
     61. U.S. Dept. of Health & Human Services/
     62. U.S. Geological Survey (USGS)/
     63. U.S. Government Printing Office (GPO) <TEL>
     64. U.S. Naval Observatory Satellite Information/
     65. U.S. Naval Research Laboratory/
     66. U.S. Senate Gopher/
     67. U.S. Small Business Administration, WV District - Via
➥Mountain.Net/
     68. U.S. Social Security Administration/
     69.  Jump to Gopher Jewels Main Menu/
     70.  Jump up a menu to Federal Agency and Related Gopher Sites/
     71. Search Gopher Jewels Menus by Key Word(s) <?>
```

2. Where to start? No question, the FBI Gopher at NASA Network Applications and Information Center looks interesting, as does the National Institute of Environmental Health Sciences. Then again, how can you avoid the Climate and Radiation Server at Goddard Space Flight Center? Later, of course, you'll be absolutely certain to go through all these Gophers in detail (sort of like that pile of unread books sitting on the study shelf), but, in the meantime, an almost depressing item makes itself instantly apparent.
3. Choose A Collection of US Government Gophers via UC Irvine. The title makes it clear that there's even more available than these 57 items Gopher already shows, or at least so it seems. It's time to dig ourselves in even further.

Warning: Just because a Gopher listing appears to offer additional resources through one of its items, don't necessarily get your hopes up. Often a Gopher site will point to a different Gopher site that, in fact, is practically the same as the one you're already in. Gophers are developed individually by any number of institutions, and their menu items point to other Gophers without taking into account that the information may well be repeated.

```
          A Collection of US Government Gophers via UC Irvine

     1.    Call for assistance...
     2.    POLITICS and GOVERNMENT/
     3.    What's new in the listing?
     4.   Definition of a "United States Government Gopher"
     5.   Federal Government Information (via Library of Congress)/
```

```
     6.  AVES: Bird Related Information/
     7.  Agency for International Development Gopher/
     8.  Americans Communicating Electronically/
     9.  Arkansas-Red River Forecast Center (NOAA)/
     10. AskERIC - (Educational Resources Information Center)/
     11. Biotechnology Information Center (UMd)/
     12. Bureau of Labor Statistics/
     13. Bureau of Transportation Statistics/
     14. Bureau of the Census/
     15. CYFERNet  USDA Children Youth Family Education Research Network/
     16. Catalog of Federal Domestic Assistance /
     17. Centers for Disease Control and Prevention/
     18. Co-operative Human Linkage Center (CHLC) Gopher/
     19. Commerce Business Daily/
     20. Comprehensive Epidemiological Data Resource (CEDR) Gopher/
     21. Consumer Product Safety Commission Gopher/
     22. Defense Nuclear Facilities Safety Board/
     23. Defense Technical Information Center Public Gopher/
     24. ERIC Clearinghouse for Science, Math, Environmental (OSU)/
     25. ERIC Clearinghouse on Assessment and Evaluation/
     26. ERIC Clearinghouses (via Syracuse)/
     27. ESnet Information Services Gopher/
     28. Economic Conversion Information Exchange Gopher/
     29. Environment, Safety & Health (USDE) Gopher/
     30. Environmental Protection Agency/
     31. Environmental Protection Agency  Futures Group/
     32. Environmental Protection Agency  Great Lakes National Program
➥Offi../
     33. Environmental Protection Agency  Great Lakes National Program
➥Offi../
     34. Extension Service, USDA/
     35. FedWorld (NTIS) - 100+ electronic government bulletin boards/
     36. Federal Communications Commission Gopher/
     37. Federal Deposit Insurance Corporation Gopher /
     38. Federal Info Exchange (FEDIX)/
     39. Federal Networking Council Advisory Committee/
     40. Federal Register - Sample access/
     41. Federal Reserve Board (via town.hall.org)/
     42. Federal Trade Commission  Consumerline/
     43. FinanceNet (National Performance Review)/
     44. Government Information Locator Service (GILS)/
     45. Government Printing Office access—trial program/
     46. GrainGenes (USDA) Gopher/
     47. GrantsNet - An Information Hub for Federal Grants Information /
     48. Information Infrastructure Task Force (DoC) Gopher/
     49. LANL Advanced Computing Laboratory/
     50. LANL Gopher Gateway /
     51. LANL Nonlinear Science Information Service/
     52. LANL Physics Information Service/
     53. LANL T-2 Nuclear Information Service Gopher/
     54. LEGI-SLATE Gopher Service /
     55. LTERnet (Long-Term Ecological Research Network)/
     56. Lawrence Berkeley Laboratory (LBL)/
     57. Library of Congress MARVEL Information System/
     58. Los Alamos National Laboratory/
     59. NASA  Network Application and Information Center (NAIC)/
     60. NASA Center for AeroSpace Information/
     61. NASA Center for Computational Sciences/
```

```
62. NASA Goddard Space Flight Center/
63. NASA Information Sources TELNET (compiled by MSU)/
64. NASA K-12 NREN Gopher/
65. NASA Laboratory for Terrestrial Physics Gopher/
66. NASA Langley Research Center  /
67. NASA Lewis Research Center (LeRC)/
68. NASA Marshall Space Flight Center  Spacelink/
69. NASA Minority University Space Interdisciplinary Network/
70. NASA Shuttle Small Payloads Information/
71. NASA Space Mechanisms Information Gopher/
72. NIST Computer Security/
73. NOAA Environmental Services Gopher/
74. NOAA National Geophysical Data Center (NGDC)/
75. NOAA National Oceanographic Data Center (NODC) Gopher/
76. NOAA Online Data and Information Systems/
77. NOAA Space Environment Laboratory/
78. NTIS FedWorld - 100+ electronic government bulletin boards/
79. National Agricultural Library/
80. National Agricultural Library Genome Gopher/
81. National Archives Gopher/
82. National Cancer Institute/
83. National Center for Atmospheric Research (NCAR) Gopher/
84. National Center for Biotechnology Information (NCBI) Gopher/
85. National Center for Education Statistics/
86. National Center for Research on Evaluation, Standards/
87. National Center for Supercomputing Applications/
88. National Center for Toxicological Research/
89. National Coordination Office for High Performance Computing and
➥Co../
90. National Criminal Justice Reference Service (NCJRS)/
91. National Geophysical Data Center (NOAA)/
92. National Heart, Lung, and Blood Institute (NHLBI) Gopher/
93. National Information Infrastructure Task Force/
94. National Institute of Allergy and Infectious Disease (NIAID)/
95. National Institute of Environmental Health Sciences (NIEHS)
➥Gopher/
96. National Institute of Mental Health (NIMH) Gopher/
97. National Institute of Standards and Technology (NIST)/
98. National Institute of Standards and Technology Gopher/
99. National Institutes of Health (NIH)/
100. National Library of Medicine /
101. National Library of Medicine TOXNET Gopher/
102. National Oceanographic Data Center (NODC) Gopher/
103. National Performance Review/
104. National Renewable Energy Laboratory/
105. National Science Foundation (STIS)/
106. National Science Foundation Center for Biological Timing/
107. National Science Foundation MetaCenter
108. National Telecommunication and Information Administration (NTIS)
➥G../
109. National Toxicology Program (NTP) NIEHS-NIH/
110. National Trade Data Bank/
111. Naval Ocean System Center (NRaD) Gopher/
112. Naval Research Laboratory/
113. Naval Research Laboratory  Central Computing Facility/
114. OSHA Salt Lake Technical Center/
115. Oak Ridge National Laboratory ESD Gopher/
116. PAVNET Online (Partnerships Against Violence)/
```

```
      117. Protein Data Bank - Brookhaven National Lab/
      118. Public Broadcasting Service (PBS) Gopher/
      119. STIS (Science and Technology Information System-NSF)/
      120. Securities and Exchange Commission "EDGAR" Gopher/
      121. Small Business Administration/
      122. Smithsonian Institution Natural History Gopher/
      123. Social Security Administration/
      124. Toxicology and Environmental Health Information Program/
      125. Tri-Service Toxicology Consortium/
      126. U.S. Agency for International Development Gopher/
      127. U.S. Bureau of Labor Statistics/
      128. U.S. Bureau of Mines Gopher/
      129. U.S. Bureau of the Census Gopher/
      130. U.S. Dept Agriculture APHIS Gopher/
      131. U.S. Dept Agriculture ARS GRIN National Genetic Resources
➥Program/
      132. U.S. Dept Agriculture Animal and Plant Health Inspection
➥Service/
      133. U.S. Dept Agriculture Children Youth Family Education Research
➥Net../
      134. U.S. Dept Agriculture Economics and Statistics/
      135. U.S. Dept Agriculture Extension Service/
      136. U.S. Dept Agriculture Food and Nutrition Information Center/
      137. U.S. Dept Agriculture National Agricultural Library Plant
➥Genome/
      138. U.S. Dept Commerce  Information Infrastructure Task Force/
      139. U.S. Dept Commerce Economic Conversion Information Exchange/
      140. U.S. Dept Commerce Economics and Statistics Administration/
      141. U.S. Dept Education/
      142. U.S. Dept Energy  Environment, Safety & Health Gopher TIS/
      143. U.S. Dept Energy  Environment, Safety & Health Hdqrs/
      144. U.S. Dept Energy  Headquarters/
      145. U.S. Dept Energy  Office of Nuclear Safety/
      146. U.S. Dept Energy Sciences Network (ESnet)/
      147. U.S. Dept Health and Human Services/
      148. U.S. Dept Housing and Urban Development/
      149. U.S. Dept Justice Gopher/
      150. U.S. Dept State Foreign Affairs Network (DOSAFAN)/
      151. U.S. Dept Transportation/
      152. U.S. Dept Transportation Bureau of Transportation Statistics/
      153. U.S. Environmental Protection Agency/
      154. U.S. Environmental Protection Agency  Futures Group/
      155. U.S. Geological Survey (USGS)/
      156. U.S. Geological Survey (USGS)/
      157. U.S. Geological Survey Atlantic Marine Geology/
      158. U.S. Government Manual (via UMich)/
      159. U.S. Government Printing Office access—trial program/
      160. U.S. House of Representatives Gopher/
      161. U.S. Information Agency/
      162. U.S. Military Academy Gopher/
      163. U.S. National Information Service for Earthquake Engineering/
      164. U.S. Navy  Naval Ocean System Center NRaD Gopher/
      165. U.S. Patent and Trademark Office Information (via
➥town.hall.org)/
      166. U.S. Securities and Exchange Commission "EDGAR" Gopher/
      167. U.S. Senate Gopher/
      168. Voice of America (Radio)/
      169. \PEG, a Peripatetic, Eclectic Gopher/
```

Note: Throughout this book, Gophers normally have been abbreviated. In this case, reproducing the entire listing is important. It demonstrates, even more than the Gopher Jewels list, the enormous range of governmental material available for browsing, perusing, downloading, and so on. Not surprisingly, given the importance placed on telecommunications by the Clinton administration, the United States has led the way in making its information publicly available, but a list like this one can take even the most jaded cynic aback. There seems to be no end to it all, and it's growing weekly.

4. Obviously, you aren't about to read everything that's available. Americans Communicating Electronically is a must-browse at some point in the next few sessions, as is the Cooperative Human Linkage Center. Even the Federal Communications Commission has a Gopher offering, and that, too, would seem to be worth checking out. That's not even counting all the NASA material that's spawning itself all over the Net. Undoubtedly, the NASA sites will offer graphics available for download, maybe even the Voyager photographs. Explore for a while, and then return to this listing.

   At this point, you know that the range of possibilities is enormous. Any student of the U.S. government probably has enough material in these various Gophers for primary research for any number of high school or early college essays, and anyone doing a research presentation can make equally good use of the material. It seems nearly endless.

5. Right now, however, you have to make a choice. At this stage, focus on material that discusses governmental activities themselves, because we have to start somewhere. So how about the U.S. House of Representatives Gopher:

```
U.S. House of Representatives Gopher

        1.  About the US House Gopher/
        2.  Educational Resources/
        3.  General Information/
        4.  Guest Register <??>
        5.  House Committee Information/
        6.  House Directories/
        7.  House Email Addresses
        8.  House Leadership Information/
        9.  House Member Information/
        10. House Schedules/
        11. House WWW Now Available-1/4/95
        12. Legislative Resources/
        13. Other Internet Resources/
        14. Visitor Information/
        15. What's New/
```

Good. It's short. Maybe we've finally found something we can get a handle on. Starting at the top, begin with some information about this Gopher site by choosing item 1. The following even shorter menu results:

```
About the US House Gopher

1.  Welcome to the US House Gopher.
2.  Welcome.au <)
3.  Internet Etiquette.
```

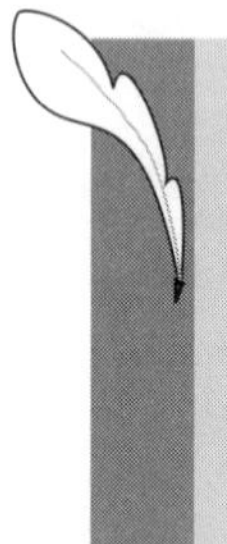

Note: Remember the general rule about Gophers. Any menu item with a slash (/) on the end represents a subdirectory; items without the slash are files. If you choose a file, it will be retrieved and displayed. For text files, this isn't a problem; the Gopher software will display it easily. For other files, however, you must set up the appropriate viewers to see or hear them. Files with extensions such as .GIF, .PCX, .JPG, and so on, are graphics files. Files with .AU, .WAV, or .MID extensions are sound files.

6. Because there's no slash (/) at the end of the lines, you know that all three of these items are files rather than further subdirectories. Because we don't have sound hardware installed, choosing the .AU file won't do any good (it's a Sun audio sound file), and we know enough about Internet etiquette not to worry about it. Read what the welcome message has to say, by choosing item 1:

```
WELCOME TO
              THE U.S. HOUSE OF REPRESENTATIVES'
                        GOPHER SERVICE

        The U.S. House of Representatives' Gopher service
provides public access to legislative information as well as
information about Members, Committees, and Organizations of
the House and to other U.S. government information resources.
It was built using the Gopher software from the University of
Minnesota.  Posting and maintaining information in Member,
Committee, and House Organization directories is the
responsibility of the individual offices.

        Since the information offered by the system will be
viewed by both Congressional staff members and users outside
the Congress from workstations with varying ranges of
characteristics and capabilities, the format of documents on
the Gopher service will, for the most part, adhere to the
"lowest common denominator" — plain ASCII text.

        The U.S. House of Representatives  does not provide
anonymous FTP or telnet.
```

Well, things are starting to cook (at least a little). Here you have at least one agency asking for feedback on its Internet offering. Of course, the name `househlp@hr.house.gov` doesn't sound overly personal, but at least it's something.

Also comforting, for those who care about such things, is that the Gopher's title (The House of Representatives' Gopher Server) actually contains the proper punctuation—an apostrophe in the right place.

7. Return to the original House menu, and this time try `General Information`.

```
                    General Information

 1.  95 Budget - USDA/
 2.  Disaster Relief Information - CSREES USDA/
 3.  The Catalog of Federal Domestic Assistance - GSA <?>
 4.  The GATT Treaty Archive - ACE/
 5.  US and World Politics - Sunsite UNC/
 6.  US House GATT Treaty <?>
```

8. Looks interesting, and we'll return later. For now, go back to the main House menu and select `House Email Addresses` (7). The following file will appear:

```
              UNITED STATES HOUSE OF REPRESENTATIVES
                 CONSTITUENT ELECTRONIC MAIL SYSTEM

        We welcome your inquiry to the House of Representatives
Constituent Electronic Mail System, a program designed to give
constituents electronic access to their elected representatives. The
nature and character of the incoming electronic mail has demonstrated
that this capability will be an invaluable source of information on
constituent opinion. We are now in the process of expanding the
project to include other Members of Congress, as technical, budgetary
and staffing constraints allow.

          Because this program is intended to provide an additional
vehicle for Members to communicate with their constitutents, it is
critical that you include your name and address in your mail message,
preferably at the top of the message. Most Congressional offices have
adequate staff resources to respond only to their constituents and your
inclusion of your full name and mailing address will insure that your
Member can identify your residence within his or her Congressional
District. Many offices are using an automatic response to all in-coming
messages, so you can expect to receive a message back from most of the
addresses to which you send a message.

        A number of House committees and leadership offices have also
 been assigned public electronic mailboxes. The names and electronic
mailbox addresses of these offices are listed below after the
information about participating Representatives.

        The Document Room of the U.S. House of Representatives has
also been assigned an electronic public mailbox. The name and
electronic mailbox address of the House Document Room is listed
below after the information about participating committees.
The House Document Room distributes House Bills, Resolutions,
Reports, Documents, and Public Laws for the 104th Congress. House
Reports, Documents, and Public Laws for the 103rd Congress are also
maintained. The public can obtain 2 copies of up to 12 different
House documents per day. Customers should include their telephone
number with their mailing address. All document orders will be
filled and mailed the same day they are received. For more
detailed information or questions, call the Document Room at
(202) 225-3456, Monday through Friday, 9 a.m. to 6 p.m.
```

Please review the list of participating Representatives below, and if the Congressional District in which you reside is listed, follow the instructions to begin communicating by electronic mail with your Representative. If your Representative is not yet on-line, please be patient.

U.S. REPRESENTATIVES PARTICIPATING IN THE CONSTITUENT ELECTRONIC MAIL SYSTEM.

Hon. Cass Ballenger
10th Congressional District, North Carolina
Rm. 2238 Rayburn House Office Building
Washington, DC 20515
CASSMAIL@HR.HOUSE.GOV

Hon. Joe Barton
6th Congressional District, Texas
Rm. 2264 Rayburn House Office Building
Washington, DC 20515
BARTON06@HR.HOUSE.GOV

Hon. Sherwood Boehlert
23rd Congressional District, New York
Rm. 2246 Rayburn House Office Building
Washington, DC 20515
BOEHLERT@HR.HOUSE.GOV

Hon. Rick Boucher
9th Congressional District, Virginia
Rm. 2245 Rayburn House Office Building
Washington, DC 20515
NINTHNET@HR.HOUSE.GOV

Hon. Jim Bunning
4th Congressional District, Kentucky
Rm. 2437 Rayburn House Office Building
Washington, DC 20515
BUNNING4@HR.HOUSE.GOV

Hon. Dave Camp
4th Congressional District, Michigan
Rm. 137 Cannon House Office Building
Washington, DC 20515
DAVECAMP@HR.HOUSE.GOV

Hon. Ben Cardin
3rd Congressional District, Maryland
Rm. 104 Cannon House Office Building
Washington, DC 20515
CARDIN@HR.HOUSE.GOV

Hon. Saxby Chambliss
8th Congressional District, Georgia
Rm. 1708 Longworth House Office Building
Washington, DC 20515
SAXBY@HR.HOUSE.GOV

```
Hon. Dick Chrysler
8th Congressional District, Michigan
Rm. 327 Cannon House Office Building
Washington, DC 20515
CHRYSLER@HR.HOUSE.GOV

Hon. John Conyers, Jr.
14th Congressional District, Michigan
Rm. 2426 Rayburn House Office Building
Washington, DC 20515
```

Several names follow, but this is enough to get the general idea. This is substantiated proof that the government is becoming Internet-savvy, with all these Representatives establishing e-mail addresses and partipating in this project. Further down the text file is a listing of committees participating in the project as well.

Task 20.2: Explore information about the U.S. budget.

General information is fine, but as its name suggests, it's merely general information. At this stage, we're getting a bit impatient for some real material, something useful and maybe worth getting angry about (that's what government information is for, isn't it?). So let's continue with our explorations from Task 20.1 in an attempt to arrive at files worth reading. This time, we'll tackle the U.S. Budget.

1. Back at the General Information menu, select the first item, the `'95 Budget`. The budget is always of interest, but the next menu shows that there may well be more available than we're actually interested in:

```
95 Budget (cyfer.esusda.gov USDA)

1.  95 Budget Table of Contents.
2.  94-02-07 The Budget Message of the President.
3.  Chapter 1 — Where We Started.
4.  Chapter 2 — What We Have Accomplished: The Clinton Economic Plan.
5.  Chapter 3a — Prosperity and Jobs .
6.  Chapter 3b — Investing for Productivity and Prosperity.
7.  Chapter 3c — Delivering a Government that Works Better and Costs ...
8.  Chapter 4 — Reforming the Nation's Health Care System .
9.  Historical Tables/
10. Information on the electronic version of the Budget.
11. Introduction — An Overview of the 1995 Budget.
12. Lists of Charts and Tables.
13. National Defense and International Affairs.
14. Personal Security: Crime, Illegal Immigration, and Drug Control.
15. Summary Tables.
16. The 1995 Proposed Federal Budget.
17. charts-95budget-tiff/
```

20

2. The `Table of Contents` can't possibly be very interesting, but the president's message might be. Besides, knowing where it is will be useful if there's ever a need to study the actual speeches related to such a controversial topic. Selecting item `2`, you can get a transcript of the entire speech.
3. Let's see what else this Gopher has to offer about the budget:

```
3.  Chapter 1 — Where We Started.
4.  Chapter 2 — What We Have Accomplished: The Clinton Economic Plan.
5.  Chapter 3a — Prosperity and Jobs.
6.  Chapter 3b — Investing for Productivity and Prosperity.
7.  Chapter 3c — Delivering a Government that Works Better and Costs ...
8.  Chapter 4 — Reforming the Nation's Health Care System.
```

It's hard not to be interested in prosperity and jobs, so check in with item `5`. Clearly, it's another rather long text file:

```
Title:Chapter 3a — Prosperity and Jobs
Author:The White House
Document-date:94-02-07
Content-Type: text/ascii charset=US ASCII


3A. PROSPERITY AND JOBS

THE ECONOMIC PROGRAM

At the time of the 1992 election, the U.S. economy was caught in a
destructive cycle of weak investment in household durables (with
unsatisfactory growth in business plant and equipment as well),
adverse consumer sentiment, and stagnant employment. To break out of
that cycle, the economy needed jobs—to add to household incomes, and
to give families the confidence to make commitments for housing and
other big-ticket consumer goods that, in turn, stimulate investment in
the business sector and build momentum for the economy as a whole.

The jobs picture was not encouraging. The unemployment rate had
risen, predictably, with the recession that began in mid-1990.
Surprisingly, however, employment remained stagnant—and the
unemployment rate continued rising—for a year after the recession
technically ended. Breaking this pattern of sluggish employment
growth would be essential to energize the recovery.

The same prescription would help toward the ultimate goal of the
President's vision for economic renewal: increasing prosperity for all
Americans. In the long run, even if every qualified job seeker can
find work with just a limited search, living standards depend upon the
factories, machines, and technology available to make our workers
productive (as well as the skills of the workers themselves).
Increased demand for big-ticket items, and hence investment goods,
would begin the process of building for the future.

The greatest resistance to this economic takeoff—the major source
of inertia—was the burden of debt service in all sectors of the
economy. With interest rates stubbornly high, much of current income
was absorbed in meeting past commitments; and future commitments for
```

```
major purchases appeared dauntingly expensive. This Administration
recognized that cutting interest rates would be crucial to stimulate
the economic recovery.


Insert chart: CHRT3A_1
```

Hmmm...a chart. Going back up a couple of menus, we discover that the charts are contained in the final menu item, `charts-95budget-tiff`. These are downloadable graphics files in .TIF format that you can retrieve if you want to construct the document in its entirety.

4. For now, however, there's no need to keep reading. You'd like easy access to the document, however, so why not save it to disk or mail it to yourself? In this case, I was using the Gopher while in an account I don't commonly use, so I decided to use the short menu that appears after every retrieved file to mail it to my normal account.

```
Press <RETURN> to continue,
<m> to mail, <D> to download, <s> to save, or <p> to print:m

1.  95 Budget Table of Contents.
2.  94-02-07 The Budget Message of the President.
3.  Chapter 1 — Where We Started.
4.  Chapter 2 — What We Have Accomplished: The Clinton Economic Plan.
 ----------------------------------------------------------------

      Mail current document to:  nrandall@watserv1.uwaterloo.ca


      [Cancel ^G]   [Accept - Enter]


 ----------------------------------------------------------------
12. Lists of Charts and Tables.
13. National Defense and International Affairs.
14. Personal Security: Crime, Illegal Immigration, and Drug Control.
15. Summary Tables.
16. The 1995 Proposed Federal Budget.
17. charts-95budget-tiff/
```

5. This time, it's back up several menus to the top of the Collection of US Government Gophers at UC Irvine, where you'll select item `2, POLITICS and GOVERNMENT`. Once there, select `National Information Infrastructure Information (via UNC)`. The NII is better known as the information superhighway. Because Vice President Gore has been trumpeting the information superhighway for months now, and because of the superhighway's potential impact on the Internet, any information about it promises to be especially interesting.

```
National Information Infrastructure Information

1.  National Information Infrastructure by Section /
2.  Boucher-Bill-to-change-NSFnet-funding (HR 1757).
3.  National Information Infrastructure - Agenda for Action (full).
4.  Technology for Economic Growth: President's Progress Report
```

20

6. Click on item `1` to yield the following menu of documents:

```
National Information Infrastructure by Section

1.  Table of Contents.
2.  Executive Summary.
3.  Agenda for Action.
4.  Benefits and Application Examples.
5.  Information Infrastructure Task Force.
6.  U.S. Advisory Council on the NII.
7.  Key Contacts
```

7. Because the interesting part to date is how the superhighway will come into being, the `Agenda for Action` sounds like the best place to start. Choose item `3` to get the following:

```
THE NATIONAL INFORMATION INFRASTRUCTURE:
AGENDA FOR ACTION

EXECUTIVE SUMMARY

All Americans have a stake in the construction of an
advanced National Information Infrastructure (NII), a seamless
web of communications networks, computers, databases, and
consumer electronics that will put vast amounts of information at
users' fingertips. Development of the NII can help unleash an
information revolution that will change forever the way people
live, work, and interact with each other:

o        People could live almost anywhere they wanted, without
foregoing opportunities for useful and fulfilling
employment, by "telecommuting" to their offices through an
electronic highway;

o        The best schools, teachers, and courses would be available
to all students, without regard to geography, distance,
resources, or disability;

o        Services that improve America's health care system and
respond to other important social needs could be available
on-line, without waiting in line, when and where you needed
them.

*************************************

The benefits of the NII for the nation are immense. An
advanced information infrastructure will enable U.S. firms to
compete and win in the global economy, generating good jobs for
the American people and economic growth for the nation. As
importantly, the NII can transform the lives of the American
people — ameliorating the constraints of geography, disability,
and economic status — giving all Americans a fair opportunity to
go as far as their talents and ambitions will take them.
```

8. There is a lot here, but again, no need to read it online. This time, rather than mailing the file, save it as a text file by typing **s**.

```
Press <RETURN> to continue,
<m> to mail, <D> to download, <s> to save, or <p> to print:s

4.  Benefits and Application Examples.
5.  Information Infrastructure Task Force.
6.  U.S. Advisory Council on the NII.
7.  NII Accomplishments to Date.
8.  Key Contacts
|------------------------------------------------
|
|
|
|           Save in file: Executive-Summary
|
|
|
|------------------------------------------------
|
```

Warning: If you're using a desktop PC as a terminal on a UNIX system, choosing Gopher's `save` command saves the file on the UNIX system's hard disk, not your own. If you want the file for personal use, you'll have to use a command such as XModem or Kermit to download it to your PC. Or, with the most recent versions of Gopher, you can use the `download` command directly, for which you must press Shift+D (not just d).

9. The only other item on the NII Gopher you want to see at this time is `Key Contacts`. Maybe, in the list, you'll find someone who might be interested in hearing of concerns and other comments.

10. Near the bottom of the `Key Contacts` section is another interesting list. Here you're given Gopher and FTP addresses for retrieving the NII Agenda package, as well as bulletin boards that also carry it. Fire up your FTP software and go see what you can find.

    You're almost at the end of your all-too-brief dalliance with material concerning the U.S. federal government. You haven't even begun to explore the Gophers or FTP sites of state or municipal governments, but keep in mind that an increasing number of government levels are adding such sites. Watch your Gopher and WWW announcements over the next year; you're certain to see a wide proliferation of government-related information, especially (once again) given the importance placed on the issue by the White House and its telecommunications policies.

11. Your last excursion takes you back to the `POLITICS and GOVERNMENT`, where you'll look at the enticing item called `White House Papers` (near the end of the listing). Here, supposedly, you'll find all kinds of officially presented government information. The first three menus look like the following, with the selected menu item once again boldfaced:

```
US and World Politics (Sunsite UNC)

1.  National Information Infrastructure Information/
2.  1992 US Presidential Campaign/
3.  Browse  White House Papers/
4.  Community_Idea_Net   proposals on how on-line databases can help l../
5.  Federal Information Resources/
6.  International Affairs/

Browse  White House Papers

1.  1993/
2.  1994/

1994
1.  Apr/
2.  Feb/
3.  Jan/
4.  Mar/
```

No matter how many online documents you might have been expecting, the following (truncated) list is almost certain to surprise. Also, remember, it's only for one month, March 1994:

```
Mar

1.  1994-02-28-President-Remarks-Welcoming-PM-John-Major-in-Pittsburgh.
2.  1994-02-28-Presidents-Public-Schedule.
3.  1994-02-28-Presidents-Remarks-in-Photo-OP-with-PM-John-Major.
4.  1994-03-01-Background-Economic-Briefing-on-4th-Quarter-GDP-and-Exp...
5.  1994-03-01-Briefing-on-Crime-Initiative-by-VP-Gore-and-AG-Reno.
6.  1994-03-01-President-Nominates-Chong-to-FCC.
7.  1994-03-01-President-Remarks-to-Dallas-Cowboys-Football-Team.
8.  1994-03-01-Presidents-Remarks-at-Wright-Junior-College-in-Chicago.
9.  1994-03-01-Presidents-Remarks-in-Photo-Op-with-House-Budget-Commit...
10. 1994-03-01-Presidents-Statement-on-Bosnian-Croat-Peace-Agreement.
150. 1994-03-25-President-Nominates-8-to-National-Council-on-Arts.
151. 1994-03-25-Presidents-Remarks-Upon-Departure-to-North-Carolina.
152. 1994-03-25-Proclamation-for-Greek-Independence-Day.
153. 1994-03-25-Statement-on-Public-Access-to-NSC-Records.
154. 1994-03-25-Statement-on-Subpoena-for-Staff-Secretary-Podesta.
155. 1994-03-28-Presidents-Statement-on-Tornado-Losses-in-the-South.
156. 1994-03-28-Statement-on-President-Conversation-with-PM-Hosokawa.
157. 1994-3-19-ABC-Childrens-Questions-with-the-President.
158. 1994-3-7-Presidents-Press-Conference-with-Chairman-Shevardnadze.
159. Presidents-Schedule-32294.
```

To get an idea of the sheer amount of information available from this one Gopher menu, the following is a short excerpt from item 157, the `ABC-Childrens-Questions-with-the-President`:

```
THE WHITE HOUSE

Office of the Press Secretary
_______________________________________________________________________
For Immediate Release                                    March 19, 1994


REMARKS BY THE PRESIDENT
IN ABC SPECIAL "ANSWERING CHILDREN'S QUESTIONS"


The East Room



11:30 A.M. EST


MR. JENNINGS:  Let's get right to it.  Kevin, how about
you?

Q  My first question is for those children who wish to
pursue a college education, what are you going to do to guarantee
that there are jobs for them when they get out of college? Today,
many adults have graduate degrees, bachelors — they have a hard time
finding jobs. They have as good a chance as those who are straight
out of high school. What are you going to do to guarantee that when
I get out of college, I have a job waiting for me?

THE PRESIDENT:  I don't know that I can guarantee it,
but I think we can make it more likely. But perhaps the main reason
I ran for president was to try to restore the economic health of the
country. And what I am trying to do is to follow policies that will
generate more jobs in America. I have tried to bring our deficit
down, get interest rates down, to create more jobs. I've tried to
open more markets to our products, and sell more American products
overseas. I've tried to train people to do the jobs of tomorrow, and
I've tried to take the technologies that we developed when we had a
big defense budget and turn them into jobs in the peacetime economy.
And in the last 13 months, since we had this meeting last, we created
over 2 million new jobs in this economy.

And let me also say, I know it's tough for college
graduates, but let me tell everyone of you one thing:  Your chances
of getting a good job are still much, much better if you first
graduate from high school, then get at least two years of further
training, and, finally, if you get a college degree. The unemployment
rate in America for college graduates is 3.5 percent. The
unemployment rate for high school dropouts is 11.5 percent.

MR. JENNINGS:  So the answer is, stay in school.

THE PRESIDENT:  So the answer is, even though it's
tougher than it has been for college graduates, you still have a much
better chance if you stay in school to have higher incomes and to
have a job.
```

Rather than read the rest at this point, why not just mail the entire file to yourself for perusing later? That's what I decided to do, as in the following:

```
Press <RETURN> to continue,
<m> to mail, <D> to download, <s> to save, or <p> to print:m

|-------------------------------------------------------------|
|                                                             |
|    Mail current document to: nrandall@watserv1.uwaterloo.ca |
|                                                             |
|-------------------------------------------------------------|
```

Task 20.3: Explore government information on the World Wide Web.

As with everything else on the Internet these days, the Web has begun to dominate the dissemination of governmental information. The Yahoo directory (`http://www.yahoo.com/`) shows well over 1500 entries under the Government heading, and Yahoo doesn't have all of them by any means. Still, we'll start there, because it's easy.

1. Using your Web browser, head for the Yahoo directory at **`http://www.yahoo.com/`**, and click on the Government hyperlink.
2. Click on the hyperlink named Legislative Branch, and then on the link called House of Representatives.
3. Click on U.S. House of Representatives. This will take you to `http://www.house.gov/`, the home page of the House, as seen in Figure 20.1.

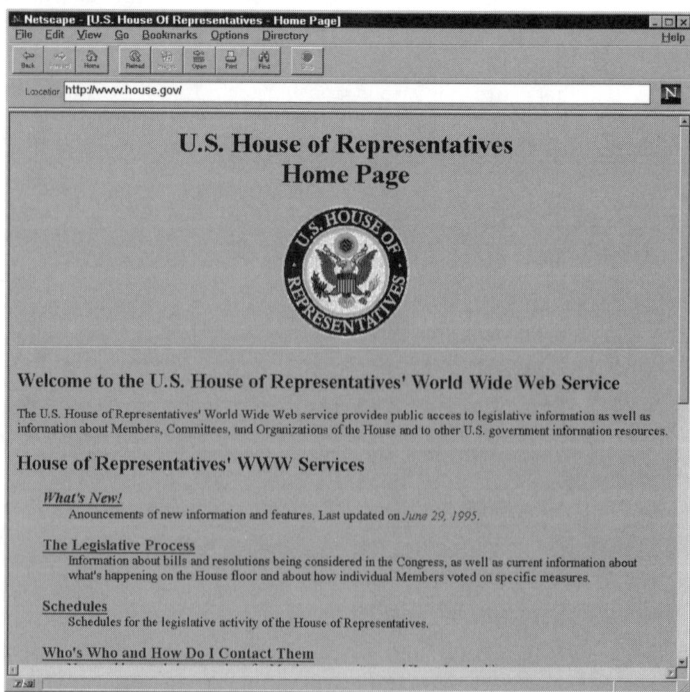

Figure 20.1.
The home page of the U.S. House of Representatives.

4. Click on What's New and tour around a bit. Then return to the home page and click on The Legislative Process. Here you'll find all kinds of useful information about activity in the House, including recent floor actions, recent bill introductions and texts, house votes and committee reports, and the complete Congressional Records. Once again, if you need this information in a hurry, or you're doing a project for business or school that requires it, this is a truly superb resource.
5. At the bottom of the page is a link called Tying it All Together. Click here to get an overview of how the legislative process works. While you're there, click on the hyperlink to the U.S. Constitution. This will take you to a full text of the Constitution, again for your research pleasure.
6. Go back to the home page and then click on Other Government Information Resources.
7. Click on the FedWorld link. This will take you to `http://www.fedworld.gov/`, the home page of the FedWorld Information Network (see Figure 20.2).

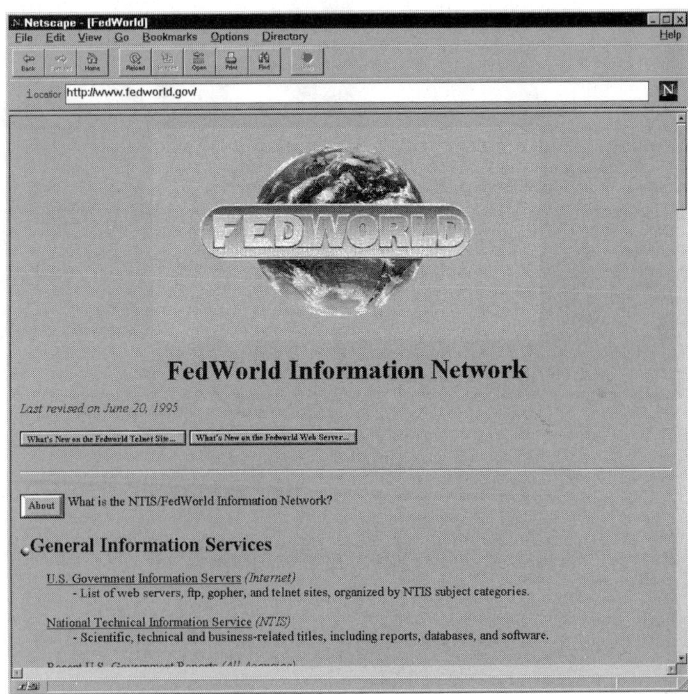

Figure 20.2.
Home page for FedWorld Information Network.

8. Click on the button labeled About. This will take you to a screen explaining what FedWorld is all about. The idea is this: the National Technical Information Service (NTIS) is working with government departments and agencies to get government information online. This makes sense, since most people have neither the desire nor

the know-how to get government info over the phone or in bookstores.

9. Go back to the FedWorld home page and click on U.S. Government Information Servers. Here, you'll see government information organized by subject. Click on Administration and Management to get an idea of what's happening. This is a long list of available information about all types of government organizations, ranging from the office of Senator Edward Kennedy to the C.I.A. Explore to your heart's content.
10. Go back to the Government Information Servers page and click on Agriculture and Food. Now click on the U.S. Department of Agriculture. This takes you to the screen shown in Figure 20.3, a well-organized Web from the USDA (`http://web.fie.com:80/web/fed/agr/`).

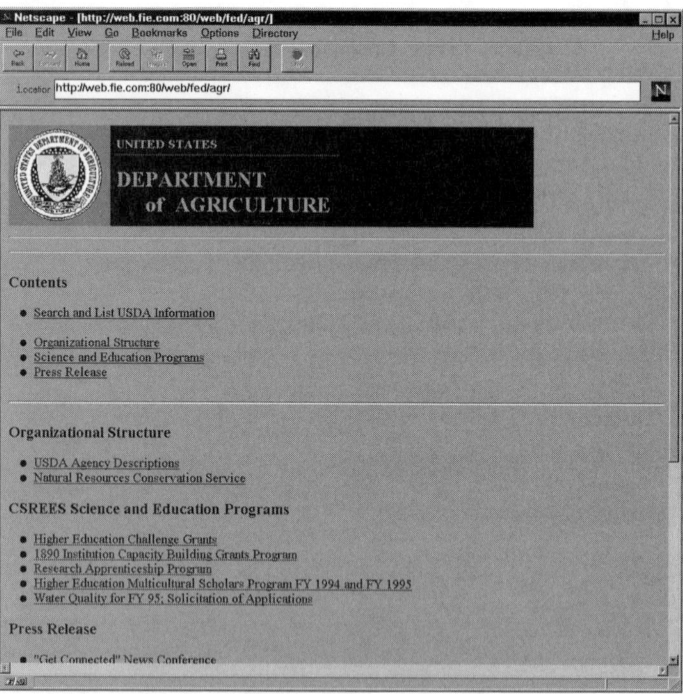

Figure 20.3.
The home page for the U.S. Department of Agriculture.

11. Return to the Yahoo page on Government. From here, click on Agencies. Explore for a while, choosing whatever agencies you'd like to see. You'll quickly realize that visiting them all would take days, and the information available is staggering. For now, click on Indian Health Service (IHS), and then click on Indian Health Service. This brings you to Figure 20.4, the Indian Health Service home page (`http://www.tucson.ihs.gov/`).

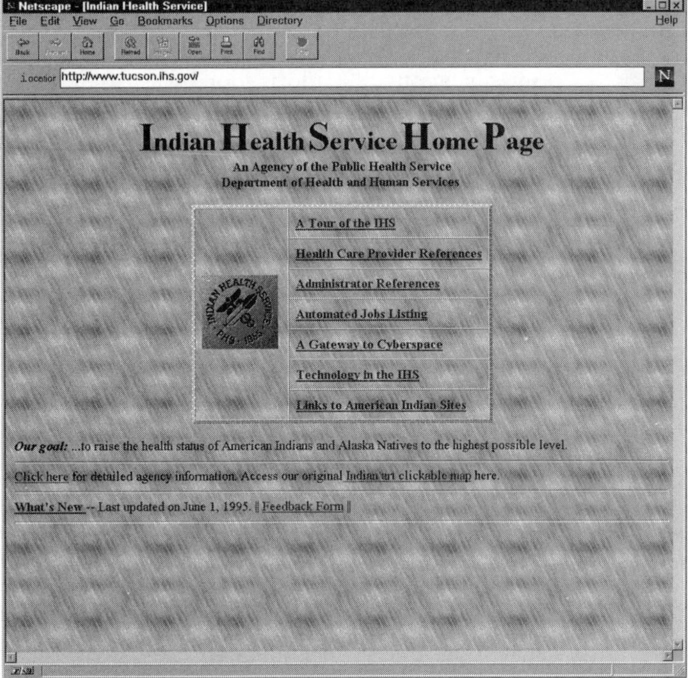

Figure 20.4.
The home page for the Indian Health Service, with advanced table design.

12. Start with the tour of this service, and then move around the site until you're familiar with its offerings. As an example, from the imagemap on the opening tour page, click on Navajo and then on Tuscon, to see the difference in information types.
13. Return to the Yahoo Government page and click on Countries. Here, you'll find roughly 200 links to governmental information in other nations. The most extensively developed is Canada, and it's well worth visiting, but click on New Zealand instead to discover their offerings.
14. From the subsequent page, click on New Zealand Government. This takes you to Figure 20.5, the home page for New Zealand government information on the Web.
15. Explore this site for a while, and then return to Yahoo and select other international government sites. One page worth seeing is the Canadian Information Explorer (nicely titled Champlain, after the 17th century explorer), which allows you to conduct searches of government info in that country. It can be found at `http://info.ic.gc.ca/champlain/champlain.html`.

The Web is filled with government information, particularly from the U.S. and Canada. Look for other nations to build their Internet presence as well, because making government information available this way makes a great deal of sense. You'll find yourself learning more about your government than you knew before, primarily because the information is easy to find and convenient to access.

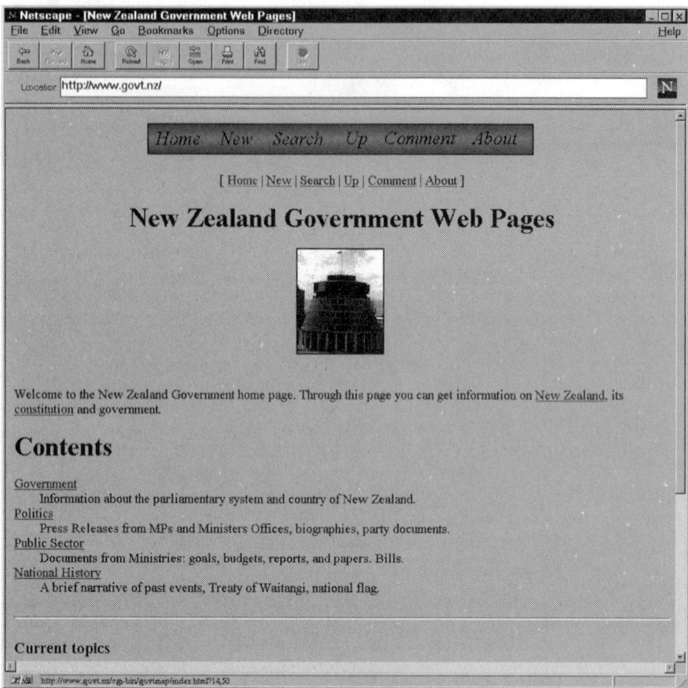

Figure 20.5.
New Zealand Government home page.

Legal Information on the Net

Legal information is also making its way to the Internet. Once again, this is an extremely valuable trend because most of us don't have the time or resources to find this information ourselves (and paying a lawyer cuts sharply into your online Internet hours). Here you'll take another brief tour of the Web, this time to get a bit of a handle on the legal information now being made available.

Task 20.4: Access Supreme Court decisions on the Web.

Supreme Court decisions in the U.S. and Canada are posted to the Internet very shortly after they're rendered. If you're following Supreme Court cases, or if you're curious to see what the Supreme Court does, you can use the World Wide Web to learn all you need to know. For everyone from law students to high school students, this information can be invaluable.

1. Using your Web browser, go to `http://www.law.cornell.edu/supct/`. This will yield Figure 20.6, the Cornell Legal Information Institute page on Supreme Court decisions in the U.S.

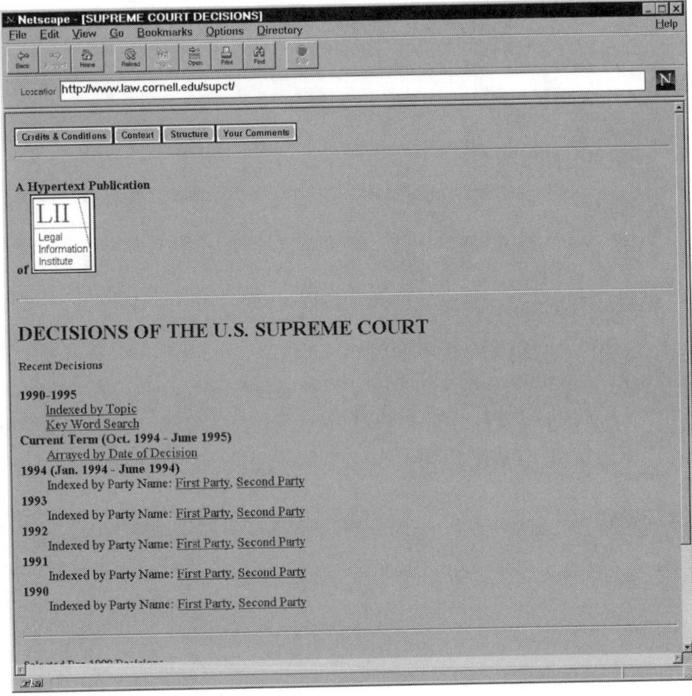

Figure 20.6.
Decisions of the Supreme Court Web page.

2. Click on the link named Indexed by Topic. Doing so gives you a subject-oriented listing of Supreme Court decisions rendered between 1990 and 1995. As an example, scroll to the D's and click on Death Penalty.
3. From the subsequent list, click on the *HARRIS vs. ALABAMA* case, Docket 93-7659. Click on the Syllabus link. This will take you directly to an FTP site and download the decision file. Following is a reproduction of the top portion of that file:

```
SUPREME COURT OF THE UNITED STATES

Syllabus

HARRIS v. ALABAMA
certiorari to the supreme court of alabama
No. 93-7659.   Argued December 5, 1994-Decided February 22, 1995

Alabama law vests capital sentencing authority in the trial judge, but
 requires the judge to "consider" an advisory jury verdict.  After
 convicting petitioner Harris of capital murder, the jury recommend-
 ed that she be imprisoned for life without parole, but the trial judge
```

```
 sentenced her to death upon concluding that the statutory aggravat-
 ing circumstance found and considered outweighed all of the miti-
 gating circumstances.  The Alabama Court of Criminal Appeals
 affirmed the conviction and sentence, rejecting Harris' argument
 that the capital sentencing statute is unconstitutional because it
 does not specify the weight the judge must give to the jury's recom-
 mendation and thus permits the arbitrary imposition of the death
 penalty.  The Alabama Supreme Court affirmed.
Held:  The Eighth Amendment does not require the State to define
 the weight the sentencing judge must give to an advisory jury
 verdict.  Pp. 4-11.
  (a)  Because the Constitution permits the trial judge, acting alone,
to impose a capital sentence, see, e.g., Spaziano v. Florida, 468
U. S. 447, 465, it is not offended when a State further requires the
judge to consider a jury recommendation and trusts the judge to
give it the proper weight.  Alabama's capital sentencing scheme is
much like Florida's, except that a Florida sentencing judge is re-
quired to give the jury's recommendations "great weight," see Tedder
v. State, 322 So. 2d 908, 910 (Fla.), while an Alabama judge is not.
```

4. Return to the Supreme Court Decision home page and scroll to the bottom. Here you'll find a link to the famous *Roe vs. Wade* abortion decision. Click on the link and you'll be taken to a hypertext version of the decision, as displayed in Figure 20.7.

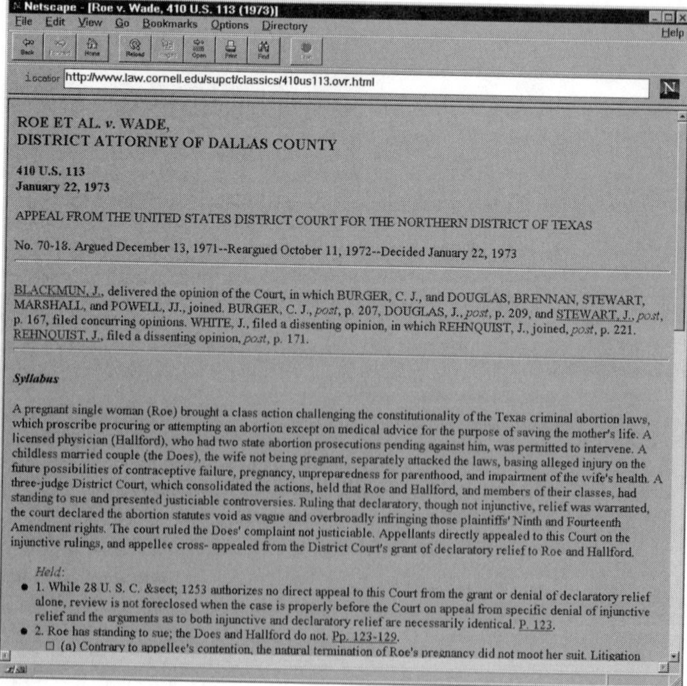

Netscape - [Roe v. Wade, 410 U.S. 113 (1973)]

Location: http://www.law.cornell.edu/supct/classics/410us113.ovr.html

ROE ET AL. *v.* WADE,
DISTRICT ATTORNEY OF DALLAS COUNTY

410 U.S. 113
January 22, 1973

APPEAL FROM THE UNITED STATES DISTRICT COURT FOR THE NORTHERN DISTRICT OF TEXAS

No. 70-18. Argued December 13, 1971--Reargued October 11, 1972--Decided January 22, 1973

BLACKMUN, J., delivered the opinion of the Court, in which BURGER, C. J., and DOUGLAS, BRENNAN, STEWART, MARSHALL, and POWELL, JJ., joined. BURGER, C. J., *post*, p. 207, DOUGLAS, J., *post*, p. 209, and STEWART, J., *post*, p. 167, filed concurring opinions. WHITE, J., filed a dissenting opinion, in which REHNQUIST, J., joined, *post*, p. 221. REHNQUIST, J., filed a dissenting opinion, *post*, p. 171.

Syllabus

A pregnant single woman (Roe) brought a class action challenging the constitutionality of the Texas criminal abortion laws, which proscribe procuring or attempting an abortion except on medical advice for the purpose of saving the mother's life. A licensed physician (Hallford), who had two state abortion prosecutions pending against him, was permitted to intervene. A childless married couple (the Does), the wife not being pregnant, separately attacked the laws, basing alleged injury on the future possibilities of contraceptive failure, pregnancy, unpreparedness for parenthood, and impairment of the wife's health. A three-judge District Court, which consolidated the actions, held that Roe and Hallford, and members of their classes, had standing to sue and presented justiciable controversies. Ruling that declaratory, though not injunctive, relief was warranted, the court declared the abortion statutes void as vague and overbroadly infringing those plaintiffs' Ninth and Fourteenth Amendment rights. The court ruled the Does' complaint not justiciable. Appellants directly appealed to this Court on the injunctive rulings, and appellee cross- appealed from the District Court's grant of declaratory relief to Roe and Hallford.

Held:

- 1. While 28 U. S. C. § 1253 authorizes no direct appeal to this Court from the grant or denial of declaratory relief alone, review is not foreclosed when the case is properly before the Court on appeal from specific denial of injunctive relief and the arguments as to both injunctive and declaratory relief are necessarily identical. P. 123.
- 2. Roe has standing to sue; the Does and Hallford do not. Pp. 123-129.
  - (a) Contrary to appellee's contention, the natural termination of Roe's pregnancy did not moot her suit. Litigation

Figure 20.7.
Hypertext version of the Roe vs. Wade *case of 1971.*

5. If you're interested in comparing the U.S. and Canadian Supreme Court decisions, try the Canadian Goverment pages at `http://info.ic.gc.ca/`.

Task 20.5: Learning of other U.S. legal matters.

The Supreme Court's decisions aren't the only legal resources available on the Internet. Far from it, in fact. In this excursion, you'll explore a small sampling of other material that's available, and from this sample, you can get an idea of where you might want to turn.

1. One of the best-maintained Internet sites for law-related material is Cornell Law School's Legal Information Institute. The LII keeps an active and growing Gopher, and they've developed a well-organized series of World Wide Web pages as well. Using your Web browser, go to the LII at **`http://www.law.cornell.edu/`**. You'll reach the screen shown in Figure 20.8.

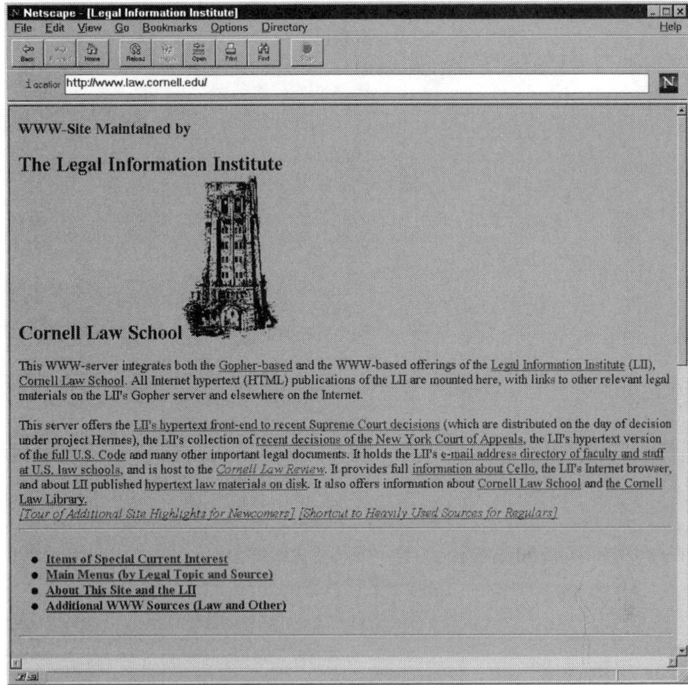

Figure 20.8.
The home page for Cornell's Legal Information Institute.

2. Scroll down the page to the link named Material Organized by Legal Topic and click. You'll see the list displayed in Figure 20.9.
3. Click on any one of these links to access the information available about that topic. This is an extremely rich source of legal information, and well worth visiting regularly. Be sure to click on the Items of Special Current Interest from the home page, to see what's making the news at the time.
4. Cornell isn't the only law school working to establish useful World Wide Web sites. In fact, the Yahoo pages list several hundred law schools on the Web, which makes the Net a good source of figuring out which law school to attend, as well as

where to obtain legal information. As shown in Figure 20.10, Indiana University's Schools of Law in Bloomington and Indianapolis have begun a service called LawTalk, featuring audio files explaining important legal issues.

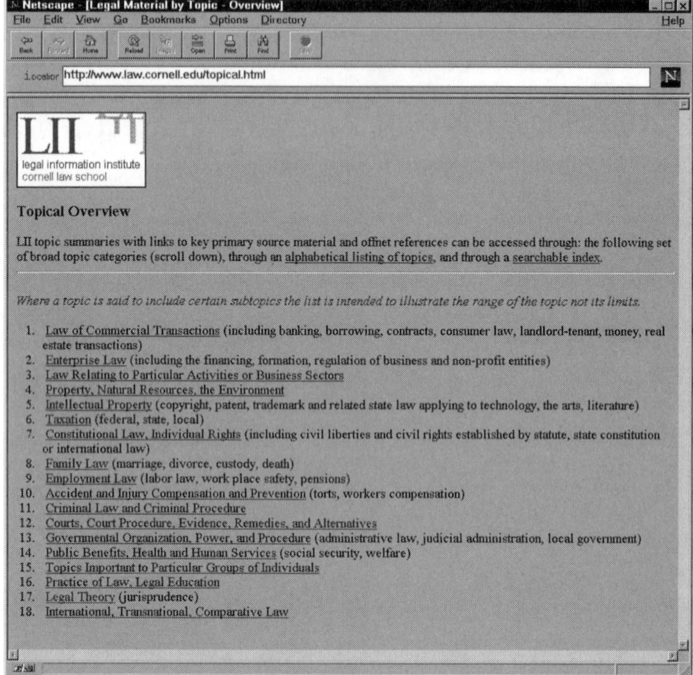

Figure 20.9. *The LII's list of available legal information by topic.*

As this home page states, all files are in .AU format (the past standard sound format for Internet audio files), and you'll need appropriate software and hardware for your computer to play them. At only a half-megabyte each, however, they're well worth downloading and hearing. Every one I've listened to is informative and well presented.

Although this excursion into legal resources could go on for days, you have to stop somewhere. Of particular interest to many Internet users is the role of the Federal Communications Commission in establishing the telecommunications regulations for the future of the information superhighway (of which the Internet is an integral part). Fortunately for us, the Indiana University School of Law at Bloomington, along with the Federal Communications Bar Association, have developed an online journal available on the World Wide Web. Entitled *Federal Communications Law Journal*, it promises to deal with a wide range of aspects regarding FCC practices and laws. Figure 20.11 shows the Web page for issue 1.

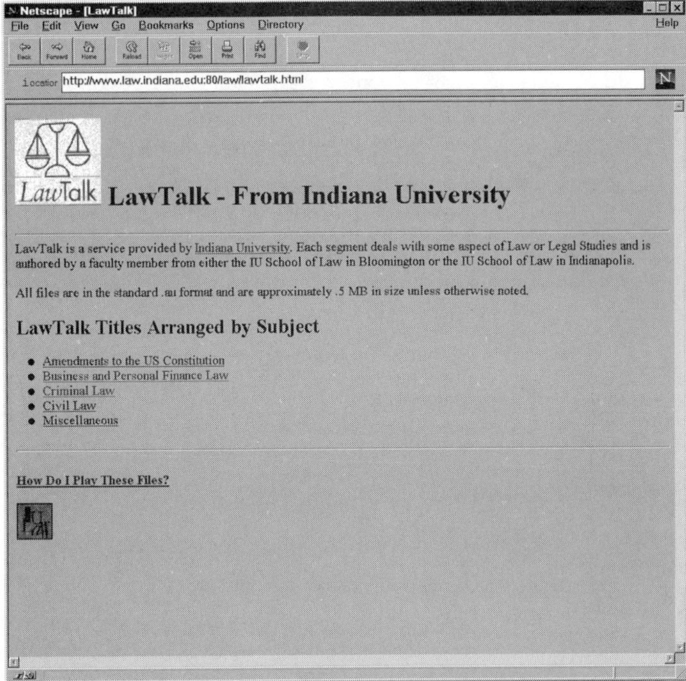

Figure 20.10.
Indiana University's LawTalk audio files.

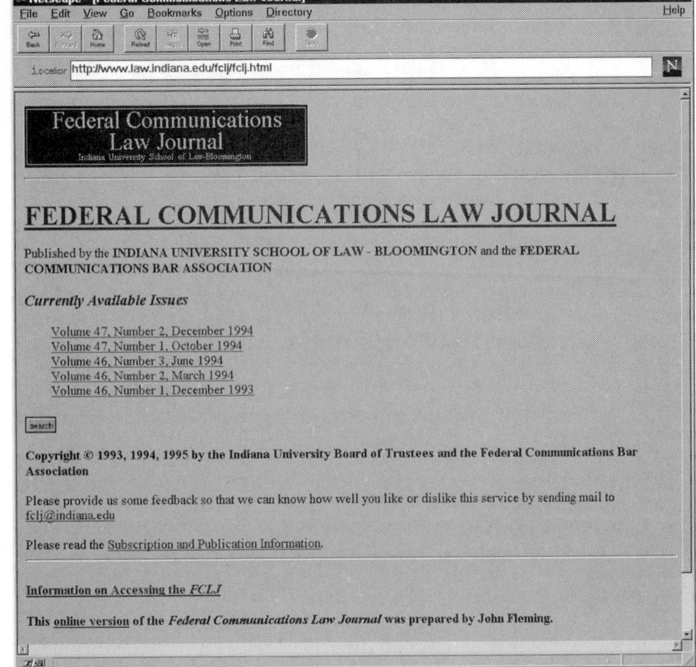

Figure 20.11.
Netscape screen showing Federal Communications Law Journal.

Summary

In this chapter, you've explored Internet resources on governments and courts. These topics are only two among a large and growing number of resources available for the researcher, the activist, or simply the concerned. The point of the chapter has been to demonstrate that there's a great deal of collaborative activity about the world's problems taking place on the Internet constantly, and to offer you a sense of where you might turn to get involved. The chapter demonstrates how the Internet can be an effective tool for educating yourself about today's crucial issues, and as such provides a virtual classroom that's arguably far better than any other form of distance education.

Task Review

In this chapter, you learned how to perform the following tasks:

- ☐ Explore U.S. government Gophers
- ☐ Examine the primary Gophers for accessing legal information
- ☐ Explore the growing number of law-related World Wide Web sites
- ☐ Find and read Supreme Court decisions
- ☐ Locate a wide range of other legal information

Q&A

Q Do state and municipal governments maintain Internet sites as well as the federal government?

A Not to the same degree, but many are starting, and some are quite far along. Of particular interest are new Gopher and Web sites developed by governments in Texas, North Carolina, and, in particular, California. New York State has some well-developed resources, as do a growing number of other states. Some municipalities are appearing online as well, with Palo Alto, California among the most interestingly presented. Often, however, community Internet access doesn't incorporate government issues, per se.

All these Gopher sites can be accessed through the University of Minnesota's main Gopher, which in turn, is almost always available as a menu item on your local Gopher. As for Web pages, keep watching the NCSA What's New Page (see Chapter 10 for details on how to access it); any interesting Web developments are noted here.

Q Will we ever see trials online?

A Who knows? Technologically, it's certainly possible, but what the legal aspects might be I really don't know. In all likelihood, any trial that can be televised could

also be done over the Net, and it's not hard to see what the benefits might be. A well-designed World Wide Web session or Gopher could include a wide range of background material, all of it accessible while you're watching the full-motion live video of the trial (live multimedia, in other words). More likely, for the time being, will be transcripts from trials, or perhaps even audio files, almost immediately downloadable. Questions of the legality of such accessibility still take precedence, however.

Q Will we ever be able to vote for our politicians this way?

A To be honest, I've never quite understood why there isn't a high-tech way of voting, even without the Internet. Every night of the week I can pick up my phone and punch in my favorite song of the day, and then have my vote tabulated with all the other listeners to determine the top 10 playlist for that evening. Why isn't this possible at election time, albeit under much more rigorous conditions?

Maybe the Internet can provide an answer. Election Gophers and Web pages could be an excellent source of background on the politicians, the issues, the platforms, and everything else that makes up a candidacy. On election day, using a variety of forms or automatic e-mail or what have you, we could cast votes, using a password drawn from our Social Security numbers. Given enough development, it could quite probably work, and it would likely solve the problem of low voter turnout. (Or maybe I'm completely missing something.)

Q Is a list of Internet government resources available on the Internet itself?

A Yes. Among the best anonymous FTP sites for such material is `una.hh.lib.umich.edu`, in the directory `inetdirsstacks`. Start with the file `government:gumprecht`, an excellent list compiled by Blake Gumprecht, Documents Librarian at Temple University. Several other excellent files are available here as well.

21

DAY 7

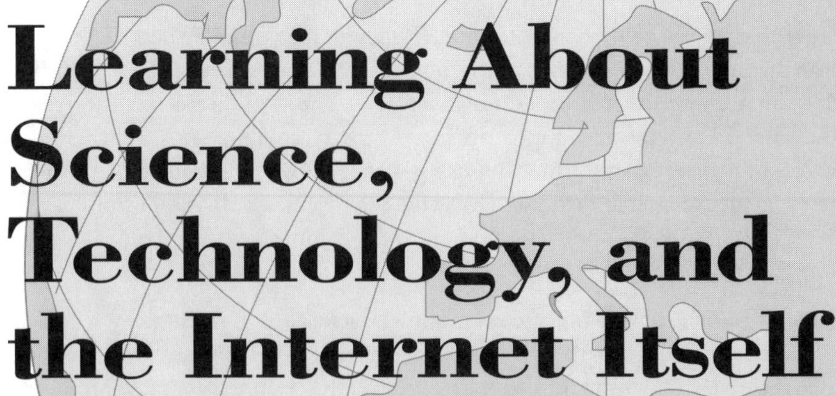

Learning About Science, Technology, and the Internet Itself

The Internet offers vast amounts of information about research projects in science and technology taking place around the globe. Furthermore, it contains a vast amount of material about the Internet itself, including guides for more productive uses of its resources. Most of the material has now gravitated to the World Wide Web, but there remains a considerable number of files and sites accessible through Gopher, FTP, and the newsgroups. This chapter examines a variety of science, technology, and Internet sites, and except for one special section, it concludes your journey through this book.

In this chapter, you will learn how to perform the following tasks:

- Use search tools to discover projects in science
- Use the World Wide Web to access these projects
- Examine projects taking place in locations around the world
- Explore projects in technology at various levels
- Access Internet guides and resources on the Net
- Use Gopher and the World Wide Web to learn about the Internet's Resources
- Join newsgroups dealing with Internet tools and issues
- Subscribe to mailing lists about the Internet and its tools
- Download Internet guides from FTP sites

Science, Technology, and the Internet on the Internet

It's hardly surprising that the scientists and technologists have established a commanding presence on the Internet. From its beginnings, the Net was oriented toward the scientific and computing communities, for two predominant reasons. The first was that scientific researchers saw the potential and the need for collaborative activity, something that only a wide area network could provide. Second, the computing specialists were needed to make the thing work and to conduct research into standards and enhancements. It wasn't until electronic mail became a fully workable application that research communities from other areas found the Internet useful.

Even knowing this, however, the sheer amount of science and technology information available for the diligent searcher is almost staggering. All the major disciplines are represented—physics, chemistry, biology, astronomy, artificial intelligence, computer interface design—and several more specialized sources are accessible as well. Gophers and FTP sites abound, and increasingly the world of science and technology research is being demonstrated and disseminated on the World Wide Web. Use of the Web is also easy to

understand. Multimedia is at the focus of contemporary computing (the computing perspective), and a greater need than ever exists for scientific research to be made publicly accessible (the scientific perspective). In fact, the Web began as a special project to allow scientists to exchange graphics-oriented material more easily.

What's also apparent is that the scientific and computing communities are leading Internet activity outside the U.S. and Canada as well. A quick look at the Web sites in Europe, Asia, Australia, the Middle East, and South America reveal that, by far, the majority of WWW activity in these places is tied to scientific research in the universities. It's no exaggeration to suggest that, just as science and technology drove the development of the Internet in the United States in the first place, so it is driving the adoption of the Net in the world's other leading research centers.

Note: The list of science and technology disciplines explored here is anything but complete or exhaustive, nor should this chapter be seen as anything beyond the smallest sampling of what's available. If I've omitted your favorite discipline or WWW site, it's because I had to stop somewhere. Trust me, I'm multi-disciplinary.

Starting Points

As you're well aware by now, the Internet has many, many starting points. For subject-oriented searches on the World Wide Web, turn to two of the best sources: the *EINet Galaxy* and the *WWW Virtual Library.* There's always Yahoo, of course, but by now, you should be getting quite tired of that truly excellent resource.

Task 21.1: Access the Science and Technology headings in the EINet Galaxy and the WWW Virtual Library.

To begin, take a look at the headings for science and technology information in two of the Web's most important meta-lists.

1. Enter the EINet Galaxy at **`http://www.einet.net/`**. Figure 21.1 shows a portion of the home page for the Galaxy. Clearly, this is an excellent place to start. Near the top of the screen you find Engineering and Technology issues, while at the bottom the subject list shows the Sciences. It's hard to go wrong from here.

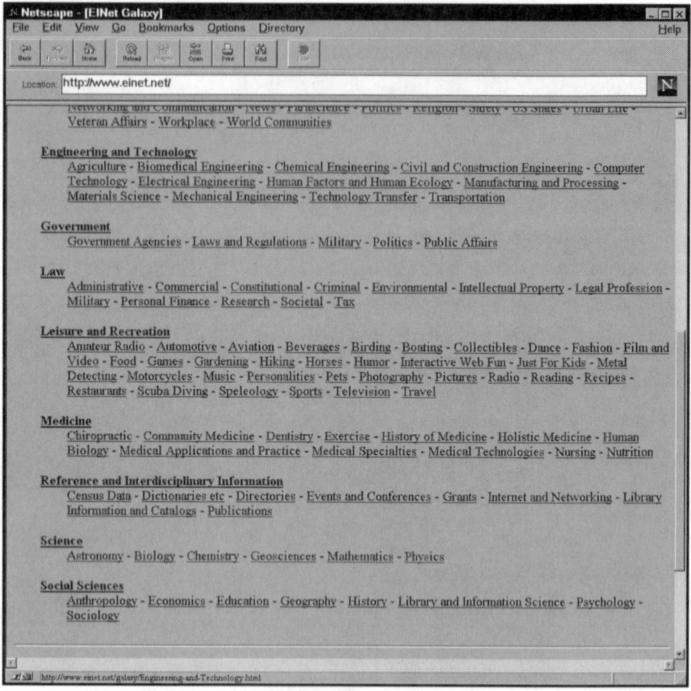

Figure 21.1.
The EINet Galaxy subject categories.

2. It's tempting to get started, but let's fire up the WWW Virtual Library first, and then work from both. If you're working with Netscape or (recent versions of) Mosaic, or some other newer browsers, you can have two browser windows going at the same time. In Netscape 1.1 or later, choose New from the File menu to launch a new window, and then switch between them as you would normally with your operating system (Alt+Tab in Windows, for example). In Mosaic for Windows (2.0beta4 or later), right-click the mouse anywhere in the document and select Spawn Mosaic from Current Page. In both cases, fill in the URL field with **`http://www.w3.org/hypertext/DataSources/bySubject/Overview.html`** to access the WWW Virtual Library. If your browser doesn't support multiple pages, go to this URL anyway, and bookmark them both for easy access.

The Library offers a subject list that is a little less conveniently designed than EINet's, but it's still extremely useful. Shown here are categories such as Astronomy, the Bio Sciences, and Chemistry; the others we need can be found by scrolling down the screen.

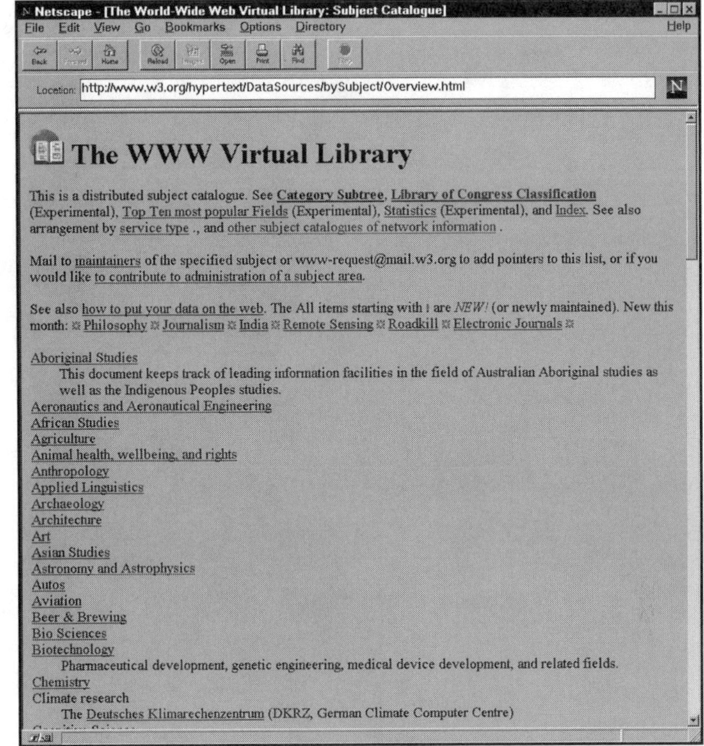

Figure 21.2.
The WWW Virtual Library subject list.

Task 21.2: Explore several astronomy pages on the Web.

Astronomy is particularly well served on the World Wide Web. In all likelihood, the reason is that astronomy lends itself well to presentation by graphics. Most of us are interested in seeing what's out there among the stars.

1. Clicking on the Astronomy link in the EINet Galaxy gives you several useful links, but the Virtual Library is more useful still. As a result, click on the Astronomy and Astrophysics link from the Library home page, to take you to AstroWeb, whose home page is shown in Figure 21.3. This is an immensely useful resource, well-organized and endlessly browsable.

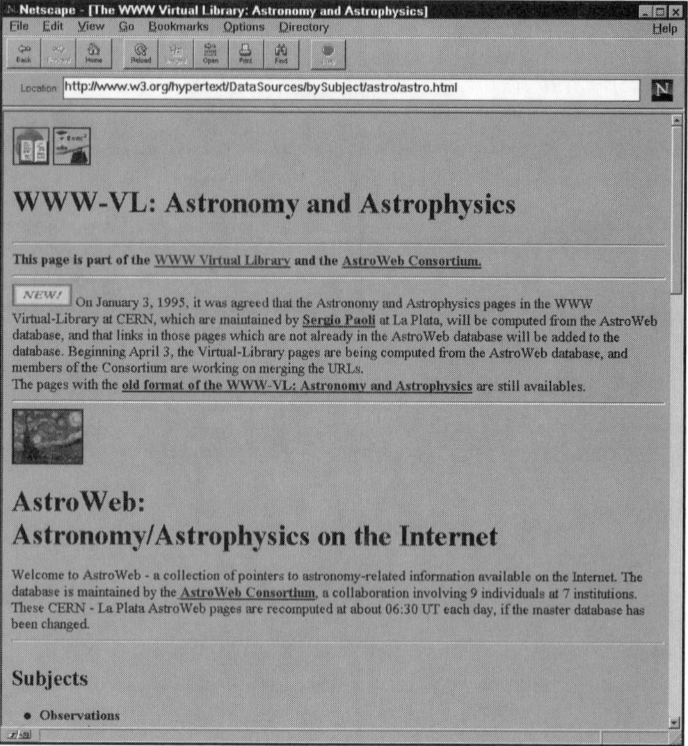

Figure 21.3.
The home page of AstroWeb from the Virtual Library.

2. There's way too much to visit here (unless you have unlimited time and Internet funding), so head for a favorite item, Space Agencies. Scroll down the page to the NASA Online Information Link; this will yield the screen shown in Figure 21.4.

   As you might expect, NASA's World Wide Web involvement is exemplary. Figure 21.4 shows the agency's fully-developed Online Information page, complete with hyperlinks to the various NASA centers and to Gopher and FTP sites as well.

   Obviously, you could spend hour upon hour searching through all this information, but just take a sampling, because you have many more sites to explore.

3. The temptation is to start with the Kennedy Space Center (if only because it's drawn most of the glory over the years), but this is an examination of research into astronomy, so give the Langley Research Center a try (`http://www.larc.nasa.gov/larc.cgi`). (See Figure 21.5.)

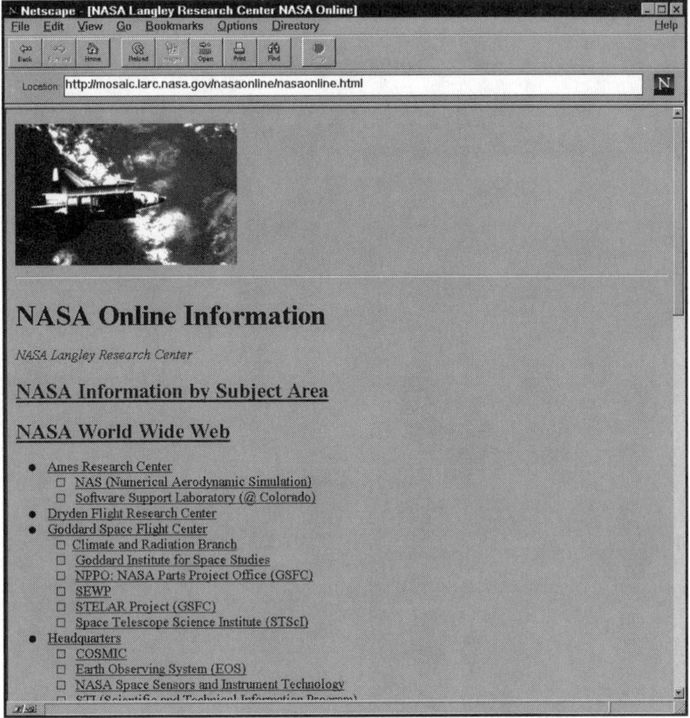

Figure 21.4.
The Online Information page from NASA, with links to several sites.

4. Where this page becomes especially useful from a research standpoint is the link named Langley Projects, Teams, and Initiatives On-Line. This link leads to a page with a long list of links to various projects, one of which is the CERES Project. The CERES Project home page contains a link to movies and audio clips about this project, as shown in Figure 21.6.

   Imagine yourself doing a project about CERES or any related space-oriented project, as a business researcher, a teacher, or a student. The amount of material at your disposal from this site alone is astounding, and this is one of many, many NASA sites. This kind of available detail continues to astonish me, no matter how many times I fire up my Web browser; from my standpoint, it's what the Net is all about.

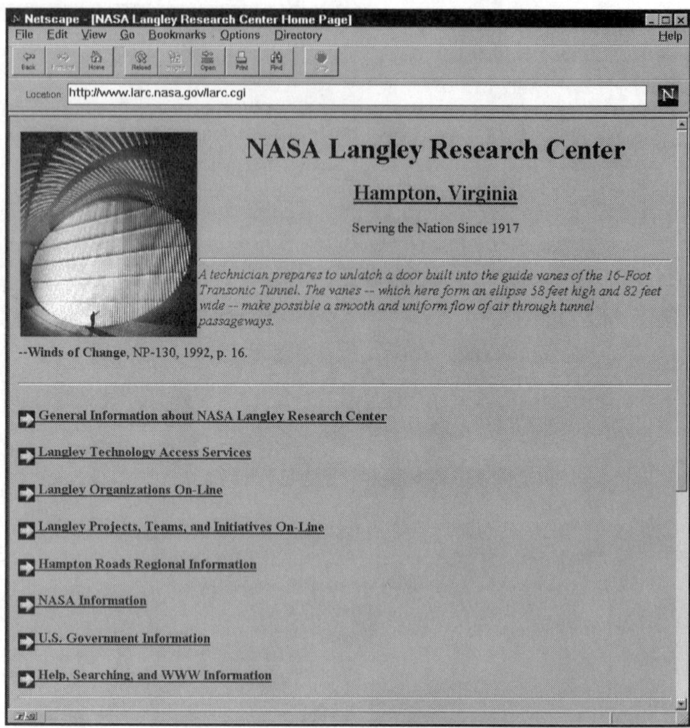

Figure 21.5.
The Langley Research Center's home page.

5. Your look at NASA's resources came nowhere near to starting, let alone finishing, but more research beckons. This time, it's the European Space Information System, accessible once again through the AstroWeb page shown in Figure 21.3.

   Enter the ESIS home page at **`http://www.esrin.esa.it/htdocs/esis/esis.html`**. From here, click on the link labeled ESIS for Astronomers, and from there click on the link called A Walk Through ESIS. This takes you to the page (`http://www.esrin.esa.it/htdocs/esis/demo/session.html`) shown in Figure 21.7.

Figure 21.6.
The movies and audio clips page from the CERES project site.

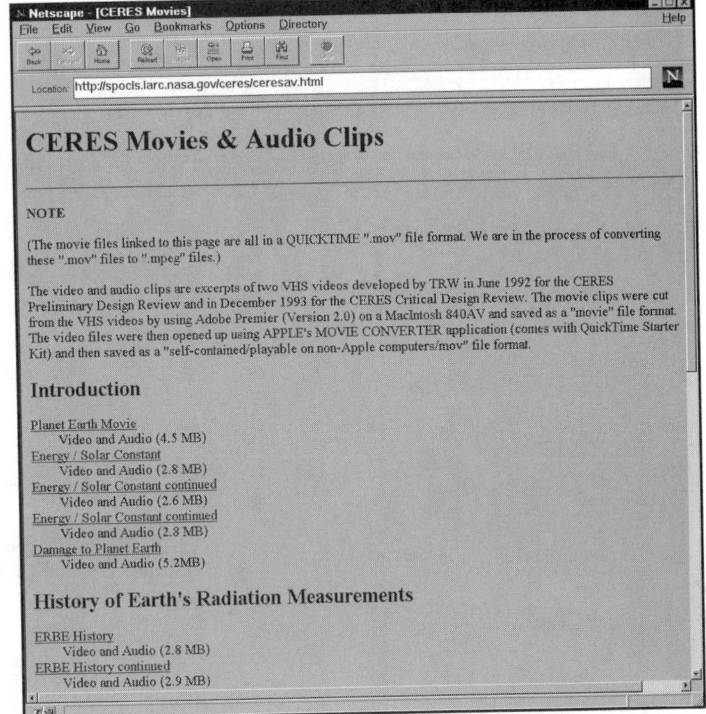

6. Actually, this is only a demo of the full ESIS interface system, but it's well worth taking a look at. Click on the Imaging button, which takes you to the colorful screen shown in Figure 21.8.

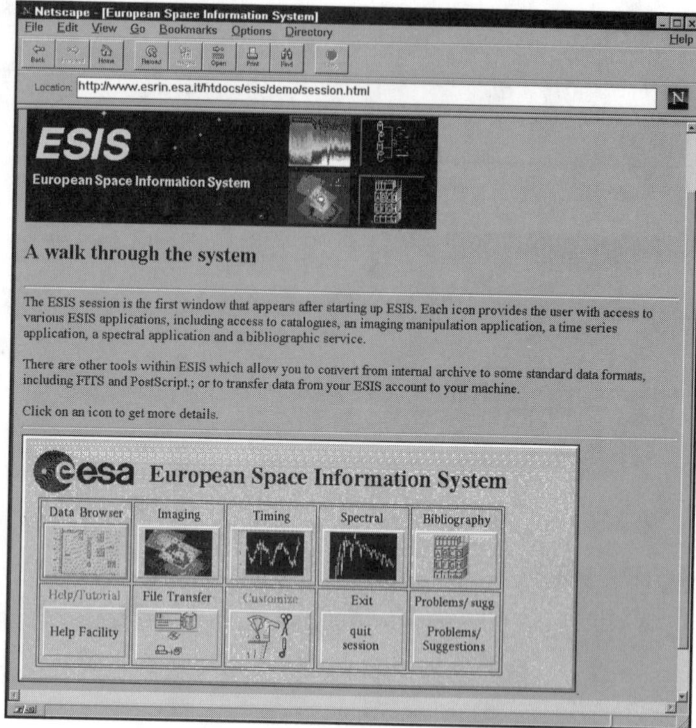

Figure 21.7.
The European Space Information System's colorful Walkthrough page.

Figure 21.8.
The imaging database main page from ESIS.

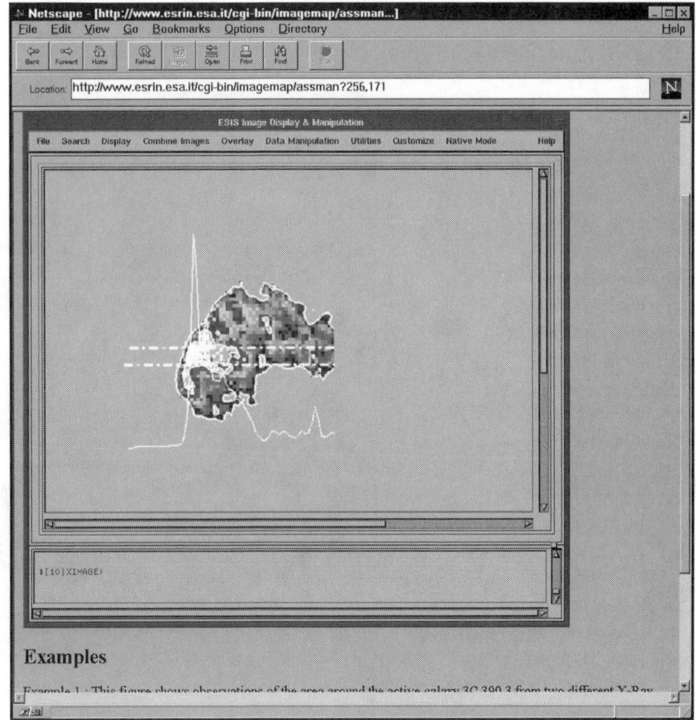

21

7. Now, scroll down the page to `Example #2`. Click here to reveal Figure 21.9, a fascinating graphic of the Andromeda Galaxy.

Figure 21.9.
The ESIS Imaging Database—one pictorial example.

Obviously, there's much, much more to the world of astronomy on the Net. Return to AstroWeb and try the Telescopes link, for example, to see how much we've bypassed. If you want to explore just one more site before going on, try the Space Telescope Electronic Information Service at `http://www.stsci.edu/`. It's superb. But there's much more science out there, so let's take a look.

Task 21.3: Explore Biology resources on the Web.

To begin your search for biology projects, turn to the EINet Galaxy. Return to the Galaxy (`http://www.einet.net/`), and click on the Biology link in the Science category. From here, you'll find links to a wide variety of Biology items, and you'll examine a select few here.

One of the most interesting science sites on the Web, especially from an educational standpoint, is the *Frog Dissection Kit.* This site not only shows how interactive the Web can be at this stage, but also how it might solve some of the problems associated with the science classroom. And it's tons of fun.

1. Enter the Frog Dissection information page at **`http://george.lbl.gov:80/ITG.hm.pg.docs/dissect/info.html`**.
2. Click on the link labeled Start Interactive program. This will take you to `http://george.lbl.gov:80/ITG.hm.pg.docs/dissect/dissect.html`, shown in Figure 21.10.

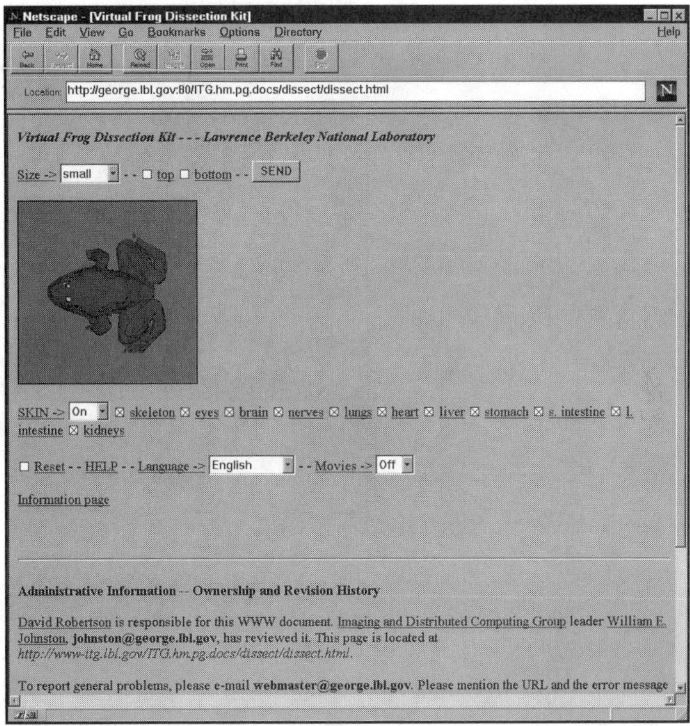

Figure 21.10.
The starting page for the Interactive Frog Dissection Kit.

3. Now enlarge the frog. Select Normal from the Size box, and click on Send. Your frog will increase in size (and download time as well). Basically, this is how to maneuver through the site; select and click on Send.
4. This time, examine the frog without its skin and with only its skeleton, brain, and large intestine showing (for no apparent reason). In the Skin box, select Off. Then get rid of the `x` beside every organ except skeleton, brain, and large intestine. Click Send to continue. You'll see the screen shown in Figure 21.11.

If you want, you can try the movie option. Many MPEG video clips are available, and as long as you're willing to wait for them to download, you'll find them useful. Whatever the case, the fact is that this site is clever and enjoyable, and that the Web could obviously be used for a variety of similar educational efforts.

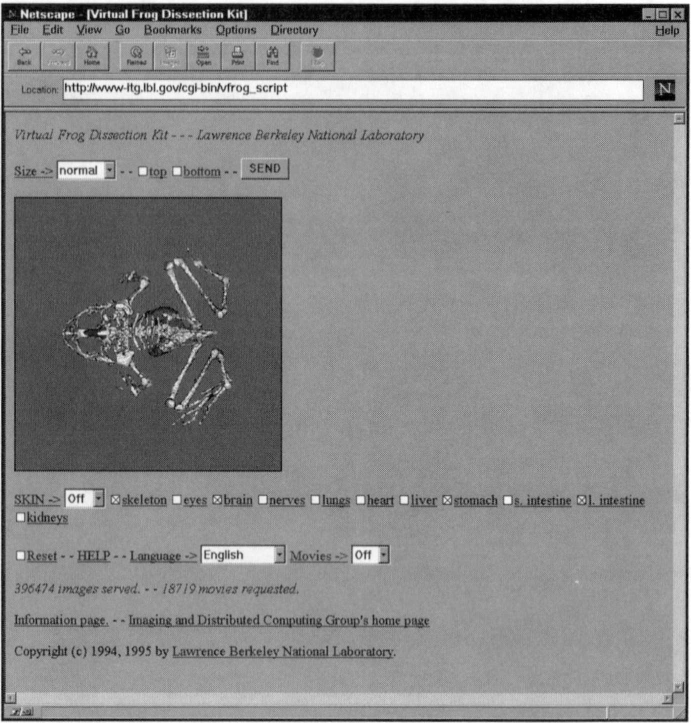

Figure 21.11.
The frog in a partial stage of dissection.

Now it's off to Australia, where the Australian National University maintains an extremely useful Bioinformatics home page. Figure 21.12 displays this page (`http: //life.anu.edu.au/`), which offers several enticing links.

From this page, it's easy to see where further searches might lead you, but in fact, it's deceptive. As Figure 21.13 shows, clicking on a topic as open-ended as molecular biology from the ANU home page brings up a page (`http://life.anu.edu.au/molbio.html`) with a significant number of additional choices.

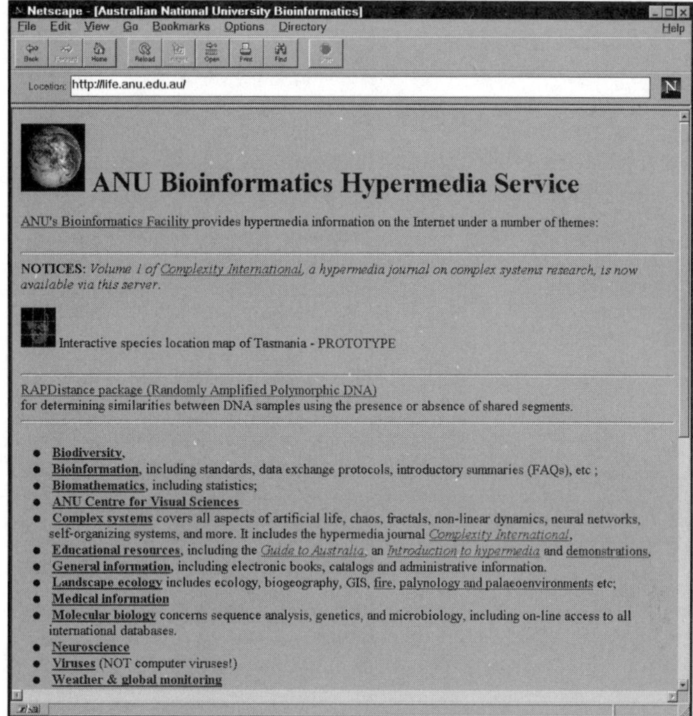

Figure 21.12.
The Australian National University: Bioinformatics home page.

Note: As you've discovered by now, this is one of the charms and the frustrations of the World Wide Web—even more, perhaps, than Gopher. Just when you think you have a handle on things, you click and encounter another array of selections. It can be overwhelming at times, especially if you're not searching for one specific item.

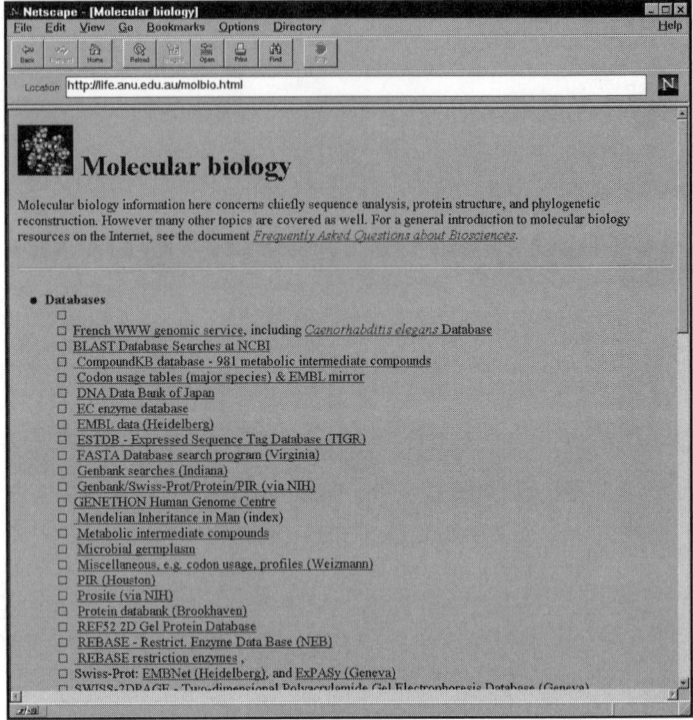

Figure 21.13.
The ANU: Molecular biology resources page.

From here, you could perform searches for the information you needed. Of course, because you're just discovering all the possibilities, you don't really need those data. The point, as with astronomy, has become very clear that there's a great deal of information for biologists to be found on the Web as well. There's more, however, as the home pages clearly show, found in Gopher sites in all parts of the Internet world.

End of biology. Time for chemistry. This is beginning to seem like a really fast survey course.

Task 21.4: Examine chemistry projects on the World Wide Web.

1. Return to the Virtual Library and click on the Chemistry link. Once again, a quick look reveals more resources than you can possibly visit. Unlike the Biology sources, however, the screen in Figure 21.14 shows primarily World Wide Web sites (`http://www.chem.ucla.edu/chempointers.html`). For your purposes, that means a wealth of graphically rich information.

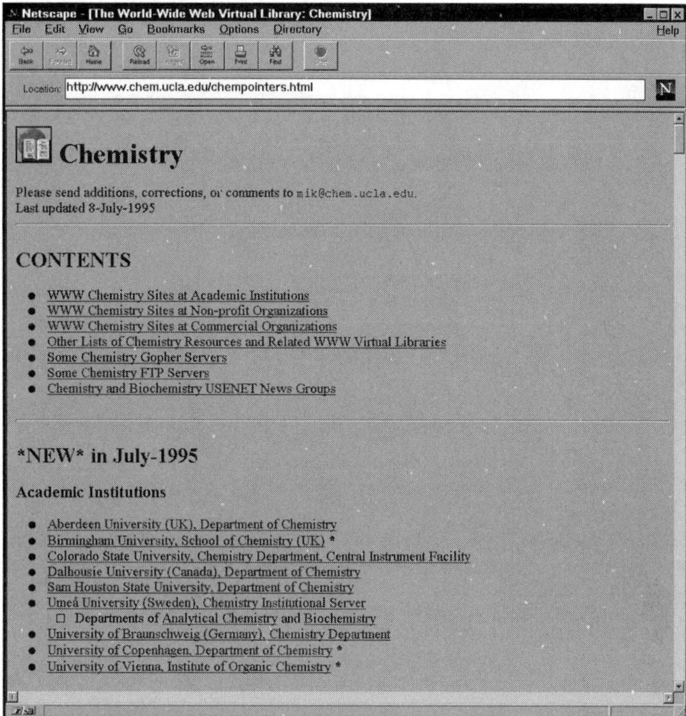

Figure 21.14.
WWW Virtual Library: chemistry-related sites.

Tip: If you're trying to determine from within Mosaic or Netscape whether the site is a WWW or Gopher server, position the cursor over an item and glance at the status bar at the bottom of the screen. If the location begins with `gopher://`, it's a Gopher site; `http://`, a WWW site. You might also see `ftp://`, `telnet://`, and `WAIS://`, which point to these types of sites.

2. A quick scan through this list shows several items from Europe, including some from the U.K. So, from France at the end of your biology excursion, it's off to the U.K. for a look at chemistry-related activities. Scroll down the page and click on the Imperial College of Science and Technology.

   The home page for the Department of Chemistry at Imperial College in London (`http://www.ch.ic.ac.uk/`) shows a tendency among European home pages toward graphics domination, as opposed to a more hypertext or simply list appearance of many North American pages (see Figure 21.15).

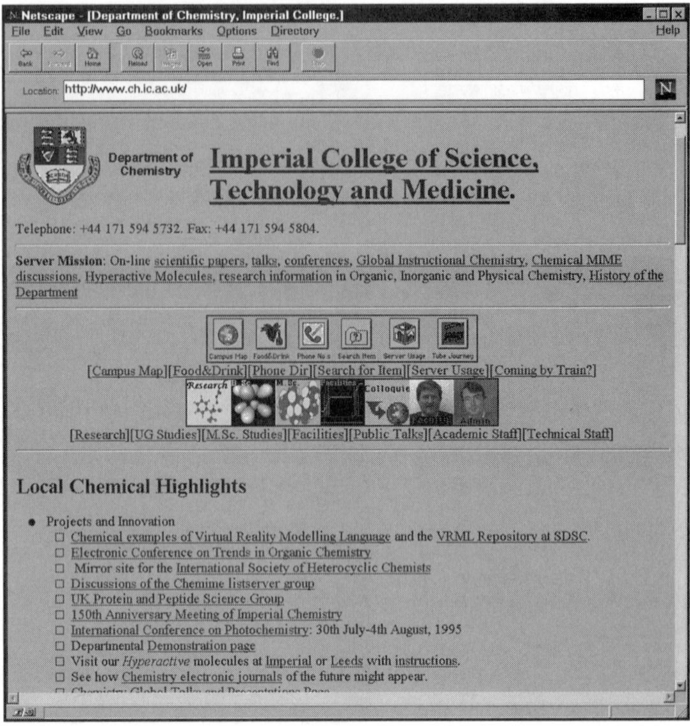

Figure 21.15.
Imperial College, Department of Chemistry home page.

3. Click on the link labeled Research Information. You'll see the nicely designed screen shown in Figure 21.16, which offers a graphic of the researchers within the department from which you can get information about ongoing research.

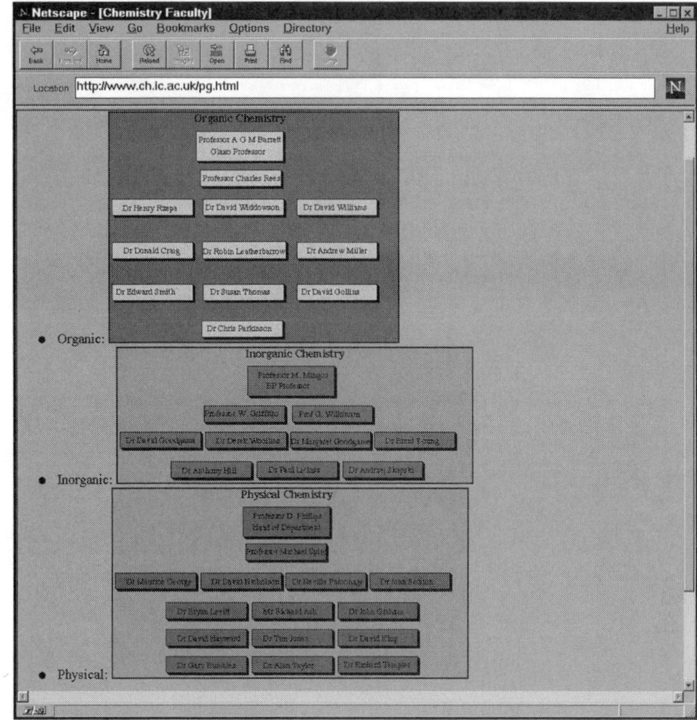

Figure 21.16.
Imperial College: a list of researchers in Organic Chemistry.

4. Another U.K. site, the University of Sheffield, offers a feature called WebElements (`http:// www.shef.ac.uk.uni/academic/A-C/chem/web-elements/web-elements-home.html`) (see Figure 21.17).

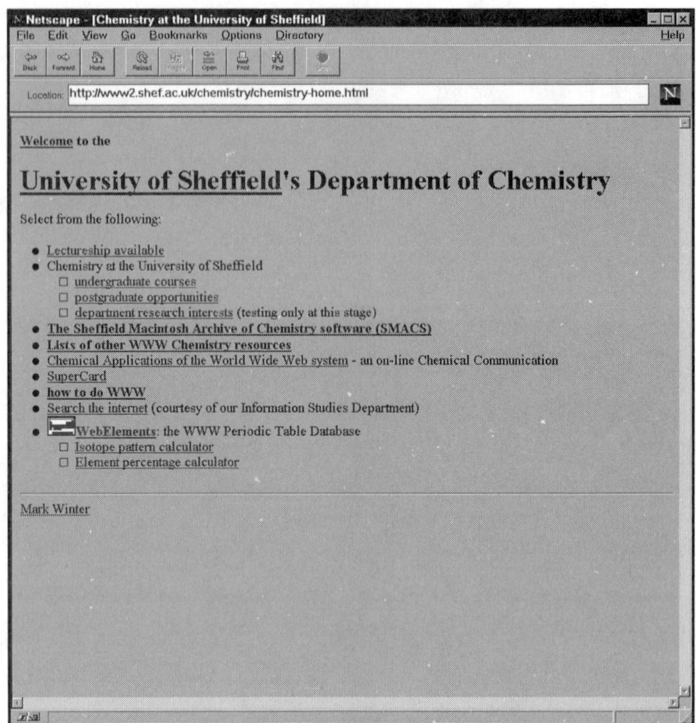

Figure 21.17.
University of Sheffield, Department of Chemistry home page.

5. Clicking on the WebElements Home Page item offers a Periodic Table Database, an Isotope Pattern Calculator, and an Element Percentage Calculator. Click on the WebElements link to reveal the periodic table of the elements shown in Figure 21.18.

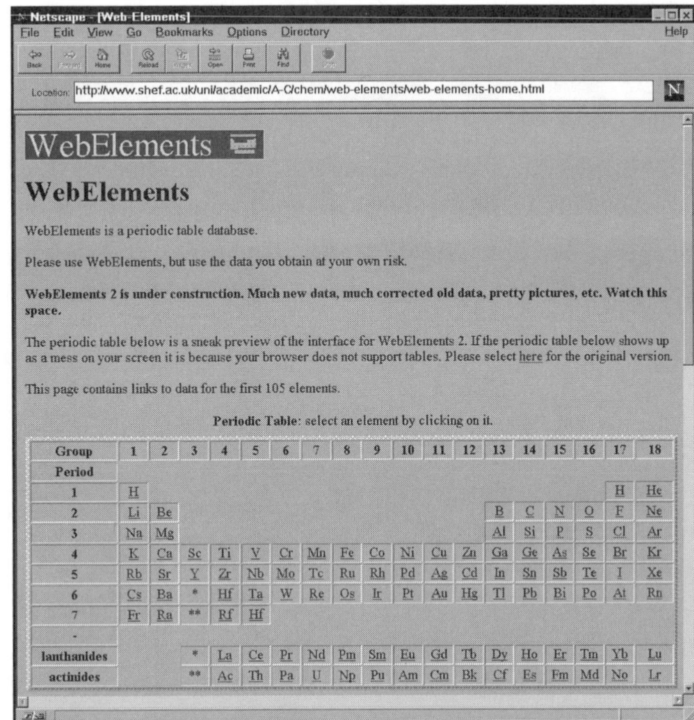

Figure 21.18.
The webElements periodic table database.

6. Now for the fun part. Choose a favorite element, click on it, and get a wealth of information. I've always been partial to sodium (it has to do with an old potato chip obsession), and clicking on `Na` yields the data.

Task 21.5: Use the Web to explore topics in Physics.

At some point in your exploration of science sites on the Web, you really have no choice but to check out what's available in Physics. Why? Because the Web was originally designed for physicists, so they deserve a special place in our Internet-filled hearts. Here are a few sites, but there are a great many more should you wish to browse further.

1. You're back to the WWW Virtual Library, and this time, into the separate list entitled Physics. Figure 21.19 shows part of the resulting page (`http://info.cern.ch/hypertext/DataSources/bySubject/Physics/Overview.html`), with several tempting sites to explore.

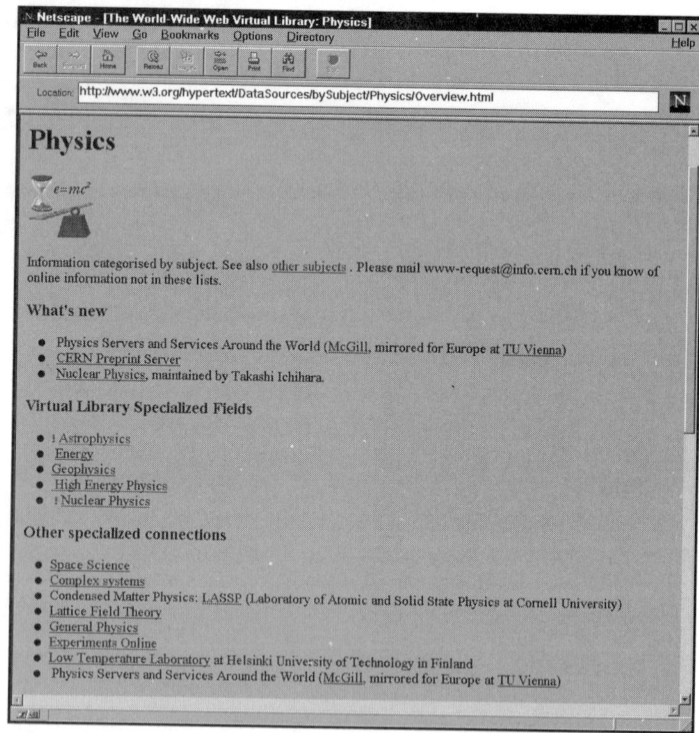

Figure 21.19.
WWW Virtual Library Physics page showing Specialized Fields section.

2. To be completely fair to the World Wide Web itself, which was founded to provide a medium of exchange for researchers in high energy physics, click on the link of that name near the top of the page. This will bring you to a page of an entire list of acronyms of HEP organizations.
3. Once again, to be fair to the Web, click on CERN. This takes you to the home page of the Web's birthplace, the European Laboratory for Particle Physics. Its home page, at `http://www.cern.ch:so/`, is shown in Figure 21.20.

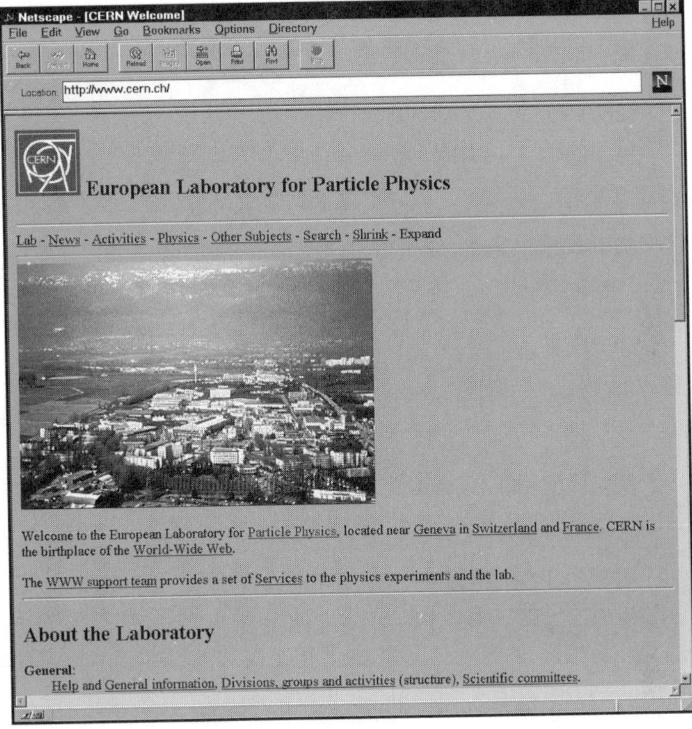

Figure 21.20.
Home page of the European Laboratory for Particle Physics (CERN).

4. Scroll down the page to the Activities section, and then click on the Research and Development link. This takes you to a page of links to research projects for CERN's latest accelerator team. Click on EAST, and then on Physics Simulation, to see what this project entails.
5. You haven't been to Germany yet, so why not now? From the University of Freiburg comes information about the OPAL experiment, as shown in the home page in Figure 21.21 (`http://hpfrs6.physik.uni-freiburg.de/opal/opal_allgemein.html`).

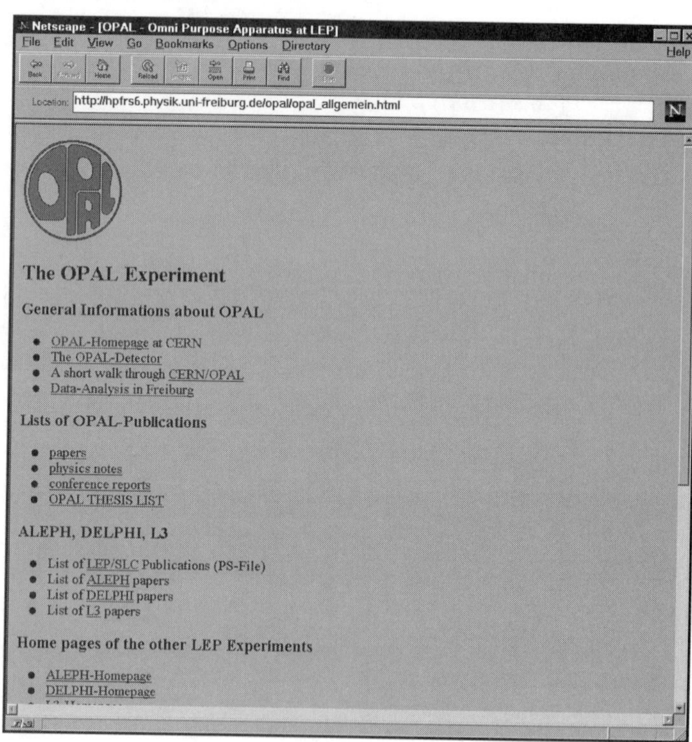

Figure 21.21.
Germany: The OPAL Experiment home page.

Clicking on The OPAL-Detector item yields Figure 21.22, an extremely well-designed WWW page with accessible explanatory text supplemented by inline graphics. From here, you can learn the basis of the OPAL project, as well as a list of the 24 institutions collaborating with Freiburg. This is clearly an impressive project and one well-articulated on the Net.

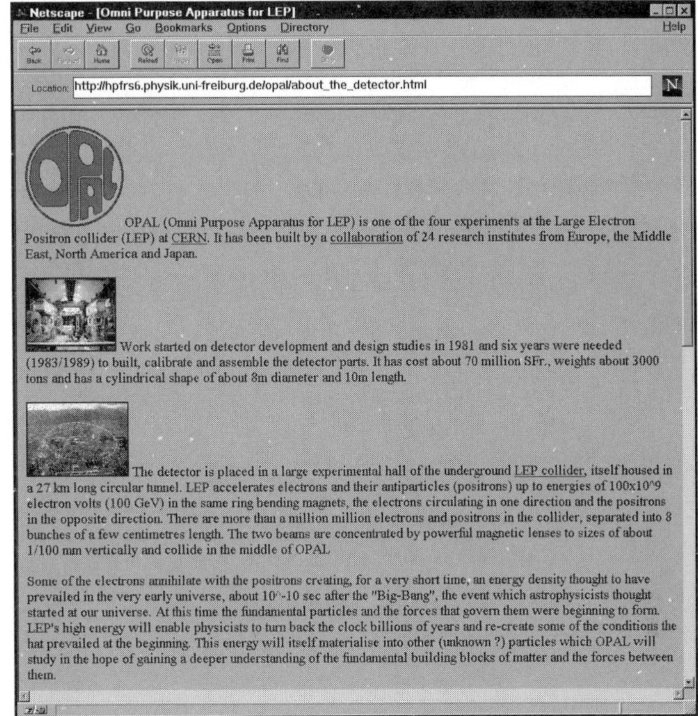

Figure 21.22.
Details about the OPAL project at Freiburg.

Task 21.6: Access science projects through Gopher.

The World Wide Web is not, of course, the only way to get information about projects and archives in the world of science. In fact, it's not even the primary method. Most of the information resides, first and foremost, in FTP and Gopher sites.

Note: As always, many of the Gopher sites offer links to FTP sites. In most cases, you can FTP directly to the site if you prefer using FTP software. As you've seen throughout this book, however, FTPing through Gopher or WWW is significantly easier, as is finding the site itself.

1. Rather than starting at Gopher Jewels, start at the well-constructed Gopher at the University of Illinois at Chicago (`gopher.uic.edu`). You first see the introductory menu, which follows:

```
1.     Gopher at UIC/ADN/
2.     What's New (1 Mar 1994).
3.     Search the UIC Campus and Beyond/
4.     The Administrator/
5.     The Campus/
6.     The Classroom/
7.     The Community/
8.     The Computer/
9.     The Library/
10.    The Researcher/
11.    The World/
```

2. This list has several items of interest, but for the purposes of this task, access item `10`, `The Researcher`. The result is the following menu:

```
The Researcher
1.     About The Researcher Menu.
2.     UIC Office of the Vice Chancellor for Research/
3.     Grants and Opportunities/
4.     Veronica: Netwide Gopher Menu Search/
5.     Aerospace/
6.     Agriculture and Forestry/
7.     Anthropology and Culture/
8.     Arts/
9.     Astronomy and Astrophysics/
10.    Biology/
11.    Chemistry/
12.    Computing and Computer Networks/
13.    Economics/
14.    Education/
15.    Environment and Ecology/
16.    Geography/
17.    Geology and Geophysics/
18.    Government, Political Science and Law/
19.    History/
20.    Language and Linguistics/
21.    Library and Information Science/
22.    Literature, Electronic Books and Journals/
23.    Mathematics/
24.    Medicine and Health/
25.    News and Journalism/
26.    Oceanography/
27.    Paleontology/
28.    Physics/
29.    Reference/
30.    Religion and Philosophy/
31.    Sociology and Psychology/
32.    Weather, Climate and Meteorology/
```

3. There is a lot to choose from, and there are several scientific disciplines. Revisit Biology to see if the resources here are as strong as those on the Web. As the next menu shows, they are as follows:

```
1.     About this directory.
2.     *= Global Biological Information Servers by Topic =*/
3.     *= Grant Abstracts Searching: NSF, NIH, DOE and USDA =*/
4.     *= Search BOING (Bio Oriented INternet Gophers) =* <?>
5.     A Biologist's Guide to the Internet/
6.     A Caenorhabditis elegans Database (ACEDB) <?>
7.     AAtDB, An Arabidopsis thaliana Database <?>
8.     ACEDB BioSci Electronic Conference <?>
9.     ACEDB, A Caenorhabditis elegans Database (1-21) <?>
10.    APIS/
11.    ATCC - The American Type Culture Collection/
12.    About Genbank.
13.    About LiMB.
14.    About Multiple Database Search.
15.    About PIR.
16.    About PROSITE.
17.    About Protein Data Bank (PDB).
18.    About SWISS-PROT.
19.    About Transcription Factor Database (TFD).
20.    American Physiological Society/
21.    Arabidopsis/
22.    Arabidopsis Research Companion, Mass Gen Hospital/Harvard/
23.    Archive of BIOSCI mailing lists and newsgroups <?>
24.    Artificial Intelligence in Systematic Biology, 1990.
25.    Association of Systematics Collections/
26.    Australian Herbaria Specimen Data Standards/
27.    Australian National Botanic Gardens (ANBG)/
28.    Australian National University Bioinformatics/
29.    BIOSCI/bionet biology newsgroups server/
30.    Base de Dados Tropical (Tropical Data Base), Campinas, Brasil/
31.    Baylor College of Medicine Genome Center/
32.    Beanbag/
33.    BioBit Archive, Oxford/
34.    BioInformatics gopher server: Weizmann Institute of Science, Israel../
35.    BioMOO, the biologists' virtual meeting place <TEL>
36.    BioSci Arabidopsis Genome Electronic Conference Archive <?>
37.    BioSci Archive, IntelliGenetics/
38.    BioSci and Other Electronic Publications/
39.    BioSci documents <?>
40.    Biodatabases from SERC Daresbury UK FTP Archive/
41.    Biodiversity Resources/
42.    Biodiversity and Biological Collections Gopher at Harvard/
43.    Bioinformatics Resource Gopher/
44.    Bioline Publications/
45.    Biological Sciences Directorate Reports/
46.    Biology FTP Archive for Macintosh (MacSciTech USA)/
47.    Biology Gopher at OSU (BCC)/
```

```
48.   Biology Journal Contents <?>
49.   Biomedical_Shareware/
50.   Bionet Newsgroups <?>
51.   Biotechnet Buyers Guide - Online Catalogues for Biology <TEL>
52.   Blocks Database (FHCRC)/
53.   Botanical Electronic News/
54.   Botanical Information/
Press ? for Help, q to Quit, u to go up a menu Page: 3/17
```

4. The bottom right of the screen tells you that these 54 items comprise a mere three of the 17 pages. You're barely a sixth of the way through the list. One area you had the option of examining on the WWW was Biodiversity, shown here in items `41` and `42`. Selecting item `42`, you arrive at the following menu:

```
Biodiversity and Biological Collections Gopher at Harvard
1.    About the Biodiversity and Biological Collections Gopher.
2.    Museum, Herbarium and Arboretum Collection Catalogs/
3.    Biodiversity Information Resources/
4.    Directories of Biologists/
5.    Biodiversity Journals and Newsletters/
6.    Curation & Management of Biological Collections/
7.    Standards Organizations and Reports/
8.    Software/
9.    Biological Images/
10.   Taxacom Services/
11.   Other Biological Gophers/
12.   Other Gopher and Information Servers (mirrored from U.Minnesota)/
13.   Top Ten Items at the Biodiversity Gopher/
```

5. In the spirit of both Dick Clark and David Letterman, the most interesting choice here simply has to be item `13`, the `Top Ten Items at the Biodiversity Gopher/`. Selecting it, you are offered the following menu:

```
Top Ten Items at the Biodiversity Gopher
1.    Harvard Gray Herbarium Index of New World Plants/
2.    Image files/
3.    Biodiversity Authority Files/
4.    Catalogs/Search by Discipline/
5.    Biodiversity Authority Files/Botany/
6.    About this Biology Image Archive.
7.    Biodiversity Database and Software Development Projects/
8.    Flora Online: Journal for Collections-Oriented Botanical Research/
9.    Collection Catalogs/Botany/
10.   Collection Catalogs/Institution/
```

6. This offers several places to go, but assume that you've been looking for images to download. Clearly, item `2` should have something to offer, and as the following menu shows, it does:

```
Image files
1.    hbia0001.jpg <Picture>
2.    hbia0002.jpg <Picture>
3.    hbia0003.jpg <Picture>
4.    hbia0004.jpg <Picture>
5.    hbia0005.jpg <Picture>
6.    hbia0006.jpg <Picture>
7.    hbia0007.jpg <Picture>
8.    hbia0008.jpg <Picture>
```

```
9.     hbia0009.jpg <Picture>
10.    hbia0010.jpg <Picture>
11.    hbia0011.jpg <Picture>
12.    hbia0012.jpg <Picture>
13.    hbia0013.jpg <Picture>
14.    hbia0014.jpg <Picture>
15.    hbia0015.jpg <Picture>
16.    hbia0016.jpg <Picture>
17.    hbia0017.jpg <Picture>
18.    hbia0018.jpg <Picture>
Press ? for Help, q to Quit, u to go up a menu Page: 1/21
```

7. Eighteen files are shown here, all in .JPG format. Again, however, look at the bottom right of the menu. This is only page 1 of a 21-page list, which means that you have access to well over 300 files. Choosing item 17 on this list (for no reason other than it's the highest prime number here—okay, I didn't say anything about a *good* reason), you can download it to your account.
8. The thing to keep in mind, as with your WWW searches in the main part of this chapter, is that this is but one graphic from one menu from a host of possible menus on one topic from one Gopher. It wouldn't take much for a diligent Gopher browser to compile a huge amount of information on the latest topics in scientific research. What you do with it, of course, remains up to you. It's there, and it's easily accessible.

That's it. You've toured the world of science. Not that there aren't another 30–40 chapters of material left to get, but for now, you at least have some idea of the vast quantity of material that's out there waiting for you to access it. There's scarcely any excuse left for not knowing the kind of scientific work that's being done all over the world.

Now it's on to technology, specifically the Internet itself.

Teach Yourself the Internet... on the Internet

No matter how many instructions, examples, or guidelines you read, learning the Internet really begins when you start sending e-mail, joining newsgroups, browsing Gophers, and doing Archie searches. So why not carry this one step further and learn the Internet from the Internet itself? This is what this chapter helps you do, by exploring online tutorials, downloading guides and instruction manuals, and finding what the experts have to say.

Like most technologies, the Internet is learned best in a hands-on manner. Admittedly, this book has been designed so that you don't actually have to be *on* the Internet to *learn* the Internet, but if you've read this far, you've already become interested enough to spring for an account and follow along. In this chapter, you'll use that account to help learn the Internet and its tools even better.

The richest source of Internet information is the Internet itself. If you want facts, statistics, suggestions, or software, turn to the Net for your needs. But it doesn't stop there. The Internet also is a rich resource for *learning* about the Internet. And that makes it a bit unusual in the world of computing. If you buy a new computer, it's unlikely that the computer itself will teach you how to use it effectively; if you buy a CD-ROM drive, you'll need all kinds of information external to the CD-ROM to get it running at all. But the Internet teaches its own, you might say, and as long as you're willing to search, there isn't much you can't find.

Warning: *Search* is the operative word here. It's true that the Net holds all kinds of useful information about how to use itself, but the help is anything but easy to find. When you know a site or two, things get considerably simpler, but getting there is much less than half the fun. Still, it's often very much worth the effort.

Task 21.7: Subscribe to mailing lists to learn about the Net.

As you might expect, those who spend their hours keeping track of what's available on the Internet use the Net's capabilities to make their findings public. One such method is the *mailing list*—as it turns out, this is the most practical way of all.

Get used to the name Gleason Sackman. If you've any interest at all in hearing about new Internet activity (and who doesn't?), you're going to read that name several times daily. That's because, starting right now, you're going to subscribe to Sackman's *net-happenings* mailing list, which is the Net's most indispensable source of new information.

1. To subscribe to net-happenings, send an e-mail message to the following address, entering the following on the first line of the message area:

```
To       : majordomo@is.internic.net
Cc       :
Attchmnt:
Subject  :
— Message Text —
subscribe net-happenings firstname lastname
```

Warning: As always, when subscribing to a mailing list (see Chapter 4), leave the `subject:` line empty, and remember to exclude your signature file.

In a few minutes or so, you'll receive a confirmation message that looks something like the following:

```
Date: Fri, 22 Apr 1994 17:45:04 -0700
From: listserv@is.internic.net
To: nrandall@watserv1.uwaterloo.ca
Cc: sackman@plains.nodak.edu
Subject: SUBSCRIBE NET-HAPPENINGS NEIL RANDALL
The net-happenings list is a service of InterNIC Information Services. The
purpose of the list is to distribute to the community announcements of
interest to network staffers and end users. This includes conference
announcements, call for papers, publications, newsletters, network tools
updates, and network resources. Net-happenings is a moderated,
announcements-only mailing list which gathers announcements from many
Internet sources and concentrates them onto one list. Traffic is
around 10-15 messages per day, and is archived daily.
```

2. From this point on, you'll start to see messages in your mailbox that let you know what's happening on the Internet. There are other such lists—the Gopher Jewels list, for example—but net-happenings often cross-posts the information from those lists anyway. In fact, most of net-happenings's information comes from other lists and newsgroups. Following is an example of what net-happenings offers:

```
Forwarded by Gleason Sackman - InterNIC net-happenings moderator
*****************************************************************

---- Forwarded message ----
Date: Sun, 17 Apr 1994 23:17:43 EDT
From: Roger R. Espinosa <roger@trillium.soe.umich.edu>
To: Multiple recipients of list EDTECH <EDTECH@msu.bitnet>
Subject: DeweyWeb: A World Wide Web Experiment in Education...

THE DEWEYWEB:JOURNEY NORTH

An experiment in using the WWW for the support of education.
----------------------------------

If you've been curious about how the World Wide Web could be used in
classrooms, and have been bugged by its one-way nature, I'm hoping you'll
take a look at:

http://ics.soe.umich.edu/

 (Or, for those who cut and paste these things:
<A HREF="http://ics.soe.umich.edu/" The DeweyWeb Experiment</A>
```

21

```
The DeweyWeb:Journey North is an experiment in building an web
environment that students can expand. Based on the World School's
Journey North activity, the primary feature of the experiment is a
series of maps which can be altered by students, as they enter in
observations of wildlife migration.
```

Tip: When you see a message such as this one, and you're interested in seeing the site mentioned, the best idea is to launch your Web, Gopher, or FTP program immediately and check it out, placing a bookmark in it if you find it useful. If you simply store or even print these pages, you'll soon find newer stuff that pushes the previous addresses into the background. If you're a user of Wollongong's Emissary software, URLs in e-mail and newsgroup messages can be clicked on to directly launch the browser.

3. Net-Happenings is the most useful list, but not the only one. Other useful mailing lists include the following:

- NEW-LIST (announcements of new mailing lists) at `LISTSERV@VM1.NODAK.EDU`
- NEWJOURN-L (announcements of new electronic journals) at `listserv@E-MATH.ams.com`
- GOPHERJEWELS (announcements of new Gophers) at `listproc@einet.net`

Task 21.8: Examine newsgroups about new Internet resources.

A number of newsgroups have the Internet as their subject matter. One, in fact—`alt.internet.services`—contains many of the same announcements found in the Net-Happenings list from Task 21.7. An important feature of the Internet newsgroups is that, obviously, they prompt considerable discussion.

1. To find newsgroups dealing with the Internet, use the search function in your newsreader. If you're using trn or rn (see Chapter 5 for how to use them), enter **`l internet`** at `trn`'s prompt:

```
alt.bbs.internet
alt.best.of.internet
alt.horror.shub-internet
alt.internet.access.wanted
alt.internet.talk-radio
ba.internet
comp.internet.library
de.comm.internet
info.big-internet
tnn.internet.firewall
```

2. Subscribe to whatever groups you're interested in. Over the course of weeks, you'll accumulate hordes of messages dealing with new Internet resources. Save the ones that seem important, or catalog them the way you want.
3. One of the groups not shown in the preceding list is the extremely popular `alt.internet.services`. This is a must-read newsgroup for anyone wanting to find out more about the Internet, even if you're already a subscriber to the net-happenings mailing list. Large numbers of messages are posted here weekly, across a very wide range of subjects.

Newsgroups provide both news about the Internet and a place to discuss that news. If you're serious about keeping in touch with Net events, by all means join a few newsgroups. Be prepared, however, to read them frequently, or you'll end up with far too many to deal with at any given time.

Task 21.9: Learn about the Internet through Gopher sites.

Newsgroups and mailing lists are excellent places to start your self-education about the Internet and its resources, but inevitably, they end up pointing you toward Gopher sites. In fact, you don't even need to access the lists to find Gopher-based information. As you've known since Chapter 8, you can browse Gophers in search of whatever you like, and finding Internet information is anything but difficult.

1. Using your Gopher browser (or the standard UNIX browser), search for any Gopher item with a title such as Internet Resources. Alternatively, you can just find the ubiquitously available Gopher Jewels items. From these items, you can browse for large amounts of Internet information, entering FTP sites and obtaining training guides, text files, and even software to help you along.
2. If you remember your Internet history from Chapter 1, you'll recall the importance of the consortium named Merit. As you might expect, Merit has its own Gopher site, which contains a wealth of data about the Net. To access this site, Gopher to **`nic.merit.edu`**.

   Figure 21.23 shows the resulting list, including some items leading directly to Internet information.

   If your purpose is to teach yourself details about the Internet itself, rather than just about Internet tools available for use, the Merit site is well worth exploring.
3. Another extremely useful site is the SunSite Gopher at the North Carolina State University. Here, you'll find a wealth of files with information about how to use the various Internet tools. The main Gopher list is shown in Figure 21.24. To reach this Gopher, use your Gopher browser to go to **`dewey.lib.ncsu.edu`**, and

then follow the path NCSU's "Library Without Walls," Reference Desk, and finally Guides (to subject literature, to Internet resources, and so on). Here you'll find the collection of documents.

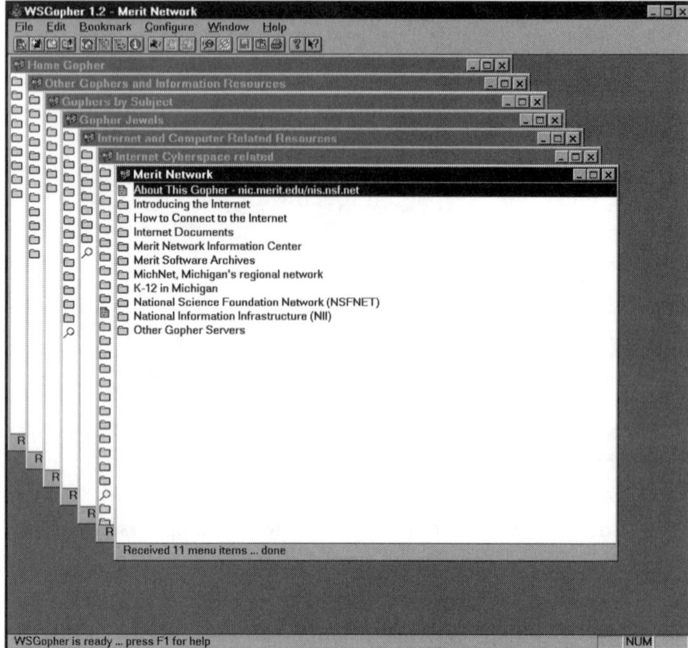

Figure 21.23.
Merit Gopher at `nic.merit.edu`.

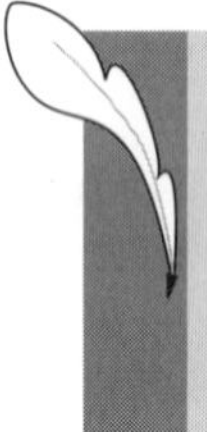

Note: SunSite is the first place you should consider when Gophering to find tutorial material, but keep in mind that not everything archived here is completely up-to-date. Some materials date from 1993 and even 1994, but earlier guides from 1990 and before are still available. Nevertheless, you can't go wrong downloading any number of these files.

4. One such guide is Big Dummy's Guide to the Internet (third item on the list), which keeps being rereleased in updated editions. This is a long, extensive, and extremely useful guide, one that more than repays the time it takes to download. Then again, it's been renamed EFF's Extended Guide to the Internet, and is available in hypertext format through the Web at `http://www.eff.org/papers/bdgtti/eegtti.html`, so maybe there's not much point downloading it here. Unless, of course, Gopher is your main Internet tool.

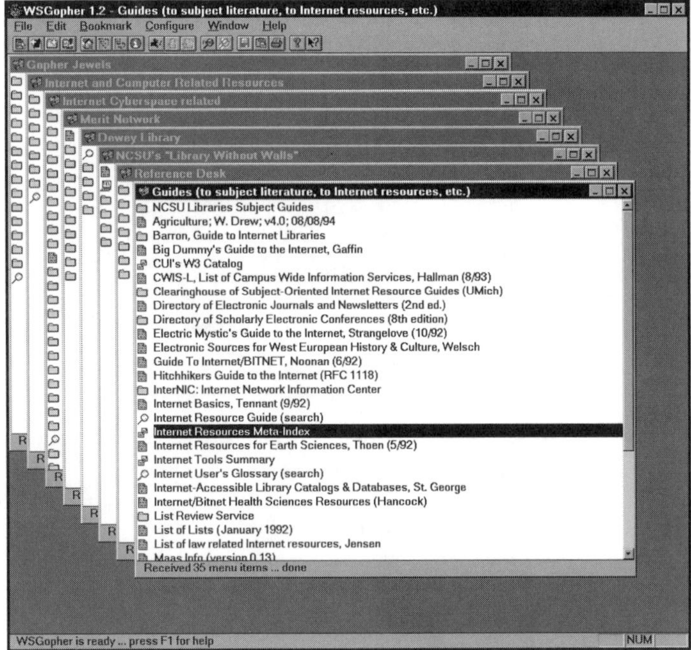

Figure 21.24.
The SunSite Gopher—guides to the Internet.

You're not restricted to North American Gopher sites if you want to learn about the Net. Several strong European sites offer information about the Internet. Among the best is the BUBL Information Service, available on the UKOLN (UK Office for Library and Information Networking) Gopher at the University of Bath, UK (`ukoln.bath.ac.uk`).

5. The BUBL (Bulletin Boards for Libraries) service contains an item entitled Internet Resources by Subject; Reference Tools, Electronic Texts, which yields the following menu:

```
1.  BUBL Beginners:Contacts, Help..Hints, News, Latest Additions, Sta/
2.  BUBL Subject Tree/
3.  Electronic Journals & Texts/
4.  Employment Resources and Opportunities/
5.  Grants Available & Competitions You Can Win/
6.  Major Networked Services/
7.  Networking Groups on the Internet/
8.  Networks and Networking/
9.  Non-Networked Groups on BUBL/
10. Reference Resources: Acronymns, Directories, E-lists, Glossaries/
11. Software for Teaching and Using to Aid Your Work/
```

6. From here, head for Networking Groups on the Internet (although some others in the menu are useful), and that choice leads you to this list (truncated here):

```
2.  Association for Progressive Communications (Connection details) -.
3.  CAUSE - Assoc for managing & using IT in HE - H2B15/
4.  CEPES-UNESCO - H2B13//
5.  CHEST - H2B12/
6.  Chemical Abstract Service STN Internet Contact - H2B08/
7.  Committee to Protect Journalists.
8.  Connect - IBM PC Users - H2B04/
9.  EARN Information Service/
10. Electronic Frontier Foundation (EFF) - H2B19/
11. Greennet - Environment - H2B03/
12. INTERNIC: The Internet Network Information Centre/
```

   Spend some time working your way through the information here, after which you'll explore some other European sites.

7. An important European network is EUnet. Gopher to the address `gopher.EU.net` to receive the following short menu:

```
1.  EUnet Country Guide/
2.  Profile: EUnet.
3.  Traveller/
```

8. The EUnet profile is worth reading, but instead, enter the `EUnet Country Guide/`, where you'll find the following:

```
1.  Austria.
2.  Germany/
3.  Greece/
4.  Ireland/
5.  Other Countries.
6.  Slovakia/
7.  Spain/
8.  Switzerland/
9.  The Netherlands/
```

9. Any of the preceding items will give you more information on EUnet, and some of the Gophers are more fleshed out than the others. One of the lesser developed (but interesting nevertheless) is Spain, which leads you to the following menu:

```
1.  Yo soy ... / I am ....
2.  Info on EUnet at Spain (goya)/
3.  Info on EUnet — Paneuropean Network Services Providers/
4.  Info on Internet/
5.  Servicios - Goya/
6.  Useful Services (worldwide)/
7.  Anuncios/
8.  pruebas/
```

10. Select the second item, `Info on EUnet at Spain (goya)/`, which yields the following short menu that demonstrates clearly that the information will be (quite naturally) in Spanish:

```
1.  Tarifas (Prices)/
2.  Informacion tecnica/
3.  GoyaHoy: anuncio de servicios accesibles via goya (eunet.es)/
4.  contratos/
```

11. In fact, the `Informacion tecnica/` item leads to this well-stocked Gopher, with several Spanish files dealing with Internet details:

```
4.  AUP: Condiciones de utilizacion de los servicios.
5.  Configuracion del correo con UUPC 1.10.
6.  Direcciones: secretaria, soporte, listas de distribucion, ....
7.  E-mail, News e IP: propaganda.
8.  E-mail: Correo electronico.
9.  FTP anonimo.
10. FTP mail: ftp anonimo via E-mail.
11. FTP: Bases de Datos on-line.
12. INDEX.
13. IP over IP.
14. Indice comentado de documentos.
15. Informacion administrativa sobre EUnet Espana / GOYA.
16. Instalacion de UUCP en una maquina UNIX via modem RTC.
17. ListServ: listas de distribucion.
```

From the tasks performed so far, it's easy to see the sheer amount of information that's available through some simple Gopher browsing. In fact, with a couple of guides downloaded and text files of Internet services information, you may think there's no reason to look any further. Wrong. There's still the World Wide Web. And that's where things really start to pick up as far as teaching yourself the Internet is concerned.

Task 21.10: Learn about the Internet through the World Wide Web.

It's no surprise that, as a teaching and information medium, the WWW has so far perhaps been best used to teach about itself and the Internet in general. The Net, after all, is a good test subject: because one of the Web's primary functions is to allow easy links to other sites, and because there's a great deal of Internet information on a wide range of sites throughout the Net, it's only natural to use the Web to point to these sites. In other words, using the Web as an Internet tutorial and resource guide makes sense because the subject matter—the Internet itself—is already available. It's a matter of designing the interface, not the material itself.

Several good Web sites provide Internet information and the potential for self-teaching. This section explores a few of them. In addition, the Extra Credit section for this chapter focuses on an extremely valuable resource, Internet Web Text. I encourage you to turn to it after you've visited these preliminary sites.

1. Access the Yahoo directory, the best of the directories for Internet links. Go to **`http://www.yahoo.com/`**, click on Computers, and then click on Internet. You'll see the screen shown in Figure 21.25.

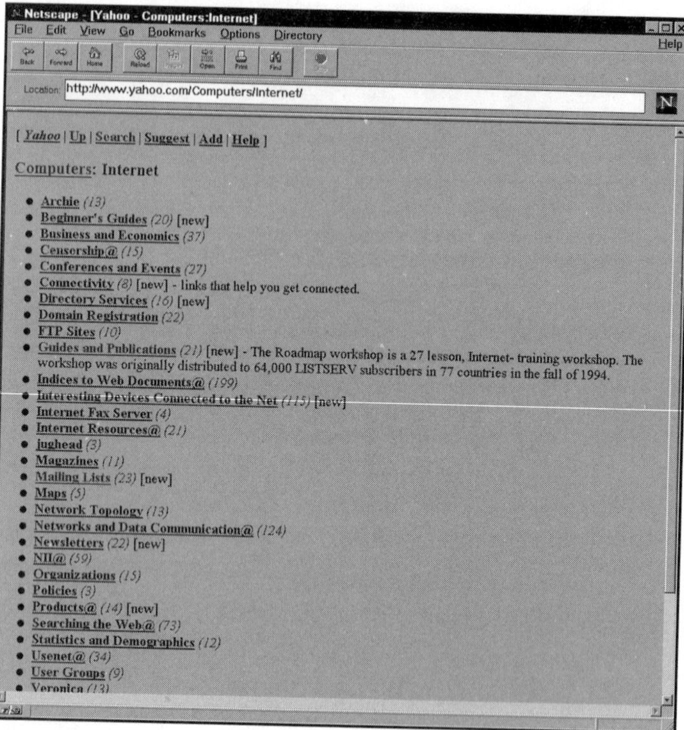

Figure 21.25.
The Internet information page from Yahoo.

2. From here, click from item to item to see where each one leads. You'll discover a truly huge array of resources about the Net, and almost endless reading. For now, click on the link named Guides and Publications, and start exploring the wide range of online guides available to you. One of them, you'll discover, is a link to the Teach Yourself the Internet Support Page, which, as you might guess, is designed expressly for you. But I won't show it here; instead, visit it yourself at `http://randall.uwaterloo.ca/tyi.html`.
3. Click on the link for the EFF's Extended Guide to the Internet. This, remember, is the renamed Big Dummy's Guide you visited in your Gopher tour earlier this chapter. You'll see the screen shown in Figure 21.26.

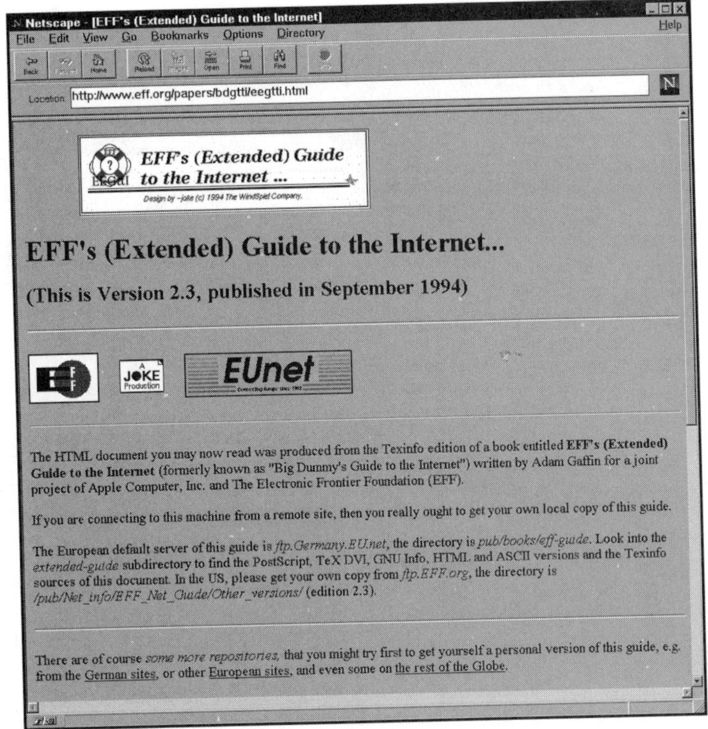

Figure 21.26.
The home page for the Electronic Frontier Foundation's Extended Guide to the Internet.

4. Return to the Yahoo Internet Guides page and click on The Online World Resources Handbook, and then click on the link named hypertext version. This is another useful guide in hypertext format, with links to a solid range of information.
5. Now it's off to the Global Network Navigator at `http://www.gnn.com`. One of the first truly well-designed WWW sites, the Global Network Navigator (GNN) offers a wide variety of Internet information and help with tools. Figure 21.27 shows GNN's home page.

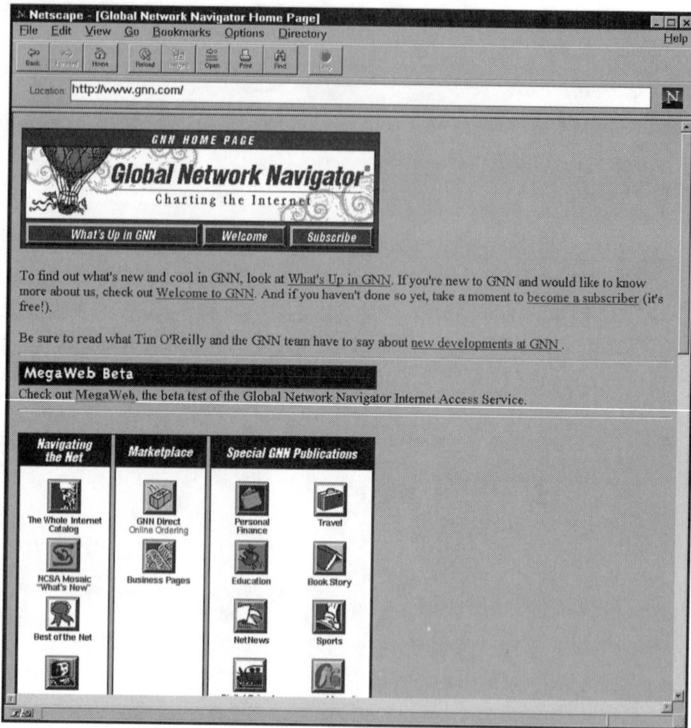

Figure 21.27.
The Global Network Navigator home page.

6. Click on any of the links in the Navigating the Net box. You've already seen the Whole Internet Catalog and the NCSA What's New page, so give Best of the Net a try. This is one of many "best-of" sites on the Web, and it offers several worthwhile links.
7. More interesting, however, are the links under Special GNN Publications. Click on NetNews to get links to articles and features about current Internet issues, one of which, Internet usage, is shown in Figure 21.28.

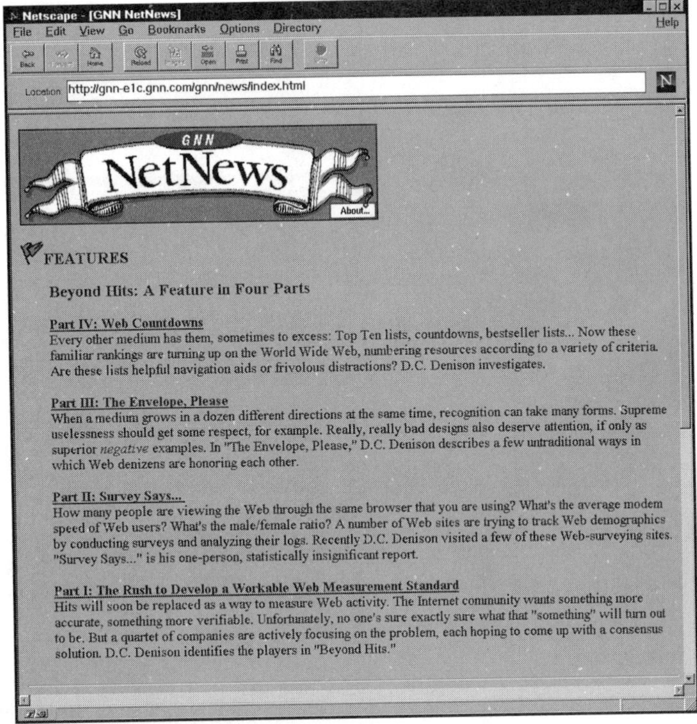

Figure 21.28.
The NetNews page from GNN.

8. Read through some of the articles, and then return to the GNN home page and click on the Digital Drive-In icon. This provides you with information about new Internet technologies, as well as a host of truly interesting material.
9. An interesting Web site promises full courses offered over the Net. The Globewide Network Academy (or GNA, as it's certain to be referred to) began posting details about a course on the Internet in early spring of 1994, with plans to begin a bit later on. The idea is that you can sign on to the course, which is a series of interactive demonstrations and hands-on activities of the various Internet tools. Go to the home page at **`http://uu-gna.mit.edu:8001/uu-gna/index.html`**. Of interest here is the concept of the *online consultant*—a real live instructor, complete with office hours, who will help you through the Internet maze.

10. Return to the Yahoo site, and check out Patrick Crispen's well-known Internet Roadmap. This is an Internet tutorial provided in a variety of formats, and the one at `http://www.brandonu.ca/~ennsnr/Resources/Roadmap/Welcome.html` is available on the Web. The home page, with several sample links, appears in Figure 21.29.

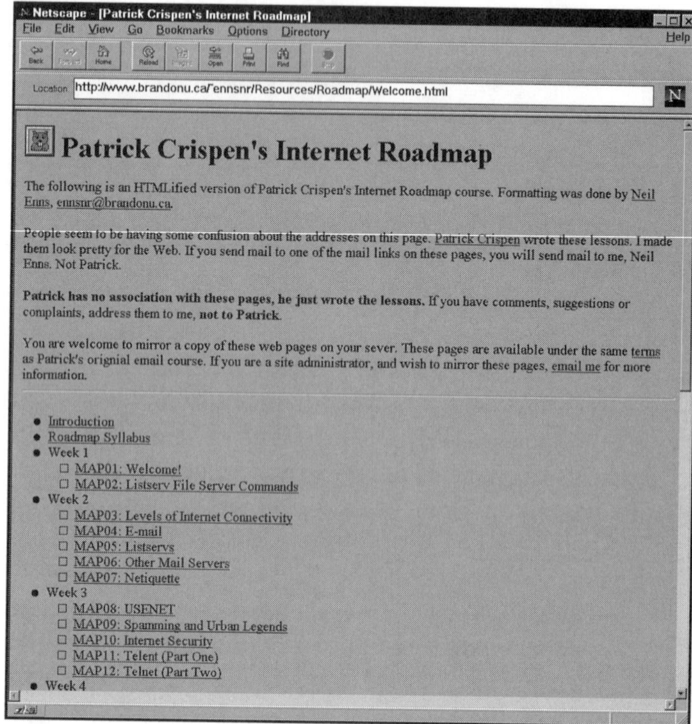

Figure 21.29.
The home page for the Internet Roadmap online tutorial.

11. Finally, if you want to learn the Internet tools from the Internet itself, plan to spend an extra few hours browsing and working with Internet Web Text, Internet Tools Summary, and Internet-CMC Page. All three are the product of John December and are featured in the Extra Credit section of this chapter.

Why are these three tools placed in Extra Credit? Precisely because they'll consume a great deal of extra time. You've already used the Internet to learn the Internet, but with December's work, you'll go far toward furthering that knowledge. Extra credit perhaps, but essential credit nevertheless.

I invite you, then, to spend another several hours teaching yourself the Internet...on the Internet. Turn to the Extra Credit section at the end of this chapter and follow a truly thorough guide. Or, head straight for the Internet Tools list at `http://www.rpi.edu/Internet/Guides/decemj/internet-tools.html` and start exploring on your own.

Summary

This chapter has provided an introduction to the projects in science being conducted throughout the world and available for perusal over the World Wide Web, and to information about the Internet itself. There's a wealth of material and knowledge offered for access and download, information that professionals in the fields, or followers (for whatever reason) of a particular branch of science can scarcely be without if they wish to consider themselves up-to-date. A great deal of collaborative research is starting to appear on the Internet, and the World Wide Web offers an excellent way for this work to be made accessible to the public. Much more of this activity is certain to find its way onto the Web as the months go by. Keeping up is going to be challenging, but that's the way it should be.

As far as technology is concerned, and Internet technologies in particular, the Internet is filled with information and advice about the Net itself. Through an extensive look at newsgroups and mailing lists, and by browsing and searching Gopher, FTP, and World Wide Web sites, you can increase your knowledge of the Net and your efficiency at using it. Already under way are hands-on workshops available over the Web, and full multimedia versions will undoubtedly follow before too long. Once you've worked your way through this book, it should be relatively easy to keep fully up-to-date on the Net and its associated tools.

Task Review

In this chapter, you learned how to perform the following tasks:

- ☐ Use search tools to discover projects in science
- ☐ Use the World Wide Web to access these science projects
- ☐ Examine projects taking place in locations around the world
- ☐ Explore projects in technology at various levels
- ☐ Access Internet guides and resources on the Net
- ☐ Use Gopher and the World Wide Web to learn about the Internet's resources
- ☐ Join newsgroups dealing with Internet tools and issues
- ☐ Subscribe to mailing lists about the Internet and its tools
- ☐ Download Internet guides from FTP sites

Q&A

Q Isn't there a problem in that we see only the successful scientific research, not the failures?

A Dissemination of research information has always been problematic in this regard. Research is funded, after all, and the funding agencies want to know everything that's going on, but for obvious reasons, nobody wants to report a continuing string of failures. Research results made available for public consumption on the Internet have already been screened, except, of course, for other researchers on the project, who have the information available through FTP in password-protected directories and sites. This is no more a problem than is the suppression of any scientific research results, and perhaps the Internet makes things a bit less suppressible. If research initiatives are announced over the Net, after all, and given their own WWW home pages and Gopher sites, then at least we can find out that they're taking place. If we're interested, we can follow their progress, and if for some reason that progress stops (or the sites disappear), we may want to follow up and find out why. Without the Internet, there isn't an easy way of even determining what kinds of projects are under way.

Q Is the Internet all I need to keep abreast of project developments?

A No, not at all. It's not even all you need to figure out which projects are being developed. There are other resources for that, and for the presentation of results. The Internet can help you locate projects and institutions about which you might want to learn much more. All centers offer packages of materials detailing their activities, and through the Net you can find out how to get these packages. They will also offer information about how to follow the results.

Q If so much Internet material is available on the Internet itself, why did I buy this book?

A Apart from helping me put my kids through university, working through this book has offered—and will continue to offer as you go along—a number of advantages over taking all your information off the Internet. The first, of course, is that it points you toward the very fact that the Net offers its own learning resources, something you might not otherwise discover. Second, you can take it with you on the plane, or you can read it while lying on the couch with a cup of tea in your other hand, neither of which you can do (without a great deal of technical resourcefulness, at least) while on the Net itself. Third, the book is formatted much more pleasantly than a long file of plain ASCII. Fourth, it's designed to move you from point to point in your explorations, which Net-based tools are only beginning to do. Finally, if you actually pay for your Internet access, the book may well be cheaper than working your way through online tutorials or downloading several files. And there is that point about my kids and university.

Extra Credit: John December's Internet Web Text

Professionally, my interest in the Internet lies in its capabilities and ramifications as a communications medium (nonprofessionally, I just like surfing). Imagine my enthusiasm, then, when I found out, through the net-happenings list discussed in this chapter, about a World Wide Web page devoted to Computer-Mediated Communication (CMC). I fired up Cello immediately to check it out (hey, this was a long time ago!).

What I found was nothing short of mind-boggling. Some guy named John December at Rensselaer Polytechnic Institute (RPI) had constructed this long, detailed Web page with a seemingly endless series of links to other sites. The links had much to do with CMC itself, and many of them pointed to Web, Gopher, FTP, and telnet sites dealing with a huge array of Internet tools. I spent hours working from this page, learning about tools I'd never even heard of.

As my Web browsing continued, I began to see December's pages referenced from a great many other pages. It turned out that the CMC and Internet Tools pages weren't the only ones he'd prepared. In fact, perhaps the most interesting of the lot was Internet Web Text, as handy an introduction to the Internet as I'd seen. Together, these pages comprised a fascinating, comprehensive reference guide to the Internet, and I decided that they had to be featured in this book.

As it turns out, I was so impressed with December's work that immediately after completing the first edition of *Teach Yourself the Internet in 21 Days*, I contacted John about collaborating on a book about the World Wide Web. He'd already been negotiating the book, and we ended up working together and with other Web experts, as well. The result was the popular *World Wide Web Unleashed*, the second edition of which you can find at your bookstore as soon as you put this book down.

Here is John December's own introduction to his immensely popular Web pages. Take it, John.

Internet Web Text

by John December

I created Internet Web Text for a graduate course in computer-mediated communication at RPI that I helped teach in the spring of 1994. My goal was to create an Internet-based interface that students could use to tap into the rich store of knowledge on the Internet and learn about it.

Having had the experience of maintaining a list of information sources about the Internet and computer-mediated communication (URL `ftp://ftp.rpi.edu/pub/communications/internet-cmc`) for more than a year and a half, I knew that the Internet itself was a rich resource for Internet information. I also knew which sources on my list were particularly helpful for particular purposes.

The Design of Internet Web Text

My design goal was to create a hypertext guide with flexible ways for users to encounter information. I wanted to link together Internet resources for orientation, guides, reference, browsing and exploring, subject- and word-oriented searching, and information about connecting with people. I wanted to create a design that would allow users to encounter the information in a variety of ways (both in list form and in narrative form) in "chunks" that did not overwhelm. I also wanted to use icons to create memory aids to help users remember the resources. I wanted to weave the whole package of information together with links so that a user could easily move from one area of the text to the other.

My resulting design meets these goals. From the front Web page (URL `http://www.rpi.edu/Internet/Guides/decemj/text.html`), I provide the user with an overview of the entire guide and links to other versions of it (see Figure 21.30). The guide itself is divided into seven subdivisions with a maximum of seven major resources mentioned in each. (Seven is a good rule-of-thumb upper limit on the number of things people can keep in mind at once.) From the front page, the user can access more information about Internet Web Text itself, release notes, and the narrative, no-icons, icons-only, and page-oriented versions of the text.

The narrative version (URL `http://www.rpi.edu/Internet/Guides/decemj/narrative.html`) presents the resources with an explanatory narrative (see Figure 21.31).

Besides the top-level narrative version, each of the seven subdivisions of the text has a narrative version of its own. In the narrative version of each subdivision, I describe seven major resources, including icons in the narrative to identify these seven resources. In addition, I provide links to supplementary or further resources that are useful, but I don't provide icons for these links in order to preserve the "major" feel of the seven major resources in each subdivision.

For each page of narrative for the seven subdivisions, I have an accompanying list version that presents only the seven major resources for that subdivision. In this way, the reader can quickly get a list of the major resources without having to read through the narrative. In this way, the list version serves as a more "expert" layer for this information.

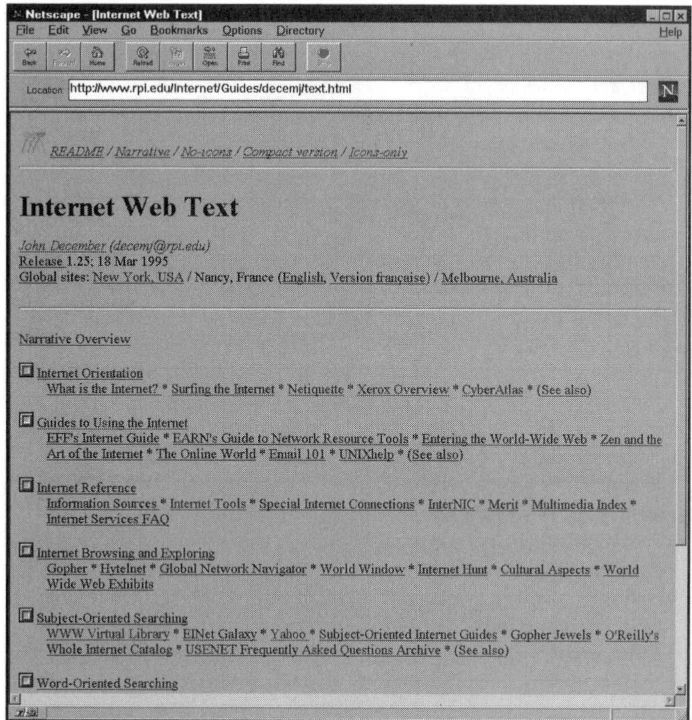

Figure 21.30.
The Internet Web Text home page.

The icons-only version of the text (URL `http://www.rpi.edu/Internet/Guides/decemj/icons.html`) presents only the icons of the major resources of the text. The icons-only version serves as a compact jumping-off point for users who are familiar enough with the resources that they can recognize them by the icons only. In contrast, the iconless version of the text presents only a list of the resources with no icons. This is particularly useful for those people who are not using a graphical browser or who do not want to bring up any icons.

Finally, I've designed links among the pages so that a reader can encounter the information using multiple paths, and jump from one version to the other. At the bottom of each list or narrative page, there is a row of icons with links to any of the seven major categories. You can go from any page-oriented list version to its corresponding page-oriented narrative version by clicking on the category title at the top of the page to the right of the category icon. Conversely, you can go from any page-oriented narrative version to its corresponding page-oriented list version by clicking on the category icon at the top of the page. The Internet Web Text icon at the top of the page will take a user to the front page of either the list-oriented version or the narrative-oriented version, depending on in what version the user is currently located. This flexibility makes it possible for a user to quickly select the way the information is presented.

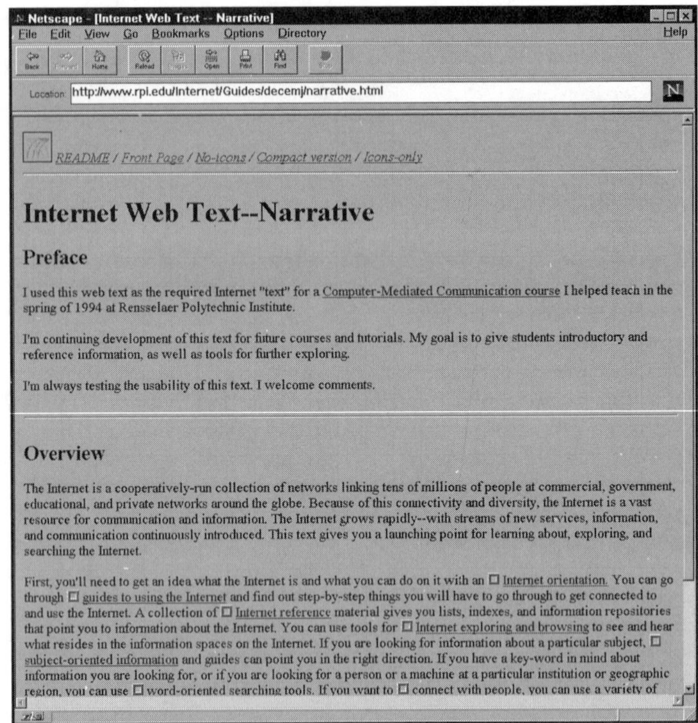

Figure 21.31.
The narrative version of Internet Web Text.

Using Internet Web Text

You can use Internet Web Text in a variety of ways. If you are an experienced user, you can probably go right to the front page and select resources from there. This front page gives direct access to all the major resources in the text. A new user to Internet Web Text or the Internet in general should first read the front page of the narrative version to become familiar with what the guide has to offer as well as the meaning of the icons representing the seven subdivisions. From there, a new Internet user should consider selecting the Internet Orientation subdivision to get acquainted with what the Internet has to offer and some basic information about it. An experienced user could view the list-only version of this same information. Beyond this orientation, the user then should select the subdivision that represents the kind of resource they are seeking (guides, reference, exploring, searching, or connecting with people).

The images in the guide can help users remember and become familiar with resources. However, it does take a while to load the images when using Mosaic or other graphical interfaces. Once the images are loaded, however, you can skip from page to page fairly rapidly and gain the benefit of having the icons. When I am going to use the text for an extended time, I usually click on the icons-only version and let all the images load while I do something else in another window. A few pages do have additional images, such as the Cultural Aspects of the Internet collection. There is currently a European mirror site for the Internet Web Text, which makes it faster for European users to load the images. I am currently working with people in Japan and Mexico to provide similar mirror sites.

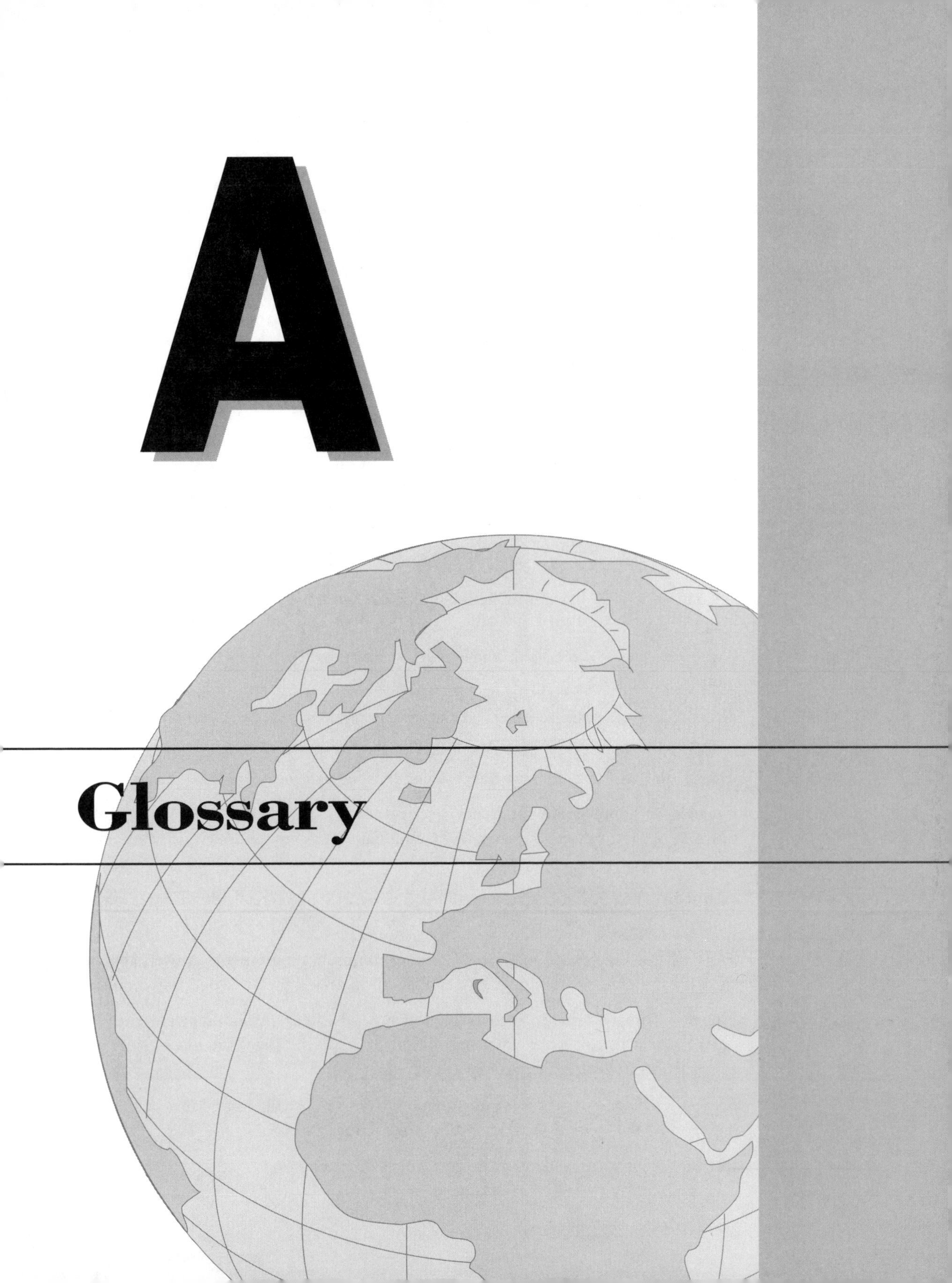

A

Glossary

Glossary

account—Your account at the bank gives you space and tools to work with your money; your account on a network gives you space and tools to work with files and data, which is really the same idea.

address—The string of characters that identifies you or an Internet file or site. My address is `nrandall@watserv1.uwaterloo.ca`, for example; yours will be in the form *`username@host.name.type`*. A Gopher site has an address such as `cwis.usc.edu`, while a World Wide Web address is in the form of a URL (see *URL*).

Archie—A search system that enables you to locate files you can then download via anonymous FTP (see *FTP*).

ASCII—The major standard for files that users on various machines can share, abbreviated as ASC. Also known as text files, which is what most ASCII files are.

binary—A file containing codes and characters that can only be used by specific kinds of software. Program files, graphic files, and formatted documents are the most common.

Cello—A graphical World Wide Web browser for Microsoft Windows

cyberspace—A broad expression used to describe the activity, communication, and culture happening on the Internet and other networks, BBSs and online services

dial-up access—As the name suggests, connecting to the Internet by dialing through a modem

direct access—Internet access that makes your computer a separate Internet node. SLIP and PPP (see both) effectively simulate direct access. See also *indirect access.*

discussion list—Another name for mailing list. See *mailing list.*

e-mail—An abbreviation for electronic mail, e-mail has become the single most used function of the Internet. It is essentially a messaging system, although it incorporates file transfer, as well.

emoticon—Pretentious name for smileys (see *smiley*), which really don't merit that much thought

FAQ (Frequently Asked Question)—A list of common questions and answers about some specific topic. They're designed to keep users from asking the same questions constantly.

Finger—A program that enables you to determine whether a specific user is currently online, or, instead, which users are currently online at a specific site. Not to be freely used in conversation at non-techie parties.

flame—To be nasty, vicious, or insulting over the Net, usually in response to an e-mail or newsgroup message that the flamer didn't like. Usually a bad idea.

freeware—Software available at no cost from FTP sites

FTP (File Transfer Protocol)—An extremely important tool that enables you to transfer files between remote computers. Its most popular Internet use is "anonymous FTP," where you log in to a remote system using the login name `anonymous` and type your full address as the password. With anonymous FTP, you don't need an account on the remote machine in order to access certain files. (Note that you can perform FTP through Gopher and the World Wide Web, or directly from the command line.)

A

Gopher—The most popular Internet browser by far, Gopher displays files and directories in a conveniently accessed list. You can perform many functions from Gopher, including telnet (see *telnet*), FTP (see *FTP*), and searches of various types.

header—The top portion of an e-mail message, showing the route taken by the message across the various networks. Unreadable by all but the most technologically unchallenged.

home page—World Wide Web page, usually the first page of an organization's or a person's Web site

HTML (Hypertext Markup Language)—The coding applied to text files that allows them to appear as formatted pages on the World Wide Web

indirect access—Internet access in which your computer is simply a terminal on a host computer, which, in turn, is directly connected to the Net (see *direct access*). Only the host computer is a separate node on the Net.

internaut—An Internet user, usually ranging toward the expert

Internet—The global network of networks that are all intercommunicable

Internetter—An Internet user, whether expert or novice

IP address—The Internet Protocol address is the numeric address of a computer on the Internet. If you have an IP address, you're essentially a separate Internet node.

Kermit—Common protocol (and program) that enables you to transfer files between your personal computer and the host computer (see *host*). See also *XModem* and *FTP*.

Listserv—A program that allows for the creation and distribution of mailing lists. See *mailing list.*

login—The process of getting connected to a networked computer. As a verb it's two words: *log in.*

login name—Your account name, to be typed when logging in to a computer (see *login*). Usually the login name is the first portion of your full Internet address (see *address*)

Lynx—A character-based World Wide Web browser for UNIX systems

mailing list—An automated message service, often moderated by an "owner," where subscribers receive postings from other subscribers on a given topic. See also *discussion list* and *newsgroup.*

meta list—Also known as meta-index or meta directory, these listings offer links to a wide variety of Web resources, and usually are sorted by topic.

Mosaic—A graphical World Wide Web browser for XWindow, Macintosh, Microsoft Windows, and Amiga systems; often used synonymously with the term World Wide Web, but that's incorrect.

MUD (Multi-User Dialog or Dimension)—Formerly called Multi-User Dungeon, a MUD is an interactive role-playing game played on the Internet. Players join the game from anywhere on the Internet by telnetting into the system where the game is stored, and then interact with each other as they play.

NCSA—The National Center for Supercomputing Applications at the University of Illinois at Champaign-Urbana, the home of the Mosaic Web browser

netiquette—Internet etiquette, consisting of things like not replying to everyone in the group when you have something to say to only one, and not dragging files from an FTP site in Mongolia when the university next door has the same stuff

Netscape—The most popular Web browser, officially known as Netscape Navigator

Netscape Communications Corporation—The company that produces Netscape Navigator and other products, and where Mosaic designer Marc Andreesen found a paying job

newsgroup—An automated message area, usually operated through Usenet (see *Usenet*), in which subscribers post messages to the entire group on specific topics. See also *mailing list.*

password—The secret string of characters assigned to your individual login name on that particular system. Typically, you're assigned a password at the same time you're given your login name, and you're expected to change the password often. It's the thing that keeps other people from accessing your account and you from accessing theirs.

PPP (Point-to-Point Protocol)—Like SLIP (see *SLIP*), a method for transferring information through serial links. The dominant protocol for Macintosh dial-up users.

protocol—The codes and procedures that make it possible for one computer to exchange data with another

search engine—An Internet search engine is a program (or set of programs) that enables you to search for specific words, phrases, or other items in a variety of ways.

secure transaction—A transaction of data on the Internet that takes place through one of several major online security systems. Secure transactions are essential for the growth of Internet commerce

shareware—Software available as a trial at no cost from FTP sites. After the trial period, users are required to register (that is, pay up), which usually gets them more features.

shell—Software that enables you interact with the UNIX operating system. Actually, there are DOS shells and other shells as well, but "UNIX shell" is a more common expression.

signature—The personalized identification at the end of an e-mail message, automatically loaded by the e-mail program

SLIP (Serial Line Internet Protocol)—Protocol that enables IP (see *IP*) to run over telephone circuits and through modems. Essential for anyone connecting through Microsoft Windows.

smiley—Dumb little line graphics consisting of a collection of keyboard characters that sort of look like a face with an expression on it when you turn your head to the appropriate angle and subsequently spill your coffee on your mouse. See also *emoticon.*

snailmail—Pejorative term used by Internetters to refer to U.S. Postal Service and the other fine postal delivery services of the world

spam—The act of excessively or over-aggressively duplicating a message (especially commercial messages) and broadcasting it to many different places on the Internet; can incite *flames* in response

subject line—The line on the e-mail message that tells you what it's about. When used well, it's indispensable. When never changed or simply ignored, it's a terrible thing.

surf—To move (virtually) from computer to computer on the Internet, usually without staying too long in any one place

TCP/IP (Transfer Control Protocol/Internet Protocol)—The combination of protocols that enable computers on the Internet to exchange data among them. TCP/IP is the *sine qua non* of the Internet today, although replacements have recently been proposed.

telnet—Important tool enabling you to log in (see *login*) to a remote computer from the one you're sitting at. (Note that you can perform telnet from Gopher or the World Wide Web, or directly from the command line.)

UNIX—Operating system specializing in customizability and multi-user capabilities. The software backbone of the Internet.

URL (Universal Resource Locator)—A standard addressing system for Internet files and functions, especially apparent on the World Wide Web

Usenet—A networking system, linked to the Internet, that houses the popular news-groups

Veronica—Search tool that provides keyword-based searches of Gopher directories and files

virtual mall—A collection of stores, services, and other sales-oriented companies on the Internet, all run from the same server and sometimes using the same shopping interface and payment systems

WAIS (Wide Area Information Servers)—A sophisticated search system designed to make searching user-friendly, efficient, and cumulative

Winsock—The necessary "sockets" for using the Internet through Microsoft Windows over a modem. You must have the Winsock software to use Windows programs such as Netscape, Mosaic, Cello, Winsock Gopher, Eudora, and so on.

World Wide Web—Hypertext-based interface to the Internet, consisting of HTML documents (see *HTML*) with built-in links to other resources. The most popular WWW browser is Netscape, with Mosaic a close second.

XModem—Very common protocol (and program) that enables you to transfer files between your personal computer and the host computer (see *host*). In general terms, you FTP files from one UNIX system to another, but if you want the file on your PC or Mac, you use XModem to get it there. See also *FTP* and *Kermit.*

Index

Symbols

A

B

C

sams
net

F

G

H

I

J-K-L

M

N

O-P

Q-R

T

U

V

W

X-Y-Z

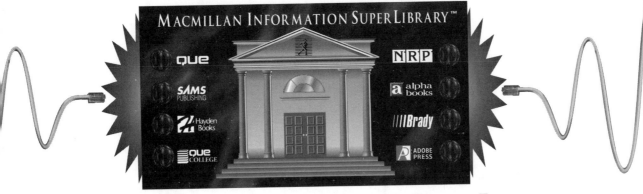

Book ISBN 0-672-30735-9